PRINCIPLES & PRACTICE *of*
MARKETING

JIM BLYTHE

PRINCIPLES & PRACTICE *of*
MARKETING

3rd EDITION

Los Angeles | London | New Delhi
Singapore | Washington DC

Los Angeles | London | New Delhi
Singapore | Washington DC

SAGE Publications Ltd
1 Oliver's Yard
55 City Road
London EC1Y 1SP

SAGE Publications Inc.
2455 Teller Road
Thousand Oaks, California 91320

SAGE Publications India Pvt Ltd
B 1/I 1 Mohan Cooperative Industrial Area
Mathura Road
New Delhi 110 044

SAGE Publications Asia-Pacific Pte Ltd
3 Church Street
#10-04 Samsung Hub
Singapore 049483

Editor: Matthew Waters
Development editor: Amy Jarrold
Editorial assistant: Nina Smith
Production editor: Sarah Cooke
Copyeditor: Elaine Leek
Proofreader: Audrey Scriven
Indexer: Silvia Benvenuto
Marketing manager: Alison Borg
Design: Francis Kenney
Typeset by: C&M Digitals (P) Ltd, Chennai, India
Printed and bound in Great Britain by Ashford
Colour Press Ltd

This edition first published 2014
Second edition published by Cengage Learning EMEA 2009

Library of Congress Control Number: 2013937185

British Library Cataloguing in Publication data

A catalogue record for this book is available from
the British Library

MIX
Paper from
responsible sources
FSC
www.fsc.org FSC® C011748

ISBN 978-1-4462-7399-9
ISBN 978-1-4462-7400-2 (pbk)

Brief contents

Contents

Part One
Concepts and contexts

Part Two
Markets and people

Part Three

Strategy and stakeholders

Part Four

Marketing in practice

List of figures

List of tables

About the author

Jim Blythe has been a Merchant Navy officer, a ladies' hairdresser, a business consultant, a rock musician, a truck driver, a company director, and an award-winning playwright before becoming an academic – he always planned on having a varied life, and likes learning new skills. Currently he is trying to learn to grow vegetables, with limited success, but he has a pilot's licence and has learned to play drums in a samba band, so the beat goes on. His next venture is to study for a degree in modern languages – having left school at 16 he thinks it's time to get the education he missed out on.

Jim has written 18 books and over 50 journal articles and has contributed chapters to eight other books. He has also written open-learning packs for international training organisations, has been a senior examiner for the Chartered Institute of Marketing, holds four real degrees and one fake one, and therefore feels somewhat irritated that he is mainly known for winning the Cardiff heat of Come Dine With Me.

Preface

Dear Reader,

First of all, thanks for buying the book! I won't have a chance to thank you in person unless you're in one of my classes, but thanks anyway... Here's some background about the book.

I wrote this book because I thought the others on the market were either far too 'academic' in tone, or were too simplistic – after all, textbooks like this are intended for grown-ups, not Primary School children. With that in mind, I have tried to give you something to think about as well as simply hold your hand through your marketing course. You'll find several features that are intended to make you think about the subject and form your own ideas: marketing is (we are told) a young discipline, so our new recruits to the marketing world should be questioning what we currently think.

This is the only major textbook which is written by just one person. I like to think this makes it consistent throughout: I have worked with other authors from time to time, and it has its pluses (not least is that it's less work, of course), but there is always the feeling that we both have to compromise a bit. Writing the whole thing myself meant that I could do it the way I wanted to, and I could use my own experience of teaching the subject to beginners to make it more lively.

I have tried to avoid all the usual case studies most marketing books use – cases and examples are taken from all over the world, and mostly I have avoided using American multinational corporations: we all know who they are and what they do, so it is probably more interesting to hear about small businesses, firms which aren't in the public eye, and companies which produce something more entertaining than soft drinks and hamburgers. All of the cases and examples I have used can be found on-line, if you want to know more: you might also check out the business press for further information.

I have also focused on services as much as physical products. As I explain in the book, nowadays there isn't much to choose between them as far as marketing is concerned, but in any case it is likely that you will be working for a service company (and probably a small business, at that) when you graduate. Of course, it's possible that you are studying marketing simply because you are really fascinated by it – but most business students study because they want a decent job at the end of it. This book is intended to help you with that noble aim.

Luckily, marketing is inherently interesting. Maybe it's because we're all consumers, maybe it's because marketing is about people, maybe it's because a lot of it is counter-intuitive. Some people study it because they think it will be some kind of instant passport to business success – outsiders often think marketers are some kind of modern-day sorcerers – but there I have to disappoint you. We can't make people buy stuff they don't want, we can only aim to offer them something they will want, and make sure they know about it and know where to get it.

Anyway, all that is in the book. I hope you enjoy it – it's supposed to be fun, honest – and that it helps you get where you want to be. There's a website and all kinds of stuff to help you remember what's in there, feel free to use it: finally, good luck with studying and (more importantly) good luck with your future career in marketing, wherever it takes you.

Jim Blythe

Acknowledgements

I would like to acknowledge the people who have helped me in writing this book. First, my friends and colleagues at Sage, Matt and Amy in particular, for their patience and support – in particular for remaining positive about me and the book during the difficult times. Second, my colleagues at the University of Glamorgan, University of Plymouth and University of Westminster for help, advice, friendship and practical guidance. Third, my wife, Sue, for bringing me tea and calming me down. Finally, I would like to thank my many students. Some were excellent scholars who asked me difficult questions and made me think, some were terrible scholars who made me work hard, some were 'class comedians' who made me laugh. Wherever you are and whatever you are doing, thanks for being such fun to work with!

Publisher's acknowledgements

The publishers would like to extend their warmest thanks to the following individuals for their invaluable feedback on the second edition and comments on draft material for the third edition.

Seamus Allison, Nottingham Business School
Adrian Bull, University of Lincoln
Rosemary Burnley, University Of Bedfordshire
Paula Durkan, University of Ulster
Al Halborg, Coventry University
Clare Halfpenny, Manchester Metropolitan University
Jan Jensen, University of Southern Denmark
Sotiris Lalaounis, University of Exeter Business School
Hannu Malkonen, University of Turku
Julie McKeown, Aberystwyth University
Raju Mulye, RMIT University
Natalie Staub, Middlesex University
Lindsay Williams, Oxford Brookes University

Guided tour

Learning objectives Highlight everything you should know or understand by the end of the chapter.

Real-life marketing Relates the chapter topic to examples from the real world to help you link theory to practice.

Preview case study Opens each chapter to contextualise what you're about to read and get you thinking about the topic through setting up a real world example.

Margin definitions Help you spot the key terms from the chapter and gives a short explanation for quick revision.

Think outside this box! Encourages you to develop your critical thinking skills, these short chatty asides offer you reflective challenges to move beyond accepted wisdom.

Summary/Key points Covers all the essential information from each chapter and summarises what you have learnt in bullet-points.

Marketing in a changing world Offers up-to-date examples of topical issues and debates in marketing practice that will help you to remain cutting edge.

Case study revisited Provides opportunity to test your learning against the preview case and read the outcome of the example.

Case study Provides yet another real world example and provides concluding questions to test your knowledge.

Further reading Suggests titles for further reading to enhance your knowledge and achieve an even better grade!

Review questions Help you test your understanding of what you have just read and provide a useful revision tool.

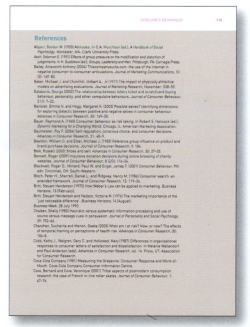

References Allow you to see what sources the author has drawn on to write the chapter and gives one example of how to provide academic references.

Companion website

Visit this website to access a wide variety of additional and very useful online resources that accompany this textbook: **www.sagepub.co.uk/blythe3e**

For lecturers:

- PowerPoint(TM) slides per chapter featuring all the key figures and diagrams from the textbook
- Instructor's manual featuring teaching notes per chapter to accompany the textbook
- Exam testbank of questions
- Guide to designing a course on marketing
- Answers to the online exercises for students

For students:

- Videos and podcasts about marketing
- Marketing employability resources and advice
- Extra case studies in addition to those in the textbook
- Guide to writing a marketing plan
- Online exercises per chapter
- Interactive multiple choice questions per chapter
- Interactive flashcards for key terms in marketing
- Pinterest page featuring useful weblinks to ads, campaigns, etc.
- RSS feed incorporating trade magazines, news websites, blogs, etc.

Part One

Concepts and contexts

This section is intended to lay the theoretical and conceptual groundwork for the rest of the book. Like any other business activity, marketing functions within a set of concepts and has a set of antecedents: this first part of the book seeks to outline the boundaries and constraints on both marketing practice and marketing thought.

Chapter 1 explains how theory from other disciplines has contributed to the development of marketing thought. Marketing is a hybrid discipline, and a relatively young one that is still building its body of theoretical research: marketing has grown from practice, and academics have sought to explain the workings of marketing by using theories already developed elsewhere.

Chapter 2 looks at marketing within the wider business world: the environment within which marketing operates, and the influence of the environment on marketing activities.

CHAPTER ①

Marketing: managing the exchange process

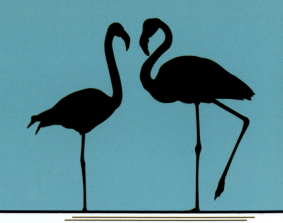

LEARNING OBJECTIVES

After reading this chapter, you should be able to:

- Compare the different definitions of marketing in common use.

- Explain marketing's role in managing the exchange process.

- Explain the importance of customers to marketing.

- Describe the relationship between marketing and other business specialisms.

- Explain the role of needs and wants in marketing.

- Describe the contribution other disciplines have made to marketing thought.

- Describe the different sub-divisions of marketing.

Introduction

Marketing is an odd kind of subject. Lecturers always have to start off by explaining what marketing is – unlike colleagues who teach engineering, accountancy, law or almost any other subject. It is a relatively new discipline, so academic debate is usually lively. It is a business function which is continually developing, with practitioners introducing new techniques and approaches at a rate that would be unthinkable for lawyers and accountants, and difficult even for engineers and designers. It is a philosophy for orientating business strategy, and it is a co-ordinating mechanism for uniting corporate activities.

Perhaps strangely (considering the powerful role of communication in marketing) the profession has generally received a bad press. Marketing has commonly been associated in people's minds with trickery and even outright lies, and there is a commonly-held perception that marketing is about persuading people to buy things they do not need or want. In fact, these criticisms are unfair: marketing is about creating value, not creating needs, and is concerned with creating and retaining customers. The ideal situation for any marketer is that customers return regularly and buy again and again – a situation that is unlikely to occur if the customers did not feel they had been fairly treated in the first place. It is well known that it is cheaper to keep an existing customer than it is to recruit a new one, and research shows that it is up to six times more expensive to recruit than to retain (Rosenberg and Czepeil 1983). Long-term customer satisfaction can only happen if the organisation offers value for money – not necessarily cheapness, but good value.

Marketing is therefore concerned with providing people with products and services which work effectively, continue to work effectively in the longer term, and are offered at a fair price. With this in mind, marketers act at the interface between the organisation and its customers. They need to co-ordinate the organisation's activities with the needs of customers, and to communicate the company's offerings to its target groups. This chapter outlines the development of marketing, and the contributions that have been made by other disciplines.

Preview case study: Pimlico Plumbers

When Charlie Mullins was only 9 years old he decided he wanted to be a plumber. He noticed that the local plumber where he lived was well-respected, had a great lifestyle, and (perhaps most importantly) had money. So Charlie began playing truant from school so he could help the plumber. When he left school at 15 with no qualifications he became apprenticed to a plumber and, within ten years, in 1979, armed only with a bag of tools and a great deal of confidence, he set up Pimlico Plumbers.

His aim from the outset was to do away with the traditional perception of plumbers: plumbers have a reputation for turning up late in a rusty van, wearing dirty overalls, and overcharging for the job. Charlie requires his team of plumbers to wear smart uniforms; they drive VW Transporters, and are required to put customer service at the top of their priorities. They are certainly not the cheapest plumbing company around – but as anybody who as waited in all day for a plumber who doesn't arrive can tell you, it often works out cheaper to pay more, and get reliability.

The company operates several BMW motorbikes, which have improved the response time on emergency call-outs. Although the bikes are not used by the plumbers themselves, they can deliver spare parts rapidly when needed – this prevents the need for another visit by the plumber, with all the associated inconvenience for the customer.

Charlie is known for being direct and outspoken – having left school at 15, he has no formal education but he has honed his business skills by being determined and by doing the job. He admits that leaving at 15 might have been a mistake – he says he should have left at 14 instead. In common with other self-made entrepreneurs such as Richard Branson and Anita Roddick, he is a skilled publicist: the vans all have plumbing-related number plates (BOG 1, B1DET, and so forth) and he is often in the news. Richard Branson is, in fact, one of his customers – as are many other celebrities.

Pimlico Plumbers charge quite a lot: if you need them to come out in the middle of the night it will cost you £200 an hour plus 20% VAT. There is no extra charge for emergency work, though, and work carried out during normal hours costs around £90 an hour – not unreasonable, for London. Pricing is entirely transparent – the rates are published on the company website, and given that the company has a response time of one hour, anywhere in London, the rates begin to look extremely reasonable.

Of course, there has been a major financial crisis in the country – so the question is, are people going to continue to be prepared to pay a premium price for a premium product?

Definitions of marketing

Unlike accountancy or the legal profession, marketing still needs to define its remit to non-marketers. There are several definitions of marketing in current use, and each suffers from some weaknesses: a universally-agreed definition of what marketing is has not yet been achieved.

American marketing guru Philip Kotler defines marketing as follows (Kotler et al. 2008: 7):

Marketing is a social and managerial process by which individuals and groups obtain what they need and want through creating and exchanging products and value with others.

This definition includes the concept of **value**, which is an important aspect of marketing. Value is the relationship between what is paid and what is received, and can be increased or reduced by marketing activities. For example, marketers can include an extra quantity of the product (10% extra free) as a way of increasing value for the customer, or (more profitably) might add an extra feature which costs the firm very little but which greatly increases the value for the customer. The problem with Kotler's definition is that it tries to include all human exchange processes, and does not differentiate between the buyer and the seller. This makes the definition very broad, and some might argue that the definition is too broad to be of much use in deciding what is marketing and what is not. For example, Kotler is apparently arguing that a parent who offers a child a trip to the zoo in exchange for tidying up his room is engaged in marketing, and (more importantly) that the child himself is also engaged in marketing. This would strike many people as being somewhat odd.

Value The benefit a customer obtains from a product.

Another aspect of the Kotler definition is the use of the terms '**need**' and '**want**'. To most non-marketers, a need is something that is essential to survival, whereas a want is something that is no more than a passing fancy. For marketers, these definitions are inadequate because there are so many products that are essential to some people, are luxuries to others, and actually dangerous for still others. For example, diabetics need insulin in order to survive, but for non-diabetics an injection of insulin could easily prove fatal. Even for the same individual, a product might be essential for survival at one time, but a luxury at another. At the extreme, if one were starving then a plate of caviar might be essential to life, but in a restaurant it would be a luxury. This is not inherently a problem with the Kotler definition, but such definitions of terms need to be addressed if the Kotler definition is to be understood and applied.

Need A perceived lack of something.

Want A specific satisfier for a need.

The Chartered Institute of Marketing uses the following definition:

Marketing is the management process which identifies, anticipates, and supplies customer requirements efficiently and profitably. (www.getin2marketing.com/discover/what-is-marketing)

This definition tries to capture a somewhat complex set of ideas concisely. The concept of putting the **customer** at the centre of the business strategy is key to marketing, and the definition also includes the idea that we are interested not in any and every customer, but only those whose needs can be satisfied profitably. Identifying customer needs and supplying products and services that satisfy those needs covers a wide range of activities from **market research** through to new product development. The definition also says that marketing is a management process; in other words it requires planning and analysis, resources, investment of money and time, and monitoring and evaluation.

Customer One who decides on payment for a product.

Market research Investigations intended to improve knowledge about customers and competitors.

On the other hand, the definition has several weaknesses. First, there is a branch of marketing which deals with non-profit organisations such as charities or government departments. Few people would argue that a campaign against child abuse carried out by the NSPCC or an anti-smoking advertising campaign carried out by the Department of Health are not marketing activities, yet they are outside the scope of the CIM definition because they are not profit-orientated. Second, the definition excludes other stakeholders such as employees and shareholders. In each case, marketers have an input in communicating with, and meeting the needs of, these groups. Third, the people whose needs are being met are not always customers – for example, a mother who buys football boots for her 10-year-old son is a customer, but it is not her needs that are being met (except in the limited sense that she needs to be regarded as a kind and generous mother).

Another commonly quoted definition is that provided by the American Marketing Association, as follows:

> *Marketing is the process of planning and executing the conception, pricing, promotion, and distribution of ideas, goods and services to create exchange and satisfy individual and organisational objectives.* (www.marketingpower.com/aboutama/pages/definitionofmarketing.aspx)

This definition agrees that marketing is a management process, and that it is about satisfying individual objectives: it also introduces the idea that marketing is about creating exchange, and that it is about meeting organisational objectives, whether this means profit or not.

The definition still suffers from a narrow focus, however. For example, marketers are often concerned about competitors, but neither of the foregoing definitions addresses this. Companies and other organisations might do an excellent job of meeting customer needs at a fair price, but still fail simply because rivals offer even better products or even better prices – or, more confusing still, might offer a product that is actually worse and more expensive, but is offered at a more convenient location or time. For example, a traveller arriving late at night in a strange town is not in a position to shop around for hotels and will probably stay at the first one with an available room.

Another definition, which includes this idea, is offered by Jobber (2003: 5):

> *Marketing is the process of achieving corporate goals through meeting and exceeding customer needs better than the competition.*

Stakeholders People who are impacted by corporate activities.

The implication of this is that all the activities of the company should be geared towards meeting customer needs rather than those of other **stakeholders**. This is not necessarily unreasonable: after all, without customers there is no business. Peter Drucker (1999) stated:

> *Because the purpose of business is to create and keep customers, it has only two central functions: marketing and innovation. The basic function of marketing is to attract and retain customers at a profit.*

From the viewpoint of the student, studying marketing is complicated somewhat by the lack of a clear definition of what marketing is. It is obviously difficult to know what to study if one does not know what the boundaries of the subject are. To clarify things a little, it may be useful to consider the development of marketing as an academic subject, and also to consider the contributions made to it by other, older disciplines.

The marketing concept

The philosophical idea underlying all marketing thought is that corporate success comes from satisfying customer needs. The idea of placing customers at the centre of everything the company does is basic to marketing thought: this idea of customer centrality is the key concept in marketing. Recent research has shown that there is a positive association between customer satisfaction and shareholder value: this is a clear vindication of the marketing concept (Anderson et al. 2004).

The marketing concept did not arrive fully formed. It is popularly supposed to have developed through a series of business orientations, as shown in Table 1.1. Some marketers have moved the concept a step further on by referring to societal marketing. Societal marketing includes the concept that companies have a responsibility for the needs of society as a whole, so should include environmental impact and the impact of their products on non-users (Kotler et al. 2008). For societal marketers, sustainability is a key issue, as well as impact assessment of the long-term results of use of the product. For example, there is an argument that car manufacturers should reduce noise pollution by making cars run quieter, but many manufacturers simply make the car more soundproof for its occupants and do not worry over much about the neighbours.

Table 1.1 Business orientations

Production orientation	A focus on manufacturing, on improving the process so as to reduce costs and increase efficiency, and on making a profit through selling large volumes of goods.
Product orientation	The focus here is on quality, and on product features. Product orientation aims to produce the best possible product with the maximum number of features.
Selling orientation	The company seeks to use aggressive and sometimes devious selling techniques to move the product. Profit comes from quick turnover and high volume.
Marketing orientation	Defining what customers want and ensuring that the company's activities are arranged in a way which will achieve customer satisfaction.

Real-life marketing: Link up with a charity

Many companies carry out charitable works, or sponsor occasional events or causes, but relatively few go the extra mile and establish a link with a charity.

If you can find a local charity whose aims fit in with your business, you could do a lot worse than form a long-term partnership. It shouldn't be too hard to find a charity that you can link in with – provided you think outside the box! Once you've established the relationship, you can offer them help with projects, give them the use of some of your facilities, maybe get your staff involved on a voluntary basis, and in return you can run joint promotions with the charity. Most charities have mailing lists – they won't give these to you, but they will almost certainly send out mailings (or e-mails) which will include some of your promotional material.

Partnering with a charity in this way improves your image, does some good for society as a whole, and helps you to promote the business at relatively little cost. The key rules for doing this successfully are:

- Choose your charity carefully. It needs to relate to your business.
- Remember it's a partnership – you have to give as well as receive.
- Never abuse the mailing list, or you will destroy the charity's carefully built reputation.

This issue has been debated by marketing academics on the grounds that marketing needs to have clear boundaries. The idea that marketing is everything, because so much human activity revolves around exchanges or the results of exchanges, is an idea that has been brought into disrepute by many academics. There are, of course, many adherents to the societal marketing concept, although it is difficult to implement in practice and few companies are in a position to adopt such an altruistic approach.

Production orientation had its beginnings at the start of the Industrial Revolution. Up until the 19th century, almost everything was hand-made and made to measure. Clothing was tailored to fit almost exactly, houses and vehicles were produced to customer specification, and relatively few items were standardised. This meant that items were relatively expensive. When machines were introduced to speed up the manufacturing process, costs dropped dramatically, so much so that prices could also be cut provided the goods could be sold rapidly. The longer the production run, the lower the costs and consequently the greater the profit: at the same time, customers were prepared to accept items that were not exactly meeting their needs, on the basis that the prices were a fraction of what they would have had to pay for the perfect, tailor-made article. For manufacturers, the key to success was therefore ever-more efficient production, but at the cost of meeting individual customers' needs.

Product orientation was a result of an oversupply of basic goods. Once everyone already owned the basic products, manufacturers needed to provide something different in order to find new customers. Better-quality products, often with more features, began to be introduced. By the late 19th century, extravagant claims were being made for products on the basis of their quality and features. Manufacturers recognised that different customers had different needs, but sought to resolve this by adding in every possible feature. The drawback is that the price of the product increases dramatically under product orientation, and customers are not always prepared to pay for features they will never use. A modern example of product orientation is the Kirby vacuum cleaner, which has a multitude of features and can clean virtually anything. The end price of the product is perhaps ten times that of a basic vacuum cleaner, a price most people are unable or unwilling to pay.

The basic difficulty with both production orientation and product orientation is that they ignore the diversity of customers and **consumers**. Customers differ from each other in terms of their needs – there is no such thing as 'the customer'.

Sales orientation assumes that people will not buy anything unless they are persuaded to do so. Sales orientation should not be confused with personal selling: salespeople do not operate on the basis of persuasion, but rather on the basis of identifying and meeting individual customers' needs.

Sales orientation, on the other hand, concentrates on the needs of the seller rather than the needs of the buyer. The assumption is that customers do not really want to spend their money, that they must be persuaded, that they will not mind being persuaded and will be happy for the salesperson to call again and persuade them some more, and that success comes through using aggressive promotional techniques.

Sales orientation is still fairly common, and often results in short-term gains. In the longer term, customers will judge the company on the quality of its products and after-sales service, and (ultimately) on value for money.

Marketing orientation means being driven by customer needs. One of the key elements of marketing orientation is that customers can be grouped according to their different needs, so that a slightly different product can be offered to each group. Differentiation (offering products that differ from each other and those of competitors) allows the company to provide for the needs of a larger group in total, because each

Production orientation The belief that corporate success comes from efficient production.

Product orientation The belief that corporate success comes from having the best product.

Consumer One who obtains the benefits from a product.
Sales orientation The belief that corporate success comes from having proactive salespeople.

Marketing orientation The belief that corporate success comes from understanding the relationships in the market.

target segment of the market is able to satisfy its needs through the purchase of the company product. The assumption is that customers actually want to satisfy their needs, and are prepared to pay money for products that do so. Using a marketing orientation to co-ordinate the firm's functions will almost always improve the firm's performance (Lyus et al. 2011).

Marketing orientation also includes the idea that customers need information about the products, advice about using the products, advice about the availability of products, and so forth. In other words, marketers believe that customer needs go beyond the basic core benefits of the product itself. For example, research has shown that American consumers no longer know how to choose fresh produce: this means that, increasingly, people seek the reassurance of a brand (even if it is the local supermarket's guarantee of quality). This has opened up opportunities for farmers and others in the food supply chain to provide the type of quality assurance modern consumers need (Stanton and Herbst 2005).

Marketing orientation also implies that customer needs are the driving force throughout the organisation. This means that everyone in the organisation, from the salespeople through to the factory workers, needs to consider customer needs at every stage. Quality control in the factory, accurate information given by telephonists and receptionists, and courteous deliveries by drivers all play a part in delivering customer value. Narver and Slater (1990) identified three components that will determine the degree to which a company is marketing-orientated: customer orientation, competitor orientation and inter-functional co-ordination.

Customer orientation is the degree to which the organisation understands its customers. The better the understanding, the better able the firm is to create value for the customers. Since value is defined by the customers and not by the firm, customer orientation means that the firm can make better offers to customers and thus receive better payments in return. Research shows that at least some consumers regard consumption as being like voting – they show approval of companies by buying their products, and avoid companies of which they disapprove (Shaw et al. 2006). Since customers manipulate products and service to increase their value, some marketers argue that value is co-created between the firm and its customers (Harwood and Garry 2010).

> **Customer orientation** The belief that corporate success comes from understanding and meeting customer needs.

Competitor orientation is the degree to which the company understands what other firms are offering to customers. These firms may be offering radically different products: the issue is whether the customer perceives the products as offering the same (or better) value. For example, a couple looking for a night out may compare the relative merits of cinemas, nightclubs, restaurants, bowling alleys, or theatres. Each of those companies is competing with the others, but the nightclub may only consider other nightclubs as competition, or the bowling alley may not recognise competition from the restaurant. Interestingly, people find the wide range of choice empowering in the long run – although initially a wider choice is actually frightening (Davies and Elliott 2006).

> **Competitor orientation** The belief that corporate success comes from understanding competitors.

Third, interfunctional co-ordination is the degree to which the internal structure of the organisation and the attitudes of its members combine to deliver marketing orientation. There is no point in marketing managers developing good ideas for improving the company's offering to its customers if the employees of the firm are prevented from delivering the promises, or are unwilling to do so.

Of course these three components can be broken down into smaller elements. Figure 1.1 shows the main elements in marketing orientation.

In order to achieve a marketing orientation, firms need to be close to their customers and consumers. For some companies this is not a problem, because they have direct contact with the ultimate consumers. Service industries such as airlines,

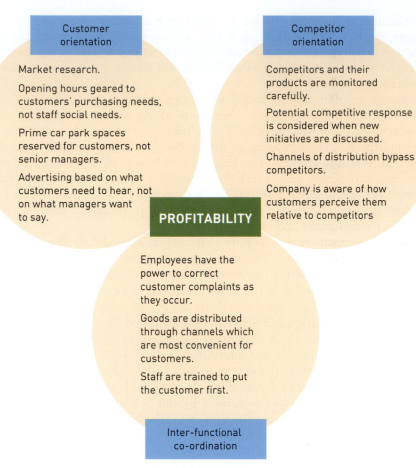

Figure 1.1   Elements in marketing orientation

End user The person or company who uses the product, without selling it on or converting it into something else.

restaurants and hairdressers have direct contact with the **end users** of their products, and can fine-tune the delivery to meet customer needs. Other industries such as the food canning industry have contact with their customers (the wholesalers and retailers who handle their products) but do not have contact with the end consumers. These companies may use market research to find out what consumers actually need, or may rely on the retailers to understand the customers and pass on their requirements.

One of the main problems in becoming marketing orientated is that other departments within the firm will find it creates conflicts. For example, the firm's marketers may identify a group of consumers who have a need for a particular set of product features. This may cause the firm's engineers a problem in developing a product with those features. Table 1.2 illustrates some of the conflicts that occur when a firm needs to consider the needs of consumers.

These conflicts can be helped by explaining the reasons for adopting a customer focus. The problem is that some people will interpret customer focus as meaning that the company should give the customers everything they want – low prices, high quality, perfect after-sales service and so forth. This is not actually what the marketing concept says: to give everything away would mean losing money, which of course is not the way to run a business. The marketing concept implies that organisations should offer a selected group of customers everything necessary to

Table 1.2   Internal conflicts with non-marketers

Situation	Problem	Resolution
Credit control	The customers may want longer credit terms. This will cause cashflow problems, which creates problems for the finance director.	Allow customers to pay extra for the credit. Marketing is not about giving customers everything they want: it is about selling customers everything they want.
New product development	Each customer wants slightly different features, but production economics rely on long production runs.	Identify groups of customers with similar needs. If the group is big enough to support a large production run, there is no problem: if the group is small, but is prepared to pay more for a custom product, again there is no problem.
Delivery service levels	Customers may want regular small deliveries (for example, car parts for small garages). This means that delivery vehicles are sometimes running with small loads, or even empty.	Arrange for a 'return load' pick-up system, or subcontract the deliveries to a parcel delivery company which can deliver to many small firms. In the motor industry, there are specialist firms called motor factors which do this.
Handling complaints	Customers may not always be satisfied with the firm and its services, which creates a problem for everyone. Some firms only respond when sued, relying on the contract to cover themselves against dissatisfied customers.	Complaints can be repeated elsewhere: word-of-mouth is a powerful medium for destroying a firm's reputation. On the other hand, research shows that complaints which are handled entirely to the customer's satisfaction actually increase customer loyalty and encourage positive word of mouth (Coca Cola Company 1981).
Purchasing of supplies	Purchasing departments can become overly-concerned with price to the exclusion of other considerations. Standardisation of components makes inputs cheaper, but reduces flexibility.	The growth of relationship marketing (see Chapter 11) and **just-in-time** purchasing has helped to bring marketers and purchasers closer together. An understanding of the reasons for retaining flexibility will, of course, help in this context.

Just in time   A supply chain management system in which the purchaser does not maintain an inventory, but instead switches responsibility for this to the supplier.

meet their needs (within the specific product category) because this is the most effective way of justifying the higher prices necessary to provide the product and make a profit.

Involving non-marketing colleagues in the process by sharing customer information with them appears to be the most powerful tool a marketer has for moving the organisation towards a marketing orientation (Korhonen-Sande 2010). Research and development managers will have applied customer information to their thinking when they were given the opportunity to access it, especially if it is integrated into the other information they have available.

There is evidence to show that satisfied customers are prepared to pay more for the products they buy – and why should this not be so? Better to pay a little more for something that meets a need than buy a cheap product that does not work (Homburg et al. 2005). Perhaps surprisingly, there is evidence to show that engineers are generally positive towards marketing and marketers (Shaw and Shaw 2003).

Think outside this box!

Some writers have taken the view that all employees are marketers now, because everybody in the organisation has a responsibility for customer satisfaction. The problem with this view is a conceptual one: if everybody in the organisation is a marketer, what role remains for the marketing managers? Presumably marketing must have some boundaries!

Customer needs

Customers in general have a set of generic needs, which marketers seek to fulfil. These are shown in Table 1.3. Customer needs therefore go beyond the product itself, and also (since customers are human beings) go beyond the simple physical needs of food, clothing and shelter.

Table 1.3   Customer needs

Type of need	Example
Current product needs	All customers for a given product have needs based on the features and benefits of the product. This also relates to the quantities they are likely to buy, and any problems they might experience with the products.
Future needs	Predicting future demand is a key function of market research. Typically, this is carried out by talking to potential and actual customers and making an assessment of likely purchase quantities. Like any other predictions of the future, the results are unlikely to be perfect, but sales forecasting is essential if resources are to be put in place to ensure that supplies are available to meet demand. Equally, over-optimistic forecasts can result in over-supply and consequent problems in getting rid of excess product. Selling off excess product at cut prices generates problems beyond the immediate loss of profit: damage to the reputation of the brand may continue for years afterwards.
Desired pricing levels	Customers will naturally want to buy products at the lowest possible prices. Pricing is not straightforward for marketers: it is not simply a matter of adding up what it costs to supply the product, adding on a profit margin and then selling the product. Customers will only pay what they feel is reasonable for the product, basing this on what they perceive to be the benefits they will get from buying the product. Customers will therefore not pay more than the 'fair' price, and charging them less is simply giving away profit. There is more on this in Chapter 14.
Information needs	Customers need to know about a product and understand what benefits will accrue from buying it. They also need to know what the drawbacks are of owning the product, but this information is unlikely to be provided by the organisation. For major purchases, customers will seek this information elsewhere. Information needs to be presented in an appropriate place and format, and should be accurate.
Product availability	Products need to be in the right place at the right time. This means that suppliers need to recruit the appropriate intermediaries (wholesalers and retailers) and to ensure efficient transport systems to move the products to the point of sale in a way that ensures they arrive in good condition, but at the same time in as economical a manner as possible.

Think outside this box!

How do we define need? Is it something without which life would be impossible? Is water a need? Maybe – but what about people who drink orange juice, beer, tea, or even Coca-Cola, but rarely drink a plain glass of water? And if water is so essential, does that mean that Evian or Perrier are essential to life?

Perhaps beer is a luxury. But beer is often the basis of a person's social life, and people who have no social life go mad, or at least a little odd. Defining whether a product is a need or a want or a luxury is really not very easy – what is a luxury to one person is a necessity to another, because people are not simply driven by their animal needs. In fact, in modern, wealthy, Western nations very few people have to be concerned about their physical needs. Most of us are much more concerned about our social and psychological needs – which is why we buy fashionable clothes, or go to the latest movies, or take up a demanding hobby.

People need many things apart from survival, and in the Western world people are wealthy enough that they can afford to meet higher-level needs.

The cliché of an artist starving in a garret is a prime example: people will often go without the basic physical necessities of life in order to self-actualise or meet aesthetic needs. A graphic instance of this occurred in Nazi concentration camps during the Second World War, when prisoners would sometimes exchange food for clothing in order to maintain appearances (Klein 2003). Likewise, a homeless person might well seek out the company of others (thus meeting a social need) without knowing where the next meal is coming from, or having a bed for the night. Having said that, it seems likely that the main preoccupation of a homeless person will be finding food and shelter, even if other needs are met along the way, and that a wealthy person is unlikely to spend much time thinking about whether their survival is threatened.

What marketers do

Marketing management is responsible for handling specific aspects of the marketing function. In practice, these functions may appear in departments other than the marketing department as such, but they are nonetheless marketing functions since they directly address customer needs. These aspects are known collectively as the marketing mix.

Several models exist for defining the marketing mix, and each model has drawbacks. One of the earliest attempts to define the mix came from McCarthy (1987 [1964]), and defined the marketing mix in terms of product, price, place and promotion. This conveniently pigeonholed everything into four categories (all starting with P) but was an incomplete picture. The 4P model has been widely criticised, not least because it has an internal orientation (it refers exclusively to the company, not the external marketplace) and it lacks personalisation (Constantinides 2006). In 1981, Booms and Bitner added three more Ps (people, process and physical evidence) to encompass the extra elements present in service industries, which after all represent the bulk of products in a modern society. This 7P model has been widely adopted, not so much for its accuracy (because like most models it omits a great deal) but because it is easy to remember and understand.

Product is the bundle of benefits the supplier offers to the purchaser. The particular set of benefits on offer will appeal to a specific group of consumers: it is extremely unlikely that any product will appeal to everyone. Even products such as Coca-Cola,

Product A bundle of benefits.

which is sold worldwide and is the world's most recognised brand name, has only a minority share of the soft drinks market. Many people simply do not like it, or think it is too expensive, or prefer other drinks which meet their needs better. Attempts to create a 'perfect' product that suits everybody are likely to result in over-complex, over-expensive products, which is why product orientation has fallen into disrepute.

Price is the total cost to the customer of buying the product. It therefore goes beyond the simple monetary costs: customers also consider the difficulty of purchase, the cost of ownership of the product, and even the 'embarrassment' factor of owning the wrong brand. Some products have psychological associations which customers find costly. However, even the financial cost of purchase is by no means simple, because there is a complex relationship between money, price and value. Price has a strategic dimension for marketers, in that there is (for most products) a relationship between price and sales volume. The lower the price, the greater the volume (in general). On the other hand, there is also a reverse relationship between price and perceived quality (the higher the price, the greater the quality). Balancing these different elements of price is a function of marketing management, not a function of financial management. Price is a fairly flexible element of the mix, since it is relatively easy to change prices in response to demand fluctuations, but continually changing prices can lead to confusion (and even suspicion) on the part of customers.

Place is the location where the exchange takes place. This may be a retail store, it may be a catalogue, it may be a restaurant, or it may be a **website**. Deciding on the appropriate place for the exchange is not merely a matter of moving goods around (although physical distribution is one aspect of the process) but is rather a strategic issue. The decisions revolve around making it as easy as possible for customers to find the goods and make the purchase, and also using channels that give the appropriate image for the product. For example, retailing a product through discount stores gives a completely different impression from retailing the same product through exclusive department stores. A final issue in place decisions is the problem of power relationships in the distribution channels. In the food industry, the major supermarkets essentially control the market, with farmers and food processing firms having to accept whatever conditions are applied by the retailers. In other industries (notably the fast-food industry), the producers have the upper hand, with retailers being compelled to accept the terms laid down.

Promotion is such a large part of marketing that it is often mistaken for the whole of marketing. Promotion encompasses all the communications activities of marketing: **advertising**, **public relations**, sales promotions, personal selling, and so forth. Promotion is not simply a hard sell, however: it is a way of meeting customers' information needs, at least in part. It is also, to an extent, persuasive in that most marketing communications emphasise the good aspects of owning products and downplay the bad aspects. In recent years promotion strategies have been thrown into turmoil by the Internet: the changes have been far-reaching, and the full implications have still to be assessed.

People are crucial to success in marketing, particularly in service industries. Customers in a restaurant are not simply buying a meal: they are buying the skill of the chef in preparing and presenting the food, the service of the waiters in delivering the food, and even the quality of the washer-up in ensuring clean cutlery and crockery. The same is true in other industries, because companies do not buy or sell products – a company is a legal fiction. People buy and sell products, sometimes on behalf of organisations, and by so doing go some way towards meeting their own needs.

Process is the set of activities that lead to delivery of the product benefits. In service industries the process of delivery makes a difference to the benefits obtained. For example, consider the process of going out for a hamburger. In a corner take-away the hamburger will be cooked to order (which means waiting a few minutes) and will

---

Price The exchange that the customer makes in order to obtain a product.

Place The location where the exchange takes place.

Website A page on the Internet designed for and dedicated to an organisation or individual.

Promotion Marketing communications.

Advertising A paid message inserted in a medium.

Public relations The practice of creating goodwill towards an organisation.

People The individuals involved in providing customer satisfaction.

Process The set of activities that together produce customer satisfaction.

be eaten either standing up in the shop or on the street walking somewhere else. The process is quick, but basic, and is useful to someone who likes freshly-cooked food but does not at present have much time for a meal. Further up the scale of service would be a hamburger chain such as McDonald's or Burger King, where the food is not as fresh but is delivered quickly and can be eaten either on the street or sitting down at clean but basic tables. This process meets the needs of someone who is in a hurry, and likes reliable food, but is not too worried that the burger might have been sitting under a warming grill for several minutes. Next up the scale might be a Hard Rock Café, where the burgers are freshly cooked and served by a waiter or waitress, where the ambience is exciting and interesting, where music is played and where the process becomes an experience. This would meet the needs of someone who has an interest in music, or is perhaps on a date or out with friends. Finally, an expensive restaurant might have waiters in jackets, soft lights and soft music, a wine list, and silver cutlery. The hamburger is now called a Vienna steak, and would suit the needs of someone who likes to know what he is eating, but is on a special date. Note that the same person could fit into each of these categories at different times, depending on the circumstances.

Real-life marketing: Ordering food on-line

The easier you make it for people to buy from you, the more likely people are to do so. Nowhere is this more true than in fast-food deliveries. If you're in the fast-food business, or in fact in any business where you deliver to customers, you're generally dealing with people who are either tired, or very busy, or possibly very lazy. The easier you make it for them, the better.

The idea comes from on-line companies such as Hungry House and JustEat. These companies operate as on-line clearing-houses for hot food deliveries. People can order on-line through the Hungry House website, can browse recommendations from other users, and can pay on-line so there is no need to part with cash. All the menus are on-line, and customers can even order from different outlets – so if someone fancies a pizza, but everybody else wants curry, the orders can be placed at the same time (though they won't necessarily arrive at the same time).

This has a lot of advantages. First, people who are tired often don't want to talk to anybody. Second, you can change your menus easily without having to reprint everything – and you won't have to waste time explaining to prospective diners that what they want is no longer available. Third, you will spend a lot less time on the telephone because the orders come through automatically and can be dealt with more easily. Fourth, the possibility of writing down the order wrongly is eliminated.

For this to work, you need to follow these rules:

- The 'website must be interactive, and as user-friendly as possible.
- People should still be able to order in the conventional way, by telephone or by arriving at your store.
- Store all orders in case of disputes – if you can send them to the delivery people's mobile telephones, so much the better.

Physical evidence The tangible proof that a service has taken place.

Physical evidence is the tangible proof that the service has been delivered. In the case of a restaurant, the food and the surroundings provide good physical evidence of the quality of the service (and probably the price, too). For an insurance company, physical evidence might be the policy documents. Physical evidence is important in services marketing because often (as in insurance) the customer is buying a promise. The policy document is therefore a reassurance that the insurance actually exists. The reverse can also be the case: the lack of physical evidence of a booking on a ticket-less airline reassures the customer that every possible cost has been cut, while the physical evidence of a modern aircraft assures the customer that essential costs have been met.

Mixing the 7Ps in the correct way should help the organisation to achieve a competitive advantage, which is of course essential to any business. However, the concept of the marketing mix has been criticised. First, the mix has been criticised on the grounds that it implies a set of sharp boundaries between its elements. In fact, each element impinges on every other element to some extent – as mentioned above, the retailer in which the product is sold gives an impression of the product, which is presumably part of its promotion. Likewise, the process of delivery of a hamburger provides different benefits in each case, so is presumably part of the product. Examples of other cross-overs abound.

Internal marketing The practice of creating goodwill among employees.

Second, the mix has been criticised because it does not cover everything that marketers do. There is nothing about **internal marketing** (the establishment of relationships and exchanges within the organisation). There is nothing about competition. There is nothing about managing long-term relationships with customers.

Third, the marketing mix concept implies that marketing is something that is done to customers, rather than something that seeks co-operation and interaction between customers and the organisation.

Fourth, the mix is almost entirely focused on consumers, whereas in fact the bulk of marketing activity is carried out between businesses (Raffia and Ahmed 1992). This business-to-business marketing is perhaps less well-researched and generally attracts less attention because it operates at a lower profile. In business-to-business marketing, success does not come from manipulation of the marketing mix components, but from establishing long-term relationships between the firms concerned. If these relationships are strong enough, they act as a barrier to entry for other suppliers (Ford et al. 1986).

These criticisms do not mean that the model is of no use. All models are an abstract of reality, and so do not give the whole picture. The model does help in considering issues or planning ways of managing the business, but it should not be treated as if it provides all the answers.

 ## Think outside this box!

Models often seem to be flawed. Any model can be criticised – and often is! So why do we use them at all? Is it possible to create the perfect model?

A model is an abstraction of reality, a simplification intended to make reality easier to understand. Therefore some things have to be left out, which means there will be gaps in our understanding, and the model may not always be easily applied in practice. We all know that a model railway is a good way of seeing how railways operate – the tracks, the carriages, the signal boxes, the points, and so forth can all be made up as miniature replicas of the real thing. But if we need to go from London to Glasgow, we need a real train!

Antecedents of marketing

Marketing has developed as a result of inputs from many other disciplines. Essentially, marketing is an applied social science, and therefore it owes a great deal to other social sciences.

ECONOMICS

An early examination of the mechanics of exchange processes came from Adam Smith. Smith was the first writer to state that the customer is king, and he outlined the law of supply and demand, which he thought explained how prices are fixed. Essentially, as the supply of a given product increases, the suppliers need to reduce prices in order to sell their goods: as the supply shrinks, customers must offer more in order to obtain the product. Higher prices will attract more suppliers into the marketplace, until the price stabilises at a point where supply equals demand, and likewise lower prices will force some suppliers out of the market.

Although this is a useful concept, it makes several assumptions that are unlikely to be true in the real world. First, it assumes that all the suppliers are providing identical products, whereas in the real world suppliers go to considerable trouble to differentiate their products from competing products. Second, the model assumes that consumers will be prepared to shop around, and will know where the cheaper products are available. Third, it assumes that no supplier (or customer) has sufficient 'clout' to affect the price, which is of course unlikely. Some examples do exist of this type of market, however: international money markets and stock exchanges are two such examples.

Smith also contributed the concept that different countries have what he called natural advantages in producing some goods, and that therefore international trade could only be advantageous since each country could produce what it could most easily and cheaply produce, and therefore maximum efficiency would result. The general principle that fair exchange leaves both parties better off is fundamental to marketing thinking: if it were not the case, trade would be impossible since one or other party would not go ahead.

Another useful contribution by economists is the concept of **elasticity of demand**. This model says that the demand for different products is affected by price to differing extents. For example, the overall demand for wedding rings or artificial limbs is unaffected by price (even though individual manufacturers' wedding rings or wooden

Elasticity of demand The degree to which people's propensity to buy a product is affected by price changes.

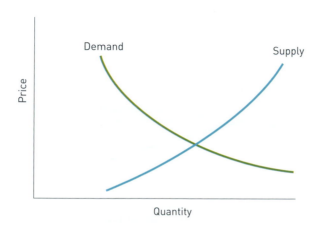

Figure 1.2 Supply and demand

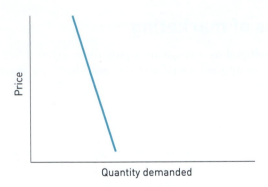

Figure 1.3   Inelastic demand curve

legs might be). Such products are said to be price inelastic. On the other hand, other products are affected seriously by very small changes in price: these are said to be price elastic. Price elasticity of demand affects the degree to which marketers can set prices relative to their competitors, and also in an absolute sense relative to other products.

An interesting point arising from the price elasticity concept is that there is no product that is totally price inelastic. In other words, there is no known product which people would buy no matter what the price charged. This is important because it means there is no single product that can truly be classed as a necessity of life – if such a product existed, it would be totally price inelastic. The corollary to this is that no product (presumably) exists that can be defined entirely as a luxury, since such a product would be totally price elastic – even a tiny rise in price would prevent any sales, since no one actually needs the product. The idea that people will not buy things that do not meet their needs is central to the marketing concept.

Economists also contributed to competition theory, which is covered in more detail in Chapter 2.

Economic choice The inability to spend the same money twice.

Finally, economists have contributed the concept of the **economic choice**. This means that money which is spent on one thing cannot be spent on another – so an individual is forced to make choices. The decision to buy one thing can be translated as a decision not to buy something else. This means that competition is by no means clear-cut: marketers are not only competing with other firms in the same industry, they are also (in effect) competing with all other ways in which consumers can spend their money. If mortgages rise, spending on consumer durables will fall, for example.

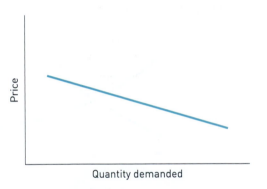

Figure 1.4   Elastic demand curve

Think outside this box!

In recent years many former government-owned enterprises have been privatised and competing organisations have been set up. In the UK, the telephone system, electricity and gas production and delivery, and even the railways were all former government monopolies, but are now privately owned and operate in competitive markets.

Yet surely all this means is that there is duplication of effort, and a degree of confusion for consumers. Train tickets are only valid on some routes, there are several competing companies providing directory enquiries, people are unable to take their telephone numbers with them if they move house, and so forth.

On the other hand, advocates of privatisation say that duplication of effort is better than no effort at all, which is too often what happens in nationalised industries. And to be fair, prices for energy have fallen, most public telephone boxes work now, and some rail companies have been investing in some very impressive rolling stock.

The problem with most economic models is that unrealistic assumptions are made for the purpose of simplifying the model. For example, economists often assume that buyers are rational, that consumers have perfect knowledge of the market, that people act in ways that maximise their welfare, and that all **brands** are essentially interchangeable. In fact none of these assumptions stands up to close scrutiny.

Brand The focus of marketing activities.

SOCIOLOGY

Sociology is the study of human beings in groups. Group behaviour is extremely important to human beings: how our friends and family see us, what we have to do to be effective employees, and what we feel about our place in society colours all our behaviour, including our purchase behaviour.

Human beings are all members of several groups, and in general wish to be part of one or more groups. In order to join or remain in a given group, individuals need to act in particular ways, and this often means buying the right items or the right services. Some examples of groups are family, friends, work colleagues, clubs or societies, and even those groups to which we belong by reason of gender or race. There are also groups to which we do not belong, and would not want to belong: for example, most of us would not want to be thought of as stupid, naïve or uneducated so we may go out of our way to learn about some subjects in order to appear knowledgeable.

An understanding of how these groups operate is essential to understanding consumer behaviour: there is more on this in Chapter 4.

PSYCHOLOGY

Psychology is the study of thought patterns of individuals. Like sociology, the contribution to marketing lies in the area of consumer behaviour. Such areas as perception, learning, motivation, attitude formation and attitude change, and our involvement with brands and products are basic to our understanding of purchasing behaviour.

Because psychology is concerned with the internal workings of the mind, it has much to tell us about communications and about how people develop relationships with the products they buy. Making those relationships more relevant and important is the role of marketing. Again, there is more on this topic in Chapter 4.

ANTHROPOLOGY

This is the study of human cultures. A culture is a set of shared beliefs, which includes religion, language, customs, child-rearing practices, gender roles and so forth. Anthropologists study the way these shared values and beliefs colour behaviour, and marketers can use this information to predict ways in which people will respond to product offerings.

Culture is particularly important in international marketing, where products are crossing cultural barriers. For example, McDonald's hamburgers are made from mutton in India, where the cow is sacred to Hindus.

All three behavioural sciences (psychology, sociology and anthropology) have considerable overlaps with each other. They mainly contribute to marketing in the areas of buyer behaviour (understanding how people make purchasing decisions and act on them) and marketing communications (understanding how people interpret and remember messages).

CORPORATE STRATEGY

Strategy is about positioning the organisation correctly for its survival and growth. Strategic thinking comes originally from military management, and much of the terminology used is the same as that of warfare. Marketers talk about campaigns, targets, capturing market share and so forth, but in fact much corporate strategy involves placing the organisation in a niche in the market where it will not upset potential competitors and attract retaliation.

The marketing strategy clearly needs to find a place within the corporate strategy, but for marketing-orientated firms the marketing strategy actually is the corporate strategy.

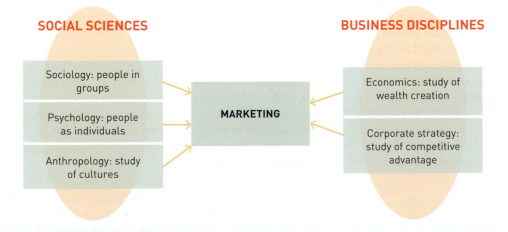

Figure 1.5 Antecedents of marketing

The scope of marketing

Marketing divides into a number of different applications, each of which will be examined in more detail in later chapters of this book. Because marketing embraces such a broad spectrum of human activity (indeed, as we saw earlier some say that marketing covers virtually everything that humans do) it is inevitable that different branches of applied marketing will emerge.

CONSUMER MARKETING

Consumer marketing is concerned with the exchange processes that take place at the end of the supply chain, at the point at which the goods and services are used up and disposed of. Because we are all consumers, this is the area that impinges on our daily lives the most, and (for many people) appears to be the whole of marketing. This view is bolstered by the way marketing is taught: examples taken from consumer marketing are most often used because they are easy to relate to.

Consumer marketing has also been the starting-point for the development of marketing theory. Because consumer markets are large, with many potential customers and competitors, the markets are complex and interesting. Companies in consumer markets see marketing as providing a suitable competitive edge, and have therefore embraced the marketing concept wholeheartedly.

Marketing theory owes much to the development of theories of consumer behaviour, which in turn derive from sociological and psychological theory. These theories have also been applied in areas other than consumer marketing.

INDUSTRIAL MARKETING

Industrial marketing examines earlier stages in the supply chain. Although the goods ultimately end up in the hands of consumers, products pass through many stages before arriving on the retailers' shelves. Industrial marketing is concerned with exchanges between organisations and is about supplies of raw materials, components and finished products.

Organisations with a marketing orientation are more successful than those without one (Avlonitis and Gounaris 1997). Business-to-business deals are, ultimately, driven by consumer demand, but ensuring that the needs of the customer business are met is an important stage in the process because it smooths out inefficiencies in the system and makes the process more effective. At the level of the individual organisation, the company that is best able to meet the overall needs of the customer company will get the business.

In fact, industrial marketing does not receive the attention it deserves. In terms of turnover, industrial markets overall are much bigger than consumer markets, yet have fewer customers, which means that order values are much larger. The success of industrial markets depends on the success of consumer markets, but the reverse is also the case: without an efficient and effective industrial supply chain, consumer needs cannot be met.

SERVICE MARKETING

A service product is one that is essentially intangible: examples include hairdressing, medical services, accountancy and insurance.

Some observers do not accept that there is a real difference between physical products and service products, and in some respects there are strong arguments in favour of this viewpoint. Any service product contains some tangible elements, and any physical product contains some service aspects. Since there are numerous examples of situations where a service product can substitute for a physical one and vice-versa, the distinction can seem to be an artificial one.

Vargo and Lusch (2004) took this idea a step further when they developed the concept of service-dominant logic (SDL). Traditional marketers took the view that people do not buy quarter-inch drills, but are actually buying quarter-inch holes: it is the outcome of the purchase that is of interest, not the physical product. SDL states that people are actually buying a hole-drilling service, in which the consumer and the producer co-operate in creating value (i.e. the holes). For Vargo and Lusch, someone who needs to have a hole drilled can buy a drill and do the work him- or herself, can hire a drill and again do the work, or can hire someone to come and drill the hole – but even in the final case, the consumer has to show the workman where to drill the hole, and has to specify what type of hole is needed, before any value is created. The implication is that nothing has any value until it is consumed (thus fulfilling a need), and therefore the consumer must be part of the value-creation process.

The implications of SDL for practical marketing are widespread: defining competition is only one area, but it is also the case that producers need to ensure that potential consumers are equipped with the necessary understanding of the product to be able to maximise the benefit of using it – in other words, to be effective co-creators of value. Academics are still exploring the full implications of service-dominant logic.

Marketing in a changing world: The growth of services

Services are certainly the big growth area. Although the UK's manufacturing output has risen by 250% since the end of the Second World War, services activity has risen even more, so that by 2013 it represented 73% of the UK economy.

Services are likely to continue to grow simply because we already have too much stuff and don't need to make any more. Service industries are generally difficult to automate, so they will employ a lot of people, and they provide the kind of experiential benefits people are looking for.

As we continue to earn a living by holding doors open for each other there may be a reduction in the emphasis on manufacturing: the problem for marketers is that the distinction between physical products and services is becoming increasingly blurred as manufacturers differentiate themselves from competitors by adding service elements, and service providers offer more physical goods to add value.

Having said that, there are differences in the way that intangible aspects of a product need to be marketed, and there are different information needs on the part of consumers. The service sector is, in most Western countries, the largest proportion of the gross national product and far and away the largest employer, so services marketing is of great importance to national prosperity. In addition, marketers of physical products have found that enhancing the services element of their products is a good way to add value for the consumer. For example, companies selling computers offer on-line support services as a way of generating extra revenue and at the same time increasing the value of the product to the consumer.

NOT-FOR-PROFIT MARKETING

Not-for-profit marketing is concerned with those organisations whose goals are something other than a profit. These include charities, hospitals, government organisations, schools, and some arts organisations. In many cases the exchange these organisations seek is not monetary at all – the government might run a campaign to discourage smoking, or to reduce drunken driving, and measure its success in terms of the number of people who quit smoking or the reduction in arrests and accidents caused by drunk drivers.

In other cases, money might change hands. Charities are becoming increasingly sophisticated at fund-raising, using TV advertising campaigns, mailings, and even telephone selling to encourage donations. Success is measured by the amount of money raised, but can also be measured in terms of raising the profile of the issues the charity was formed to address. For example, the UK children's charity the NSPCC (National Society for the Prevention of Cruelty to Children) runs advertising campaigns aimed at encouraging people to report cases of child abuse. This advertising also helps with fund-raising. In either case, profit is not the motive: as a charity, the NSPCC is non-profit-making.

Non-profit organisations that adopt a marketing orientation are more effective in achieving their organisational missions, in satisfying their beneficiaries, and in building a strong reputation with peer groups (Modi and Mishra 2010).

SMALL BUSINESS MARKETING

Much marketing theory (and practice) focuses on large organisations. Small businesses have specific problems of their own, largely related to their limited resources and non-specialist management. Someone running a small business has to be the marketer, the financial director, the personnel manager, the chief production manager, and the head of research and development. Because many small businesses come into existence because the owner has a particular expertise in producing something (whether this is haircuts, hamburgers or electronic components) small businesses tend to have a production or product orientation.

INTERNATIONAL MARKETING

The conceptual basis for international marketing has recently gone through a transformation in which a distinction has been drawn between the international and the global.

International marketing implies an emphasis on producing goods in one country and selling them in another, perhaps with some local assembly in the destination country. Global marketing implies a wider vision in which the company sources raw materials and components in a variety of countries, manufactures in a variety of countries, and markets its goods in the same or different countries.

Globalisation of business has been a major issue in world politics, since fully globalised companies are difficult to control and can often act as if they are above government intervention. Also, there are issues about the homogenisation of cultures and the erosion of national diversity as globalised companies force local businesses to close down. There is perhaps a responsibility on marketers to seek ways of minimising the damage from globalisation while maximising the economies of scale and other advantages that come from addressing global markets.

Globalisation The view of the world as a single market and single source of supply.

One of the key drivers for globalisation is the identification of **market segments** that cross national boundaries. This allows for the development of products with very specific features that appeal to only a tiny proportion of the population, since even a segment representing 0.01% of the world's population is numbered in the hundreds of thousands. Thus a producer will obtain economies of scale in manufacturing for this segment, whereas the same segment (on a national basis) would not support development of the product.

Market segment A group of people having similar needs.

In order to operate in global markets (or international markets) firms need to adapt the marketing mix to meet local conditions. For most global firms, this means making compromises. On the one hand, a single marketing message means that the firm benefits from economies of scale in its marketing activities, on the other hand a single message will not appeal to the diversity of cultures that exist worldwide.

Chapter summary

Marketing is a young discipline, yet it has captured the imagination of managers and academics alike. As a result, there is a lively debate about the nature and scope of marketing – which means in turn that definitions of what marketing is and what it should be are still emerging.

For some people marketing is about managing exchange. For others, it is about meeting customer needs at a profit (or in ways that lead to other organisational objectives). For still others, marketing is everything that businesses do, and for yet others marketing is what marketers do. All these definitions have some degree of truth in them.

The key issue in practice is that marketers should not try to please everybody. A marketer should be content to meet some of the needs of some of the customers most of the time – trying to do more is unlikely to be practical.

However marketing is viewed, whether as a quick fix, or a function of the business, or as the guiding philosophy of the business, there is no disagreement that companies need to take care of their customers. As Sam Walton, charismatic founder of Wal-Mart (the world's biggest retailer), once said:

There is only one boss – the customer. And he can fire everybody in the company from the chairman on down, simply by spending his money somewhere else.

 Key points

- There is no single definition of marketing in common use.
- Marketing is about exchange.
- Marketers put the satisfaction of customer need at the centre of everything they do.
- Marketing often conflicts with other business specialisms.
- People's needs go far beyond mere survival.
- Marketing draws from many other disciplines, including economics, sociology, anthropology, psychology and corporate strategy.
- Marketing sub-divides into specialist areas such as services marketing, non-profit marketing and so forth, each of which has its own set of parameters and techniques.

Review questions

1. Describe how exchange theory makes trade possible.
2. Which behavioural sciences have contributed to marketing theory?
3. What are some of the practical difficulties in becoming truly customer-centred?
4. What is the difference between needs and wants?
5. What are the problems of defining marketing as being simply the management of exchange?
6. What is the difference between product orientation and production orientation?
7. What are the major drawbacks of the 7P model?
8. What problems might arise in defining who the customer is in a non-profit market?
9. Why might some people feel that globalisation is a bad thing?
10. Explain price elasticity of demand.

Case study revisited: Pimlico Plumbers

Running a premium-price business in the middle of a worldwide depression might be thought a difficult task, but Pimlico Plumbers have not only survived, they have actually expanded.

In 2008 the company expanded to Marbella, where the rich and famous have holiday homes. The Marbella operation works in exactly the same way as the London one, covering the coast from Marbella to Buenavista. The Marbella operation has its own website, and work is carried out in accordance with Spanish building regulations.

In London, meanwhile, the company continues to grow, and to recruit more people. With 200 people in the workforce, Pimlico Plumbers is still recruiting everyone from office assistants through to qualified tradesmen: Charlie Mullins seeks out people who have experience (preferably through apprenticeships) as well as qualifications – he is certainly not a man who looks for book-learning, but rather looks for good people who know what they are doing.

Publicity is handled by Max Clifford, and the company has featured on TV shows such as Britain's Best Young Plumber and Secret Millionaire. The company employed Britain's (reputedly) oldest worker, Buster Martin, who worked for the company until his death in 2011 at the age of 104. Charlie Mullins claimed in an interview for French TV that employing Buster Martin had increased business by 36% due to the publicity.

In early 2013 Charlie Mullins said in a press release that in the previous year the company had had its best November ever, turning over £1.7m in one month. This was due, he said, not to the bad weather, but to people investing in their homes rather than moving house. Company turnover is more than £18m a year and growing – so clearly Pimlico Plumbers must be doing something right!

Case study: Avacta Group PLC

Avacta Group is a small biotech company based in Wetherby, Yorkshire. The company produces high-end biological testing systems for the pharmaceutical industry and the veterinary market.

Avacta was founded by scientists: the CEO, Dr Alastair Smith, is a scientist with a world reputation. The company has close links with university science departments.

The company operates in three main areas: first, and perhaps most importantly, it produces a device called the Optim 1000 which can tell drug companies whether the new products they are developing will ultimately be successful. This has a tremen-

dous commercial advantage for the pharmaceutical companies – new drugs are extremely expensive to develop, and more than 90% of them do not survive the rigorous testing procedures required by government regulators worldwide. If the companies know early on in the process that the drug will not be successful, the saving can easily run into millions of dollars.

The company's second product, the AX-1, is a desktop blood-testing machine. It can test blood, saliva or serum for a wide variety of conditions, providing rapid results for many conditions without the need to send samples to a laboratory. The benefits are again enormous – apart from the cost implication, which is in itself considerable, the machine reduces the risk of samples becoming contaminated or lost (or worse, mixed up with another sample). At the time of writing the machine is under test for the veterinary market, but should be launched in 2013. The reason for marketing the equipment to vets is that the regulations are much less stringent for animals than for humans: this means the product can be launched and used much more quickly and easily than would be the case for humans. However, the company expects that, once the equipment has been proven to work on animals, a human version can be developed and launched relatively easily. Currently the equipment is used for allergy testing, but other tests will be added as the product is developed further.

A third exciting development for the company is the artificial manufacture of antibodies. Antibodies are widely used in medical research, but are extremely expensive since they have to be derived from living people or animals. The cost is therefore around $1m per gram. Artificial antibodies are extremely complex to produce, but hundreds of times cheaper, which means that some medical research becomes a great deal cheaper as a consequence. The company hopes that the new development will give a boost to cancer research as well as improving the efficiency and range of operations of the Optim 1000 and the AX-1 devices.

Companies in the biotech area can easily find themselves caught up in the excitement of a new scientific breakthrough without truly understanding the business implications of what they are doing. Avacta seems to be avoiding this trap very neatly – the products have a known market, they fulfil a customer need very effectively, and they have clear advantages over what has gone before. The potential market is huge: the biopharmaceutical market is estimated to be worth $200bn worldwide, so if Avacta captured even a fraction of one-hundredth of a per cent of that market the company would be catapulted into the big league immediately.

Questions

1. What is Avacta offering to customers?
2. What needs does the AX-1 meet?
3. Which orientation does Avacta appear to have?
4. What conflicts might there be between Avacta's researchers and marketers?
5. How might Avacta go about setting prices?

Further reading

The material in this chapter is covered in introductory marketing texts rather than dedicated textbooks. For the arguments in favour of 'marketing is everything' see Philip Kotler, Gary Armstrong, John Saunders and Veronica Wong, *Principles of Marketing* (Harlow: FT Prentice Hall, 2008).

For contributions from economics, John Sloman and Mark Sutcliffe have written *Economics for Business* (Harlow: FT Prentice Hall, 2010), which ties economic theory to the real world of business in a way that is interesting and relevant.

For contributions from the behavioural sciences, there are many books on psychology, sociology and anthropology, but you may want to read Chapter 3 first as there is much more on these topics in that chapter.

References

Anderson, Eugene W., Fornell, Claes and Mazvancheryl, Sanal K. (2004) Customer satisfaction and shareholder value. *Journal of Marketing*, 68 (4): 172–85.

Avlonitis, G. and Gounaris, S.P. (1997) Marketing orientation and company performance: industrial vs. consumer goods companies. *Industrial Marketing Management*, 26 (5): 385–402.

Booms, B.H. and Bitner, M.J. (1981) Marketing strategies and organisation structures for service firms. In J.H. Donnelly and W.R. George (eds), *Marketing of Services*. Chicago, IL: American Marketing Association. pp. 47–52.

Coca-Cola Company (1981) *Measuring the Grapevine: Consumer Response and Word-of-Mouth*. Coca-Cola Company Consumer Information Centre.

Constantinides, E. (2006) The marketing mix revisited: towards 21st century marketing. *Journal of Marketing Management*, 22 (3/4): 407–38.

Davies, Andrea and Elliott, Richard (2006) The evolution of the empowered consumer. *European Journal of Marketing*, 40 (9/10): 1106–21.

Drucker, P.F. (1999) *The Practice of Management*. London: Heinemann.

Ford, D.H., Hakansson, H. and Johanson, J. (1986) How do companies interact? *Industrial Marketing and Purchasing*, 1 (1): 26–41.

Harwood, Tracy and Garry, Tony (2010) 'It's mine!' Participation and ownership within virtual co-creation environments. *Journal of Marketing Management*, 26 (3/4): 290–301.

Homburg, Christian, Koschate, Nicole and Hoyer, Wayne D (2005) Do satisfied customers really pay more? A study of the relationship between customer satisfaction and willingness to pay. *Journal of Marketing*, 69 (2): 84–96.

Jobber, D. (2003) *Principles and Practice of Marketing*. Maidenhead: McGraw–Hill.

Klein, Jill G. (2003) Calories for dignity: fashion in the concentration camp. *Advances in Consumer Research*, 30 (1): 34–7.

Korhonen-Sande, Silja (2010) Micro-foundations of market orientation: influencing non-marketing managers' customer information processing. *Industrial Marketing Management*, 39 (4): 661–71.

Kotler, P., Armstrong, G., Saunders, J. and Wong, V. (2008) *Principles of Marketing*, 5th European edn. Harlow: FT Prentice Hall.

Lyus, David, Rogers, Beth and Simms, Christopher (2011) The role of sales and marketing integration in improving strategic responsiveness to market change. *Journal of Database Marketing and Customer Strategy Management*, 18 (1): 39–49.

McCarthy, E.J. (1987 [1964]) *Basic Marketing: A Managerial Approach*, 9th edition. Homewood, IL: Irwin.

Modi, Pratik and Mishra, Debiprasad (2010) Conceptualising market orientation in non-profit organisations: definition, performance, and preliminary construction of a scale. *Journal of Marketing Management*, 26 (5&6): 548–69.

Narver, J.C. and Slater, S.F. (1990) The effects of a market orientation on business profitability. *Journal of Marketing*, 54 (4): 20–55.

Raffia, M. and Ahmed, P.K. (1992) The marketing mix reconsidered. *Proceedings of the Marketing Education Group Conference*, Salford, pp. 439–51.

Rosenberg, I.J. and Czepeil, J.A. (1983) A marketing approach to customer retention. *Journal of Consumer Marketing*, 2: 45–51.

Shaw, Deirdre, Newholme, Terry and Dickson, Roger (2006) Consumption as voting: an exploration of consumer empowerment. *European Journal of Marketing*, 40 (9/10): 1049–67.

Shaw, Vivienne and Shaw, Christopher T. (2003) Marketing: the engineer's perspective. *Journal of Marketing Management*, 19: 345–78.

Stanton, John L. and Herbst, Kenneth C. (2005) Commodities must begin to act like branded companies: some perspectives from the United States. *Journal of Marketing Management*, 21 (1/2): 7–18.

Vargo, Stephen L. and Lusch, Robert F. (2004) Evolving to a new dominant logic for marketing. *Journal of Marketing*, 68 (Jan.): 1–17.

More online

To gain free access to additional online resources to support this chapter please visit:
www.sagepub.co.uk/blythe3e

CHAPTER ②
The marketing environment

CHAPTER CONTENTS

LEARNING OBJECTIVES

After reading this chapter, you should be able to:

- Explain the nature of the business environment, and the relationship between the firm and its environment.

- Understand the problems of dealing with the micro and macro environments.

- Describe the relationship between the elements of the business environment.

- Explain the effects of demographic change on marketing.

- Discuss the nature and sources of competition.

- Explain how technological change can transfer between industries.

Introduction

No business operates in a vacuum. Decisions are made within a context of competition, customer characteristics, behaviour of suppliers and distributors, and of course within a legislative and social framework. People working within organisations are contributing to the welfare of society and of each other, and obtaining satisfaction of their own needs in return: this complex network of exchanges results in a better standard of living for everybody.

From a marketing viewpoint, managing the exchange process between the firm and its customers comes highest on the list of priorities, but it would be impossible to carry out this function without considering the effects of customer-based decisions on other people and organisations. A stakeholder is any individual or organisation affected by the firm's activities – neighbours, suppliers, competitors, customers, even governments – and all of these will have some input into marketing decisions, either directly or indirectly.

Some environmental factors are easily controlled by managers within the firm, whereas others cannot be changed and must therefore be accommodated in decision-making. In general, the larger the firm, the greater the control over its environment: on the other hand, large firms often find it difficult to adapt to sudden environmental changes in the way that a small firm might.

In order to assess the impact of different environmental factors, managers first need to classify them.

Preview case study: Costain West Africa

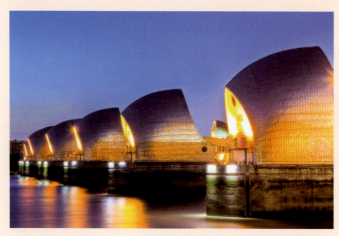

Costain is a major international civil engineering company. Founded in Liverpool in 1865, the company became one the largest British civil engineering companies in the ensuing years. Costain was involved in building the Mulberry harbours used on D-Day, the Channel Tunnel, the Thames Barrier, Hong Kong's airport, and many other large-scale construction projects. At one time Costain operated in 25 countries, but during the 1990s the company contracted and began to concentrate on the UK market, due to the recession that heralded the decade.

Costain West Africa was originally founded in 1948, to take over the Holt construction business. The company became fully independent of Costain UK when the parent company began its partial withdrawal from overseas markets: Costain West Africa is quoted on the Nigeria Stock Exchange, and is the largest construction company in Nigeria, if not in the whole of sub-Saharan Africa.

Any company in the construction business is likely to be affected by recessions and financial crises: major capital projects are frequently put on hold when money runs short, because an organisation can always cope for another year or two without its new headquarters, and the new bridge can always wait – after all, it wasn't always there, was it? So many construction companies face hard times – as do their suppliers and subcontractors. Costain West Africa was affected by the financial crisis of 2008 as much as any other organisation, but managed to survive and even flourish.

Surviving a financial crisis is no mean feat – but Costain West Africa met this sudden shift in the marketing environment with a uniquely African approach.

Macro environment Factors that affect all the firms in an industry.

Micro environment Factors that affect one firm only.

Internal environment Factors that operate within the organisation.

External environment Factors that operate outside the organisation.

Classifying environmental factors

Factors within the environment can be classified in a number of ways. First, the environment can be considered in terms of those elements that affect all firms within the industry (the **macro environment**), as opposed to those elements that affect only the individual firm (the **micro environment**). In general, the macro environment is difficult to influence or control, whereas the micro environment is much more within the firm's control.

The environment can also be classified as internal or external. The **internal environment** comprises those factors that operate within the firm (the corporate culture and history, staff behaviour and attitudes, the firm's capabilities) and the **external environment** comprises those elements that operate outside the firm (competition, government, customers). A problem for firms lies in deciding where

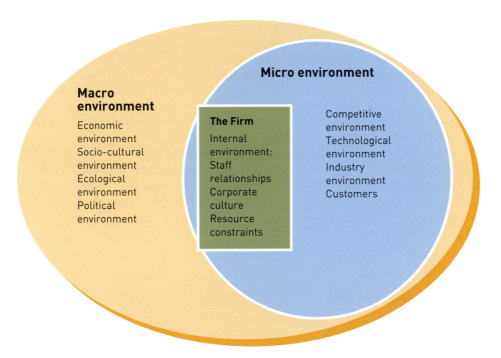

Figure 2.1 Environmental factors

the boundaries lie: for a truly customer-orientated company, customers might be considered as part of the internal environment, for example. Figure 2.1 shows how these factors relate. In effect, the firm operates within a series of layers of environmental factors, each of which has a greater or lesser impact on the firm's marketing policies. As a general rule, the further out the layer is, the more difficult it is for the firm to control what is happening: only the very largest firms have control, or even influence, on the macro environment.

The macro environment

The macro environment comprises those factors which are common to all firms in the industry. In many cases the same factors affect firms in other industries. Government policy, the economic climate and the culture within the countries in which the firms operate are common factors for all firms, but will affect firms differently according to the industries they are in.

In some cases there will be overlap between the micro environment and the macro environment. For example, a very large, global firm operating a subsidiary in a small country might regard the government of the country as part of the micro environment, since it is possible for the firm to control what the government does. This has certainly been the case with major fruit-importing companies operating in Central America. On the other hand, although competitors are usually regarded as part of the micro environment, a firm which is large enough to control an industry might be regarded as part of the macro environment by smaller firms in the same industry.

ECONOMIC ENVIRONMENT

The economic environment is basically about the level of demand in the economy. Most national economies follow the boom-and-bust economic cycle: every seven or eight years the economy goes into **recession**, which means that the production of

Recession A situation in which gross national production falls for three consecutive months.

goods and services shrinks and unemployment rises. A recession is a period of three consecutive months or more in which output shrinks, and the consequences may or may not be serious: during periods of recession, consumers are likely to postpone major purchases such as washing machines or new carpets due to uncertainty about employment security, and (by the same token) businesses will cut back on capital expenditure for such items as new factories or machinery. Borrowing is likely to reduce as consumers and firms become less confident about their ability to repay, and consequently demand drops still further.

In most cases recessions 'bottom out' within a few months or a year, but the financial collapse of 2008 created a worldwide recession in which many economies failed to recover for more than five years after the initial crisis. Governments tried many different measures to restart the world economy, but with little success.

Think outside this box!

If governments are so poor at controlling the economy, wouldn't it be better to leave things well alone and let Nature take its course? After all, there are so many factors to take into account in the way the economy works – people's confidence, the availability of manufacturing capacity, the activities of other countries and companies, and so on. Governments in the 19th century only concerned themselves with the defence of the realm and the internal security of its citizens – running the army and the police is a big enough task, surely!

On the other hand, the 19th century was marked by revolutions and rioting throughout Europe as starving people revolted against their governments. Maybe having a job and putting food on the table is a security issue after all.

Governments have a fine balancing act to perform in ensuring that the economy remains stable, and thus provides citizens with a good standard of living and a degree of confidence about the future. The problems caused by the financial crisis of 2008 have far exceeded government power to control: even when several governments act together, the situation can only be managed partially. In recent years, governments have controlled the economy largely by setting interest rates, and by controlling their own taxation and expenditure regimes. Both of these have a strong impact on marketers, because they affect people's willingness to spend on consumer goods and also (for firms that deal directly with the government) affect the size of the potential market. Non-profit organisations may feel the effects even more strongly, since many are funded from government grants and contracts, which may be cut back in times of austerity.

Within the European Union (EU) the common agricultural policy is an example of government intervention. The EU intervenes in agricultural markets, buying up and stockpiling food in order to maintain prices and smooth out supplies. However, this policy has resulted in the so-called 'wine lakes' and 'butter mountains' when continuing surplus production is bought and stockpiled, until eventually it has to be dumped on world markets or destroyed. On the other hand, the EU specifically prohibits governments from favouring their own national suppliers when ordering such items as computers or office equipment – all such tenders must be thrown open to suppliers in all member states.

Economic changes can be monitored in several ways. The business press typically provides informed analysis of economic changes, and national treasury officials in most countries also produce impact assessments. These are of variable quality according to the countries concerned. In some countries the assessments are as objective as it is possible to make them, since this allows companies and individuals to make informed judgements. In other countries the treasury produces distorted reports for reasons of political expediency, in order to support the party in power. Some universities and business schools also publish information and forecasts based on their own econometric models, and these may offer a different perspective from those forecasts produced by the government.

SOCIO-CULTURAL ENVIRONMENT

Socio-cultural forces fall into four categories, as follows:

1. **Demographic** forces. Demography refers to the structure of the population, in terms of factors such as age, income distribution, and ethnicity.
2. **Culture**. This refers to differences in beliefs, behaviours and customs between people from different countries.
3. Social responsibility and ethics. Derived in part from culture, ethical beliefs about how marketers should operate affect the ways in which people respond to marketing initiatives.
4. **Consumerism**. The shift of power away from companies and towards consumers.

The relationship between these elements is shown in Figure 2.2. These relationships will be explained in more detail throughout this section.

Demographic forces are affected by variations in the birth-rate and death-rate, by immigration and emigration, and by shifts in wealth distribution, which may be caused by government policies. The demography of Western Europe has shifted dramatically over the past fifty years as the birth-rate has fallen and improvements in medical care have pushed the average age of the population sharply upwards. The birth-rate in Western Europe as a whole is now lower than the death-rate, so that the population would be shrinking were it not for immigration from Eastern Europe and the Third World. In some countries the situation is approaching

Demographics The study of the structure of the population.

Culture The set of shared beliefs and behaviours common to an identifiable group of people.

Consumerism The set of organised activities intended to promote the needs of the consumer against those of the firm.

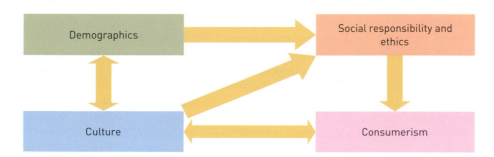

Figure 2.2 Socio-cultural environment

crisis point: for example, Spain has introduced a policy of contacting expatriate Spaniards in Latin America and encouraging them to return home. The Spanish government estimates that it needs 10,000 immigrants per annum to maintain the population.

The problem of depopulation and an ageing population is that many of the older people are retired, and therefore need to be supported by the productive members of society.

An influential report prepared for the EU in 2002 showed that the 15 member states (at that time – there are now 25 members) had experienced considerable immigration, virtually no outmigration, and dramatically reduced birth-rates. Coupled with the increased life expectancy (now around 75 for men, and 81 for women) the net result has been a reduction in the under-25 age group and increases in both the working population and the elderly population. These changes have happened over a thirty-year period from the mid-1970s (Cruijsen et al. 2002). The report goes on to say that entry by the new Eastern European member states will change this pattern in the short term, since these countries have lower life expectancies. During the 1990s (following the collapse of Communism in Europe) Eastern European countries have themselves experienced demographic shifts, notably a dramatically reduced birth-rate. These demographic shifts are thought to be the result of worsening health care, fear over job security, and less healthy lifestyles. The authors expect the following demographic shifts as a result of expansion:

1. Population decline will occur several years sooner.
2. Population ageing will be slightly suppressed.
3. Population dejuvenation (reduction in under-25s) will become stronger in future decades.
4. Expected decline of the working population will hardly change.

So far, experience has borne out these findings. There have been dramatic shifts in populations (several million Poles have emigrated to other EU states, for example), so there has been no decline in the working population of the original 15 member states.

From a marketing viewpoint, these changes offer both opportunities and threats. Clearly products aimed at a youth market are likely to decline, whereas products aimed at older people will be in greater demand. In practice, however, this may lead to surprises: for example, an assumption that almost all 70-year-olds have mobility problems may have been true thirty years ago, but improved health care and healthier lifestyles probably mean that most 70-year-olds in the 21st century are as fit as 50-year-olds were in the 1960s. The increase in the elderly population is not expected to peak out until the 2040s, and even this assumption depends on limited improvements in health care and the life expectancy of the very old – in other words, it assumes that people will not live much beyond 100 years old (Cruijsen et al. 2002).

A further demographic change (general to Europe) is the increase in single-person households. This has come about through an increase in the divorce rate and increasing affluence: young people no longer live with their parents until they marry, as was the case in the 1950s. At the other end of the age scale, large numbers of widowed elderly people continue to live in the former marital home. In several EU countries single-person households now represent the largest category of household: the UK's 2011 census revealed that single-person households had increased from 17% of all households in 1971 to 31% in 2011. Two-person households represented 32% of all households, making those two categories far and away the greatest proportion of households in the UK (Census 2011).

Real-life marketing: Think small

Most companies like the idea of being big. Retailers especially like to have big, well-stocked shops: a wider range of merchandise means more opportunities to sell something, after all. As in other aspects of marketing, though, you should be prepared to do something the others aren't doing – and thinking small has certainly been a success story for some firms.

The idea is to use small outlets, for example at railway stations and airports, to sell a limited range of goods that all fall into a particular category. This idea is used by firms such as Tie Rack and Sock Shop, who locate in high-footfall areas such as transport hubs. These companies pay a relatively low rent because the premises are very small, but they have a high turnover because people know they can get what they want quickly and easily – someone who has just spilled coffee down his tie can buy another one for that important meeting, for example.

For the idea to work, you should follow these rules:

- Think outside the box.
- Look for a resource that is currently unused or at least under-used.
- Specialise! This is essential for small firms – only very large firms can afford to be all things to all people.
- Don't try to compete head-on with the big companies.

The implications for marketing are widespread. For house builders, smaller homes and starter homes (e.g. flats) will show increased demand. This may mean that smaller models of domestic appliances will be more popular, that pack sizes of cereals and other foods will be smaller, that furniture will be smaller and perhaps more adaptable (for example futons, which convert from sofas to beds) and that security devices will be more popular as more people leave their homes unattended when they go to work. Such a rapid increase in single-person households represents a major challenge for many marketers since it implies a considerable shift in market demand for almost every consumer product.

Income distribution and wealth concentration are also part of the demographic structure. Income is a somewhat fluid concept: pre-tax income does not mean a great deal, since an individual's salary may be heavily or lightly-taxed according to the country concerned and the level of income of the individual. Disposable income is the income remaining after income tax and other deductions, but of course this is not the end of the story – basic household expenses need to be met such as mortgages, local authority property taxes, household bills and so forth. This leaves an amount which the individual can spend in any way he or she chooses: this is called discretionary income. There is, of course, a conceptual problem here in distinguishing between necessities and discretionary purchases. Housing is an example – a relatively wealthy person might choose to live in a small house, and thus have an extremely small mortgage and a correspondingly high discretionary income. Someone else might decide to live in a large house, and have very little discretionary income as a result. In either case, the choice of house was freely-made, so the house purchase might be considered in the same way as the purchase of a particular brand of bread or make of car. Clothing is even more problematical – wearing some kind of clothing is obviously essential, but the fashion industry is founded on the basis of attracting discretionary income, so the line between necessity and discretionary purchase is somewhat blurred.

CULTURAL ENVIRONMENT

The cultural environment refers to the shared set of beliefs and behaviours prevalent within the society in which the company operates. These include language, religious beliefs, customary ways of working, gender roles, purchasing behaviour, gift-giving behaviour, and so forth. Social behaviour and cultural attitudes play an enormous role in determining consumer behaviour, but they also play a role in commercial purchasing behaviour and in the way staff behave and expect to be treated by employers.

Socio-cultural issues manifest themselves in several ways, affecting both the external and the internal environments of the organisation. For example, a company operating in Thailand will need to consider the role of Buddhism in Thai life, including the fact that most Thai men spend several years as monks at some point in their lives. This would be a surprising entry on the CV of a Western employee, but would be normal in Thailand, and indeed regarded as commendable. Also, Thais have the concept of *sanuk*, meaning 'fun', which is applied equally in the workplace as in private life. This means that Thais might expect to spend part of their working day cracking jokes or even singing songs. This can be a difficult aspect of Thai life for Western managers.

Further examples of cultural issues are shown in Table 2.1.

Culture can also dictate the ways people spend their discretionary income. For example, Irish people spend a high proportion of their incomes on alcoholic beverages (around double the UK figure). This does not necessarily mean that Irish people drink more alcohol than their UK counterparts – in part the figures reflect lower incomes in Ireland and higher taxes on alcohol (Euromonitor 2004). It does, however, reflect the importance that drinking has in the Irish culture: Irish

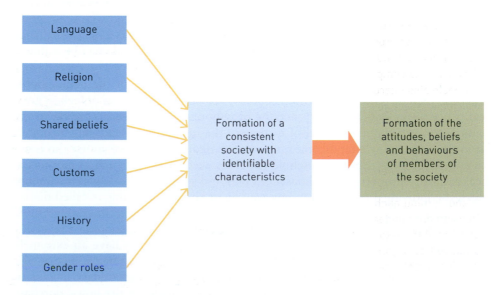

Figure 2.3 Cultural effects

Table 2.1 Cultural issues in the marketing environment

Example	Explanation
Time sense	In many agrarian countries (and warmer countries in general) each day is regarded as being essentially the same as the one before and the one after. Therefore it does not matter if tasks are not completed today: tomorrow is another day. In Northern, industrialised countries each day is regarded as unique, so that lost time is regarded as being lost forever.
Gift-giving behaviour	While gift-giving behaviour is common throughout human societies, the occasions on which it happens are not. The Onam festival in Kerala, Christmas in the UK and the United States, Twelfth Night in Spain and Portugal, and O-Chugen in Japan are all examples of general gift-giving seasons, but they happen at different times of year and have different traditions behind them.
Meanings of symbols.	In advertising, a busy person denotes success to someone from the UK or United States. To an African, the same symbol denotes someone who has no time for others and is selfish.

social life centres around the pub, whereas in the UK social life tends to centre on the home.

Changes in taste and fashion are also a component of the cultural environment. Fashions in food, clothing and even ideas can affect marketing effort.

Real-life marketing: Talk the customer's language

Although we might imagine that we're all speaking the same language, there are many subtleties about language that we might have missed. Communication is not that straightforward – it isn't the linear process we imagine (we say something, the other person hears it, now they know it) because people interpret what they hear and compare it with past experience.

People also interpret by considering the source as well – and that will really affect your communication, because people don't trust marketers!

When the Department of Transport in the UK wanted to reduce accidents among teenage pedestrians, their research showed that teenagers were often involved in accidents while not paying attention to traffic – wandering into the road while texting a friend, filming each other on mobile phones, and so forth. So the Department handed out 14 mobile phones to groups of teenagers and asked them to film their usual activities: the final advert was produced by a group from Stoke Newington in London, with only the final crash scene being filmed using a stunt artist and stunt

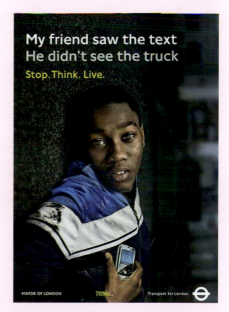

(Continued)

(Continued)

driver. By using the same imagery and language the teenagers themselves used, the ad was hard-hitting without being patronising.

In practice, you need to follow these rules:

- Don't try to guess what the target audience's language is. Otherwise you will end up with a 'Hey, kids, road safety's cool!' – type of patronising message.
- Don't talk down to your audience. They are not idiots.
- Remember that people think about communications – don't assume that once you have said something, they will simply accept it as true.
- Remember that people consider the source of communications – try to make it sound as if it's people like themselves.

Another aspect of culture that evolves over time is the change in lifestyle expectations. In the 21st century few people would consider living without a telephone, television, refrigerator, car, bank account and credit cards. Yet in 1960 each of these product categories was owned by a minority of the UK population. At that time it was common for a whole street to have only one or two homes with a TV set, and perhaps one telephone. In 2013 the vast majority of UK homes have more than one television set, and the advent of cellular phones means that many households have several telephones as well.

Referring back to Figure 2.2, culture and demographic change are interrelated. Culture dictates the aspirations of the population, which in turn dictate some of the changes in income, education and lifestyle. Movement of population also influences culture, as new influences are brought in by immigrant groups – one has only to consider the influence of Indian immigration into the UK on British eating habits, or the equivalent effect in the Netherlands of Indonesian immigration.

Think outside this box!

Earlier on it was mentioned that the Spanish government needs to attract 10,000 immigrants a year to maintain its population balance. All very well, but what about the effect on Spanish culture? In the Middle Ages Spain was invaded from Morocco, and many of the current icons of Spanish culture (flamenco, olive oil, architectural style) were actually Moorish in origin. The great monuments of Spain (the Alhambra, the walled city of Toledo) date from Moorish times.

Can we expect the same level of cultural change from new waves of immigrants? Should we worry about this? Is this type of change something to be feared – or is it a natural part of human development? After all, if the native Spaniards found that cooking with olive oil rather than pig grease made the food taste better, isn't that a positive cultural change?

There is more on cultural issues in Chapter 3.

POLITICAL AND LEGAL ENVIRONMENT

Political influences affect businesses in two main ways: first, political parties have policies that are often put into legislation, which clearly must be obeyed. Second, the ruling party sets the general tone of behaviour in the country as a whole, and in government departments in particular. This subtle change in the national culture will also affect business.

The political environment is usually regarded as including the regulatory environment, whether such regulation emanates from the government or from industry-based bodies. Some examples of government controls in business are as follows:

1. Patent legislation. Governments set the rules about what may and may not be patented, and for how long. In high-tech industries such as bioengineering or software design, intellectual property may represent the bulk of the firm's assets. Changes in patent (and copyright) law can have profound effects. This is particularly an issue in the international arena, since there is no such thing as a world patent: products must be patented in each country separately, and in some countries (notably Taiwan) few products are patentable, so that companies are left open to having their products copied at a fraction of the cost of the 'genuine' product.

2. Taxation. Apart from the general taxation regime on corporations, governments often impose selective taxation on specific products in order to manage demand and raise revenue. This is particularly a problem in the alcoholic drinks industry and the tobacco industry, but in recent years changes in the classification of different products in respect of VAT has had a marked effect on some firms. As with patent legislation, taxation varies from one country to another and therefore firms need to be particularly careful when entering foreign markets.

3. Safety regulations. Products need to conform to national safety regulations. Within the EU many attempts have been made to co-ordinate the wildly differing safety laws in the member states, but to no avail: finally, the EU has adopted the stance that any product that is legal in one member state will be legal in all member states unless the governments concerned can demonstrate that there is a very real danger to human or animal life.

4. Contract law. Governments can, and do, amend contract law although much contract law is developed through the decisions of law courts. In the UK, contract law is looser than it is in the United States: in America the written agreement is the basis of the law, whereas in the UK verbal contracts are as binding as written contracts. There is, of course, the problem of proof in the case of verbal contracts. The main area of government intervention in contract law has been in the field of consumer protection, where the contract between the consumer and the retailer is often regulated to compensate for the perceived imbalance of power between individual consumers and large companies.

5. Consumer protection legislation. Apart from contract law, mentioned above, governments often enact legislation designed to protect consumers. In the UK there are several hundred laws relating to consumer protection, covering everything from credit agreements to the quality of goods sold. In general, the old principle of *caveat emptor* (let the buyer beware) is no longer necessary since retailers are required to ensure that goods are of a suitable quality for the purpose for which they are intended, are being sold at prices that are transparent and reasonable, and can be returned if they are faulty or (often) when the customer changes his or her mind.

6. Control of opening hours. In the UK, the opening hours of retail shops are limited only on Sundays, when shops may open for six hours only (with exemptions for small businesses). In other countries tougher restrictions apply: in particular, retail hours in Germany are still heavily limited by law. In the past the opening hours of German retailers were even more restricted, the net result of which was the development of one of the largest mail order markets in the world.

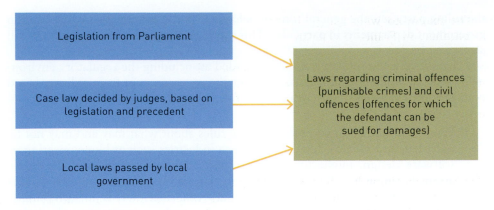

Figure 2.4   Sources of law

A change in the political nature of the government can make considerable changes in the general tenor of the law. Left-wing governments traditionally increase the number of laws and restrictions on businesses (taking the hand of government approach to ethics described in Chapter 10), whereas right-wing governments tend to reduce restrictions on business (taking the invisible hand approach – again see Chapter 10 for more on this).

The enforcement of legislation is usually left to specialist bodies such as the Office of Fair Trading and the Trading Standards Institute. Trading standards are enforced at local authority level, with each council in the UK having its own trading stand-ards department. In the United States the same function is carried out by the Better Business Bureau (BBB), which is a non-profit body funded by businesses themselves. Businesses fund the BBB in order to keep the rogue operators out – honest businesses are then able to compete on a level playing field.

The legal environment is created in two ways: first, by government legislation, and second by case decisions made by judges. Case law is created when legislation is put into action: the law is often unclear, and individual circumstances mean that judges (and magistrates) need to clarify matters, usually by referring to other cases that have been decided already. This system of referring to other examples ensures a degree of consistency in decision-making, but of course each case is different in some way, which is why they need to be argued out in court.

Local government

Local government does not pass laws as such (although there may be some local bye-laws affecting businesses) but often has the role of enforcing national laws. Local authorities also deal with such issues as planning permission and the zoning of busi-ness activities (retail parks, residential areas and manufacturing areas).

In most cases planning permission presents few problems that marketers need to worry about, but areas that have caused difficulties for marketers include plan-ning permission for signs and displays, the location of billboards, and the zoning of out-of-town retail parks. On the one hand, small businesses tend to oppose the creation of large retail parks since they represent serious (and sometimes fatal) competition, but on the other hand such retail parks offer an opportunity for large firms to grow.

The extent to which such regulations affect firms varies from one country to another: in France it is relatively easy to obtain permission for large out-of-town stores or hypermarkets, and a reasonable compromise has been worked out between the hypermarkets and local businesses whereby small businesses are given space within the hypermarket complex. In Italy, on the other hand, restrictions are extremely strict and hypermarkets have great difficulty in obtaining permission to build.

The European Union

The European Union has the role of trying to co-ordinate business law throughout the member states in order to ensure a fair and competitive environment for businesses operating within the EU. Ultimately, the intention is that businesses will be able to compete on an equal basis throughout the EU, but the problems are all but insuperable and it will be some time before there is a single body of regulation covering all member states. Some of the issues are as follows:

1. Technical standards. Although most EU countries use the metric system, Britain and Ireland use the imperial system, which is almost entirely incompatible with the metric system. Simply changing the sizes of such items as plumbing fittings and electrical wiring is not enough – most of the buildings in both countries were built using imperial measures, which means that any repair work or alterations need to be carried out either using imperial size components or using conversion fittings where one system joins another. At a more subtle level, the specifications for wiring, plumbing, strength of bricks and so forth vary among member states. Even the television broadcasting systems differ – video recordings made in the UK will not play on Spanish televisions, although they will on French and German systems. Building regulations differ between member states, and even such things as the threads on screws and bolts differ, so that British fixings manufacturers need to retool their factories to be able to do business on the Continent.

2. Frontier controls. These have largely been abandoned since 1993, when the European Single Market came into existence. However, Customs officers still have the right to stop vehicles and check for illicit goods, some of which might seem surprising. For example, there is no problem shipping computers, gemstones and alcoholic drinks across European borders but there is a problem shipping bananas between the UK and Germany. Immigration controls are in place for non-EU citizens, but the difficulty of policing all the former frontiers means that in most cases immigration officers rely on spot checks and occasional tip-offs to catch illegal immigrants.

3. Safety standards. Common criteria for safety and health have been agreed, but only at a somewhat minimal level. Provided a product conforms to basic EU safety regulations it is given the CE mark and is legal for sale anywhere in the EU. However, such products may not meet the safety standards of products manufactured in the target country.

4. Currency fluctuations. The introduction of the Euro for most member states has meant that companies operating between Eurozone states no longer have to consider the risks of currency fluctuations. A company doing business between the UK and France has to take account of the possibility that the pound might strengthen or weaken against the Euro, and must therefore fix the price of the goods to allow for the possibility of a fluctuation, or must buy or sell currency in

advance in order to minimise the risk of losing money on the contract. Companies dealing between (say) France and Spain do not have this problem, because all prices and costs are calculated in Euros. Sweden, Britain and Denmark were not members of the Euro at the time of writing: in September 2003 Sweden overwhelmingly rejected membership as a result of a national referendum. In fact, members of the Euro have found that it has brought problems as well as benefits: soaring prices in Germany, an unwelcome influx of holiday-home buyers in southern Spain, price rises in France, and increased smuggling of cigarettes throughout the EU have all followed on from the single currency.

5. Advertising. The EU has made some progress towards harmonising advertising regulations, but apart from introducing a Europe-wide ban on tobacco advertising in broadcast media (TV and radio) there are no regulations that apply throughout the EU.

Database marketing Using a list of customers or potential customers stored on a computer to drive the marketing effort.

Telephone selling The practice of using telephone communications as a personal selling medium rather than face-to-face meetings.

Meanwhile, the EU continues to seek ways of unifying marketing law. It would seem likely that the main successes will happen in the new media such as the Internet, **database marketing**, **telephone selling** and so forth, simply because national laws in member states are only in their infancy and therefore will need only minimal changes.

Marketing in a changing world: The European Union

The European Union was originally conceived as a single trading bloc in which goods, capital, labour and enterprise could move freely between the nations, with a common external tariff barrier. As time has gone on, it has become much more: it now regulates a great deal of what happens within member states, and aims to create a single set of ground rules for all firms throughout the 27 member states.

Although the EU has had a rough ride during the financial crisis, with the very real threat of members leaving (either because they had no money, or because they had money and didn't want to share it), it seems fairly unlikely that it will break up. The benefits of membership are too great.

From a marketing viewpoint, greater integration has a number of possible consequences. Industry tends to be more regulated in Northern Europe than is the case in the UK, for one thing. For another, as the continent becomes more integrated it will compete better against the United States and the Far East (led by Japan). As new trading blocs emerge, the EU should be strong enough to resist outside incursions into its markets. The emphasis is therefore on co-operation with other European firms in the same business, rather than competition. The future almost certainly lies in being part of a big trading bloc, with large companies able to fight their corner.

REGULATORY BODIES

Some regulatory bodies are government-sponsored and government-run. Most of them are established as independent bodies, in other words they operate without direct involvement from politicians. These are sometimes called QUANGOS, meaning quasi-autonomous non-governmental organisations. They have a specific task to perform within a limited set of guidelines, and are therefore able to act much more quickly than a government department could. Here are some examples of UK QUANGOS:

1. Oftel. This is the organisation responsible for regulating the telecommunications industry. Since the privatisation and deregulation of the telephone system in the 1980s, several hundred companies have established themselves in the telecommunications market at some level or another, from major landline and satellite providers like British Telecom through to small companies providing answering services.

2. Ofgas. This organisation is responsible for controlling gas suppliers. Ofgas is concerned with selling practices in the industry, billing problems, difficulties encountered when switching suppliers, and disputes between suppliers. Part of the problem for Ofgas has been the practice of doorstep selling energy services, using salespeople who are unsalaried and who rely on the commissions they get for converting customers. In some cases these salespeople have been less than ethical in their approach to selling, sometimes telling outright lies or even forging signatures. The difficulty for Ofgas is that part of its remit is to encourage vigorous competition between suppliers (Benady 1997).

3. Independent Television Commission. In conjunction with its sister organisation, the Radio Authority, the ITC controls commercial broadcasting. Both organisations have the responsibility for issuing licences to broadcast, and have several responsibilities. First is to ensure that programme content meets generally-agreed standards of good taste. Second, both are charged with the responsibility of ensuring that the broadcast media do not fall under the control of too small a group of people, so mergers and acquisitions between broadcasters are carefully scrutinised. Third, and perhaps most importantly for marketers, both organisations have responsibility for monitoring and approving broadcast advertising. This includes ensuring that advertising appears at appropriate times (considering that children might be watching or listening), that advertising content is within the bounds of good taste, and that advertising is clearly differentiated from programming. The ITC is also responsible for monitoring **product placement**. At one time, any reference to a brand name was not allowed, but the impossibility of removing brands from feature films made this ruling unworkable. The current position is that brands can be shown, but the programme makers are not allowed to accept money for including a specific brand (unlike the film industry, where movies are frequently funded by brand owners).

Product placement The use of branded products in TV programming or movies.

4. Office of Fair Trading. This government organisation has two remits: first, to protect consumers and explain their rights, which it does through advertising campaigns and occasional leaflets, and second to ensure that businesses compete and operate fairly. The OFT tends not to become involved in individual consumer problems, but lays down guidelines and occasionally becomes involved in test cases. In other words, the OFT might become involved in a general problem of unsafe imports from a foreign country, but would not become involved in a case of a customer who has bought faulty double glazing.

5. Monopolies and Mergers Commission. The MMC has the responsibility for preventing companies from exercising undue power in the marketplace due to having an excessive share of the market. This does not mean that a monopoly or near-monopoly is not allowed: it merely means that the MMC will monitor such situations carefully to ensure that the company or companies involved do not abuse their power, for example by fixing prices at too high a level or by preventing other companies from entering the market. For example, the washing-powder market is entirely controlled in the UK by Unilever and Procter and Gamble. Because of the high cost of the plant and equipment needed to make washing powder, other firms cannot economically enter the market, so the MMC monitors the situation to ensure that the two giant firms do not exploit their position.

In the voluntary sector there are many regulatory bodies that have been set up by industries themselves. In many cases, this has been seen as a way of forestalling government intervention: if the industry does not have its own regulatory body, the government might well step in to establish one. This is the case with the Advertising Standards Authority and the British Board of Film Censors.

The ASA is probably the voluntary organisation that most impinges on marketers. However, it has no statutory powers to compel advertisers or media such as newspapers and television to comply with its rulings. In practice, the ASA operates on the basis of complaints received, and will act even if only a few complaints come in. The ASA will examine the advertisement concerned, interview the advertisers and their creative people if necessary, and then decide whether the complaint is justified. If the complaint is upheld, the ASA will request the advertiser to withdraw the advertisement. If the advertiser refuses, the ASA will ask the media not to run the advertisement. These requests are rarely refused – in the event that they are, the Office of Fair Trading does have the power (under the Control of Misleading Advertisements Regulations 1988) to apply for a legal injunction to prevent the advertisement being shown, but this is rarely invoked since no one in the industry wants the expense of litigation or, indeed, to encourage government intervention.

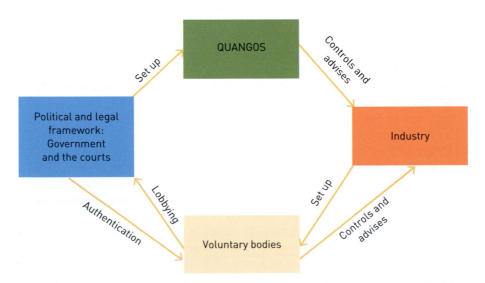

Figure 2.5   Regulatory bodies

Think outside this box!

If an organisation is set up by an industry, presumably it is funded by that industry and its management is appointed by the industry. So how can such a body have any credibility at all? How can it possibly bite the hand that feeds it by seeking to regulate the activities of its founders?

Maybe the founders of these organisations felt that they were pure in heart themselves, but that the rogues needed to be regulated. All well and good – but everyone's a rogue sometimes. Might there not be a danger of the leading firms being treated more leniently than the small guy struggling to get established by whatever means present themselves?

One of the problems the ASA faces is that it has no authority to vet advertisements before they go out. Thus by the time the ASA has acted, the advertisement has already been seen, and the publicity surrounding its withdrawal often means that the advertisement achieves a much greater impact than it otherwise might have done. Benetton in particular have been accused of exploiting this situation by deliberately producing highly provocative advertisements in the certain knowledge that the ASA will issue a request for their withdrawal.

Many industries have **trade associations** which police the activities of members. If a firm is a member of a trade association, this provides some reassurance for potential customers because the trade association will have a code of conduct which its members are expected to adhere to, and which usually provides some redress for disappointed consumers or sanctions against rogue members. Attempts have been made by some trade organisations to co-ordinate their codes of practice across Europe, but given the widely differing consumer protection laws and systems in different countries this is proving somewhat problematical.

Trade association A group of companies in the same industry, set up to look after the collective interests of the group.

INFLUENCING THE MACRO ENVIRONMENT

For smaller firms, the macro environment usually has to be accepted as it is. Large firms are able to influence some aspects of the macro environment, however. Advertising campaigns can affect the country's culture in at least a small way, although in most cases this happens more by accident than by design. For example, some advertising slogans have found their way into everyday conversation (Compare the Market's Meerkat says 'Simples!', which is one example from the UK, and the saying 'an apple a day keeps the doctor away' began life as a promotional slogan for apple farmers in the 1900s). This can be seen as an example both of the power of advertising to enter the national consciousness, and also the fulfilment of an advertising copywriter's dream.

However, in most cases advertising has only a superficial influence on culture. The main influence that large firms have on the macro environment lies in the area of **lobbying** government for changes in the law, and in playing leading roles in the regulatory bodies. This type of influence is not restricted to businesses, however: pressure groups and even individuals can also lobby government, even at the simple level of speaking to the local Member of Parliament.

Lobbying Making representations to politicians with the aim of changing legislation.

For smaller firms, the chances of making any material change to the macro environment are minimal. The best way of having some effect is to join a trade organisation or other pressure group. In some countries, politicians can be sponsored by pressure groups and in others pressure groups sponsor political parties in order to receive favourable treatment at a later stage when the party is in power. In the UK, sponsorship of political parties is subject to careful monitoring to ensure that this does not unduly influence legislation, but in practice the Labour party is largely financed by trade unions and the Conservative party is largely financed by big business. This sponsorship will inevitably affect the thinking of politicians.

The micro environment

The micro environment comprises those elements of the environment that impinge on the firm and usually its industry, but do not affect all firms in all industries. The micro environment is composed of the following elements:

- The competition. In a sense, all firms compete with all other firms for consumers' limited spending power. For most practical purposes, though, consideration of the competition is limited to firms providing similar solutions to the same customer problem.
- Technology. Major technological changes such as the advent of satellite communications or cellular telephones clearly affect most industries. Such radical technological advances are relatively rare, though – most technological change happens in small increments. In most cases technological change only affects a relatively small sector of the economy: for example, a new manufacturing process for aluminium will have some effect on any firm or customer using aluminium products, but the firms most affected will be aluminium refiners.
- Industry structure and power relationships. This may be related to competition, but equally encompasses supply chains and strategic alliances between firms. Some industries operate in a highly-competitive manner, while others are more co-operative: for example, funeral directors tend to be fairly co-operative with each other, whereas estate agents are highly competitive.
- Customers. The pool of customers, the nature of them, the different segments of the market made up of people with slightly different needs, will all affect the firm. For example, a law firm specialising in corporate law will have a very different customer base from that of a firm specialising in house conveyancing. The difference in customer type will affect almost everything about the firm, from the design and location of its offices through to its recruitment policy.

THE COMPETITION

Competition is a fact of life in any business. There is no such thing as a product that has no competition, because each product (from the consumer's viewpoint) represents a way of solving a problem. Before the product existed, people almost always had some other way of solving the problem: it may not have been as effective, but it existed. For example, television was certainly a radical technological breakthrough, and from the engineering viewpoint it had no competitors. There was, at the time, no other way of transmitting pictures electrically and instantaneously over a long distance. From the consumer's viewpoint, though, television was simply another entertainment device, which was perhaps more convenient than the cinema which it replaced (or the theatre before that) but did not represent a very major change.

Competition can vary greatly between industries, however. As we saw in Chapter 1, competition can be categorised as a **monopoly** (in which one firm controls the market), an **oligopoly** (in which a few large firms control the market between them), **perfect competition** (in which no single buyer or seller can significantly influence the market) and **monopolistic competition**, in which companies offer products that are sufficiently different from each other as to constitute monopolies in the short term. The main types of competition are shown in Table 2.2.

Monopoly A situation in which one company controls the market.

Oligopoly A situation in which a group of companies control the market between them.

Perfect competition A state of affairs where everyone in the market has perfect knowledge and no one buyer or seller can influence the market.

Monopolistic competition A situation in which one company exercises a strong influence in the market, but other companies still enter the market and compete effectively.

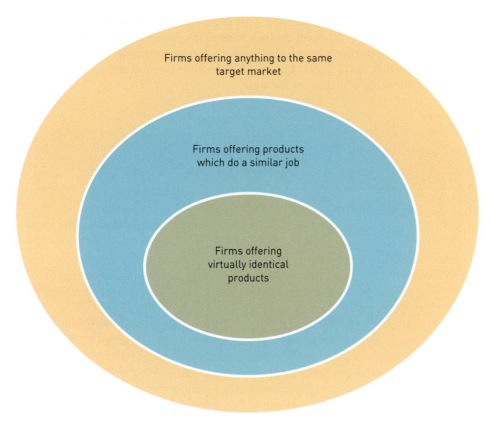

Figure 2.6 Levels of competition

Table 2.2 Competition

Type of competition	Explanation
Perfect competition	This is a condition where there are many suppliers none of whom is large enough to control the market, many customers who also cannot individually influence the market and a product that is homogeneous, i.e. does not differ from one supplier to another. Perfect competition also assumes that all parties have complete knowledge of the market. In practice, this type of competition does not exist, apart from a few special cases such as the international money markets.
Oligopoly	An oligopoly exists when a few companies control the supply of goods. Oligopolies almost always fix prices, either by agreeing prices between themselves (a practice which is illegal in most countries) or by being very careful not to start a price war by undercutting each other.
Monopoly	This is a circumstance in which one company supplies the entire market. Very few monopolies exist, since they almost invariably lead to companies setting excessively high prices and earning excessively high profits. In most countries monopolies are carefully regulated, and even prevented, by government intervention. However, there are cases where a monopoly is almost inevitable – the railway systems in most countries are monopolies, for example.
Monopolistic competition	This occurs when companies differentiate their products sufficiently that they can be considered as monopolies, at least in the short term (until competitors copy the differentiating features). This is the commonest type of competition.

Much business strategy is concerned with establishing the firm in a suitable competitive position (there is more on this in Chapter 10). Too-rapid growth may lead to unwelcome attention from major firms, whereas too-slow growth may lead to being left behind by other small firms. Equally, a large firm cannot afford to be complacent: new challengers will arise all the time.

Real-life marketing: Don't compete!

In business, we often use the language of warfare: we talk about campaigns, capturing markets, beating the competition and so forth. This is fine unless you are a small firm: your chances of beating a large firm are minimal.

There has long been a tradition of co-operating with non-competitors – for example, takeaway food outlets co-operating with DVD rental outlets – but a more recent trend has been to co-operate with competitors. Even large companies do this – car makers Seat, VW and Ford co-produce the Ford Galaxy/Seat Alhambra/VW Sharan, which is essentially the same car.

For example, when Communism collapsed in Eastern Europe, there was a fear that Western Europe would be flooded with cheap cars from the East. Skoda in particular was seen as a threat – although under Communism its cars had become clunky and unreliable, it had at one time been an upmarket manufacturer on the lines of BMW. Most manufacturers braced themselves for a competitive onslaught – but not Volkswagen. VW co-operated with Skoda, providing it with new technology and better manufacturing processes. Skoda is now a serious manufacturer again, but VW owns it and takes its profits that way, even though the two companies operate entirely independently.

To do this in practice, you should be careful about the following:

- Ensure that both parties gain – you have to bring something to the party as well.
- You aren't allowed to collude in order to share out the market between you – the monopolies regulators are watching! For small firms this won't be a problem, of course.
- You should try not to cannibalise each other's markets.
- You don't need to buy out the competitor – you can agree to co-operate in all sorts of other ways.

Competitor analysis can be carried out using Porter's Five Forces Model (Porter 1990). This model offers a way of assessing the likely strength of competition in any given market. The five forces are as follows:

1. The bargaining power of suppliers. If suppliers have strong bargaining power, the competitive pressure will be greater.
2. The bargaining power of customers. Customers with strong bargaining power will be more demanding and can set one supplier against another. This will make the competition fiercer.
3. The threat of new entrants. If it is easy for new companies to set up in the same business, the competition will be strong: if it is difficult for new firms to enter the market, the existing firms can become complacent.
4. The threat of substitute products and services. If close substitutes are readily available, the competition will be stronger. For example, pizza delivery companies recognise each other as competition, but the business is extremely competitive because of the existence of many other types of takeaway food.

5. Rivalry among current competitors. In some industries firms will have a 'live and let live' approach, which reduces competition. This is particularly the case in oligopolistic markets, and in markets that are well-established. In new or rapidly-growing markets such rivalry will tend to be stronger and therefore the competition will be stronger.

The bargaining power of suppliers, if high, can seriously reduce industry profits and thus make the competition stronger. The bargaining power of suppliers is determined by the factors shown in Figure 2.7.

If there are few suppliers, the buyer has very little room for bargaining. Suppliers in such circumstances can operate oligopolistically, setting the terms for business between them. For example, hairdressing businesses in the UK have a choice of only six or seven suppliers of hairdressing products. Most hairdressing businesses are small, owner-managed concerns with very little buying power, so they are unable to bargain effectively with their suppliers.

Suppliers' products cannot always substitute for each other. A typical example is the motor industry: spare parts for Ford cars will not fit Toyotas and vice-versa, so the garage business is forced to buy from a small group of suppliers. Likewise, in the computer software industry some software will not run on certain operating systems.

Vertical integration of the industry refers to the degree to which the supply chain is owned or controlled by a few firms. A highly integrated industry (for example the oil industry, where a few companies control everything from extraction through refining and distribution to the petrol forecourt) does not allow many opportunities for competitors to enter.

The importance of buyers to the supplier is about the extent to which a buyer represents a strategic opportunity for the supplier. Large buyers such as major retailers may control the market – for example, the toy industry is largely controlled by Toys R Us. In general, though, the evidence is that few companies bother (or are able) to develop their suppliers effectively (Wagner 2006).

> **Vertical integration** A situation in which one company controls or owns suppliers and customers throughout the supply chain.

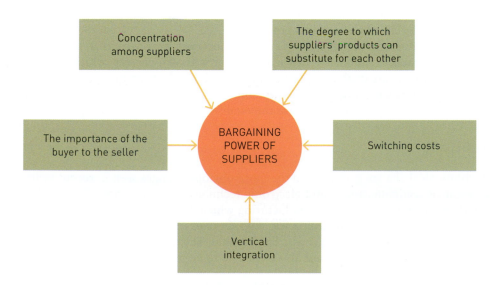

Figure 2.7   Factors in the bargaining power of suppliers

Finally, if it would be expensive to switch from one supplier to another, the suppliers occupy a strong position. This is the case for firms such as Microsoft, since switching from Microsoft systems might well mean making changes to hardware, retraining staff, redesigning administrative systems and so forth.

The bargaining power of customers is determined in much the same way as the bargaining power of suppliers, except that the deciding factors work the other way round.

New entrants to a market can pose a threat for the established companies, but the danger of new firms being able to enter the market is limited by the following factors:

Economies of scale Cost savings resulting from large production runs.

Differentiation Factors that distinguish one product from another.

Switching cost The expenditure of money and effort resulting from changing from one product to another.

1. **Economies of scale**. If the industry is such that production can be carried out efficiently only on a very large scale, entry will be less likely. For example, modern steel production operates efficiently only when steel is produced in very large quantities.
2. Product **differentiation**. If the products are very similar, new entrants can easily produce copies. If, however, the existing companies have managed to create highly differentiated products (either by strong branding or by using patented technology) it becomes difficult for new companies to establish a foothold in the market.
3. Capital requirements. If the capital outlay needed to enter the market is large, few companies will be able to raise the necessary money, especially without a track record in the industry. For example, for many years the major airlines had little or no serious competition. The cost of buying a fleet of aircraft was prohibitive. However, in recent years the wide availability of good second-hand aircraft has allowed niche operators such as Ryanair and easyJet to enter the market.
4. **Switching costs**. If it would be prohibitively expensive for the customers and consumers within the industry to change suppliers, new entrants will be unable to gain a toehold in the market. This is a strong barrier to entry.
5. Access to distribution channels. If the industry has already integrated the distribution network (the supply chain), new entrants will be unable to obtain distribution. This is a critical determinant of success in markets that are geographically large, such as the United States: the key issue for any new firm is obtaining distribution for its products.
6. Cost advantages independent of scale. Sometimes firms within an industry will have access to supplies of raw materials, or will own patents, which mean that newcomers are unable to produce competing products at an economical price. Of course, sometimes it is the newcomer that has the new patent or access to sources of supply, in which case the established firms may have a problem.

TECHNOLOGY

Technological change goes beyond the more obvious changes seen in recent years as a result of communications and electronic technology. For example, Toyota developed new technology for car manufacturing which enabled them to retool a factory to produce a new model in only a few days, instead of the six months or so it took their American and European rivals. This meant that the firm were able to make better use of capital equipment and also were able to be much more flexible in meeting changes in the market.

A technological change can transform an industry. Most of the products in common use today did not exist 100 years ago: refrigerators, televisions, dishwashers,

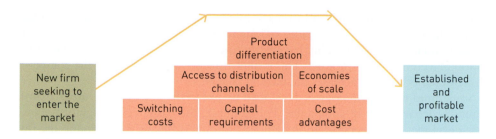

Figure 2.8   The market entry mountain

telecommunications satellites, microwave ovens, jet aircraft, computers, frozen foods and many others. The pace of technological change appears to be increasing, as more firms invest in research and development and ideas are more rapidly disseminated due to improved communications. For example, Sony now estimate that a new electronic device has a life of around three months before its replacement will be produced – whether the replacement is produced by Sony or by a competitor is irrelevant to the consumer, so the firm is forced to develop new products that will hurt the sales of its existing products.

The effects of this technological explosion are widespread for the firms concerned. As a threat, the possibility of competitors developing products that will wipe out existing products on the market is very real. All new products replace something else, since people almost always have an existing solution for a real problem. Transistors replaced the thermionic valve over a period of only a few years, computers have virtually eliminated the carbon-paper industry, and digital music players such as the iPod have gone a long way towards replacing CDs, as CDs have replaced vinyl records (and of course vinyl records replaced shellac 78 rpm records, which replaced wax cylinders).

A further problem is that the new technology might arise in an apparently unrelated industry. It would have been impossible for postal services to have recognised the threat from new computer technology in the 1970s, but the advent of cheap personal computers has led in turn to the Internet revolution, and the explosion in e-mailing. This has undoubtedly had a marked effect on postal services worldwide, as people send e-mails rather than writing letters. Equally, the development of electronic watches virtually destroyed the Swiss watch making industry, which relied on mechanical technology and did not have the necessary expertise or technological infrastructure to make the necessary changes.

Maintaining a technological lead requires firms to make heavy investments in research and development. This in turn means that the investment must be repaid from sales of the product – and given the shorter product life cycles involved, the payback must be very high. This means either that the profit margins per unit of product must be high, or the market must be very large. This is why most companies in rapidly changing markets such as electronics have adopted a global marketing approach. This is the only way these firms can access a large enough market to be able to obtain the necessary returns on their capital.

Because of the domination of large, globalised firms in high-technology areas, smaller firms find themselves unable to compete effectively. This has resulted in a number of cross-border collaborations. In some cases these have worked well, especially in relatively low-tech industries such as vehicle design and building, but in others the results have been less than exciting.

In most cases companies tend to make minor improvements to existing products rather than aim to make complete redesigns. Sometimes these improvements are made to their own products, but frequently companies will produce a 'me-too' adaptation of a competitor's product. This is likely to lead to a response by the competing firm, which of course increases the pace of change.

Sometimes new technology is developed by university researchers rather than by research departments of companies. For example, the basic technology of the laser was developed at universities in the United States and Russia, even though the final working model was developed at Hughes Laboratories. Even then this revolutionary device had no discernible purpose – it was four or five years before anyone was able to make practical use of lasers. This is an example of the value of pure research (research that has no immediate practical value).

In some cases technological development is delayed by legislation. New drugs need to go through extremely rigorous testing and in some countries (notably the United States) product liability legislation places a strict liability on manufacturers to ensure that their products are safe. This is another reason for producing 'me-too' products: the competitor has already dealt with the safety issues.

INDUSTRY ISSUES

Any competitive act must be considered in the light of possible retaliation. The structure and nature of the industry is crucial in understanding the possible results of any actions. The intensity of competitive response will depend on the following factors:

1. The degree of concentration in the industry. The fewer the competitors, the greater the likelihood of an oligopoly.
2. The rate of growth of the industry. Rapidly growing industries are usually less stable than established industries, with greater fall-out of companies that are unable to adapt quickly enough. This means that marketers must be very quick to respond to competitors, and be prepared for rapid retaliation in turn.
3. The degree of differentiation. If the products are essentially the same (for example, petrol) the nature of competition shifts to other factors. In some cases the other factor is price, but this is a dangerous way to compete because it squeezes profit margins. Marketers generally aim to compete on service or product features rather then price.
4. Cost structures. If fixed costs are high (for example because the industry is capital-intensive) profits are dependent on maintaining a high level of sales. The airline industry is a prime example: airlines cannot afford to have planes flying half-empty, so they are prepared to discount seats in order to maintain efficiency. Effective marketing means having systems in place to accommodate this.
5. Investment structures. If the industry is one in which new investment is made in sizeable chunks, new entrants will make a strong impact on existing firms until demand catches up. For example, if there are three hotels in a town and a fourth one opens up, the impact will be substantial, at least in the short term.
6. Competitive information. If firms in the industry can inform themselves easily about what their competitors are doing, oligopolistic behaviour is the likeliest outcome. On the other hand, some industries (such as farming) operate in almost total ignorance of what other farmers are planting this year, which leads to occasional surpluses or shortages.

7. Strategic objectives of competitors. In some industries, the firms have strategic objectives that do not conflict with other firms in the industry. For example, Ford does not compete strongly with Rolls-Royce because they are aiming at different sections of the car market.
8. Cost of leaving the industry. In some industries, capital assets that have a theoretical book value in the millions may have little or no second-hand value, and thus any firm that leaves the industry will have to leave behind its assets, and thus go bankrupt. Mining and steel production are examples.

The industry environment may be controlled by sources of supply, or by a lack of customers: for example, the oil industry is controlled in large part by the OPEC countries, who are the producers of petroleum. In the past, the oil companies ran the industry, but during the 1970s the oil-producing countries realised that they held the real power if they were prepared to act together, and they have controlled the world price of oil ever since. At the other end of the supply chain, aircraft manufacturers have relatively few potential customers. Most of the world's airlines are too small to be able to afford new aircraft, so manufacturers can only approach a relatively small number of major national airlines. Equally, there are relatively few large aircraft manufacturers in the world.

Internal environment

The firm's internal environment is the internal culture, staff relationships and resource constraints that colour all of the activities and decisions made by the organisation.

All firms operate with limited resources. Firms create competency in what they do by making appropriate combinations of the resources at their disposal: the more effectively the resources are deployed, the better the firm will do in the competitive environment. Ensuring that the internal environment is working well is an important aspect of management: it is not always part of the marketing manager's remit, but it is (at the conceptual level) marketing.

STAFF RELATIONSHIPS

The relationships between staff within the organisation are key in ensuring an effective working environment. While there are many areas of staff relationships that are outside the control of managers, management should be able to create an environment in which staff relationships can flourish.

Organisations have, in general, two structures that work in parallel. The **formal structure** is shown on the organisation chart, and shows where each person fits into the overall hierarchy. This structure shows who is answerable to whom, and which department is responsible for which set of activities. People in the formal structure have specific job titles and, usually, fairly clearly defined responsibilities to the organisation.

The **informal structure**, on the other hand, is not shown on any organisational chart. It comprises the friendships and alliances which are struck up by people who share a lift home, or who have lunch together every day, or who meet at the photocopier or coffee machine. The informal structure cuts right across the organisation chart, and is often more powerful in running the organisation than is the formal structure. Where the formal structure lays down exactly what people should be doing, the informal structure allows people to be flexible in what they do. Problems that have been unaccounted-for in the organisational chart can be

Formal structure The official relationships between members of an organisation.

Informal structure The unofficial relationships between members of an organisation.

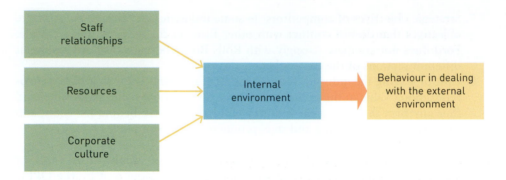

Figure 2.9   The internal environment

solved by people who can call in a favour from a friend in another department. For this reason, managers should encourage the informal structure to develop – it provides a flexibility of response in a changing world. Research shows that joint reward systems and social networking are the two most important factors in reducing conflict between marketers and others within the company (Chimhanzi 2004). In many organisations, fostering the informal structure is seen as an internal marketing responsibility.

CORPORATE CULTURE

Culture is a set of shared rules and beliefs. Within organisations, beliefs will develop, and a corporate culture will eventually emerge. Corporate culture has been called 'the way we do things round here' and it can be a powerful influence on staff behaviour. Research shows that people are able to have one set of beliefs outside work, and an entirely different set of beliefs in the workplace. However, corporate culture and personal ethics should not be too widely separated: staff need to feel that they are working for an ethical organisation (see Chapter 3 for more on this).

Developing the appropriate corporate culture is a lengthy process, since people change slowly. Often the beginning of a corporate culture is the firm's mission statement, in which the company lays down its long-term aims and overall beliefs. In some cases, a charismatic leader will be able to impose a corporate personality on the organisation, but this type of corporate culture sometimes dies with the founder.

RESOURCE CONSTRAINTS

All organisations suffer from a lack of resources, but of course some suffer more seriously than others. What is more important is the way the organisation uses its resources and plays to its strengths. As an analogy, a good cook can take flour, butter, apples and so forth and make an apple pie. A great chef can take the same ingredients and produce a delicious confection – but a bad cook can produce an inedible mess. The resources plus the management input constitute what the marketer has to work with, and no matter how wonderful the marketing campaign being planned, and no matter how effective it would be, the plan cannot work if the organisation does not have the necessary resources.

Marketers are frequently faced with the frustrating situation in which senior managers will cut the marketing budget because business is bad. Marketers naturally respond by saying that cutting the marketing budget is the worst possible solution, since it will inevitably lead to a further loss of business, but if this argument does not work the marketers are forced into a situation of having to achieve the same results with less resources. This often calls for considerable creativity.

Chapter summary

The environment within which the business operates clearly affects marketing plans. Marketers are always looking outwards, mainly towards the customers and competitors who make up the market, but they also need to consider the internal environment because this is where the resources come from to maintain a marketing plan.

Key points

- No business operates in a vacuum.
- The macro environment is largely uncontrollable: the micro environment is much more susceptible to influence or control.
- The elements of the environment overlap, and also impinge on each other.
- Interest rates are the main tool of government control of the economy, since globalised business means that most governments are too small to influence the world economy.
- The ageing populations of most industrial countries are often well-off: they represent an opportunity, not a threat.
- Judges create law by making decisions on specific cases.
- Competition may be indirect: it may not even come from the same industry.
- Technological change can also come from unrelated industries.

Review questions

1. How might a rise in the rate of inflation affect marketing policy?
2. How might a toy manufacturer respond to the changing demography of Europe?
3. Which industries might be affected by the discovery of an anti-ageing drug?
4. How might a large company and a small company differ in their dealings with a government regulatory body?
5. How might governments respond to a cross-border merger between two major steel companies?
6. What might be the effect on food retailers of the increase in single-person households?
7. How might a pizza delivery service define its competition?
8. How might a company develop a positive corporate culture?
9. Why do most companies tend to take an incremental approach to innovation?
10. Why would an industry spend time and money to establish its own regulatory system rather than allow the government to do so?

Case study revisited: Costain West Africa

Sub-Saharan Africa is an interesting continent, culturally speaking. There is a sense of collective responsibility, which is often sadly lacking in northerly countries – Africans look after each other.

Costain West Africa managed to survive the sudden financial crisis because the company has a foothold in both the public and the private sector. It is rare for both sectors to be in trouble at once, so Costain managed to switch efforts back and forth between its government projects (for example working on the Jebba–Kano railway line) and its private-sector projects (building an eight-storey apartment building in Abuja). The result was that the firm came through the crisis well – but unfortunately many of its suppliers and subcontractors hit financial difficulties as their funding dried up.

Costain West Africa's response was to provide lines of credit to these crucial suppliers. This meant they could keep their heads above water until the crisis eased, and would then be well-placed to take advantage of any new growth in the Nigerian economy. Of course this benefited Costain West Africa as well, since without suppliers and subcontractors the company would be unable to function, but it is an approach few Northern companies would have taken. Costain West Africa also announced that the company would be funding the training of local men as construction workers, since the crisis meant that foreign workers could no longer be brought into the country.

Costain West Africa has a strong commitment to sustainable, socially-responsible business, but there is no doubt that helping others through the crisis has benefited the company very directly.

Case study: Ladbroke's

Gambling is, of course, a vice – yet many of us enjoy the occasional bet, and for a lot of people it's almost a way of life. As a business, it's often regarded as recession-proof, because people will sometimes try to win their way out of financial troubles. Gambling offers people a degree of hope in troubled times, so bookmakers can see a rise in business during financial crises.

Ladbroke's had its beginnings in the 19th century, acting as a horse agent. During the early part of the 20th century the company was limited to taking bets only at racecourses – off-course gambling was illegal. Then in 1961 the UK government made off-course betting shops legal, and a gambling revolution swept the country. Although restrictions were tough, and licences to run betting shops were difficult to obtain, this move regularised what was happening anyway – instead of people dealing with illegal back-street bookmakers, the industry was out in the open and could be regulated. In 2005, the UK government legalised advertising for betting shops, and again there was a increase in business. The legislation also allowed for on-line gambling (which cannot be controlled anyway, since the Internet is global) which gave another boost to the industry.

During the 1980s and 1990s the company diversified into other leisure businesses: it bought DIY chain Texas Homecare in 1986, selling it on to Sainsbury's PLC in 1995: in 1999 it bought the Stakis hotel chain and rebranded it as Hilton. These ventures were partly successful in that the company turned a profit on their resale, but eventually the firm reverted to its roots, and is now Britain's largest bookmaker, and overall the largest bookmaker in the world. Ladbroke's is an innovative company – it was the first bookmaker to offer a loyalty card, it was among the first to set up on-line gambling (from its office in Gibraltar), and it was the first company to introduce fixed-odds football betting. In 2010 the company announced that its staff would act as call centre operators during quiet times, as a way of maximising efficiency: rather than relocate the company's call centre to Gibraltar, as at least one rival had done, incoming calls were routed to betting shops all over the country so that staff could take bets over the phone. This greatly increased the efficiency of the operation since staff time was used more effectively, and in any case telephone betting was going into decline as a result of a greater emphasis on on-line betting.

Sometimes this creativity has a downside – the company's advertising has been the subject of complaints from the Advertising Standards Authority, some of which were upheld.

The company has a liking for expanding by acquisition: a failed takeover of on-line sporting bookie Sportingbet in 2011 was caused by a change in the Turkish regulatory framework. The Turkish government introduced a ban on on-line gambling in 2007, but of course this only applied to companies with a base in Turkey: Sportingbet simply moved its Turkish operation to the Channel Islands, but there were still regulatory problems since the intention of the Turkish authorities was to make on-line gambling impossible for Turks. Sportingbet therefore planned to sell the Turkish operation so that the merger with Ladbroke's could go ahead, but Ladbroke's legal team decided that the risk of regulatory fallout was too great – in other words, they were afraid that the Turkish government might yet be able to impose sanctions on the company for illegal gambling.

Another takeover, this time of 888.com (another on-line gambling rival) also failed when the parties could not agree a price. Market watchers agreed that the gambling industry was ripe for takeovers – but Ladbroke's seemed to keep missing the bus. Nevertheless, corporate disappointment was considerably mollified by an impressive leap in profits from the company's gaming machines, which are sited in pubs, clubs and cafes throughout the country. The appetite for takeovers was not diminished, either – in January 2013 the company announced a takeover bid for Irish on-line gambling company Betdaq. This company operates a system whereby gamblers can place bets directly with each other, with the bookmaker taking a cut of the bet.

Ladbroke's has certainly ridden out many storms during its long existence. Changes in regulations, economic ups and down, mergers and acquisitions have all contributed to the company's history. As a member of the FTSE 250 the company has the prestige and success usually accorded only to major manufacturing or retail companies: gambling has certainly come out of the shadows and into the mainstream.

Questions

1. How have regulatory changes affected Ladbroke's?
2. How has the company responded to volatility in the marketplace?
3. How has technology played its part in Ladbroke's planning?
4. What should Ladbroke's do to reduce risk in future?
5. What competitive pressures are there on Ladbroke's?

Further reading

This is a somewhat specialised area, with relatively few books dedicated solely to the marketing environment. However, here are some possibilities.

Adrian Palmer and Bob Hartley, *The Business and Marketing Environment* (Maidenhead, McGraw–Hill, 1999). This gives a comprehensive coverage of the marketing environment and the management issues surrounding it.

The UK's Chartered Institute of Marketing also publish several study guides on the marketing environment, geared towards the CIM Diploma examinations (www.cim.co.uk/Home.aspx).

References

Benady, D. (1997) Ofgas must dispel advertising hot air. *Marketing Week*, 4 December, pp. 19–20.

Census 20011. Office for National Statistics. www.ons.gov.uk.

Chimhanzi, Jacqueline (2004) The impact of integration mechanisms on marketing/HR dynamics. *Journal of Marketing Management*, 20 (7/8): 713–40.

Cruijsen, H., Eding, H. and Gjatelma, T. (2002) Demographic consequences of enlargement of the European Union with the 12 candidate countries. Statistics Netherlands, Division of Social and Spatial Statistics, Project Group European Demography, January.

Euromonitor (2004) *Alcoholic Drinks in Ireland*. London: Euromonitor.

Porter, M.E. (1990) How competitive forces shape strategy. *Harvard Business Review*, 57 (2): 137–45.

Wagner, Stephan M. (2006) Supplier development practices: an exploratory study. *European Journal of Marketing*, 40 (5/6): 554–71.

More online

To gain free access to additional online resources to support this chapter please visit:
www.sagepub.co.uk/blythe3e

Part Two

Markets and people

This section takes the theoretical underpinnings of marketing further and aims to show how marketing relates to the people it serves: the consumers, the firms, the employees and other stakeholders. Markets are the aggregate of consumers, suppliers and competitors: this section is concerned with techniques for dealing with all these elements, and especially with the people who make up these groups.

Chapter 3 covers consumer behaviour. Consumers are at the centre of everything marketers do, so the importance of understanding their behaviour cannot be overstated. We are all consumers, of course. This chapter includes the theoretical underpinning derived from behavioural sciences, and connects this to real-world purchasing behaviour.

Chapter 4 is concerned with business-to-business marketing. There are differences between the ways people behave when they are buying for themselves or their families, and the ways they behave when buying on behalf of the firms they work for: this chapter shows how these differences manifest themselves in a business-to-business environment.

Chapter 5 is concerned with information-gathering. Good information about the market is a prerequisite for any decision-making; marketing research is the term for all the methods used for collecting and analysing data in order to generate knowledge.

Choosing which customers to do business with is important when trying to allocate corporate resources. Chapter 6 looks at segmenting (dividing the marketing into groups of people with similar needs) and targeting (deciding which groups to approach). The chapter also covers positioning, which is about putting the brand into the correct place in the consumer's mind relative to competing brands.

For many people, marketing is all about communications. Of course, advertising and so forth are the most visible parts of marketing: Chapter 7 outlines the basic communications theories that underpin marketing communications, and also introduces some of the techniques that marketers use.

Chapter 8 looks at foreign markets. International marketing and globalisation have become hot topics in recent years – as has opposition to globalisation. This chapter looks at some of the theory and debate surrounding international marketing, and also examines the practical aspects of entering overseas markets.

CHAPTER ③
Consumer behaviour

LEARNING OBJECTIVES

After reading this chapter, you should be able to:

- Describe the decision-making process.

- Explain the role of emotion in the decision-making process.

- Explain the role of information processing in decision-making.

- Describe the trade-offs in information collection and processing.

- Understand the role of goals in motivating purchasing behaviour.

- Develop ways of handling complaints.

- Understand learning processes.

- Explain the role of social groups in influencing behaviour.

- Explain how perception operates.

- Explain the role of self-concept in consumer motivation.

Introduction

Consumer behaviour consists of all the activities people undertake when obtaining, consuming and disposing of products and services (Blackwell et al. 2001). Studying consumer behaviour involves looking at what influences people to behave in particular ways when obtaining products, using them and disposing of them.

Understanding the way people think when they go about their purchasing behaviour is a key factor in successful marketing. The motivations, decision-making processes and post-purchase behaviour of consumers are useful when seeking to persuade people to choose one product rather than another, and to encourage people to recommend products to their friends.

In terms of studying marketing as an academic discipline, consumers are at the heart of any consideration of business policy. Understanding consumer behaviour is central to communications planning, to strategy planning and to segmentation and targeting. Reading this chapter will introduce you to the key issues and ways of thinking that inform everything marketers do.

Preview case study: Riverford Organics

In recent years there has been an ever-increasing interest in food. In some cases this has led to people becoming better chefs: in other cases it has led to people taking a greater interest in the source of their food. Food scares have abounded – tales of food grown artificially, of genetically modified foods, of the various sprays and fertilisers used, and a great many stories about the way supermarkets treat fresh produce so that it has a longer shelf-life. Not unnaturally, this has led some people to mistrust the food industry and look elsewhere for their nourishment.

Not everybody can grow their own, of course – many do not have the time or the gardening skill to have an allotment and grow their own vegetables. Hence the rising interest in organically grown vegetables and meat. Organic farmers have to adhere to strict regulations laid down by the Soil Association regarding fertilisers, pesticides and the source of seeds, and in the case of meat they must adhere to regulations about feeding, housing and caring for the animals. This goes a long way towards inspiring confidence in consumers, but does not answer the questions raised by the distribution networks.

This is where Riverford Organics comes in. Riverford started out from Guy Watson's farm in Devon. Guy decided to start growing organic vegetables in the 1980s, but needed to find a way of getting them to consumers. In 1993 he hit on the idea of arranging direct deliveries of boxes of vegetables, straight to the end consumer. At first he supplied only local people – family and friends living within a few miles of his farm. The idea soon caught on, though, and he began supplying people further away.

Eventually, Guy recruited four other farmers with the same ethos, and now Riverford supplies most of England and South Wales, delivering almost 50,000 boxes of vegetables a week. Recently, they found a farm in the Vendée, in France, which is able to supply fresh vegetables during the British 'hungry gap' (early spring) when there are few vegetables around – the winter vegetables having finished, and the early summer ones not being ready yet.

The decision-making process

Psychology The study of thought processes.

Sociology The study of behaviour in groups.

Economics The study of supply and demand.

Anthropology The study of culture.

The study of consumers draws from other scientific disciplines: **psychology**, **sociology**, **economics** and **anthropology** among them.

Many different models have been developed for illustrating the consumer decision-making process. An early model was that of John Dewey (1910). Dewey's model is as follows:

1. A difficulty is felt.
2. The difficulty is located and defined.
3. Possible solutions are suggested.
4. Consequences are considered.
5. A solution is accepted.

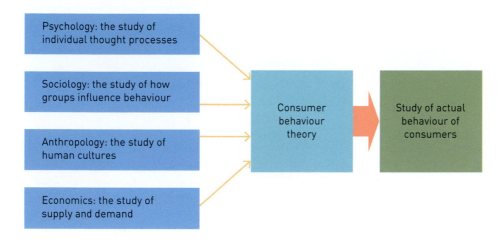

Figure 3.1 Contributions to studying consumers

This model is, of course, somewhat simplistic. In most cases, people do not go through such an elaborate and considered process. Many purchases are made without apparent conscious thought – people often buy as a result of unexplained impulses, or simply fall in love with a product for no apparent reason. Later, Engel, Kollat and Blackwell developed the EKB model of consumer behaviour, which later became the CDP (Consumer Decision Process) model, and which follows seven stages (Blackwell et al. 2001). These are:

1. Need recognition. The individual recognises that something is missing from his or her life.
2. Search for information. This information search may be internal (remembering facts about products, or recalling experiences with them) or external (reading about possible products, visiting shops, etc.)
3. Pre-purchase evaluation of alternatives. The individual considers which of the possible alternatives might be best for fulfilling the need.
4. Purchase. The act of making the final selection and paying for it.
5. Consumption. Using the product for the purpose of fulfilling the need.
6. Post-consumption evaluation. Considering whether the product actually satisfied the need or not, and whether there were any problems arising from its purchase and consumption.
7. Divestment. Disposing of the product, or its packaging, or any residue left from consuming the product.

The similarity between Dewey's model and the CDP model is obvious, and similar criticisms apply, but both models offer a basic outline of how people make consumption decisions. People do not buy unless they feel they have a need (see Chapter 1 for a definition of what constitutes a need). A need is felt when there is a divergence between the person's actual state and their desired state. The degree of difference between the two states is what determines the level of motivation the person feels to do something about the problem, and this will in turn depend on a number of external factors.

For example, a driver who is late for an appointment may feel thirsty, but not thirsty enough to stop somewhere for a drink and thus make himself even later. The thirst would have to become unbearable, or the appointment would have to be unimportant, for the driver to deviate from the purpose of the trip.

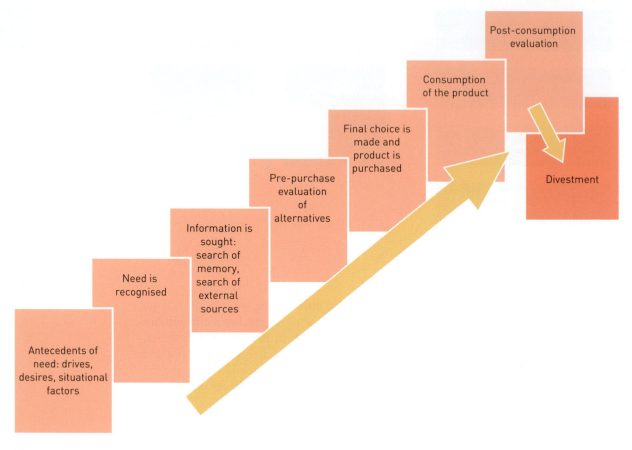

Figure 3.2   Decision-making process

Desired state The situation the individual wishes to be in.

Actual state The situation the individual is currently experiencing.

There are two possible reasons for a divergence between the **desired state** and the **actual state**: either the actual state has changed, or the desired state has changed. In practice, it is rare for the actual and desired states to be the same, but most people will tolerate a small discrepancy: if the actual and desired states were the same, the person would be perfectly happy and have everything he or she could want, which is unlikely in an imperfect world.

Causes of the shift in the actual state could be either of the following (Onkvisit and Shaw 1994);

Assortment depletion Using up resources or wearing out products.

1. **Assortment depletion**. Consumption, spoilage, wear and tear, or loss of a possession from the person's assortment of goods will cause a shift in the actual state.
2. Income change. An upward change in the individual's income will allow more purchases to be made: likewise, a downward shift in income will cause a reduction in the amount or quality of goods that can be purchased. The same applies to a windfall such as a lottery win or inheritance, or a sudden unexpected expense such as a lawsuit or accident.

Marketers have little control over the actual state of consumers. Causes of shifts in the desired state, on the other hand, often result from marketing activities. New information will often change a person's expectations because he or she becomes aware that there may be a better solution to his or her consumption problems than that

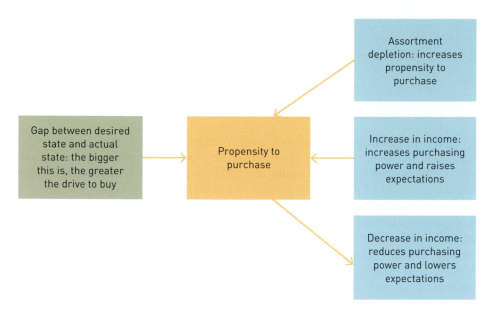

Figure 3.3   Influences on the propensity to purchase

currently being used. Marketers are often able to supply this new information through an advertisement or a news story about the product, or even through encouraging word-of-mouth. Much of what marketing is about is changing consumers' desired states by showing them products that will solve their needs better than the products they are currently using.

In some cases a shift in the actual state also leads to a shift in the desired state. For example, someone who receives a pay rise may develop new aspirations – having been perfectly happy driving a small basic car, the individual suddenly develops the desire to own a luxury car, for example. Previously the luxury car was not even under consideration because it would be totally out of reach, but the possibility of being able to buy it leads to the desire to own it, through a re-evaluation of the individual's desires.

Psychology of complication
The desire to make one's life more complex and therefore more interesting.

Think outside this box!

Marketers are often accused of creating needs where no needs previously existed. This they hotly deny – needs were there before marketing, after all!

And yet marketers do raise aspirations – nobody knew they needed a BMW until it was invented, nobody needed the electric toothbrush, nobody needed a computer in their living-room, let alone in their washing machine.

On the other hand, nobody needed houses until they were invented – caves were perfectly adequate. Nor did we need fire, or spears, or bread. So at what point do we say that we have progressed far enough in making our lives more comfortable and convenient?

The **psychology of complication** states that people seek to complicate their lives: the **psychology of simplification** states that people seek to simplify their lives. In fact, at different times in our lives we may seek a more complex, interesting and stimulating

Psychology of simplification
The desire to make one's life simpler and therefore less demanding.

life (psychology of complication) while at other times we will find life too difficult and look for ways of simplifying our existences (psychology of simplification). Product purchases play a role in both systems (Hoyer and Ridgway 1984).

Pre-purchase activities

Having recognised the need, people will undertake a series of pre-purchase activities. The information search may be internal or external: for most routine purchases, people need only remember which brand they usually buy, and even for less-frequent purchases people often already know a lot about the product category and even the brands involved.

External search Looking for information in places other than memory.

In other cases, for example with high-value or infrequent purchases, consumers often need to carry out an **external search**. This probably means obtaining information from the Internet in the first instance: but newspapers, brochures, TV programmes, friends, salespeople and helplines may also be used. This information, combined with what is already known, completes the information search.

Sometimes an individual will set out with a belief that he or she already knows enough to be able to make the purchase, but is then confronted with new information at the point of purchase. For example, the last time an individual might have bought a stereo system could have been ten years previously: such a person would not necessarily be aware of the advances in technology that have occurred in the interim, and may be confronted by a huge array of new systems. This would cause that individual to re-assess his or her level of knowledge and return to the information search stage of the process.

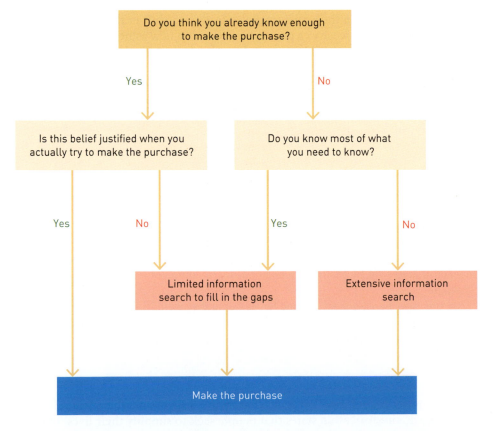

Figure 3.4 Information search

Information search efforts are not usually very extensive, even when major purchases are being considered. This is because of the amount of time and effort that needs to be expended when carrying out an extensive search. In fact, there is evidence to show that information overload will reduce consumers' propensity to buy (Keller and Staelin 1987). Confusion can easily be created: research shows that consumer confusion has three dimensions, based on a similarity with other information, information overload, and the ambiguity of information (Walsh et al. 2007). Confusion caused by information overload is not uncommon when searching the Internet, simply because there is so much information available (as well as misinformation and downright lies). Such confusion obviously makes decision-making much harder, and also creates a degree of unease for consumers. This has been the source of success for comparison websites such as Confused.com and Comparethemarket.com. People certainly go to considerable efforts to avoid marketing communications, flipping past the advertisements in magazines and switching channels to avoid TV advertising. There is more on this in Chapter 7.

Assortment adjustment is the act of entering the market to replenish or exchange the assortment of goods the consumer owns. People recognise that their assortment of products is not what it should be in order to meet their needs (i.e. solve their day-to-day problems). Assortment adjustment can be programmed or unprogrammed: programmed assortment adjustment is about the habitual daily purchases that do not require much thought. Unprogrammed assortment adjustment needs much more thought, and refers to buying products that are new to the consumer. Non-programmed assortment adjustment falls into three categories, as follows (Onkvisit and Shaw 1994):

> **Assortment adjustment** Changing the proportions of products owned in order to increase satisfaction.

1. **Impulse purchases**. These are not based on any plan, and happen because the consumer is confronted with a stimulus, usually chancing to see something appealing. In fact, impulse purchases are not necessarily as impulsive as might be supposed, and impulse buying has been further divided into four categories (Stern 1962). Pure impulse is based largely on the novelty of the product, reminder impulse relates to products that have been left off the shopping list, suggestion impulse relates to products which fulfil a previously unfelt need, and planned impulse occurs when the individual has gone out to buy one type of product or one brand, but is prepared to be swayed by special offers or new ideas. Typically, impulse buyers are also variety seekers: impulse buying often happens as an antidote to boredom (Sharma et al. 2010). There is some evidence that the Internet encourages impulse buying – it is certainly the case that people often give to charities on impulse when surfing the Internet (Bennett 2009).

> **Impulse purchases** Purchases made without apparent conscious thought.

2. **Limited problem-solving** takes place when the individual is already familiar with the product class and merely wants to update his or her available information. Limited decision-making is probably the most common form of unprogrammed assortment adjustment, because most people are familiar with the product categories they buy, even if they are unfamiliar with new brands or new models of the products.

> **Limited problem-solving** Routine purchasing behaviour.

3. **Extended problem-solving** takes place when the product category is new to the consumer. For example, someone who has never owned a notebook computer would need to gather a great deal of information and see a lot of machines before making a decision.

> **Extended problem-solving** Non-routine purchasing behaviour.

FACTORS AFFECTING THE SEARCH FOR INFORMATION

The information search will be affected by a number of factors connected with the individual's situation. Assortment adjustment can take the form of either **replenishment**

> **Replenishment** Replacing products that have been worn out or used up.

		Value of the information	
		High	Low
Cost of obtaining the information	High	People are prepared to pay, albeit reluctantly	Extremely unlikely that people will pay for information
	Low	People will obtain the information readily	People may not even try to obtain the information

Figure 3.5   Trade-offs between cost and value of information

Extension Increasing the number of products owned.

or **extension**. Replenishing the assortment (i.e. replacing worn-out or used items) requires the least information, since the consumer already knows what works and what does not. Extending the assortment requires much more information, since it implies learning about products the consumer does not currently own.

The perceived value of the information is important in deciding whether it is worthwhile to collect it. For example, an information search on the Internet may be a very useful exercise provided it does not lead to paid-for sites. Some people would be prepared to pay for information about a potential purchase, whereas others would not. The relevance of the information is also a factor. If it has been a long time since the last purchase of the product category, new information might be highly relevant. Provided the consumer was happy with the last purchase, the internal information will be regarded as relevant, so there will be no need to seek out new information. In other words, if it ain't broke, don't fix it.

Real-life marketing: Tesco

When Tesco introduced its loyalty card in 1995, the company little knew what a huge set of marketing problems – and a huge set of marketing solutions – the card would create. The card users win Clubcard points every time they use the card, so they present the card every time they shop at Tesco: Tesco has a fairly complete record of each customer's purchasing behaviour, because the checkouts store the information and pass it to the central computer.

At first, Tesco saw this as an opportunity to draw customers' attention to products they were not, at present, buying. Customers were mailed special offers geared individually and based on products they were not currently putting through the checkouts. This meant that someone who always buys basic ingredients for cooking would be sent offers for ready meals, customers who apparently never buy bread would be sent vouchers for money off bread purchases, and so forth. Unfortunately, these vouchers were rarely redeemed – presumably an enthusiastic amateur chef would be unlikely to buy ready meals, and someone allergic to bread would hardly be swayed by a money-off voucher.

Nowadays Tesco sends vouchers which offer products that are close to, but not exactly, what the consumer usually buys. This 'If you like that, you will probably like this' approach has paid off in a big way: Tesco's loyalty card is one of a very few such cards that really does inspire loyalty. This is because the company has ensured that it is customer-centred, not centred on what the store wants to sell. In 2004, Tesco announced record profits – perhaps not a coincidence?

If you're going to create a loyalty scheme like this, here are the rules:

- Keep good records of your loyalty scheme customers. The idea is to have as much detail as possible on them – home address, e-mail address, phone number, anything they are prepared to let you have. Obviously you'll be keeping a record of their purchases.
- Promote products that they like and already buy, rather than trying to shift them onto buying new things. People don't want a sales pitch when you're pretending to be a friend.
- Treat the loyal customers as individuals – don't send out blanket communications to all of them, customise each one.

The perceived risk of the transaction refers to the possibility of unforeseen consequences (Bauer 1960). The risks fall into four categories:

1. **Physical risk**. Buying the wrong product might cause injury.
2. **Financial risk**. The product might prove to be a waste of money.
3. **Functional risk**. The risk that the product will not do the job for which it is intended.
4. **Psychosocial risk**. The purchase might prove to be embarrassing. This is especially true of such items as clothing.

All of these risks reduce as knowledge increases, so if the perceived risk is high the information search is likely to be more extensive.

The **perceived cost of the search** is the degree to which the consumer has to commit resources to the search. These resources are not necessarily only financial: for example, an individual might ask a friend for help, and thus incur a social obligation to repay the favour at a later date. In some cases, the cost of making a full search might exceed the perceived risk of making a wrong purchase – for low-value items this is almost always the case. For example, buying the wrong type of shirt might result in a financial and social loss, but the financial loss is small and the social loss can be minimised by not wearing the shirt. Few people would expend a great deal of effort on an information search in these circumstances.

The perceived cost breaks down into time costs, money costs, and psychological costs. Highly paid people might have a greater appreciation of the value of time, and might be prepared to spend money in order to save time. Poorer customers may be more prepared to shop around in order to save money (Urbany 1986).

Money costs are the out-of-pocket expenses of searching. Comparing the prices of olive oil between supermarkets is relatively cheap, but few consumers would cross the Channel to see if the oil is cheaper in France or Spain.

Physical risk The danger of physical harm as the result of a purchase.

Financial risk The danger of losing money as the result of a purchase.

Functional risk The risk that a product or service will not provide the expected benefits.

Psychosocial risk The danger of looking foolish as a result of a purchase.

Perceived cost of search The degree to which an individual believes that an information search will be too arduous or expensive.

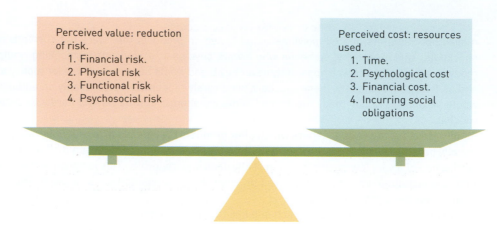

Figure 3.6   Risk management balance

The psychological cost of the information search includes frustration, the stress of finding the information or shopping around, talking to salespeople, and generally giving a lot of emotional energy to the search. Sometimes, of course, the search itself becomes pleasurable – many consumers enjoy shopping as an entertainment, and certainly many people enjoy Internet searches, even when they are not ready to buy yet. This can be a more important motivator than an actual need to buy something (Bloch et al. 1986).

Situational factors Elements of the immediate surroundings that affect decision-making.

Situational factors also affect the extent of the information search. In an emergency, for example a burst water pipe, few people would spend much time telephoning around several plumbers and comparing quotations for doing the work. Other situational variables might include product scarcity and the lack of available credit.

Since each consumer is an individual, individual characteristics play a part in the information search. Some people enjoy shopping around, others are bored by it: more importantly, most people like shopping for some categories of goods and not for others.

GOALS

Goal An objective.

Establishing a **goal** is the outcome of being motivated to do something about a problem. The basic outcome that the individual seeks to achieve is called an end goal, but it may be preceded by several sub-goals that lead to the end goal. For example, a simple goal hierarchy for buying a second-hand car might look like this:

1. Find out which car would best suit the individual's needs.
2. Find out which is the cheapest way of financing the purchase.
3. Find out who has the right type of car at the right price.
4. Go and buy the car.

In order to act on this basic plan of action, the person will have to establish a series of subsidiary goals, with matching activities. This 'route map' to buying the car might look like this:

1. Buy a used-car guide.
2. Decide which models look as if they might meet the need.
3. Decide what prices are within an acceptable range.

4. Telephone banks and loan companies for loan quotes.
5. Buy the local paper.
6. Call up anybody who seems to have the right kind of car, call round and buy the right one.

An inexperienced car buyer may need to establish a more elaborate and lengthy plan, such as this:

1. Decide to buy a car.
2. Ask around among family and friends to find out which car might suit the purpose. An experienced car-owner among this group might point out needs which the actual consumer had not thought of – a lack of experience sometimes translates into a lack of knowledge about one's own needs.
3. Look on-line for more information to fill in any gaps in knowledge, and verify the advice obtained from friends.
4. Go to used-car showrooms to examine the alternatives.
5. Find a helpful salesperson who appears honest and trustworthy.
6. Explain the needs to the salesperson.
7. Listen to the salesperson's advice, perhaps with a knowledgeable friend on hand to assess the value and honesty of the advice.
8. Make the purchase decision, based on the closeness of fit between the salesperson's description of the car and the needs that have been identified.
9. Buy the car.

Experienced people tend to use shorter lists of sub-goals because they are able to cut out some of the stages. In the case of inexperienced buyers, the risk involved is greater, so they will go to some trouble to reduce the risk to a minimum. The degree of risk perceived by the consumer depends on two factors. First, the seriousness of the possible damage caused by buying the wrong product, and second, the likelihood that the negative consequences will occur. For example, a failed climbing rope would (possibly) kill the person using it, but the possibility of failure is fairly remote.

For experienced buyers, the decision process will be much faster. For example, when older drivers buy new cars they consider fewer brands and dealers, and are more likely to choose long-established brands with which they are familiar (Lambert-Pandraud et al. 2005).

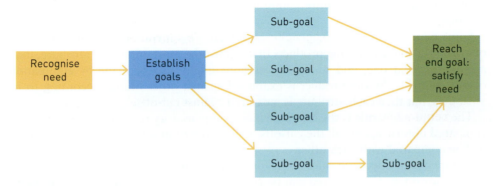

Figure 3.7 Goal hierarchies

Making the choice

Having recognised the need and collected the information, the customer is in a position to make the final choice of product. Making a final choice can be hard work – sometimes people end up making a bad choice simply because they get tired of trying to work out the best course of action (Baumeister 2004). People often begin by establishing a **consideration set**, which is the group of products any of which would provide an acceptable solution. The consideration set is usually small – only two or three choices – because too much choice leads to an inability to decide, or choice paralysis (Shankar et al. 2006). From a marketer's viewpoint, it is important to ensure that the company's product is in the consideration set, and this is actually the purpose of most advertising.

> **Consideration set** The group of products that might be capable of meeting a need.

The consideration set is established from the information obtained in the information search. People will often use decision rules (**heuristics**) when establishing the consideration set – for example, someone may have a rule that they never buy Eastern European cars. This would mean that Skoda, Dacia, and Lada would have no chance of being included in the consideration set. Another type of heuristic is a **cut-off**, by which the individual sets the limits of the decision. A cut-off may be based on price, i.e. no product above (or below) a particular price will be included, but equally a cut-off could be based on time (someone may not be prepared to consider any holiday that involves a flight of more than two hours) or product characteristics (no stereo will be considered that does not provide quadraphonic stereo).

> **Heuristic** A decision-making rule.

> **Cut-off** A filtering device that involves deciding the outer limits of acceptability for a given product's characteristics.

Judging product quality is often a result of **signals**. A signal is a surrogate for knowing what the characteristics of the product actually are. For example, the retailer's reputation would be a signal for the quality of the products on offer. Price is often used as a signal: people assume that the higher-priced products must be higher quality, even when there is no **objective** evidence to support this. Of course, if the consumer is able to inspect the product in detail, or has other evidence of the quality of the product, signals are less important. For on-line shoppers, signals become extremely important since it is not possible to examine the product until it has been delivered, at which point it might be embarrassing (or impossible) to return it.

> **Signal** A feature of the product or its surrounding attributes which conveys meaning about the product.
> **Objective** Not subject to bias from the individual.

Heuristics can be categorised as **compensatory** or **non-compensatory**. Compensatory heuristics can be offset against each other, whereas non-compensatory heuristics cannot. For example, someone may be prepared to accept a longer flight when going on holiday, because all the other characteristics of the holiday are exactly what is wanted. On the other hand, someone who becomes airsick if the flight is longer than two hours might be entirely unprepared to compromise on this aspect of the decision.

> **Compensatory** Of a heuristic, one that allows negative features to be offset against positive features.
> **Non-compensatory** Of a heuristic, one that does not allow a positive feature to offset a negative feature.
> **Lexicographic** A hierarchy of heuristics.

Some people adopt a **lexicographic** approach. This involves creating a hierarchy of attributes, and comparing products first against the most important attribute, then against the next one, and so forth. Decisions might also be made by elimination of aspects, whereby the product is examined against other brands according to its attributes, but then each attribute is measured against cut-offs.

> **Conjunctive** Heuristics that are considered together.

The **conjunctive** rule is the last of the non-compensatory rules. Here each brand is compared in turn against all the cut-offs. Only those brands that survive this process will be compared with each other.

Compensatory decision rules allow for trade-offs between attributes. This means that disadvantages in one area can be compensated for by advantages in another. The simple additive rule means that the individual makes a simple total of the product's positive attributes, and compares this with a similar tally for other

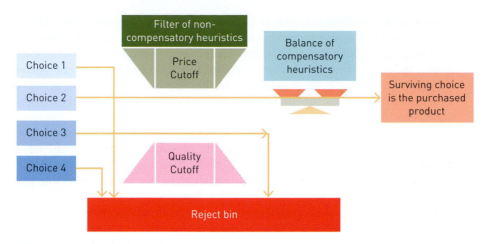

Figure 3.8   Decision rules

products. The weighted additive approach gives greater weight to some aspects than to others, and the phased decision strategy involves using rules in a sequence. This means that the individual might use non-compensatory heuristics such as cut-offs to reduce the number of options, then use a weighted additive rule to make the final choice between the remaining products.

Two more special categories of decision rule exist. First, people may use a constructive decision rule. This means that the rule must be established from scratch whenever a new situation is encountered. If the rule works, the consumer will store it in their memory for use in the future when a similar situation arises. Second, affect referral is the process whereby consumers use a standard attitude (often based on emotional reasons) to make a decision. For example, someone may have a dislike of Japanese products, based on a negative experience with a Japanese person. This type of rule is usually non-compensatory.

In fact, the bulk of consumer decision-making is not made in such a calculated manner. People decide their purchases at least as much on emotion as on logic, and rationalise the decision afterwards. Current thinking is that complex decisions are made as a series of waves of thought and action, in other words a multi-phase, non-linear process occurs (Lye et al. 2005).

Consumption of the product

Consumption of products appears at first sight to be an obvious area of consumer behaviour. However, from a marketing viewpoint, there are several issues around consumption which merit closer attention. For example:

1. When is the product consumed? In some cases this is known in advance – concert tickets, restaurant bookings, and visits to the hairdresser or dentist are all pre-booked. In other cases the time of consumption is implied, as with breakfast cereals, summer holidays, and take-away meals (which are consumed soon after purchase). In some cases marketers can increase sales by focusing on consumption rather than on purchase – for example, encouraging people to eat breakfast cereal as a snack, or to take holidays at non-traditional times.

2. Where is the product consumed? Products might be consumed in public, in private, or while doing something else. Consider the beer market. Some beer is consumed in bars and pubs, often on draught: some beer is consumed at home, indoors. Some beer is consumed outdoors, on picnics or when participating in an activity such as fishing or cricket. Each type of consumption has different implications for marketers – in particular, what type of container the beer is packed in, and what the implications are for branding. Beer consumed in the home while watching TV may be a supermarket own-brand, but the same individual might order a specific prestige brand in a pub, where friends can see what is being ordered. Beer carried on a picnic is easier to carry if it is in a can or a plastic bottle rather than in a heavy, breakable glass bottle.

3. How is the product consumed? Products have frequently been reinvented dramatically by purchasers (for example, using coffee filters to stop compost from leaking out of a plant-pot, or using coffee to transport earthworms on fishing trips) (Wansink 2004). Apart from these uses, which are clearly far-removed from those the producer had envisaged, consumers may have other consumption habits. For example, it is useful to know whether people use rice as a side-dish or as an ingredient in dishes such as paella. In a paella, people often use unbranded rice (except in Spain, where the rice is regarded as a key ingredient in the success of the dish). As a side-dish, people are more likely to have a favourite rice brand, believing that the flavour is more important when it is not disguised by other ingredients. In either case, knowing that someone has found a new way to use the product is useful, since the producer can disseminate this knowledge to other consumers.

4. How much is consumed? Identifying which type of person is a heavy consumer, which type is a moderate consumer, which type is a light consumer, and which type is a non-consumer can be extremely useful. Producers have to decide whether they can identify potential heavy users in the population of non-users, but may find it equally useful to try to convert light users into heavy users.

Figure 3.9 shows how these consumption behaviours relate.

During the act of consumption, the individual makes a judgement about the experience. This is a post-purchase evaluation, leading to a decision about whether the product was satisfying or not – in other words, whether the product fulfilled the consumer's expectations. A critical part of this evaluation is the feelings experienced during consumption: these can vary from fear through excitement, pleasure, relief, boredom and anger to guilt and regret. These feelings should be appropriate to the product, or a further purchase is unlikely. If the experience is largely emotional, the outcome will be evaluated by feelings: unsurprisingly, if the experience is largely practical, mental calculation is more important in evaluation (Hsee and Rottenstreich, 2004).

For example, compare the feelings illustrated in Table 3.1. In each case the feeling is the same, but the situation is different – and would result in a different propensity to repurchase.

Pre-purchase expectations fall into three categories:

● Equitable performance. This is the performance one could reasonably expect, given the cost and effort involved of obtaining the product (Woodruff et al. 1983).
● Ideal performance. What the customer hoped the product would do (Holbrook 1984).
● Expected performance. What the customer expects the product will actually do (Leichty and Churchill 1979).

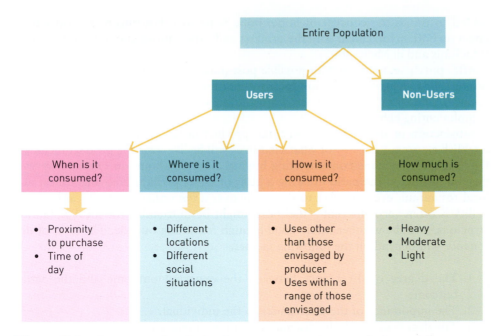

Figure 3.9   Consumption behaviour: users and usage (adapted from Blackwell et al. 2001)

Table 3.1   Feelings versus situations

Feeling	Situation One	Situation Two
Fear	White-knuckle ride at a theme park. In this situation, fear is fun because it provides the consumer with the confidence which comes from overcoming it, and also adds some excitement to his or her life.	Steering failure while driving one's new car on a motorway. In this case, the fear is genuinely life-threatening. It is not part of the expected benefits of the product.
Boredom	An afternoon spent game-fishing, when no fish were caught. Someone who books a game-fishing trip expects the thrill of the chase, the battle between angler and fish, and some impressive photographs to take home. Without the fish, all that results is a long ride on a boat.	An afternoon spent at a meditation centre. Here, boredom is the desired outcome, a chance to clear the brain and recharge the batteries. If the afternoon were exciting, it would not serve its purpose.
Anger	A football match where the referee makes a series of unfavourable decisions. Part of the pleasure of football matches is being able to shout at the referee – anger over something which is unlikely to affect one's lifestyle is part of the fun, releasing tension which may have built up as a result of not being allowed to shout at (say) the boss.	A hairdressing salon when the hairstyle has gone seriously wrong. In this circumstance, anger arises because there is probably not much that can be done to put matters right. In this case, anger is not part of the expectation.
Pain	At the dentist's, patients expect to feel some pain. Pain is seen as an acceptable part of the process, because there is a long-term benefit.	Almost any other location or consumption experience. People do not bargain for being hurt by the products and services they buy.

Added to this is the concept of hope: hope is positive but uncertain, and has an effect on both involvement with the product and expectations about its performance (MacInnis and deMello 2005).

After purchase, there are four possible post-purchase emotional states (Santos and Boote 2003): delight, satisfaction (positive indifference), acceptance (negative indifference), and dissatisfaction. Each will generate different levels of complaining or complimenting behaviour.

Perceptual map The individual's view of competing products.

Satisfaction or dissatisfaction with the product arises because consumers try to establish a **perceptual map** of what their lives will be like with the product included. For example, someone contemplating buying a holiday home in France may well imagine sitting on the patio drinking a glass of wine, perhaps enjoying a meal at a local restaurant, even chatting to the locals over a *vin ordinaire* at a local bar. The reality is often very different – the locals might be unfriendly, the local restaurant atrocious, and the weather rarely good enough for sitting outside. The level of dissonance will depend on the following factors:

1. The degree of divergence between the expected outcome and the actual outcome.
2. The importance of the discrepancy to the individual.
3. The degree to which the discrepancy can be corrected.
4. The cost of the purchase, in both time and money.

Compulsive consumption An obsessive need to buy and use products.

In some cases the results of the consumption experience are so positive that the consumer becomes 'hooked' on consumption. This may take the form of excessive consumption of a specific product (e.g. alcohol, chocolate, fatty foods etc.) or it may take a more general form, with the individual becoming a 'shopaholic' (O'Guinn and Faber 1989). **Compulsive consumption** has been defined as those practices that, though undertaken to bolster self-esteem, are inappropriate, excessive, and disruptive to the lives of those who are involved (Faber et al. 1987). There is also evidence that compulsive behaviour in one area (for example buying lottery tickets and scratchcards) is linked to other addictive behaviours (such as smoking) (Balabanis 2002).

Post-purchase evaluation The process of deciding whether the outcome of a purchase has been appropriate or not.

In general, **post-purchase evaluation** will be positive if the consumer's expectations were met or exceeded, and negative if these expectations were not met. Positive post-purchase evaluations will encourage repeat buying and positive word-of-mouth recommendations to other potential consumers. Note that the objective experience is

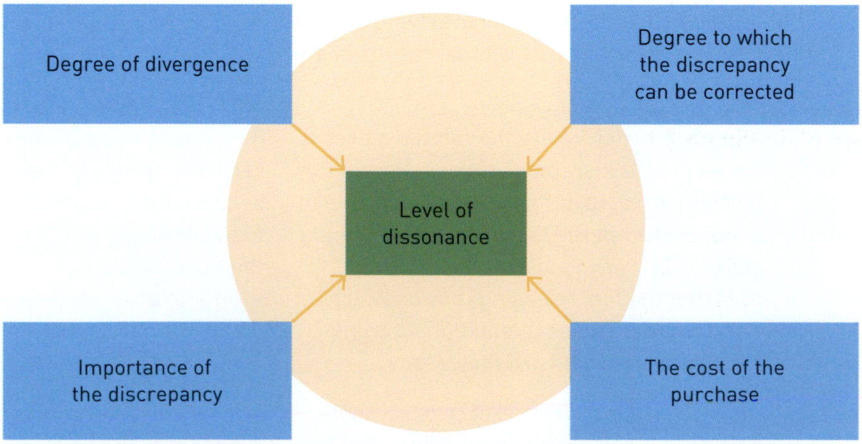

Figure 3.10 Factors in dissonance

only partly relevant – what matters is whether or not the customer's expectations were met. This means that over-hyping a product may result in short-term sales as a result of the consumer's pre-purchase expectations being high, but will damage sales in the long run as consumers are dissatisfied, and may tell others about their experience.

Think outside this box!

Apparently people sometimes enjoy complicating their lives, and sometimes enjoy simplifying them. Sometimes they like to be frightened, sometimes they like to be reassured. Sometimes they will tolerate pain as part of the process, more often they will regard pain as being the last thing they bargained for.

Everybody is different, and indeed everybody's mood shifts at different times: so how can marketers have any control whatsoever over post-purchase dissonance? One person leaves the white-knuckle ride excited and eager to go again – another person leaves the same ride threatening to sue the theme park.

Maybe it's about managing expectations. Provided the customers have a clear idea of what they are getting, they surely don't have any cause for complaint. Yet at the same time, marketers need to promote the products – encourage people to believe that products will meet their needs! So maybe it's also about managing the aftermath – having a good complaints procedure in place.

In practice, not every dissatisfied customer will complain. Some people will feel that it is not worth the trouble (especially if the problem is a minor one), some people will blame other factors, and so forth.

There are four general approaches that people take to reduce post-purchase dissonance:

1. Ignore the dissonant information and look for positive information about the product. (For example, the stereo system may not sound as good as one expected, but it looks really good.)
2. Distort the dissonant information. (It sounds a lot better than the one you had before.)
3. Play down the importance of the issue. (As long as it plays so you can hear the beat, it hasn't got to be perfect.)
4. Change one's behaviour. (Sell the stereo and buy something else, listen to the radio instead.)

If post-purchase dissonance does occur, consumers will use three general approaches to complain (Singh 1988):

1. **Voice responses**. The customer comes back to the provider to complain or seek redress. Sometimes people are reluctant to seek a confrontation, so do not voice a complaint: this is especially true of older people (Grougiou and Pettigrew 2009). This means that firms should make it as easy as possible for people to voice complaints, because this is a great deal less damaging than the alternatives.
2. **Private responses**. The customer generates negative word-of-mouth by talking to family and friends about the negative experience. In some cases, consumers have set up websites to disseminate complaints about the company (Bailey 2004).
3. **Third-party responses**. The customer goes to a lawyer or consumer champion to take up the case on their behalf.

Voice responses Complaints made directly to the supplier.

Private responses Complaints made to friends or family about a product or company.

Third-party responses Complaints made via lawyers or consumer rights advocates.

Obviously the firm and the customer may well not agree on the legitimacy of the complaint: managers sometimes feel that the consumer wants something for nothing, or may even feel that there is an implied personal criticism in the complaint (Cobb et al. 1987). As the level of complaints increases, the willingness of managers to listen decreases (Smart and Martin 1991), presumably because they grow tired of hearing the same old problems. However, the way the complaint is handled affects satisfaction and dissatisfaction, and some research shows that **loyalty** will actually increase if the complaint is handled to the customer's satisfaction – in other words, customers whose complaints are handled well become more loyal than those who did not have a complaint in the first place (Coca-Cola Company 1981).

Loyalty The tendency to repeat purchase a brand.

Real-life marketing: Let your customers write the invoice

Many companies will knock a bit off the bill if a customer complains – but how many companies will let the customer decide how much the goods are worth? What better way to stop complaints before they start, though!

Here's the idea, from a real company. Granite Rock supplies gravel for the building industry. They have an interesting and possibly unique approach to customer complaints – the invite customers NOT to pay the invoice.

On the back of each invoice is a statement to the effect that, if the customer is not satisfied with Granite Rock's performance (e.g. a delivery of gravel was late and held up construction), the client should deduct something from the invoice and only pay Granite Rock what they think the company has earned.

In practice, few customers feel the need to do this – and Granite Rock's trusting attitude means that many minor transgressions are simply forgiven. The end result is an increase in trust, and an increase in business – what is more, Granite Rock's customers are prepared to pay (on average) 6% more for their gravel than they would have to pay competing firms. The additional security of dealing with an honest company, prepared to admit its mistakes, is something worth paying extra for, even in an industry where the low bid typically gets the business.

If you want to try this, here are the key points:

- Tell the customer what you think the job's worth, and invite them to disagree. Most of the time they won't.
- Do a good job – or you get nothing!
- Be sure your employees understand how the whole thing works.
- Abuse is possible – so be wary of customers who continually deduct from the invoice. You can always stop supplying them – and you're probably better off without a customer like that anyway, because sooner or later they will cheat you, whatever you do.
- Monitor what the scheme is costing – but remember to allow for any increased business due to greater customer trust.
- This works best in business-to-business markets, but any market where you aim for a long-term relationship with the customer is ripe for this approach.

Third-party responses almost always occur after the consumer has been dissatisfied with the outcome of a voice response. Any lawyer will confirm whether the consumer has already complained directly to the company, since a court case is unlikely to succeed if the company has not had the opportunity to put matters right. The likelihood of a complaint being made depends on the following factors (Day 1984):

1. The significance of the consumption event in terms of product importance, cost, social visibility and time required in consumption. Consumers are unlikely to bother to complain if the product was cheap and unimportant, and unlikely to last long anyway.
2. The consumer's knowledge and experience in terms of the number of previous purchases, level of product knowledge, perception of ability as a consumer, and previous complaining experience. Consumers who have complained in the past are more likely to do so in the future: consumers with substantial knowledge of the product category are more likely to complain if things go wrong.
3. The difficulty of seeking redress. Customers are unlikely to complain if the product was purchased a long way away, or if complaining would take too much time and trouble. Some low-cost providers make it extremely difficult to contact the company – they have no e-mail address, and telephone calls are charged at a premium rate. Other firms make it easy to comment on products by providing on-line feedback forms and subsidised call centre lines.
4. The probability that a complaint will lead to a positive outcome (Halstead and Droge 1991). Complaints are more likely if the customer believes that the company is reputable, or has a guarantee. Also, customers are less likely to complain if the problem is perceived as being incapable of being put right or compensated for.

The growth of the so-called compensation culture in the UK has led to a marked increase in third-party complaints. Partly this is due to the removal of restrictions on no-win-no-fee litigation, and partly due to increased expectations on the part of consumers.

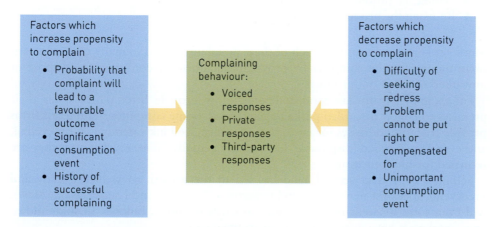

Figure 3.11 Complaining behaviour

From the viewpoint of a marketer, voice complaints are by far the least damaging. A voice complaint can be dealt with privately, and the supplier can retain a degree of control: also, a well-handled complaint results in a more loyal customer. Marketers should, at least in theory, encourage people to voice their complaints.

In some cases, consumers **boycott** the company and its products and encourage others to do the same. Four factors predict boycott behaviour (Klein et al. 2004):

1. The desire to make a difference, in other words to teach the company a lesson.
2. Scope for self-enhancement: the desire to make oneself feel important and powerful against the company.
3. Counterarguments that inhibit boycotting: friends saying that it will make no difference to the company, or that boycotting the product only means doing without it, and so forth.
4. Cost to the boycotter of constrained consumption: managing without the product may be harder on the boycotter than it is on the company.

Complaint behaviour is something that most marketers will seek to address, since it is central to establishing a long-term relationship with customers and is also crucial in establishing a good reputation with the target customer base.

Disposal

Getting rid of the product after it has been consumed (or at least getting rid of what is left of the product) is the final stage in the consumption process. Consumers and marketers have become more concerned about disposal in recent years due to the increased interest in environmental issues.

Disposal may take any of the following forms:

- Simply dumping the product or its packaging into the environment, either in an uncontrolled way (throwing packing into the street) or in a controlled way (via local refuse disposal arrangements).
- Recycling the product.
- Selling the product second-hand.
- Re-using the product in a novel way.

Marketers have an input into each of these possibilities, and in many cases can earn extra money for the company by providing facilities for consumers to dispose of unwanted or worn-out products.

For example, many fast-food companies now provide litter patrols near their premises to collect discarded packaging and food. Some computer peripherals firms provide freepost addresses for customers to return used ink cartridges for recycling, and even the so-called 'disposable' cameras are actually 70% recycled after they are returned for film processing.

Selling the product second-hand has led to the growth of websites (eBay and Freecycle), specialist newspapers and magazines (*Free-ads*, and *Exchange and Mart*), and even some amateur marketing such as cards in shop windows. In some industries, marketers have instituted trade-in arrangements.

Marketing in a changing world: Do it yourself recycling

Most people are familiar with the idea of sending bottles, cans, papers and plastics to the recycling unit. It has become a part of normal life to recycle, and we feel less guilty about being rampant consumers if we recycle.

Some people take things a step further, though. They would rather give something away so that someone else can get some use out of it than dump the item in the recycling bin. There are several websites devoted to this, not to mention those where people can sell used items. Those who take the products from the sites are not necessarily doing so for financial reasons: in many cases it is the moral aspect of not wasting natural resources that prompts them to use second-hand goods.

Even further down this route are Freegans – people who raid supermarket skips for out-of-date packed food. Thousands of tons of perfectly edible food are dumped daily because it has passed its sell-by date, so Freegans salvage this and use it. Unfortunately, this practice is illegal – taking stuff from a rubbish bin is stealing.

From a marketing viewpoint, the potential consequences might be fairly devastating. The second-hand book business has been all but destroyed by charity shops, and clearly there will be less new stuff sold if people are recycling old stuff. On the other hand, waste is a moral issue, and recycling is certainly here to stay, at least for the foreseeable future.

Re-using products or packaging has become popular in some circles in recent years: many people keep the containers that take-away foods come in, and use them for the freezer: some companies encourage this behaviour by providing packaging that lends itself to re-use. For example, French mustard manufacturers typically package their product in glass containers that can be used as wine glasses afterwards. More novel uses for discarded products include use as garden ornaments or containers, and even as part of artworks.

Influences on the buying decision

In 21st century Western society, people are faced with a vast range of possible ways of meeting their consumption needs. The variety of goods on offer, and the unprecedented wealth of industrial society, allow people to make extremely wide choices in satisfying their needs and the needs of their families. The basic necessities of life have long ago been taken care of – people are now catering to higher-level needs.

For a supplier to make its voice heard amidst the almost overwhelming clamour of competitors, an understanding of what would sway customers one way or the other is clearly important. Individuals buy not only because they have a specific practical need for a product at a given moment: they also buy because they have social, psychological and cultural needs, needs that go beyond the merely physical needs for food, shelter, and warmth.

Psychological influences include **perception**, **attitude** and **motivation**. Sociological influences are about group behaviour: the respect of one's friends and colleagues, and the influence of families. Cultural influences refer to religion, language, and the shared beliefs and customs of the culture the individual is part of.

Perception The process of building up a mental map of the world.

Attitude A learned tendency to respond in a consistent manner to a specific stimulus or object.

Motivation The force that moves an individual towards a specific set of solutions.

Attitude formation and change

A great deal of marketing communication (possibly even the majority of it) is aimed at either changing people's attitudes, or encouraging specific attitudes to form among a target audience. The theory of attitude formation and change is therefore crucial to effective marketing communication.

Attitude is defined as a learned predisposition to respond to an object or class of objects in a consistently favourable or unfavourable way (Allport 1935). Attitudes represent what we like and dislike, so attitude determines to a large extent what people will and will not buy. Dismantling the definition, we find that:

1. Attitude is learned, it is not instinctive. We develop attitudes largely through experience, but partly through the experience of others, communicated through conversation or writing.
2. Attitude is a tendency to respond, it is not the response itself. Attitude does not always lead to action – someone might hate the boss, but not actually do anything about it.
3. Attitude is consistent over time. People tend to keep their attitudes intact unless some major new experience or information changes them.
4. Attitudes can be favourable or unfavourable. Since attitudes have a strength, an attitude is a vector: it has both strength and direction.
5. There is an implied relationship between the person and the attitudinal object. The object of the attitude could be a product, a person, or an idea: the word 'object' is used here in the sense of 'objective'.

Attitudes cannot be observed: they can be inferred from behaviour, or might be determined by market research, but often attitudes are hidden from the observer (and may even be unclear to the holder of the attitude).

Cognition The rational component of attitude.

Conation Intended behaviour.

Affect The emotional component of attitude.

Attitude has three dimensions: **cognition**, **conation** and **affect**. Cognition is what is known about the attitudinal object, in other words the facts about it. Affect is the emotional component of attitude, and is composed of what is felt about the object. Conation is the person's intended behaviour, resulting from holding the attitude.

Conation is only intended behaviour – it is not the behaviour itself. Someone may, for example, intend to change bank accounts on hearing that the bank has acted unethically in some way, but may find (on mature reflection) that switching to another bank is too much trouble. The attitude itself has not been affected by this, merely the outcome.

The components of attitude interact in complex ways. Provided the three elements are in balance, the attitude is stable and is unlikely to change. Purchase intention is strongly linked to attitude, and some studies indicate that attitude to product is affected by attitude to the advertisements for it (Homer and Yoon 1992).

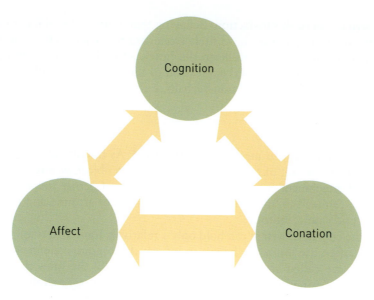

Figure 3.12   Stable attitude

The traditional (and possibly intuitive) view of attitude is that attitudes are formed in a sequence, i.e. that knowledge (cognition) comes first, then emotional elements develop (affect) followed by behaviour (conation). In fact it has been shown that attitudes form in no particular order: someone can fall in love with, or take an instant dislike to, an attitudinal object without knowing anything substantial about it. In this way, affect can precede cognition (Zajonc and Markus, 1985). Equally, someone might act on impulse to buy something that looks interesting, then learn about it and form an attitude later.

 Think outside this box!

Attitude seems to be a complex area. We don't know how a person's attitude formed, we don't know what it might lead to, and it's difficult to change anyway. So why not just ignore it, and go on how people actually behave? After all, people are not always rational anyway – they buy products they didn't really want, and form attitudes later!

Or should we perhaps be finding groups with positive attitudes towards our products and going to them? Why bother trying to change attitudes at all? In short, which is better – leave attitudes alone and just sell to people who like our products anyway, or go out and find people to whom we would like to sell, and try to change their attitudes?

Attitude contains components of **belief** and opinion, but it is neither. Attitude differs from belief in that belief is neutral, and does not include connotations of good or bad. Belief is only concerned with the possession (or otherwise) of an attribute, and is usually based on a judgement of the available evidence. Attitude contains an emotional element, and evaluates whether the existence or otherwise of an attribute will

Belief An understanding that an object possesses a particular attribute.

result in satisfaction or dissatisfaction. Believing that a luxury hotel has a reputation for comfort, for example, may be entirely irrelevant to a backpacker, and therefore not form part of his or her attitude to the hotel. Attitude differs from opinion in that opinion is an overt, vocalised expression of an attitude. Attitude is not always expressed, and may be expressed non-verbally, but opinion is always expressed.

ATTITUDE FORMATION

Attitude formation is by no means straightforward. As has already been seen, attitudes can form as a result of finding out facts about an object, as a result of forming an emotional attachment to an object, or as a result of acting towards an object. Each of these can lead to 'filling in' the other elements of attitude and thus forming a complete, and stable, attitude.

Salient belief An understanding that an object possesses a relevant attribute.

Because the cognitive system can hold only a relatively limited amount of information, people often use just a few beliefs to inform the cognitive element of attitude. These beliefs are called **salient beliefs**, and are usually the ones the individuals believes to be most important. Salient beliefs could, of course, merely be the beliefs that were most recently presented (Fishbein and Ajzen 1975).

The degree to which people form cognitions about attitudinal objects depends on their capacity to process information and also on the degree of attention they are prepared to give to the process. An ability to process information depends partly on intelligence and partly on existing knowledge of the product type. For example, someone who is a real computer buff will have a greater ability to process information about new software than someone who is a novice with computers, even though each person might be of equal intelligence.

The overall attitude is the result of formulating many attributes of the object. The multiattribute model (Fishbein 1963) attempts to explain how the consumer's salient beliefs help to form the final attitude. The model proposes that the attitude towards the product is based on the summed set of beliefs about the product's attributes, weighted by the evaluation of those attributes. These attributes could include factors that are not directly part of the product, for example celebrity endorsement, slogans, relationships with charities, charisma of the company's founder, and so forth. The multiattribute model has remained one of the key concepts in attitude, but has been criticised because of its reliance on cognition as the starting-point of attitude.

Forming a belief set about the object may result in a qualified attitude: for example, a restaurant may score highly on its food and service, but low on its atmosphere, which would make it a good place for a quick meal when one does not feel like cooking, but a bad place when one has a romantic dinner for two planned.

Attitudes clearly affect behaviour. Fishbein's (1980) theory of reasoned action says that individuals consciously evaluate the consequences of different behaviours and choose the one that will lead to the most favourable consequences. Beliefs about the intended behaviour and the likely outcome are what colours attitude, according to Fishbein: the theory assumes that consumers perform a logical evaluation procedure for making decisions about behaviour, based on their attitude towards the behaviour, which derives from attitudes towards the brand.

Fishbein's model seeks to combine the internal influences on attitude with external influences. All of us are influenced by what other people think (there is more on this later in the chapter), so our attitudes towards other people and their expectations of us will affect what we do in the same way as our attitudes towards the behaviour itself will affect our behaviour. The model seeks to combine these factors into one unified explanation of behaviour.

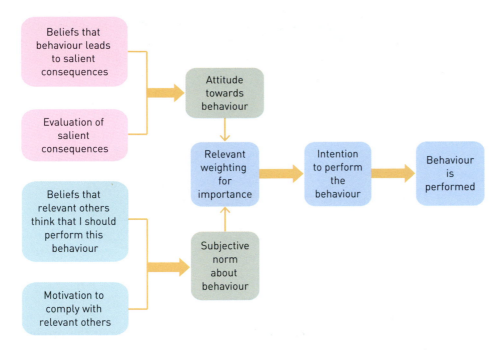

Figure 3.13   The theory of reasoned action (from Fishbein 1980)

Of course, the model assumes that people are rational, which is often not the case: emotions affect attitude, and also affect behaviour, so that people often act in ways that would not be predicted by their stated attitudes.

Attitudes can also be formed primarily through the affective route, or even through behaviour: they are not always formed as a result of conscious thought. People are not always rational: they form attitudes and opinions based on gut feeling, sometimes in the face of strong objective evidence to the contrary. A theory has been developed which states that there are two routes to attitude formation: the **central route**, which operates through cognition, and the **peripheral route**, which operates through affect (Petty and Cacioppo 1986). The elaboration likelihood model (Petty et al. 1983) proposes that, in any situation, the person's level of involvement and ability to process information will be the key factors in determining which route predominates. If involvement is high, and processing ability is also high, the central route will predominate. If on the other hand involvement is low and processing ability is low, the peripheral route is likely to predominate. In this case, the person will be influenced by cues that are incidental to the object in question (Chaiken 1980).

More recent studies have shown that peripheral processing may also influence consumers' beliefs as well as their feelings (Miniard et al. 1990). This implies that peripheral processing supplements, rather than replaces, central processing.

Central route Cognitive approach to changing behaviour.

Peripheral route Affective approach to changing behaviour.

CHANGING ATTITUDES

Attitude change is one of the key objectives of marketing communication. If an attitude is stable, it is extremely difficult to change – each element of the attitude supports every other element. The starting-point of any attitude change is therefore to destabilise the attitude. Attitudes can be destabilised by attacking any of the components. Changing the way a person feels about a product

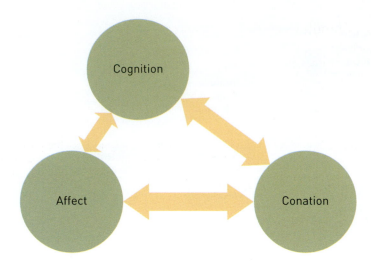

Figure 3.14   Unstable attitude

is likely to be as effective as changing some of their beliefs about the product, and marketers even try to change people's behaviour (for example, by offering free samples or test drives) in order to destabilise the attitude. Very strongly held attitudes are unlikely to be changed greatly, but weakly held attitudes can certainly be shifted.

There are four ways of changing attitudes using the central route. These are:

1. Add a new salient belief. New facts about the product can change attitudes – for example, if a report from the Health and Safety Executive shows that the product is dangerous.
2. Change the strength of a salient belief. If the salient belief is a negative one, it can be discounted or played down: if it is a positive one, it can be emphasised. For example, a restaurant customer may have a low level of belief in the cleanliness of the kitchen, so the proprietor could allow the customer to visit the kitchen, or could fit a window so that customers could see into the kitchen.
3. Change the evaluation of an existing belief. For example, the reliability of a car may seem unimportant against the cost, but the manufacturer or dealer might point out that reliable cars cost a lot less to run because they need less servicing and fewer new components.
4. Make an existing belief more salient. Customers might believe, for example, that the waiters in a restaurant are friendly, but not regard this as particularly important until a friend points out that friendly staff make the evening more pleasant.

Inconsistency between the three components of attitude comes about when a new stimulus is presented. When presented with a new stimulus, people have three ways of dealing with it, as shown in Table 3.2.

The three elements of attitude are so closely linked that a change in one element will almost always lead to a change in the others (Rosenberg 1960). Teasing out the individual factors in the attitude can be a time-consuming and conceptually difficult process: this is because so many factors go to make up an attitude, and in some cases

Table 3.2 Stimulus defence mechanisms

Defence mechanism	Explanation
Stimulus rejection	The individual simply ignores the stimulus, discounting the new information. By rejecting the new information, the individual is able to maintain the status quo and leave the attitude unchanged.
Attitude splitting	Here the individual only accepts the part of the new information that does not create an inconsistency. For example, someone might accept the truth of the new information, but regard it as a special case which does not apply to the actual situation.
Accommodate the new attitude	The individual accepts the stimulus as fact, and changes his or her attitude accordingly.

the attitude will be affected by halo effect (sometimes also known as horns effect). Halo effect is the tendency to believe that, if one aspect of the product is good, then all other aspects are also good. Horns effect is the opposite side of the coin – if one aspect is bad, all aspects are bad.

Drive, motivation and hedonism

Drive is the force that makes a person respond to a need. It is caused by the drift from the desired state to the actual state – the starting-point for recognising a need. If the drive state is at a high level, the individual becomes motivated to do something to correct the situation.

> **Drive** The force generated in an individual as a result of a felt need.

Allowing a gap to develop between the desired and actual states can be stimulating and enjoyable. Working up an appetite before a meal makes the meal more enjoyable, and achieving a goal may simply lead to developing a new goal. People often enjoy planning something more than they enjoy the actual experience (Raghunathan and Mukherji 2003).

Most people have a level at which this type of stimulation is enjoyable and stimulating, and not yet unpleasant. This is called the **optimum stimulation level**, or **OSL**. If external stimulation goes above the OSL, the individual will seek to meet the need: if stimulation is below the OSL, the person will seek to increase the stimulation and bring it back up to the OSL.

> **Optimum stimulation level (OSL)** The level at which the gap between the desired state and the actual state has not yet become unpleasant.

The OSL varies from one individual to another, but research shows that people with high OSLs like novelty and risk-taking, whereas those with low OSLs prefer the tried and tested (Raju 1980). In general, people with high OSLs tend to be younger.

Motivation derives from drive. A drive only has quantity, whereas a motivation is directed towards a specific group of solutions. Much marketing effort is aimed at developing drives, but even more is aimed at developing motivations towards a specific product or group of products. Motives can be classified as shown in Table 3.3.

The current view of motivation is that there is a balance between the rational and emotional elements of motivation. There can be little doubt that emotion plays a large part in buying decisions, partly through the formation of attitudes. Also, needs can be classified into utilitarian needs, which are about the objective, functional

Table 3.3   Classification of motives

Primary motives	The reason that leads to the purchase of a product class. The consumer may feel a need to buy a new car to replace a worn-out one.
Secondary motives	The reasons behind buying a specific brand. The consumer may have reasons for buying a Mercedes rather than a BMW.
Rational motives	These are based on reasoning, or a logical assessment of the situation. The consumer may have decided that the new car should be able to carry three children and their paraphernalia, and should fit the garage.
Emotional motives	These motives have to do with the consumer's feelings about the brand. This may include considerations such as what the neighbours might think of the car, what the car looks like, and how it feels to drive it.
Conscious motives	Motives of which the customer is aware.
Dormant motives	Motives operating below the conscious level. The car buyer may not be consciously aware that a sudden urge to buy a sports car is actually about approaching middle age, not about a need for transport.

Hedonic needs Needs that relate to the pleasurable aspects of ownership.

aspects of life, and **hedonic needs**, which are about the pleasurable or aesthetic aspects of the products (Holbrook and Hirschmann 1982). It is common for both types of need to be considered in the same purchase decision: car purchase is a good example, since the practical aspects of owning a car are moderated by the pleasurable aspects of driving a car which is smart, comfortable, fast and so forth. People sometimes move towards hedonic needs as a result of shocking events: for example, after a near-death experience people who normally look after their bodies tend to diet and exercise more, whereas people who have low body esteem tend to relax their diets and eat things they enjoy (Shiv et al. 2004).

Hedonic aspects of the product are often the main distinguishing feature between it and its competition. For example, car manufacturers design car doors so that they close with a satisfying 'thunk': this serves no useful purpose, but it does give the impression that the car is a solid machine. Heinz use turquoise for the label on their baked beans cans because it contrasts well with the colour of the beans, emphasising the orange colour of the sauce: the foil seals on jars of coffee

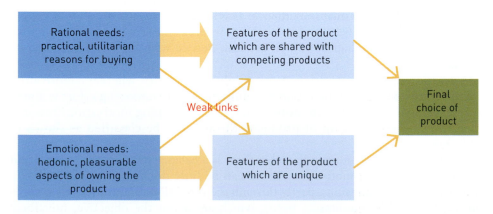

Figure 3.15   Balance between rational and emotional needs

are pleasurable to pop, and websites use cartoon images for their Help sections. In some cases these hedonic aspects have been a by-product of packaging decisions, but in many cases the hedonic aspects of the product have been added at the design stage.

Advertising often uses hedonic imagery to promote products. Chocolate, beer, cars and even laundry products are promoted by emphasising fun, luxury, comfort, or excitement – all of which are hedonic aspects of the products concerned.

Involvement

Involvement is the perceived importance or personal relevance of an object or event. In consumer terms, it is the degree to which the individual feels attached to the product or product category. For example, a professional musician may have a strong attachment to a particular brand of guitar string, whereas an amateur may not be so concerned since his or her livelihood does not depend on making choices of that nature.

Involvement Emotional attachment to a product.

Involvement is an important concept in marketing, since it relates strongly to repeat purchases. Involvement has both **affective** and **cognitive** elements, and is a part of attitude theory. High involvement comes about if the consumer feels that the product attributes are strongly linked to end goals or values: lower levels of involvement occur if the attributes of the product link only to function, and low levels occur if the attributes are irrelevant to the consequences. High involvement purchases are the ones that figure most in the purchaser's lifestyle.

Affective Relating to emotional factors.

Cognitive Relating to rational factors.

Table 3.4 compares the different levels of involvement and how these impact on the decision-making process. High-involvement customers are difficult to persuade – they are unlikely to be moved by advertising, or even by persuasive sales pitches (Keisler et al. 1969).

Involvement can be extremely complex: a study carried out with members of a major art gallery in the UK found six characteristics of involvement, as follows (Slater and Armstrong 2010):

- Centrality and pleasure. This relates to the enjoyment of the artworks, but could equally apply to the pleasure of driving a luxury car, or of wearing designer clothes.
- Desire to learn. In the art gallery context, this means the mental stimulation of the artworks, but could apply equally to almost any hobby.
- Escapism, both spiritual and creative. This is about getting away from everyday concerns for a while.
- Sense of belonging and prestige. This could equally apply to the luxury car or the designer clothes mentioned earlier – identifying with a respectable institution or brand is important to many people.
- Physical involvement. The act of visiting the gallery and walking around it is part of the pleasure.
- Drivers of involvement. This refers to the internal needs the individual has to become part of something.

Personal sources The means–end knowledge stored in an individual's memory.

Levels of involvement are influenced both by **personal sources** and **situational sources**. Personal sources (also called intrinsic self-relevance) are the means–end knowledge stored in the individual's memory, and are influenced both by the individual's personality and by the product characteristics. If the individual thinks that

Situational sources Sources of involvement derived from immediate social or cultural factors.

Table 3.4 Comparison of involvement levels

High involvement	Medium involvement	Low involvement
Attributes strongly linked to end goals: for example, the quality of a hotel's catering may be strongly linked to the success of a wedding reception held there.	Attributes only link to function: hotel catering for a dinner when one is travelling on business need only be adequate.	Attributes irrelevant to consequences: provided the hotel offers a clean room, other attributes (such as a gym or a swimming-pool) probably will not matter much.
Important to get it right first time: a wedding reception only happens once!	Need to have reasonably reliable results: provided the food is cooked and presented adequately, it does not need to be Michelin-star standard.	Results perceived to be the same whichever product chosen: most business hotels are very similar.
Consumer has in-depth knowledge and strong opinions: most people would take great care to investigate all the alternatives when planning a wedding.	Consumer has knowledge of the product group, no strong feelings: business travellers usually do not develop strong feelings about the hotels they stay in.	No strong feelings, knowledge of product group irrelevant: if the traveller is only looking for somewhere to sleep, most hotels will be fine, and only the price will be relevant.
Discrepant information ignored or discounted: once the reception has begun, any minor failings may well be ignored.	Discrepant information considered carefully: if the meal is poor, the traveller may well complain.	Discrepant information ignored: probably most information, apart from the cleanliness of the room and the price, will be ignored. The traveller may not even pay too much attention to the name of the hotel.

the characteristics of the product relate strongly to life goals, or reflect strongly on the individual as a person, the intrinsic self-relevance will be high.

Situational sources of involvement relate to the immediate social or physical surroundings of the consumer. Social circumstances refer to the potential embarrassment factor of being seen wearing the wrong clothes, or driving the wrong car. Physical factors relate to the use of the product in the 'real world'. For example, referring back to the climbing rope mentioned earlier, a climber might revise her view of the importance of reliability if the rope should break halfway up a rock face.

Real-life marketing: Form a club

People like to belong to things. Harley–Davidson owners join HOG (Harley Owners' Group), people join fan clubs and supporters' clubs for their favourite bands or teams, people join hobby clubs. Belonging to clubs is powerful – and you should not be slow to capitalise on this.

The idea was taken up by Kimberley–Clark, This company makes disposable nappies (called Huggies) in various types: there are boys' ones, girls' ones, pull-up ones for potty training, and so forth. So Kimberley–Clark formed a club called the Huggies Club.

This club is open to expectant mothers and new mothers, and provides a set of forums where they can discuss the problems of motherhood with others. The site genuinely belongs to the mothers – Kimberley–Clark does not interfere at all – and mothers are free to discuss whatever they like. Much of the site is available for free, but mothers wanting to post comments or access the whole site need to register by providing their details: the expected delivery date for the baby, their address and contact details, address of their usual supermarket, and so forth. In exchange, mothers are given a coupon to be redeemed against Huggies products.

If you're going to try this, here are some guidelines:

- Don't be tempted to take over the site to plug your products – people already know who you are and what you do; there's no need to harass them into leaving.
- Don't abuse people's trust – use the information they give you very carefully, and of course keep it to yourself.
- Give a small reward for providing the information. It makes people feel good about you, and it doesn't cost much.
- Recruit the first members yourself, otherwise there will be no one to interact with.
- Publicise the club off-line as well as on-line – on your packaging is a good place to start, or (in the case of Huggies) on something designed for expectant mothers.

Sometimes marketers are able to emphasise the environmental sources of involvement in order to increase the consumer's involvement in the product. Clothes retailers can advise on appropriate dress for special occasions, and outdoors shops often offer advice on the necessity of buying the right equipment for outdoor pursuits such as camping or mountaineering.

Consumers frequently develop close relationships with brands, partly because the brand reflects their self-image. Cigarette smokers often become fiercely loyal to their brands, although research shows that most smokers are unable to distinguish their own brand of cigarette in a blind taste test. Car drivers develop close relationships with their cars, often talking to the car and even giving it a name. People can be categorised according to their involvement level (see Table 3.5) but of course this categorisation only applies to particular product categories – someone may be extremely loyal to a specific brand of gin, but not care what brand of tonic goes in it. Equally, someone may be intensely loyal to a brand of tomato ketchup and have no loyalty at all to a car manufacturer: price is not relevant to involvement. Research shows that pre-teen children often link snack foods to lifestyle values, and become highly involved with their favourite brands (Dibley and Baker 2001).

Involvement is a function of loyalty, and therefore is of interest to marketers who seek to increase repeat purchases. There is strong evidence to indicate that it is approximately six times cheaper to retain an existing customer than it is to win

Table 3.5   Categories of consumer according to involvement

Brand loyalists	Strong affective links to a favourite brand. Usually they tend to link the product category to the provision of personally-relevant consequences. These are people who go for the 'best brand' for their needs, but also feel that the product category itself is an important part of their lives.
Routine brand buyers	Low personal sources of involvement, but have a favourite brand. These consumers are more interested in the types of consequences associated with regular brand purchases (it is easier to buy the same one each week, and it is at least reliable). They are not necessarily looking for the 'best brand': a satisfactory one will do.
Information seekers	Have positive means–end information about the product category, but no one brand stands out as superior. These consumers use a lot of information to help them find a suitable brand from within the product category.
Brand switchers	Low brand loyalty, low personal involvement. These people do not see that the brand used has any important consequences, even if the product category is interesting. Usually they do not have a strong relationship with the product category either. This means that they are easily affected by environmental factors such as sales promotions.

Source: J. Paul Peter and Jerry C. Olson, *Understanding Consumer Behaviour* (Burr Ridge, IL: Irwin, 1994)

a new one, and considerable effort on the part of many companies has gone into establishing systems for winning back customers who have defected to the opposition (Rosenberg and Czepeil 1983).

Learning and perception

Learning is not only about classroom-type learning. Most behaviour is learned as a result of external experiences; most of what people know (and almost certainly many of the things they are most proud of knowing) they learned outside school. People learn things partly through a formalised structure of teaching and partly through an unconscious process of learning by experience.

Learning is highly relevant to marketing, since consumers are affected by the things they learn, and much consumer behaviour is based on the learning process. Persuading consumers to remember the information they see in advertisements is a major problem for marketers: people are often able to remember the advertisement, but not the brand being advertised, for example.

Learning is defined as the behavioural changes that occur over time relative to an external stimulus condition (Onkvisit and Shaw 1994). According to this definition, activities are changed or originated through a reaction to an encountered situation. We can therefore say that someone has learned something if, as a result, their behaviour changes in some way.

The main conditions that arise from this definition are as follows:

1. There must be a change in behaviour (response tendencies).
2. This must result from an external stimulus.

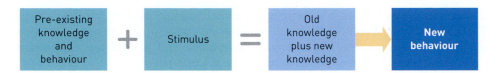

Figure 3.16   Development of learning

Learning has not taken place under the following circumstances:

1. **Species response tendencies**. These are instincts, or reflexes; for example, the response of ducking when a stone is thrown at you does not rely on your having learned that stones are hard and hurt the skin. Learning has not taken place under those circumstances.
2. **Maturation**. Behavioural changes often occur in adolescence due to hormonal changes (for example), but again this is not a behavioural change as a result of learning.
3. Temporary states of the organism. Whilst behaviour can be, and often is, affected by tiredness, hunger, drunkenness, etc. these factors do not constitute part of a larger learning process (even though learning may result from those states; the drunk may well learn to drink less in future).

Academic study of learning has two main schools of thought: first, the stimulus–response approach, which further subdivides into **classical** and **operant conditioning**, and second, cognitive theories, where the conscious thought of the individual enters into the equation.

CLASSICAL LEARNING THEORY

The classical theory of learning was developed by, among others, the Russian researcher Pavlov (1927). Pavlov's famous experiments with dogs demonstrated that automatic responses (reflexes) could be learned. What Pavlov did was present a dog with an **unconditioned stimulus** (in this case, meat powder) knowing that this would lead to an **unconditioned response** (salivation). At the same time Pavlov would ring a bell (the **conditioned stimulus**). After a while the dog would associate the ringing of the bell with the meat, and would salivate whenever it heard the bell, without actually seeing any meat. This mechanism is shown in Figure 3.14.

Classical conditioning occurs in humans as well. Many smokers associate having a cup of coffee with having a cigarette, and find it difficult to give up smoking without also giving up coffee. Repetitive advertising jingles or **strap lines** become associated with the brands concerned, and the four-note tune (the sound logo) associated with the Intel computer chip is recognised worldwide.

For this to work it is usually necessary to repeat the stimulus a number of times in order for the **conditioned response** to become established. The number of times the process needs to be repeated will depend on the strength of the stimulus and the receptiveness (motivation) of the individual. Research has shown that, although conditioning has been reported for a single conditioning event (Gorn 1982), perhaps as many as 30 pairings may be required before conditioning is maximised (Kroeber-Riel 1984).

Behaviours influenced by classical conditioning are thought to be involuntary. If the doorbell rings, it is automatic for most people to look up, without consciously thinking about whether somebody is at the door. Most people are familiar with

---

Species response tendencies Automatic behaviour as a result of instinct rather than learning.

Maturation The development of the organism over time.

Classical conditioning The instilling of automatic responses in an individual by repetition of stimulus and reward.

Operant conditioning The instilling of automatic responses via the active participation of the individual.

Unconditioned stimulus A stimulus that would normally produce a known reaction in an individual: this stimulus is offered as part of the conditioning process.

Unconditioned response The existing automatic response of the individual to an unconditioned stimulus.

Conditioned stimulus A stimulus offered at the same time as an unconditioned stimulus, with the intention of creating an artificial association between it and the unconditioned response.

Strap line The slogan at the end of an advertisement.

Conditioned response A response that results from exposure to a conditioned stimulus.

the start of recognition that sometimes occurs if a similar doorbell is rung during a TV drama. Classical conditioning also operates on the emotions: playing Christmas music will elicit memories of childhood Christmases, and advertising that portrays events from the recent past will generate feelings of nostalgia.

Another factor in the effectiveness of classical conditioning is the order in which the conditioned stimulus and the unconditioned stimulus are presented. In **forward conditioning** the conditioned stimulus (CS) comes before the unconditioned stimulus (US). In the case of conditioning via an advertising jingle, forward conditioning would mean that the product would be shown before the music was played.

In **backward conditioning** the US comes before the CS. Here the music would be played before the product is shown. **Simultaneous conditioning** requires both to be presented at the same time.

It appears that forward conditioning and simultaneous conditioning work best in advertising (McSweeney and Bierley 1984). This means that it is usually better to present the product before playing the popular tune, or play both together; the responses from this approach are usually stronger and longer-lasting.

Extinction occurs when the conditioned stimulus no longer evokes the conditioned response. This occurs in the ways shown in Table 3.6.

Generalisation happens when a stimulus that is close to the existing one evokes the same response. Pavlov found that a sound similar to the bell he used could also stimulate salivation, and it is often the case that a similar brand name can evoke a purchase response. A very common tactic in marketing is to produce similar packaging to that of one's competitor in order to take advantage of the generalisation effect. For an example of this, observe the similarity in the packaging between Tesco Premium coffee and Nescafé Gold Blend (there is more on this in Chapter 12).

Discrimination is the process by which we learn to distinguish between stimuli, and only respond to the appropriate one. Consumers quite quickly learn to distinguish between brands, even when the design of the packaging is similar. Advertisers

Forward conditioning The conditioned stimulus comes before the unconditioned stimulus.

Backward conditioning The unconditioned stimulus comes before the conditioned stimulus.

Simultaneous conditioning The conditioned stimulus and the unconditioned stimulus are offered at the same time.

Extinction The gradual weakening of conditioning over time.

Generalisation The tendency for the individual to react in several ways to the conditioned stimulus.

Discrimination The ability to distinguish between similar stimuli.

Table 3.6 Extinction of conditioning

Reason for extinction	Example	Explanation	Techniques to avoid extinction
The conditioned stimulus is encountered without the unconditioned stimulus.	The product is shown without the background music.	Seeing the product without the music tends to reduce the association of the music with the product; other stimuli will replace the music.	Ensure that all the advertising uses the same music, or imagery associated with the music.
The unconditioned stimulus is encountered without the conditioned stimulus.	The background music is heard without the product being present.	In this case, other stimuli may be evoked by the music; it will become associated with something other than the product.	Either ensure that the music is not played anywhere other than when the product is being shown, or ensure that the product is available when the music is played. For example, ensure that the club has an ample supply of the drink you are advertising.

will often encourage discrimination by pairing a positive US with their own product, but not with the competitor's product. Classical conditioning is responsible for many repetitive advertising campaigns, and for many catchphrases that are now in common use.

Classical conditioning assumes that the individual plays no active role in the learning process. Pavlov's dogs did not have to do anything in order to be 'conditioned', because the process was carried out on their involuntary reflex of salivation. Although classical conditioning does operate in human beings, people are not usually passive in the process; the individual person (and most higher animals, in fact) is able to take part in the process and co-operate with it or avoid it. This process of active role-playing is called operant conditioning.

OPERANT CONDITIONING

Here the learner will conduct trial-and-error behaviour to obtain a reward (or avoid a punishment). Burris F. Skinner (1953) developed the concept in order to explain higher-level learning than that identified by Pavlov. The difference between Pavlov's approach and the operant conditioning approach is that the learner has a choice in the outcome; the modern view of classical conditioning is that it also involves a cognitive dimension. In other words, Skinner is describing a type of learning that requires the learner to do something rather than be the passive recipient of a stimulus; and the modern view is that even Pavlov's dog would have thought 'Here comes dinner' when the bell rang.

The basis of operant conditioning is the concept of **reinforcement**. If a consumer buys a product and is pleased with the outcome of using it, then he or she is likely to buy the product again. This means that the activity has had a positive reinforcement, and the consumer has become 'conditioned' to buy the product next time. The greater the positive reinforcement, the greater the likelihood of a repeat purchase.

If the reward works, the consumer will try to think of a way to make it even better: 'If a little will help, a lot will cure'. This can lead to over-indulgence in food or alcohol, or indeed almost any other pleasurable activity. Typically this will happen if the consumer's need cannot be totally met by the product, but will be helped; a person with a serious psychological problem may well find that alcohol helps, but doesn't cure. An increasing intake of alcohol will never result in a complete meeting of the person's psychological needs because eventually sobriety will begin to set in again.

Reinforcement Increasing the strength of learning by rewarding appropriate behaviour.

Think outside this box!

Operant conditioning appears to suggest that we are all simply acting on the basis of what is pleasurable, or gratifying. But isn't this a rather depressing view of human beings? Don't people ever do things just to help others, even when it might be damaging to their own self-interest? Do we never give to charity without an ulterior motive?

Or perhaps the warm glow we get from helping others is also part of operant conditioning. Maybe we hope that self-sacrifice will be our ticket to happiness – and that the reward of generosity is knowing that we have achieved the moral high ground.

On the other hand, maybe we should be admiring of people for whom altruistic behaviour is gratifying. After all, there are enough people around who appear to find anti-social behaviour gratifying, so why not accept that there is something in altruism after all?

Airline loyalty schemes are aimed at reinforcing the frequent flyers, whose loyalty is desirable since they are likely to be the most profitable customers. The airlines offer free flights to their most regular customers, and for many business travellers these free flights offer an attractive reason for choosing the same airline every time.

Figure 3.17 shows three forms of operant conditioning. In the first example, positive reinforcement, the individual receives a stimulus and acts upon it. This action works, and the individual gets a good result; this leads to the behaviour being repeated if the same antecedent stimulus is presented at a later date. For example, in India many historic attractions have ladies-only ticket queues. The chivalrous Indian men form a very long queue to buy their tickets, while the Western tourists send their wives to buy the tickets at the ladies-only queue. This behaviour is rewarded by a shorter wait, so tourists quickly learn that this is the best way to buy tickets and repeat the process at any other opportunity.

The second example in the diagram shows a negative stimulus; this time the operant behaviour relieves the problem, and again the individual has learned how to avoid bad consequences when faced with a difficulty.

The third example shows how punishment fits into the learning process. If the operant behaviour leads to a bad result, for example the other people queuing become angry at the queue-jumping tactic, the individual won't try that tactic again. The problem with punishment as a motivator is that it may lead to the individual not visiting the attraction, or avoiding the product, in future.

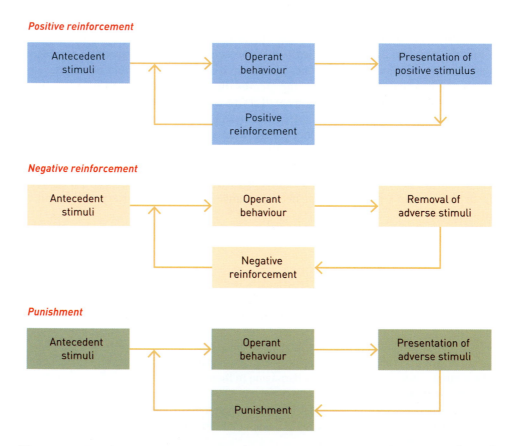

Figure 3.17   Operant conditioning (adapted from Stanley M. Widrick (1986) Concept of negative reinforcement has place in classroom. *Marketing News*, 20: 48–9)

Real life marketing: Make it fun!

If it's fun for people to buy from you, they are much more likely to do so. Humour is always good – but if you can hit on something that encourages people to pass on the message, so much the better. This is the basis of viral marketing: on-line jokes that people pass to their friends. But there's nothing to stop you doing fun things off-line as well.

Radisson Hotels hit on a great idea for doing this. Radisson are mainly business hotels, and business travellers often spend a lot of time away from their friends and family. They also tend to spend a lot of time in their rooms – it isn't much fun wandering around a strange city on your own. So Radisson supplied each room with a plastic duck to play with in the bath. The duck came with a note saying that the duck was a gift, the guest could take it home or have it mailed to someone in its own special crate, for a nominal postage charge. The charge was actually enough to cover the cost of the duck, the crate, and the postage, but against the cost of a room at the Radisson it was a negligible amount.

Soon hundreds of thousands of Radisson ducks were being mailed to children, wives, girlfriends, grandchildren, work colleagues, friends, bosses and business associates, all with the Radisson logo on them. Apart from raising the firm's profile, it also conveyed an image of a friendly, fun place to stay – a business hotel with a sense of humour, in fact. This contributed to a strong growth in the chain's family trade, which helped fill the hotels at weekends.

The rules for this type of promotion are:

- Do something that is fun.
- Make it easy for your customers to tell other people about it.
- If possible, have something tangible attached to the experience, so that it remains memorable.
- Be careful that the message 'We like to have fun' fits with your brand image.

Operant conditioning does not necessarily require a product purchase; marketers will frequently give away free samples in the hope that a positive experience from using the product will encourage consumers to purchase in future. Likewise, car dealers always offer a test drive.

Operant conditioning is helpful in explaining how people become conditioned, or form habits of purchase; however, it still does not explain how learning operates when people become active in seeking out information. To understand this aspect of learning, it is necessary to look at the cognitive learning process.

COGNITIVE LEARNING

Not all learning is just an automatic response to a stimulus. People analyse purchasing situations taking into account previous experiences, and make evaluative judgements.

Learning is part of this, both in terms of informing the process as a result of earlier experiences, and also in terms of the consumer's approach to learning more about the product category or brand.

When considering cognitive learning, the emphasis is not on what is learned (as in stimulus–response theories) but on how it is learned. Classical learning and operant conditioning theories suppose that learning is automatic; cognitive learning theories assume that there is a conscious process going on.

The classical and operant theories assume that what goes on inside the consumer's head is a 'black box' in that we know that a given stimulus will prompt a particular response, but for most practical purposes we have no real way of knowing what is happening inside the black box. Within the cognitive learning paradigm, however, we are concerned with what happens inside the box, and we try to infer what is going on by analysing behaviour and responses from the individual. Figure 3.18 illustrates this.

The black box contains the cognitive processes; the stimulus is considered in the light of the individual's memory of what has happened in the past when presented with similar stimuli, his or her assessment of the desirable outcome and an assessment of the likely outcome of any action. Following this processing the individual produces a response.

Cognitive learning expertise has five aspects:

- Cognitive effort
- Cognitive structure
- Analysis
- Elaboration
- Memory

Cognitive effort The degree of effort the consumer is prepared to put into thinking about the product offering.

Cognitive structure The way information is fitted into the existing knowledge.

Elaboration The structuring of the information within the brain, and adding to it from memory in order to form a coherent whole.

Memory The mechanism by which learned information is stored.

Cognitive effort is the degree of effort the consumer is prepared to put into thinking about the product offering. This will depend on such aspects as the complexity of the product, the consumer's involvement with it, and the motivation for learning.

Cognitive structure is about the way the consumer thinks, and the way the information is fitted into the existing knowledge.

The analysis of information is firstly concerned with selecting the correct, relevant information from the environment, and secondly with interpreting the information correctly in order to obtain a clear action plan.

Elaboration is the structuring of the information within the brain, and adding to it from memory in order to form a coherent whole.

Memory is the mechanism by which learned information is stored. In fact, nothing is ever truly forgotten; information will eventually become irrecoverable by the conscious mind (forgotten) but the brain still retains the information and can be stimulated to recall it, either by hypnosis or the association of ideas.

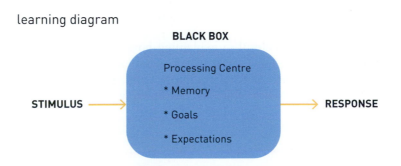

learning diagram

BLACK BOX

Processing Centre

* Memory

STIMULUS → * Goals → RESPONSE

* Expectations

Figure 3.18 Cognitive learning

Cognitive learning processes are important to marketers since they are helpful in predicting consumer responses to advertising. Hoch and Ha (1986) say that consumers view advertisements as tentative hypotheses about product performance that can be tested through product experience. Early learning about a product will affect future learning; this is called the **law of primacy**. For this reason first impressions count for a great deal.

Advertising will tend to be ignored if there is unambiguous objective evidence to hand. If the evidence is ambiguous or unobtainable at first hand (as is often the case) advertising appears to have an effect on consumer perceptions.

Learning from experience is a four-stage process, as Table 3.7 shows. In most cases people prefer to learn by experience, especially for major product purchases; few people would buy a car without having a test drive first, and still fewer would buy from the Internet unless they were people with previous direct experience of the car. It is for this reason that on-line retailers usually have a no-quibble money-back guarantee; if this were not the case, few people would be prepared to buy on-line rather than visit a high-street shop where they can see and feel the goods.

There are also three moderating factors in the cognitive learning process:

1. **Familiarity** with the domain. This is the degree to which the consumer has pre-existing knowledge of the product category.
2. Motivation to learn. If the purchase is an important one, or the possible effects of making a mistake would be serious, the consumer is likely to be highly-motivated to obtain as much information as possible.
3. **Ambiguity** of the information environment. If the information is hard to get, contradictory, or incomprehensible this will hinder the learning process. Sometimes consumers will give up on the process if this is the case.

Law of primacy The law that states that early learning about an object will colour future experiences of the object and future interpretations of that experience.

Familiarity The degree to which an object is known.

Ambiguity The degree to which stimuli can be interpreted in different ways.

Table 3.7 Learning from experience

Stage	Explanation	Example	Marketing response
Hypothesising	Developing a rough estimate of what's available.	Getting information from a friend, reading advertising material or brochures.	Have clearly-written brochures and advertising, without too much jargon.
Exposure	Obtaining direct experience of the product.	Visiting a shop to try the product and ask questions about it.	Ensure that the product is on display, and allow plenty of opportunity for hands-on testing.
Encoding	Making sense of the information.	Translating the information, understanding what the product is and does in terms which fit in with previous experience.	Have sales people who can explain things in lay terms, and who do not frighten the customer off by using too much technical language.
Integration	Fitting the new information into the existing knowledge bank.	Thinking about the new information gained about the product, and discarding previous misconceptions.	Ensure that customers feel able to come back for further explanations if they still have problems. Make sure that customers understand everything before leaving the shop.

How motivated are consumers to learn?	What do consumers already know?	How much can experience teach?	
		Little (high ambiguity)	**A lot (low ambiguity)**
HIGHLY MOTIVATED	**Unfamiliar**	Learning is most susceptible to management	Learning is spontaneous, rapid and difficult to manage
	Familiar	Formation of superstitious beliefs is possible. Existing beliefs inhibit suggestibility	
WEAKLY MOTIVATED	**Unfamiliar**	Learning is slow to start and difficult to sustain, but is susceptible to management	Learning is difficult to initiate and once started difficult to manage
	Familiar	Complacency inhibits initiation of learning, so experience is unresponsive to management	

Figure 3.19   Moderating factors in cognitive learning (from Hoch, S.J. and Deighton, J. (1989) Managing what consumers learn from experience. *Journal of Marketing*, 53 (April): 1–20)

Figure 3.19 illustrates these moderating factors in terms of classifying readiness to learn from experience.

Cognitive theories recognise that consumers influence the outcome in an active manner, so the learning process is not always easy for an outsider (i.e. a marketing person) to manage. This may be some of the reason why new products fail so frequently; weak motivation to learn about new products leads to difficulty for marketers in starting the learning process.

Cognitive learning has five elements, as follows:

1. Drive. Drive is the stimulus that impels action. The impulse to learn can be driven by a fear of making an expensive mistake, or by a desire to maximise the benefits of the purchase.
2. **Cue**. This is some external trigger that encourages learning. It is weaker than a drive, is external and is specific. For example, a public service such as the Health and Safety Council might exhort employers to send for a leaflet on safety in the workplace. Sometimes firms will use advertisement retrieval cues to trigger responses.
3. **Response**. This is the reaction the consumer makes to the interaction between a drive and a cue.
4. Reinforcement. Purchase response should be rewarded with a positive experience of the product. The object of reinforcement is to ensure that consumers associate the product with certain benefits.
5. **Retention**. This is the stability of the learned material over time, or in other words how well it is remembered. (The opposite of retention is extinction).

Learned responses are never truly unlearned. The brain remembers (stores) everything, but rather like a computer with a faulty disk drive it may not always

Cue An external trigger that encourages learning.

Response The reaction the consumer makes to the interaction between a drive and a cue.

Retention The stability of learned material over time.

be able to recall (retrieve) everything. Also, the human memory is huge; the *Encyclopaedia Britannica* contains 12,500 million characters, but the brain has a 125,000,000 million characters storage capacity. This is enough storage to hold 10,000 *Encyclopaedia Britannica*s, which makes the human brain easily the world's most powerful computer (*Business Week* 1990).

PERCEPTION

Human beings have considerably more than five senses. Apart from the basic five (touch, taste, smell, sight, hearing) there are senses of direction, sense of balance, a clear knowledge of which way is down, and so forth. Each sense is feeding information to the brain constantly, and the amount of information being collected would seriously overload the system if one took it all in. The brain therefore selects from the environment around the individual and cuts out the extraneous noise.

In effect, the brain makes automatic decisions as to what is relevant and what is not. Even though there may be many things happening around the individual, the person is unaware of most of them; in fact, experiments have shown that some information is filtered out by the optic nerve even before it gets to the brain. People quickly learn to ignore extraneous noises. For example, as a visitor to someone else's home you may be sharply aware of a loudly ticking clock, whereas your host may be entirely used to it and unaware of it except when making a conscious effort to check that the clock is still running. Therefore the information entering the brain does not provide a complete view of the world.

When the individual constructs a world-view, he or she then assembles the remaining information to map what is happening in the outside world. Any gaps (and there will, of course, be plenty of these) will be filled in with imagination and experience. The cognitive map is therefore not a 'photograph'; it is a construct of the imagination. This mapping will be affected by the following factors:

1. **Subjectivity**. This is the existing world-view within the individual, and is unique to that individual.
2. **Categorisation**. This is the 'pigeonholing' of information, and the prejudging of events and products. This can happening through a process known as **chunking** whereby the individual organises information into chunks of related items (Miller 1956). For example, a picture seen while a particular piece of music is playing might be chunked as one item in the memory, so that sight of the picture evokes the music and vice versa.
3. **Selectivity** is the degree to which the brain is selecting from the environment. It is a function of how much is going on around the individual, and also of how selective (concentrated) the individual is on the current task. Selectivity is also subjective; some people are a great deal more selective than others. Sometimes people select information simply because they assume it will be useful – this appears to be true of novel names for paint colours (Miller and Khan 2003).
4. Expectations lead individuals to interpret later information in a specific way. For example, look at this series of numbers and letters:

A 13 C D E F G H I
10 11 12 13 14 15 16

Subjectivity The unique world-view within the individual.

Categorisation Filing information alongside similar information in the memory.

Chunking The mental process whereby information is stored alongside connected information.

Selectivity Selecting from external stimuli.

5. In fact, the number 13 appears in both series, but in the first series it would be interpreted as a B because that is what the brain is being led to expect. (The B in this typeface looks like this: **ƀ**)

6. Past experience leads us to interpret later experience in the light of what we already know. This is called the Law of Primacy by psychologists. Sometimes sights, smells or sounds from our past will trigger off inappropriate responses; the smell of bread baking may recall a village bakery from twenty years ago, but in fact the smell could have been artificially generated by an aerosol spray near the supermarket bread counter.

An example of cognitive mapping as applied to perception of product quality might run as follows. First, the consumer uses the input selector to select clues and assign values to them. For quality, the cues are typically price, brand name, and retailer name. There are strong positive relationships between price and quality in most consumers' perceptions, and brand name and quality; although the retailer name is less significant, it still carries some weight. For example, many consumers would feel confident that Harrod's would sell higher-quality items than the local corner shop, but might be less able to distinguish between Sainsbury's and Tesco.

Subjective Appertaining to the individual; influenced by or derived from personal taste or opinion.

The information is **subjective**, in that the consumer will base decisions on the selected information. Each of us selects differently from the environment, and each of us has differing views. For example, illiterate people have different cognitive approaches as well as different heuristics: they tend to be swayed more by pictorial evidence, and prefer concrete reasoning (Viswathanan et al. 2005). Likewise, people tend to assess information as being stronger when it is framed within a short timescale – saying that more than 1000 people a day die of smoking is more powerful than saying that 440,000 people a year die of it (Chandran and Menon 2003).

Information about quality will be pigeonholed, or categorised; the individual may put Jaguars in the same category as BMWs, or perhaps put Sony in the same slot as Hitachi.

Selectivity will depend on how much is going on in the environment, on the individual's interest and motivation regarding the subject area, and on the degree of concentration the individual has on the task in hand. People with a highly developed ability to concentrate select less from the environment, because they are able to 'shut out' the world much more. In a cluttered environment, the use of colour will reduce search times because it cuts through the selection process better (Jansson et al. 2004).

Expectations of quality play a huge part; if the individual is expecting a high-quality item, he or she will select evidence which supports that view and tend to ignore evidence that does not. Past experience will also play a part in quality judgement. If the consumer has had bad experiences of Japanese products, this might lead to a general perception that Japanese products are poor quality.

Weber's Law states that the size of the least detectable change depends on the size of the stimulus. This means that a very intense stimulus will require a bigger change if the change is to be perceived by the consumer. For example, 20 pence off the price of a morning newspaper is a substantial discount, and would attract attention in advertising, whereas 20 pence off the price of a BMW would go unnoticed. Clearly at this level of intensity (a price of a few pence compared with a price of thousands of pounds) Weber's Law may not work very precisely (Britt and Nelson 1976), but in the middle range of prices the Law appears to work well. Incidentally, reducing the price from £10 to £9.99 is very noticeable even though the actual reduction is only 0.01% of the initial price. The important element here is that the reduction should be noticeable. There is more on pricing in Chapter 14.

Weber's Law also applies to product differentiation. The Law can be applied to determine how much better the product has to be for the difference to be noticeable (Britt 1975), or conversely to determine how similar the product needs to be to be indistinguishable from the leading brand.

It should be noted here that perception and reality are not different things. There is a popular view that perception somehow differs from reality; in fact, reality only exists in the heads of individuals. If there is an objective reality, it is not accessible to us as human beings; we have only what our senses tell us, and for each of us reality is different because each of us selects and synthesises in a different way.

From a marketing viewpoint, the fact that perception is so nebulous and individual a thing is probably helpful in the long run. People's views of products and services rely heavily on perceived attributes, some of which have no objective reality; the difficulty for marketers lies in knowing what will be the general perception of the members of the market segments with whom we are attempting to do business.

Peer and reference groups

A group is two or more persons who share a set of norms and whose relationship makes their behaviour interdependent. A **reference group** is 'A person or group of people that significantly influences an individual's behaviour' (Beardon and Etzel 1982). The reference groups provide standards or norms by which consumers judge their attitudes and behaviour.

Reference group A group from which one takes behavioural cues.

Originally groups formed for the purpose of co-operating on survival activities. Because human beings could co-operate in such activities as hunting, food-gathering and defence from predators, we were able to increase the chances of survival for the species as a whole. Interestingly, this still appears to hold true; social researchers have reported that socially isolated people have mortality rates between 50% and 300% higher than people who are strongly integrated into groups (Koretz 1990).

Most people prefer to fit in with the group (to a greater or lesser extent). This is either through politeness or through a desire not to be left out of things. Particularly with groups of friends, people will 'go along with the crowd' on a great many issues, and will tend to adopt the group norms regarding behaviour and attitudes (Asch 1951).

Reference groups fall into many possible groupings; the following list is not intended to be exhaustive.

Primary groups are composed of those people we see most often: friends, family, close colleagues. A primary group is small enough to permit face-to-face interaction on a regular basis, and there is cohesiveness and mutual participation which result in similar beliefs and behaviour within the group.

Primary group The group of people who are closest to the individual.

Secondary groups are composed of people we see occasionally, and with whom we have some shared interest. For example, a trade association or a sports club would constitute a secondary group. These groups are correspondingly less influential in shaping attitudes and controlling behaviour, but can exert influence on behaviour within the purview of the subject of mutual interest.

Secondary group A group to which one belongs but which one does not relate to on a regular basis.

Aspirational groups are the groups the individual wants to join. These groups can be very powerful in influencing behaviour, because the individual will often adopt the behaviour of the aspirational group in the hopes of being accepted as a member.

Aspirational groups Groups an individual would like to be a member of.

Dissociative group A group to which one would not wish to belong.

Formal group A group with a known, recorded membership list.

Informal group A group that does not have a fixed membership list or known rules.

Automatic group A group to which one belongs by virtue of birth. Also called a category group.

Dissociative groups on the other hand are those groups with which the individual does not want to be associated. This can have a negative effect on behaviour; the individual avoids certain products or behaviours rather than be mistaken for somebody from the dissociative group. Like aspirational groups, the definition of a group as dissociative is purely subjective.

Formal groups have a known list of members, very often recorded somewhere. An example might be a professional association, or a club. Usually the rules and structure of the group are laid down in writing; there are rules for membership and members' behaviour is constrained while they remain part of the group. However, the constraints usually apply only to fairly limited areas of behaviour.

Informal groups are less structured, and are typically based on friendship. An example would be an individual's circle of friends, which only exists for mutual moral support, company, and sharing experiences. Although there can be even greater pressure to conform than would be the case with a formal group, there is nothing in writing.

Automatic groups are those groups to which one belongs by virtue of age, gender, culture or education. These are sometimes also called category groups. Although at first sight it would appear that these groups would not exert much influence on the members' behaviour, because these are groups that have not been joined voluntarily, it would appear that people are influenced by a group pressure to conform. For example, when buying clothes older people are sometimes reluctant to look like 'mutton dressed as lamb'. Sometimes people prefer to buy and wear second-hand clothes, either for nostalgic reasons or to show how thrifty they are (Roux and Korcha 2006), and shoes have been shown to carry many symbolic aspects (Belk 2003). Also, religion influences shopping behaviour even for apparently 'neutral' products such as television sets (Essoo and Dibb 2004).

The above categories of group are not mutually exclusive. A dissociative group could also be an informal one; a formal group can be a secondary group (and often is) and so forth. For example, one may not wish to become friends with a group of drunken hooligans (who see themselves as an informal group of friends having a good time). Likewise the golf club could be a place of refuge to which one retreats to have a quiet drink with like-minded people, as well as a place where golf is played.

Real-life marketing: Tribalism

Some recent thinking has likened groups to tribes. Neo-tribalism applies to primary groups and, to an extent, to secondary groups, but the emphasis on consumption is in the linking powers of the product rather than its utility as a product. For example, the France Telecom pager, Tatoo, has been marketed in a tribal way by using in-line roller skaters as an example tribe. Roller skaters are used in the firm's promotion, with events being organised for them and advertising built around them, even though (of course) the company's target market is much wider. The approach has been highly successful, but attempts by other firms to cash in on the idea have not always worked. Caisse d'Epargne, a French bank, tried launching a savings account called Tribu, but it was a complete failure because the account had no specific linking features (Cova and Cova 2001).

If you're going to encourage tribes, you need to:

- Identify the primary group – the group of friends and family.
- Ensure that your product helps the tribe to function better as a tribe.
- Identify the other products the tribe uses so that you can identify tribe members and find other things they would like to buy.

Table 3.8   Group influence

Type of Influence	Definition	Explanation	Example
Normative compliance	The pressure exerted on an individual to conform and comply.	Works best when social acceptance is a strong motive, strong pressures exist from the group, and the product or service is conspicuous in its use.	Street gangs require their members to wear specific jackets, or other uniforms. The members want to be accepted, the pressure to wear the jacket is great, and the jacket itself is a conspicuous badge of membership.
Value-expressive influence	The pressure that comes from the need for psychological association with a group.	The desired outcome is respect from others; this pressure comes from the need for esteem, rather than from the need to belong.	A businessman in a tailored suit is expressing a set of values suitable to the groups with which he is associated. At other times, he may wear entirely different clothing – perhaps golfing wear – to fit in with a different group.
Informational influence	The influence arising from a need to seek information from the reference group about the product category being considered.	People often need to get expert advice and opinion about their product choices. This can often be provided by the appropriate reference group.	Many professional organisations and trade bodies offer their members free advice about useful products for their businesses. Clearly a recommendation on, say, computer software for a hairdressing business would be well-received if it came from the Hairdressers Federation.

Source: After Engel, Blackwell and Miniard (1995)

Reference groups affect consumer choice in three ways, as shown in Table 3.8. Of the three influences, **normative compliance**, is probably the most powerful. The source of normative compliance lies in operant conditioning; the individual finds that conforming behaviour results in group approval and esteem, whereas non-conforming behaviour results in group disapproval. Eventually the 'good' behaviour becomes automatic and natural, and it would be difficult to imagine any other way of doing things. The principles of good moral behaviour are not absolutes – they are the result (in most cases) of normative compliance with a reference group.

Normative compliance The pressure to conform to group norms of behaviour.

Think outside this box!

If moral behaviour is simply the result of normative compliance, where does that leave the world's major religions? Each one lays down a moral code, often on the basis of a set of laws for reasonable behaviour towards other people.

Or is it possible that the framers of such laws operate by considering what is reasonable group behaviour? Are they, in fact, setting out normative compliance parameters? Perhaps more to the point – if normative compliance is so powerful, why do we need such guidelines at all?

Of course, the pressure to conform will only work on someone who has a strong motivation to be accepted. If the pressure is coming from an aspirational group, this is likely to be the case; if, on the other hand, the pressure is coming from a dissociative group, the reverse will be the case and the individual will not feel under any pressure to conform. For example, most law-abiding citizens would comply with instructions from the police, and would usually go out of their way to help the police. Criminals, on the other hand, might avoid helping the police even in circumstances where their own crimes were not at issue.

The conspicuousness of the product or service is also crucial to the operation of normative compliance. For example, if all the individual's friends vote Labour the person might be under some pressure to do likewise, but since the ballot is secret nobody will know if he or she votes Conservative instead, so there is little pressure for normative compliance. Likewise, if one's friends all drink Stella Artois lager one may feel under pressure to do the same, but might be happy with supermarket own-brand when having a beer in the back garden at home.

Inner directed Motivated by forces originating within the individual.

Normative compliance is in decline in the Western world due to the shifting social paradigm towards a more **inner-directed** society (McNulty 1985). The reduction in face-to-face interaction may be leading to this move away from normative compliance; increasingly people communicate by impersonal means such as telephone, e-mail and social media such as Facebook and Twitter. Whether this is a cause of the paradigm shift or one of its effects is difficult to decide at present, but research by the Future Foundation indicates that people with a greater sense of independence, less concerned about material wealth and more concerned about experiences, and more idealistic (dubbed high-I people) are much more prolific users of the new communications technologies (Howard and Mason 2001).

The reference group will not exert influence over every buying decision. Even in circumstances where group influence does come into play, the consumer will be influenced by other variables such as product characteristics, standards of judgement and conflicting influences from other groups. Table 3.9 shows some of the determinants of reference group influence.

The effectiveness of the role model in modelling behaviour will depend on the personal characteristics of the role model. Attractive models will be imitated more than unattractive ones, successful-looking models are given more credence than unsuccessful-looking ones, and a model who is perceived as being similar to the observer is also more likely to be emulated (Baker and Churchill 1977). There is also some evidence to show that observers are more likely to identify with role models who have some difficulty in completing the modelled task (Manz and Sims 1981).

Other research seems to indicate that poor people are more influenced by informal reference groups, while wealthier people are more influenced by formal groups. The research was conducted with expectant mothers who were choosing maternity services, which is of course a high-involvement decision in virtually all cases. This may have had some effect on the findings (Tinson and Ensor 2001).

The family

Of all reference groups, the family is probably the most powerful in influencing consumer decision-making. The reasons for this are as follows:

1. In the case of children, the parental influence is the earliest, and therefore colours the child's perception of everything that follows.
2. In the case of parents, the desire to do the best they can for their children influences their decision-making when making purchases for the family. Clear examples

are the purchase of breakfast cereals such as Ready Brek, and disposable nappies, where the marketing appeal is almost invariably based on the comfort and well-being of the baby.

3. In the case of siblings, the influence comes either as role model (where the sibling is older) or as carer/adviser (where the sibling is younger).

Visible Able to be seen by others.

Non-universal ownership Not owned by people who are not members of the group.

Table 3.9 Determinants of reference group influence

Determinant	Definition	Explanation	Example
Judgement standards	The criteria used by the individual to evaluate the need to conform.	Judgement standards are *objective* when the group norms are obvious and when the group approach is clearly the sensible course of action. The standards are *subjective* when it is not clear which is the most sensible course of action.	Decisions of the government are often portrayed as being unanimous. This is to protect the illusion that the ruling party is united, since discord is often seen as a sign of weakness.
Product characteristics	The features of the product that are salient to the group influence.	The two main characteristics necessary for group influence to work are that the product should be **visible**, and that it should stand out (**non-universal ownership**).	Designer T-shirts have the designer's name written prominently across the front. This is often the only distinguishing feature of the product.
Member characteristics	The traits of the group member which make him or her more or less susceptible to group pressures.	People vary considerably in the degree to which they are influenced by the pressures from the group. Some people remain fairly independent, where others conform habitually. Personality, status and security all seem to play major roles in determining whether an individual will conform or not.	It transpires that university students are much more likely to conform with group norms than housewives (Park and Lessig 1977). This is possibly because the university students are young, poor and often away from home so have a greater need to belong.
Group characteristics	The features of the group that influence individuals to conform.	The power of the group to influence the individual varies according to size, cohesiveness and leadership. Once the group is bigger than three members, the power to influence levels off. This is probably because the group has difficulty reaching a consensus. Likewise, the stronger the leadership the greater the influence, and the greater the cohesiveness the stronger the influence, because the group reaches a clear decision.	Most smokers take up the habit as a result of peer group pressure when they are aged around 12 or 13. If a child's friends are strongly anti-smoking, the influence from marketers and even family background is likely to be much less.
Role model	An individual whose influence is similar to that of a group.	A role model is a hero, a star, or just somebody the individual respects and admires, and wishes to imitate.	Imitating film stars has a long history. When Clark Gable removed his shirt in the 1930s to reveal that he was not wearing a vest, sales of vests plummeted. More recently, it has been reported that teenage girls are using Botox in imitation of celebrities.

Within the UK, a family is usually defined in narrow terms – the parents and their offspring. However, in most families there will also be influences from uncles, aunts, grandparents and cousins. While these influences are often less strong in UK households than they might be in some other countries where the extended family is more common, the influences still exist to a greater or lesser extent. One of the changes currently occurring throughout Western Europe is the increase in the number of single-person households; there is, of course, a difference between a household and a family. A further change, coming about through the tremendous increase in the divorce rate, is the growing number of single-parent families.

There is also a problem here with terminology. Traditionally, studies of the family have referred to the male partner as the husband, and the female partner as the wife. The increasing number of families in which the parents are not married has rendered this approach obsolete; even the definition of what constitutes a family is in doubt, because of the many different forms of relationship that have emerged, such as households in which both partners are of the same sex. The traditional family group of a married couple and their children now accounts for less than 20% of households in the UK, for example (Office for National Statistics 2013).

From a marketing viewpoint, the level of demand for many products is dictated more by the number of households than by the number of families. The relevance of families to marketing is therefore much more about consumer behaviour than about consumer demand levels.

In terms of its function as a reference group, the family is distinguished by the following characteristics:

1. Face-to-face contact. Family members see each other every day or thereabouts, and interact as advisers, information providers, and sometimes deciders. Other reference groups rarely have this level of contact.
2. Shared consumption. Durables such as fridges, freezers, televisions and furniture are shared, and food is collectively purchased and cooked (although there is a strong trend away from families eating together). Purchase of these items is often collective; children even participate in decision-making on such major purchases as cars and houses. Other reference groups may share some consumption (for example, a model railway club may hire a workshop and share tools) but families share the consumption of most domestic items. In some cases, products are handed down from one generation to another, reinforcing family values and traditions (Curasi 2011; Hartman and Kiecker 2004).
3. Subordination of individual needs. Because consumption is shared, some family members will find that the solution chosen is not one that fully meets their needs. Although this happens in other reference groups, the effect is more pronounced in families.
4. Purchasing agent. Because of the shared consumption, most families will have one member who does most, or all, of the shopping. Traditionally, this has been the mother of the family, but increasingly the purchasing agent is an older child of the family – even pre-teens are sometimes taking over this role. The reason for this is the increase in the number of working mothers – women who work outside the home – which has left less time for shopping. This has major implications for marketers, since pre-teens and young teens generally watch more TV than adults and use the Internet more, and are therefore more open to marketing communications.

The above characteristics can also serve as a definition of a family. Whatever the composition of its members, the above list constitutes a convenient way of identifying what constitutes a family and what does not.

Family decision-making is not as straightforward as marketers have supposed in the past. There has been an assumption that the purchasing agent (e.g. the mother) is the one who makes the decisions, and while this is often the case, this approach ignores the ways in which the purchase decisions are arrived at.

Role specialisation is critical in family decision-making because of the sheer number of different products that must be bought each year in order to keep the family supplied. What this means in practice is that, for example, the family member responsible for doing the cooking is also likely to take the main responsibility for shopping for food. The family member who does the most driving is likely to make the main decision about the car and its accessories, servicing, fuelling and so forth; the family gardener buys the gardening products, and so on.

Product category affects role specialisation and decision-making systems. When an expensive purchase is being considered, it is likely that most of the family will be involved in some way, if only because major purchases affect the family budgeting for other items. At the other end of the scale, day-to-day shopping for toilet rolls and cans of beans entails very little collective decision-making. Where the product has a shared usage (a holiday or a car) the collective decision-making component is likely to increase greatly. Conversely, where the product is used predominantly by one family member, that member will dominate the decision-making even when the purchase is a major one (the family chef will make most of the decisions about the new cooker, for example).

The family may well adopt different roles according to the decision-making stage. At the problem-recognition stage of, for example, the need for new shoes for the children, the children themselves may be the main contributors. The mother may then decide what type of shoes should be bought, and the father may be the one who takes the children to buy the shoes. It is reasonable to suppose that the main user of the product might be important in the initial stages, with perhaps joint decision-making at the final purchase.

Other determinants might include such factors as whether both parents are earning. In such families, decision-making is more likely to be joint because each has a financial stake in the outcome. Some studies seem to indicate that family decision-making is more likely to be husband-dominated when the husband is the sole earner, whereas couples who are both earning make decisions jointly (Filiatrault and Ritchie 1980). Males also tend to dominate highly technical durable products (e.g. home computers).

Conflict resolution tends to have an increased importance in family decision-making as opposed to individual purchase behaviour. The reason for this is that, obviously, more people are involved each with their own needs and their own internal conflicts to resolve. The conflict resolution system is as laid out in Table 3.10.

Influence of children on buying decisions

First-born children generate more economic impact than higher-order babies. Around 40% of babies are first-borns; they are photographed more, they get all new clothes (no hand-me-downs), and get more attention all round. First-born and only children have a higher achievement rate than their siblings, and since the birth-rate is falling there are more of them proportionally. More and more couples are choosing to have only one child, and families larger than two children are becoming a rarity. Childlessness is also more common now than it was thirty years ago.

Children also have a role in applying pressure to their parents to make particular purchasing decisions. The level of 'pester power' generated can be overwhelming, and parents will frequently give in to the child's demands (Ekstrom et al. 1987).

Table 3.10   Conflict resolution in families

Resolution method	Explanation
Persuasion through information exchange	When a conflict occurs, each family member seeks to persuade the others of his or her point of view. This leads to discussion, and ultimately some form of compromise.
Role expectation	If persuasion fails, a family member may be designated to make the decision. This is usually somebody who has the greatest expertise in the area of conflict being discussed. This method appears to be going out of fashion as greater democracy in family decision-making is appearing.
Establishment of norms	Families will often adopt rules for decision-making. Sometimes this will involve taking turns over making decisions (perhaps over which restaurant the family will go to this week, or where they will go on holiday).
Power exertion	This is also known as browbeating. One family member will try to exert power to force the other members to comply; this may be a husband who refuses to sign the cheque unless he gets his own way, or a wife who refuses to cook the dinner until the family agree, or a child who throws a tantrum. The person with the most power is called the **least dependent person** because he or she is not as dependent on the other family members. Using the examples above, if the wife has her own income she will not need to ask the husband to sign the cheque; if the other family members can cook they can get their own dinner; and if the family can ignore the yelling toddler long enough eventually the child will give up.

Source: Adapted from Onkvisit and Shaw 1994

Least dependent person The individual with the most power in a group.

Children often develop sophisticated negotiating techniques in order to get their own way, highlighting the benefits of purchase and forming coalitions with siblings or parents (Thomson et al. 2007). There is also some evidence to show that children regard pester power as a game – the aim is to exert power over the parents, rather than simply get something out of them (Lawlor and Protheroe 2011).

Although the number of children is steadily declining, their importance as consumers is not. Apart from the direct purchases of things that children need, they influence decision-making to a marked extent. Children's development as consumers goes through five stages:

1. Observing
2. Making requests
3. Making selections
4. Making assisted purchases
5. Making independent purchases

In some cases children have the role of teaching their parents about new products (Ekstrom 2007). For example, many parents ask their children to help with such new products as mobile telephones and DVD players. Young teenage children are often more aware of such issues as healthy eating and environmentalism, and are therefore likely to try to exert pressure on their parents over such issues (Nancarrow et al. 2011).

Children have to learn to be effective consumers, and this training comes mainly (but not only) from the parents. Parents who are too strict with their children, or who insist on making all the decisions (even when they are being essentially indulgent), will create dependent adults who are unable to make their own consumption decisions (Rose et al. 2002). Families also develop consistent purchasing behaviours through the generations – children often buy the same brands they remember from their childhoods, for example (Epp and Arnould 2006).

Self-concept

Self-concept is the individual's feelings about him- or herself. Beliefs about ourselves are often the main drivers in what we buy: we buy things that enhance our image of ourselves, both in our own eyes and in the eyes of others.

Each of us projects a **role** that is either accepted or rejected by other people. In effect, we are each playing a part: Erving Goffman (1969) originally conceived this as the **dramaturgical analogy**, that life is theatre and that each of us uses props, costume, script and make-up to play our roles. We even have a backstage area, where our most intimate friends and family see us. If our role is accepted by others, we are rewarded with applause: if it is rejected, we are made to feel awkward by those around us.

Self-image has four components:

1. **Real self**. This is the objective self that others observe.
2. **Self-image**. This is the subjective self, as we see ourselves.
3. **Ideal self**. The person we wish we were.
4. **Looking-glass self**. The way we think other people see us.

Recently, the concept of **worst self** has been added. This is the negative aspect of self, and is usually the self that people seek to reduce within themselves (Banister and Hogg 2003). Each of these components has purchasing implications. The real self drives conspicuous consumption of cars, fashion, hairdressing and all the outward manifestations of self. Self-image drives purchases of goods that fit the values and lifestyle of the individual, both conspicuously and inconspicuously. Ideal self drives self-improvement purchases such as education, cosmetic surgery, musical instruments and self-help books. Looking-glass self is a reflection of real self, so similar drives will result.

Self-concept has been shown to drive people's behaviour on holiday. Some people clearly behave very differently on holiday from how they do at home, almost becoming new people: this reflects in the type of holiday purchased and the types of activities undertaken (Todd 2001).

Self-concept is, like attitude, learned and purposeful. It is also stable over time, within limits, and is unique to the individual.

Self-concept One's view of oneself.

Role The position one has in the group.

Dramaturgical analogy The view that life is essentially theatrical in nature.

Real self The objective self that others observe.

Self-image The subjective self: the person we think we are.

Ideal self The person we wish we were.

Looking-glass self The way we think other people see us.

Worst self The negative aspects of one's personality; the aspects we wish to overcome in ourselves.

Chapter summary

If consumers are at the centre of everything that marketers do, consumer behaviour should be the starting-point in developing any marketing strategy. Consumer behaviour is not especially different from any other type of human behaviour: most behaviour is aimed at making life more convenient and comfortable. For human beings, this includes ensuring that we fit in with the people around us, and do not attract ridicule or abuse from them. Human behaviour is complex, and involves many exchanges at many different levels. It is those exchanges which marketers seek to influence and facilitate.

Key points

- People are not entirely rational when making purchasing decisions – emotional issues are also involved.
- The less the individual knows about the product, the longer the problem-solving behaviour will take.
- The cost of obtaining information will be weighed against the value of the information.
- Goals operate in hierarchies: establishing an end goal will lead to establishing a set of sub-goals.
- Complaints should be encouraged, because a voiced complaint is easier to deal with and less damaging than either private complaints or third-party complaints.
- Operant conditioning involves action on the part of the person being conditioned.
- Families have the greatest influence on behaviour, but other groups are also important.
- Perception is both analytic and synthetic, but generates the only reality the individual has.
- Self-concept is one of the most important non-rational drivers for consumer behaviour.

Review questions

1. What is the reason for developing a hierarchy of goals?
2. How does drive relate to motivation?
3. Under what circumstances would you expect someone to undertake an extensive external search?
4. Why do people become involved with specific brands?
5. What is the role of self-concept in buying fashion wear?
6. What are the factors that relate to the length of an information search?
7. What is the difference between conation and behaviour?
8. Why are families an important influence on decision-making?
9. Why is perception described as being both analytic and synthetic?
10. How might a service firm (such as a restaurant) minimise the perception of risk?

Case study revisited: Riverford Organics

Supermarkets have been quick to respond to the organic revolution, and many now offer at least some organic vegetables. Generally, these cost around 10% more than the equivalent factory-farmed vegetables, but obviously many people feel that it's worth paying the extra. Notably, however, the vegetables on offer are not always seasonal – which indicates that they have been imported, often from a long way away (some are even flown in from Africa). The vast majority of British consumers would not be able to say with any certainty which vegetables are in season at which time of year, of course, because vegetables of all types have been available all year round for at least 30 years now.

A drawback of Riverford boxes is that they contain whatever is available, so people have to be creative in their cooking and able to use what's there rather than follow recipes. Although

Riverford tries to ensure that some popular vegetables (for example onions and potatoes) are available in every box every week, it clearly is not possible to guarantee that (say) turnips or lettuces will be available every time. In fact, there is unlikely ever to be a box with both in, since they are not in season at the same time.

The twin problems of lack of knowledge of seasonality and an inability to cook without a recipe mean that Riverford has had to put some effort into re-educating people. This has been done in two ways: first, the company runs a restaurant called the Field Kitchen at its Devon farm, and second they put recipes in the veg boxes so that people know what to do with their seasonal veg. The Field Kitchen has a touring version (housed in a yurt), and also there are Riverford Cooks around the country who will explain seasonality and demonstrate cooking methods. The company has also published two cookbooks, one called *Riverford Farm Cookbook*, the other called *Every Day and Sunday*.

Riverford has been a commercial success, despite the boxes being 20% cheaper than supermarket organic vegetables – but for Guy Watson, the most important outcome is that the word has spread about organic produce. Consumers are more aware of what is available, and how to use it: the need which was once confined to a very few people, and which was regarded as somewhat cranky, has moved into the mainstream, with more converts to the organic cause every day.

Case study: Buying a car

The UK has one of the biggest traffic problems in the world. It's a relatively small country to have 22 million cars on the road – more than one car per household on average – and yet owning a car is regarded as almost as important as owning a home. Partly this is due to an expensive and inadequate public transport infrastructure for the bulk of the country, but partly it is a cultural issue – people just love to own a car. Outside London (which does have an efficient public transport system) 70% of people travel to work by car, with about one-third of these trips taking people into already-congested urban centres. In all, people travel 78 billion miles a year, just getting to and from work by car. Each year around two and a half million new cars are sold in the UK, but the used car market is much bigger: according to the Society of Motor Manufacturers and Traders, around seven and a half million used cars change hands every year. This only refers to cars – around another million and a half other vehicles change hands each year as well.

Almost everybody in the UK uses cars (even people who do not drive are regularly driven around by car owners). Buying a used car is a familiar process for most people, yet it is still fraught with risk – a car represents a large investment, and the technical aspects of cars are too complex for most people to grasp fully. A typical car owner might have to make the difficult purchase decision twenty times in a lifetime of motoring; even someone who keeps each car for a long time might make ten or twelve purchases. At the same time, technology is moving forward: vehicles are becoming more complex, new features are added each year, and some favourite features disappear.

It has been said that buying a car is the second most financially important decision you can make. Not true, according to the website Top Gear. They say that 'You are much more likely to flush cash down the toilet on a used car' than on buying a house. This is because a car is a very visible product – one's choice of car says a lot about one's status, personality, financial security, and so forth. The website, owned by the magazine of the same name, goes on to offer a step-by-step guide to buying a second-hand car, including advice on some tax-efficient ways of buying.

The guide is comprehensive – it advises on what to buy, when to buy, where to buy and what to look for when checking the car's history and paperwork. It advises on how to negotiate with sellers, how to pay for the car in the most cost-effective and secure way, and even provides a lengthy checklist for inspecting the car. A key piece of advice is to take a friend with you when buying, partly because the extra pair of eyes might spot something the buyer has missed, and partly because having someone else around provides moral support in any negotiating situation.

Top Gear is not alone in offering this type of advice. Yahoo! have their own advice system for used car buying, as have motoring organisations such as the Automobile Association and the Royal Automobile Club. Even *Times Online* has an advice section for used car buying, complete with the obligatory checklist and finance advice.

It seems that almost everybody offers advice on buying cars, despite the huge environmental and financial cost associated with them. Car purchase will continue to be an important part of UK consumer behaviour, and people will continue to be grateful for any help.

Questions

1. What is the role of the peer group in car purchase?
2. Why are there so many websites offering help with buying used cars?
3. How might the average person reduce risk when buying a car?
4. Why is used car purchase so risky?
5. What would you expect the purchase process for a car to encompass?

Further reading

The very large number of books on consumer behaviour make it difficult to make specific recommendations: many of the texts are American, and should be treated with a degree of caution, since American consumption behaviour is not necessarily the same as that of other countries in the world. Having said that, much of the quoted research in consumer behaviour is American.

Here is a selection of texts:

Richard P. Bagozzi, Zeynep Gurhan-Canli and Joseph R. Priester, *The Social Psychology of Consumer Behaviour* (Buckingham: Open University Press, 2002). This is an erudite and academically advanced text for those who are interested in the deeper issues underlying consumer behaviour.

Jim Blythe, *Consumer Behaviour*, 2nd edn (London: Sage, 2013). This text gives a more detailed account of consumer behaviour than is possible here.

James F. Engel, Roger T. Blackwell and Paul W. Miniard, *Consumer Behaviour* 10th edition (Cincinnati, OH: South-Western, 2005). This text is by the same writers who developed one of the most widely quoted models of consumer behaviour. The text is comprehensive, well argued and also readable and interesting.

References

Allport, Gordon W. (1935) Attitudes. In C.A. Murchison (ed.), *A Handbook of Social Psychology*. Worcester, MA: Clark University Press.

Asch, Solomon E. (1951) Effects of group pressure on the modification and distortion of judgements. In H. Guetzkow (ed.), *Groups, Leadership and Men*. Pittsburgh, PA: Carnegie Press.

Bailey, Ainsworth Anthony (2004) Thiscompanysucks.com: the use of the Internet in negative consumer-to-consumer articulations. *Journal of Marketing Communications*, 10 (3): 169–82.

Baker, Michael J. and Churchill, Gilbert A., Jr (1977) The impact of physically attractive models on advertising evaluations. *Journal of Marketing Research*, November: 538–55.

Balabanis, George (2002) The relationship between lottery ticket and scratchcard buying behaviour, personality, and other compulsive behaviours. *Journal of Consumer Behaviour*, 2 (1): 7–22.

Banister, Emma N. and Hogg, Margaret K. (2003) Possible selves? Identifying dimensions for exploring dialectic between positive and negative selves in consumer behaviour. *Advances in Consumer Research*, 30: 149–50.

Bauer, Raymond A. (1960) Consumer behaviour as risk taking. In Robert S. Hancock (ed.), *Dynamic Marketing for a Changing World*. Chicago, IL: American Marketing Association.

Baumeister, Roy F. (2004) Self-regulation, conscious choice, and consumer decisions. *Advances in Consumer Research*, 31: 48–9.

Beardon, William O. and Etzel, Michael J. (1982) Reference group influence on product and brand purchase decisions. *Journal of Consumer Research*, 9: 184.

Belk, Russell (2003) Shoes and self. *Advances in Consumer Research*, 30: 27–33.

Bennett, Roger (2009) Impulsive donation decisions during online browsing of charity websites. *Journal of Consumer Behaviour*, 8 (2/3): 116–34.

Blackwell, Roger D., Miniard, Paul W. and Engel, James F. (2001) *Consumer Behaviour*, 9th edn. Cincinnati, OH: South-Western.

Bloch, Peter H., Sherrell, Daniel L. and Ridgway, Nancy M. (1986) Consumer search: an extended framework. *Journal of Consumer Research*, 13: 119–26.

Britt, Steuart Henderson (1975) How Weber's Law can be applied to marketing. *Business Horizons*, 13 (February).

Britt, Steuart Henderson and Nelson, Victoria M. (1976) The marketing importance of the 'just noticeable difference'. *Business Horizons*, 14 (August).

Business Week, 28 July 1990.

Chaiken, Shelly (1980) Heuristic versus systematic information processing and use of source versus message cues in persuasion. *Journal of Personality and Social Psychology*, 39: 752–66.

Chandran, Sucharita and Menon, Geeta (2003) When am I at risk? Now, or now? The effects of temporal framing on perceptions of health risk. *Advances in Consumer Research*, 30: 106–8.

Cobb, Kathy J., Walgren, Gary C. and Hollowed, Mary (1987) Differences in organisational responses to consumer letters of satisfaction and dissatisfaction. In Melanie Wallendorf and Paul Anderson (eds), *Advances in Consumer Research*, vol. 14. Provo, UT: Association for Consumer Research.

Coca-Cola Company (1981) Measuring the Grapevine: Consumer Response and Word-of-Mouth. Coca-Cola Company Consumer Information Centre.

Cova, Bernard and Cova, Veronique (2001) Tribal aspects of postmodern consumption research: the case of French in-line roller skates. *Journal of Consumer Behaviour*, 1: 67–76.

Curasi, Carolyn F. (2011) Intergenerational possession transfers and identity maintenance. *Journal of Consumer Behaviour*, 10 (2): 111–18.

Day, Ralph L. (1984) Modelling choices among alternative responses to dissatisfaction. In Thomas Kinnear (ed.), *Advances in Consumer Research*, vol. 11. Provo, UT: Association for Consumer Research.

Day, Ralph L., Brabicke, Klaus, Schaetzle, Thomas and Staubach, Fritz (1981) The hidden agenda of consumer complaining. *Journal of Retailing*, 57 (Fall): 86–106.

Dewey, John (1910) *How We Think*. Boston, MA: DC Heath and Co.

Dibley, Anne and Baker, Susan (2001) Uncovering the links between brand choice and personal values among young British and Spanish girls. *Journal of Consumer Behaviour*, 1 (1): 77–93.

Ekstrom, Karin M. (2007) Parental consumer learning or 'keeping up with the children'. *Journal of Consumer Behaviour*, 6 (4): 203–17.

Ekstrom, Karin M., Tansuhaj, Patriya S. and Foxman, Ellen (1987) Children's influence in family decisions and consumer socialisation: a reciprocal view. In Melanie Wallendorf and Paul Anderson (eds), *Advances in Consumer Research*, vol. 14. Provo, UT: Association for Consumer Research.

Engel, James F., Blackwell, Roger D. and Miniard, Paul W. (1995) *Consumer Behaviour*, 8th edn. Fort Worth, TX: Dryden Press.

Epp, Amber M. and Arnould, Eric J. (2006) Enacting the family legacy: how family themes influence consumption behaviour. *Advances in Consumer Research*, 33: 82–6.

Essoo, Nittin and Dibb, Sally (2004) Religious influences on shopping behaviour: an exploratory study. *Journal of Marketing Management*, 20 (7/8): 683–712.

Faber, Ronald J., O'Guinn, Thomas C. and Krych, Raymond (1987) Compulsive consumption. In Melanie Wallendorf and Paul Anderson (eds), *Advances in Consumer Research*, vol. 14. Provo, UT: Association for Consumer Research. pp. 132–5.

Filiatrault, P. and Ritchie, J.R.B. (1980) Joint purchasing decisions: a comparison of influence structure in family and couple decision making units. *Journal of Consumer Research*, 7 (September): 131–40.

Fishbein, Martin (1963) An investigation of the relationships between beliefs about an object and the attitude towards that object. *Human Relations*, 16: 233–40.

Fishbein, Martin (1980) An overview of the attitude construct. In G.B. Hafer (ed.), *A Look Back, A Look Ahead*. Chicago, IL: American Marketing Association.

Fishbein, Martin and Ajzen, Icek (1975) *Belief, Attitude, Intention and Behaviour: An Introduction to Theory and Research*. Reading, MA: Addison–Wesley.

Goffman, Erving (1969) *The Presentation of Self in Everyday Life*. Harmondsworth: Penguin.

Gorn, Gerald J. (1982) The effects of music in advertising on choice behaviour: a classical conditioning approach. *Journal of Marketing*, 46: 94–101.

Grougiou, Vassiliki and Pettigrew, Simone (2009) Seniors' attitudes to voicing complaints: a qualitative study. *Journal of Marketing Management*, 25 (9/10): 987-1001.

Halstead, Diane and Droge, Cornelia (1991) Consumer attitudes towards complaining and the prediction of multiple complaint response. In R. Holman and M. Solomon (eds), *Advances in Consumer Research*, vol. 18. Provo, UT: Association for Consumer Research.

Hartman, Cathy L. and Kiecker, Pamela (2004) Jewellery – passing along the continuum of sacred and profane meanings. *Advances in Consumer Research*, 31: 53–4.

Hoch, Stephen J. and Ha, Young-Won (1986) Consumer learning: advertising and the ambiguity of product experience. *Journal of Consumer Research*, 13: 221–33.

Holbrook, Morris B. (1984) Situation-specific ideal points and usage of multiple dissimilar brands. In Jagdish N. Sheth (ed.), *Research in Marketing*, vol. 7. Greenwich, CT: JAI Press.

Holbrook, Morris P. and Hirschmann, Elizabeth C. (1982) The experiential aspects of consumption: consumer fantasies, feelings and fun. *Journal of Consumer Research*, 9: 132–40.

Homer, Pamela M. and Yoon, Sun-Gil (1992) Message framing and the interrelationships among ad-based feelings, affect and cognition. *Journal of Advertising*, 21 (March): 19–33.

Howard, Melanie and Mason, Jane (2001) 21st century consumer society. *Journal of Consumer Behaviour*, 1: 94–101.

Hoyer, William D. and Ridgway, Nancy M. (1984) Variety seeking as an explanation for exploratory purchase behaviour: a theoretical model. In Thomas C. Kinnear (ed.), *Advances in Consumer Research*, vol. 11. Provo, UT: Association for Consumer Research.

Hsee, Christopher K. and Rottenstreich, Yuval (2004) Music, pandas, and muggers: on the affective psychology of value. *Journal of Experimental Psychology: General*, 2004, 133: 23–30.

Jansson, Catherine, Marlow, Nigel and Bristow, Matthew (2004) The influence of colour on visual search times in cluttered environments. *Journal of Marketing Communications*, 10 (3): 183–93.

Keisler, C.A., Collins, B. E. and Miller, Norman (1969) *Attitude Change: A Critical Analysis of Theoretical Approaches*. New York: John Wiley.

Keller, Kevin Lane, and Staelin, Richard (1987) Effects of quality and quantity of information on decision effectiveness. *Journal of Consumer Research*, 14:200–13.

Klein, Jill Gabrielle, Smith, N. Craig and John, Andrew (2004) Why we boycott: consumer motivations for boycott participation. *Journal of Marketing*, 68 (3): 92–109.

Koretz, Gene (1990) Economic trends. *Business Week*, 5 March.

Kroeber-Riel, Werner (1984) Emotional product differentiation by classical conditioning. In Thomas C. Kinnear (ed.), *Advances in Consumer Research*, vol. 11. Provo, UT: Association for Consumer Research.

Lambert-Pandraud, Raphaelle, Laurent, Gilles and LaPersonne, Eric (2005) Repeat purchase of new automobiles by older consumers: empirical evidence and interpretations. *Journal of Marketing*, 69 (2).

Lawlor, Margaret-Anne and Prothero, Andrea (2011) Pester power – a battle of wills between children and their parents. *Journal of Marketing Management*, 27 (5/6): 561–81.

Leichty, M. and Churchill, Gilbert A., Jr. (1979) Conceptual insights into consumer satisfaction and services. In Neil Beckwith et al. (eds), *Educators Conference Proceedings*. Chicago, IL: American Marketing Association.

Lye, Ashley, Shao, Wei, Rundle-Thiele, Sharyn and Fausnaugh, Carolyn (2005) Decision waves: consumer decisions in today's complex world. *European Journal of Marketing*, 39 (1/2): 216–30.

MacInnis, Deborah J. and deMello, Gustavo E. (2005) The concept of hope and its relevance to product evaluation and choice. *Journal of Marketing*, 69 (1): 1–13.

Manz, Charles C. and Sims, Henry P. (1981) Vicarious learning: the influence of modelling on organisational behaviour. *Academy of Management Review*, 6: 105–13.

McNulty, W. Kirk (1985) UK social change through a wide-angle lens. *Futures*, August.

McSweeney, Frances K. and Bierley, Calvin (1984) Recent developments in classical conditioning. *Journal of Consumer Research*, 11: 619–31.

Miller, Elizabeth Gelfand and Khan, Barbara E. (2003) Shades of meaning: the effect of novel colour names on consumer preferences. *Advances in Consumer Research*, 30: 11–13.

Miller, George A. (1956) The magical number seven, plus or minus two: some limits on our capacity for processing information. *Psychological Review*, 63 (2): 81.

Miniard, Paul W., Bhatla, Sunil and Rose, Randall L. (1990) On the formation and relationship of ad and brand attitudes: an experimental and causal analysis. *Journal of Marketing Research*, 27 (Aug): 290–303.

Nancarrow, Clive, Tinson, Julie and Brace, Ian (2011) Profiling key purchase influencers: those perceived as consumer savvy. *Journal of Consumer Behaviour*, 10 (2): 102-10.

Office for National Statistics (2013) www.ons.gov.uk/ons/dcp171776_302210.pdf (accessed June 2013).

O'Guinn, Thomas C. and Faber, Ronald J. (1989) Compulsive buying: a phenomenological explanation. *Journal of Consumer Research*, 16: 151–5.

Onkvisit, Sak and Shaw, John J. (1994) *Consumer Behaviour, Strategy and Analysis.* New York: Macmillan.

Park, C. Whan and Lessig, V. Parker (1977) Students and housewives: susceptibility to reference group influence. *Journal of Consumer Research*, 4: 102–10.

Pavlov, Ivan P. (1927) *Conditioned Reflexes.* Oxford: Oxford University Press.

Petty, Richard E. and Cacioppo, John T. (1986) Central and peripheral routes to persuasion: application to advertising. In Larry Percy and Arch Woodside (eds), *Advertising and Consumer Psychology.* Lexington, MA: Lexington Books.

Petty, Richard E., Cacioppo, John and Schumann, David (1983) Central and peripheral routes to advertising effectiveness. *Journal of Consumer Research*, 10 (Sept): 135–46.

Raghunathan, Raj and Mukherji, Ashesh (2003) Is hope to enjoy more enjoyed than hope enjoyed? *Advances in Consumer Research*, 30: 85–6.

Raju, P.S. (1980) Optimum stimulation level: its relationship to personality, demographics and exploratory behaviour. *Journal of Consumer Research*, 7: 272–82.

Rose, Gregory M., Dalakis, Vassilis, Kropp, Fredric and Kamineni, Rajeev (2002) Raising young consumers: consumer socialisation and parental style across cultures. *Advances in Consumer Research*, 29: 65.

Rosenberg, Milton J. (1960) An analysis of affective-cognitive consistency. In Milton J. Rosenberg et al. (eds), *Attitude Organisation and Change*. New Haven, CT: Yale University Press.

Rosenberg, I.J. and Czepeil, J.A. (1983) A marketing approach to customer retention. *Journal of Consumer Marketing*, 2: 45–51.

Roux, Dominique, and Korcha, Michael (2006) Am I what I wear? An exploratory study of symbolic meanings associated with second-hand clothing. *Advances in Consumer Research*, 33: 28–35.

Santos, Jessica and Boote, Jonathan (2003) A theoretical exploration and model of consumer expectations, post-purchase affective states and affective behaviour. *Journal of Consumer Behaviour*, 3 (2): 142–56.

Shankar, Avi, Cherrier, Helene and Canniford, Robin (2006) Consumer empowerment: a Foucauldian interpretation. *European Journal of Marketing*, 40 (9/10): 1013–30.

Sharma, Piyush, Sivakumaranb, Bharadhwaj and Marshall, Roger (2010) Exploring impulse buying and variety seeking by retail shoppers: towards a common conceptual framework. *Journal of Marketing Management*, 26 (5/6): 473–94.

Shiv, Baba, Ferraro, Roselina and Bettman, James R.(2004) Let us eat and drink, for tomorrow we shall die: mortality salience and hedonic choice. *Advances in Consumer Research*, 31: 118–21.

Singh, Jagdip (1988) Consumer complaint intentions and behaviour: definitions and taxonomical issues. *Journal of Marketing*, 52 (1): 93–107.

Skinner, B.F. (1953) *Science and Human Behaviour.* New York: Macmillan.

Slater, Alix and Armstrong, Kate (2010) Involvement, Tate, and me. *Journal of Marketing Management*, 26 (7/8): 727–48.

Smart, Denise T. and Martin, Charles L. (1991) Manufacturer responsiveness to consumer correspondence: an empirical investigation of consumer perceptions. *Journal of Consumer Affairs*, 26 (Summer): 104–28.

Stern, Hawkins (1962) The significance of impulse buying today. *Journal of Marketing*, 26 (2): 59–60.

Thomson, Elizabeth S., Laing, Angus W. and McKee, Lorna (2007) Family purchase decision making: exploring child influence behaviour. *Journal of Consumer Behaviour*, 6 (4): 182–202.

Tinson, Julie and Ensor, John (2001) Formal and informal referent groups: an exploration of novices and experts in maternity services. *Journal of Consumer Behaviour*, 1 (2): 174–83.

Todd, Sarah (2001) Self-concept: a tourism application. *Journal of Consumer Behaviour*, 1 (2): 184–96.

Urbany, Joel E. (1986) An experimental examination of the economics of information. *Journal of Consumer Research*, 13: 257–71.

Viswanathan, Madhubalan, Rosa, Jose Antonio and Harris, James Edwin (2005) Decision-making and coping of functionally illiterate consumers and some implications for marketing management. *Journal of Marketing*, 69 (1): 15–31.

Walsh, Giafranco, Hennig-Thurau, Thorsten and Mitchell, Vincent-Wayne (2007) Consumer confusion proneness: scale development, validation, and application. *Journal of Marketing Management*, 23 (7/8): 697–721.

Wansink, Brian (2004) How resourceful consumers identify new uses for old products. *Journal of Family and Consumer Science*, 95: 4.

Woodruff, Robert B., Cadotte, Ernst R. and Jenkins, Roger J. (1983) Modelling consumer satisfaction using experience-based norms. *Journal of Marketing Research*, 20 (Aug): 296–304.

Zajonc, Robert B. and Markus, Hazel (1985) Must all affect be mediated by cognition? *Journal of Consumer Research*, 12 (December): 363–4.

More online

To gain free access to additional online resources to support this chapter please visit:
www.sagepub.co.uk/blythe3e

CHAPTER ④
Business-to-business marketing

LEARNING OBJECTIVES

After reading this chapter, you should be able to:

- Explain the pressures that influence industrial buyers.

- Explain the role of the decision-making unit.

- Explain the role of customers in driving the reseller market.

- Describe approaches to government markets.

- Show how industrial markets can be divided.

- Describe the different types of buying situation, and the factors that are involved for making buying decisions within those situations.

- Understand the role of team selling in industrial markets.

Introduction

Organisational buying is often supposed to be more rational and less emotional than consumer purchasing behaviour. However, it would be wrong to assume that organisational buying is always entirely rational: those responsible for making buying decisions within organisations are still human beings, and do not leave their emotions at the door when they come to work, so it seems unrealistic to suppose that they do not have some emotional or irrational input in their decision-making.

Businesses, government departments, charities and other organisational purchasers actually represent the bulk of marketing activities, yet much of the attention in marketing is focused on business-to-consumer markets rather than on business-to-business markets. The reasons for this are obscure, but may have much to do with the fact that we are all consumers and can therefore relate more easily to consumer marketing issues.

This chapter looks at the ways organisational buyers make decisions, and also at some of the influences buyers are subject to.

Preview case study: BHP Billiton

BHP Billiton is the world's largest mining company, and also the world's third-largest company as measured by market capitalisation. The company is based in Australia and the UK, and is quoted on stock markets in both countries.

Broken Hill Proprietary was incorporated in 1865, to exploit the colossal mineral wealth around Broken Hill, an area of outback in New South Wales. Broken Hill is a mining town to beat all mining towns – even the streets are named after minerals (Argent Street, Sulphide Street, Chloride Street), and the slag heap towers 100 feet high to the east of the town. The town (like many outback towns) is one of contrasts, however: many artists live there, due to the quality of the outback light, and it has a major Flying Doctor base.

BHP grew dramatically during the 20th century, as industrial countries absorbed huge amounts of Australia's mineral wealth: the company went into steel production in 1915, at Newcastle, New South Wales, and began exploring the Bass Strait for oil in the 1960s. Overseas expansion followed, with the Ok Tedi copper mine in Papua New Guinea: the company was successfully sued by local inhabitants due to the environmental damage caused by the mining operations. BHP was luckier with the Escondida copper mine in Chile and the Ekati diamond mine in Canada.

Billiton was a Dutch company formed in 1860 to exploit mineral wealth in Indonesia, which was at the time a Dutch colony. As time went by, the company established a smelting operation in the Netherlands, and extended its mining operations worldwide: the company ran aluminium smelters in South Africa and Mozambique, coal mines in Australia, and base metals mines in South America. In 2001, the company merged with BHP to form BHP Billiton.

During the early part of the 21st century the merged company developed a strong market in China. Following on from the relaxation of communist ideology in China and the encouragement of free enterprise and foreign trade, Chinese industry has burgeoned. Low costs, plus management expertise brought in from capitalist enclaves Hong Kong and Macau, have resulted in an exponential surge in Chinese-made goods, with a consequent demand for raw materials. BHP Billiton was therefore ideally placed to supply this demand, since the company can provide almost any kind of mineral from its various mines, and indeed almost any type of refined metal from its smelters around the world. BHP Billiton began talks to take over rival Rio Tinto, but the deal was abandoned in 2008, partly as a result of the world financial crisis.

The decision-making unit

Decision-making unit (DMU) A group of people who, between them, decide on purchases.

There are very few cases where an industrial purchasing decision is made by only one person. Even in a small business it is likely that several people would expect to have some influence or input into the purchase decision. Because of this, the decision-making process often becomes formalised, with specific areas of interest being expressed by members of the **decision-making unit (DMU)**, and roles and responsibilities being shared. This group is also called the buying centre, and it cannot be identified on any company organisation chart: it varies in make-up from one buying situation to another. Individuals may participate for a brief time only or be part of the group from conception to conclusion.

The DMU is thought to contain the following categories of member (Webster and Wind, 1972):

- **Initiators**. These are the individuals who first recognise the problem.
- **Gatekeepers**. These individuals control the flow of knowledge, either by being proactive in collecting information, or by filtering it. They could be junior staff who are told to visit a trade fair and collect brochures, or a personal assistant who sees his or her role as being to prevent salespeople from 'wasting' the decision-maker's time.
- **Buyers**. The individuals given the task of sourcing suppliers and negotiating the final deal. Often these are purchasing agents who complete the administrative tasks necessary for buying. These people often work to a specific brief, and may have very little autonomy, even though they may be the only contact a supplier's salespeople have at the purchasing organisation.
- **Deciders**. These are the people who make the final decisions, and may be senior managers or specialists. They may never meet any representatives of the supplying companies. Deciders generally rely heavily on advice from other members of the DMU.
- **Users**. These are the people who will be using the products that are supplied: they may be engineers or technicians, or even the cleaning staff who use cleaning products. Their opinions may well be sought by the deciders, and in many cases the users are also the initiators.
- **Influencers**. These people 'have the ear of' the deciders. They are trusted advisers, but from the supplying company's viewpoint they are extremely difficult to identify. Influencers may be employed by the purchasing firm (for example, engineers, information systems managers or research managers) or they may be consultants (for example, architects, acoustics and safety consultants). An **influencer** might even be the decider's golf partner, old college friend, or teenage son.

These categories are not, of course, mutually exclusive. A User might also be an Influencer, or a Gatekeeper might also be an Initiator. The categories were originally developed to explain purchasing within families – which may be an example of the apparent similarities between business-to-business marketing and consumer marketing.

In fact, the members of the DMU are affected both by rational and emotional motivations. Salespeople are well aware that buyers are affected by their liking or dislike for the suppliers' representatives, and buyers will often be working to their own agendas: for example, a buyer might be seeking a promotion, or might feel threatened in terms of job security, or may be conducting a vendetta with a colleague. Any of these influences might affect a buyer's behaviour, but all of them would be difficult or impossible for a supplier's salesperson to identify correctly and act upon.

The relationship between buyers and salespeople is often complex, and perceptions shift according to the stage of the buying process (Claycomb and Frankwick 2010). In the awareness phase, joint problem-solving between buyers and salespeople actually increases buyer uncertainty, but as the relationship develops through the exploratory and expansion phases buyers will invest more in the relationship and uncertainty decreases. In any event, the degree to which salespeople are customer-orientated strongly affects supplier success in the market (Singh and Koshy 2011).

Initiator The person who first recognises a problem.

Gatekeeper The person who controls the flow of information.

Buyer The person who negotiates the purchase.

Decider The person who has the power to agree a purchase.

User The person who uses the product.

Influencers Staff who can affect the way customers are treated even though they have no direct access to them.

Influencer The person who has the ability to sway the judgement of a decider.

Figure 4.1   Relationships in the DMU

In general, members of a decision-making unit tend to be more risk-averse than do consumers. This is because the DMU members have more to lose in the event of a wrong decision: for a consumer, the main risk is financial, and even that is limited since most retailers will replace or refund goods purchased in error. For the industrial purchaser, however, a serious purchasing mistake can result in major negative consequences for the business as well as loss of face at work, in shattered promotion dreams, or even in dismissal in serious cases. The professional persona of the industrial buyer is liable to be compromised by purchasing errors, which in turn means that the buyer will feel a loss of self-esteem.

Real-life marketing: Getting decision-makers together

Because there are usually several decision-makers involved in any major buying decision, salespeople often have to talk to a lot of different people if they are to make a sale. Often the decision-makers have conflicting agendas – so there may be a problem in getting them together to thrash out their differences and come to an agreement.

One example comes from the introduction of long-life lightbulbs. When they first came out they were much more expensive than the traditional bulbs they replaced, which caused a problem for companies selling them to business customers. Maintenance managers liked the bulbs because they would save on the cost of replacing them (which can be expensive in, say, a warehouse where the lights are 30 feet above floor level) but they were only given a small budget for buying bulbs. Finance directors could increase the budget, but simply referred salespeople to the maintenance managers, since it was a maintenance issue. Obviously the two managers had to get together to talk – but how to do it?

Osram, a major bulb manufacturer, had the solution. They mailed out small cashboxes to the finance directors, with a note to say that the box contained something that would save the firm thousands a year, but the key was with the maintenance managers. The maintenance managers were sent the keys, with a note to say that the box was with the finance director. Clearly one or other manager would contact the other simply out of curiosity – and inside the box was a calculation showing how the bulbs would save the company a small fortune.

To make this work in practice, you need to do the following:

- Identify which decision-makers you need to get together, and personalise the approach.
- Do your homework – tell them how it will benefit THEIR company (not some general 'example' company), and if possible explain how it will benefit them as individuals.
- Make certain that they can only access the information by getting together. The cashbox idea is one: a simple jigsaw might be another, or a memory stick with a password on it might also work.
- Make the whole thing intriguing and fun – using a tangible item is good, especially if it is relevant to the person's role in the firm.

Determining the relative power of each member of the DMU for each purchasing situation is a difficult task. Ronchetto et al. (1989) identify these characteristics of individuals who may be most influential in a DMU:

- important in the corporate and departmental hierarchy
- close to the organisational boundary
- central to the workflow
- active in cross-departmental communications
- directly linked to senior management

It should be obvious that purchasing managers are most important in repetitive purchases while the CEO will become heavily involved in unique, costly and risky buying decisions.

As a result of this increased risk, industrial buyers use a variety of risk-reducing tactics (Hawes and Barnhouse 1987). These are as follows, and are presented in order of importance:

1. Visit the operations of the potential vendor to observe its viability.
2. Question present customers of the vendor concerning their experience with the vendor's performance.
3. Multisource the order to ensure a backup source of supply.
4. Obtain contract penalty clause provisions from the potential vendor.
5. Obtain the opinion of colleagues concerning the potential vendor.
6. In choosing a vendor, favour firms that your company has done business with in the past.
7. Confirm that members of your upper management are in favour of using the vendor as a supplier.
8. Limit the search for, and ultimate choice of, a potential vendor only to well-known vendors.
9. Obtain the opinion of a majority of your co-workers that the chosen vendor is satisfactory.

Buyers are affected by individual, personal factors as well as environmental and organisational factors. Personally they exhibit many of the same influences on the buying decision that consumers have: the desire to play a role, for example, may cause a buyer to be difficult to negotiate with as he or she tries to drive a hard bargain. The desire for respect and liking may cause a buyer to want to give the order to a salesperson

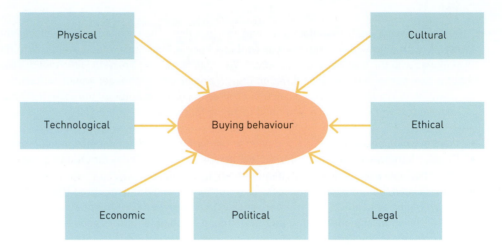

Figure 4.2   Environmental influences on buyer behaviour

who is exceptionally pleasant or helpful, and to deny the order to a salesperson who is regarded as being unpleasant or pushy. Business buyers are likely to be affected by some or all of the following environmental influences (Loudon and Della Bitta 1993):

1. Physical influences. The location of the purchasing firm relative to its suppliers may be decisive, since many firms prefer to source supplies locally. This is especially true in the global marketplace, where a purchasing company may wish to support local suppliers, or may prefer to deal with people from the same cultural background. In many cases, buyers seem almost afraid to source from outside their own national boundaries, even when rational considerations of cost and quality would make the foreign supplier the better bet.
2. Technological influences. The level of technological development available among local suppliers will affect what the buyer can obtain. The technology of the buyer and the seller must also be compatible: in global markets this often presents a problem, since international technical standards remain very different for most products. Despite efforts within the European Union to harmonise technical standards, Europe still does not have standardised electrical fittings, plumbing fittings or even computer keyboards. Many European firms find it easier to trade with former colonies thousands of miles away than deal with countries within the EU, simply because the technical standards of the former colonies are identical with their own.
3. Economic influences. The macroeconomic environment is concerned with the level of demand in the economy, and with the current taxation regime within the buyer's country. These conditions affect buyers' ability to buy goods as well as their need to buy in raw materials: if demand for their products is low, the demand for raw materials to manufacture them will also be low. On a more subtle level, the macroeconomic climate affects the buyer's confidence in the same way as it affects consumer confidence. For example, a widespread belief that the national economy is about to go into a recession will almost certainly make buyers reluctant to commit to major investments in stock, equipment and machinery. In a global context, the fact that countries enter and leave recessions at different times will affect the timing of marketing efforts on the part of vendors. At the microeconomic level, a firm experiencing a boom in business will have greater ability to pay for goods and a greater level of confidence.
4. Political influences. Governments frequently pass laws affecting the way businesses operate, and this is nowhere more true than in international trade. Trade

sanctions, trade barriers, specifically non-tariff barriers, preferred-nation status and so forth all affect the ways in which buyers are permitted or encouraged to buy. In some cases, governments specifically help certain domestic businesses as part of an economic growth package. The political stability of countries is also a factor that vendors need to take account of.

5. Legal influences. Laws often lay down specific technical standards, which affect buyer decisions. Buyers may be compelled to incorporate safety features into products, or may be subject to legal restrictions in terms of raw materials. Often, vendors can obtain a competitive advantage by anticipating changes in the law.

6. Ethical influences. In general, buyers are expected to act at all times for the benefit of the organisation, not for personal gain. This means that, in most cultures, the buyers are expected not to accept bribes, for example. However, in some cultures bribery is the normal way of doing business, which leaves the vendor with a major ethical problem – refusing to give a bribe is likely to lose the business, but giving a bribe is probably unethical or illegal in the company's home country, especially now that the OECD Anti-Bribery Convention has been widely adopted. As a general rule, buyers are likely to be highly suspicious of doing business with a salesperson whom they perceive as acting unethically – after all, if the salesperson is prepared to cheat on his or her employer, he or she cannot be trusted not to cheat on the buyer.

7. Cultural influences. Culture establishes the values, attitudes, customary behaviour, language, religion, and art of a given group of people. When dealing internationally, cultural influences come to the forefront: in the UK it might be customary to offer a visitor a cup of tea or coffee, whereas in China it might be customary to offer food. Dim Sum originated as a way for Chinese businessmen to offer their visitors a symbolic meal, as a way of establishing rapport. Beyond the national culture is the corporate culture, sometimes defined as 'the way we do things round here'. Corporate culture encompasses the strategic vision of the organisation, its ethical stance, and its attitudes towards suppliers among other things. In addition, many businesspeople act in accordance with their professional culture as well (Terpstra and David, 1991). Each of these will affect the way business is done.

Organisational factors derive from the corporate culture, as well as from the strategic decisions made by senior management within the firm. Organisational policies, procedures, structure, systems of rewards, authority, status, and communication systems will all affect the ways buyers relate to salespeople. Figure 4.3 shows the main categories of organisational influences on the buyers' behaviour.

Think outside this box!

The expansion of the European Union in 2004 was hailed (rightly) as an historic event, reuniting Europe peacefully for the first time in its long and bloody history. For business, the expansion was expected to bring great rewards in terms of bigger markets and a greater choice of suppliers.

Yet many firms still preferred to deal with countries thousands of miles away, where the technical standards were the same. So why not create closer links with these countries? Why did Britain, for example, join the EU and reject its former empire just at the time when transportation costs had fallen dramatically? Surely the wider range of climate, availability of raw materials, and greater diversity of the Commonwealth made it a better bet?

Or perhaps the Commonwealth countries (for the most part) are so poor that they have no choice but to sell to us anyway – and we need to ally ourselves with the rich rather than with the poor!

Figure 4.3   Organisational influences on buyer behaviour

Buying tasks differ greatly between firms, but may also differ significantly within firms. For example, the buying task for a supermarket clearly differs from that for a manufacturing company, since the supermarket intends to sell on the vast majority of its purchases unchanged whereas the manufacturer is largely concerned with sourcing components and raw materials. Within this generalised structure the supermarket has other variations in the buying task: the buyers' approach to buying canned goods will be totally different from the approach used to buy fresh produce such as vegetables or fresh fish. Equally, the manufacturer will have a different approach when buying basic raw materials versus buying components, and a different approach again when buying lubricating oil or business services or new factory premises. The purchasing tasks will affect the buyer's thinking and negotiating approach, usually so seriously that firms will have separate buyers for each type of buying task.

Structure of the organisation falls into two categories: the formal structure is what shows on the organisation chart, and the informal structure is what actually dictates staff behaviour in most cases. The informal structure is the network of social obligations, friendships and internal liaisons that influence day-to-day behaviour. The formal organisation structure determines such issues as the degree of centralisation in purchasing decision-making, the degree to which buying decisions follow a formal procedure (i.e. how constrained by the rules the buyers are), and the degree of specialisation in buying for different purposes or different departments in the organisation.

The informal structure dictates such issues as rivalry between buyers, 'brownie points' (recognition by management for jobs done well), co-operation between buyers in maintaining each other's status in the eyes of the boss, and so forth. The maze of informal relationships can be extremely complex, especially for a salesperson observing it from the outside, but often forms a key element in the success or failure of key-account selling. Key-account salespeople therefore spend considerable effort in finding out about internal alliances and rivalries in client firms – they have to use these effectively if they are going to persuade a disparate group of people to agree on buying a product. There is more on personal selling and key-account management in Chapter 17.

In the global context, the informal structure is subject to many cultural influences – the Oriental concern with gaining or losing face, for example, can be a crucial factor in doing business. The informal structure is also important in determining who will be the influencers in the DMU; some colleagues' opinions may be regarded as more trustworthy than others, for example.

The technology within the organisation may act to control or circumvent much of the buyers' role. For example, computer-controlled stock purchasing, particularly in a just-in-time purchasing environment, will prevent buyers from being able to negotiate deals and in many cases removes the buyer from the process altogether. Models for inventory control and price forecasting are also widely used by buyers, so that in many cases the negotiating process is virtually automated with little room for manoeuvre on the part of the buyer. In these circumstances the selling organisation needs to go beyond the buyer to the other members of the DMU in order to work around the rules. More technology-minded companies are likely to use electronic communications systems (e-mail being only one example) more: technology-mediated communications have a positive, direct effect on future intentions to buy, but of course this is mediated by factors of trust and commitment (McDonald and Smith 2004). E-commerce in business-to-business marketing relies on the following factors (Claycomb et al. 2005):

1. Compatibility with existing systems.
2. Co-operative norms with customers.
3. Lateral integration within the firm.
4. Technocratic specialisation.
5. Decentralisation of information technology.

The characteristics of the people involved in the organisation will, in part, determine the organisational culture, but will in any event control the interpretation of the rules under which the purchasing department operates. At senior management level, the character of the organisation is likely to be a function of the senior management, and in many cases the organisation's founder will have stamped his or her personality firmly on the organisation's culture. Virgin is clearly an offshoot of Richard Branson's personality, as The Body Shop is an offshoot of Anita Roddick's.

Think outside this box!

We frequently hear about the global village, and about the convergence of cultures, and about a new world order in which we accept and understand each other's cultures. So why is it necessary to consider cultural issues when we are marketing products and services? Surely the goods speak for themselves – does crude oil have a cultural value, or does a stamp mill have a cultural connotation?

Shouldn't buyers be prepared to accept and understand cultural differences? Otherwise how are we to do business? Or perhaps the buyers arrogantly believe that the sellers should adapt their approach to meet the buyers' culture – thus possibly missing out on getting the best deals for their organisations.

If we get clashes between corporate cultures within the same country, how much worse will the clashes be in globalised markets?

Classifying business customers

A business customer is one who is buying on behalf of an organisation rather than buying for personal or family consumption. For the purposes of discussion, we usually talk about organisations as the purchasers of goods, but of course this is not the case: business customers, in practice, are human beings who buy on behalf of organisations.

Organisations might be classified according to the types of buying and end use they have for the products. Table 4.1 shows the commonly accepted classifications.

Table 4.1   Classification of buying organisations

Type of organisation	Description
Business and commercial organisations	These organisations buy goods which are used to make other goods, and those that are consumed in the course of running the organisation's business. These organisations buy foundation goods and services used to make other products, facilitating goods and services, which help an organisation achieve its objectives, and entering goods and services, which become part of another product.
Reseller organisations	Resellers buy goods in order to sell them on to other organisations or to final consumers. Typically, resellers will be wholesalers or retailers, but they may also be agents for services, for example travel agents or webmasters who act as facilitators for other firms.
Governmental organisations	Governments buy everything from paperclips to aircraft carriers through their various departments. Because national and local government departments operate under specific rules, a different approach from that for businesses is usually required.
Institutional organisations	Institutional organisations include charities, educational establishments, hospitals and other organisations that do not fit into the business, reseller or government categories. These organisations may buy any of the products but they are used to achieve institutional goals, usually to provide services.

Reseller organisation A firm that buys goods in order to sell them on to other firms or consumers.

OEM Original-equipment manufacturer.

Aftermarket See MRO.
MRO Maintenance, repair and overhauling company.

BUSINESS AND COMMERCIAL ORGANISATIONS

Business and commercial organisations can be segmented as **OEM**s (original-equipment manufacturers), users and **aftermarket** (**MRO**) customers. OEMs buy foundation, entering and facilitating goods including machinery and equipment used to make products and which are incorporated directly into the final product. For example, computer manufacturers may buy machine tools to make computer cases and also buy silicon chips from specialist producers: the chips are incorporated into the final product, but the same type of chip might be incorporated in computers from several different OEMs. The Intel Pentium chip is an example.

For OEM buyers, the key issue will be the quality of the products or services. Such buyers are usually operating to fairly exact specifications laid down by their own production engineers and designers: it is unlikely that the supplying firm will be able to do very much to have the specification changed. This means that introducing a new product to an OEM will be a lengthy process, since the supplying company will need to establish a long-term relationship with the customer in order to become involved at the design stage for the new products.

User customers buy products that are used up within the organisation, either as components in their own equipment or to make the equipment perform properly, for example lubricating oils or cleaning products. These products are not re-sold, but may be bought in considerable quantities. Obviously some of these are service products – accountancy or legal services, cleaning services, maintenance or building services are all contained within the firm and not resold.

Aftermarket customers are those involved in the maintaining, repairing and overhauling (MRO) of products after they have been sold. For example, in the elevator business, independent contractors not affiliated with the original manufacturer

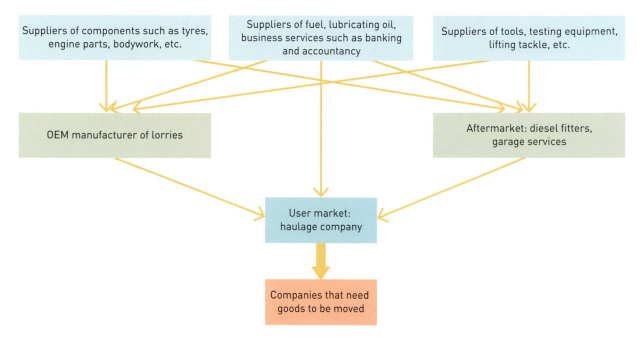

Figure 4.4   Types of purchase

perform most MRO. These contractors buy the components, supplies and services they need wherever they can find them.

The classification split between OEM, users and aftermarket customers is only relevant to the supplier. OEMs can also be user customers for some suppliers. For example, a plastic moulding company may sell components to an OEM and plastic tools to a user as well as plastic replacement parts to an aftermarket organisation: in some cases these may even be the same organisation. Buying motivations for each type of purchase are clearly very different.

In Figure 4.4, the same suppliers sometimes provide goods or services for several firms in the supply chain. In some cases there will be considerable crossover between firms.

RESELLER ORGANISATIONS

The majority of manufactured goods are sold through reseller organisations such as retailers and wholesalers. Intermediaries provide useful services such as bulk breaking, assortment of goods, and accumulation of associated product types: due to increased efficiencies resulting from these services, intermediaries tend to reduce overall prices for the final consumer. Cutting out the middleman usually reduces efficiency and tends to increase prices as a result; although there is a popular view that disintermediation reduces prices by cutting out the intermediaries' mark-ups.

Reseller organisations are driven almost entirely by their customers. This means that they will buy only those products they perceive to have a ready market: there is therefore a premium on employing buyers who have a clear understanding of marketing. Unlike the OEM buyers, there is little need for resellers to understand the technical aspects of the products they buy – they merely need to feel confident that the ultimate consumers will want the products.

Reseller organisations carry out the following basic functions:

1. Negotiation with suppliers.
2. Promotional activities such as advertising, sales promotion, providing a salesforce, etc.
3. Warehousing, storage and product handling.
4. Transportation of local and (occasionally) long-distance shipments.
5. Inventory control.
6. Credit checking and credit control.
7. Pricing and collection of price information, particularly about competitors.
8. Collection of market information about consumers and competitors.

For manufacturers, this places a premium on establishing close, long-term relationships with resellers. Shared information, as part of an integrated channel management strategy, becomes crucial to forward planning.

There is more on retailers and wholesalers in Chapter 20.

GOVERNMENT ORGANISATIONS

Government and quasi-government organisations are major buyers of almost everything. In some markets, the government is heavily involved in industry, and may hold monopolies on some products. For instance, all insurance in India is a government monopoly and the oil industry in Mexico is controlled by PEMEX, a quasi-government entity; tobacco is a government monopoly in Spain. Governments are thought to be the largest category of market in the world, if all levels of government are included in the equation. The structure of government varies from one country to another: for example, in Spain there is the national government based in Madrid, the regional governments (e.g. the Junta de Andalucía), the provincial governments (e.g. Provincia de Granada) and the local town halls (e.g. Ayuntamiento de Ugijar). Sometimes these local town halls group together to form an alliance, which carries out mutually beneficial activities such as tourism marketing or funding a local swimming pool, but frequently they will act independent of one another within the frameworks of their own jurisdictions.

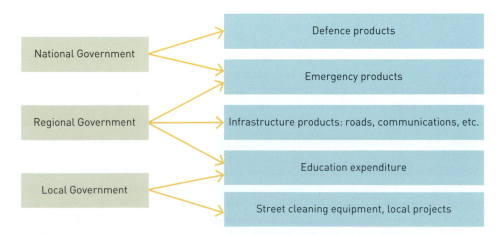

Figure 4.5   Tiers of government and their typical purchases

Because of the strict rules under which most government organisations operate, special measures are often needed to negotiate deals. In particular, government organisations are characterised by the tendering system, in which firms are asked to bid for contracts which are then usually offered to the lowest bidder. From a supplier's viewpoint, this can be seriously counterproductive since the lowest price is likely to be also the least profitable price, so selling firms will often try to circumvent the process by ensuring that they become involved before the tender is finalised. In this way it is often possible to ensure that the tender is drawn up in a way that favours the proactive firm over its competitors, thus ensuring that competitors either do not bid at all, or bid at too high a price.

Marketing in a changing world: Contracting out

Many government departments now contract out parts of their function to private firms. The process is even further advanced in local authorities, which now contract out areas such as road maintenance, cleaning and back office business processes.

The most extreme example so far was a move by Suffolk County Council to contract out everything – from rubbish collection to social services – thus saving the council several million pounds a year. The move was overturned after protests by local residents, but the council is still contracting out a great many services, often to charities.

In the longer run, this is a trend that is likely to continue. Council workers have had strong unions which have negotiated generous pay and pension packages, which councils might well prefer to circumvent by getting rid of the staff. For marketers wishing to sell to government, though, the situation has become complicated because they now have to deal with a larger number of providers. On the other hand, they will probably not come up against the usual local authority bureaucracy, which is of course one of the reasons contracting out saves money.

In some cases governments need to purchase items that are not available to the general public or to other businesses. Military hardware is an obvious example: clearly ordinary businesses are not allowed to buy tanks or fighter planes. On a more subtle level, goods such as handguns are not permitted for private organisations in the UK, but can be sold to the army or the police force. Some types of computer software are only appropriate for use by the tax authorities, and academic research is, in general, paid for entirely by the government in the UK. From a marketing viewpoint, these specialist markets present an interesting challenge, since in some cases the products need to be tailored to a specific government or a specific government department. This may mean that there is considerable scope for negotiation, but since the contract might still have to go out to tender, the company may find that it has merely wasted time unless it can demonstrate that no other company can carry out the work.

Real-life marketing: Influencing the influencers

In many institutional markets the people who make the decisions about what to buy aren't the same people who make the actual purchase. Health professionals, for example, don't buy drugs, but they do determine which patients get which drugs. Pharmaceutical companies therefore employ 'missionary' salespeople to call on doctors and others to encourage them to prescribe specific medicines.

This happens in other markets – architects don't buy building materials, government buildings inspectors don't do construction work, and TV chefs don't sell particular cuts of meat. What you need to do is identify who in the government department lays down the rules and specifications which others must adhere to – that's the person you have to influence. In practice, this requires you to:

- Identify the influencers in your market. You can sometimes do this by asking your contact in the department if there is anyone he or she would normally have to consult.
- Influence your influencers by personal approach if at all possible – this is what key-account salespeople do.
- Be subtle – influencers are good persuaders themselves and they can spot others a mile off!

In some circumstances, governments may issue a 'cost-plus' contract, in which the organisation is given a specific task to carry out and bills according to the cost of the contract plus an agreed profit margin. In the early days of space research this type of contract was common, since it was impossible to predict what the costs might be when dealing with an unknown set of circumstances. More recently these contracts have fallen into disrepute since they reward inefficiency and waste.

INSTITUTIONAL ORGANISATIONS

Institutions include charities, universities, hospital trusts, and non-profit organisations of all types, schools, and so forth. In some cases these are government-owned but independent for purposes of purchasing and supply (for example secondary schools), in other cases they are totally independent (for example registered charities). The traditional view of these organisations is that they are chronically under funded and therefore do not represent a particularly munificent market, but in practice the organisations actually have a very substantial aggregate spending power.

Because budgets are almost always very tight, the marketing organisation may need to be creative in helping the institution to raise the money to buy. For example, a firm that produces drilling equipment may find it has a substantial market at Oxfam, since Oxfam drills wells in many arid regions of the developing world. Oxfam relies on public generosity to raise the money to buy the equipment, so the manufacturer may find it necessary to part-fund or even manage a fundraising campaign in order to make the sale.

Suppliers are often asked to contribute to charities, in cash or in products. This may not always be possible, since the supplier's only market might be the charities, but in some cases firms may find it worthwhile to supply free products to charities in order to gain PR value, or sometimes in order to open the door to lucrative deals with other organisations. For example, a charity working in a developing country might be prepared to field-test equipment which could then be sold to a government department in the same country.

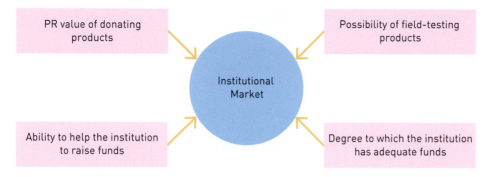

Figure 4.6   Factors in institutional marketing

Think outside this box!

We are often told that marketing is about managing the exchange process, yet government departments and many institutions seem to lay down the ground rules from the start. Marketers have to play by the buyer's rules to be in the game at all – so how can they possibly be managing the process? Pushed from one set of constraints to the next, it would seem that the average marketer is just a pawn in the buyers' hands!

Yet maybe that is how it should be, if customers are at the centre of everything we do. Not to mention that the management process itself could be construed as a clearing-house for pressures rather than as a directive force – in a sense, no manager is actually in control, so why should marketers be any different?

The value chain

The first element in building customer relationships is the value the customer receives from the end product. In the past, marketers have tended to consider the product as being that which comes from a manufacturer, is passed through wholesalers and retailers, and eventually lands with the end consumer. This view has been superseded to an extent by a holistic view, which examines the whole chain of events from raw material extraction through to the store shelf. This chain is called the **value chain**, because it is the means by which value is delivered to the end consumer in exchange for money.

Value chain analysis examines the ways in which organisations add value to the products as they pass along the chain. This involves analysis of the organisations themselves, and also the interactions between suppliers and distributors within the chain. Value chain analysis recognises that each organisation within the chain adds value to the product: this is an obvious proposition, since they would not be able to become part of the chain unless the other members thought that they had something to offer, yet people often talk of 'cutting out the middleman' as if these organisations were not adding value. Each increment of value added to the product needs to be greater than the cost of adding it, otherwise that particular member of the chain is not operating efficiently and will either be cut out of the chain or will be unable to show a profit and will disappear. Much of the efficiency gained by effective firms lies in their ability to manage the linkages between themselves and other organisations in an effective manner.

Value chain The firms involved in the process of turning raw materials into products.

Value chain analysis Assessment of ways in which organisations add value to the products they handle.

The implications of this are as follows:

1. Value creation requires co-operation from all the members of the chain. Whether this comes about through a negotiated co-ordination of activities or market forces does not matter greatly: the organisations rely on each other either way.
2. Those in the chain must consider the needs of other chain members if the process is to work to mutual advantage.
3. Cost improvement and efficiency improvements will benefit everyone in the chain in the long run, but most especially will benefit the individual member because there is no need to renegotiate with other members in order to reap the benefits.
4. There is therefore a premium on managing the value chain within the firm itself.
5. There is a fundamental reliance on the contribution of people.

This management of the interfaces between organisations is also a manifestation of relationship marketing. Developing good working relationships with suppliers and customers means changing the organisation's working patterns to adapt to the needs of the other organisations, and also considering their profitability as well as the company's own profitability.

Within the value chain, there exist the categories of activity shown in Table 4.2 (Porter 1985). All of these activities must be carried out by some (or even all) of the members of the chain. Very few companies undertake all the activities in the value chain, from raw material extraction through to final retailing of the product: a

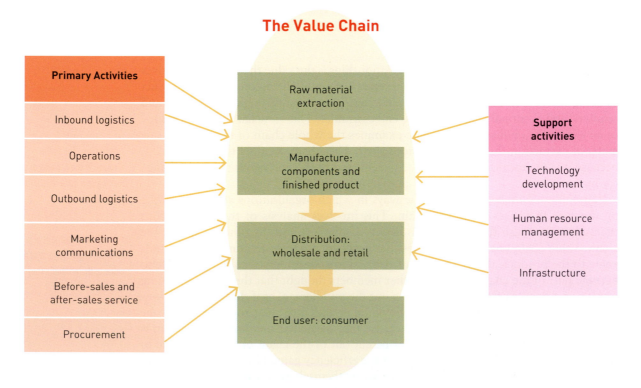

Figure 4.7   The value chain

Table 4.2 Primary and support activities in the value chain

	Activity	Explanation and examples
Primary activities	Inbound logistics	Activities concerned with receiving, storing and distributing raw materials and components.
	Operations	Transforming inputs into outputs. Raw materials into components, or components into finished products.
	Outbound logistics	Collection, storage and delivery to customers. This might be undertaken by a delivery or warehousing firm.
	Marketing communications	Functional aspects of marketing. Making customers aware of the product, and fine-tuning the offering.
	Before-sales and after-sales service	Activities that maintain or enhance product value. For example, repair services are often contracted out.
	Procurement	Processes involved in obtaining the necessary resources for the primary activities. Raw material and equipment purchase, acquisition of office space, etc.
Support activities	Technology development	Technological advances in product or process, or even in resource improvement, may be subcontracted.
	Human resource management	The activities involved in developing an effective workforce. Hiring, training, motivating and rewarding.
	Infrastructure	Planning, financing, quality control, information management, communication and so forth.

notable exception is the major oil companies, which explore for oil, drill for it, refine it, package it and retail its products. Even these companies will subcontract some of their activities – for example, oil well fires are typically handled by outside specialist companies. In most cases, activities within the most efficient value chains are handled by specialist firms – for example, the food industry often works through a large number of intermediaries, each supplying specialist skills, which means that the value chain operates very efficiently. Hence a can of tuna, which has been handled by perhaps eight members of a value chain, can retail for one euro, or less than a pound.

Many of the activities might be contracted out to other members of the supply chain: for example, technological advances often come as a result of research grants to universities. Identifying the **core competences** needed for each member of the value chain (and for the chain as a whole) is a process that will vary from one industry to another, so that (for example) an accountancy firm that has a core competence in dealing with performing artists such as musicians and actors will not have the same level of expertise when dealing with small manufacturing businesses.

The value chain is supported by four core activities:

1. **Procurement.** Acquiring the inputs used in the value chain is a key function: inputs must be of the right quality, the right quantity, and at the right price but they must also be delivered at the right time. Procurement is concerned with anything used in the course of providing marketing inputs, servicing inputs, or materials used for outbound logistics.

Core competences The central, most important aspects of the company's abilities.

Procurement Obtaining goods to be used in production or running the organisation.

2. Human resource management. This is the function of recruiting, training and rewarding staff members in the organisation.
3. Technology development. This includes know-how, research and development, product design, and process improvement work.
4. **Infrastructure**. This includes working spaces (factories, offices mines, etc.), the organisational structure of the firm, the financial and operational control systems, and the feedback systems used by management.

Infrastructure The physical resources available to the firm for logistical processes.

Each of the activities in the chain might lead to a competitive advantage. In some firms it is only the marketing that really distinguishes the product: in other value chains, the reliability of **outbound logistics** might be the deciding factor (especially if the customer operates a just-in-time purchasing system). However, one of the problems of value chain analysis, from a marketer's viewpoint, is that marketing becomes relegated to a function within the system, rather than the over-riding philosophy of the organisation. For a marketer, marketing should be the guiding philosophy in everything the firm does, from purchasing through to human resources and on into outbound logistics.

Outbound logistics Controlling the flow of the product from the organisation to its customers.

In some cases the value chain becomes a **value network**. Rather than a linear process in which raw materials progress through to consumers' homes in a straight line, with value being added at each stage, firms might contribute collectively to one stage, be suppliers to one stage of the process and customers of another, and products might move back and forth between network members. This is illustrated in Figure 4.8. In this example, a chemicals manufacturer supplies raw materials to a cleaning products manufacturer, and also to a plastics moulding company. The plastics company supplies to a wholesaler, and to an electrical goods manufacturer. The cleaning products company supplies industrial cleaning products to the manufacturers in the network, and consumer products via the wholesaler, who also handles some of the products from the electrical goods manufacturer. The electrical goods manufacturer supplies products to the other companies and also supplies consumer products through the wholesaler and direct to the retailer.

Value network The group of organisations that collectively add value to raw materials.

Furthermore, each separate company in the chain has relationships with many other companies, in other words each firm is involved in several value chains at once. Adapting the firm's practices to each value chain becomes difficult or impossible – especially if members of one supply chain feel that they are being unfairly dealt with compared with members of another value chain. Obviously in such circumstances the management of the process relies heavily on developing close relationships within the network, on communicating effectively and openly between members, and on developing a high degree of trust between the members of the chain.

For firms in global markets, many relationships in many different countries need to be considered. The value network may be different for each major customer – for example, Taylor Woodrow may form alliances with many companies in order to carry out a major construction project: intelligent managers know when to co-operate with competitors and when to compete. Marketing alliances of all kinds have been developed to serve customers. These may focus on a product or service, promotion, logistics, or joint pricing (Kotler 2003).

As the relationship deepens, the emphasis shifts from single transactions through to co-operation, and the nature of the problems being addressed by the partners also shifts (Wilson 1993). At the beginning of the relationship, the parties tend to be concerned with product-based problems: design, specifications, performance and so forth. As the relationship deepens and the product problems are resolved, the parties tend to concentrate more on process issues – delivery times, relation to the value-creation processes of the customer. When the relationship is fully developed the parties become more concerned about facilitation, in other words the way in which

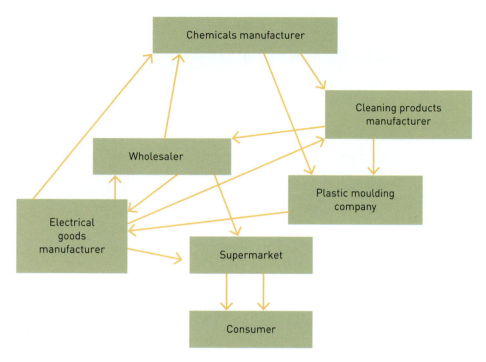

Figure 4.8   Value network

business is carried out between them. At this point, the companies might be so close as to be almost indistinguishable to an outside observer. This has been described as the PPF model (Product, Process, Facilitation).

In 1995 Millman and Wilson developed the KAM (key-account management) stages of development model, which identified six stages of development in dyadic relationships. This model was later combined with the PPF model to shown how the problem-solving aspects link to the stages of development (Wilson 1999). This combined model is shown in Table 4.3.

The process of developing these relationships is a slow one; it would normally take several years to work through the process from initial contact to synergy, but the rewards make it worth the effort. The more efficiently the value chain (or value network) operates, the more likely it is that the partners in the chain will reach their strategic objectives. Developing the relationship is a worthwhile exercise for smaller, weaker firms: research shows that such firms can thrive in relationships with larger firms if they can develop high levels of trust (Narayandas and Rangan 2004).

Inevitably relationships will occasionally end. There are six basic types of ending for relationships, as follows (Michalski 2004):

1. Forced. This is a situation where the relationship is dissolved by outside forces, for example government monopoly regulators.
2. Sudden. Here, one or other of the partners breaks off the relationship without warning.
3. Creeping. The partners gradually move their attention and business elsewhere.
4. Optional. An alternative set of relationships is offered.
5. Involuntary. One or other partner is compelled to withdraw.
6. Planned. The partners understand that there must be a separation, and they carry it out in the most equitable manner possible.

Table 4.3   KAM stages of development model

Stage of development	Objectives	Strategies
Pre-KAM: the relationship has not yet started: each partner is looking for the other.	Define and identify strategic account potential. Secure initial contact.	Identify key contacts and decision-making unit. Establish product need. Display willingness to address other areas of problem.
Early-KAM: The partners have made a start on doing business together.	Account penetration. Increase volume of business. Achieve preferred supplier status.	Build social network. Identify process-related problems and signal willingness to work together to provide cost-effective solutions.
Mid-KAM: The partnership is established and working well, the partners are looking for ways to make it even more effective.	Build partnership. Consolidate preferred-supplier status. Establish key account in-house.	Focus on process-related issues. Manage the implementation of process-related solutions. Build inter-organisational teams. Establish joint systems. Begin to perform non-core management tasks.
Partnership-KAM. The partners are operating in a highly-integrated way, dividing the work and the profits by mutual agreement.	Develop spirit of partnership. Build common culture. Lock in customer by being external resource base.	Integrate processes. Extend joint problem-solving. Focus on cost reduction and joint value-creating opportunities. Address key strategic issues of the client. Address facilitation issues.
Synergistic-KAM. At this point the companies are virtually indistinguishable. They operate almost entirely together.	Continuous improvement. Shared rewards. Quasi-integration.	Focus on joint value creation. Create semi-autonomous project teams. Develop strategic congruence.
Uncoupling-KAM. This can occur after any stage: the partners decide that the relationship is not working, and they go their separate ways.	Disengagement.	Withdrawal.

KAM. key-account management.

Following the world financial crisis, many suppliers downsized with the result that buyers defected elsewhere: the defections, in general, caused a greater financial loss than was saved by the downsize and thus downsizing is likely to be counter-productive (Williams et al. 2011).

Suppliers are often reluctant to end relationships even if the relationship is unprofitable: this may be because the companies have little understanding of how to manage relationships (Helm et al. 2006). If customers do end the relationship, it may be easier to win back the defectors rather than gain new customers from the 'never-bought' group because they already have some positive feelings about the brand as well as some negatives, but they will need to be handled very differently (Bogomolova and Romaniuk 2010).

Contracts provide the governing structure of relationships, especially in the early stages and the dissolution stages (Traynor and Traynor 2004) but it is the personal relationships between the individuals in the firms which decide the nature of the business relationship. For relationship marketers in business-to-business environments, products cease to be bundles of benefits as such, but become relational processes in which an overall value is created (Tuli et al. 2007).

Total quality management

The intention behind total quality management is to ensure that the firm and its associates do the right things at the right time at every stage of the value chain. The theory is that if every stage of the process is carried to the highest standards, or at least the appropriate standards, the outcome will be a product or service of the appropriate quality. The problem with this is that it does not take account of the customer's expectations, but instead relies on the firm's view of what constitutes a high-quality process. This means that the company will have difficulty in deciding at what level to pitch the quality assurance at each stage of the process.

The main contribution total quality management has is in the reduction of waste, and consequently a reduction in costs, because finished products will not need to be rejected due to component failures. The concept of zero-defect manufacture has led to dramatic cost savings in some industries, but apart from the cost savings has relatively little effect on marketing issues.

Buyers' techniques

Buyers use a wide variety of techniques according to the buying situation they are faced with. The buying situations are generally divided into three types:

1. **Straight rebuy**. This is a situation where the buyer is buying the same product in very much the same quantities from the same supplier. For example, an engineering company might buy the same quantity of components from its suppliers each month. In these circumstances the buyer needs no new information, and does not need to engage in much negotiation either. Prudent buyers may occasionally look at other possible sources of components in order to ensure that no new technology is available or that other suppliers are not able to supply the same components more cheaply, but in general the order placement is automatic. In many cases the buyer establishes an electronic data interchange (EDI) link with a supplier or establishes automatic buying procedures through the Internet and orders are handled without any human interface. If the product is of minor importance, or represents a low commitment in terms of finance or risk, the buyer will not undertake any information search and will probably simply order the goods. This is called causal purchasing, because it results automatically from a cause such as low stock levels. For example, a buyer for a large engineering firm probably spends very little time deciding on brands of paper for the photocopier. On the other hand, buying copper cable might be a routine purchase, but the buyer might monitor the market for alternatives occasionally. Such buying is called routine low-priority buying because it has a lower priority than would be the case if an entirely new situation were being faced. The company is unlikely to get into serious trouble if it pays 10% more than it should for cable, for example.

   Straight rebuy A repeat purchase with no modifications.

2. **Modified rebuy**. In this situation, the buyer re-evaluates the habitual buying patterns of the firm with a view to changing them in some way. The quantities ordered, or the specification of the components, may be changed. Even the supplier may be changed. Sometimes these changes will come about as a result

   Modified rebuy A repeat purchase where some changes have been made.

of environmental scanning, in which the buyer has become aware of a better alternative than the one currently employed, or sometimes the changes will come about because of marketing activities by the current suppliers' competitors. Internal forces (increases or decreases in the demand for components) might trigger a renegotiation with suppliers or a search for new suppliers. In any event, the buyer is faced with a limited problem-solving scenario in which he or she will need to carry out some negotiation with existing or new suppliers, and will probably need to seek out new information as well. In a modified rebuy situation a buyer may well require potential suppliers to bid against each other for the business: the drawback of this approach, however, is that it often results in damaging the relationship with existing suppliers that may have been built up over many years.

New task A purchase that has no precedent.

3. **New task**. This type of buying situation comes about when the task is perceived as being entirely new. Past experience is therefore no guide, and present suppliers may not be able to help either. Thus the buyer is faced with a complex decision process. Judgemental new task situations are those in which the buyer must deal with the technical complexities of a product, a complex evaluation of alternatives, and negotiating with new suppliers. Strategic new task situations are those in which the final decision is of strategic importance to the firm – for example, an insurance company in the market for new record-keeping software will be investing (potentially) hundreds of thousands of pounds in retraining staff, and in transferring existing records, not to mention the risks of buying software that is unable to cope with the tasks it is required to carry out. In these circumstances, long-range planning at director level drives the buying process, and the relationship with the suppliers is likely to be both long term and close.

From the viewpoint of the business marketer, the main chance of winning new customers will come in the new-task situation. The risks for buyers involved in switching suppliers are often too great unless there is a very real and clear advantage in doing so: such an advantage is likely to be difficult to prove in practice. In the new task situation, potential suppliers may well find themselves screened out early in the process, and will then find it almost impossible to be reconsidered later.

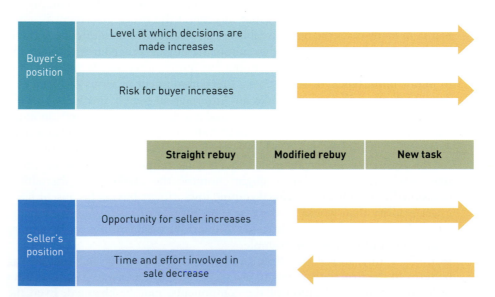

Figure 4.9   Trade-offs in type of buying situation

The buygrid framework

Organisational buying can be seen as a series of decisions, each of which leads to a further problem about which a decision must be made (Cardozo 1983). From the viewpoint of the business marketer, it is possible to diagnose problems by examining the sequence of decisions – provided, of course, the decision sequence is known to the marketer. Marketers can identify the stage at which the firm is currently making decisions, and can tailor the approach accordingly.

The industrial buying process can be mapped against a grid, as shown in Figure 4.10. The most complex buying situations occur in the upper left portion of the framework and involve the largest number of decision-makers and buying influences. This is because new tasks require the greatest amount of effort in seeking information and formulating appropriate solutions, but also will require the greatest involvement of individuals at all levels of the organisation, each of whom will have his or her own agenda.

The buygrid framework has been widely criticised, however. Like most models it tends to oversimplify the case. As in consumer decision-making, the sequence may not be as clear-cut as the model implies, and events may take place in a different order in certain circumstances. For example, a supplier might approach a firm with a solution for a problem it didn't know it had, thus cutting out several stages of the process: the firm may well recognise the need and the problem, but

Stage	Buying Situations		
	New Task	Modified Rebuy	Straight Rebuy
Anticipation or recognition of a problem (need) and a general solution			
Determination of characteristics and quantity of needed item			
Description of characteristics and quantity of needed item			
Search for and qualification of potential sources			
Acquisition and analysis of proposals			
Evaluation of proposals and selection of supplier(s)			
Selection of an order routine			
Performance feedback and evaluation			

Figure 4.10   The buygrid framework (from the Marketing Science Institute Series, *Industrial Buying and Creative Marketing*, by Patrick J. Robinson, Charles W. Faris and Yoram Wind. Copyright 1967 by Allyn and Bacon Inc., Boston)

will probably not need to acquire proposals and select a supplier since the supplier is already on board with a solution. Second, suppliers go to great lengths to differentiate themselves from competitors as effectively as they can, so that the buyer may not have any other potential suppliers of the exact product on offer. Third, the model assumes a rational approach to purchasing that is often simply not there. Finally, the boundaries between new task, modified rebuy and straight rebuy are by no means clear-cut.

Real-life marketing: Startling the buyer

Because buyers are no more rational than anyone else, it can pay you very well to do something that marks your company out as different from the others, especially in a situation where you're pitching competitively for a job. Advertising agencies are especially good at doing this – after all, if they can't promote themselves, how can they promote the client's business? But the principle applies to any company – in any business-to-business situation where you are up against direct competition, you can learn a lot from advertising agencies.

When Saatchi and Saatchi were pitching for the Toyota account, they had three Toyota cars suspended from its office building. Having three cars hanging off the side of a London office block not only made the newspapers – it also seriously impressed the Toyota executives when they arrived for their meeting. Needless to say, they won the account.

You can't always hang cars off your building, but you can use some imagination and daring to achieve a startling result. You should:

- Determine what will most interest your customers.
- Take the fight to the customer – put the promotion where they will see it, outside their premises if necessary.
- Do something unusual – you can't startle somebody unless you are very daring.

Because buyers are influenced by both rational and emotional considerations, the potential supplier needs to be aware of the buying motives of each member of the decision-making unit. What is more, each member of the DMU will apply different criteria for judging which suppliers should be included and which excluded (Kelly and Coaker 1976): the finance director might emphasise low prices, whereas the chief designer might be concerned with product quality, and the production engineer with reliable delivery. The buyer might be concerned with the relationship with the supplier's salespeople. In many cases, brand equity is less important than issues of price and delivery (Bendixen et al. 2004).

In the case of key-account management, this problem of dealing with different members of the DMU is often overcome by taking a team approach to the sale. While the **key-account manager** handles the initial contact and the management of the process, other specialists are brought in to deal with financial aspects, technical aspects, and so forth. In this way each member of the DMU is speaking to someone with whom he or she has a common language and a common understanding of the conceptual environment within which each specialty operates. In some cases the number of people working on the account can become large: when IBM were dealing with Lloyd's Bank (one of the Big Four UK banks) they had over 100 people working on the account, and set up a special branch office in the Canary Wharf area to be near Lloyd's head office.

Key-account manager Someone charged with the task of managing the relationship with a strategically important customer.

There are three types of business net (Moller and Svahn 2004):

1. Stable. These are networks which are perhaps still growing, but they are following a predictable course.
2. Established. These networks are fixed and relatively unchanging: the rules are known by the members.
3. Emerging. These networks are still growing and changing.

The internal culture of the firm (and the external culture, in an international context) affects the nature of each of these network types.

Managing the network means identifying the key network, developing a strategy for managing the individuals who operate within the network and developing methods at the operational level for managing those actors (Ojasalo 2004). The responsibility for managing the actors is often divided between the members of the selling team.

Value analysis

Value analysis is a method of evaluating components, raw materials and even manufacturing processes in order to determine ways of cutting costs or improving finished products. Value-in-use is defined as a product's economic value to the user relative to a specific alternative in a particular application (Kijewski and Yoon 1990). Value-in-use is the price that would equate to the overall costs and benefits of using one product rather than using another.

For example, consider a comparison between delivery vans. One type of van is cheap and spare parts are also cheap, but it tends to be less reliable and has to be serviced every 10,000 miles. The other type is almost twice as expensive, but is extremely reliable and has service intervals at 20,000 miles. At first, it seems as if the calculation would simply be a matter of adding up the total running costs of each type of van, and comparing the total cost against the purchase cost. However, this does not take account of the cost of losing deliveries as a result of a breakdown, or of the views of the drivers, or of the resale value of the vans when they are replaced. For some firms, absolute reliability in use is worth a very great deal – for others it is less important. It is the value-in-use to the firm that is important.

Because some buyers do use this type of calculation to assess alternative solutions to existing problems, the astute marketer will be prepared with the full arguments in favour of the new solution, including all the relevant factors that make the product more attractive. On the other side of the coin, astute purchasers will involve potential suppliers in the discussions and in the value analysis process (Dowst and Raia 1990).

Value analysis A method of evaluating components, raw materials and even manufacturing processes in order to determine ways of cutting costs or improving finished products.

EVALUATING SUPPLIER CAPABILITY

Purchasers also need to assess the capability of potential suppliers to continue to supply successfully. This is a combination of assessing financial stability, technical expertise, reliability, quality assurance processes and production capacity. In simple terms, the purchasing company is trying to ensure that the potential supplier will be in a position to keep the promises it makes. Business customers that track the performance of suppliers gain a competitive advantage because they are better able to manage the supply chain (Bharadwaj 2004).

Table 4.4   Assessing suppliers

Attribute	Assessment method
Technical capability	Visit the supplier to examine production equipment, inspect quality control procedures and meet the engineering staff.
Managerial capability	Discuss systems for controlling processes, meet the managerial staff, and become involved in planning and scheduling supplies.
Financial stability	Check the accounts filed at Companies House or other public record office, run a credit check, examine annual reports if any.
Capacity to deliver	Ascertain the status of other customers of the supplier – would any of these take priority? Assess the production capacity of the supplier, warehouse stocks of the product, reputation in the industry.

Table 4.4 illustrates some of the ways in which buyers can assess potential suppliers. Whilst these methods are better than nothing, in most cases they rely on judgement on the part of the purchaser, who may not in fact have the necessary expertise to understand what the supplier's capability really is.

Think outside this box!

The methods of assessment shown in Table 4.4 all rely on some kind of judgement on the part of the buyer. Even the financial figures filed at the company record office require interpretation – and may even have been 'massaged' to make the company look more financially viable than it actually is.

So why bother with what is, after all, a somewhat time-consuming exercise? Presumably a rogue supplier would have little difficulty in pulling the wool over the eyes of a buyer who probably lacks the engineering training to understand what is in front of him or her. On the other hand, an honest supplier would probably provide the 'warts and all' picture that might well lose the contract. Maybe buyers would be better advised to go for the supplier who looks the worst – at least we know they are being honest with us!

EVALUATING SUPPLIER PERFORMANCE

Even after the contract is awarded, the purchasing company is likely to need to review the supplier's performance periodically. In some cases, suppliers have been known to relax once the contract is awarded, and of course the circumstances of the buying organisation are likely to change considerably in the course of what will be a lengthy relationship.

The basic evaluation methods are as outlined in Table 4.5. All of these methods involve some degree of subjectivity; in other words, each method requires buyers to make judgements about the supplier. The fact that the outcomes are expressed in numbers gives each method a spurious credibility. Those involved in evaluation exercises of this nature should be aware that the evaluation exercise itself should be evaluated periodically, and the criteria used by the various individuals involved need to be checked.

Table 4.5 Evaluation approaches

Approach	Explanation
Categorical plan	Each department having contact with the supplier is asked to provide a regular rating of suppliers against a list of salient performance factors. This method is extremely subjective, but easy to administer.
Weighted-point plan	Performance factors are graded according to their importance to the organisation: for example, delivery reliability might be more important for some organisations than for others. The supplier's total rating can be calculated and the supplier's offering can be adjusted if necessary to meet the purchasing organisation's needs.
Cost-ratio plan	Here the buying organisation evaluates quality, delivery and service in terms of what each one costs. Good performance is assigned a negative score, i.e. the costs of purchase are reduced by good performance: poor performance is assigned a positive score, meaning that the costs are deemed to be greater when dealing with a poor performer.

Think outside this box!

Much of the emphasis in the preceding sections has been on the purchaser's evaluation of suppliers. But what about the other way round? Customers are not always plaster saints – some are late payers, some impose unreasonable restrictions, some reject supplies for the flimsiest of reasons, and some are just plain unpleasant to deal with.

So should suppliers have their own systems for assessing purchasers? Should we just grovel at the feet of any organisation willing to buy our goods – or should we stand up and be counted? After all, without supplies no company can survive – so presumably we are equally important to one another.

Maybe this is really the purpose of segmenting our markets – and what is really meant by segmentation.

In fact, suppliers tend to adapt more often than do purchasers when there is an ongoing relationship (Brennan et al. 2003). This is due to the relative power each has (buyers being more powerful in most circumstances) and managerial preferences. Suppliers that are market-orientated tend to develop a greater **customer intimacy**, which also may drive suppliers to change (Tuominen et al. 2004). Buyers that are themselves market-orientated tend to become more loyal to their suppliers (Jose Sanzo et al. 2003).

Categorical plan An approach to valuing suppliers based on salient performance factors.

Weighted-point plan A method of evaluating suppliers based on factors that are of greatest importance to the company.

Cost-ratio plan A method of evaluating suppliers based on the costs of doing business with them.

Customer intimacy The degree to which a firm is close to its customers.

Chapter summary

Buyers have a large number of influences on their decision-making. At the very least, buyers have their own personal agendas within the companies they work for: in the broader context, a wide range of political, environmental and technological issues will affect their decision-making. The end result is likely to be a combination of experience, careful calculation and gut feeling.

Key points

- Buyers are subject to many pressures other than the simple commercial ones: emotions, organisational influence, politics and internal structures are also important factors.
- The decision-making unit (DMU) or buying centre is the group of people who will make the buying decision. Roles and composition of DMUs vary widely.
- Business and commercial organisations are likely to be swayed most by past experience with a vendor, product characteristics and quality.
- Resellers are driven by their customers.
- Institutional markets may need special techniques to help them afford to buy the products.
- Markets can be divided into those buyers who buy products designed to make other products or will incorporate the purchase into their own products (original equipment manufacturers); those who consume the product in the course of running their businesses (user markets); or those who serve the aftermarket.
- A purchase may be a straight rebuy, a modified rebuy, or a new task. These are given in order of increasing complexity, and do not have discrete boundaries.
- A team approach to buying usually dictates a team approach to selling.

Review questions

1. How would you expect a government department to go about buying a new computer system?
2. How might internal politics affect a buyer's behaviour?
3. What factors might be prominent in the buying decision for cleaning materials?
4. What factors might a supplier take into account when evaluating a purchasing company?
5. How might the directors of a company go about setting standards for evaluating suppliers? What objective criteria are available?
6. What are the main problems with evaluating supplier performance?
7. How should a seller approach a government department?
8. What are the main differences between marketing to commercial organisations and marketing to charities?
9. How might a seller find out who the influencers are in the DMU?
10. How might a seller act to reduce the risk for the buyer?

Case study revisited: BHP Billiton

The crisis has treated BHP Billiton fairly kindly. Some plants have been closed down or downsized, but in the main the company has continued to grow, largely because of its very diversified markets. It does business in most parts of the world, and demand for its products holds up well because as one country is in crisis, another one booms. Even a global recession has not fazed the company – in effect, it is too big and too diversified to fail.

The company made a strong commitment to the Chinese market, since Chinese GDP was forecast to triple within the next twelve years. Corresponding figures for the European Union and United States were still good, but not on the same scale: BHP Billiton also saw opportunities in Brazil and Russia, but in both cases these countries have substantial natural resources of their own, and the mining companies to exploit them.

Much of BHP Billiton's focus tends to be on the supply side, because the world's resources are running out and therefore demand will probably continue to outstrip supply: however, the company needed to find new outlets for aluminium since this is the commonest metal in the earth's crust and is therefore in good supply, despite being difficult to smelt. For BHP Billiton, marketing consists not so much in finding new customers, but in finding the raw materials they need – the company is geared around matching supply and demand, rather than encouraging a greater demand. This means that the company has a somewhat different perspective than most, and provides a new way of thinking about marketing.

Case study: Tyron Automotive Group Ltd

Tyron Automotive Group Ltd manufactures, distributes and services a comprehensive range of safety systems for vehicle tyres. The main customers for the systems are police forces, security companies, emergency services, armies, trucking companies and even the general public via a system of distributors. The products allow the vehicle to continue to be driven even if the tyres burst or are shot out.

Founded in 1979, Tyron developed, in conjunction with Avon Tyres, the first commercially available products for steel drop centre rims as a direct result of a request from the UK's Ministry of Defence to overcome the immobilisation of vehicles by having the tyres shot out or deflated by running over booby-traps. These first 'well filler' bands were sold throughout the world, primarily to military, government and security organisations. The systems vary from an economical 'run-flat' system that allows the vehicle to continue for a short distance so that the driver does not lose control in the event of a blowout, through to military systems that allow the vehicle to be driven for 50 km or more on flat tyres. The latest version of the Tyron product can cope with a blowout at 150 mph, and is expected to be a big seller to police forces.

The company was founded in 1979, and in 1984 it allowed its patented products to be manufactured under licence. This gave the company a worldwide presence, but in late 1990 these licensing agreements ran out, leaving Tyron with a major gap in its marketing programme. From 1991 to 1993 the company made considerable efforts to develop new products, working closely with tyre, wheel and vehicle manufacturers, and investing substantial sums of money in new plant and machinery to produce the improved products. The difficulty the company faced was in finding suitable distribution for the products, especially in foreign markets.

The company's salesforce eventually recruited more than 1000 distributors throughout England, Wales and Scotland: typical distributors are tyre-fitting companies, caravan suppliers, automotive parts suppliers and garages. These are mainly small firms, but they ensure a very wide distribution throughout the mainland UK: there is even one distributor in Northern Ireland. These distributors fit the systems to existing customers' vehicles.

For international sales, the company eventually contacted Trade Partners UK, through its local chamber of commerce. Trade Partners UK (TPUK) is a government organisation set up to help small firms to export. TPUK provided training for Tyron's salesforce, and also arranged for the company's managing director, Tony Glazebrook, to attend two trade fairs – Meplex in Dubai, and Intersec. The second of these trade fairs was followed up by a visit to Australia and New Zealand under the guidance of TPUK's export experts, the trade attachés of the British embassies in those countries.

As a result of these initiatives, Tyron appointed several new distributors in the Middle East, resulting in immediate orders worth over £110,000 each. This is a substantial sum for a firm employing only ten people. The company went on to appoint distributors in France, Benelux, Australia, Trinidad and Tobago, Germany, the United States, Indonesia, Singapore, Sweden and Oman. These lead distributors are expected in turn to appoint sub-distributors within their own regions and countries (although the US distributor has yet to leave California). Recruiting sub-distributors is a slow process, and in some cases the national distributors have made little progress, but in the long run the company expects substantial growth from these foreign distributors.

As time has gone by, the company has gone from strength to strength – Tyron systems are now available to the general public, but the company developed an all-terrain run-flat tyre for military vehicles in 2008, and in 2009 it launched a super-strong alloy wheel for 4x4 and cash-carrying vehicles. This wheel allows the vehicle to be driven for 50 km with all four tyres flat, on or off-road, so that security vehicles can escape from would-be robbers even if the tyres have been shot out.

Tyron tends to be a product-orientated company, so the help given by TPUK has proved invaluable. Managing director Tony Glazebrook said, 'Getting help from Trade Partners is the best business decision I ever made.'

Questions

1. Tyron is relying heavily on distributors. What other methods might be appropriate?
2. What are the advantages for Tyron of using overseas distributors rather than setting up a subsidiary in the target country?
3. How might Tyron's dealers respond to the news that the company is seeking to have the systems fitted as original equipment?
4. For a major market such as the United States, how might Tyron speed up the process of acquiring distributors?
5. What other approaches might Tyron have for dealing in the United States?

Further reading

There are many books on business-to-business marketing, including:

Jim Blythe and Alan Zimmerman, *Business to Business Marketing Management,* 2nd edition (Abingdon: Routledge, 2013). This book takes a global perspective on B2B marketing.

Chris Fill and Karen Fill, *Business to Business Marketing: Relationships, Systems and Communications* (Harlow: FT Prentice Hall, 2004). This is a comprehensive, readable textbook written from a marketing management perspective.

Mark Whitehead and Chris Barrat, *Buying for Business: Insights into Purchasing and Supply* (Chichester: John Wiley, 2004). This is a view from the other side. Written as a guide for practitioners, the book takes the buyer's viewpoint.

References

Bendixen, Mike, Bukasa, Kalala A. and Abratt, Russell A. (2004) Brand equity in the business to business market. *Industrial Marketing Management*, 33 (5): 371–80.

Bharadwaj, Neeraj (2004) Investigating the decision criteria used in electronic components procurement. *Industrial Marketing Management*, 33 (4): 317–23.

Bogomolova, Svetlana and Romaniuk, Jenni (2010) Brand equity of defectors and never boughts in a business financial market. *Industrial Marketing Management*, 39 (8): 1261–8.

Brennan, Ross D., Turnbull, Peter W. and Wilson, David T. (2003) Dyadic adaptation in business-to-business markets. *European Journal of Marketing*, 37 (11): 1636–65.

Cardozo, Richard N. (1983) Modelling organisational buying as a sequence of decisions. *Industrial Marketing Management*, 12: 75.

Claycomb, Cindy and Frankwick, Gary (2010) Buyers' perspectives of buyer–seller relationship development. *Industrial Marketing Management*, 39 (2): 252–63.

Claycomb, Cindy, Iyer, Karthik and Germain, Richard (2005) Predicting the level of B2B e-commerce in industrial organisations. *Industrial Marketing Management*, 34 (3): 221–34.

Dowst, S. and Raia, E. (1990) Teaming up for the 90s. *Purchasing*, 108: 54–9.

Hawes, J.M and Barnhouse, S.H. (1987) How purchasing agents handle personal risk. *Industrial Marketing Management*, 16: 287–93.

Helm, Sabrina, Rolfes, Ludger and Gunther, Berndt (2006) Suppliers' willingness to end unprofitable customer relationships. *European Journal of Marketing*, 40: 366–383.

Jose Sanzo, Maria, Leticia Santos, Maria, Vasquez, Rodolfo and Alvarez, Luis I. (2003) The role of market orientation in business dyadic relationships: testing an integrator model. *Journal of Marketing Management*, 19: 73–107.

Kelly, P. and Coaker, J.W. (1976) Can we generalise about choice criteria for industrial purchasing decisions? In Bernhardt, K.L. (ed.), *Marketing 1776–1976 and Beyond*. Chicago, IL: American Marketing Association. pp. 330–3.

Kijewski, V. and Yoon, E. (1990) Market-based pricing: beyond price–performance curves. *Industrial Marketing Management*, 19: 11–19.

Kotler, Philip (2003) *Marketing Management*. Upper Saddle River, NJ: Prentice Hall.

Loudon, D. and Della Bitta, A. (1993) *Consumer Behaviour: Concepts and Applications*. New York: McGraw–Hill Education.

McDonald, Jason B. and Smith, Kirk (2004) The effects of technology-mediated communication on industrial buyer behaviour. *Industrial Marketing Management*, 33 (2): 107–16.

Michalski, Silke (2004) Types of customer relationship ending processes. *Journal of Marketing Management*, 20 (9/10): 977–99.

Millman, T. and Wilson, K.J. (1995) From key account selling to key account management. *Journal of Marketing Science*, issue 1.

Moller, Kristian and Svahn, Senja (2004) Crossing east–west boundaries: knowledge sharing in intercultural business networks. *Industrial Marketing Management*, 33 (3): 219–28.

Narayandas, Das and Rangan, V. Kasturi (2004) Building and sustaining buyer–seller relationships in mature industrial markets. *Journal of Marketing*, 68 (3): 63–77.

Ojasalo, Jukka (2004) Key network management. *Industrial Marketing Management*, 33 (3): 195–205.

Porter, M.E. (1985) *Competitive Advantage.* New York: Free Press.

Ronchetto, John R., Jr; Hutt, Michael D. and Reingen, Peter H. (1989) Embedded influence patterns in organizational buying systems. *Journal of Marketing*, 53 (4): 51–62.

Singh, Ramendra and Koshy, Abraham (2011) Does salesperson's customer orientation create value in B2B relationships? Empirical evidence from India. *Industrial Marketing Management*, 40 (1): 78–85.

Terpstra, Vern and David, Kenneth (1991) *The Cultural Environment of International Business*, 3rd ed. Cincinnati, OH: South-Western.

Traynor, Kenneth and Traynor, Susan (2004) A comparison of marketing approaches used by high-tech firms: 1985 versus 2001. *Industrial Marketing Management*, 33 (5): 457–61.

Tuli, Kapil R., Kohli, Ajay K. and Bharadwaj, Sundar G. (2007) Rethinking customer solutions: from product bundles to relational processes. *Journal of Marketing*, 71 (3): 1–17.

Tuominen, Matti, Rajala, Arto and Moller, Kristian (2004) Market-driving versus market-driven: divergent roles of market orientation in business relationships. *Industrial Marketing Management*, 33 (3): 207–17.

Webster, F.E. and Wind, Y. (1972) *Organisational Buying Behaviour*. Englewood Cliffs, NJ: Prentice Hall.

Williams, Paul, Khan, M. Sajid and Naumann, Earl (2011) Customer dissatisfaction and defection: the hidden costs of downsizing. *Industrial Marketing Management*, 40 (3): 405–13.

Wilson, K.J. (1993) A problem centred approach to key-account management. *Proceedings of the National Sales Management Conference*, Atlanta, GA.

Wilson, K.J. (1999) Developing key account relationships: the integration of the Millman–Wilson relational development model with the problem-centred (PPF) model of buyer–seller interaction in business-to-business markets. *Journal of Selling and Major Account Management*, 1 (4).

 More online

To gain free access to additional online resources to support this chapter please visit:
www.sagepub.co.uk/blythe3e

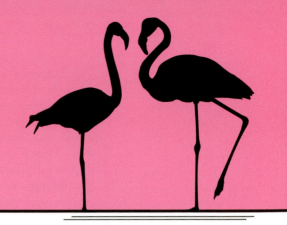

CHAPTER ⑤

Marketing research and information systems

LEARNING OBJECTIVES

After reading this chapter, you should be able to:

- Explain the role of marketing research in decision-making.

- Describe the different sub-divisions of marketing research.

- Explain the benefits of secondary research and primary research.

- Describe what is meant by qualitative and quantitative research, and explain the benefits of each.

- Explain the differences between planning and execution.

- Describe the most common techniques of marketing research.

- Explain some of the ethical issues raised in carrying out marketing research.

Introduction

As with any other business function, marketing relies heavily on information. Some of this information already exists, buried within corporate records, and some of it needs to be collected from outside sources. These outside sources might be organisations that routinely collect market information and publish reports, or it may be necessary to collect data directly from consumers. Marketers need to decide which information-generating method is most appropriate, and which will be most cost-effective in generating the right information at the right price.

There is a degree of confusion in academic circles about what constitutes market research and what constitutes **marketing research**. A possible way of distinguishing between the two terms is to consider market research to be concerned with finding out about markets (customers, competitors, suppliers, market conditions in general), whereas marketing research takes the broader approach of researching anything that might be of use to a marketer. This debate overlaps into the debate about the boundaries of marketing. The American Marketing Association defines marketing research as follows:

Marketing research Information-gathering for the purpose of improving the organisation's effectiveness.

The function that links the customer, consumer and public to the marketer through information – information used to identify and define marketing opportunities and problems: generate, refine, and evaluate marketing actions: monitor marketing performance: and improve understanding of marketing as a process. Marketing research specifies the information required to address these issues: designs the method for collecting information: manages and implements the data-collection process: analyses the results: and communicates the findings and their implications. (AMA 1987)

Marketing research therefore looks beyond the immediate market and includes monitoring systems for marketing plans, identification of opportunities and threats, identification of what information is needed, and takes account of past experience and future expectations as well as looking at the present situation.

All business decisions involve an element of risk: the purpose of marketing research is to minimise the risk.

Preview case study: Avios

Avios is a reward programme operated by British Airways, and was formerly known as Airmiles. People can collect Avios points simply by shopping at specific retailers or by flying with BA or its partner airlines. Points can be redeemed for flights, or can be used as part-payment for flights with the remainder of the fare being paid in cash.

The appeal of the scheme is clear – people collect points simply by shopping in their usual places, and every so often they are able to have a flight to somewhere nice. Avios is more than just a loyalty scheme – it is a sales promotion scheme as well, and (for BA) it is a scheme that increases passenger numbers and revenue. However, it seems that some people are collecting the points and then not redeeming them, in fact some people even go to the trouble of calling BA's call centre or visiting the website without actually making a booking.

At first sight this may not matter – but BA were concerned that they are running a scheme that does not appeal to some people, and what is more some people would have been redeeming some points and paying cash for the rest of the fare, so they were in fact depriving BA of revenue by not booking. If Avios are the currency of the airline, why are people calling in or entering the website without booking?

At first BA went the standard route of hiring in a research agency to run a questionnaire-type survey to find out what was going wrong. This did turn up some useful information, but fell short of finding out the true answer. Something more creative needed to be done.

Types of marketing research

Marketing research divides into broad groupings. There are six main groupings (Proctor 2000), with some subgroupings (see Figure 5.1). These groupings are not mutually exclusive: aspects of each area of marketing might well be researched within the same study.

Figure 5.1   Components of marketing research

CUSTOMER RESEARCH

Confusingly, this is also sometimes referred to as market research. **Customer research** is concerned with the motivations and behaviour of customers, their geographical or demographical spread, their number and spending power, and their creditworthiness.

Customer research provides information on the market and market segment size, trends in the market, brand shares, customer characteristics and motivation, and competitor brand shares. It also provides information on the positioning of brands in the customers' minds.

Customer research Investigations into the behaviour of purchasers of the product.

ADVERTISING RESEARCH

Advertising research is about measuring the success (or otherwise) of advertising campaigns or other promotional exercises. It provides marketers with information on the most appropriate media to use, the most effective type of campaign to use, and the most effective design for the advertising. Because advertising research also looks at the motivations and perceptions of customers, it overlaps to an extent with customer research: understanding the impact of advertising on customers is of obvious benefit, especially when one considers the cost of running a major campaign.

Advertising research Investigations into the effectiveness and potential effectiveness of marketing communications.

PRODUCT RESEARCH

Product research is used to test new product ideas on potential customers. Often this type of research is carried out at the concept stage, even before a prototype is available: this avoids the company investing in an expensive research and development programme for products that have no market. Product research can also provide an assessment of the strengths and weaknesses of a firm's products against those of its competitors.

Once a prototype is available, the product can be test-marketed with a group of potential users to find out whether any final flaws exist which can be ironed out

Product research Investigations intended to generate knowledge that can be used to inform new product development.

before the product is launched. Even at this late stage, research is useful because it often points up problems (or strengths) that are not apparent at the concept stage.

Product research also looks at the packaging of a product. This includes the appeal to the end consumer, the effectiveness of the packaging in protecting the product from the environment and vice versa, and the acceptability of the packaging to distributors, wholesalers, retailers and so forth.

DISTRIBUTION RESEARCH

Distribution research Investigations into the effectiveness of different outlets for products.

Finding the most effective distribution channels is by no means an obvious exercise. Research can help to identify which distributors will be of most assistance, which have the appropriate facilities for the product, and which are best connected to the end users.

Distribution research also considers **physical distribution** – the best location for warehouses, the best type of delivery systems, and so forth.

Physical distribution The movement of products along the value chain from producer to retailer and ultimately to the consumer.

SALES RESEARCH

Sales research Investigations into aspects of the personal selling function, including the performances of individual salespeople.

The effectiveness of the salesforce can be the key factor in making or breaking a company. **Sales research** helps to assess the effectiveness of individual salespeople, of different sales techniques, and of different management techniques. It helps to ensure that sales territories are of approximately the same value in terms of sales potential, and can also help ensure that the right salespeople are working in the right territories.

Sales research can also be used for establishing the right type of remuneration mix, and the right type of training programme for salespeople. It therefore has a role in internal marketing.

MARKETING ENVIRONMENT

Environment research Investigations into the external factors that impinge on the organisation's activities.

Environment research looks at the political, economic, social and technological factors that affect marketing decision-making. Trends in the population, possible effects of proposed legislation and the likely effects of new technology are all within the remit of environmental research.

Knowing which factors are relevant and how they may impact on the firm and its marketing activities is of obvious importance.

Applied marketing research

Preliminary research Investigations intended to outline the dimensions of a problem.

Exploratory research Investigations intended to identify problems.

Conclusive research Investigations intended to provide answers to problems.

Field research Investigations carried out in the marketplace.

The first stage of applied marketing research is often **preliminary research** intended to identify the dimensions of a problem. Understanding which factors go to make up the problem is only part of what companies need to know – they also need to know which other problems exist that may not yet have been identified. Preliminary research is often known as **exploratory research**, because it sets out to examine unknown territory in terms of the information available to the firm.

Conclusive research is carried out in order to support (or refute) the theories generated by the preliminary research. Conclusive research is intended to generate conclusions – this may or may not always be possible. Conclusive research may use data that have already been collected, or may use **field research** in which new data are collected, or it may require a combination of both.

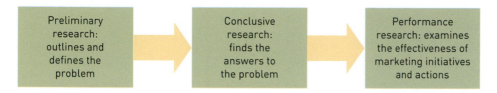

Figure 5.2 Applied marketing research

Performance research examines the effectiveness of marketing initiatives and actions, and therefore (in effect) provides information about whether the previous market research has been correctly carried out and interpreted. If the performance research shows that the company is not achieving its objectives, it is possible to make corrections and re-examine the nature of the original problem – this may, in turn, lead to a revision of the previous preliminary and conclusive research.

Think outside this box!

If we don't know what the problem is, how do we know we have a problem at all? Is preliminary research really necessary? Surely what we don't know about can't hurt us, so why go looking for trouble?

Or is it better to identify potential threats before they become unmanageable? What we don't know may not hurt us – until the problem becomes so huge we can't miss it!

Marketing information systems

A **marketing information system** provides a continuously updated stream of information on which decisions can be based. It has been defined as:

> *A system in which marketing information is formally gathered, stored, analysed and distributed to managers in accord with their informational needs on a regular planned basis. (Jobber and Rainbow 1977)*

Marketing information systems are built around the needs of managers, and should be designed to supply up-to-date information in a timely manner. A marketing information system consists of four elements: **internal continuous data**, **internal ad hoc data**, **environmental scanning** and marketing research.

Internal continuous data may consist of sales records, customer records, profitability calculations, customer feedback (positive and negative) and other management records such as individual performance records for employees (e.g. salespeople). In many cases this information is already being collected by individuals within the firm, but is not being brought together in an appropriate form for the purposes of marketing management. In other cases, the information is not being collected at all – many firms, for example, calculate the profitability of each product in the range, but for a marketing manager it might be a great deal more useful to calculate the profitability of each market segment.

Marketing information systems Mechanisms for providing a constant flow of information about markets.

Internal continuous data Information supplied by systems within the organisation on a constant basis.

Internal ad hoc data Information supplied by systems within the organisation for a specific purpose.

Environmental scanning Continuous monitoring of external factors that might impinge on the organisation's activities.

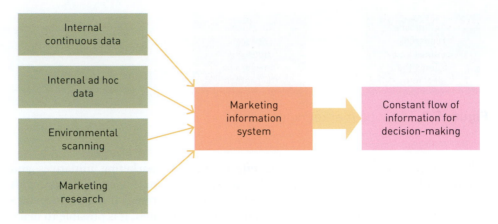

Figure 5.3   Marketing information system

Internal ad hoc data are collected on an occasional basis for a specific purpose. For example, marketers might want to monitor the sales of a specific product following the introduction of a 'budget' version, with a view to seeing whether the cheaper product cannibalises sales of the original product. The marketing information system should already be capturing sales of the original product, so there should be little difficulty in providing the necessary information.

Environmental scanning was mentioned in Chapter 2. Monitoring the news media (and especially the trade press) for potential threats and opportunities is part of the marketing information system, but other potential sources of information about the marketing environment should not be ignored; reports from staff, especially salespeople, can be invaluable in monitoring what is going on in the outside world.

Marketing research forms the final element of the marketing information system, and is used when specific answers to a specific problem need to be found. In this sense, marketing research fills in the gaps in the marketing information system.

Collecting such data is only the first stage, however: for raw data to become information these must be analysed and interpreted. Sophisticated marketing information systems are able to do at least some of the analysis automatically, although interpretation is likely to remain beyond the capability of computers for some time yet.

A good marketing information system will provide regular reports, or even real-time information on screen, to enable marketers to know what is happening in the marketplace. This allows managers to adjust tactics, formulate new policies, and keep ahead of the competitors. The evidence is that the ability to measure marketing performance has a significant positive effect on the firm's performance, profitability, stock returns and (not surprisingly) the status of marketing within the firm (O'Sullivan and Abela 2007).

Data types

Data can be collected in many ways, but these fall into four main types, as shown in Table 5.1.

Qualitative data can also be secondary or primary data, and likewise quantitative data can be primary or secondary. Figure 5.4 shows some examples in each category.

Research data can come from custom-designed studies, tailored to meet the specific needs of the firm, from syndicated studies that are carried out on behalf of a

Table 5.1   Data typology

Primary data	Data that are collected from an original source, for example by running a questionnaire survey or by interviewing respondents.
Secondary data	Data that are second-hand. These are data that have been collected by someone else (for example, a commercial market research company) and which already existed before the problem was identified.
Quantitative data	Data that can be expressed numerically, for example in terms of percentages. This type of research is good for finding out what people do in terms of purchasing behaviour, but is not good for finding out why they do it.
Qualitative data	Data that cannot be expressed in numbers, for example interviews. This type of research is effective for finding out why people behave in the ways they do, but is not so good for finding out what people in general do.

	Secondary data	Primary data
Qualitative data	• Company reports • Complaint letters • Sales reps' reports	• Focus groups • In-depth interviews • Written responses
Quantitative data	• Past sales figures • Published market research • Customer records	• Questionnaire surveys • Observations • Experiments

Figure 5.4   Categories of data

Primary data Information collected first-hand for a specific purpose.
Secondary data Information collected second-hand: information that was originally collected for a different purpose from that for which the researcher now wants to use it.
Quantitative data Information that can be expressed numerically.
Qualitative data Information that cannot be expressed numerically.

group of firms (often competitors), or from standardised studies that are carried out by commercial research firms such as Mintel and sold to anyone who may find them useful.

Applied market research has undergone considerable change in recent years. Twenty years ago, commercial applied research usually consisted of questionnaire research, in which researchers would go out with clipboards and stop people in the street to ask them questions. This approach has largely been abandoned in the 21st century – qualitative research (**focus groups**, depth interviews and so forth) have proved to be more reliable and to provide better insights into people's intentions and behaviour. The results are obtained much more quickly, and it is also cheaper since it requires a lot fewer people than questionnaire studies.

Focus group Respondents brought together to discuss a research question in a controlled and structured manner under the guidance of a researcher.

Planning for research

The first stage in any planning process is to determine what the problem actually is. Defining the problem enables planners to focus their efforts more precisely and therefore avoid being drawn into researching areas that might be interesting but have little immediate relevance.

A goal-orientated approach to problem definition was suggested by Rickards (1974). This is shown in Table 5.2.

Table 5.2   Problem definition

Stage	Example
Stage One: Write down a description of the problem.	Problem: Our product line is becoming outdated, and we need to create something new.
Stage Two: What do we need to accomplish?	We need to find out what people would like to see in a new product.
Stage Three: What are the obstacles?	Potential customers may not know what they would like in a new product. Competitors also have vigorous new-product programmes.
Stage Four: What constraints must we accept to solve the problem?	We have limited funds, we do not know which groups of people might be interested in our product.
Stage Five: Redefine the problem, taking into account the previous answers.	We do not understand our customers' needs adequately, and we do not know what other potential customers may exist.

Having recognised the problem, managers need to consider whether carrying out research is a sensible option anyway. Sometimes the cost of the research will exceed any possible benefits that may accrue, so the managers need to decide whether the potential pay-off justifies the outlay. For example, a small restaurant may decide to offer a new main course. The cost of carrying out a survey to find out whether the meal would prove popular would be far in excess of simply adding it as a 'special' for a few weeks to see what the response of diners is.

Decision tree A diagrammatic representation of the route a manager must take to reach a decision.

The decision whether or not to carry out research can be based on a simple **decision tree**, as shown in Figure 5.5. The problem with this approach is that it gives a spurious credibility to the decision. In fact the decision tree is itself based on a set of judgements, but the impression given is that the outcome is objective. Management cannot know in advance how much the research is going to be worth: many research projects have proved to be worthless because the research question was wrong, or the research itself was poorly executed. Even worse, some projects have proved to be counter-productive because they have taken the company in entirely the wrong direction.

A further problem that arises is that those responsible for a new idea are often reluctant to carry out the research because they have such faith in the idea they are unwilling to accept the possibility that it will not work.

Having decided that research is necessary and worthwhile, a detailed plan needs to be drawn up. A useful starting-point is to hold discussions with the people who will be using the results of the research. Obviously there is a risk of producing a research exercise that tries to achieve too many objectives, but this is better than producing a research exercise that does not achieve the necessary objectives.

Research plan An outline of the steps that must be taken in gathering information systematically.

The **research plan** is an outline of the design, execution and monitoring of a study. The plan is not set in concrete – it can be changed, but the intention is that it provides a clear set of guidelines for those who will actually carry out the research, and those who will benefit from the findings. The plan contains a statement of the

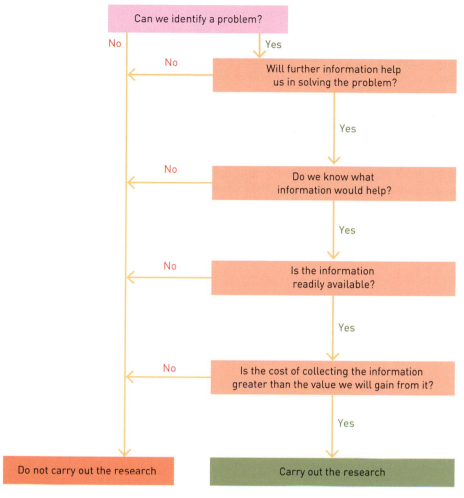

Figure 5.5   Decision tree for evaluating research

company's problem, and the proposed means of collecting information to help solve it. The plan leads on to the research proposal, which is a statement of the plan including the need for the research and an assessment of the costs and benefits that will attach to it. The proposal is usually used to obtain approval of the plan from the various decision-makers involved in the problem and its solution.

The research plan and proposal will state exactly how the data are to be collected, analysed and interpreted in order to create the information the firm needs.

If the budget allows (bearing in mind that marketing research is an expensive exercise) it is good practice to use more than one research method to examine the problem. This is called triangulation: the purpose of the exercise is to reduce the risk that one or other method will provide a false result. By looking at the problem from different angles and with different methods, the researchers should be able to pick up on any errors in the research design or execution. There is more on triangulation later in the chapter.

OBTAINING INFORMATION: SECONDARY SOURCES

Secondary sources of information are those that already exist. In many cases, the information the firm needs has already been collected by someone else, often for some other purpose. Provided this information can be bought, or is published some-where, the firm may not need to carry out its own research at all.

The main advantage of **secondary research** is, of course, cost. Secondary research is almost always cheaper than **primary research**, even when it has to be paid for. When it is already published in a readily available form in libraries or on the Internet, the advantage is clear.

The drawback with secondary research is that it often does not fit exactly with the firm's problem. Sometimes managers need to be creative in combining and interpreting information from secondary sources in order to create usable information.

Secondary sources include newspapers, journals, websites, published research, books, academic journals, government reports, commercial research, European Union reports and research conducted by trade associations.

Secondary research Research that has already been carried out (often by someone else for another purpose) and is available to the researcher for the current project.

Primary research Research that is carried out from scratch for a specific project.

Real-life marketing: The Internet

The Internet probably contains nearly all the information you will ever need about almost anything – the problem lies in sorting out the truth from the lies and distortions. Much of what appears on the Internet is biased, and is intended to sell you something – especially the free content. To sort out fact from fiction, you need to apply the following rules:

- If the site is sponsored by a company, ask yourself what that company hopes to gain from running it.
- Find another source that can back up what you are reading.
- Find out how they conducted the research – and if it isn't made clear, it's probably because there is some unreliability about the information.
- Be sceptical – nobody puts stuff on the Internet without a reason. If it seems too good to be true, it probably is!

Another source of secondary data is internally generated information. Sales records often yield detailed data about customer behaviour: how often customers buy, how much they buy in any one order, where the customers are geographically, even what their delivery preferences are. Many firms have separate records of their customers' behaviour, held in different departments: for example, the sales manager may have records of which customers are difficult to sell to, which are likely to be increasing their orders in the near future, and which are likely to be going bankrupt. The invoicing department will know which customers are bad payers and which are habitual complainers, the shipping department will know where the customers are, and so forth. Combining this information could give a very clear picture of which customers are the most rewarding and which should be downgraded or dropped altogether.

OBTAINING INFORMATION: PRIMARY SOURCES

Primary research is carried out with the aim of generating original data. This means data that have not been collected before, and which serve to fill a gap in the firm's knowledge. Primary research should only be carried out after secondary sources have been exhausted. This helps to minimise the cost by avoiding a re-invention of existing data. In marketing research, primary data can be collected in many ways: postal

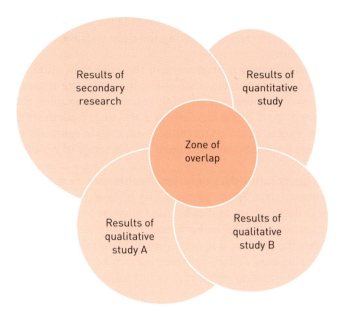

Figure 5.6 Triangulation

Triangulation Using more than one research method to answer the same question in order to reduce the chances of errors.

surveys, street questionnaires, interviews, focus groups and so forth. Some of these will generate quantitative data, some qualitative data. Some studies will use more than one method in order to triangulate on the problem or examine different aspects of the same problem.

Triangulation means using different methods to focus on the same problem in order to confirm the accuracy of the answers. For example, a firm might run a questionnaire survey to find out how many people shop in a particular shopping mall, then send an observer to the mall in order to count the number of people passing through. This type of study allows the researchers to confirm that the questionnaire has been properly carried out, which may have a bearing on the reliability of any other questions contained in it.

Using different methods to attack different parts of the problem is also common. For example, a researcher might run a focus group to find out what the dimensions of the problem are, then use the results to design and run a questionnaire survey to find out how common the focus group's opinions are among the general population. Equally the reverse might happen – the researchers might run a questionnaire survey which tells them how people behave, then run a focus group to find out why.

Quantitative data are data that can be expressed numerically. Quantitative data can be collected by any of the following methods:

1. Questionnaires. These are quick to administer and analyse, but difficult to design.
2. Interview surveys. Similar to questionnaires, these surveys are carried out by interviewers. This ensures that respondents understand the questions, and also helps to ensure that they answer all of these appropriately.
3. Observation. Observing what people do and counting the numbers who behave in specific ways is a non-intrusive form of research. For example, a researcher might observe how many people enter a retail store, at what times

of day, and to which shelves they go first. This could be extremely useful in managing the store, in terms of setting the right staffing numbers or laying out the store efficiently.

4. **Test marketing**. Putting a product onto the market in a limited geographical area, or with a few customers, enables the firm to gauge responses.
5. **Panels**. Many commercial marketing research companies recruit panels of respondents who participate regularly in marketing research studies in exchange for payment. Panels might be recruited from a wide range of individuals, who report on their buying behaviour across a wide range of products.

Test marketing Offering a product to a small group of consumers in order to judge the likely response from a large group of consumers.

Panel A permanently established group of research respondents.

Other sources of quantitative data exist, and techniques exist to extract numerical results from qualitative data. In the vast majority of cases, however, quantitative data collection means collecting a set of standardised answers to standardised questions. In this way, the researcher is able to make statements such as '43% of respondents said that they would buy the product if it were available from their local supermarket, but only 8% would buy by mail order'. Provided we can be confident of this result, this is a useful piece of information: what it does not tell us is why people prefer to buy from the supermarket.

SAMPLING

In most cases, it is not possible to ask everybody their opinions. Occasionally the number of potential respondents (for example, the number of people who might be expected to be in the market for a given product) is small enough that all of them can be questioned: this is called a census survey. In the vast majority of cases, however, the number of potential respondents is so large that only a small number of them can be included.

Sampling Selecting appropriate respondents for research.

Sampling from among all the potential respondents is therefore essential, but it is fraught with risk. How can we tell that the people being asked their opinions are the same in most essential aspects as the people who have not been asked? Such problems are susceptible to statistical analysis. At its most basic level, we can be fairly sure that if we ask one person's opinion the answers are unlikely to be representative of the population as a whole, since people differ widely in their opinions: on the other hand, if we ask everybody then we know that the opinions will be absolutely accurate. It follows, therefore, that the larger the number of people whose opinions are included, the more reliable the results will be. In practice, reliable

Figure 5.7   Sampling

results can be obtained from relatively small samples, depending on the scale of the effect being measured: if the difference between two groups is large, the sample can be smaller, whereas if we are looking for subtle differences the sample size will need to be much larger.

Sampling types are shown in Tables 5.3 and 5.4. Table 5.3 shows probability samples, in which the inclusion or exclusion of respondents is largely a matter of chance, and therefore does not suffer from the bias of the interviewer. Non-probability sampling seeks to avoid the potential pitfalls of probability sampling by deliberately choosing the sample. There are three forms of non-probability sampling, as shown in Table 5.4.

A derivative of judgement sampling is the **Delphi** technique. Delphi uses a small sample of experts to give their opinions. Initially, each expert is asked to give an

Delphi A system of research under which opinions are sought iteratively from experts.

Table 5.3   Types of probability sample

Type of sample	Description	Advantages and disadvantages
Simple random sample	All members of the population have an equal chance of being included.	Will provide a good cross-section of individuals, but in practice it is extremely difficult to achieve true randomness. Often an apparently random approach is biased because we do not have a complete list of every member of the population. The major difficulty is that some people will refuse to participate in research, and are therefore left out of the study – which means the sample is no longer random.
Random walk sampling	Respondents are chosen on the basis of a 'random walk' around the area. Interviewers are given a route chosen at random and told to question (for example) every tenth household.	This method is simple to administer, but is not truly random.
Stratified random sample	The population is divided into mutually exclusive groups (for example by income or age) and interviewers are instructed to take a random sample from within each group.	This ensures that each group is represented in the final sample, for example to ensure that minority groups are adequately represented, but again is not truly random and is subject to errors in deciding what the stratifications should be.
Cluster sample	Clusters are chosen using a range of measures – geographical, income, age (for example). Individuals within the clusters are chosen at random.	Useful in cases where the population being studied is very large. Again, this method is not truly random, but does produce a representative sample.
Systematic sampling	Sampling units are chosen from the sampling frame at a uniform rate. For example, a business directory might be used, and every tenth firm sampled from it. In order to maintain randomness, the start point should be chosen at random, so if choosing every tenth respondent the start point should be a number between one and nine.	Again, this method works well for large populations. Care needs to be taken to ensure that the list of respondents being used is not affected by number – if companies are grouped in tens in some way, the sample will be seriously biased, for example.

Table 5.4   Non-probability sampling

Sample type	Description	Advantages and disadvantages
Quota sampling	The researcher starts with the knowledge of how the population is divided, and instructs the interviewers to obtain data from a set number of representatives from each group.	The sample will be representative, provided the researcher really does know the structure of the population. Unfortunately, it is easy to make errors and miss out important factors.
Convenience sampling	A convenience sample has no sample design. The researcher simply interviews anyone who is available.	This method wins quick results, and often gives as good an outcome as a complex sampling method. Convenience samples often happen by accident when the researcher is actually trying to obtain a random sample, but has a high number of people who refuse to participate.
Judgement sampling	The researcher selects a group of people who are believed (for whatever reason) to have opinions that are representative of the population at large.	Judgement samples obviously rely on good judgement on the part of the researcher. If he or she is wrong about the representativeness of the group chosen, the results will be seriously biased: on the other hand, judgement samples often give excellent results simply because they do include the people whose opinions count.

Quota sampling Selecting respondents according to a set of prearranged parameters.

Convenience sampling Selecting respondents by availability, without regard to the characteristics of the respondents.

Judgement sampling Selecting respondents according to criteria established by the researcher.

Bias Errors in research results caused by failures in the research design or sampling method.

opinion on a given topic, then the opinions are consolidated into a report which is circulated to the participants for further comment. The comments are then also consolidated and circulated, until either a consensus is reached or the experts agree to differ. Delphi is a widely used method for obtaining usable opinions from a small group of people – it does not work well for larger groups, because the range of opinions becomes too unwieldy.

Sampling **bias** accounts for much of the inaccuracy in market research. Researchers often think they have taken a representative sample when in fact they have not, and often researchers are fooled into thinking that a large sample is a substitute for a representative sample. Statistical tools exist to help decide whether the sample was big enough, but there are no tools that can check on a researcher's judgement, good or otherwise.

Real-life marketing: Sports Council for Wales

Getting the sampling wrong can really mess up your research – as can the idea that you can 'knock up a little questionnaire'. When the Sports Council for Wales wanted to investigate sports participation in the principality, it set up a simple survey. Interviewers stood outside the sports centres and stopped people at random, asking them how often they participated in sport, which sports they enjoyed most, and so forth. The Sports Council were amazed to find that a huge proportion of the respondents stated that they were frequent, enthusiastic participators in all kinds of sport. In fact, the reported results showed that participation in sport exceeded the capacity of the facilities available, if the results were projected across the population of Wales.

When the Sports Council called in a professional marketing research agency to explain the problem, the answer was obvious. By conducting the survey outside the sports centres the interviewers had picked up a large number of people who were either on their way in or on their way out of the sports centres. The sample was so biased the survey was effectively useless, and had to be conducted again from scratch.

If you're doing this kind of research, ask yourself the following questions:

- Does everybody in your target group have an equal chance of being included in the survey? Probably not – so what are you going to do about it?
- Does the sample you have collected look like a microcosm of the world? Check against an independent source, such as the national census, for this.
- Do the results look silly? If they do, you may have a bad sample.
- Are your interviewers being entirely honest with you? How do you know?

Errors in sampling also occur because of non-response. Often people refuse to participate, which means that the researcher is forced to assume that people who do not participate are the same in all important respects as those who do participate. This is a considerable leap of faith – people who participate may have more time to spare, may be more likely to want to please the interviewer, or may simply be more interested in the subject matter of the research.

Think outside this box!

There seem to be so many sources of bias in sampling, we might wonder whether any research is reliable. What we cheerfully think is a random sample turns out to be non-random, and we might only find this out when we come to analyse the results, after spending thousands of pounds paying people to stand on street corners questioning passers-by.

Not to mention the non-response problem, and the false-response problem. Opinion polls taken at the time of general elections have proved to be unreliable simply because people lie to the researchers about which way they intend to vote.

So should we just stop invading people's privacy in this way? After all, a nosy question deserves a short answer. On the other hand, understanding the market better means that we can plan products better, which should lead to a better life for everybody. Perhaps responding to marketing research should be made compulsory!

QUESTIONNAIRE DESIGN

Questionnaires might be intended for self-completion, that is, without the researcher being present, or for completion as part of a survey in which the researcher asks the questions and fills in the answers. Self-completion questionnaires are used if the respondents are geographically separated, or if the researcher is concerned that respondents might be influenced by the presence of the researcher and give inaccurate answers. They are also often used if the survey is to be conducted using a very large sample of respondents: an interviewer survey involving several thousand people would be too time-consuming to undertake.

The major drawback of self-completion questionnaires is that there is little or no control over the respondent (who can lie much more easily when completing a questionnaire than when answering questions from another person), there is no control over who actually fills in the questionnaire (in the case of B2B research a personal assistant might fill in the form rather than the executive it is aimed at), and the response rate tends to be very low, of the order of a few per cent in many cases. This means that the researcher may be in the position of assuming that the non-respondents are the same as the respondents, at least as far as any relevant characteristics are concerned. This is not always the case – for example, consider the lower literacy levels currently prevailing in many countries. Many people rarely read or write anything, and therefore are unlikely to complete the questionnaire: the fact that they are only semi-literate may well be a relevant factor in the research.

Researchers often use the total design method, first outlined by Dillman in 1978. This has the following stages:

1. Identify aspects of the survey process affecting quantity or quality and design them for the best response.
2. Develop an administrative survey plan to accomplish the survey in complete detail.
3. Reward the respondents: this can take the form of positive regard, written appreciation, using a consultative approach, supporting his or her values, offering a tangible reward, or even just providing an interesting questionnaire.
4. Reduce the costs to the respondent. This means making the task appear brief, reducing the effort required, eliminating embarrassing questions, eliminating subordination, and eliminating any monetary costs.
5. Establish trust with the respondent. Provide a token of appreciation in advance, identify with a known and reputable organisation, and build on other exchange relationships.

Following a total design approach will greatly increase the response rate, though of course care must be taken not to compromise the research merely in order to win a large number of respondents.

	Large numbers of respondents	**Relatively small numbers of respondents**
High risk of interviewer bias	Self-completion questionnaires	Self-completion questionnaires
Interviewer bias not regarded as an important risk	Telephone surveys	Face-to-face interviewer surveys

Figure 5.8 Factors indicating appropriateness of questionnaire delivery methods

Self-completion surveys are often used by restaurants and hotels to obtain feed-back from customers. Most people are reluctant to complain in hotels and restaurants unless there is something seriously wrong, or the problem is one that can easily be put right. Self-completion questionnaires left on tables or in rooms can allow people to comment in a non-threatening way, and can also direct people's attention to the areas the firm is trying to improve. The drawback to this type of survey is that the respondents are self-selecting – only those who have a complaint or are highly delighted are likely to take the time to fill in the questionnaire, so a quantitative analysis of the responses is likely to be of little use. Incidentally, some marketers regard anything less than a 'highly satisfied' score on these cards as a criticism that should be dealt with as if it were a complaint.

Surveys where the researcher is present have the advantage that the researcher can probe for answers if the respondent is unclear, and can also explain any ambiguities in the questions. They have the drawback that the researcher's body language or manner of speech might encourage the respondent in a particular direction, thus biasing the results of the survey, and they are much more labour-intensive than postal surveys and therefore much more expensive.

Marketing in a changing world: Paid respondents

It used to be the case that people would be fairly happy to co-operate with market researchers. Maybe people had more time, or maybe they were simply happy to discuss their opinions about things – but times have changed.

People are very much aware of the value of information – after all we read about it all the time, and people are well-educated and marketing-savvy. A whole industry has grown up around this, whereby people are paid to respond to market research questionnaires, getting as much as £5 a time for completing them. This obviously adds to the cost of carrying out surveys, but there are advantages – for one thing, it is possible to choose respondents carefully so as to obtain a representative sample. For another thing, people are more likely to be honest in their responses, since they have a certain moral obligation to do so and would probably not want to be dropped from the panel for lying. Also, people will actually respond fully, not get halfway through the questionnaire and give up, or leave out questions they don't want to answer.

When dealing with the modern, perhaps more materialistic, world paying respondents is likely to become the norm.

Telephone surveys occupy a half-way point between street surveys and self-completion questionnaires. Telephoning individuals and asking a series of questions has the advantage of being quick and relatively cheap, while ensuring that the right person is contacted and any ambiguous questions can be explained. The main drawback is that many people find it intrusive and will not respond, or respond with false answers in order to sabotage the research. A further problem is that many people now do not have landline telephones at all, relying on cell phones, for which there is no easily accessible national directory. These people are effectively excluded from any telephone survey, which may bias the results. This is not a problem when dealing with most business surveys, but may be in cases where (for example) salespeople form the target group of respondents.

Real-life marketing: SurveyMonkey

For small firms, the cost of carrying out market research can be prohibitive. Also, analysing quantitative research is not all that straightforward: simply totting up who said what isn't going to tell you anything, you need to run cross-tabulations and statistical tests to ensure that what you are being told is reliable.

Help is at hand. SurveyMonkey is an on-line survey design system which allows you to create and run a survey questionnaire. You can set up a survey using pre-prepared questionnaire templates, choosing from more than 20 different types of question. The surveys are run on-line, so all you need to do is recruit your respondents and let them fill in the survey in their own time.

Simple surveys can be conducted for free, but larger or more complex ones need to be paid for. The software automatically runs the analysis, so you get the results back very quickly: if you're running a service business like a hairdressing salon or a hotel you can set up a computer and get people to fill in the survey while they are waiting. Surveys can be made engaging and fun to do, as well.

If you're using SurveyMonkey or any similar service, you need to be aware of the following:

- Because the survey is conducted on-line, you can't always be sure that the person filling in the form is actually the respondent you want.
- You still have to write the questions yourself – and that is not easy!
- Always pilot any survey first – you will almost always pick up something that you have done wrong in the design or the sampling.
- Get the design right and the results will follow.
- Not everybody is comfortable on-line – make sure that isn't going to bias your results.
- The bigger the sample, the more reliable (as a general rule). Around 200 respondents is probably right for most purposes.

Designing questionnaires is by no means easy. The first stage is to ensure that the problem to be tackled is clearly defined: it is all too easy to ask questions that are not relevant, and either over-extend the questionnaire so that respondents will not complete it, or create problems when it comes to analysing the results. On the other hand, leaving out questions that are relevant may result in incomplete and misleading results.

The questionnaire needs to be structured in three main parts: the introduction, the body of the questionnaire and the demographic or basic data about the respondent. The introduction explains what the questionnaire is about, how the information will be used, and what the researcher's policy is on confidentiality (usually a reassurance that the results will not be disclosed to a third party). This introduction should be brief and to the point: it should also seek to persuade the respondent to complete the questionnaire.

The body of the questionnaire should address the issues that the researcher is interested in. These are the basic questions for which the research was designed. The final part of the questionnaire should be about the respondents themselves: in the case of consumer surveys, these may be demographic questions (age, gender, income level, and so forth) or in an industrial survey they may be questions about the firm, its turnover, the business it is in, number of employees, and so forth. These questions are intended to allow the researcher to analyse the data according to respondent type. These questions are usually put at the end of the questionnaire because they are generally considered to be sensitive: the received wisdom is that people are more likely to complete these questions when they have already invested some time in answering the earlier questions.

The questions themselves need to have the following characteristics:

1. They should address the problem itself.
2. They should not be leading questions, in other words they should not favour one answer over another or give any clue as to what the researcher wants to hear.
3. They should be broad enough to accommodate a range of opinions, but narrow enough to be easy to analyse.
4. Each question should be discrete, i.e. it should not require more than one answer.

The entire questionnaire should, of course, be written in simple and unambiguous language. Jargon, slang and unusual idioms should be avoided, and any terminology that might be offensive or incomprehensible to possible respondents should not be used.

The following checklist is a useful way of ensuring that the questions are appropriate.

1. Is the question necessary? If the question does not address the research problem, it should be removed.
2. Will the respondents understand the question? Questions may address areas that are not within the respondent's experience, or may be phrased in such a way that respondents cannot grasp the underlying concept.
3. Does the respondent have the necessary information to answer the question? For example, asking the chief buyer of a firm what the firm's annual expenditure is on salaries may not produce any answer. The respondent's memory may not be good enough ('how many chocolate bars did you buy last year?' is unlikely to be answered accurately), or the respondent may not have the necessary language skills to be able to formulate an answer.
4. Is the respondent willing to answer the question? Some questions are embarrassing or may seem intrusive: for example, people typically overstate their incomes on questionnaires rather than lose face by stating their true incomes. Respondents might be persuaded by a statement to the effect that an honest answer is essential to the accuracy of the research, but in many cases these questions can be removed or substituted without affecting the research adversely.

Closed questions Enquiries to which there will be only a small range of possible answers, usually yes or no.

Open questions Enquiries to which there might be a wide range of possible answers.

Dichotomous question An inquiry that can only be answered 'yes' or 'no'.

Negative questions ('Don't you think that …') are confusing and are likely to lead to biased answers. Hypothetical questions can also lead to hypothetical answers, although there are circumstances where they can help overcome embarrassment.

Questionnaires usually use **closed questions**, where the answer is already reduced to only a few choices. This is because it is difficult to analyse **open questions**. For example, if a respondent is asked 'On average, how often do you shop in the city centre?' the question might have any number of answers. If the question is followed by a list such as 'Every day, once a week, once a month, once a year, less often' the responses will be categorised in a way that allows for easy analysis. A **dichotomous**

question is one in which the answer can be only yes or no, which is of course the easiest type to analyse.

A problem in designing any research instrument is that respondents do not always reply accurately. For example, there is evidence that the fact that people are being surveyed affects their intentions to buy: the correlation between latent intention and subsequent purchase behaviour is 58% greater among surveyed consumers than it is among non-surveyed consumers (Chandon et al. 2005).

PROJECTIVE TECHNIQUES

Projective technique A research method that invites respondents to say what they think another person might answer to a specific question or problem.

Overcoming embarrassment in questionnaires can be difficult. For example, asking people about their sexual orientation, personal hygiene purchases, attitudes towards their employer, or racial attitudes is likely to lead to inaccurate responses. **Projective techniques** can help to overcome this problem by asking people to respond as if they were someone else. At least in theory, the individuals respond with their own attitude, since they are unlikely to have a very clear knowledge of what other people's attitudes are.

Think outside this box!

If people are embarrassed or made to feel uncomfortable when answering questions, why are we asking the questions at all? It's not a very nice way to make a living, and in any case a snoopy question deserves a lying answer! If people are uncomfortable with the questions, they are likely to give false answers – which doesn't help anybody.

On the other hand, maybe that's what a projective technique is all about. Making people feel more comfortable about helping with the research – which is ultimately going to benefit them anyway, if it means that we can met their needs better.

For example, someone might be asked what they think their work colleagues think about the boss, or what the average person thinks about people from another ethnic group. These questions might be asked in a fairly direct manner, or respondents might be asked to complete a sentence or say what a cartoon character might be saying. Projective techniques are useful, but often result in data that are difficult to analyse. As a way of reaching hidden attitudes, they are often the only option, however.

For example, in Figure 5.9, the character on the left is expressing an opinion which may not be one that everyone would be prepared to admit to in public (more controversial topics might include racism, sexual preferences or drug-taking). The respondent is invited to write in the response they would expect the other character to make to this statement. Responses might differ according to whether the respondent is told that the other character is male or female, and one might expect some differences in the answers given by men as opposed to women. There would also be differences if respondents were asked what the second character might be thinking, rather than what the character is saying.

ANALYSING QUESTIONNAIRES

Data, in themselves, do not provide answers: they must first be analysed. The questionnaire should be designed so that the answers can easily be entered into a computer and totalled, but totalling does not equal analysis either.

Figure 5.9 Thematic apperception test

For example, a survey of 6000 adults might show that 34% of them regularly shop in out-of-town stores. This is vaguely interesting, but is not as useful as breaking down the sample according to demographic data. This might tell us that 74% of people aged between 50 and 60 shop in out-of-town stores, and since this group are likely to be the wealthiest members of society we now have something more important to go on. If we could also say that people with household incomes in excess of £50,000 a year shop in out-of-town stores, we have something very useful. This type of cross-tabulation is basic to analysis.

Researchers also need to be confident that the analysis is meaningful, and that the differences between different groups of respondents are real, and not just the result of a chance combination. There are several ways of checking this using statistical tools that calculate the size of the difference between the groups, the overall sample size, and the size of the group concerned. In general, the larger the sample size the more accurate the findings are likely to be. Table 5.5 shows the commonest methods for establishing statistical significance.

Table 5.5 Measures of statistical significance

Measure	Explanation
Student's t-test	Invented by a mathematician whose pen-name was The Student, this test measures the probability that an observed difference between two groups is the result of chance. It returns a percentage called a confidence interval (CI): if this is (say) 95%, the test says that the researcher can be 95% confident that the difference is real, and not the result of a sampling error.
Mann–Whitney U test	This compares two groups where the data are ordinal, i.e. expressed as rankings.
Wilcoxon or Signed Rank test	This is used where two matching samples are being compared using ordinal data.
Kruskal–Wallis test	Compares more than two independent samples using ordinal data.
Chi-square test	Used in checking whether cross-tabulated data are statistically significant, in other words if data that are distinguished by more than one variable show differences that are unlikely to have occurred by chance.

Having analysed the questionnaire, the researcher needs to consider interpreting the results. Interpretation means explaining what the results mean – it includes explaining why the results might have come about, what they say about respondents, and examining all the possible implications for the management of the firm. Interpretation is largely a matter of judgement, and different researchers might interpret the same data in different ways. For example, a finding that young people tend to live in small houses or apartments is probably a reflection of their incomes rather than a preference for small houses. It may also indicate their childless state, or even a low number of possessions and therefore a lower requirement for space. Questionnaires are not generally good for finding out definitive answers to this type of question, so researchers need to consider carefully what the answers actually mean. An alternative is to use qualitative research to back up the findings.

Questionnaire-based research has been criticised in other ways. Filling in questionnaires is a specific type of behaviour that has rules of its own: in order to understand consumers' responses to questionnaires, we may need to understand their behaviour towards the questionnaire itself (Grunert 2003). Also, Wefeld (2003) has criticised questionnaire surveys for the following reasons:

1. There is insufficient emphasis on external validity.
2. There is an implicit belief in the rationality of consumers which is not borne out in the real world.
3. Samples are often not representative due to high refusal rates.
4. Distortion and bias creep in because respondents will often give an answer rather than appear ignorant.

Think outside this box!

If questionnaires are so poor as a research instrument, why use them at all? After all, they are difficult to design, time-consuming to administer, and you need a degree in mathematics to interpret the results.

On the other hand, they do give a broad view of the opinions and behaviour of a lot of people at once. It would take years to run depth interviews with the thousands of people some questionnaire surveys deal with – and by that time the data would be no use anyway!

Observation and experiment

One of the drawbacks of questionnaire research is that it relies on self-reports, i.e. people are being asked to report on their own behaviour and attitudes. This may not give accurate results for the following reasons:

1. People often cannot remember what their behaviour has been. For example, someone who is asked how many times they have bought a specific brand of biscuits this year is unlikely to remember accurately: and even a frequent-flying businessman may not remember how many flights he has taken in any given year.
2. People may be reluctant to admit to their behaviour. A heavy drinker who is asked about his or her alcohol intake is very likely to understate the amount, due to embarrassment or fear of being criticised.

3. If asked about their future behaviour, people may honestly provide an answer that they believe in but subsequent events prevent them from carrying out the proposed action. Future purchase intentions are notoriously inaccurate: an individual may intend to buy (for example) a new washing machine but in the event not have the money to do so.

Observing people's actual behaviour as it happens overcomes these problems. Three conditions exist for successful observation. First, the things to be researched must be observable. Attitudes, motives, emotions and so forth cannot be researched by observing behaviour. Second, the event must occur frequently or be predictable. Observing house purchases is unlikely to be very rewarding, although observing people's behaviour when they view properties might be feasible by accompanying the estate agent to viewings. Third, the event must be completed over a short period of time.

There are of course exceptions. **Longitudinal studies** (studies carried out over a long period of time) have been carried out by observation – for example, Piaget's famous experiments and observation of child development – but in most cases lengthy observations are difficult or impossible to carry out.

Observation needs to be carried out as far as possible without the knowledge of the people being observed. This can raise ethical problems regarding privacy – for example, there would be no ethical problem in counting how many people enter a shopping mall, but there may be a problem in following people around to see where (and if) they shop, and there would certainly be an ethical problem attached to observing known individuals (e.g. people selected as part of a sampling process) without their knowledge. On the other hand, people typically act differently if they know they are being observed, which will affect the results. There is more on ethics in Chapter 10.

When setting up an observation, the observers need to be briefed carefully. In the case of an unstructured observation, the observers need to note everything and draw

> **Longitudinal study** Research that is carried out over a lengthy time period.

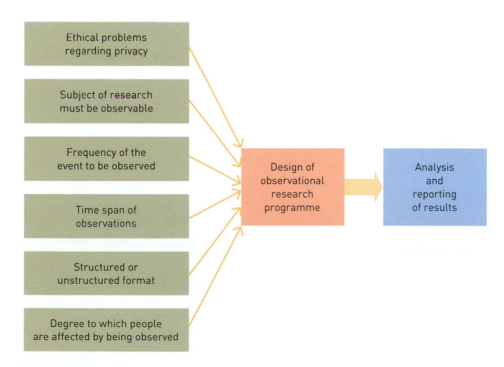

Figure 5.10 Issues in carrying out observations

conclusions: unstructured observations work in much the same way as unstructured interviews or focus groups, in which the researcher does not know what might come of the research exercise. In the case of a **structured observation**, the observer is told what to look for, and is given a checklist. Structured observations are most often used for hypothesis testing, i.e. in situations where the researcher has a clear idea of what to look for.

Structured observation A marketing research technique that involves directly watching consumer behaviour.

Real-life marketing: Fisher–Price

Researching children is always difficult, especially if they are of pre-school age. They can't fill in a questionnaire or join a focus group panel, after all, so observation is an important way of researching their likes and dislikes.

Fisher–Price is a subsidiary of Mattel, the world's largest toy manufacturer. At the company's headquarters in Chicago there is a free crèche for pre-school children, and (of course) the toys are all made by Fisher–Price. What the toddlers neither know nor care about is that they are being observed by researchers all the time – how they play with the toys, which ones are the favourites, which ones become boring after a few minutes, which ones are worth fighting over, and so forth. This observational research is invaluable to the company in developing new toys.

You can use this idea in other contexts – watch how people behave in a coffee shop, for example, or how people interact with the waiters in a restaurant. If you're going to try this yourself, you should keep the following in mind:

- People sometimes behave differently when they are being watched.
- You can video people, but only if they know you're doing it – if you have a sign up saying that the premises are under video surveillance, that should put you in the clear.
- Get somebody else to observe as well – interpreting behaviour is a matter of judgement, you may find other people interpret things differently.
- Make notes as you go along, and if you have a video recording play it through a few times to check that you really did see what you thought you saw.
- Get a book on body language. It will help a lot!

Unstructured observations are often video-recorded to allow for more careful analysis of (for example) body language, but structured observations can often be carried out using a tick sheet.

A common type of observation used in retail environments is to use '**mystery shoppers**'. These are observers who pretend to be ordinary customers, and who take note of such issues as staff courtesy, store layouts and cleanliness, store traffic and so forth. In some cases the retailer sends the mystery shopper to the company's own stores in order to check that management and staff are doing their jobs effectively, but more often the mystery shoppers are sent to competitors' shops in order to pick up useful ideas from the competition.

Mystery shoppers A marketing research technique whereby the researcher pretends to be a customer.

EXPERIMENTS

In order to meet all three of the conditions for observation outlined above (observability, frequency and short-term completion), researchers may conduct an **experiment**. This enables the observation to happen under controlled conditions. In general, the subjects of experiments are well aware that they are part of a research study, but it is possible to conduct experiments without the subject being aware of the exact nature of the experiment. In recent years this type of experiment has sometimes been seen as unethical, however – there is a view that subjects should be willing, informed participants. For example, a retailer might want to find out whether customers are dishonest or not, and arrange for cashiers to give each customer slightly too much change. Observers could then see which customers return the excess change and which do not. There would certainly be an ethical problem with this type of research, because it involves setting a trap for the customers. Some customers might simply not have checked their change, but would be listed on the research as being dishonest – clearly an unfair description.

Experiment A research technique in which a controlled situation is used to determine consumer response to a given stimulus.

Experiments should have three components: first, the subject of the experiment, sometimes called the **dependent variable** or the test unit; second, the change that is imposed on the subject, also called the **independent variable**; and third, the results that relate to the change introduced by the independent variable, also called the outcome or observation.

Dependent variable The stimulus that is applied to generate a response.

Independent variable The response resulting from a dependent variable.

In an experiment the researcher manipulates selected independent variables and measures the effect of these manipulations on the dependent variables (Proctor 2005). This means that the researcher will observe what happens under one set of circumstances, then change one of the circumstances and see what the effect is on the outcomes. For example, a researcher wanting to test which of two instruction manuals is the clearer for the assembly of a piece of furniture might give a copy of each to two separate individuals and observe how quickly each can assemble the furniture. Carrying out this experiment with a number of people would give a clear idea of which wording is the most effective, and where the problems might arise.

Experiments (and indeed all research) should have both internal and external validity. **Internally valid** experiments are those in which the independent variable is solely accountable for the changes observed in the dependent variable – in other words, the change the researcher introduced accounts for the change in the subject of the experiment. This is by no means certain: sometimes other factors will creep

Internal validity A condition where a research exercise provides evidence that supports what the exercise was intended to discover.

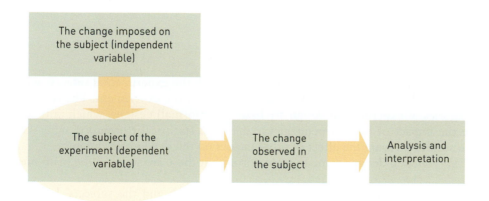

Figure 5.11 Components of experiments

in (or are already present) and the results become invalid. For example, in the experiment described above the experimenter might believe that it is the wording of the instructions which generates the difference between the two groups, whereas in fact the different wordings have caused the printer to re-arrange the diagrams into a more easily-understood format in one instruction leaflet. Thus it would be the change in the diagrams, and not in the wording, which accounts for the differences.

External validity A condition where a research exercise would generate the same results if it were repeated elsewhere.

External validity refers to the generalisability of the results, in other words whether the experiment's outcomes will work out under real-world conditions. Sometimes experiments are carried out under such carefully controlled conditions (in an attempt to ensure internal validity) that the results do not apply in the real world, when other factors are present. The problem for the researcher is that internal validity is best ensured by conducting the experiment under laboratory conditions, whereas external validity is best assured by conducting the experiment under field conditions. In some cases the research is conducted under both conditions in an attempt to ensure both internal and external validity.

Outside factors that may affect the validity of the experiment include the following:

1. Repeated testing. If the experiment is conducted with the same group of participants over and over again, the participants become used to the research method, and learn too much about the research topic to be able to react in the same way as someone would who was new to the research.
2. Interviewer bias. Sometimes the personality of the researchers will affect the outcomes because the research participants respond differently to different people.
3. Maturation. If research is being conducted over a period of time, the participants mature or change. These changes may easily be mistaken for effects of the research.
4. History. Current events outside the laboratory can affect the way participants behave. For example, research on responsiveness to advertising for cars would be affected by a large increase in the cost of fuel, or by a new tax on large cars.

Mortality The tendency for respondents to disappear over time.

5. **Mortality**. Over a period of time, participants drop out of the research, sometimes through actually dying, but more often through boredom, change of circumstances, or simply becoming too busy to participate.
6. Selection errors. Like other sampling errors, selection of the wrong participants will affect the research outcomes adversely.

Regression effect The tendency for extremes to move towards the middle in longitudinal studies.

7. **Regression effects**. If the subjects for the experiment are chosen on the basis of a test (for example, a personality test), those at the extremes will often tend (over time) to move towards the middle. This is in part due to maturation and history effects.

These factors tend to cause errors, but can often be overcome (controlled) by using an appropriate experimental design.

EXPERIMENTAL DESIGNS

The experimental design defines the way in which the experimental subjects will be treated, and the ways of measuring the outcomes of the experiment. The two broad categories of experimental design are basic (or informal) designs, which only measure the impact of the independent variable, and statistical (formal) designs which also seek to measure the effect of other factors on the dependent variable.

Experimental designs come in many forms, but these are some of the main ones:

1. After-only design. Here the stimulus is applied, and the subjects' behaviour afterwards is measured. This design does not examine the subjects' behaviour beforehand, so it is difficult to know whether the change of behaviour came about as a result of the stimulus, or whether it would have happened anyway. In some cases this may not matter – for example, a marketer might place

money-off coupons in different newspapers, and measure which newspaper returned the most coupon redemptions.

2. Before–after without control. Here the researcher measures the subjects' behaviour, applies the stimulus, then re-measures the behaviour to see whether there has been a change. For example, sales for a given period might be recorded, then a sales promotion put in place, and sales after the period measured. Clearly the problem with this design is that part of the change might have come from some other factor unconnected with the promotion. Other factors might have increased (or reduced) sales, so that the researcher ends up either overstating or understating the effect of the promotion.

3. Before–after with control. In this design, the researcher applies the stimulus to one group and not to another so that most outside factors can be compensated for. For example, a company might record sales from two comparable parts of the country, apply the sales promotion in only one part, and see whether the change in the area where the promotion was offered is greater than the change in the area where the promotion was not offered.

4. After-only with control. In some cases, testing before applying the stimulus is difficult. For example, if an advertising agency wants to test the effectiveness of an advertisement for chocolate bars, the fact of questioning people about their chocolate-eating behaviour will sensitise them to the advertisement and their responses will not be spontaneous. With an after-only experimental design, the advertisement could be shown to one group (preferably buried among a group of advertisements for other products), then both groups can be questioned about their chocolate-buying intentions. Any differences should be due to the advertisement, provided the groups are well matched.

5. Ex-post-facto design. Here the groups are selected after the stimulus has been applied. For example, a market researcher might conduct a street survey in which people are asked whether they have seen a particular advertisement. Those who have seen the advert become the experimental group, while those who have not become the control group. Differences between the groups should be due to the advertisement. In practice, this type of study is difficult to carry out well because people are often unable to remember what they have and have not seen – most advertising operates below the conscious level.

6. Four-group six-study design. This design was pioneered by Solomon during the Second World War as a way of testing the effects of training films on soldiers. The problem was that questioning soldiers prior to showing them the films made them pay more attention to the films: also, if they knew they were to be questioned afterwards, they paid more attention. Anecdotal evidence suggested that most of them, left to their own devices, slept through the films. Solomon's design involved selecting four similar groups of soldiers. One group was tested before the film and not afterwards, one group was tested afterwards, one group was tested both before and after, and one group was tested twice without being shown the film. In this way, it was possible to check what the effects were of being tested before the film, being tested after the film, and of being tested more than once. This allowed Solomon to calculate the effect of the film, with the effects of the experiment 'tuned out'.

7. **Time series** design. This design assumes that the researcher will have access to the same group of people for a long period of time, and that the testing itself will not affect the outcome. For example, a market research company might recruit a panel, perhaps of several thousand people, who record their purchases (or their TV viewing, or their leisure time activities, as appropriate) over a long period. Stimuli such as sales promotions, advertising, special offers and so forth may be offered during this period, and the effects measured on the group as a whole. Because of the long time-scales involved, and the participatory nature of the exercise, effects arising from history, maturation and regression tend to be minimised.

Time series Analysis that shows how the situation has progressed over a period, carried out in order to predict likely future trends.

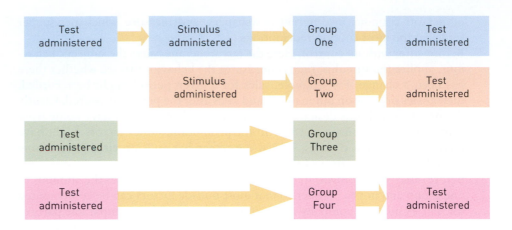

Figure 5.12   Four-group six-study design

STATISTICAL DESIGNS

These designs use statistical techniques to assess the outcomes of the experiment. Statistical tools can be used to analyse the variance between the experimental groups and determine which of the changes come from the intended stimulus and which from extraneous factors.

A randomised design means that the stimulus is applied to participants (subjects) on a completely random basis. This should spread the effects of any other influences so as to ensure that any changes are the results of the stimulus, not of accidental influences.

Randomised block design is used when the researcher suspects that another major influence might affect the results. For example, leading up to Christmas 2003, exceptionally mild weather in the UK affected people's Christmas expenditure: it took longer for people to get into the Christmas spirit, and as a result some retailers panicked and slashed their prices (and profits) in order to clear Christmas stocks quickly. Unseasonable weather can be a major influence on behaviour and outcomes. For example, cutting prices might increase sales, but so might any one of a large number of factors. To allow for unseasonable weather, the researcher might run random tests across blocks of time – one in the spring, one in the summer, one in the winter, and so forth. Differences between the blocks might relate to the seasonal weather.

Latin square design allows researchers to isolate two major external influences. Each influence is laid out on one or other axis of a square and the variables entered in the boxes. The main problem with the Latin square is that it is expensive and complex to analyse. In circumstances where the cost is not a major consideration, and where the situation faced by the researcher is also complex, it can be well worth conducting a Latin square design.

Factorial design is used when the researcher suspects that some of the factors may also act on each other. A factorial design is likely to be of the same general type as a Latin square or randomised block study, but it uses more complex variance analysis to analyse the results.

The main problem with experiments in general is that they are undertaken under artificial conditions, with many of the possible influences deliberately left out in order to ensure validity. This means that the applicability of the results in the real world is limited – often the results are not generalisable to reality. One type of experiment that avoids these problems is test-marketing, in which the product is offered within a limited geographical area for a period of time to see how acceptable it is to the potential customers.

	Influence One		
	Variable One	Variable Two	Variable Three
Influence Two	Variable Two	Variable Three	Variable One
	Variable Three	Variable One	Variable Two

Figure 5.13 Latin square design

Test marketing certainly gives a clear idea of the product's acceptability under real conditions, but it has the drawback of alerting competitors to the existence of the product. Also, test marketing does not save the company the cost of developing the product and the marketing campaign – both of which are major elements in the cost of launching a new product. Thus test marketing has limited benefits in most cases. An exception might be in retailing, where a store chain could order a small amount of a product and sell it through one or two of its stores, rolling it out nationally at a later date if it is successful.

Analysing and interpreting quantitative data

Analysis is concerned with arranging the information in such a way that it acquires meaning. Interpretation is concerned with extracting usable recommendations from the data.

Analysis goes beyond simply listing the data. For example, a questionnaire survey may indicate that 20% of the respondents regularly buy the product, 35% occasionally buy it, and the remainder never buy it. The same questionnaire may show that 52% of the respondents are men, 48% are women, 10% are aged between 20 and 30, 23% aged between 31 and 40, 45% aged between 41 and 50, 18% aged between 51 and 60, and the remainder are over 60. Although this information is accurate and interesting, it does not mean much unless the researcher analyses it to show how many women aged 20–30 regularly buy the product, or how many people over 60 are occasional users. Also, it would appear that the sample is somewhat biased, since the age proportions do not correspond to those in the census. This means that the results of the analysis are likely to be inaccurate when taken as a whole, that is, if conclusions are drawn based on (say) gender.

The first step in analysis is to edit the data. This means removing any anomalous or inaccurate data. Obviously it does not mean removing data that do not agree with the researcher's preconceptions, but it does mean removing (for example) questionnaires where the respondent has obviously just ticked all the left-hand boxes in order to get the task out of the way (or, worse, to sabotage the research). The intention is to eliminate errors, which come either from mistakes made by the interviewer or from mistakes or untrue statements from the respondents.

In some cases, computers can be used to detect inconsistencies. For example, if a respondent has indicated that he or she never uses a product, but then goes on

Please read the statements below, then place a tick in the column which most closely matches your attitude to the statement. Tick Column One if you agree strongly with the statement, Column Two if you agree, and so forth with Column Five indicating that you disagree strongly with the statement.	1	2	3	4	5	Office use only
People who drive four-wheel-drive vehicles are selfish.	/					1
People should consider others when they choose a new car.	/					1
Cars are an essential part of modern life.		/				2
Cars are a luxury.					/	5
Cars are responsible for much of the high standard of living we enjoy.		/				2
Cars should be restricted in use because they damage the environment.				/		4
We should be seeking alternatives to car use.		/				2
People will never give up their cars.		/				2

Figure 5.14   Sample questionnaire

to discuss the product in some detail, there is clearly an error somewhere. If the questionnaire is being completed on-line, the computer can pick up this error as it is being made, and advise the respondent accordingly.

The next stage in analysis is to enter the data into a suitable software package. This allows responses to be grouped according to the answers given. Typically, questionnaires should have a coding frame in one of the margins. Answers can be numbered in the coding frame so that they become easier to enter into the computer for analysis. Figure 5.14 shows how this works in practice.

In Figure 5.14, the researcher has converted the answers into numbers, which are entered in the final column. This makes entering the data into a computer much easier, and less prone to mistakes (this is particularly true if the researcher has to enter several hundred responses into a computer, or if a number of people will be working on data entry).

The next stage is to create tables of data. It is not sufficient merely to total the answers to each question: the researcher will be looking for groups of respondents who tend to answer in the same way, so cross-tabulations will be necessary. For example, in the case of the questionnaire used in Figure 5.14, respondents who are strongly against four-wheel-drive (4x4) vehicles might be expected to answer the other questions differently from the way those in favour of 4x4s would answer. For a motor manufacturer, a breakdown of attitudes of each group to the other factors in the questionnaire would be a great deal more useful than simply knowing how many people like 4x4s and how many do not.

Finally, the data need to be interpreted in order to extract meaningful information. Interpreting data is an area that requires considerable judgement, plus a degree of objectivity. For example, an American newspaper reported that there were more African-Americans in jail than there were in college. In itself, this statistic is perfectly true: however, the same is true of Anglo-Saxon Americans. When the comparison is made between black prisoners of college age and black students, it turns out that there are half a million black students compared with 200,000 black prisoners of the

Table 5.6 Statistical tools

Statistical tool	Purpose
Analysis of variance	Measures the degree to which the results vary from each other.
Correlation analysis	Measures the degree to which one variable is affected by another.
Rank order correlation	Measures the degree to which different aspects of the data end up being put into the same order by respondents.
Regression analysis	Establishes the relationship between different factors in the data.
Multivariate analysis	Establishes the relationships between a large number of variables, stating which of the variables accounts for the greatest amount of the observed variation in the outcomes.
Cluster analysis	Identifies similar entities from among a group of characteristics shared by the entities.
Factor analysis	This group of techniques reduces the data and summarises these into a group of factors which account for the observed variance to a greater or lesser extent.
Conjoint analysis	This set of techniques analyses the degree to which a change in one variable affects changes in another variable.
Multidimensional scaling	MDS is aimed at producing a visual set of relationships between different attributes based on a set of scales.

same age – still a shocking statistic, but with rather different implications from the one reported earlier (Grapentine 2004a).

STATISTICAL ANALYSIS

A detailed account of all the techniques of statistical analysis which are available is beyond the scope of this chapter. Having said that, statistical tools are used to extract meaning from raw data, and to indicate the reliability of the data. Table 5.6 shows some of the statistical tools in current use.

These techniques (and many others) are available on computer software packages such as SPSS, Excel and Minitab.

Qualitative research

Although much marketing research is carried out through surveys, the drawbacks of survey research are such that many researchers are using qualitative techniques instead of, or as well as, quantitative methods.

Qualitative research cannot usually be expressed in numerical terms. Typically, qualitative research results in expressions of opinion, and is usually therefore verbal. Qualitative techniques include the following:

1. Open-ended interviews. Respondents are asked an open-ended question (for example, 'What do you think of Cornish pasties?') and are then encouraged to talk freely about the topic. The responses could range from a discussion of the flavour and nutritional value of Cornish pasties to a discussion of the history of Cornish tin-mining. The problem for the researcher lies in deciding whether

this is a digression or whether it is leading up to a relevant point – if the respondent is about to say something like 'The crusts had to be tough enough to survive being dropped down a mineshaft, so I never eat them' that would be relevant. A discussion of mine closures and consequent redundancies among miners probably would not.

2. Group discussions or focus groups. A group of people who have an interest in the subject or are typical of the expected target market are brought together and invited to discuss a particular topic. The advantage of a focus group is that members will often trigger ideas in each other, and thus develop a wider-ranging set of responses. In many cases, focus groups will be allowed to test prototypes or experience a promotion of some sort: these are called experiencing focus groups, and appear to work best if the group is given verbal information as well as experiencing the event (D'Astous and Kamou 2010).

3. Analysis of written documents. Respondents may be asked to write down their opinions on the topic under discussion. This has the advantage that they do not need to make statements directly to other people about subjects that may be embarrassing or otherwise hard to discuss. Other written documents (for example, letters of complaint) might be analysed as part of the secondary research carried out ahead of the primary research.

Qualitative data are useful for exploratory research. If the researcher has little or no idea which are the topics of importance within the research problem, a focus group or a series of depth interviews will reveal what questions to ask. The topics the respondents discuss most often will be the ones of importance, and questionnaire questions can be suitably framed to find out the extent to which the views of the group apply to the general population. In other words, qualitative research defines the dimensions of the problem, and quantitative research finds out the size of those dimensions. As shown in Figure 5.15, either method can help with answering research questions,

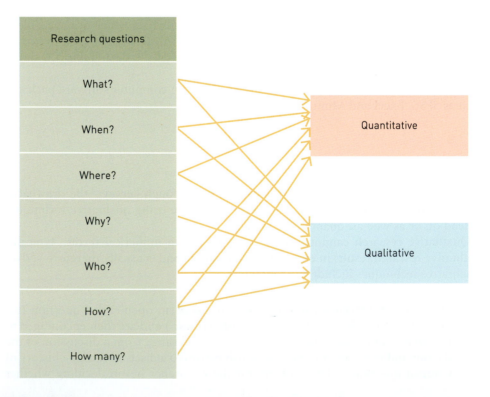

Figure 5.15   Qualitative versus quantitative research

but quantitative research cannot answer 'why' questions very easily, and qualitative research cannot answer 'how many' or 'how often' questions very easily.

Alternatively, qualitative research can be used after quantitative research as an aid to explaining the outcomes. A focus group might be briefed by telling them that '74% of people aged between 50 and 60 shop in out-of-town stores' before asking them 'Why do you think that might be?' If the focus group is drawn from that age group, they are very likely to be able to give some ideas as to why this behaviour occurs. In any event, they are more likely to be able to provide an answer than a 35-year-old researcher.

Focus groups are not without their problems, however. First, much focus group research is carried out with people who do not, in fact, form a group (Rook 2003). The groups are usually recruited as individuals, and may have met for the first time on the day of the discussion. Second, researchers often try to cover too much ground in a short period of time: perhaps because the research has been commissioned by an ambitious client, researchers may ask up to 40 direct questions of the group within an hour, which gives little time for discussion or reflection. Third, people often lie in focus groups: they may give socially acceptable answers in a group situation (especially when in the presence of a group of strangers), they may seek to please the researcher, there may be insufficient time to build trust, or they may give superficial replies about topics they have never considered and have little interest in (Zaltman 2003). Systems do exist to tell whether someone is lying in a focus group (Grapentine 2004b), but such systems are of little help against someone who is an accomplished liar.

Real-life marketing: Biasing respondents

Biasing respondents is easy when you're doing qualitative research.

The story goes that a radio station commissioned some focus group research to find out what people liked and disliked about the station. The researchers duly recruited a focus group, and decided that the group should be kept in the dark about who was paying for the research, in order to avoid biasing the results. They therefore planned to ask the group about radio stations in general, and three local FM stations in particular.

Unfortunately, on the day of the focus group interview two executives from the station turned up in reception, and in front of the waiting focus group members announced 'Hi. We're from the XYZ Radio station, we're here to observe the focus groups.' Not only had they given away the name of the commissioning company, but also the group members now knew who they were. The researchers had no choice but to pay off the focus group respondents and cancel the research – an expensive error for the radio station!

To avoid this type of scenario, follow these rules:

- Don't tell people who the research is for, unless you want them to voice their complaints very directly – in which case, you might as well just talk to your customer service people or your receptionist.
- Don't answer questions from respondents – always turn it round to ask them what they think. You already know what you think!
- Always check the transcripts for statements which seem to be 'political' from people who have an axe to grind.

Analysing qualitative data can be complex. It is possible to extract numerical results from these, but in general it would be meaningless to make statements such as '25% of respondents expressed doubt about the company's efficiency' since the sample sizes are usually too small for such a statement to have any significance.

How a researcher analyses the data will depend on the framework within which he or she is operating. A typical approach is to look for key words or phrases in transcripts of people's statements, as in Figure 5.16. The word 'quality' might be regarded as a key word, for example, and frequency counts of the word might give an indication of how important quality issues are to the respondents.

The key themes in the following transcript have been highlighted. This is an interview with a buyer for a major supermarket chain.

"Actually, people often think that the sales people and the buyers are enemies. We're not. We're more like, sort of, helping each other. We have to buy product, that's our job, I have to have product lines my customers want to buy. Reps come in here to sell their stuff, and OK they want to sell what they have to sell, but if it's any good and we can use it, sure I'll buy it. What I don't like is if they get pushy, because if my customers won't buy it then I don't want it. I'm really acting as a sort of agent for the consumers, they're the ones paying my salary, if I don't please them then that's me on my bike. On the other hand, if a rep can show me something we can sell, then that's good, I'm grateful, I'll take his arm off. I mean, we'll have to agree terms and so on, but why not? It's my job. Just like selling is his job. Sometimes they want to push it on merchandising – you know, shelf space, displays. OK, the more we sell the better, but I have other lines to fit in, I have to make them understand that, once they understand that then we can talk."

The key themes are:

1. Job/professional issues. (In red)
2. Controlling the process. (In green)
3. Roles. (In blue)

Obviously these categories are arbitrary, and depend on the researcher's judgement: equally, it is sometimes difficult to see which category a statement should go in. However, themes do emerge from this type of analysis.

Figure 5.16   Analysing qualitative data

Searching for key phrases might be more problematic, since respondents may express the same concept in different ways. Selecting key themes from an initial read-through of the data might generate a large number of themes which can then be reduced to a smaller number of related themes: a second read through the data would allow the researcher to assign each phrase in the transcripts to one or other of the themes and thus develop an overview of the areas that concern respondents. This allows the researcher to understand the dimensions of the problem.

Although computer programs can help take the tedium out of analysis, it is important to recognise that the interpretation of qualitative research is very much an intellectual task, and therefore falls to the researcher. Using a computer may seem to be more objective as a method of research analysis, but the bottom line is that the computer is controlled by the researcher, not the other way round.

Internet research

In recent years the Internet has become a widely used medium for conducting research. Qualitative research has been carried out using chat rooms to conduct virtual focus groups, and questionnaires have been e-mailed to existing customers. Automated survey websites such as SurveyMonkey.com have appeared, making it easy to carry out mass surveys on-line, and even to analyse the data automatically. Some websites include self-completion surveys, often offering prizes for completing the questionnaire.

Real-life marketing: Form a panel

If you need to carry out qualitative research frequently for whatever reason (for example, if you often introduce new products) you might want to consider having a permanent group of people who are prepared to respond at a moment's notice.

Insight Express is a consultancy specialising in on-line market research. Their approach is simple – they have a group of people who are prepared to comment on-line at any time on almost any subject. They are paid for doing so, so they are happy to respond and are likely to be fairly honest about it, too, not wishing to lose the job. Responses are very fast, and because it's on-line there's no need to make transcripts – responses can be analysed by computer fairly easily.

If you're doing this yourself, you should:

- Recruit a representative sample. Check their profiles against your target market, so that you have somebody from each of your customer types.
- Pay them. If you don't, they will soon get tired of responding to you, and will in any case just provide the briefest responses they can. Free product might work well for you.
- Feed back to them what you found out and how you used the information. This helps keep them involved, and in any case might result in more responses.
- Keep track of the membership profile – you might have to recruit new members as your customer base changes.

The advantage of carrying out research on the Internet is that it is extremely cheap in comparison with other methods, and it frequently results in a very high number of responses. This can, however, give a spurious credibility to the results. The percentage of respondents on the Internet is approximately 4%, which is low: the large number of respondents is due to the extremely large number of people who see the questionnaire (Grandcolas et al. 2003). The people who respond are extremely unlikely to be identical to the 96% who did not respond, although whether the differences are material to the research will depend on what is being researched. Grandcolas et al. (2003) surmised that non-respondents may have ignored the survey because of several possible reasons: they may be poor typists, or perhaps less Web-literate than respondents, or they may have less time, or may be using a dial-up connection for which they pay by the minute.

Sampling errors are considered to be the major cause of problems with Internet surveys (Ray 2003), since around 40% of households do not have Internet access. It is dangerous to assume that those who do not have Internet access are the same as those who do – they are likely to have lower incomes, be older, and be less well educated. A further sampling problem arises if respondents are rewarded: some people are suspicious of rewards, especially if being asked for personal information, while more materialistic people are prepared to volunteer information (Ward et al. 2005).

Chat rooms also have a self-selecting sample base, which can lead to bias. A virtual focus group can be conducted with a group selected by the researcher, simply by using e-mails in which the comments go to all members. This method is advantageous because all the comments are recorded and the transcript is, in effect, already made.

In designing Internet-based surveys, researchers need to be aware of some of the general issues surrounding website design. For example, screen colour affects people's willingness to wait for material to download (Gorn et al. 2004), so the wrong colour might lead to a higher refusal rate as potential respondents log off rather than wait (relaxing colours give the impression that the wait is longer than it actually is).

There is little doubt that using the Internet will revolutionise marketing research. Three main areas have been identified as being particularly susceptible to change: sampling, marketing stimulus presentation and reporting (Wyner 2003). Sampling becomes easier in some ways because of the huge number of potential respondents: it is possible to find quite large numbers of obscure types of individual if necessary. Stimuli can be presented visually, aurally or in writing on-line: although this is not as good as, for example, giving someone a prototype of a new product to handle, it is certainly the next best thing. Finally, analysis and reporting of results can be largely automated. It is no longer necessary to enter data manually, which is a great saving in labour costs and time.

For Internet research to be successful, the software needs the following attributes (Deal 2003):

1. There should be direct and simple facilities for developing appropriate, flexible and attractive questionnaires.
2. Relatively easy fielding of questionnaires, including considerations of security and integrity control.
3. Ability to perform basic analysis.

There is some evidence that the widespread practice of paying people to participate in Internet-based surveys has created a group of professional respondents (Gillin and Sheppard 2003). There are obvious implications for this in terms of honesty of response and the quality of the sample.

Creating the report

The final stage of the research project is to create and present a report. The report should outline the background to the research (the research problem), the way in which the research was conducted and the rationale for doing so, the outcomes in terms of responses, the results (suitably analysed) and the interpretation of the results. The report should conclude with an outline of some recommendations for management, both in terms of an action plan resulting from the research and in terms of recommendations for any further research. The report should (in an ideal world) contain a statement regarding the limitations of the study.

In practice, many marketing research projects result in a less than fully frank report. Commercial marketing research companies may not be prepared to admit to their failings, and (worse) some researchers will only provide the company with good news, suppressing any findings that may be unpopular. Managers who commission research should therefore examine the research method used as carefully as is feasible, and not simply rely on the bottom line.

A typical report is structured as follows:

1. Executive summary. This is at the beginning of the report, and allows executives to grasp the findings and recommendations quickly. It includes the basics of the research method (for example, how many respondents participated, and of what type), the main findings and the resulting recommendations.
2. Introduction. This includes the background to the research, the people involved and any acknowledgements.
3. Research methods and methodology. This includes the thinking behind the choice of method as well as a description of what was done and how it was done. The type of study, the purpose of the study, a description of the respondents and reasons for their inclusion, the sample design, data collection method, and an example of the questionnaire (or other data-collection device).
4. Analysis and findings. The analytical approach adopted, tables and figures showing the results, and explanatory text.
5. Recommendations arising from the research results.
6. Limitations of the research.
7. Appendices containing any technical details or in-depth material regarding the data collection or analysis.

Chapter summary

Marketing research supplies the information managers need to make decisions. Knowledge is power: without a continuous, timely and accurate flow of information about the external (and internal) environment marketing managers would be working entirely in the dark.

For marketers, all research is ultimately directed at meeting consumer needs better. Research will tell them what consumers want and need, what is already being supplied by competitors, and what the consumers think of what they are being offered. Ultimately, the purpose of marketing research is to minimise risk in making business decisions. Using research to answer specific problems, marketing information systems to provide continuous updates and by triangulating on problems managers can ensure the best possible basis on which to plan ahead.

Key points

- Marketing research supplies the information on which decisions are made.
- Marketing research can be divided into customer research, advertising research, product research, distribution research, sales research and marketing environment research.
- Secondary research is cheaper than primary research but less well-tailored to the company's needs.
- Qualitative research is good for finding out people's deeper motivations, but does not have the statistical rigour of qualitative research.

(Continued)

(Continued)

- Research planning is based on what we need to know and how we are able to find it out. Execution is based on objectivity and avoidance of bias.
- Although questionnaire surveys are very common, focus groups, in-depth interviews, observation and experiments also have their place in marketing research.
- Secondary research is second-hand research – someone else collected it, usually for another purpose, but it can be recycled for the current purpose.
- Primary research is new, original research that is intended to be exactly tailored to find out information relevant to the company carrying it out.
- Research must be conducted honestly, and with respect for the individuals who have volunteered their time and trust to respond.

Review questions

1. What is the difference between secondary and primary research?
2. What is the difference between preliminary research and conclusive research?
3. Which would be more suitable for preliminary research: qualitative or quantitative research?
4. How would a manager decide whether a piece of research is worth carrying out?
5. What are the main sources of inaccuracy in research?
6. What are the main drawbacks of questionnaires?
7. What ethical problems arise when conducting experiments?
8. How does triangulation improve the reliability of research?
9. What are the advantages of secondary research over primary research?
10. How can marketing information systems help in decision-making?

Case study revisited: Avios

BA's agency linked their survey software, Confirmit, to the Epiphany software being used by BA's call centre. This enabled the agency to send out survey requests to respondents the day after the call had been made, and to personalise the survey to the individual. This had the further advantage that the surveys could be drastically shortened – only the most directly relevant questions needed to be included because the respondents' details were already largely on file. The personalised questionnaires only needed to cover aspects that were as yet unknown.

An interesting spin-off was that response rate rose dramatically to 35%. This is exceptionally high: but because people were not being asked questions to which BA already knew the answers, they were happier to respond to the remaining questions.

The results were a surprise. The company had assumed that availability of flights was probably the key reason for people failing to book, but in fact price and perception of value for money were more important. Availability was an issue, but it came third behind the others. A further spin-off was that some respondents were prepared to talk to salespeople about booking hotels and other peripherals: although the research was not primarily aimed at making sales directly, this certainly added to its value.

The importance of talking to people direct about their needs, and of keeping the survey questionnaire short and to the point, was strongly demonstrated in the course of this research.

Case study: Mintel

Commercial market research is the cornerstone of business decision-making, and Mintel is at the sharp end of providing it. The company produces detailed industry reports at regular intervals, and few marketing departments are without at least one Mintel report.

Since the late 1970s, when Mintel began by researching the food and drinks industries, the company has produced regular reports on all industries. These reports are sold to interested parties: regular subscribers include SmithKlineBeecham and Associated Newspapers.

As time has gone on, Mintel have expanded from providing 'blanket', one-size-fits-all industry reports which, useful as they are as secondary research, often do not provide the detail some companies need. Mintel can provide tailored advice to marketing departments through their research consultancy, and have specialist databases such as the Global New Products Database, which covers food, beverages, toiletries, over-the-counter pharmaceuticals and household goods in all major global markets. The site offers more than just a brief description: each product is accompanied by an informative editorial on the market and the product's fit within it.

Mintel Menu Insights tracks 350 restaurant chains, 150 independent restaurants, 50 top chefs, 25 beverage-based restaurants and 5 buffet restaurants to provide an overview of trends in the restaurant industry. The site provides information on prices, menu changes, ingredients and even preparation methods to give a comprehensive overview of trends in eating out. One recent highlight is the launch of Brix chocolate, specially made to go with specific wines: Mintel report that Brix (a Gia Brands product) has a different formula for each type of wine, and will be sold through off-licences.

Of course, none of this comes cheap – information is expensive to create, because the cost of the original research is high, and the reports are very comprehensive. A typical report costs around £1500, but this is a small price to pay considering that the cost of running a dedicated primary research exercise to find out the same information is likely to cost upwards of £30,000. Granted, the Mintel report may not provide exactly the answer the firm needs, but it often provides most of them, and many firms can easily make up the shortfall from their internal sources, without ever using primary research.

Data are collected through interviews, questionnaires and trawls of secondary sources such as government statistics. Trade research includes interviews with senior managers in the industry and trawls of the trade press. Analysis is carried out by Mintel's own core of statisticians and analysts to create the final report, which includes informed editorial analysis as well as statistical tables. The reports all follow the same basic format, as follows:

- Executive summary
- Market drivers
- Market size and trends
- Market segmentation
- The supply structure
- Advertising and promotion
- New product trends
- Retail distribution
- Consumer attitudes and purchasing habits
- Forecast and future

Reports are designed to cover the next five years, so the data should remain usable for a long enough period for most firms' planning. From the viewpoint of almost any major firm, using Mintel reports really does not require much thinking time – they are an obvious asset in any firm's planning. Using other Mintel services to fine-tune the information is also likely to be a great deal more cost-effective than running a dedicated primary research exercise – after all, Mintel's staff are extremely highly skilled in the collection of data and the creation of information.

Questions

1. What are the main advantages of using Mintel reports?
2. What disadvantages might there be in using Mintel reports?
3. Why would a firm carry out primary research, even after buying a report?
4. How might Mintel expand its market?
5. What research methods might complement Mintel's own approach?

Further reading

David Carson, Audrey Gilmore, Kjell Gronhaug and Chad Perry, *Qualitative Marketing Research* (London: Sage, 2001). This text provides a very comprehensive and erudite guide to qualitative research.

Don A. Dillman, Jolene D Smyth and Leah Milani, Christian, *Internet, Mail and Mixed-Mode Surveys: The Tailored Design Method*, 3rd edn (Hoboken, NJ: John Wiley, 2009). Dillman was the inventor of total design, and he has applied the same thinking to Internet surveys. This is a book aimed mainly at practitioners, but is an extremely useful reference work for anyone engaged in marketing research.

Tony Proctor, *Essentials of Marketing Research*, 4th edn (Harlow: FT Prentice Hall, 2005). This book gives a good overview of current marketing research practice.

References

AMA (American Marketing Association) (1987) New market research definition approved. *Marketing News*, 21 (2 January).

Chandon, Pierre, Morwitz, Vicki G. and Reinartz, Werner J. (2005) Do intentions really predict behaviour? Self-generated validity effects in survey research. *Journal of Marketing*, 69 (2): 1–13.

D'Astous, Alain and Kamau, Estelle (2010) Consumer product evaluation based on tactile sensory information. *Journal of Consumer Behaviour*, 9 (3): 206–13.

Deal, Ken (2003) Do-it-yourself internet surveys. *Marketing Research*, 15 (2): 40–2.

Dillman, D. (1978) *Mail and Telephone Surveys: The Total Design Method*. New York: Wiley.

Gillin, Donna L. and Sheppard, Jane (2003) The fallacy of getting paid for your opinions. *Marketing* Research, 15 (3): 8.

Gorn, Gerald J., Chattopadhyay, Amitava, Sengupta, Jagdeep and Tripathi, Shashank (2004) Waiting for the web: how screen colour affects time perception. *Journal of Marketing Research*, 41 (2): 215–25.

Grandcolas, U., Rettie, R. and Marusenko, K. (2003) Web survey bias: sample or mode effect? *Journal of Marketing Management*, 19 (5/6): 541–61.

Grapentine, Terry (2004a) Fuzzy math. *Marketing Research*, 16 (1): 4.

Grapentine, Terry (2004b) To tell the truth. *Marketing Research*, 16 (1): 4.

Grunert, Klaus D. (2003) Can we understand consumers by asking them? *Marketing Research*, 15 (2): 46–48.

Jobber, D. and Rainbow, C. (1977) A study of the development and implementation of marketing information systems in British industry. *Journal of the Marketing Research Society*, 19 (3): 104–11.

O'Sullivan, Don, and Abela, Andrew V. (2007) Marketing performance measurement ability and firm performance. *Journal of Marketing*, 71 (2): 79–93.

Proctor, Tony (2005) *Essentials of Marketing Research*, 4th edn. Harlow: FT Prentice Hall.

Ray, Nina M. (2003) Cyber surveys come of age. *Marketing Research*, 15 (1): 32–7.

Rickards, T. (1974) *Problem Solving through Creative Analysis*. Aldershot: Gower.

Rook, Dennis W. (2003) Out of focus groups. *Marketing Research*, 15 (2): 10–15.

Ward, Steven, Bridges, Kate and Chitty, Bill (2005) Do incentives matter? An examination of on-line privacy concerns and willingness to provide personal and financial information. *Journal of Marketing Communications*, 11 (1): 21–40.

Wefeld, John P. (2003) Consumer research in the land of Oz. *Marketing Research*, 15 (1): 10–15.

Wyner, Gordon A. (2003) Reinventing research design. *Marketing Research*, 14 (4): 6.

Zaltman, G. (2003) *How Customers Think: Insights into the Mind of the Market*. Cambridge, MA: Harvard University Press.

More online

To gain free access to additional online resources to support this chapter please visit:
www.sagepub.co.uk/blythe3e

CHAPTER ⑥
Segmentation, targeting and positioning

CHAPTER CONTENTS

LEARNING OBJECTIVES

After reading this chapter, you should be able to:

- Understand the basic concept behind segmentation.

- Explain the role of marketing research in segmenting markets.

- Describe some of the commonest methods of segmenting markets.

- Explain the role of targeting.

- Explain the potential strategic issues in targeting.

- Explain what positioning implies for customers.

- Understand the key features of successful positioning.

Introduction

Segmentation Dividing the market into groups of people with similar needs.

Targeting Choosing which segments to service.

Positioning Placing the product in the appropriate location in the consumers' perceptual maps.

Segmentation is about separating the overall market into groups of customers with similar needs. **Targeting** is about developing variations on the basic product to meet the needs of these different groups. Segmentation can be defined as the grouping of individuals or organisations with similar needs, those needs being capable of being met by a single product offering.

Targeting also implies deciding which groups of customers are the best ones to aim for. A basic tenet of business (and of life in general) is that it is impossible to please everybody. This means that marketers need to consider which segments they cannot please, and which they can, and then decide which of these segments will also be profitable.

There are very few products that please everybody – in fact, it is difficult to think of any. Even products such as Coca-Cola, which has penetrated soft-drink markets in almost every country on the planet and is the world's most recognised brand, only has a minority share of the world's soft drinks market. Marketers therefore seek to position their products appropriately relative to competitors: **positioning** is, of course, in the minds of consumers.

The relationship between segmentation, targeting and positioning is shown in Figure 6.1.

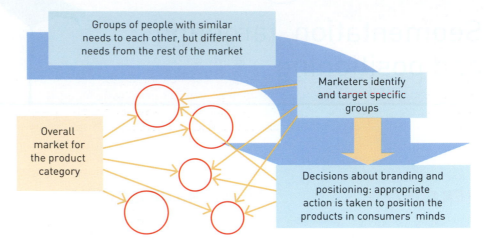

Figure 6.1   Segmentation, targeting and positioning

Preview case study: Verdié

Verdié Voyages is a French company based in Rodez, in southern France. The company was founded by Yves Verdié, and operates package holidays in Europe and the rest of the world.

Typically, French people tend to holiday within France. It is a country with a very wide range of terrain and is large enough to have noticeable climate changes – in the north the climate is much like Britain's (after all, the UK is only 20 miles from Calais), whereas the Midi is on the Mediterranean, with a correspondingly warm climate. The country has plenty of mountains – skiing in the Alps and Pyrenees, and the hiking country of the Massif Central. City breaks obviously include Paris, but also the cathedral cities of Chartres and Rouen, the castles of the Loire, and the very Spanish-orientated Perpignan.

Perhaps because of this propensity to stay within France (where the food and language are familiar and it is easy to drive to one's holiday destination) French people are more likely than British people to go for the security of a package holiday, where there is someone to help out if things go wrong, and the experience can be sanitised somewhat. However, the market breaks down into a number of different segments which Verdié Voyages tries to address.

There is the standard package holiday, where someone books for a specific hotel in a specific country for a stay of one or two weeks. Then there is the adventure holiday, where someone travels around a country staying in different hotels, seeing sights or trying new experiences., There is also the short-break holiday to a city or a specific event, and there are educational trips for schoolchildren and students. Verdié tries to suit all those markets.

Interestingly, Rodez is a centre for tour operators – there are five within this one small town, and relatively few elsewhere in France. The reasons for this are unclear, but may be a result of people leaving a company to set up on their own – not uncommon in a country where jobs are hard to get.

Segmentation

The purpose of segmenting the market is to ensure, as far as possible, that resources are directed at those individuals or organisations that are likely to yield the best returns. All firms operate with limited resources: taking a 'scattergun' approach to marketing activities rather than aiming at specific groups will inevitably waste those resources.

In Figure 6.2, the market for a service is broken down into groups with different ideas of what they want. The largest group is the one looking for a low-price, no-frills service – but of course low prices often go hand-in-hand with low profits. The group who are prepared to pay for exceptional quality is small, but probably more profitable as individuals. The company has to decide where its own strengths lie in terms of meeting customer expectations, and then decide whether it is able to meet the needs of its chosen target group better than the competition can do it.

The concept is, of course, much more straightforward than the practice. Deciding the basis on which the market should be segmented is only part of the problem – for example, one might assume that only young people visit nightclubs, and therefore target accordingly. However, it is actually the case that nightclubs cater for single people (most of whom are young, admittedly) but by targeting young people the nightclub might miss out on the growing number of divorced people in their thirties, forties and even fifties who might be customers. Since these people often have a great deal more money than their younger counterparts, the nightclub could miss out on a lucrative area of business.

Addressable and interactive media (about which there is more in Chapter 18) mean that segments can be very small indeed, and even self-selecting (Bailey et al. 2009). This makes life simpler in some ways, since the segment will choose itself, and harder in other ways, since it is difficult to know what to offer the market and even harder to estimate potential demand.

Total market

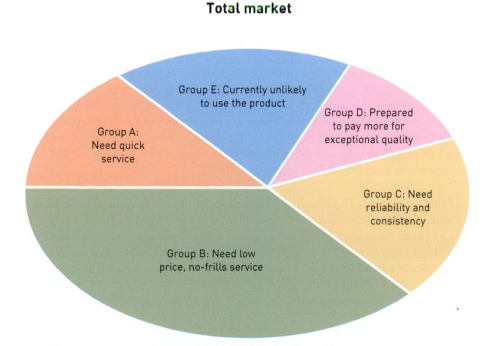

Figure 6.2   Basic segmentation example

Real-life marketing: Keep your eggs in one basket

Mark Twain famously said that a wise man keeps all his eggs in one basket – and then watches that basket! If you look for the right segment for your firm, you can direct your resources towards that segment and avoid wasting effort, time and money on side-issues.

Young's Home Brew is a specialist wholesaler dealing only in products for people who like to make their own wines and beer. Their website offers advice to end consumers even though Young's deals through retailers – this makes it easier for people to buy and use the products and reinforces Young's position in the market. By being the recognised expert, Young's has shut out much of the competition, and is therefore the market leader in their chosen segment. This is a great strategy for a small firm, because it focuses limited resources very accurately and it also avoids a head-on collision with the big players in the market. You wouldn't pick a fight with a nightclub doorman – so why do it in business?

To make this work in practice, you need to:

- Resist the temptation to try to please everybody.
- Be sure that you really are the expert.
- Make sure everybody involved understands your expert status – consumers, intermediaries, suppliers, in fact everyone.
- Use the Internet, but why not also let your local TV and radio stations know that you are an expert? If something comes up in the news about your area of expertise, they are very likely to ask you to comment on-air.

Targeting might involve developing appropriate variations on the product (or new products), considering approaches to promoting the product to the different segments and positioning the product against competitors in the same market.

Ultimately, the firm will want to use its segmentation policy to develop differential market strategies. Each segment will require a different approach, since each segment has different needs and characteristics and will therefore be interested in different aspects of the product offering. If the segmentation differs from that of the competition, the firm will be able to offer a product more closely tailored to the needs of the segment and will therefore obtain a competitive advantage.

Segmentation operates at four levels, as follows:

1. Mass marketing. The idea behind mass marketing is to produce something that almost everyone would want, then produce it in vast quantities at low prices and promote it heavily to gain a market share. This approach is all but impossible to carry out in the modern world, because the markets are so diverse and consumer expectations have risen. Production has also become more efficient, so that the cost difference between the mass-produced, mass-marketed item and the more tailored product is smaller than it once was. Wealthy consumers, which includes almost everybody in the Western world, can easily afford the very tiny extra cost of a more customised product.
2. Segmented markets. Here the company seeks to identify substantial groups of individuals with similar needs, and aims to satisfy those needs. Competition

will tend to be reduced by targeting a segment, and the company is able to direct resources more effectively.

3. **Niche marketing**. Niche marketers focus on small subgroups within the larger segments and produce very carefully targeted products. The advantage of doing this is that the company is able to reach a group which is too small for larger firms to approach, and therefore will not experience much competitive pressure: the firm will also be able to operate with much less capital, since promotion will not need to be as powerful as it would if the company were competing against major firms for share of voice. Niche marketers usually get to understand their customers so well that they are able to charge a premium price for their products, and the approach is so successful that large companies sometimes also target niches within their overall market segment.

Niche marketing Serving a small segment.

4. **Micromarketing**. This is the practice of tailoring products and marketing programmes to suit specific individuals and circumstances. For example, Dell Computers will produce a computer to the purchaser's specifications, within certain limits. Ultimately, micromarketing takes us full circle, to the days when craftsmen made everything to the customers' specifications – tailor-made clothing and furniture was, at one time, the norm. Micromarketing enables us to use modern production techniques to achieve similar outcomes. Mass customisation is the ability to prepare individual, custom-made products through a mass-production process. For example, Vision Express opticians manufacture the lenses on-site so that a customer can have an eye test, choose the frames for his or her new spectacles, and walk out with the finished product within an hour. In many cases people are not prepared to pay the increased cost of such good service, however (Bardacki and Whitelock 2004).

Micromarketing Tailoring a product to a specific customer's needs.

As the product becomes more customised, one would expect that customers would be prepared to pay more for it, so there is a trade-off between the extra cost of providing a more tailored product and the extra price that customers are prepared to pay. If the premium is small and the costs are large, the customisation is unlikely to be worthwhile. This calculation can be a difficult one for marketers to make – and research shows that many practitioners have real difficulty in segmenting in practice (Dolnicar and Lazarevski 2009).

Each level of segmentation has its own advantages and disadvantages, but in general consumers are expecting a much higher standard of service than they previously have, and given the globalisation of world markets, consumers have a great deal more

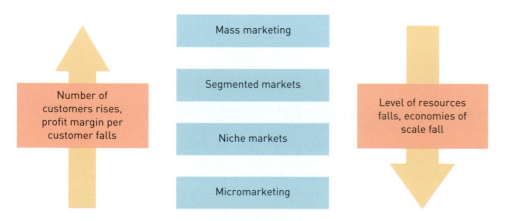

Figure 6.3 Segmentation trade-offs

choice and variety than they have had before. People (understandably) want to be treated as individuals, and the marketer who ignores this does so at his or her peril.

Segmenting the market

The starting-point for successful segmentation is good market research. Understanding the needs of customers, and the characteristics of those customers the firm wants to reach, is basic to deciding how to meet those needs. Segmentation occurs in three stages, as follows:

1. An understanding of the needs of the various customers in the total market needs to be developed. This happens through market research, and sometimes through internal knowledge within the firm (for example reports from salespeople). There is more on market research in Chapter 7.
2. Customers are grouped according to their needs and characteristics. This can be a complex operation, since it is sometimes difficult to be clear about what the salient characteristics of the customers are (see the nightclub example above). There are a great many ways to segment the same market, and companies that are able to view markets from a fresh perspective are often able to find new ways of grouping customers. These new groupings may mean new advantages for customers, and a competitive advantage for the firm.
3. Groupings are selected for targeting. Segmentation implies rejecting groups that are unprofitable, or do not otherwise fit with the firm's strategic plans. For example, a firm may identify a lucrative market but be unwilling to compete directly with a major firm that already serves that market. Wiser counsels may dictate that the firm targets a different group which would not pose a threat to the industry leaders.

Grouping people into segments can be carried out in a large number of ways, but the generally accepted view is that segmentation of consumer markets can be based on the following:

1. Behavioural factors, i.e. on what people actually do with the product or with related products.
2. Psychographic factors, i.e. the way people think, their hopes and fears, and so forth.
3. Profile factors, i.e. what kind of people we are dealing with, in terms of wealth, work, income, lifestyle and so forth.

Think outside this box!

There seems to be a view that people can be pigeonholed: that our reactions to marketing stimuli can be predicted, programmed, manipulated and filed away. Yet we all think of ourselves as individuals – making independent, even quirky, decisions without caring what other people think of us.

So which view is right? After all, it's easy to find examples of people acting like sheep, following the crowd: and it's also easy to find people who follow the same routines day in and day out. Most people eat the same thing for breakfast every day, wear the same style of clothing, choose the same type of food in restaurants. On the other hand, people enjoy having a change now and then, doing the unexpected, and acting on impulse. If that's the case, how can we possibly expect to segment a market?

In practice, these different approaches are not mutually exclusive, and marketers often use more than one segmentation variable in order to focus on a very specific part of the market.

Behavioural segmentation

Basing segmentation on consumers' behaviour can be straightforward, but may also lack subtlety. For example, a manufacturer of fishing rods may not feel a need to know much about potential consumers in terms of their ages, incomes, or attitudes: the fact that they go fishing is sufficient. Within that, the manufacturer might want to know what type of fish the angler is after, or on what occasions he or she goes fishing, but all of these questions operate within the behavioural segmentation area.

The main behavioural bases for segmentation are as follows:

1. Benefits sought. Different people look for different things, even in the same product category. For example, some people buy a car because they need transport from one place to another, for themselves and their luggage. Others may be seeking the prestige which comes from driving an up-market car, and still others might be looking for hedonic aspects of the product (the fun of driving from one place to another). Sampson (1992) called these people (respectively) functionality seekers, image seekers, and pleasure seekers.

2. Purchase occasion. Some people might buy the product as a regular purchase, others might only buy as an occasional treat. For example, forty years ago chicken was regarded as something of a luxury in the UK, and would only occasionally be eaten as a Sunday dinner – the staple of British Sunday dinners was beef. However, some people ate chicken frequently, either because they were wealthy enough to do so or because they considered the extra cost to be worthwhile. The same argument applies to lamb in the 21st century – it is one of the most expensive of meats, but to its aficionados it is worth every penny. Another type of purchase occasion relates to gift giving. The greater part of sales of aftershave is made to women: aftershave lotion is typically given as a gift, and relatively little is bought by men for their own use. Purchase occasion might also relate to situational factors: buying a new car battery might be a result of awareness that the old battery is gradually becoming less efficient, or it may be the result of a sudden failure of the battery far from home. Purchase occasion may result in the same consumer buying different versions of the same product at different times. For example, someone might stay in a four-star hotel when travelling for business purposes, but stay in a crumbling old bed-and-breakfast when on holiday, because such places have more character. Equally, going out for a meal when one is too tired to cook results in a very different choice of restaurant from that chosen for a wedding anniversary or a first date.

3. Purchase behaviour. This could relate to time of purchase, place of purchase, quantities bought on each occasion, degree of willingness to buy innovative products, and so forth. For example, books may be bought in a bookshop, in a newsagent's, in a charity shop, in a street market, or over the Internet. Each type of purchase behaviour may be typical of the consumers concerned, but may not relate to other characteristics – the fact that someone enjoys bargain-hunting in a charity shop or second-hand book stall does not necessarily mean that he or she is poorer than someone who buys books on the Internet, for

instance. Brand loyalty is also an element in purchase behaviour: if there is a group of consumers who regularly switch from one brand to another according to the price, this has implications for the marketing approach. On the other hand, if there is a group of consumers who remain loyal to the product no matter what happens, the thrust of the marketing effort will lie in identifying and recruiting these people.

4. Usage. Consumers may be heavy users of the product category, medium users, light users, ex-users, or non-users. Non-users are not, of course, consumers of the product but may represent an opportunity if the supplying company can find out why they are non-users. Equally, light users and medium users can be encouraged to use more of the product – although this is almost certainly the easier option, many firms still concentrate on finding new users for their products from among the non-user category. For many firms, the obvious tactic is to target heavy users and try to steal these customers away from competing firms. This tactic is dangerous if all the firms in the market are targeting heavy users, however, because the competitive pressure might prove too intense. In those circumstances, a firm might be better to target light or medium users. A neglected area of marketing is customer win-back, in which ex-users are brought back into the fold. An ex-user, after all, already knows all about the product and the company, and may have defected to the competition for a reason that can easily be corrected.

5. Buyer readiness stage. Some people are closer to buying the product than are others. People may be unaware of the product, others may be aware but not yet interested, others are aware and interested but do not yet need the product, others have an interest and a need but no money, and finally there are those who are actually in the market for the product. Being aware of these stages is important for firms selling major items such as houses or cars. Someone who recently moved house is unlikely to be in the market for another house, but after (say) seven or eight years a move is a likely option. Likewise, a couple who have recently started a family may well be interested in moving to a larger house, or a house with a garden. Contacting people (for example by mail) when they are at the wrong stage of readiness is irritating and therefore counter-productive, whereas a contact at the right stage is helpful and useful.

6. Attitude towards the product. In some cases, the non-user's attitude towards the product is so hostile there is really very little point in trying to change it. For example, in political marketing it is well-known that the committed Labour (Socialist, Democrat) or Conservative (Christian Democrat, Republican) supporter is unlikely to change. Political campaigners know that there is little point in spending time either on committed supporters or on sworn enemies: better by far to concentrate on the 'floating voters' who might be swayed by argument. Also, some Party supporters may want a greater involvement than merely voting – some will want to help with the election campaign, or contribute money to support the campaign, or become Party members.

Geographic segmentation

The area where people live can have a marked effect on their purchasing behaviour. An obvious example is the effect of climate – people in cold countries need to spend

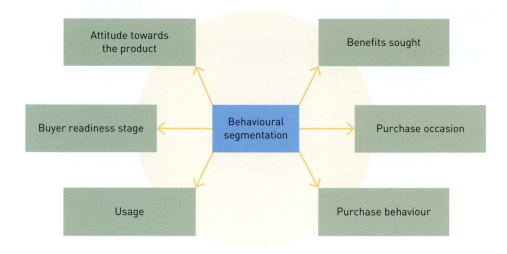

Figure 6.4   Behavioural segmentation

more on warm clothing, home insulation and heating products than do people in warm countries. The reverse is true for air conditioning, sun lotion, solar heating and barbecues. Less obvious examples are the effects of culture and the effects of location on shopping habits.

Culture is frequently geographically linked. Language tends to be a strong influence in linking people together, and language tends to be specific to particular localities. For example, research has shown that Europe can be divided into five regions for the purpose of selling cars: the north (Scandinavia), the north-west (UK, Iceland, Belgium and Holland), the centre (Germany, Switzerland and Eastern Europe), the west (France and the French-speaking areas of Belgium and Switzerland) and the south (the Mediterranean countries). Each region tends to have its own attitudes to car purchase and ownership: the centre, for example, is more concerned about pollution than are the other regions, and the south region is more concerned about value for money. Cultural issues can be a basis for segmentation on their own – for example, African Americans sometimes wear African-style clothing to identify themselves with Africa, even though most of them are unlikely ever to visit Africa (DeBerry Spence and Izberk-Bilgin 2006).

Geographic segmentation can be taken to a micro level as well. One of the best-known examples of localised geographic segmentation is **ACORN**, a system for classifying consumers according to their postcodes. ACORN stands for A Classification of Residential Neighbourhoods, and it seeks to categorise households according to the type of housing that predominates within their postcode area. ACORN classifications are used by retailers to determine which products are the best to stock, by home-improvement companies to know which areas are likely to be the most in need of the product, and by direct mail companies to know which areas are likely to be most receptive to mailings. Insurance companies are also able to tell which type of housing is most likely to result in claims.

The ACORN classifications are as shown in Table 6.1. The basic assumption underpinning ACORN is that the area one lives in has a strong influence on one's purchasing behaviour, partly because it relates to income level, partly because it relates to a local culture (the assumption being that similar types of people live in the same area) and partly because the type of housing one lives in has an effect on household purchases such as furniture and home improvements.

ACORN A geographical segmentation method: A Classification Of Residential Neighbourhoods.

Table 6.1 ACORN classifications

Main grouping	Sub-groups
A: Lavish lifestyles	1. Exclusive enclaves 2. Metropolitan money 3. Large house luxury
B: Executive wealth	4. Asset-rich families 5. Wealthy countryside commuters 6. Financially comfortable families 7. Affluent professionals 8. Prosperous suburban families 9. Well-off edge of towners
C: Mature money	10. Better-off villagers 11. Settled suburbia, older people 12. Retired and empty-nesters 13. Upmarket downsizers
D: City sophisticates	14. Townhouse cosmopolitans 15. Younger professionals in smaller flats 16. Metropolitan professionals 17. Socialising young renters
E: Career climbers	18. Career-driven young families 19. First-time buyers in small, modern homes 20. Mixed metropolitan areas
F: Countryside communities	21. Farms and cottages 22. Larger families in rural areas 23. Owner occupiers in small towns and villages
G: Successful suburbs	24. Comfortably-off families in modern housing 25. Larger family homes, multi-ethnic 26. Semi-professional families, owner-occupied neighbourhoods
H: Steady neighbourhoods	27. Suburban semis, conventional attitudes 28. Owner-occupied terraces, average income 29. Established suburbs, older families
I: Comfortable seniors	30. Older people, neat and tidy neighbourhoods 31. Elderly singles in purpose-built accommodation
J: Starting out	32. Educated families in terraces, young children 33. Smaller houses and starter homes
K: Student life	34. Student flats and halls of residence 35. Term-time terraces 36. Educated young people in flats and tenements
L: Modest means	37. Low-cost flats in suburban areas 38. Semi-skilled workers in traditional neighbourhoods 39. Fading owner occupied terraces 40. High occupancy terraces, many Asian families

Main grouping	Sub-groups
M: Striving families	41. Labouring semi-rural estates 42. Struggling young families in post-war terraces 43. Families in right-to-buy estates 44. Post-war estates, limited means
N: Poorer pensioners	45. Pensioners in social housing, semis and terraces 46. Elderly people in social rented flats 47. Low income older people in smaller semis 48. Pensioners and singles in social rented flats
O: Young hardship	49. Young families in low cost private flats 50. Struggling young people in mixed tenure 51. Young people in small, low-cost terraces
P: Struggling estates	52. Poorer families, many children, terraced housing 53. Low income terraces 54. Multi-ethnic, purpose built estates 55. Deprived and ethnically diverse in flats 56. Low income large families in social rented semis
Q: Difficult circumstances	57. Social rented flats, families and single parents 58. Singles and young families, some receiving benefits 59. Deprived areas and high-rise flats
R: Not private households	60. Inactive communal population 61. Business addresses without resident population

Think outside this box!

Most of us live in cities. Even the relatively few people who live in rural areas (at least in Western Europe and the United States) live what is essentially an urban life – even farmers shop in supermarkets rather than grow their own food. Part of the advantage of living in a city is the variety of experience that cities provide – the entertainment facilities, the restaurants, the variety of people we can mix with, and so forth. The whole point of living in a city is that we are *not* like our neighbours – so how does ACORN work?

Even more to the point, what about community workers who have to live in run-down areas as part of their jobs? What about university lecturers who act as wardens in student accommodation halls? What about caretakers who live in office blocks?

Perhaps ACORN provides a general overview of who is likely to live in a given area, but there may be plenty of exceptions!

Lifestyle choices are often geographically based. For example, American and Australian washing machines are almost always top-loading, whereas UK washing machines are typically front-loading. Because houses are bigger in Australia and the United States, people have spare space for the easier-to-load top-loaders, whereas in the UK (and most of the rest of Europe) front-loaders are more convenient because they fit under a kitchen worktop. In hot countries people tend to live outside more, so there is less emphasis on furniture and home décor.

Demographic segmentation

Demographics is concerned with factors such as age, gender, sexual orientation, family size, family life cycle stage, income, occupation, education, religion, ethnicity and nationality. Demographic factors are probably more widely used than any other factors for segmentation purposes, probably because the data are relatively easy to collect. Needs, wants and usage rates also correlate closely with demographic variables: for example, the wealthier an individual is, the more likely he or she is to consume almost any product one cares to mention. On the other hand, some demographic information can be misleading – age is particularly prone to this, but other demographic information can also be misinterpreted. For example, a product may appear to appeal to better-educated people, but in fact the appeal is to people with higher incomes. Since better-educated people tend to have higher incomes, the two factors can easily be confused.

AGE SEGMENTATION

Some consumer needs and wants change with age. As people grow older, they will become more concerned with pensions and investments, for example. Physical changes such as greying hair, weight increase and increasing numbers of wrinkles also offer marketing opportunities, and in old age mobility is also likely to lessen. Age is not an adequate segmentation variable in itself, however, since the relationship between age and behaviour is far from linear (Simcock et al. 2006). Age segmentation is sometimes carried out somewhat crudely, for example by categorising everyone over 65 as one group. This implies that a 65-year-old man has something in common with his 87-year-old mother, which is of course extremely unlikely.

At the other end of the scale, age segmentation is widely used in the children's toy market, and of course babies' and children's clothing is almost always designated by age rather than size. However, age is not the whole answer – apart from the obvious divergence in clothing as children leave the baby stage, their interests in toys is also gender-specific to a large extent. As children develop interests of their own, and become more individual in their needs, other factors become more important than age. For example, Disneyland Paris know that around 20% of children would not want to visit the theme park under any circumstances, even though the majority of children would love a visit.

A more subtle effect of segmentation by age is that different age groups have had different life experiences. People in their 80s and older remember living through the Second World War, people in their 70s were teenagers during the 1950s, people in their 60s remember Vietnam War protests, people in their 50s spent their early working lives in Thatcherite Britain, people in their 40s grew up with the telecommunications revolution, and people in their 30s are faced with a longer working life than previous generations. These life experiences are particularly useful when tailoring communications because (for example) music from the specific era can be used to trigger memories. Some products also rely on nostalgia – DVDs, compilation albums of music from specific decades or 'best of' musicians who were popular at the time, and even DVDs or videos of newsreel events are all aimed at specific age groups.

GENDER

Segmentation by gender is not as clear-cut as it once was. Gender roles have shifted dramatically in the last thirty years, with men taking on more household tasks and women working outside the home and developing careers. For example, the highly successful advertising campaign for Flash cleaning products features a man doing the cleaning: the ads use the strap line 'Flash does the hard work so you don't have to', and implies that the man is cleverly gaining favour with his wife by cleaning the bathroom. Research by Mintel shows that 28% of men take major responsibility for cooking, 20% take responsibility for all the laundry, and 40% of men aged 55 plus do at least half the grocery shopping. Men still take the bulk of the responsibility for gardening and DIY tasks, although women are encroaching on these traditional male preserves.

It seems likely that these trends will continue. While there are many older households in which the traditional gender division of household tasks continues, most younger couples have a more equal division of labour, and certainly younger women usually expect to have careers rather than 'pin money' jobs, which means that household tasks need to be shared equally. The statistics may also be skewed by the number of women who remain at home to care for small children, and therefore carry out more household tasks.

Astute marketers have taken note of these changes. Power-tool manufacturers now offer smaller, lighter power tools with women in mind: the Black and Decker Mouse sander is an example. Instructions for assembling flat-pack furniture no longer assume that the reader will have studied woodwork in school, and men are shown cooking, cleaning and shopping in TV advertising.

Having said that, there are still products that are gender-specific, simply because of physical differences between men and women. Added to these there are products that tend to be aimed at one gender because social mores still dictate some gender roles. For example, facial make-up for men is still somewhat rare in Western societies, and relatively few women take up boxing. The old gender roles may be eroding, but there will probably always be some products that meet the needs of one gender better than they do the other.

Think outside this box!

OK, so gender roles have changed. Why do we care? Is it still an issue whether we show a man doing the hoovering, or a woman fixing the car? Haven't we moved beyond this need to make a conscious effort about gender stereotyping?

Or have we even gone too far the other way? Some advertising is derogatory to men, showing women rescuing them from their own folly, or implying that men are incapable of carrying out simple household tasks. Should such advertising be subject to the same protests that eventually removed advertising which demeaned women? A simple test for whether an advertisement is sexist is to reverse the genders and see what happens.

Maybe it's men's turn to be demeaned in this way. But to be fair, the current generation of men is not responsible for past gender stereotyping, and anyway two wrongs don't make a right!

Within the gender debate there is also the question of sexual orientation. Homosexual people (gays) have specific characteristics from a marketing viewpoint: in general, gay people tend to be wealthier, and have fewer outgoings since they are less likely to have dependent children. In the UK, homosexuals' disposable income is referred to as the Pink Pound, valued at around £6bn a year; in the United States it is known as the Dorothy Dollar and is estimated to be worth around $350bn a year (BBC News 1998). This has meant that gays have been targeted as a group by financial institutions and by information services, clubs and even holiday companies such as Pink Pound Travel. Gays are estimated to represent about 4% of the population, although this figure is doubtful because of a reluctance to 'come out' or identify oneself as gay, due to the prejudice and stigma which still attaches to homosexuality in some quarters. Research carried out in Scotland for the Glasgow-based Beyond Barriers organisation indicated that two-thirds of gay people had been verbally abused or threatened.

Male homosexuals in the UK earn on average 23% more than the national average, have twice as many credit cards as the general population, and spend more than the average on entertainment (BBC 1998).

INCOME

Segmenting by income is widely practised, although it is not as simple as might first appear. For example, an individual may have a high income coupled with high outgoings, or vice versa. Income segmentation is often used for goods such as cars, luggage, holidays and fashion items.

There is an assumption that rich people spend more money, and this is not unreasonable: the difficulty lies in deciding what a rich person would regard as being a desirable item. Income actually says very little about an individual's tastes and interests, and even less about what such people regard as value for money. Rich people are often very careful with their money – not surprisingly, since this is how many of them became rich in the first place.

Some firms have managed to grow successful on marketing to the poorer end of the market. Retailers such as Aldi and Lidl target less affluent market segments, offering basic products at knock-down prices in basic surroundings. By having a lean organisation, narrow product ranges, cheap store locations and a no-frills approach to store design these companies have minimised their costs and can offer heavily discounted products. During 2008, as the recession began to take effect and food prices rose, these stores reported substantial increases in business from middle-class consumers looking for ways to economise.

RELIGION, ETHNICITY AND NATIONALITY

At first sight, these factors would seem to have little bearing on consumption behaviour. In truth, their influence is limited and often affects only a small part of the consumer's purchasing behaviour, but each of the three factors has some effect.

For example, religion will have an effect on the purchase of religious artefacts and, in some cases, affects diet. Jewish people and Muslims avoid pork, Buddhists avoid meat in general, Jains and Parsees are strictly vegetarian, and many Catholics still eat fish on a Friday although this is no longer a requirement of the faith.

Ethnicity Cultural background.

Ethnicity is a combination of culture and race. The cultural element of ethnicity has clear effects on people's eating habits, clothing and even entertainment. The physical differences that go with racial characteristics may have some effect on purchasing: darker-skinned women use different cosmetics, and the characteristics of hair differ between black, Asian and white people, which means that slightly different formulations of hair care product are needed. In recent years some ethnic segmentation has become blurred because marketing activities have caused culture swapping: people have adopted products aimed at other cultures (food and clothing being good examples) and therefore ethnic segmentation for these products is no longer realistic (Jamal 2003; Lindridge 2010).

Nationality is a legal state rather than an ethnic state, so has relatively little effect on purchase, but in global markets it is common to segment by nationality. This is because different legal restrictions apply within different countries. There exists a limited number of products that apply only to people of a particular nationality – flags, patriotic symbols and legal services for example.

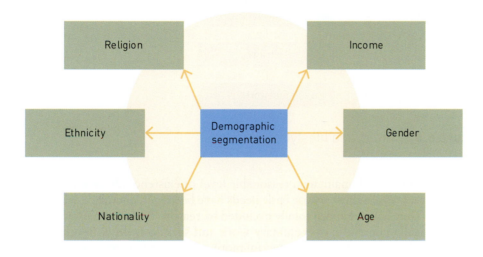

Figure 6.5 Demographic segmentation

Psychographic segmentation

People can be divided into groups according to lifestyle or personality characteristics. Lifestyles are both created by products and dictate which products will be bought: someone who owns a penthouse has a different lifestyle from someone who owns a farm, but those dwellings are products as well as lifestyle determinants.

Lifestyle segmentation has the major advantage that it relates directly to purchasing behaviour. It has been said that marketing delivers a lifestyle, so looking at consumers in terms of their chosen way of life seems logical on the face of it. One well-known lifestyle segmentation method is the VALS structure, shown in Figure 6.6.

Outer directed Taking one's cue from the behaviour of others.

The VALS structure postulates nine different lifestyle positions. At the poorer end of the scale, people are need-driven: they are concerned with survival, security and belonging. In the zone of the double hierarchy, wealthier people can be divided into the **outer-directed** (those whose main motivation derives from the respect or admiration of others) and the inner-directed (those whose main motivation derives from an inner drive).

Finally, the theory postulates that people at the top of the hierarchy (the wealthiest or most secure people) have an integrated set of values and a balanced lifestyle.

Survivors Those people who struggle to maintain any kind of lifestyle.

At the bottom of the hierarchy, **survivors** are those people who can barely make ends meet. They are struggling to maintain any kind of lifestyle and live in poverty. Slightly further up are the **sustainers**, who might typically be in a difficult position

Sustainers People who have very limited incomes, but can still maintain a basic standard of living.

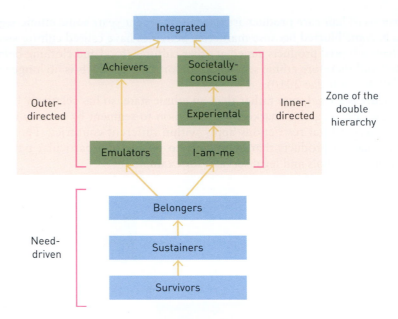

Figure 6.6   Values and lifestyles (VALS)

Belongers People who seek to join groups in society.

Societally conscious Cause-oriented people who become involved in charitable work.

Achievers People who seek respect by buying appropriate products.

financially but can still maintain a reasonable level of existence above the subsistence point. **Belongers** are those whose basic needs have been met, and who seek to belong to society. They have not been totally excluded by reason of their circumstances: they would typically join clubs, do voluntary work and seek to fit in with other people. The need to belong can be a very powerful motivator – members of a football fan club often resist buying anything outside the group (Richardson and Turley 2006).

Inner-directed people divide into the I-am-me group, who seek to live their own lives regardless of what others think, the experiential group, who seek new experiences, and the **societally conscious** group, who seek to do good in the world. Because these groups are less concerned about what others think of them, they are unlikely to buy goods simply because of the brand. The I-am-me group tend not to be heavy consumers, but are often creative. The experiential group are customers for travel, concerts, interesting foods, restaurants, cinema, and theatre. The societally conscious group are cause-orientated people who enjoy getting involved in charity work or political parties (Donnelly 1970).

Among the outer-directed people the emulators seek to copy other people, taking their cue from their neighbours. They are susceptible to suggestion from marketers, since they are keen to find out what is currently in fashion. **Achievers**, on the other hand, seek respect from other people and are therefore prime buyers of status-symbol products such as designer clothing, branded goods and visible purchases such as cars (Zhinkan and Shermohamad 1986). People with an integrated set of values like to be respected, but do not let this drive their lives: they are often wealthy, and care about other people, but have their own set of drivers.

Another possible segmentation method, still in its infancy, is the concept of interpretive communities. These are subcultures sharing a way of interpreting messages (and of course brands) (Kates 2002). Interpretive communities can only be identified by the way they process information, so they are difficult to identify except by running an advertisement and seeing who responds to it. For example, it is known that some people prefer to interpret messages visually, some prefer kinaesthetic (tactile) interpretations, while others process information aurally. Each group will respond to advertising differently (Skinner and Stephens 2001).

PERSONALITY CHARACTERISTICS

Segmenting by personality has a certain appeal about it, because personality changes only slowly over a long period of time. The difficulty lies in identifying a group of people with similar personality traits and targeting them successfully. For example, an insurance company might wish to target people with the personality traits of being security-minded, of being afraid of burglary and of owning enough valuable objects to make the policy a large one. Such individuals would probably be careful to lock their houses, would have secure door and window locks and probably a burglar alarm, would be highly motivated to buy a policy and would be prepared to pay a lot for it. Unfortunately there is no easy way to target such a group: there is no single advertising medium directed at these people.

Psychologists have developed many ways of grouping people according to personality types. The mother and daughter team of Kathryn Briggs and Isabel Myers developed the Myers–Briggs Type Indicator (Briggs and Myers 1962), which has four personality dimensions, as follows:

- Extrovert/Introvert.
- Sensing/Intuitive.
- Thinking/Feeling.
- Judging/Perceptive.

Each of these dimensions represents a continuum rather than a dichotomy, and each of us can be placed somewhere within those dimensions. At the extremes, an extrovert-sensing-feeling-judging person is warm-hearted, talkative and popular, and likes harmonious relationships. Such a person is likely to enjoy meals out, evenings with friends and romantic encounters. An introvert-intuitive-thinking-judging person is likely to be quiet, intelligent, cerebral and reclusive. Such a person is likely to enjoy the Internet, computer games, reading and learning.

Horney (1945) defined people across three dimensions:

- **Compliant**. Moves towards people, has goodness, sympathy, love, unselfishness and humility. Tends to be over-apologetic, over-sensitive, over-grateful, over-generous, and over-considerate in seeking love and attention.
- **Aggressive**. Usually moves against people. Controls fear and emotions in a quest for success, prestige and admiration. Needs power, exploits others.
- **Detached**. Moves away from people. Conformity is repugnant to the detached person. Distrustful of others, these people are self-sufficient and independent, and value intelligence and reasoning.

There is some empirical evidence to show that these categorisations have some effect on people's buying behaviour. For example, it has been shown that compliant people use more mouthwash and toilet soap, and prefer branded products; aggressive people use more cologne and aftershave. Detached people show low interest in branding (Cohen 1967).

The main way of targeting by personality characteristics is to use similar types of individual in the advertising, so that the product is modelled (see Chapter 3). Thus a product aimed at extrovert people would show extroverts using the product.

Although personality traits can be linked to consumer behaviour, the problem lies in the sheer number of traits that have been identified. It has been estimated that there are some 18,000 personality traits (Allport and Odbert 1936), and since each of these is interdependent, study of a few traits in isolation is unlikely to yield any concrete results (*Marketing News* 1985).

Compliant Someone who moves towards people, has goodness, sympathy, love, unselfishness and humility.

Aggressive Someone who usually moves against people and controls fear and emotions in a quest for success, prestige and admiration.

Detached Someone who moves away from people, is self-sufficient and independent.

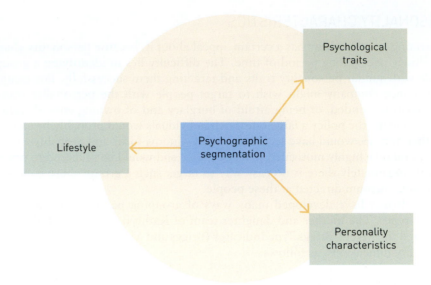

Figure 6.7   Psychographic segmentation

A relatively recent concept is that of the 'savvy' consumer. These are people who have an in-depth understanding of consumption possibilities. They have the following characteristics (McDonald and Uncles 2007):

1. They are competent in technology, especially communications technology.
2. They are competent in interpersonal networking.
3. They are good at on-line networking.
4. They are marketing-literate, in other words they understand how marketers are trying to influence them.
5. They are empowered by their own self-efficacy.
6. They are empowered by the expectations of firms, because they understand how to manipulate marketers.

Savvy consumers pose a special challenge to marketers because they know how to manipulate situations to their own advantage. This is particularly a problem in personal selling, for example in a retail store.

Marketing in a changing world: Segments of One

Nobody likes to be pigeonholed, least of all by a commercial organisation. The Internet allows us to be as individual as we like, and in fact we can define ourselves in all kinds of ways. Social networking sites allow segments to be built up from groups of people who have organised themselves into segments – we don't have to take a large market and break it down, we can build it up from individuals.

There is, however, a further factor on the horizon. People expect more and more from firms, and are looking for the perfect product. In a world in which information about products is not only freely available but also virtually jumps out at us, people can (and do) expect personal treatment.

Producers can, given modern manufacturing techniques, supply customised products. If this trend continues, people will expect tailoring in everything they buy, from cars to dishwashers. This may be the biggest challenge facing producers twenty years from now.

Segmenting business markets

Segmentation methods and criteria differ between consumer markets and business-to-business markets, for the following reasons:

1. Consumer markets are characterised by customers who are either the end user of the product or are very close to the end user. Business markets are characterised by buyers who do not themselves use the product.
2. The number of potential customers in business markets is almost always smaller, so there is likely to be a greater degree of customisation necessary.
3. Psychographic and demographic variables are almost entirely inappropriate.

Business marketers should be careful about applying consumer segmentation techniques directly to business markets. Unrefined use of consumer segmentation techniques can lead a business marketer in the wrong direction.

Many firms define a market segment by product type or product size. This overly simplistic approach can have dire consequences, because it is product-focused rather than customer-focused. In the United States computer hard disk drive (HDD) industry, suppliers identified customers for 14-inch drives as mainframe computer manufacturers, users of 8-inch drives as mini-computer makers, customers for 6.25-inch drives as personal computer manufacturers and for 2.5-inch drives as portable and laptop suppliers. Many firms focused on one or few segments and were unable to move into new segments as technology converged. A number of leading US HDD firms such as Memorex, Control Data and DEC were eventually forced to leave the HDD business. In the HDD business, the leading Japanese firms continue to be the major suppliers, as they have been for the past twenty years (Chesbrough 2003).

Another common error business marketers make in segmenting is simply accepting the definition of an entire industry as one segment. For instance, a manufacturer of train control equipment might say 'we sell to electrified railways' and classify the Santiago Subway or London Underground in the same category as a surface electrified railway in India. The most obvious differences (such as the product being used underground as opposed to being used in full exposure to the elements) would thus be ignored. Some managers err on the other side of the spectrum, thinking about their segments in too narrow a fashion. They may think only about a particular industry dominated by a few major firms and not about new segments that could use their product that are entirely unrelated to the primary target segment.

Think outside this box!

If a whole industry is not a segment, then what is? If we define our segment as smaller than the whole industry, how do we decide who we are *not* going to sell to? And isn't that a little stupid anyway? If another firm in the same industry wanted to buy our products, are we going to throw them out on their ears? Or if a firm from another industry wants to buy, what do we say? Do we tell them their money isn't good enough for us? Obviously not – so what are we saying?

Is segmentation about who spends their money with us – or is it about how we spend our money?

SEGMENTATION VARIABLES

Business marketing segmentation variables can be divided into two main categories, as shown in Table 6.2.

Table 6.2   Segmentation variables

Identifier (a priori)	Response profile (a posteriori)
Demographic	**Vendor product attributes**

- Industry classification
  - Firm type – OEM, end user, aftermarket (MRO)
  - Company size
  - Geographic location
  - Financial info/credit rating
	- Overall value
	  - Product quality
	  - Vendor reputation
	  - Innovativeness
	  - On-time delivery
	  - Lowest cost

Operations	**Customer variables**

- Technologies used
  - Level of use – heavy, light, non-user
  - Centralised/decentralised purchasing
	- DMU (buying centre) makeup
	  - Purchase importance
	  - Attitude toward product
	  - Corporate cultural characteristics (innovativeness)

Product required	**Application**
- Custom ↔ Standard	- End use - Importance of value in use
Purchasing situation	**DMU/Buying centre personal characteristics**

- Buying situation – new task, modified rebuy, straight rebuy
  - Current attitude toward our firm
  - Relationships
	- Risk tolerance
	  - Loyalty to current vendor
	  - Age
	  - Experience
	  - Education

Source: Adapted from: Cardozo 1980; Day 1990; Kotler 2003; Malhotra 1989; Rao and Wang 1995

Identifiers The major variables in segmentation, which can be listed without carrying out extensive research.

In the first category, called **identifiers** by Day (1990), firms attempt to pre-establish segments a priori, that is before any data are collected. These are the more traditional segmentation variables because the data are easier to obtain through observation of the buying situation or from secondary sources. Some researchers call these macro variables. As can be seen from Table 6.2, they include demographic, operations, product required and purchasing situation variables related to current or potential customer market segments.

Day (1990) also identified response profile characteristics, 'unique to the product or service … based on attributes and behaviour toward the product category or specific brands and vendors in that category'. These include specific vendor attributes such as overall value offered, product quality, vendor reputation, on time delivery and so on. In addition, customer variables such as the makeup of the decision-making unit (or buying centre), the importance of the purchase to the subject segment, and the innovativeness of the firms in this potential segment are examined. Another important aspect of the response profile technique is to review applications to determine how products are used. Finally, personal characteristics may be included to define a particular segment. These include variables related to individuals in the buying centre such as risk tolerance, loyalty, age, education and experience. These variables are often referred to as a posteriori, or after the fact variables, in which a 'clustering approach' is used to gather like customers together based on their particular needs. Some researchers call these micro variables.

Looking at the usefulness of the two basic segmentation approaches as measured against the tests for a good segment, Malhotra (1989) claims the identifier approach is better than the response profile approach in terms of measurability and accessibility since it is easy to find and reach the segments that already have established data classifications. He feels this method is particularly good for institutional markets where the number of establishments is small and the number of variables is large. On the other hand, Malhotra believes that using the response profile or clustering approach will produce more responsiveness from a particular segment since the marketing mix will be closely tailored to the specific needs of the segment identified.

Generally speaking, business marketers have used identifiers in segmenting their customers. The major reason for this is simplicity. With the Internet, it is easy to get the kinds of information needed to segment markets using the identifier approach.

Use of the response profile approach is a subject of much discussion in the literature. While there is general agreement that the customer's view of vendor attributes or how the decision-making unit is constituted or the risk tolerance of key members of the DMU is invaluable segmentation information, there is little agreement about how widespread this approach is.

Dibb and Simkin (2001) identified three major categories of barriers to segmentation: infrastructure, process and implementation. These can be further sub-divided into culture, structure and resources. Table 6.3 shows the key segmentation barriers, and some possible approaches to overcoming them.

Senior management must strongly support the process, develop the proper communications channels, establish adequate budgets and set up training for people who will be assigned to do the process but may not have the necessary education or skills.

During the process, marketers need to identify the segmentation steps, get the education gaps filled, then collect the data through internal and external sources. Those involved need to ensure that they stay on target, so that senior management know that the segmentation is going to fit into the overall corporate strategy.

The most widely accepted approach to segmentation is that proposed by Bonoma and Shapiro (1984). They describe the nested approach, starting with very general, easily available information and moving to the most specific variables which, incidentally, are the most difficult to obtain information about. (See Figure 6.8.)

The first and most obvious step is to group companies by industry classification. Industry classifications give a firm a start on a grouping of customers and prospective customers into potential segments – there are several systems in use. In the United States the NAICS system is used (originally introduced after the North American Free Trade Area was created to include Mexico and Canada), but in Europe the United Nations' ISICAEA system is more common.

Many firms simply divide their customers into heavy, medium and light users, the so-called A-B-C division. This may be useful for assigning salespeople to particular accounts, but is a poor substitute for the full segmentation process. Using firm demographics also includes dividing customers into types (OEM, user and aftermarket) and grouping them by company size, geographic location and specific financial factors such as credit worthiness.

Classifying customers as OEM (original equipment manufacturer), end user or aftermarket (or MRO: maintenance, repair and operations) gives important clues to their commonalities. An OEM buys components, systems, equipment and materials. In the case of components, these enter the OEM's final product, whereas materials are consumed in the manufacturing of their products. OEMs often purchase many different items to develop a particular product and frequently brand the product with their own name. Users obviously put the product to use. For instance, John

Table 6.3   Diagnosing and treating key segmentation barriers

Problems	Infrastructure	Process	Implementation
Culture	• Inflexible, resists new ideas • Not customer focused • Doesn't understand segmentation rationale	• Not committed to sharing data/ideas • Lack of 'buy in' • No fit with corporate strategy planning	• Product focus • Insufficient belief in the process • Unwillingness to change current segmentation
Structure	• Lack of intra-functional communications • Low senior management interest or involvement • Entrenched organisational structures	• Misuse of segmentation process	• Poor demarcation of responsibility • Ineffective communications of segmentation solution • Poor senior management involvement
Resources	• Too few or untrained people • Insufficient budgets	• Inadequate data available • Insufficient budgets • Too few or untrained people	• Lack of alignment of budgeting with segmentation • Insufficient time allowed
Solutions	Prior to process: • Find available data • Identify people/skills • Get senior management support • Develop communications • Establish adequate budgets • Train people – basic segmentation skills	During process: • Specify segmentation steps • Fill gaps in education/skills • Collect data – internal and external • Establish regular communications meetings • Review for fit with corporate strategy	Facilitate implementation: • Identify and communicate findings • Make changes to plans and programs • Identify changes required to culture and structure • Specify budgets, responsibilities and timing to roll out solutions • Develop method for monitoring roll out

Source: Based on Dibb and Simkin 2001

Deere tractors are used by farmers while Deere itself is an OEM (Hlavacek and Ames, 1986). The aftermarket includes firms who offer add-on products, repair services or replacement parts. Often, a producer may sell its product or services to all three of these firm types, but each is a separate and different segment since requirements will probably be quite different (There is more on this in Chapter 4.)

A second step involves more understanding of customer operations. In this step, the marketer would determine which technologies potential customers are employing, whether they are heavy or light users of the product to be offered, whether they purchase in a centralised or decentralised way, and specifically what product requirements customers have, ranging from standard to custom products.

A third step is to look at the purchasing situation – whether for this firm this purchase is a new task, a straight rebuy or a modified rebuy, whether the potential customer has positive attitudes toward the firm and what relationships have been established by the marketing firm with potential customers.

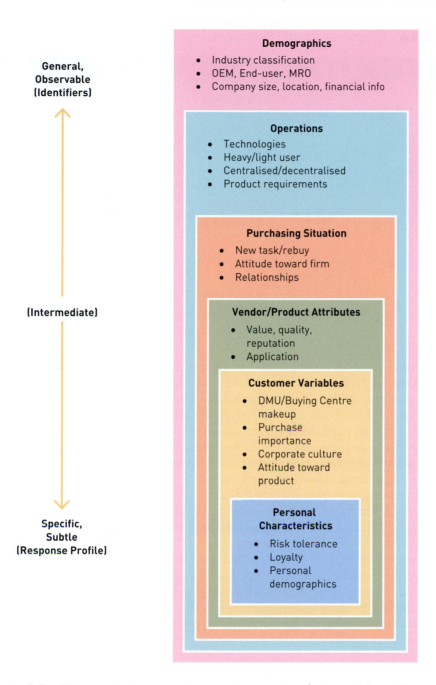

General,
Observable
(Identifiers)

(Intermediate)

Specific,
Subtle
(Response Profile)

Figure 6.8 The nested approach to segmentation (adapted from Bonoma and Shapiro 1983)

The fourth step is to determine what commonalities there are among potential customers. For instance, one customer group may be price-sensitive where another emphasises delivery, and still a third product quality (however that is defined). For instance, a motor engineer might regard the rapid delivery of spare parts as being far more important than a low price, since a delay in repairing a car might cost a great deal more in lost revenue. Another aspect of the vendor attribute would be the application in which the product may be used.

Table 6.4   Classification of customers

Type of customer	Description
OEM	Original equipment manufacturer. These customers buy manufacturing equipment, raw materials and components to make into finished products. Examples would be car manufacturers or consumer durables manufacturers.
End user	These customers use up the product entirely in the course of running the business. For example, a company will use cleaning materials, energy, copier paper, office furniture and so forth without incorporating any of these items into the finished products which it sells.
Aftermarket (MRO)	Maintenance, repair and operations companies provide services to companies and consumers. For example, a computer repair company will use spare parts, tools and transport to repair or replace defective parts.

Customer variables may be harder to identify. First and most important would be the makeup of the buying centre or DMU. Included here would be the importance of this purchase to the firm, the corporate culture, including the attitude toward innovation, and finally the attitude toward the product area. The most difficult variables to obtain are personal characteristics of individuals in the DMU. These include age, experience and education, loyalty to current vendor and risk tolerance. In nearly every industrial market, firms tend to stay with suppliers who have proved reliable: therefore the attitude toward the firm (as well as loyalty and tolerance for risk) will be important segmentation characteristics.

Robertson and Barich (1992) proposed a simple approach to segmentation based only on the purchase decision process. In this case, the authors claim that identifying potential customers as **first-time prospects**, **novices** and **sophisticates** yields all the segmentation information needed. First-time **prospects** are firms who see a need for the product, have started to evaluate possible suppliers, but have not yet purchased. Novices are customers who have purchased the product for the first time within the last 90 days and sophisticates have purchased the product before, and are now ready to rebuy or have recently repurchased. Their different needs are as follows:

- First-time prospects are seeking honest salespeople who know and understand their business, a vendor who has been in business for some time, and they usually negotiate for a trial period.
- Novices are looking for technical support, training and knowledgeable sales reps.
- Sophisticates are seeking compatibility with existing systems, customised products, a successful record from the supplier, speed in sorting out problems, and post-sales support. The main advantage of this simplified approach is the ability to implement it with the salesforce, which is often the major hurdle for effective segmentation implementation.

Segmenting by customer benefits is recommended as the most effective approach and Rao and Wang (1995) found that identifiers do not correlate very well with

Novices Customers who have purchased the product for the first time within the last 90 days.

First-time prospects Potential customers with whom the company has never done business before.

Sophisticates Customers who have purchased the product before and are ready to rebuy or have recently repurchased.

Prospects People who have a need for a product and the means to pay for it.

profile or benefit sought variables. While these authors endorsed the nested approach to segmentation, they emphasised the importance of understanding specific customer benefits for the most effective segmentation.

NEED TO RE-SEGMENT

Since business market segments change quickly, it is important to re-segment frequently. Changes in competition, technological advances, economic downturns or upswings and consolidation of an industry make re-segmentation essential from time to time. Once a firm begins to look at its existing segmentation on a regular basis, it may find it necessary to establish new segments for the most effective use of its marketing efforts. Managements should avoid being 'married' to the current segmentation and hold open the possibility of re-segmenting. It is a management task to question the assumptions that underlie the current segmentation on a regular basis.

GLOBAL SEGMENTATION

Segmentation strategy is not limited to any one country. Sophisticated business marketing firms look across countries for commonalities of market segments. For instance, ICI Nobel Explosives offers mining explosives across various countries to similar customer types, co-ordinating its activities in each country by segment and offering product and sales activities accordingly (Gillespie et al. 2004). The same segmentation procedure described in Figure 6.8 can be used across various countries except that the data are much more difficult to get and developing common measures is often a real obstacle. Despite this, Schuster and Bodkin (1987) found that more than 40% of firms they surveyed gathered segmentation information for the following macro variables: geographic location, company size, usage, buying strategy, end market and decision-making stage. More than 40% of firms gathered data for the following micro variables: product attributes, purchase importance, attitudes and personal characteristics.

In business markets, it is not unusual to find commonalities among customers throughout the world. Electric utilities require the same products whether they are located in Kuala Lumpur or Caracas. A firm selling switchgear to electric utilities must look to a worldwide customer base in order to get the economies of scale necessary to be a global competitor. According to Yip (2003), customers can be segmented according to their purchasing patterns. **Global customers** are quite willing to purchase products outside their domestic markets and tend to have global control of purchasing from headquarters. The way the product is used also gives clues to the segmentation of the market.

Yip defines **national global customers** who use suppliers from around the world but employ the products in one country. **Multinational global customers** also buy from suppliers in many countries, but they use the products in many countries as well. Management should look for commonalities among customers using the segmentation process described in the earlier part of the chapter rather than accept that minor differences make serving one segment across countries too difficult to achieve. There are many benefits to serving multinational customer segments, not only including economies of scale, but also moving rapidly to world class product and service offerings, making further expansion even easier.

Targeting

Targeting is a process of choosing a segment or segments, deciding on a tactical approach to marketing the products to that segment, and developing the tactics into practical actions.

Global customers Firms that are willing to purchase products outside their domestic markets and tend to have global control of purchasing from headquarters.

National global customers Customers who source products globally but use them only within their national borders.

Multinational global customers Customers who source products globally, and also use the products globally.

For a segment to be viable, it must have the following characteristics:

- It must be definable, or measurable. There must be some way of identifying the members of the segment and knowing how many of them there are.
- It must be accessible. This means it must be possible to communicate with the segment as a group, and get the products to them as a group.
- It must be substantial, i.e. big enough to be worth targeting.
- It must be congruent. The members must have closely similar needs.
- It must be stable. The segment should not change substantially over time, either in its needs or in its membership.

The three key criteria are accessibility, substance and measurability, but it is important to look at the causes underlying the segmentation.

Freytag and Clarke (2001) offer a segment selection process, as illustrated in Figure 6.9. This process requires that a firm compare the potential segments it may serve, estimating future attractiveness, resource demands and fit with firm strategy. First, the firm should decide whether this particular segment will be growing at a suitable rate, is large enough and profitable enough to serve. In addition, the firm

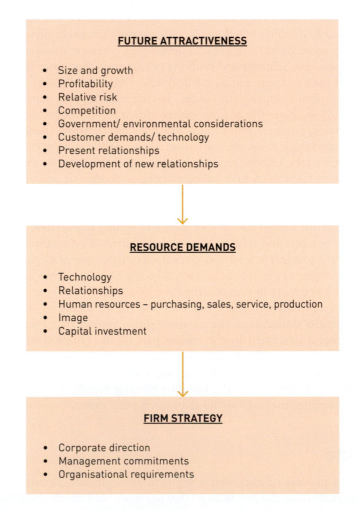

Figure 6.9   Segment selection process (adapted from Freytag and Clarke 2001)

should assess the competition and the risk, and understand any governmental or environmental concerns, what demands customers may have and how serving this particular segment may affect present and future relationships with current and future customers. Second, the firm must look at demands on its resources in technology, relationships, human resources in each of the functional areas, image, capital investment and product development required. Finally, the firm should examine whether this new segment is congruent with its present or future strategy related to the overall corporate direction, management's commitment and organisational requirements required to implement the strategy.

Real-life marketing: Pick the segments nobody else wants

When bank robber Willie Sutton was asked (on his way to prison) why he robbed banks, he supposedly said 'Because that's where the money is.' It's tempting to go for the biggest or wealthiest segments of the market because that's where the money is, but of course everybody else is going there as well.

If you go for a less popular option, you can often capture the whole segment yourself. For example, Saga tapped into the market for holidays for over-60s. Everybody else assumed that older people would be surviving on small pensions and would not want to travel much anyway – but Saga noticed that

many older people have substantial occupational pensions, are often fit and healthy, and at last have the time to see the world. The company moved away from the coach trips to Blackpool or the Lake District that were targeted at old people, and began taking them on cruises up the Amazon, train rides through the Rockies, and walking holidays in the Picos de Europa.

The company recognises that some elderly people might have trouble carrying luggage, or might need special medical care, and may well want to supplement (say) a tour of Australia with a few weeks' visit to relatives there. Therefore Saga trips are flexible, but they certainly aren't cheap and they certainly aren't boring.

If this idea appeals to you, here are some tips:

- Know your segment. Get to understand their needs in detail.
- Find a segment nobody else wants – even people with very little money still buy something.
- Look for opportunities to widen the range of products you can offer to your chosen segment. It's knowing the segment that counts, not your knowledge of the products.

Bonoma and Shapiro (1983) recommend choosing segments using two major criteria: Customer Conversion Analysis and Segment Profitability Analysis. The first simply means the attempt by a manager to determine how many of potential prospects in a particular segment can be converted into customers and how large that served segment will be. This is based upon the number of prospects in a market (the density) which can be reached for a particular marketing expenditure.

Product life cycle The process of launch, growth, maturity and decline which products are thought to go through.

Segment Profitability Analysis is an attempt to determine the contribution margin per pound invested to serve that segment. Bonoma and Shapiro recommend combining these approaches to determine which segments a firm ought to serve. To decide on which market segments to target, a firm would decide whether a segment is attractive, whether it has the resources to serve that segment, and whether serving that segment fits with the its overall objectives.

A firm may choose to apply undifferentiated marketing, which means focusing on commonalities among all segments, but in essence attempting to serve the entire market with only one marketing mix. This is found most often in the earliest stages of a **product life cycle** when undifferentiated product will be accepted by customers because there is no other choice. Think for a moment of the early days of the personal computer market industry. Early personal computers were very heavy, very slow and had limited software capabilities. Yet many firms purchased large numbers of these personal computers because the productivity increases of their employees outweighed the difficulties of finding specific computers that satisfied their corporate needs. Undifferentiated marketing usually only lasts as long as competition is limited.

When a firm decides to use differentiated marketing, it designs specific marketing mixes to serve each segment. Obviously, differentiated marketing costs more than undifferentiated marketing and can only be justified when the results outweigh the cost. In order to differentiate its marketing, the firm changes the balance of the marketing mix elements (see Chapter 1) in order to vary its offering.

It is important to remember that not all marketing mix elements have to be changed to serve each segment. In many cases the same product, price and promotion may serve two different segments where the only variation required is distribution or service.

For firms with very limited resources the only choice may be *concentrated marketing*. In this case a firm concentrates on one or very few segments. The idea is to build a dominant position in that segment. For example, a firm manufacturing highly sensitive, low-light level television cameras focuses its efforts on industrial applications of unauthorised entry or pilferage. Here again, the marketing mix must be carefully set to serve the specific segment(s) chosen. This is perhaps the most risky targeting strategy since the possibility exists that the segment may experience economic difficulties or choose to use a substitute product. Firms using the concentration strategy must be vigilant about the possibilities of new segments.

Positioning

Positioning essentially means developing a theme that will provide a 'meaningful distinction for customers' (Day, 1990). The concept of positioning was strongly advanced by Ries and Trout (2001). They stated that many products already have a distinctive position in the mind of the customer, and that these positions are difficult to dislodge. For instance, IBM might be thought of as the world's largest and most competent computer company.

There are eight generic factors which are used in positioning products, as follows (Blankson and Kalafatis 2004):

1. Top of the range.
2. Service.
3. Value for money.
4. Reliability.

5. Attractiveness.
6. Country of origin.
7. Brand name.
8. Selectivity.

These elements in a positioning strategy are not mutually exclusive, but obviously a firm cannot emphasise all of the factors because such a claim would lack credibility. For example, claiming to offer the best service, best country of origin and best value for money might sound unlikely (depending on one's definition of value for money).

Trout and Ries say that competitors have three possible strategies they may follow. First, the firm may choose to strengthen its current leadership position by reinforcing the original concepts that lead to the first position in the mind of the customer. Second, to establish a new position – 'cherchez les creneaux' – looking for new openings in a market. Third, to attempt to de-position or re-position the competition. Ries and Trout claim that customers establish a ladder for each product category in their minds. On these ladders, buyers establish possible suppliers as first, second or third level. This can offer an opportunity for positioning. Their most famous example of this comes from the car hire business and the car hire company, Avis. When Avis entered the market, Hertz held an unassailable position as the premier car rental firm. Avis was one of many other competitors, but Avis chose to position themselves as 'Number 2' which at that time was an unoccupied position. This immediately catapulted Avis to a position as an important competitor despite the reality that it was no larger than any of the other competitors fighting for a piece of the market with the pre-eminent Hertz. This is also known as establishing the 'against' position – Avis placing themselves against Hertz.

Research shows that when people compare brands, the position of the product within the overall brand (for example, the best or worst model within the Ford range of cars) is more important than differences between competing brands (the difference between Ford and Renault). This implies that people tend to look at the overall, umbrella brand before they decide on products within the brand (LeClerc et al. 2002).

Treacy and Wiersema (1993) offer three value disciplines – operational excellence, customer intimacy or product leadership. They recommend that a firm should try to become a 'champion' in one of these areas while simply meeting industry standards in the other two.

Often, positioning is based upon a series of perceptual maps. An example is shown in Figure 6.10. This example shows two important variables, the horizontal axis for initial price and the vertical axis for technical assistance. The lower right-hand corner of this matrix is probably a poor position to be in – in this quadrant, a firm would be offering a high initial price with only adequate technical assistance, an offering that is unlikely to appeal.

Let us assume that three firms are in the market. Firm A is a low-priced firm offering little technical assistance. Firm B is a higher-priced firm with very good technical assistance. The management of Firm C may see an opportunity to stake out a position as a somewhat lower-price offering than B with somewhat better technical assistance than A. (It might be noted here that a firm which could occupy the upper-left quadrant offering low initial price and very good comprehensive technical assistance might win many more customers than either A, B, or C. In the real world, though, this can't be done – technical support must be paid for somehow.)

A critical point is that customers must place value on the variables being examined. In our example, if the customers had no particular need for technical assistance this perceptual map would be virtually useless. However, if Firm C's market research shows

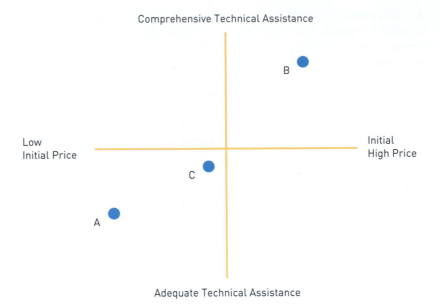

Comprehensive Technical Assistance

B

Low
Initial Price

Initial
High Price

C

A

Adequate Technical Assistance

Figure 6.10   Perceptual map

that technical assistance and initial price are critical variables in the decision-making process this map is quite useful in helping develop a position that can be clearly communicated to potential customers. In political markets there are five technical features of the political campaign: national policy, local policy, leaders, values and candidates. In fact, though, voters are most often swayed by service features – the degree to which their MP is supportive in the community, and so forth (Baines et al. 2003).

A special consideration for international positioning is the country of origin effect. Buyers have already established perceptions of country capabilities, i.e. 'German engineering' develops positive associations. Country of origin has less effect in consumer markets: a Canadian study showed that 93% of consumers did not know the country of origin of the product they had just bought, and of the 5.5% who did know, only 2% thought that the knowledge might have played a part in their decision (Liefeld 2004). On the other hand, if the country of origin has a poor reputation this can have a strong negative effect on positioning (Martin et al. 2011).

Positioning a brand relies on four factors (the four Cs of positioning):

1. Clarity. It must be obvious to the consumers (or customers) what the brand is and where it sits relative to other brands.
2. Credibility. The position must be logical and believable – an obviously cheap and basic product cannot position itself as a premium brand. The reverse is also true – few people would believe that a well-designed and well-made product can be sold for a low price: most people would suspect a catch!
3. Consistency. Whatever position is adopted, the marketers must maintain a consistent brand message.
4. Competitiveness. Successful positioning should mean that the company is not trying to occupy a position already taken by a competitor – it is far better to find a position that is currently not subject to competition.

Provided the company has a brand message that is clear, consistent, credible and competitive the positioning will be successful and the brand will sell.

Re-positioning

If a current position has been rendered useless by competitor pressure or customer indifference or because the results of the firm are less than expected, new positioning is necessary. Day (1990) suggested a four-step process, as follows:

1. Identify alternative positioning themes.
2. Screen each alternative according to whether it is meaningful to customers, feasible (given the firm's capabilities and customers' perceptions), offers a sustainable competitive advantage, and fits with corporate objectives.
3. Choose the position that satisfies the criteria, and is also popular within the organisation.
4. Design the programmes needed to implement the new positioning.

The main test in this approach is to be sure that alternatives are meaningful to customers, feasible, and superior to what competitors offer.

Real-life marketing: Lucozade

Sometimes a brand continues to be targeted at a shrinking segment, or at least one that is less attractive than another segment. Repositioning takes effort and expense, because you will have to educate a totally new audience for the product, but it can pay off really well.

Lucozade used to be a product marketed to people recovering from a serious illness. The glucose gave them a quick energy boost, and the bubbles stimulated their digestions: as a way of nourishing someone with a depressed appetite it was very effective. The problem was that the population was getting healthier, so there were fewer convalescents around to drink the stuff.

The company therefore repositioned Lucozade as a sports drink, using Olympic athlete Daley Thompson in its advertising. Small PET bottles were used rather than the big pint bottles the product previously came in, and distribution shifted from pharmacies to supermarkets. Now, relatively few people remember the original use of the drink.

If you want to reposition your brand, you have to:

- Be sure that you are happy to lose the existing segment. You can't occupy two positions at once.
- Be clear about the position you want to occupy.
- Anticipate retaliation from competitors who are already established in the position you want to occupy.
- Keep all your marketing consistent with the new position.

Repositioning carries risks, because the firm will have to abandon the existing segment in order to focus on the new one. If the new positioning does not work, then it is likely to be difficult or even impossible to regain the old position. On the other hand, if the firm is targeting a shrinking segment, the product will eventually fail anyway: moving the brand to a different segment would save it, under those circumstances.

Designing the programmes to implement the chosen position can be a complex task requiring cooperation from all functional areas in the firm and sometimes requiring product and service modifications as well. Once a position is chosen, a firm must clearly communicate this position in a consistent way. The best positioning is simple to communicate: 'the fastest, the oldest or the most technically competent' are easy messages to communicate through advertising, public relations and especially through the salesforce. It is especially important that a simple position be established when a firm is to communicate in many languages and across many cultures. Reducing the position to its irreducible simplest form will make it easy for the salesforce to communicate what the company stands for and this is a critical ingredient in global success. Choosing the right position is the culmination of all the market segmentation and targeting work which has been discussed in this chapter.

Chapter summary

Choosing the right customers, for the right reasons, and presenting the product in the right way is how a competitive advantage is achieved, no matter what the industry. Segmenting markets is key to allocating marketing resources effectively. Understanding which customer characteristics are most relevant in predicting their propensity to buy the firm's products is a matter of executive judgement, based on clear market research.

Targeting is the process of choosing which segments of the market will be most helpful to the company in achieving its strategic objectives. No company can please everybody, but more importantly no company should try to do so: choosing which customers are too expensive, too troublesome, or too unprofitable to service is as important as choosing which are the most attractive customers.

Positioning the brand in consumers' minds is the final stage in establishing a presence in the market. Correct positioning ensures that customers are not disappointed when they buy the product, and also that the target customers will prefer the product over rival firms' products, thus ensuring long-term success for the company.

 Key points

- Segmentation is about dividing the overall market into groups of people with similar needs.
- The starting-point for segmentation is good market research.
- Targeting implies choosing who *not* to do business with.
- The chosen target is not necessarily the most profitable: there could be strategic reasons for marketing to a particular segment.
- Positioning means providing a meaningful distinction for customers.
- Customers must place value on the variables on offer if positioning is to succeed.
- Positioning relies on clarity, credibility, consistency, and competitiveness.

Review questions

1. Why would someone be prepared to pay £500 a night for a hotel room on one type of trip, and only £50 a night on a different trip?
2. What are the benefits of segmentation?
3. Why should a firm deliberately turn away potential customers?
4. What are the potential problems in targeting a wealthy segment?
5. How does positioning work?
6. What are the key bases for segmenting a market?
7. How might the market for entertainment segment?
8. When should a company consider repositioning a brand?
9. What are the potential dangers of repositioning a product?
10. How might targeting be carried out in the restaurant business?

Case study revisited: Verdié

Verdié approaches each of its segments with a different proposition. Their *Version Découverte* is aimed mainly at students and schoolchildren, and can be tailored around the specific needs of the group – in the main, the purpose of the trip is to improve students' language skills, so popular destinations include the UK, the United States, South Africa and Australia. Verdié employ bilingual staff to liaise with hotels, private households and attractions such as museums etc. in the host countries. In some cases students are accommodated with families in those countries, in other cases they might be accommodated in hostels or hotels.

The *Version Liberté* looks much like any other package holiday – it includes flights, transfers to hotels, and some on-site support by the firm's agents, but mainly people are left to enjoy their leisure time as they wish (probably centred around the hotel swimming-pool or the beach). Many of these trips are arranged within France – the company offers trips to the Alps and Pyrenees as well as Spain and Morocco. Hotels are classified as budget, '*bien-être*' (which means well-being and includes hotels with spas and gyms), '*charme*' (which means 'charm' and includes boutique hotels and hotels which are themselves an experience) and '*famille*' (for child-friendly hotels with facilities for children).

The *Version Exploration* provides adventure trips for small groups. Some of these are very adventurous – camping in the Sahara, boat trips on the Niger River, crossing the Serengeti in a 4x4, and so on.

The company also offers the *Version Fêtes et Carnavals*, which is aimed – often seasonally – at short-break clients. These take people to Christmas markets in Austria, to Spanish fiestas, shopping in New York, and many other destinations.

For all these segments of the market, the company tries to live up to its branding: '*Voir le monde, pas comme tout le monde*', which means 'See the world, but not like everybody else'. (Of course it sounds much better in French!)

Case study: FirstDirect

FirstDirect was established in 1989 as Britain's first virtual bank. A subsidiary of Midland Bank (later HSBC), FirstDirect had no high street branches, but instead operated entirely by telephone and post (there was no Internet in 1989, at least not for the vast majority of people).

The new bank was a radical departure in an industry that had always traded on its traditional, solid image. In fact it represented a very risky proposition indeed from a marketing viewpoint, because the concept of telephone banking did not exist – people were used to visiting a physical, bricks-and-mortar branch if they needed to deposit or withdraw cash, or indeed do anything with their banking. The idea of being able to arrange a loan, set up a standing order or direct debit, or open a new account purely over the telephone was one for which the public was entirely unprepared. FirstDirect therefore needed to consider who would be prepared to make the switch – and, even more so, who would see the new bank as a breath of fresh air.

FirstDirect looked at the type of person who would find it difficult to get to a bricks-and-mortar branch, and also at the type of person who would have enough income to be attractive to a bank. The final aspect of FirstDirect's segmentation and targeting was to look for people who would be open to new ideas, and would respond positively to a new type of banking.

The result was a target audience profile of young urban professionals earning somewhere above the national median income. At the time, this group were popularly known as yuppies – young urban professionals – and would certainly respond well to the new idea. The typical FirstDirect customer would be a Channel 4 viewer, would be educated to degree level or the equivalent, an employee with a regular salary going into his or her bank account, and a home-owner. Of course some people slipped through the net – the occasional self-employed plumber may have opened an account – but FirstDirect had a clear target segment in mind.

The company used a quirky approach to promoting the new bank. TV adverts ran simultaneously on Channel 4 and regional ITV stations, one channel showing the positives of FirstDirect and the other channel showing the negatives of existing banks. Viewers were advised to choose which ads they wanted to see, and switch channels accordingly. This interactive approach was completely new territory in 1989 – remember the Internet had only just been invented, and was still a toy for academics and military forces to play with, not something the public had access to.

FirstDirect took its first telephone call at 12.01 am on 1 October 1 1989, and handled over 1000 calls in the first 24 hours. Call centre staff are friendly and helpful – they are not restricted as to how much time they spend with a customer, they are empowered to solve most customer problems, and pretty much everything a customer needs to do can be handled over the telephone with the exception of some loan agreements that require a physical signature (this is a UK banking regulation).

By 1991 FirstDirect had 100,000 customers, but growth after this was rapid: four years later the customer base passed the half-million mark, and as of 2012 it had 1.16 million. Other banks have tried to copy the format, but with limited success – often their call centres are unable to match FirstDirect's professional, friendly and capable staff, and in any case distance banking is peripheral to their core business, so will naturally have less attention and resources devoted to it. FirstDirect pioneered Internet banking and mobile telephone banking, and are among the first to have a presence in social media. This commitment to the technology means that the bank continues to appeal to its target audience – young, educated people who are good earners and are tech-savvy. Perhaps this is why FirstDirect is the bank that is most often recommended by its customers.

Questions

1. Why target a yuppie market?
2. What might have been the thinking behind the concurrent advertising on different channels?
3. Why are the call centre staff given so much empowerment?
4. Why might FirstDirect be the most widely-recommended bank by its customers?
5. Why can't other banks simply copy the format?

Further reading

Books purely on the subject of segmentation and targeting are not all that common: all introductory marketing texts cover the principles. Having said that, there are some segmentation texts available: here is a selection:

H.B. McDonald and Ian Dunbar, *Market Segmentation: How to Do It, How to Profit From It* (Oxford: Butterworth Heinemann, 2004). This is a textbook with a strong practitioner bias. Although it is aimed at marketing professionals, it is academically rigorous and also fairly readable.

Michael Wedel and Wagner A. Kamakura, *Market Segmentation: Conceptual and Methodological Foundations* (Dordrecht, Kluwer Academic Publishers, 1999). This is a much more academic text, replete with theory.

References

Allport G.W. and Odbert, H.S. (1936) Trait names: a psycholexial study. *Psychological Monograph* 47: 211 (Princeton, NJ: American Psychological Association).

Baines, Paul R., Worcester, Robert M., Jarrett, David and Mortimore, Roger (2003) Market segmentation and product differentiation in political campaigns: a technical feature perspective. *Journal of Marketing Management*, 19: 225–49.

Bailey, Christine, Baines, Paul R., Wilson, Hugh and Clark, Moira (2009) Segmentation and customer insight in contemporary services marketing practice: why grouping customers is no longer enough. *Journal of Marketing Management*, 25 (3/4): 227–52.

Bardacki, Ahmet and Whitelock, Jeryl (2004) How ready are customers for mass customisation? An exploratory investigation. *European Journal of Marketing*, 38 (11/12): 1396–416.

BBC News (1998) Business: The economy and the pink pound, 31 July. news.bbc.co.uk/1/hi/business/the_economy/142998.stm [accessed 3 September 2013].

Blankson, Charles and Kalafatis, Stavros P. (2004) The development and validation of a scale measuring consumer/customer derived generic typology of positioning strategies. *Journal of Marketing Management*, 20 (1): 5–43.

Bonoma, Thomas V. and Shapiro, Benson P. (1983) *Segmenting the Industrial Market*. Lexington, MA: D.C. Heath Co.

Bonoma, Thomas V. and Shapiro, Benson P. (1984) Evaluating market segmentation approaches. *Industrial Marketing Management*, 13 (4): 257–68.

Briggs, K. and Myers, I. (1962) *Manual: The Myers–Briggs Type Indicator.* Princeton, NJ: Educational Testing Service.

Cardozo, Richard N. (1980) Situational segmentation of industrial markets. *European Journal of Marketing*, 14 (5/6): 264–76.

Chesbrough, Henry W. (2003) Environmental influences upon firm entry into new sub-markets: evidence from the worldwide hard disk drive industry conditionally. *Research Policy*, 32: 659–78.

Cohen, J.B. (1967) An interpersonal orientation to the study of consumer behaviour. *Journal of Marketing Research*, 6 (August): 270–8.

Day, George S. (1990) *Market-Driven Strategy: Process for Creating Value*. New York: The Free Press.

DeBerry-Spence, Benet and Izberk-Bilgin, Elif (2006) Wearing identity: the symbolic uses of native African clothing by African Americans. *Advances in Consumer Research*, 33 (1):193.

Dibb, Sally and Simkin, Lyndon (2001) Market segmentation: diagnosing and treating the barriers. *Industrial Marketing Management*, 30 (8): 609–25.

Dolnicar, Sara and Lazarevski, Katie (2009) Methodological reasons for the theory/practice divide in market segmentation. *Journal of Marketing Management*, 25 (3/4): 357–73.

Donnelly, J.H. (1970) Social character and the acceptance of new products. *Journal of Marketing Research*, 7 (Feb): 111–13.

Freytag, Per Vagn and Clarke, Ann Hojberg (2001) Business to business market segmentation. *Industrial Marketing Management*, 30 (6): 473–86.

Gillespie, Kate, Jeannet, Jean-Pierre and Hennessey, H. David (2004) *Global Marketing: An Interactive Approach*. Boston, MA: Houghton Mifflin.

Hlavacek, James D. and Ames, B.C. (1986) Segmenting industrial and high-tech markets. *Journal of Business Strategy*, 7 (2): 39–50.

Horney, K. (1945) *Our Inner Conflict*. New York: WW Norton.

Jamal, Ahmed (2003) Marketing in a multicultural world: the interplay of marketing, ethnicity and consumption. *European Journal of Marketing*, 37 (11): 1599–620.

Kates, Steve (2002) Doing brand and subculture ethnographies: developing the interpretive community concept in consumer research. *Advances in Consumer Research*, 29 (1): 43.

Kotler, Philip (2003) *Marketing Management*. Upper Saddle River, NJ: Prentice Hall.

LeClerc, France, Hsee, Christopher K. and Nunnes, Joseph C. (2002) Best of the worst or worst of the best? *Advances in Consumer Research*, 29 (1): 59–61.

Liefeld, John P. (2004) Consumer knowledge and use of country-of-origin information at the point of purchase. *Journal of Consumer Behaviour*, 4 (2): 85–96.

Lindridge, Andrew (2010) Are we fooling ourselves when we talk about ethnic homogeneity? The case of religion and ethnic subdivisions amongst Indians living in Britain. *Journal of Marketing Management*, 26 (5/6): 441–72.

McDonald, Emma K. and Uncles, Mark D. (2007) Consumer savvy: conceptualisation and measurement. *Journal of Marketing Management*, 23 (5/6): 497–517.

Malhotra, Naresh K. (1989) Segmenting hospitals for improved management strategy. *Journal of Health Care Marketing*, 9 (3): 45–52.

Marketing News (1985) 13 September, p. 56.

Martin, B.A.S., Lee, M.S.W. and Lacey, C. (2011) Countering negative country of origin effects using imagery processing. *Journal of Consumer Behaviour*, 10 (2): 80–92.

Rao, Chatrathi P. and Wang, Zhengyuan (1995) Evaluating alternative segmentation strategies in standard industrial markets. *European Journal of Marketing*, 29 (2): 58–75.

Richardson, Brendan and Turley, Darach (2006) Support your local team: resistance subculture and the desire for distinction. *Advances in Consumer Research*, 33 (1): 175–80.

Ries, Al and Trout, Jack (2001) *Positioning: The Battle for Your Mind*. New York: McGraw–Hill.

Robertson, Thomas S. and Barich, Howard (1992) A successful approach to segmenting industrial markets. *Planning Review*, Nov–Dec: 4–48.

Sampson, P. (1992) People are people the world over: the case for psychological market segmentation. *Marketing and Research Today*, November: 236–44.

Schuster, Camille P. and Bodkin, Charles D. (1987) Market segmentation practices of exporting companies. *Industrial Marketing Management*, 16 (2): 95–102.

Simcock, Peter, Sudbury, Lynn and Wright, Gillian (2006) Age, perceived risk and satisfaction in consumer decision-making: a review and extension. *Journal of Marketing Management*, 22 (3/4): 355–77.

Skinner, H. and Stephens, P. (2001) Speaking the same language: an exploratory study into the relevance of neuro-linguistic programming to effective marketing communications. 6th International Conference on Corporate and Marketing Communications, Queen's University Belfast.

Treacy, Michael and Wiersema, Fred (1993) Customer intimacy and other value disciplines. *Harvard Business Review*, 71 (1): 84–93.

Yip, George S. (2003) *Total Global Strategy II*. Upper Saddle River, NJ: Prentice Hall.

Zhinkan, G.M. and Shermohamad, A. (1986) Is other-directedness on the increase? An empirical test of Reisman's theory of social character. *Journal of Consumer Research*, 13 (June): 127–30.

More online

To gain free access to additional online resources to support this chapter please visit:
www.sagepub.co.uk/blythe3e

CHAPTER ⑦
Integrated marketing communications

LEARNING OBJECTIVES

After reading this chapter, you should be able to:

- Explain how people interact with marketing communications.

- Understand the interactive nature of communication.

- Explain the role of redundancy in communication.

- Describe the role of culture in communication.

- Explain the sources of miscommunication.

- Describe the taxonomy of marketing communication.

- Explain the role of personal factors in communication.

- Explain the difference between, and the role of, push and pull strategies.

- Explain the role of negotiation in budget-setting.

- Explain how competition affects communication strategies.

- Describe the problems of integrating marketing communications.

Introduction

Marketing communications are the most visible part of marketing. Everyone is familiar with advertising, mailings, press releases, messages on T-shirts, spam e-mails, and so forth. It is common to say that people are bombarded with advertising – but in fact this is not really true.

Human beings like to communicate. Conversation is still the most popular form of entertainment for the majority of us: we communicate with each other via telephone, newsprint, billboard, e-mail, television, radio, text message, and probably by jungle drum and sign language if nothing else is available. As a species, we love to exchange information, to argue, to persuade and to influence others. Communication about products and services is part of that mass of communication, and marketers are simply joining in with everyone else in the process. For marketers, communication about products and services is not just an entertainment, it is also a profession and a livelihood. Although communication is a major part of marketing, it is not the whole story: just as there is more to being a human being than just communication, there is more to being a marketer than just advertising.

This chapter examines the theoretical context of marketing communications. Beginning with theories of communication, the chapter continues into the structure and current thinking about the management of marketing communications.

Preview case study: Budweiser

Budweiser is a light lager produced by Anheuser-Busch in the United States, and brewed under licence in several other countries. The beer owes its lightness in part to the fact that it is brewed using up to 30% rice, rather than the barley used for most beers. The company was formed in 1864, when Adolphus Busch went into partnership with his father-in-law, Eberhard Anheuser. Busch owned a brewery supply company, whereas his father-in-law owned a brewery. The company prospered until 1920, when Prohibition banned alcohol from the United States: the ban remained in force until 1933, at which point Anheuser Busch began brewing again.

The product had to be adapted, however. American taste in beer had shifted – although alcohol was technically illegal during Prohibition, huge quantities were smuggled in or were brewed at home (illegally). The imported beers and home-brews were sweeter than traditional lagers, so Anheuser Busch instituted a promotional campaign in which they challenged drinkers to drink Budweiser for a week – if they weren't completely satisfied, the company was happy for them to go back to their original beer.

The Second World War created another hiatus, with the company having to abandon its customers on the West Coast due to restrictions on railroad freight. After the war, though, business boomed again – the country was wealthy, having come out of the war with very little loss and a great deal of gain in terms of export markets. Returning soldiers were eager for the good life after four years of war, and the beer market boomed.

The Budweiser brand, in common with other beer brands, is associated with fun and good times. In the early 20th century the company commissioned a song called 'Under the Anheuser Bush' which had a limited commercial success, but which put the company name on the airwaves of America. In later years, the Budweiser brand has been promoted using computer-generated frogs (Bud, Weis and Er), and a series of ads built around the word 'Whassup?' These have passed into popular American culture and can often be heard used in humorous contexts by Americans.

From the viewpoint of any brewer, however, the holy grail of marketing has to be a young audience, preferably one that is educated and affluent. Targeting this audience has become the challenge of the 21st century for Budweiser.

Communication theory

Communication is one of the most human of activities. The exchange of thoughts that characterises communication is carried out by conversation (still the most popular form of entertainment in the world), by the written word (letters, books, magazines and newspapers) and by pictures (cartoons, television and film).

Communication has been defined as a transactional process between two or more parties whereby meaning is exchanged through the intentional use of symbols (Engel et al., 1994).

Breaking down this definition, we see that communication is intentional (a deliberate effort is made to convey information), that it is a transaction (the participants are all involved in the process, even if they do not make a response), and it is also symbolic (words, pictures, music and other sensory stimulants are used to translate thoughts into something that can be understood by the other person of people). People are not telepathic, so all communications require concepts to be translated into symbols to convey the required meaning.

This means that the individual or firm issuing the communication must first reduce the concepts to a set of symbols that can be passed on to the recipient of the message; the recipient must decode the symbols to get the original message. In fact, the parties must share a common field of experience which includes a common view of what the symbols involved actually mean.

A well-known and widely used model of communication was developed by Schramm in 1948 and revised in 1971. This model is shown in Figure 7.1. The Schramm model views communication as a process that takes place between a sender and a receiver: there will also be a message, and a medium through which the message can be transmitted. The receiver may have a method of sending feedback on the message, to confirm that the message has been correctly received and understood, but noise and interference will affect both the ability of the message to get through, and the content of the message.

The sender's field of experience and the receiver's field of experience must overlap, at least to the extent of having a common language, but in fact the overlap is likely to be much more complex and subtle in most marketing communications. Advertisements typically use references from TV shows, proverbs and common sayings: they often make puns or use half-statements which the audience are able to complete because they are aware of the cultural referents involved. This is why foreign advertising often seems unintentionally humorous, or even incomprehensible.

Noise is the surrounding distractions present during the communications process, for example someone walking into the room during a commercial break. Interference is a deliberate attempt to distract the audience's attention with intelligent communications. For example, a car driver may be distracted away from a radio advertisement by another car cutting in (noise) or by seeing an interesting billboard (interference). For most marketing purposes the difference is academic.

The Schramm model is useful, but it suffers from a number of weaknesses. First, it is essentially a one-step model of communication. This is rather over-simplified; Katz and Lazarsfield (1955) postulated a two-step model in which the messages are

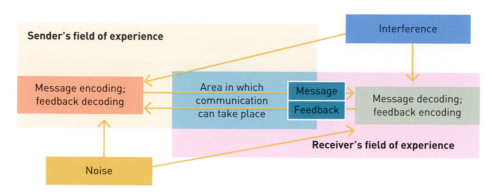

Figure 7.1 Schramm model of the communication process

filtered through opinion leaders, for example magazine journalists, which alters both the content of the message and its impact on the receiver. Many marketing messages are filtered in this way, because the messages need to appear in a medium that might itself become part of the message. For example, an advertisement placed in a tabloid newspaper undoubtedly has a very different impact from that of the same advertisement placed in a glossy magazine. The image of the medium affects the credibility of the message.

Redundancy In communications, sending a message by more than one route, to ensure a correct delivery.

Second, in most cases the message reaches the receiver via several routes. Sending the same message by more than one route is called **redundancy**, and is a good way of ensuring that the message gets through. Figure 7.2 shows this diagrammatically. In the diagram, the sender sends almost identical messages via different routes. The effect of noise and interference is to distort the message, and the opinion leader will moderate the message, but by using three different routes the meaning of the message is more likely to get through.

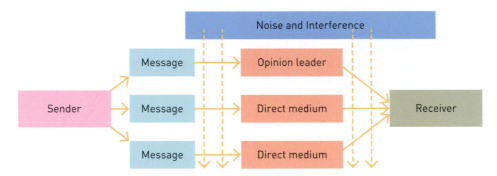

Figure 7.2   Redundancy in communication

At first sight, this would be a good reason to integrate marketing communications, but in practice the message will tend to shift according to the route being used, which makes integration difficult. Because of the selective nature of perception (see Chapter 3), a radio advertisement is likely to have a different impact from that of a TV advertisement, and (even more so) from that of a press advertisement. Current thinking is that different media cannot deliver the identical message, so integrating communications may therefore be more about delivering different parts of the same message rather than delivering the same message in several different ways.

Think outside this box!

If people are interested in the subject matter of the message, presumably they will pay attention to it. If they are not interested, presumably they will not act upon the message even if they are forced to hear it. So why do we need to worry about noise, interference, and so forth? Why not just put out messages, and assume that people will take in the ones they are interested in and ignore the ones that are irrelevant?

Or is this a naïve view? Maybe people don't know whether they will be interested or not until after they have heard the message – so maybe we have to hammer it at them to get a result. Then again, is this really the way to treat our potential customers?

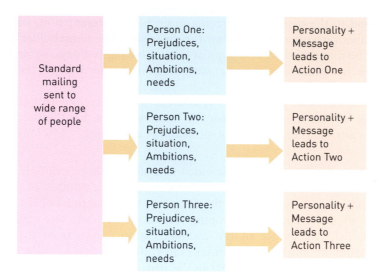

Figure 7.3   Message plus person equals action

A further criticism of the Schramm model is that it tends to assume that the receiver is passive in the process. Human beings are not radio transmitters and receivers: they think about what they send and receive, adding the message to what is already known. The Schramm model does not address issues of persuasion, or even of outright lying. Furthermore, the model assumes that the receiver is either listening or is not listening, whereas in practice people may be listening only part of the time. In other words selective attention will distort the message. Frequently communications are conducted as a dialogue of the deaf, in which each person wishes to make his or her point without actually listening to the other person's statements, or at best is only picking up part of what is being said (Varey 2000). Despite these shortcomings, the Schramm model is not only widely taught, but is also widely accepted as the expected model. People tend to imagine that what they say will be taken at face value, when of course this is unlikely to be the case. Consequently, people will exaggerate, omit negative facts and overstate the case in order to persuade other people to adopt their point of view. This is particularly true in the organisational context, where much communication is 'political', i.e. aimed at creating an impression in the mind of the receiver.

Figure 7.3 illustrates how a standard message sent to a group of people will produce a different response from each person, because the message is added to the existing prejudices, needs, situation and ambitions of the specific individual. The actions that arise from the message will be different for each person.

For example, consider what happens when a householder receives an offer of a free holiday in exchange for attending a presentation on timeshare apartments. The householder might respond in any of the following ways:

1. Throw the mailing away, perhaps without reading it. The householder's view of reality is that timeshare salespeople are unethical, and that timeshare is at best poor value for money and at worst fraudulent.
2. Respond to the mailing by agreeing to go to the presentation, having no intention of buying a timeshare but simply attending in order to win the free holiday. The householder's view is that the timeshare company is stupid, and is 'fair game' for being exploited.

3. Respond to the mailing by agreeing to go to the presentation, with an open mind about whether or not to buy the timeshare. The householder's view here might be that timeshare is a popular way of buying holidays, so perhaps there are benefits attached to it: either way, the householder will win the holiday, so it is a 'win–win' proposition.

4. Examine the exact wording of the address on the envelope to find out which mailing list was used. Reality for the householder is that the timeshare company is not smart enough to outwit its target customers.

There are undoubtedly other possible outcomes, but the above example shows how the message sent out by the timeshare company creates a number of possibilities, most of which are not desirable for the company. Only the third of the above four outcomes is what the company is hoping for, and is the only one covered by the Schramm model. Acceptance of the communication comes from the recipient's choice, not from the initiator's intentions (Varey 2000).

Furthermore, emotion plays a part in the processing of information. Memory is stimulated by advertisements that produce powerful emotions (Baird et al. 2007), in some cases to the extent that bland messages are not processed at all. The effect appears to be stronger in women than in men, for reasons that are not clear.

Recently, an alternative view of the communication process has emerged. Communications theorists such as Deetz (1992) and Mantovani (1996) see communication as a co-operative process in which meaning is developed between individuals. Their joint perception of the world is developed through a co-construction of meaning, in which dialogue acts as the mediating device. In this model, communication is not something that is done to recipients: it is something that is shared with recipients. Research shows that people prefer interactive communications (Vlasic and Kesic 2007), probably because one-way communications are boring, and also somewhat patronising compared with a dialogue of equals.

An analogy for this is shown in Figure 7.4. Reality is represented as a pool of shared meaning into which people have an input. Each person adds something to the

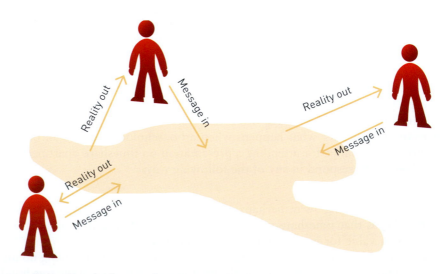

Figure 7.4   Pool of meaning

pool, and each person takes something out of the pool: what is put in is not necessarily the same as what is taken out, because each individual only takes what he or she wants from the pool. Also, what is put in is mixed with everything else in the same pool, so that the input is transformed.

If this alternative view of communication is accepted, it has far-reaching implications for marketers. In particular, the approach to marketing communications on the Internet is likely to be affected dramatically, since the Internet is above all an interactive medium: meaning is co-created and refined by the interactions between the website owner and the visitor, so that entirely new meanings are developed.

The hierarchy of communication effects

Communications are unlikely to create all their impact at once. Successive exposures to a communication will, if all goes well, move the recipient up a 'ladder' as shown in Figure 7.5. At the bottom of the ladder are people who are completely unaware of the product in question; at the top of the ladder are those who actually purchase the product. A problem with this model is that it implies that the process is invariably linear. This is not necessarily the case; an individual can become aware of a product and form an instant liking for it, without having detailed knowledge of it. Equally, people often buy products on impulse and form an opinion about them afterwards.

Having said that, the hierarchy of effects model is helpful in planning communications campaigns, since different communications methods and styles can be used according to the consumer's level on the hierarchy. For example, when a new product is introduced (or a product is introduced into a new market) few of the target audience will know anything about it. Establishing the brand name in people's consciousnesses is therefore a realistic first move in the communications process. Later on in the campaign, more detail about the product can be introduced, and finally some more persuasive arguments might be used to encourage people to buy.

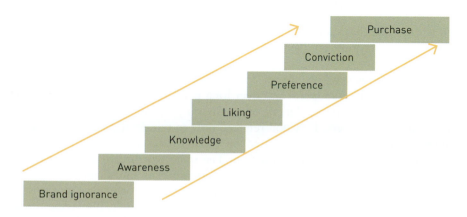

Figure 7.5   The hierarchy of communications effects

Real-life marketing: Getting noticed on Google

A different hierarchy of effects model operates in e-marketing, or at least that's what we might be led to believe. Marketing on the Internet seems to follow rules of its own, and communications is no exception. Apparently 85% of visitors to websites are taken there by search engines such as Google or Lycos, which means that the websites need to be attractive to search engines, not necessarily to visitors.

Search engines such as Google are increasingly gearing up to search for strings rather than keywords, because relatively few people now type in a single keyword when making a search. Single key words give far too many results for the average person to handle, so instead of typing in, say, 'mortgage' the searcher types in 'mortgage rates'. Even this gives too many results, so a searcher might type in 'lowest mortgage rates UK' or 'lowest mortgage rates first time buyers UK' to limit the search to the areas he or she is interested in.

From the viewpoint of the people running Google, teaching the machine to recognise strings is good business. The better the searches, the less time people spend on-line tying up resources and the more Google are able to charge their subscribers. The better the leads the search engine delivers, the happier the subscribers are and the more money everybody makes.

Once again the key to the whole process lies in understanding what the customers do when they search the Internet. Which is, of course, a marketing problem – unfortunately, the research into this area is still far from complete.

To get this to work for you in practice, you should do the following:

- Choose strings that accurately describe what you do. This will move you up the list and avoids irritating people who actually want something else.
- Remember that you don't want the maximum number of hits – you want the maximum number of leads.
- Use cookies to track the hits. You can then tailor what you do in order to maximise success for the visitor to your site.

Signs and meaning

A sign is 'anything that stands for something (its object) to somebody (its interpreter) in some respect (its context)' (Peirce 1986). Signs fall into three categories, as shown in Table 7.1.

The most obvious symbols are, of course, words. Words only have meanings as they are interpreted by people – and over long periods of time, even words change their meanings. For example, 'great' originally only meant 'large' but is now commonly used to denote 'good'. 'Cool' referred only to temperature fifty years ago – it moved through meaning 'well-presented' or 'capable' to a current meaning signifying agreement with a proposed plan of action. The same words can also have different meanings in different languages: in Portuguese, *mais* means 'more', whereas in French the word means 'but': in Spanish *mas* means 'more', but in Portuguese it means 'but'. Considering that these three languages are closely related, one can imagine the wide range of meanings a word might have in all the languages of the world.

Denotative Having the same meaning for everybody.
Connotative Having a unique meaning for an individual.

Meanings of words can be **denotative**, i.e. having the same meaning for everybody, or **connotative**, i.e. having a meaning that is unique to the individual. Although

Table 7.1   Categorising signs

Type of sign	Definition	Example
Icon	A sign that looks like the object, or represents it visually in a way that most people would relate to.	A drawing of a tractor would represent the countryside and farming to most people.
Index	A sign that relates to the object by a causal connection.	A sweaty manual worker going into a bar would symbolise beer to most people: we are all familiar with the idea of becoming thirsty after working hard.
Symbol	An artificial sign which has been created for the purpose of providing meaning.	Most people would recognise the intertwined arrows used to denote recyclable or recycled materials. This conveys an image of 'greenness' to the products it appears on.

everybody knows what a 'ship' is (denotative), some individuals can become seasick and might associate 'ship' with the discomfort experienced when at sea (connotative).

Because connotative meanings vary among individuals, marketers need to develop empathy with their target audiences. This is easiest when the marketer and the audience are as similar as possible in terms of background and outlook. Semiotics, syntactics and semantics are fields of study that enable us to ensure that the correct meanings are attributed to symbols.

SEMIOTICS

Semiotics is the study of sign systems. It is really more of a theoretical approach than an academic discipline (O'Sullivan et al. 1983). Spoken language is used as the main example of a sign system, but semiotics is not limited to language. Semiotics assumes that meaning can only be derived socially, so it agrees with the alternative view of communications described earlier. Communication is seen as an interaction between the reader and the text: texts are created by reworking signs, codes and symbols within the particular sign system in order to generate myths (stories that are not founded on evidence), connotations and meanings. The social process involved in communication is assumed to generate pleasure as well as cognitive, rational outcomes.

For example, a film (or indeed a TV advert) uses the sign systems of the spoken word, the actions of the actors, the music of the soundtrack, and the conventions of direction and production to generate its meaning. People seeing the film filter the information and add it to their pre-existing attitudes, knowledge and prejudices in order to create a meaning. In this sense all communication is interactive to the extent that the observer edits and mutates the meanings offered. This is why people often have heated discussions about the meaning of films, the motivations of the characters, and (of course) whether or not they enjoyed it.

Semiotics is an attempt to show how meaning is produced within a social context, implying that meaning is not produced by an individual but is subject to power plays, struggle and interpretation, much like any other social interaction.

SYNTACTICS

Syntactics is about the structure of communications. Symbols and signs will change their meanings according to the syntax, or contexts, in which they appear. For example, a road-safety poster showing a 10-year-old girl holding her father's hand to cross the road has a different meaning from that of the same 10-year-old holding her 4-year-old brother's hand. The girl means something different in each poster; in the first instance she is the protected person, in the second she is the protector, but there are greater connotations of vulnerability in the second example, which might make this poster more effective in alerting drivers to the dangers of children crossing the road.

Equally, the same word can have different meanings in different sentences, or the whole advertisement can acquire a different meaning when seen in different locations.

SEMANTICS

Semantics is often thought to be about the study of meaning, but in fact it is concerned with the way words relate to the external reality to which they refer.

In fact, communication is carried out in many other ways than the verbal or written word. Only 30% of communication is conveyed by words; people communicate by pictures, non-verbal sounds, smell, touch, numbers, artefacts, time and kinetics. Most of these media are used by marketers – for example, women's magazines sometimes have scratch-and-sniff cards which contain new fragrances. Charities often send out free pens to prospective donors so that they can more easily fill in direct debit contribution forms: the gift of a pen also places the recipient under a small social obligation to make a contribution.

Table 7.2 shows some of the ways these silent communications methods are used by marketers.

In Figure 7.6, semantics overlaps into reality because it is about the relationship between words and reality. The words become the reality in the minds of listeners. Semiotics feeds into syntactics, and thus the message is formulated: derived from reality, and moderated by the meanings and structures imposed by the composer of the message, the message becomes something new that is part reality, part messenger and part receiver.

Table 7.2 Silent communications

Medium	Example
Numbers	Heinz 57 Varieties is an example. There must have been a time when HJ Heinz produced exactly 57 varieties of canned food, but the range is very much larger than that now, and was very much smaller when the brand was established. The number implies a wide range of products.
Space	An image of people standing close together implies that they are good friends; likewise an image of wide open spaces implies freedom. Car advertising often uses this imagery.
Artefacts	Images of what people own imply their social status. Some artefacts (aircraft, cars, ships) might imply travel.
Time	An image of a clock's hands moving on might imply stress and pressure, or it might imply ageing.
Kinetics	People who are walking (or running) imply a fit and active lifestyle; those who are gesticulating with their hands imply intellectual discussion, or argument.

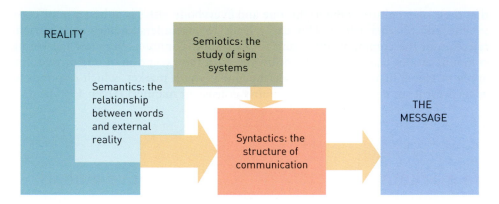

Figure 7.6 Semiotics, semantics and syntactics structuring communication

Silent languages and culture

The main problem with silent languages is that they are not culturally universal. Most body language does not transfer well to other cultures, even when the cultures are otherwise close. Well-known examples are the two-fingers sign, which is highly insulting to British people but which can denote merely 'two' in the rest of Europe; the thumb and index finger circle which denotes 'OK' to Americans but which is a rude gesture in Brazil; and showing the soles of the feet to Thais, which is again insulting. Other examples are more subtle. Japanese people tend to show their emotions less in public than do Americans, Indians tend to regard shabby or torn clothes as denoting poverty whereas North Europeans often associate this with independence and freedom, and numbers that are considered lucky in some cultures are neutral in others (Costa and Pavia 1992). Hong Kong and Shanghai Banking Corporation (HSBC) have made good use of these differences in their advertising, explaining that the bank has exceptional local knowledge and understands these cultural differences.

Think outside this box!

World communications are very well established, and people are not all that stupid. Surely if the message we are conveying is 'Please buy this product', which is what most marketing communications are about, most people would get the idea. Buying and selling is straightforward enough, isn't it?

So why worry about culture? If people know that they are looking at a German company's advertisements, or a Japanese company's ads, they *know* that these people are foreigners, and they will make allowances. In fact, mistakes in language and so on are often charming rather than offensive.

Could it be that we are being over-sensitive?

The problem arises because of **ethnocentrism**, which is the practice of assuming that others think and believe as we do. Ethnocentrism is one of the few features of human behaviour that belongs to all cultures; the tendency is for people to believe

Ethnocentrism The belief that one's own culture is superior to others.

that their own culture is the 'right' one and everybody else's is at best a poor copy (Shimp and Sharma 1987). This easily leads to misunderstandings and outright rejection of the communication, and is remarkably common. Very few marketing communications can be applied worldwide, with the exception of one or two that apply to global markets (for example the global youth market, which responds to adverts for jeans and music CDs in a fairly consistent manner) (Steen 1995).

Real-life marketing: If you're on the Web, you're global!

Almost all businesses nowadays have a website and in most cases it's interactive – but it's easy to forget that your website can be accessed from anywhere in the world. This has dangers as well as benefits: on the one hand, you might pick up business from anywhere between Vladivostok and Valparaiso, but on the other hand the potential for miscommunication is much greater.

Banco Mare Nostrum is a small Spanish bank which is able to offer Euro-denominated accounts to foreigners. All you need is a certificate of non-residence from the Spanish authorities and your interest is paid tax-free. The bank's website operates in both Spanish and English, with other languages shortly to follow. However, the translations have not always worked perfectly – some banking terms simply do not exist in other countries, and sometimes the legal and technical aspects of banking in Spain do not come across well. Having said that, the bank has had a great deal of new business, especially from British holiday-home owners.

If you're on the Internet, which almost certainly you are, you need to keep these factors in mind:

- Check that you don't have features, terms or pictures that might be offensive to people from other cultures (this is far from easy!)
- Consider whether slogans and strap lines will mean the same to foreigners – even if they are English-speaking, this might be a problem (we're all familiar with differences between US English and British English, but what about South Africans?)
- Always use a native speaker to translate your website.
- Think about how foreigners might use your product – bicycles are sports equipment in the UK but basic transport in India, for example.

National cultural differences can sometimes be identified: the main researcher quoted in this context is Hofstede (1984), who researched 6000 respondents in many countries in order to find national differences in culture. This research is, however, now seriously out of date: world communications and extensive migrations have eroded national differences to the extent that generalisations cannot be easily made.

Symbols differ from one culture to another. British marketers might use a lion to symbolise patriotism, whereas French marketers would use a cockerel and Americans would use a bald eagle. Advertisements transfer cultural meanings into products (McCracken 1986).

Miscommunication

Failure to communicate can arise from several different causes. In essence, these can be categorised under the following headings:

- Implication. Recipients sometimes read meanings into communications, due to their previous experiences, attitudes and prejudices.

- Distortion. Interference or noise from outside can change the message.
- Disruption. The circumstances surrounding the message, or deliberate acts by the recipient, can change the message.
- Confusion. If the message is ambiguous, the recipient may find it confusing.
- Agreement/Disagreement. If the sender and the receiver have different perspectives, there may be disagreement as to the meaning of the message.
- Understanding/Misunderstanding. Sometimes cultural issues (especially of language) or differences in perception mean that the message is simply misunderstood.
- Personal transformation. If the recipient is not prepared to change, the message may have little or no effect.

Each of these sources of miscommunication is present in marketing communications, as they are in interpersonal communications; the marketing implications of each are outlined in the following sections.

IMPLICATION

The implications of a communication are the meanings that are placed on it by the recipient. Miscommunication often arises between individuals because the communication raises unpleasant implications, and therefore the message is not stated clearly enough; for example, an employer telling staff that there might be redundancies might only intend to raise the possibility, but some staff will take it that their jobs are about to end, while others might take it that their own jobs are safe and others are under threat. Equally, marketing communications can fail because of implications. The implications of a message are peculiar to the individual: a mass communication will have different implications for each person who receives it, but marketers have to deal with people in the mass most of the time and therefore need to guess what the implications might be for most of the customers, not for a few individuals.

The main elements of implication are shown in Table 7.3.

DISTORTION

Internal distractions and external interference often lead to distortions in the meaning of the message. For example, an individual may believe that German products

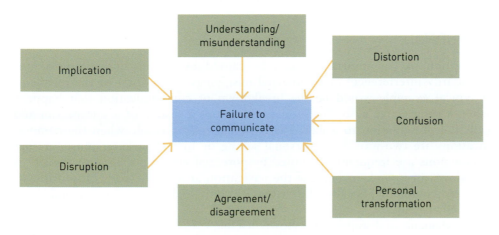

Figure 7.7 Causes of communication failure

Table 7.3   Elements of Implication

Element	Explanation
Assumption	If the message is unclear, the receiver tends to 'fill in the gaps' by making assumptions about the message. These assumptions are subject to positive or negative slanting, may or may not be open to inspection and revision in future, and may turn out to be true or false when the recipient tries to act on them.
Inference	The recipient may add extra ideas to the message as received, adding information from memory. This can happen even when the message itself is clear and no misunderstanding is involved.
Expectation	Expectations about the communication may affect the meaning even before the message is delivered. People often respond to what they expected to hear, rather than what was actually said.
Reflection	Consideration of past communications affects the recipient's behaviour towards future communications. This is similar to expectation and inference.
Attribution	In the case of interactive communications, there will be a jointly produced outcome, but each party will attribute the outcome differently. For example, a salesperson may attribute a failed sale to the sales resistance of the customer, whereas the customer may attribute the failure to the salesperson's irritating manner.
Metacommunication	Metacommunication is about how things are said rather than what is being said. In marketing communications, metacommunication is manifested in two ways; the style of the communication (for example, different styles of press release) or in the type of communication (television advertising as opposed to mailings).
The search for common ground	If there is no overlap between the sender's and recipient's fields of experience the communication will fail. In most cases, both parties are likely to seek the common ground in which communication takes place; the sender because of a need for the message to get through, the recipient because of curiosity about the message content.

are well-engineered, and from this will be biased towards all German products. The messages conveyed by adverts for German goods will be distorted by this internal distraction. Table 7.4 shows the main elements of distortion.

DISRUPTION

Disruption of communications can be caused by outside interruptions (not necessarily interference) or by internal misgivings on the part of the recipient. A typical example would be the breakdown of communication that happens when a prospective customer suddenly develops a dislike of a salesperson and calls the presentation to a halt. Disruption is only possible when the communications are two-way, as in personal selling or Internet transactions. Internet transactions are frequently curtailed by potential customers because the site is too slow to respond, or because the navigation around the site is too difficult, or (most commonly) because the customer is only seeking information and is not yet ready to buy.

The elements of disruption are shown in Table 7.5.

Table 7.4   Elements of distortion

Element	Explanation
Interference	To understand the message, the recipient must be able to concentrate on it to some extent. Other incoming messages may be inadvertently included in the interpretation of the main message, or may distract the recipient so that pieces of the main message are missed. The concept of interference relates mainly to the Schramm model described earlier: the 'pool' model of communication includes extra communications of this nature as part of the content of the pool.
Bias	Bias does not imply a malicious or negative mindset; it can simply mean that the recipient is likely to interpret the message in a particular way. Ideological, ethnocentric or egocentric biases all contribute to the distortion of messages because all messages are added (in whole or in part) to the information in an individual's memory.
Miscalculation	Miscalculation occurs when the information presented is wrongly interpreted through a mistake in cognition. Sometimes this comes about through simple stupidity or mistakes; sometimes it comes about through a desire for an alternative truth to prevail. In marketing communication terms, a customer might misinterpret the terms of a special offer because he or she is unable to meet the true conditions and is hoping that other, simpler, conditions would be acceptable.
Pseudo-communication	Some communications are intended to cover up a true state of affairs, in order to preserve appearances. Without actually lying about the true state of affairs, the communication is nonetheless a distortion of the truth. This is very much in accordance with Deetz's theories on political communication: for Deetz, the majority of communications within organisations fall into this category (Deetz 1992).

CONFUSION

Confusion arises from distortion, mistakes, disruption and conflict. Conflicting information about a product (for example, from a salesperson on the one hand and from a friend on the other) creates confusion in the mind of the recipient. Avoidance of confusion is one of the main driving forces behind the integration of marketing communications: if everyone tells the same story, the possibilities for conflict and confusion are reduced dramatically.

The elements of confusion are shown in Table 7.6.

AGREEMENT/DISAGREEMENT

Disagreement occurs when the recipient understands but does not accept the message. The message might be discounted because of a bias against the source, or because of the style of the message, or because the recipient has a different frame of reference from that of the sender.

Table 7.7 shows the elements of agreement and disagreement.

UNDERSTANDING AND MISUNDERSTANDING

There is always a risk of misunderstanding; part of the problem is that it is often impossible for the recipient of a message to know that there is a misunderstanding,

Table 7.5 Elements of disruption

Element	Explanation
Unmanageable circumstance	The feeling that the situation is outside one's control can lead to disruption. For example, a complex mail-order form may never be completed because the customer feels unable to control the situation.
Relational instability	The consistency of people's behaviour derives from the type of situations they find themselves in. In an unfamiliar or awkward situation (for example, a young man meeting his girlfriend's parents for the first time) the recipient may not be able to respond to the messages being offered.
Conversational irregularities	Conversation normally involves statements, assessment of the meaning of the statements, and responses. If statements meet with inappropriate or undesired responses the communication breaks down and is disrupted. For example, if a customer writes to complain about the company and in return receives a sales pitch for another product, the dialogue breaks down.
Lack of reciprocity	Life is a matter of give and take, and if (for example) a salesperson is clearly not prepared to give ground or allow the customer a chance to make a point, the dialogue will break down.
Mutual misconstruction	This applies to personal encounters where the participants are unable to translate their interpretations of self and other into a coherent vocabulary. The root of the problem is an inability to understand why someone else's viewpoint appears sensible to them; this can cause problems in negotiations.
Threat of dissolution	The knowledge that the relationship might end is one that can affect both parties. This is particularly relevant in business-to-business markets, where a disruption of supply can be as important to a customer as the disruption of income would be to the marketer. Without any stated threat by either party, the nature of the communications between them will be affected by the knowledge of their relationship (see Chapter 11 for more on relationship marketing).

at least until it comes time to act on the information. Minimising misunderstanding is clearly of importance to marketers, since misunderstandings are a common cause for complaints against firms.

Sometimes basic disagreements lead to misunderstandings, sometimes it is the other way round. It is certainly easier to determine whether people agree with each other than whether they really understand each other, especially since people will sometimes act as if they understand each other in order to reach an agreement more quickly. Understanding is a construction of the mind; there are degrees of understanding, and the process of interpretation is (potentially) inexhaustible.

The elements of understanding are shown in Table 7.8.

PERSONAL TRANSFORMATION

The willingness of the recipient to be open-minded about the communication, and to be prepared to change, is of paramount importance. If the recipient of the message has already decided that the communication is not going to make any difference, then (in effect) he or she will not be listening to the message.

Elements of personal transformation are shown in Table 7.9.

Table 7.6   Elements of confusion

Element	Explanation
Conflict	Disputes between the parties will almost always create confused communications, especially in negotiating situations. Tension tends to result in an overstatement of positions, and attempts to resolve the conflict can also distract attention from the main issues. In many marketing situations the existence of serious conflict will disrupt the communication rather than merely confuse it, however.
Ambiguity	If the communication can be interpreted in two different ways it is ambiguous. This commonly happens in advertising, where the message is often so brief and so loaded with cultural connotations that it is easily misinterpreted.
Equivocation	If two messages are received that conflict with each other there is equivocation. Integrating marketing communications will reduce this problem, but it will always be present to some extent.
Vagueness	There will always be some uncertainty in communications, but some communications are so vaguely constructed that the meaning is lost. As the level of uncertainty increases, the frames of reference need to be expanded and the individual becomes confused.
Paradox	A paradox is a logical impossibility that creates confusion. For example, a sales promotion with an expiry date that has already passed (perhaps due to a printing error) will create confusion.
Contradiction	Similar to equivocation and paradox, contradiction is the appearance of irreconcilable differences in the communications received. Again this can be overcome to some extent by integrating marketing communications.

Table 7.7   Elements of disagreement

Element	Explanation
Relational ties	If the relationship between the parties is not a close one, disagreement is more likely. This is part of the reason for the increasing emphasis on relationship marketing.
Commonality of perspectives	If there is a foundation of consensus between the parties there will be a common perspective applied to discussions. This greatly increases the likelihood of agreement between parties.
Compatibility of values	If the personal value systems of the participants are close, there is less scope for disagreement. Marketers (especially salespeople) will often go to considerable trouble to establish a rapport with customers.
Similarity of interests	If both parties stand to gain from the encounter, the interaction is likely to lead to agreement. Common experience and common goals both lead to closer agreement on other issues.
Depth of involvement	The importance of the issues under discussion will influence the degree to which the parties become involved. As involvement increases, so do the possibilities for both agreement and disagreement. A greater depth of involvement is more likely to lead to agreement in the long run, though, because the parties are less likely to withdraw from the discussions prematurely.
Quality of interaction	The quality of interaction is affected by the levels of agreement or disagreement. Disagreement will make the interaction unpleasant, and therefore more likely to terminate early.
Equality of influence	The party with the greatest power in the relationship will be able to enforce agreement from the other party. If the relationship is one of equals, then genuine agreement is more likely, and a more lasting relationship becomes possible.

Table 7.8 Elements of understanding

Element	Explanation
Recognition of intent	It may not be possible to be sure of the other party's intentions, but having a clear recognition of them will help in understanding.
Multiple perspective taking	The more opportunity the recipient has to examine the information from different angles, the less likely it is that a misunderstanding will occur.
Warrants and reasons	When an observation leads to a conclusion, the explanatory mechanism is called a warrant. This is the reasoning process the individual goes through to arrive at an understanding. Reasons are the elements that serve as the basis for the warrant to operate on.
Tests of comprehension	The true measure of understanding is the degree to which the knowledge is effective when used to predict outcomes in the real world. Sometimes comprehension can be tested without making a commitment; for example, a consumer may call a helpline to check that the terms of a special offer are as they appear to be.
Code switching	The ability to understand is greatly improved if the participants are able to switch from one style of communication to another. Integration of marketing communications helps this process because it allows the dialogue to continue in a different way. Code switching is an element in redundancy; sending the message via different routes and using different codes will usually improve comprehension.
Synchrony and alignment of communicative styles	Synchronisation means that both parties follow through the dialogue at the same pace; alignment means that they follow through each stage together without being sidetracked. Understanding is improved if both parties can remain synchronised and aligned throughout the exchange.
Working through problematic concerns	More commonly found in personal selling situations, a preparedness to work through problems together is more likely to lead to mutual understanding. For this to happen both parties must perceive a mutually-beneficial end goal.
Mutual struggle to minimise miscommunication	If both participants are prepared to make an effort to understand each other's viewpoint, accurate communication is more likely to result.

Table 7.9 Elements of personal transformation

Element	Explanation
Receptivity to change	An individual who is not open-minded is unlikely to be receptive to communications; confusion is likely to result.
Supportive communication	Communications that support a customer through a change of attitude are usually helpful; this is why salespeople will often leave information about the products with a customer.

Perhaps the best way of minimising miscommunication is to ensure that the participants are motivated to seek understanding. Motivating the recipients to want to understand and learn from the communications is as important as (for example) motivating salespeople to go out and tell the story, or motivating creative people in advertising agencies to come up with a clever campaign.

Think outside this box!

It seems that there is so much that can go wrong with communications it's amazing we can speak to each other at all. Is it really worth bothering with all this stuff? Why not just drop the whole idea, put the goods in the shops where people can get at them, and wait to see what happens?

After all, some companies operate very well without advertising at all – British Home Stores in the UK is one example. Maybe marketing communications are as likely to go wrong as to go right!

Elements of the communications mix

Marketers have many tactics at their disposal, and the best marketers use them in appropriate ways to maximise the impact of their communications activities. A very basic taxonomy of promotional tools is the four-way division into advertising, public relations, sales promotion and personal selling. This taxonomy is really too simplistic; each of the elements subdivides further, and there are several elements which don't readily fit into these categories. For example, T-shirt slogans are clearly communications, but they are not advertising, nor are they really public relations; yet T-shirts with brand logos on, or even adaptations of brand logos, are a common sight and can be considered as marketing communications.

Marketing in a changing world: Clutter cutting

Marketing communications, and indeed communication in general, has gone through a sea-change over the past twenty years or so. The existence of mobile telephones and e-mail has meant that people are not only able to be in communication with everyone else all the time, but they are also expected to be in communication. Twenty years ago, if someone went on holiday they would effectively be out of communication for the entire time they were away. Only very senior, important people would leave the telephone number of their hotel in case of emergencies – most people disappeared and were not heard of again until they came back. Now, people are expected to collect e-mails and take their mobiles with them, and will be contacted while they are away.

The problem here is that people become more resistant to communication, and more resentful. Having an e-mail from a work colleague is irritating enough, but one from a cinema telling you what films are on next week (when you can't go anyway) is infuriating. Cutting through this extra layer of resistance is likely to become even more challenging for marketers in future, and they will try to become even more creative in cutting through the clutter. However, eventually marketers and others will have to find ways of cutting back on the clutter altogether, otherwise people will simply switch off most of the time.

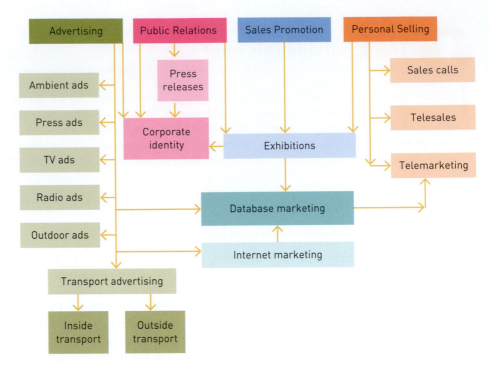

Figure 7.8   A taxonomy of marketing communications

Table 7.10 lists some of the elements of the mix. This list is unlikely to be exhaustive, and there is also the problem of boundary-spanning; some elements of the mix go beyond communication and into the realms of distribution (telemarketing and home shopping channels for example) or even into new product development (as with the websites that allow students to sell successful essays to other students). Each of these elements is dealt with in more detail elsewhere in the book.

The range of possible tools at the marketer's disposal is obviously large; creating a good mix of communications methods is akin to following a recipe. The ingredients have to be added in the right amounts at the right time, and treated in the right way, if the recipe is to work. Also, one ingredient cannot substitute for another; personal selling cannot, on its own, replace advertising, nor can public relations exercises replace sales promotions. Figure 7.8 shows how the above elements of the mix relate to each other. The interconnections between the various elements shown in Figure 7.8 are not the only ones; each marketing communication affects every other in some way or another.

Structuring the communication mix

Structuring the communication mix will differ from one firm to another, and indeed from one promotion to another within the same firm. Developing effective marketing communications follows a six-stage process, as follows:

1. Identify the target audience. In other words, decide who the message should get to.
2. Determine the response sought. What would the marketer like the audience to do after they get the message?

Table 7.10   Elements of the communications mix

Element	Description
Advertising	A paid insertion of a message in a medium.
Ambient advertising	Any message that forms part of the environment – for example messages placed on items such as bus tickets, stamp franking, till receipts, petrol pump nozzles and so forth.
Press advertising	Any paid message that appears in a newspaper, magazine, or directory.
TV advertising	Commercial messages shown in the breaks during and between TV programmes.
Radio advertising	Sound-only advertisements broadcast on radio.
Outdoor advertising	Billboards, bus shelters, fly posters etc.
Transport advertising	Posters in stations and inside buses and trains.
Outside transport advertising	Posters on buses and taxis, and in some countries the sides of trains. British Airways have even carried other companies' logos on the tail planes of aircraft (though not, of course, those of other airlines).
Press releases	News stories about the firm or its products.
Public relations	The planned and sustained effort to establish and maintain goodwill and mutual understanding between an organisation and its publics (Institute of Public Relations 1984).
Sponsorship	Funding of arts events, sporting events etc. in exchange for publicity and prestige.
Sales promotions	Activities designed to give a temporary boost to sales, such as money-off coupons, free samples, two-for-the-price-of-one promotions etc.
Personal selling	Face-to-face communications between buyers and sellers designed to ascertain and meet customers' needs on a one-to-one basis.
Database marketing	Profiling customers onto a database and sending out personalised mailings or other communications to them.
Telemarketing	Inbound (helpline, telephone ordering) or outbound (telecanvassing, teleselling) telephone calls. There are legal restrictions on outbound telemarketing.
Presence website	A website that acts as an advertisement, offering no interaction or ordering capability. Such websites only contain a telephone number or e-mail link; they are increasingly rare as firms become more Internet-literate.
Interactive website	A website that offers the capability to order goods or to engage in a dialogue with the firm.
Spamming	Sending out mass e-mail messages, usually (but not always) to a consenting mailing list (i.e. people who have asked for the mailings in some way, or who are voluntary members of a mailing list). In some countries there are legal restrictions on spamming, and sometimes irate Internet users will retaliate in ways the spamming companies do not like.
Short-message texting	Messages sent out to the mobile telephones of consenting members of a mailing list. These range from sports results services to travel offers to telephone banking.
Direct-response TV advertising	Using TV adverts linked to inbound telephone operations to sell goods.
Exhibitions and trade fairs	Companies take stands at trade fairs to display new products, meet consumers and customers, and raise the company profile with interested parties.
Corporate identity	The overall image that the company projects; the company's 'personality'.
Branding	The mechanism by which marketing communications are co-ordinated.

3. Choose the message. Write the copy, or produce an appropriate image.
4. Choose the channel. Decide which newspaper, TV station, radio station or other medium is most appealing to the audience.
5. Select the source's attributes. Decide what it is about the product or company that needs to be communicated.
6. Collect feedback. For example carry out market research to find out how successful the message was.

Communication is often expensive: full-page advertisements in Sunday colour supplements can cost upwards of £11,000 per insertion, and a thirty-second TV ad at peak time can cost £30,000 per station. It is therefore worthwhile spending time and effort in ensuring that the message can be understood by the target audience, and is reaching the right people. Figure 7.9 shows how the communication mix operates. In the diagram, messages from the company about its products and itself are transmitted via the elements of the promotional mix to the consumers, employees, pressure groups and other **publics**. Each of these groups receives the messages from more than one transmitter, so the elements of the mix also feed into each other thus reducing conflict. The choice of method will depend upon the message, the receiver and the desired effect.

Publics The groups of people with whom the organisation interacts.

The problem with this view of the promotional mix is that it is very much tied to the Schramm model of communication, which assumes that recipients are passive. For example, a recipient may feel perfectly comfortable with seeing a TV advertisement for the firm's products, less comfortable about receiving a mailing, and extremely uncomfortable about being telephoned at home. This will vary between different people – some people resent having their favourite programme interrupted by advertising, and prefer to have a mailing from a company they deal with frequently.

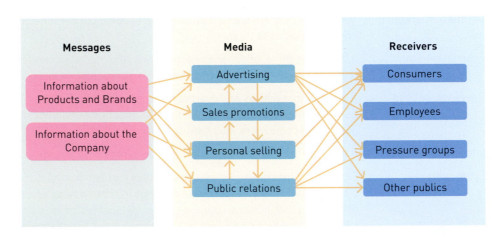

Figure 7.9   The promotional mix

Mechanisms of personal influence

Overall, word-of-mouth influence is much stronger than advertising or other marketer-produced communications. For marketers, then, the problem lies in knowing how to use word-of-mouth to its best advantage. Table 7.11 offers some comparisons and strategies.

Table 7.11 Using word-of-mouth

Strong influence	Weak influence	Tactical suggestions
Seeker initiates conversation with source	Source initiates conversation with seeker	Advertising could emphasise the idea of 'Ask the person who owns one'. Network marketers could emphasise a more advisory role for their salespeople rather than a strongly proactive approach.
Negative information	Positive information	Because marketers are uniformly positive about the product, the seeker is more alert to any negatives. The essential thing for marketers to do is to ensure that any complaints are dealt with immediately and thoroughly.
Verbal communication is stronger for thinking and evaluation.	Visual communication is stronger for awareness and stimulation of interest.	Where appropriate, marketers could encourage satisfied customers to show their friends the product; this tactic is often used for home improvement sales, where customers are paid a small reward or commission for introducing friends to the product. This is also the basis for party-plan selling, e.g. Tupperware and Anne Summers.

Real-life marketing: Viral marketing

Many websites encourage visitors to involve their friends. 'E-mail this site to a friend' buttons became commonplace, and eventually firms began to add value to the site by including games and puzzles, and even jokes, to encourage site visitors to enrol their friends onto the site. This approach helped to overcome the major problem of Internet marketing – making your voice heard through the clutter of almost 4 billion websites worldwide.

The challenge is to find a reason for someone to forward the weblink to a friend. Panasonic found one way when they launched their Lumix camera range. A key feature of the camera is its 10X optical zoom, operating through a 28mm lens. TV advertising showing various national monuments being compressed to fit the picture had a great impact, but the product needed more, so Panasonic commissioned Inbox Digital to create an on-line game called Lumix World. The game is based on an 18-hole crazy golf course played around nine World Heritage Sites. Players can zoom in and out (as if they were using the camera) and also win prizes (redeemable against purchasing the camera): the key element is that players can compete against a friend (or indeed a stranger). The website attracted over a million visitors, most of whom found out about the site through friends.

To do this yourself, follow these rules:

- The game must be professionally produced – which will cost money.
- The game must connect to the product in some way, not just act as a vehicle for plugging the brand name.
- You will need to include other promotions, either to drive people to the site or to make them act on buying the product.
- There should, of course, be a tell-a-friend button, but better still it should be possible for friends to compete.
- It should be humorous – people like to give their friends a good laugh.

It is not usually possible to rely entirely on word of mouth, but marketers should take steps to stimulate it as a promotional tool. Advertising should be interesting and involving, perhaps even controversial so that debate ensues. It is not true to say that any word-of-mouth will be good for a company, but it is certainly true to say that controversy and debate will increase brand awareness. These do not always enhance brand image, however.

FORMULATING A STRATEGY

As in any other issue in marketing, the first step in formulating a strategy is to find out what the target customers are looking for. In communications terms this means finding out which magazines they read, which TV stations they watch, what their leisure activities are, whether they are interested in football or opera or horse racing, and so forth. Marketing research has the main role here. Consumers not only consume products, they also consume communications media; knowing which media the target customers consume enables the astute marketer to target communications accurately, which avoids wasting the budget on trying to communicate with people who have no need for the product.

Strategy must be integrated across the whole range of marketing activities; it must be formulated in the light of good analysis of the environment; and it must include a feedback system so that the strategy can be adapted in the light of environmental changes. Strategy is influenced by organisational objectives and resources, competitor activities, the structure of the market itself and the firm's willingness to make changes and take risks.

PUSH VS PULL STRATEGIES

Push strategy Promoting to channel intermediaries in order to 'push' products through the distribution channel.

Pull strategy Promoting to end users in order to 'pull' products through the distribution channel.

Two basic strategic alternatives exist for marketing communications. **Push strategy** involves promoting heavily to wholesalers, retailers and agents on the assumption that they will, in turn, promote heavily to the end consumers. In this way the products are pushed through the distribution channel. **Pull strategy** involves promoting heavily to end users and consumers to create a demand that will pull the products through the distribution channel. Push strategies place the emphasis on personal selling and sales promotion, whereas pull strategies tend to place the emphasis on mass advertising. The two strategies are not mutually exclusive, but rather represent opposite ends of a spectrum (see Figure 7.10). Most campaigns will contain elements of both.

Table 7.12 shows the functions that need to be carried out when planning the communications campaign.

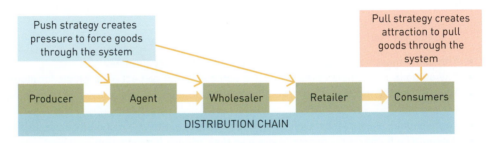

Figure 7.10   Push versus pull strategies

Table 7.12 Communications planning functions

Planning function	Explanation
Situation analysis	1. Demand factors. These include consumer needs and decision-making processes, cultural and social influences on demand, product category and brand attitudes, individual differences between consumers. 2. Identify the target. It is better to approach a small segment of the market than to try to use a 'scattergun' approach on everybody. 3. Assess the competition; other products, possible competitor responses, etc. 4. Legal and regulatory restrictions that might affect what we are able to do.
Defining the objectives	Deciding what the communications are supposed to achieve. It is essential here to give everybody associated with the campaign (salesforce, advertising agency, etc.) a clear brief: 'We want to raise awareness of the product to 50% of the adult population' is a measurable objective. 'We want to increase sales as much as possible' is not measurable since we do not know how far sales can be increased, so there is no way of knowing whether the aim has been achieved.
Setting the budget	Setting the right level of budget is important, but setting it on the right basis is even more important. There is more on this later in the chapter.
Managing the elements of the mix	Media planning. This is about deciding which media will carry the communications. There are two main decision areas; the **reach** (number of potential consumers the communication reaches) and the **frequency** of coverage (number of times each consumer is exposed to the communication). In advertising, the decision is frequently made on the basis of cost per thousand readers/viewers, but this doesn't take into account the impact of the ad or the degree to which people will actually read or watch it. Briefing the sales force. Deciding whether it is to be a push or pull strategy, choosing the PR and support communications.
Creating the platform	Deciding the basic issues and selling points that the communication must convey. This clarifies the agency briefings, or at least clarifies the marketers' thinking on producing the communications.

Budgeting

Having decided the overall plan for the promotional campaign, the marketer needs to decide what the organisation can afford. The level of noise from advertising **clutter** means that (unless the creative people are very creative indeed) companies must spend a certain minimum amount simply to be heard, so there is likely to be a minimum level below which there is no point in spending any money at all. Table 7.13 illustrates some methods for setting budgets.

In the real world, marketers will usually adopt a combination strategy, using several of the above methods. Even an objective-and-task approach might begin by looking at what the competition are spending (comparative parity approach) if only to determine what the likely spend would have to be to overcome clutter. Likewise, a marketer may be part-way through a campaign and be told by the finance department that no more money is available (or perhaps be told that more than anticipated is available) and will switch to an all-you-can-spend policy.

Reach Number of potential consumers a communication reaches.

Frequency Number of times each consumer is exposed to the communication.

Clutter Excessive advertising.

Table 7.13   Promotional budgeting methods

Method	Explanation	Advantages	Disadvantages
Objective and task method	Identify the objective to be achieved, then determine the costs and effort required to achieve those objectives.	This is logical, and links to the firm's strategic goals.	The marketing research needed for this method is expensive, and outcomes are hard to predict.
Percentage of sales method	The planner simply allows a fixed percentage of the company's sales to be used for promotion. This is a very common method of budgeting.	Simple to calculate, also ensures that, if sales drop off, costs also drop.	Is based on the false premise that sales cause promotion, rather than promotion causing sales. It would be more logical to increase expenditure if sales fall.
Comparative parity method	The marketer matches expenditure to that of the competitors. Thus the firm does not lose ground if a competing firm increases its budget.	This method should maintain the firm's position relative to the competitors, reducing wasted expenditure.	The method is not customer-orientated, and also means that competitors are setting the firm's budgets.
Marginal approach	Marketer only spends up to the point where any further spending would not generate enough extra business to justify the outlay.	This method should maximise profits since no excess spending would result.	Given the changing nature of markets, this method is almost impossible to calculate.
All-you-can-afford method	The marketer spends whatever money can be spared from other activities. Often used by small businesses when starting out.	Company cannot become over-committed or run into trouble by relying on sales that do not, in the end, materialise.	This means that expenditure bears no relationship to the state of the marketplace. Also, it means that marketers have to fight for budgets with colleagues within the firm, which causes resentment and also means that the size of budget depends on office politics, not on the needs of the company and its customers.

Think outside this box!

Budgeting seems to be somewhat hit-and-miss. After all, we can't be rigid about how much money will be available – the customers have control over that. Then there is the problem of bargaining power: some of our colleagues are much better at bargaining, some are the managing director's office poodles, some simply shout the loudest. So they might get the funding while we have to put up with what we can get.

Maybe marketers need to develop the kind of rigid systems the accountants have, where everything is accurately calculated (or at least, that's what they tell us) and there is no argument. Maybe marketing hasn't reached that level of sophistication – but isn't it time it did so?

Planning the campaign

Whether this stage comes before or after the budget-setting will depend on whether the marketer is adopting an objective-and-task policy or not. In most cases, though, planning the campaign in detail will come after the budget is known and agreed; few companies give the marketing department a blank cheque for promotional spending. Campaigns can be carried out to achieve many objectives. A new product launch is often an objective, but in most cases the products will be in the maturity phase of the product life cycle.

Image building campaigns are designed to convey a particular status for the product, and to emphasise ways in which it will complement the user's lifestyle. For example, Audi use the slogan 'Vorsprung durch Technik' which means 'Progress through technology' as a way of showing that their cars are at the cutting edge of technology.

Product differentiation campaigns aim to show how the product is better than others by emphasising its differences. In most cases this will take the form of the **unique selling proposition** or **USP**. The USP is the one feature of the product that most stands out, and is usually a feature that conveys unique benefits to the consumer. Mature products often only differ very slightly from each other in terms of performance, so a USP can sometimes be identified only in terms of packaging, distribution, or a prestigious brand. The USP will be effective only if it means something to consumers – otherwise the effect on the buying decision will be negligible.

Positioning strategies are concerned with the way consumers perceive the product compared with their perceptions of the competition (see Chapter 3 and Chapter 6).

Direct response campaigns seek an immediate response from the consumer in terms of a purchase, or a request for a brochure, or a visit to the shop. For example, a retailer might run a newspaper campaign which includes a money-off coupon. The aim of the campaign is to encourage consumers to visit the shop to redeem the coupon, and the retailer can easily judge the effectiveness of the campaign by the number of coupons redeemed.

The different types of campaign are summarised in Figure 7.11.

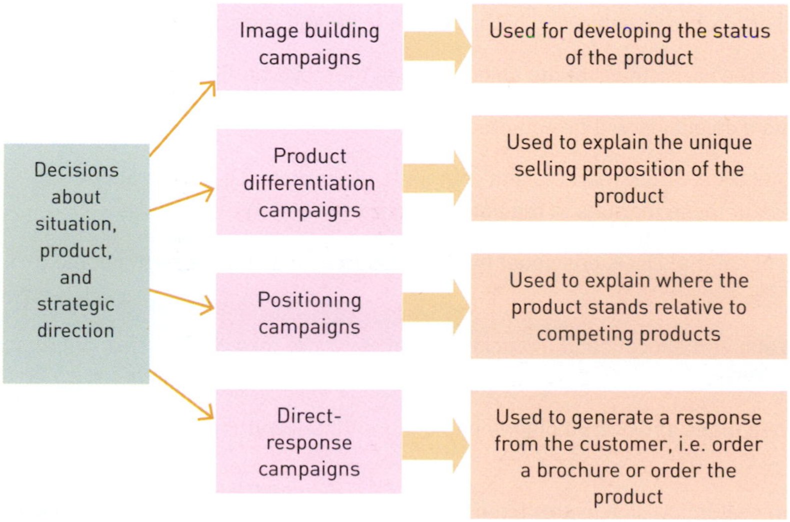

Image building A type of campaign that is conducted for the purpose of conveying a specific perception of a product in the minds of customers.

Product differentiation A type of campaign that emphasises the differences between a product and competing products.

Unique selling proposition (USP) The factors that distinguish a product from its competitors.

Direct response A type of advertising campaign that contains a method for the consumer to contact the supplier immediately and directly.

Figure 7.11 Types of campaign

Tactical considerations

Most of the tactics of marketing involve creativity on the part of practitioners, so it is virtually impossible to lay down any hard and fast rules about approaching different marketing problems. There are also a large number of alternative approaches available. However, the following might prove to be useful guidelines:

- Marketers should always try to do something that the competition hasn't thought of yet.
- It is important to consult everybody who is involved in the day-to-day application of the plans. Front-line people such as salespeople, receptionists, telesales operators and so forth are particularly important in this respect.
- Most marketing activities do not produce instant results, but results should be monitored anyway.
- The messages given to the consumers, the middlemen, the suppliers, and all the other publics should be consistent.
- Competitors are likely to make some kind of response, so marketers should try to anticipate what the response might be when formulating plans.

The SOSTT+4Ms structure for planning gives a useful checklist for ensuring that the elements of strategy and tactics are brought together effectively. Table 7.14 shows how the structure works.

Cost-effectiveness will always be an issue in promotional campaigns, and it is for this reason that there has been a growth in direct marketing worldwide (see Chapter 8). The accurate targeting of market segments made possible by computer technology has enabled marketers to refine the approach, and hence increase the

Table 7.14   SOSTT+4Ms

Element	Description
Situation	Current position of the firm in terms of its resources, product range, and markets.
Objectives	What the company hopes to achieve in both the long term and the short term.
Strategy	Decisions about the correctness of the objectives and their overall fit.
Tactics	How the strategic objectives will be achieved.
Targets	Formalised objectives, target markets and segments of markets. Decisions about the appropriateness of these markets in the light of the firm's strategic objectives.
Men	Both genders, of course! Decisions about human resources; having the right people to do the job.
Money	Correct budgeting and allocation of financial resources where they will do the most to achieve the overall objectives.
Minutes	Time-scales, deadlines and overall planning to ensure that everything happens at the right time.
Measurement	Monitoring and evaluation of activities to ensure that they remain on course and work as they should.

response rate. Marketers now talk in terms of response rates from promotions, not in terms of contact numbers.

Cutting through advertising clutter is a perennial problem. Most people skip past marketing communications, so marketers need to be creative in finding ways of making the communication eye-catching. Irritating or annoying slogans are often remembered better than others, and using variations on slogans also helps to make them more attention-getting (Rosengren and Dahlen 2006). Whether this approach makes people more likely to buy as a result is debatable, however.

Putting it all together

To make the best use of the promotional effort it is worth spending time planning how the communications will fit together. The mix will need to be adapted according to what the product is and how the company wants to promote it, as well as according to the characteristics of the customers.

The elements marketers need to consider (summarised in Figure 7.12) are:

- Size of budget.
- Size of individual order value.
- Number of potential buyers.
- Geodemographic spread of potential buyers.
- Category of product (convenience, unsought, shopping, etc.)
- What it is the firm is trying to achieve.

It is impossible to achieve everything all at once, so marketers will often plan the campaign as an integrated package. For example, Table 7.15 shows a product launch strategy designed to maximise penetration of a new food product.

Carrying out this kind of planning needs the co-operation of all the members of the marketing team. It is no use having the PR people doing one thing, and the

Figure 7.12 Factors in promotional planning

Table 7.15   Example of a promotional calendar

Month	Activity
May	Press release to the trade press; retailers.
June	Sales campaign to persuade retailers to stock the product. The aim is to get 50% of retailers stocking the product, so the salesforce will tell them a big advertising spend is forthcoming. Begin a **teaser campaign** (see Chapter 15).
July/August	Denouement of teaser campaign. Promotion staff appear in major retail outlets offering free samples. Press releases to cookery writers, possibly reports on daytime TV if product is newsworthy enough.
September/October	Once 50% retailer penetration has occurred, start the TV campaign. Brief the advertising agency to obtain maximum brand awareness.
January/February	Begin a new campaign to inform consumers about the brand. Possibly use money-off sales promotion, linked promotions, etc. Review progress so far using market research. Possibly issue some press releases, if the product is innovative enough, to the business/cookery press.

Teaser campaign An advertising campaign in two stages: the first stage involves a message which in itself is meaningless, but which is explained by later advertisements in the second stage.

salesforce doing something else that negates their efforts. If the campaign is to be effective it is important that all the team members are involved in the discussions so that unrealistic demands are not made of them.

Integration of marketing communications

Integration of marketing communications has become a 'hot topic' among marketing academics and practitioners alike, and this is being extended to include all corporate communications (Nowak and Phelps 1994). The need for integration is shown in the following factors (Borremans 1998):

1. Changes in the consumer market.

   o The information overload caused by the ever-increasing number of commercial messages.
   o Advertising in the mass media is increasingly irritating.
   o Media fragmentation.
   o Increasing numbers of 'me-too' products, where the differences between brands are minor.
   o Complexity and change in fast-moving consumer goods markets, with increased distances between suppliers and consumers making it harder for suppliers to establish a consistent image.
   o Increasing media attention on the social and ethical behaviour of companies, putting goodwill at a premium.

2. Changes in the supplier market:

   o Multiple acquisitions and changes in structure in and around corporations.
   o Interest of management in short-term results.
   o Increased recognition of the strategic importance of communication.
   o Increased interest in good internal communications with employees.

To these should be added the paradigm shift caused by the Internet: this has placed power firmly in the hands of consumers, who expect to find out information for themselves rather than wait passively for an advertiser to tell them what to do.

Integration aims to reduce ambiguity and increase the impact of messages emanating from the firm, and also should reduce costs by reducing duplication of effort. There are, however, barriers to integration (Petrison and Wang 1996); the following factors tend to mean that integration would actually detract from the effectiveness of communications.

- Database marketing allows customers to be targeted with individually tailored communications.
- In niche marketing and micromarketing, suppliers can communicate with very small and specific audiences, using different messages for each group.
- Specific methods and working practices used for different communication tools will affect the message each transmits.
- Corporate diversification means that different branches of the company need to send different messages.
- Different international (and even national) cultures mean that a single message comprehensible to all is difficult to achieve without producing 'lowest common denominator' messages, which have a low impact.
- Existing structures within organisations mean that different departments may not be able or willing to 'sing the same song'. For example, salespeople have to deal with customers as individuals: they may not agree with the advertising department's ideas on what customers should be told.
- Personal resistance to change, managers' fear of losing responsibilities and budgets. This is particularly true of firms that have adopted the brand manager system of management.

In practice promotional mix elements often operate independently (Duncan and Caywood 1996), with specialist agencies for PR, advertising, exhibitions, corporate identity, branding, etc. all working in isolation. Because each department or agency has its own budgets and concerns, integration may not happen simply because each wants to fight for its own part of the campaign, even when they understand that the needs of the campaign dictate that another department should have precedence.

There are nine types or levels of integration, as shown in Table 7.16 and Figure 7.13: note that these do not necessarily constitute a process, or represent stages of development, and indeed there may be considerable overlap between the types.

Part of the reason for separating the functions is historical. Traditionally, marketing communications were divided into **above the line** communications and **below the line** communications. Above the line means advertising; below the line means everything else. This division came about because of the way advertising agencies are paid: they receive commission by the media in which they place the adverts (usually the rate is 15% of the billing) and/or fees paid by the client. Traditionally, any paid-for advertising attracted commission (hence above the line) and any other activities such as PR or sales promotion were paid for by fees (hence below the line). As time has gone by these distinctions have become more blurred, especially with the advent of **advertorials** (advertisements that look like editorials), which are usually written by journalists, and with **ambient advertising**, the Internet and other new media that do not attract commission.

Above the line Advertising for which the advertising agency obtains a commission from the media.

Below the line Promotional tools for which the advertising agency charges the client.

Advertorials Advertisements that are written in the style of editorials (not to be confused with press releases).

Ambient advertising Advertising that becomes part of the environment.

Table 7.16   Levels of integration

Level of integration	Explanation
Awareness stage	Those responsible for communications realise that a fragmented approach is not the optimum one.
Planning integration	The co-ordination of activities. There are two broad approaches; functional integration, which co-ordinates separate tools to create a single message where appropriate, and instrumental integration, which combines tools in such a way that they reinforce one another (Bruhn 1995).
Integration of content	Ensuring that there are no contradictions in the basic brand or corporate messages. At a higher level, integrating the themes of communication to make the basic messages the same.
Formal integration	Using the same logo, corporate colours, graphic approach and house style for all communications.
Integration between planning periods	Basic content remains the same from one campaign to the next. Either basic content remains the same, or the same executional approach is used in different projects.
Intra-organisational integration	Integration of the activities of everyone involved in communication functions (which could mean everybody who works in the organisation).
Inter-organisational integration	Integration of all the outside agencies involved in the firm's communication activities.
Geographical integration	Integration of campaigns in different countries. This is strongest in large multinationals which operate globally, e.g. the Coca-Cola Corporation (Hartley and Pickton 1997).
Integration of publics	All communications targeted on one segment of the market are integrated (horizontal integration) or all communications targeted on different segments are attuned (vertical integration).

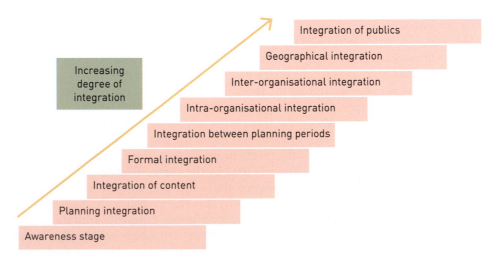

Figure 7.13   Ladder of integration

Real-life marketing: Integrating your communications

One way of co-ordinating communications is to use off-line methods to direct people to the corporate website. Nine West Shoes came up with a good idea for doing this. Shoes are not necessarily the most exciting of products, and for sure most people would not spend time at the computer researching websites about them unless they were looking for something special. What Nine West did was mould the Web address into the soles of the shoes. If anyone left a shoeprint (after stepping in a puddle, for example) the footprint promoted the website. Using one medium to promote another isn't new – 'as seen on TV' used to be a popular sign in retail shops – but Nine West have found a cheap and innovative way of driving visits to their website.

If you're going to integrate your communications in the real world, you need to do the following:

- Integrate the message at all levels in the firm, from the managing director to the cleaners. People talk when they leave work.
- All outgoing communications should have the same visual standards.
- Your overall strategy should be made clear to everybody.
- Start with a zero budget and add to it when you know what you have to do – of course, your finance director might have something to say about it if the budget gets too big!
- Always use the same artwork.
- Be prepared to change if it isn't working – for which you need a good information system, of course.

Overall, the advantages of integrating communications almost certainly overcome the drawbacks, since the cost savings and the reduction of ambiguity are clearly important objectives for most marketers. There is, however, the danger of losing the capacity to tailor messages for individuals (as happens in personal selling) or for niches in the market, and there are certainly some major creative problems attached to integrating communications on a global scale.

International marketing communications

Single communications strategies rarely work for firms in the global arena. In fact, the few exceptions are so notable that they are used as examples time and again – McDonald's, Coca-Cola, Levi jeans – and nearly all are American. It is possible that the overwhelming influence of Hollywood in exporting American culture worldwide means that people in most countries are able to understand American cultural references (the Coca-Cola 'Holidays are Coming' illuminated trucks, for example) in a way that would not work for, say, the Brazilian gaucho or the Japanese samurai. Even within these examples, there are differences between campaigns in different countries: McDonald's produced a completely new campaign for the 2012 Olympics, for example.

There is some common ground between countries, and there are identifiable international markets: the market for women's magazines has expanded in Europe as a result of deregulation, and magazines such as *Hello!* (originally *Hola!* in its native

Table 7.17 Basic international strategies

Strategy	Explanation
Same product, same communication	Can be used where the need for the product and its use are the same as in its home market.
Same product, different communication	Can be used where the need for the product differs in some way, but the basic method of use is the same, or when the cultural references differ. For example, fish sauce is often considered an exotic product in Western Europe, but is a regular purchase item in Oriental countries.
Different products, same communication	Sometimes the product formula has to change to meet local conditions, but the communication can remain the same. For example, the formulation of chocolate is different for hot countries due to the low melting-point of cocoa butter, but this need not affect the advertising.
Different product, different communications	Applies to markets with different needs and different product use, for example greetings cards, or electrical appliances.

Spain) have managed to cross over successfully. This means that some print advertising within those magazines should also be able to make the transition.

The main reason for standardising communications is cost. It is clearly much cheaper to produce one advert and repeat it across borders (perhaps changing the language as necessary) than it is to produce separate adverts for each country. However, the savings are most apparent in producing TV adverts, where the costs of production can easily approach the costs of airtime. This is not the case with press advertising, so the pressure to internationalise is less apparent.

There are four basic strategies for international communications, as shown in Table 7.17 (Keegan 1984).

Most successful international campaigns are run on TV, which enables the advertiser to minimise or even omit words altogether. Standardising press communications is more difficult due to language differences. Some difficulties in this connection are subtle – some languages such as Arabic and Hebrew read from right to left, which can significantly alter the meaning of before-and-after pictures.

The following tips for translating advertising copy have been identified (Majaro 1982):

1. Avoid idioms, jargon or buzz-words.
2. Leave space to expand foreign language text (Latin languages take 20% more space than English and Arabic may need up to 50% more space).
3. Check local legal requirements and codes of conduct.
4. Ensure that the translators speak the everyday language of the country in question. The Spanish spoken in Spain and Latin America differs, as does UK English and American English, or French French and Belgian French. (For obvious reasons, people who are not native speakers of the language should never be used.)
5. Brief the translators thoroughly so that they get a feel for the product, its benefits, the customer and competition. Do not just hand over the copy and expect it to be translated.
6. Check the translation with customers and distributors in the local market. This also gives local users the opportunity of being involved and raising any criticisms of the promotional materials before they are published for use.
7. Re-translate the materials back into English as a 'safety check'. They may not come back exactly as the original version, but there should be a reasonable commonality.

	Same promotion	Different promotion
Same product	Need and use similar to home market	Need similar, use different
Different product	Need different, use similar	Need and use both different from home market

Figure 7.14   Cultural and product trade offs in international markets

There are many (probably apocryphal) stories about translations of brand names and slogans that have gone horribly wrong; Pepsi's 'Come Alive with Pepsi' translating as 'Come Back from the Grave with Pepsi', or the Vauxhall Nova translating as 'Doesn't Go' in Spanish; any regular traveller will be aware of humorous (or obscene) brand names on foreign products.

Provided a universally recognisable icon is available, and it is possible to produce meaningful hooks in each language, it should be possible to produce good internationalised press advertising. Certainly factual information (e.g. 'Open Sundays') should translate fairly easily, so sought communications are presumably more likely to transfer easily.

A major headache for marketers is establishing meaningful websites. Since a website might be accessed from anywhere in the world, cultural differences need to be minimised – but at the same time, the site needs to have impact if it is to stand out from all the competing sites. Since some of these sites will be from the native country of the person accessing the site, they will inevitably be more appealing (or at least more comprehensible) than foreign websites. Even when the language is the same, cultural referents may differ in ways that make the site hard to understand. Additionally, websites may be accessed accidentally by foreigners, so website designers need to be aware of this. Often, websites contain contact telephone numbers that are devoid of the international dialling code, so that it becomes difficult or impossible for the observer to know which country the website originates in, and which offers are available. For example, someone in Cardiff, Wales, may be looking for new curtains and may pick up a retailer in Cardiff, New South Wales, Cardiff by the Sea in California, or Cardiff, Canada. Although these retailers might offer free delivery, each would need to make clear how far they were prepared to go to meet this promise.

Marketing in a changing world: HSBC

The Hong Kong and Shanghai Bank (HSBC) is one of the world's leading banks, with branches throughout the world. It uses a single global website as a portal through which customers can approach their local, national banks, and prides itself on its cultural sensitivity.

Each country in which HSBC operates has its own website and its own promotional campaigns, tailored to local needs: the bank even tailors its products to local needs (for example, in Saudi Arabia the bank offers Islamic banking, which conforms to the laws laid down in the Koran). Offering a Visa card that conforms to Shariah principles is clearly some achievement. In some cases the products offered in some markets would contravene the law in other markets – the special bank accounts for women offered in some Muslim

(Continued)

(Continued)

countries, the 100% car loans offered in the UK, some of the investment packages offered in Australia, to name but a few. HSBC calls itself the world's local bank, and it is in the realm of marketing communications that it makes this most obvious.

The bank allows its executives in each country to plan their own marketing campaigns, but under the umbrella of 'the world's local bank'. In the UK, the bank uses images from throughout the world which demonstrate cultural differences – the grasshopper which is a pest in the United States but a delicacy in China, the various methods people use for curing headaches, the different items that denote good luck around the world. The bank's TV advertising follows the theme, showing the meanings of different gestures in different parts of the world.

Some of the communications are aimed at investors, some at personal banking customers, some at business customers: what the bank has as its strength is the ability to target so many different groups and persuade them all that they are dealing with the world's local bank.

If you're in the position of trading globally (and who isn't, since the Internet is a global entity), you need to do your homework.

- Check your website for cultural gaffes – you might have something on there that people would find offensive, even if you didn't mean it to be.
- If possible, get somebody from the local culture to check for you. In the UK this shouldn't be too difficult because the country is already multicultural, but you may have *a lot* of checking to do!
- Allow your local people in the overseas markets some autonomy in tailoring the approach – provided they retain the overall strategy and underlying message.

Researching the effectiveness of communications

Having developed and implemented the strategic and tactical plans, the next stage is to gather feedback as to the effectiveness of the communication. Much of the emphasis on measures of effectiveness centres around advertising, since it is a high-profile activity and often a very expensive one. Four elements appear to be important in the effectiveness of advertising: awareness, liking, interest and enjoyment. There is a high correlation between brand loyalty and brand awareness (Stapel 1990); likeability appears to be the single best predictor of sales effectiveness since likeability scales predict 97% of sales successes (Biel 1989); interest clearly relates to likeability (Stapel 1991); and enjoyment appears to be a good indicator in advertising pre-tests (Brown 1991).

For many years effectiveness was measured in terms of sales results, the premise being that the purpose of advertising is to generate sales. The problem with this view is that sales can result from many other activities (personal selling, increased efforts by distributors, increased prosperity and so forth) so that it is difficult to assess the importance of advertising in the outcomes. A more recent view has been that the role of advertising is to communicate – to change awareness and attitudes (Colley 1961). This view crystallised as the DAGMAR model (Defining Advertising Goals, Measuring Advertising Results) (Colley 1961). DAGMAR implies that concrete and measurable communication objectives should be set for advertising, rather than sales

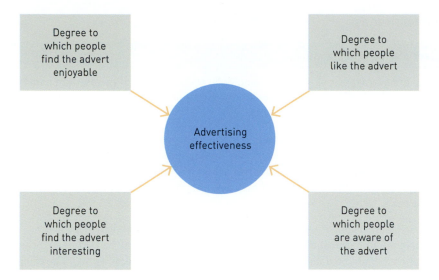

Figure 7.15 Factors in advertising effectiveness

turnover goals. Thus the outcomes that are measured are usually things like awareness, brand recognition, recall of content and so forth.

DAGMAR has been criticised on the grounds that it tends to lead planners to find out what can be measured easily, then set that as a goal (Broadbent 1989). The simple objectives that can be measured do not tell the whole story of major-brand success; advertising does other things that are hard to measure, such as encouraging brand loyalty or increasing word-of-mouth communication between consumers themselves.

Advertising effectiveness can be assessed by market research, by returned coupons and (sometimes) by increased sales. The last method is somewhat risky, however, since there may be many other factors that could have increased the sales of the product. Table 7.18 shows some common techniques for evaluating advertising effectiveness.

Any testing must be *valid* (i.e. it must measure what it says it measures) and *reliable* (i.e. it must be free of random error). A reliable test would provide consistent results every time it is used, and a valid test would enable the marketer to predict outcomes reasonably accurately. In order to ensure that this is the case, a set of principles called PACT (Positioning Advertising Copy Testing) have been established (*Marketing News* 1982). A good advertising testing system should:

1. Provide measurements that are relevant to the objectives of the advertising.
2. Require agreement about how the results will be used in advance of each specific test.
3. Provide multiple measurements because single measurements are generally inadequate to assess the advert's performance.
4. Be based on a model of human response to communication – the reception of a stimulus, the comprehension of the stimulus, and the response to the stimulus.
5. Allow for consideration of whether the advertising stimulus should be exposed more than once.
6. Recognise that the more finished a piece of copy is the more soundly it can be evaluated. It should also require as a minimum that alternative executions be tested to the same degree of finish.
7. Provide controls to avoid the biasing effects of the exposure content.
8. Take into account basic considerations of sample definition.
9. Demonstrate reliability and validity empirically.

Table 7.18   Advertising effectiveness

Technique	Description and explanation
Pre-tests	These are evaluations of the advertising before it is released. Pre-tests are commonly carried out using focus groups; research shows that this is the commonest method used by advertisers (Eagle et al. 1998).
Coupon returns, or enquiries	The advertiser counts up the number of enquiries received during each phase of an advertising campaign. This allows the marketing management to judge which media are working best, provided the coupons have an identifying code on them. This method assumes that it is the advertising that is generating the sales, which may or may not be the case.
Post-campaign tests (post-tests)	The particular testing method used will depend largely on the objectives of the campaign. Communications objectives (product awareness, attitude change, brand awareness) might be determined through surveys; sales objectives might be measured according to changes in sales which can be attributed to the campaign. This is difficult to do because of other factors (changes in economic conditions, for example) which might distort the findings.
Recognition tests and recall tests	In recognition tests, consumers are shown the advertisement and asked if they recognise it. They are then asked how much of it they actually recall. In an *unaided* recall test the consumer is asked which adverts he or she remembers seeing recently; in an *aided* recall test the consumer is shown a group of ads (without being told which is the one the researcher is interested in) and is asked which ones he or she has seen recently.

Advertisements can be tested on two dimensions: those related to the advertisement itself, and those related to its contents. Since these two issues are sometimes difficult for the consumer to separate there is no real certainty as to which is actually being tested.

PRE-TESTING AND POST-TESTING

Pre-testing the advertisement to assess whether it is likely to be effective has a mixed history. There has been considerable debate as to whether it is really possible to predict whether an advert will work or not, and there is of course no certainty about this even when sophisticated copy-testing methods are used. Testing almost certainly reduces the risk of producing an ineffective advert, and it is better to find this out before expensive space is booked in the media, and possibly before an inappropriate message is sent out.

Post-testing is concerned with researching the effectiveness of the advert after it has appeared. Finding out whether the advertising has been effective in achieving the objectives laid down is much easier if clear objectives were set in the first place, of course, and if the advertising agency was given a clear brief.

LABORATORY TECHNIQUES

Testing can be carried out in the field or in the laboratory; most pre-tests are carried out in laboratory conditions. Table 7.19 shows some of the available techniques.

Table 7.19 Laboratory techniques for testing advertising effectiveness

Technique	Explanation
Consumer juries	Groups of consumers are asked to judge whether they think the advertisement will work. This has the advantage that consumers (presumably) know what affects them most. The drawback is that they will sometimes 'play expert', trying to guess how other people would react to the advertisement rather than giving their own reactions.
Focus groups	A moderator conducts a loosely structured interview with six to twelve respondents simultaneously. The respondents tend to trigger comments from each other, so that a range of ideas is elicited. These data are qualitative; it is not usually possible or desirable to express this numerically, but it does raise issues effectively.
Portfolio tests	Respondents are shown test adverts (those the researcher wants to test) and control adverts (adverts whose effectiveness is already known) and asked to score them. The researcher can then compare the scores of the test adverts with the control adverts and see whether the test adverts will be as effective. This method may also mean that respondents try to 'play the expert'.
Readability tests	The copy is analysed for readability without consumer interviewing. The foremost method is the Fleisch formula (Flesch 1979). Readability is assessed by determining the average number of syllables per hundred words, the length of sentences, the human interest content, and the familiarity of words. Results can be compared with predetermined norms for the target audience.
Physiological measures	Eye cameras can be used to record the route an individual's eye takes when seeing an advert. This can be unreliable; lingering on one part of the advert might denote interest, or it might denote incomprehension. Galvanic skin response and pupil dilation response measure different aspects of interest; pupils dilate and the electrical resistance of the skin decreases when an object of interest appears.

Laboratory measures at first appear scientific and therefore objective, but this is often not the case. While the researcher might be able to maintain objectivity, it is unlikely that the subject (respondent) will and knowledge of the artificiality of the situation is likely to cloud the respondent's judgement. Furthermore, the results of (for example) a galvanic skin response or pupil dilation response still need to be interpreted. Interest or excitement at seeing an advertisement does not necessarily stem from the communication itself, and almost certainly does not translate into the achievement of the communications objectives.

Chapter summary

Communication is a very common human activity – some might even argue that it is a defining activity of human beings. Marketers are no exception, but marketers communicate about products and services on a professional basis. Communication is about establishing a common understanding of how the world works, and consumers are not passive in this process. Marketers therefore need to consider the personalities of their target audience, and the ways in which the messages will be interpreted – these interpretations may differ greatly from the message the marketers thought they were sending.

Key points

- People are not radios: they consider and interpret marketing messages in light of their previous experience.
- Communications are rarely one-way.
- Redundancy in communication helps ensure the clarity of the message.
- Meaning is derived from the message plus the personality of the person receiving it.
- Signs are not culturally universal.
- Miscommunication is common due to misunderstanding, implication, distraction, confusion and distortion.
- Marketing communication is a great deal more than just advertising, public relations, personal selling and sales promotion.
- Push strategies emphasise promotion to the distribution chain; pull strategies emphasise promotion to consumers. Most campaigns contain elements of both push and pull.
- Budgeting is more about negotiation than about the needs of the campaign.
- Marketers should aim to do things that their competitors are not doing.
- Integration of marketing communications is difficult because different departments and agencies will each have different ideas.
- Integration is also difficult because each medium will inevitably colour the message.

Review questions

1. How might distortion affect the integration of a campaign?
2. How does the pool of reality model differ from the Schramm model?
3. What is the main drawback of post-testing?
4. What are the main criticisms of the Schramm model of communication?
5. What is meant by semantics?
6. How might ethnocentrism affect a communications campaign?
7. What are the main ways of stimulating word-of-mouth communication?
8. What is the difference between a push strategy and a pull strategy?
9. What are the advantages and disadvantages of integrating marketing communications?
10. How might symbols lead to miscommunication?

Case study revisited: Budweiser

One of the key issues for Anheuser Busch lay in ensuring that Budweiser would appeal to a younger audience, and continue to do so as the century progressed. Television advertising certainly helped in keeping the brand name in the public eye – but the company knew it would have to do more if Bud was going to appeal to the Internet generation.

The company therefore produced a series of adverts intended for the Internet. These appeared on YouTube and included one of a young couple on a horse-drawn sleigh, parked in a beautiful snowy forest clearing: the romance of the scene is spoiled by the horse, which appears to have a flatulence problem. This type of advert would not, of course, be allowed on TV (at least not in the United States) but it quickly 'went viral' as friends e-mailed the link to each other. The appeal to a young male audience was obvious, and people e-mailed it to friends who would appreciate the humour – in other words, other young men.

Other advertisements featured a man's pet chimpanzee trying to seduce the man's girl-friend, a man accidentally going into the wrong room in a beauty parlour and having a bikini wax instead of the expected massage, and a newly invented 'extending arm for reaching your Bud' malfunctioning dramatically at a football match.

Many of these adverts only appeared on social media, and were billed as 'banned' – which of course increased their appeal. Some years after their release, many are still circulating, and certainly many millions of people have seen them. The cost is of course well below that of television advertising, and the impact is greater because the message goes exactly to the target audience.

Case study: Pay-day lenders

Most of us will find, at some time, that we run out of cash before the next pay-day. The 'too much month left at the end of the money' phenomenon is well known – especially to those on small incomes, who are often very close to the edge anyway. Even a minor crisis can tip them over – which is where pay-day lenders step in.

A pay-day lender is a firm that offers people short-term unsecured loans. The loan is supposed to be repaid by the next pay-day, so will only (in theory) be needed for a few days or a couple of weeks at most. Loans are typically very small – even a loan of a few hundred pounds would be rare – and the loan terms are equally short. However, the administrative costs are high, and defaults are also a feature of pay-day lending, so charges may look high. For example, a loan of £60 taken over a period of two weeks will cost around £15 in charges and interest, which equates to an annual interest rate of over 4000%. Pay-day lenders point out that this is an unfair comparison, because the loans are taken out over a short period – the shorter the period, the higher the annual rate would be.

Of course, pay-day lenders have a serious image problem: it's easy for news media and regulators to focus on the 4000% APR rather than on the very reasonable £15. Pay-day lenders have been equated with loan sharks, and during the financial crisis they have been involved in further controversy as debt advice charities report that they have seen a doubling in the number of people seeking advice because of pay-day debt. Some under-age borrowers have managed to convince the lenders' automated systems that they are eligible to borrow, and there have been cases of people taking out 80 or more such loans, borrowing from one lender to repay another until the debt reaches astronomical levels.

In fact, pay-day lenders' profits are not excessive. The administrative costs of operating a large number of small debts, coupled with a relatively high default rate (higher than a bank would experience, anyway) mean that the companies do not earn much more than would a normal bank lender.

Pay-day lenders rely heavily on their websites for promotion, since borrowers use the website to make an application for the loan. Most pay-day lenders explain very clearly that the loans are only intended as a short-term, emergency solution – not for long-term financial commitments. By law, they are required to show the annual percentage rate of interest in a prominent position – given the flexible nature of the loans, this has to be calculated on a case-by-case basis in real time. All the lenders agree to get the money to the borrower's bank account the same day (often within minutes of the application) and the application process is, in general, extremely quick. Someone deciding to take out a pay-day loan will usually have the money within an hour or two.

Other promotion includes television: some ads are jokey (Wonga uses puppets of elderly people joking about borrowing money), some are serious (QuickQuid shows a woman worrying over how she is going to pay the bills), some are reassuring and cosy (PayDay First's ad shows people enjoying the new things they have bought – a man putting up shelves with his new cordless drill, a woman dressing her son in his new school uniform, a young man on stage with his new guitar). This advertising is intended to drive people to the company website, where everything is explained in more detail.

The problem is, of course, that no matter how careful the companies are to emphasise the need for caution, and the need to pay off the loan when it is due, and the need to avoid using a short-term loan to mask a long-term problem, people who are desperate for the cash (for whatever reason) are likely to throw caution to the winds. Many of those who use pay-day lenders are likely to be less than astute financially, and are unlikely to read the small print. This creates a major communications problem for the lender – especially if pay-day lenders are to avoid being regulated (or even banned altogether) by the government.

Questions

1. How do pay-day lenders integrate their communications?
2. Why do people apparently ignore much of the information on the pay-day lenders' websites?
3. How might pay-day lenders avoid the risk of government intervention?
4. How might the use of TV advertising affect people's perception of the product?
5. If pay-day lenders are not making excess profits, why is their image so poor?

Further reading

There are many books on marketing communications; the following represent only a small sample:

Chris Fill's *Marketing Communications: Contexts, Strategies and Applications* (Hemel Hempstead: FT Prentice Hall, 2001) is a classic student textbook on communications.

P.R. Smith and Ze Zook, *Marketing Communications: Integrating Offline and Online with Social Media*, 5th edn (London: Kogan Page, 2011) is very much a practitioner's text, putting theory second to practice. On the other hand, it is extremely comprehensive.

A book that provides a much deeper theoretical background than the others, but does not ignore practice, is Patrick de Pelsmacker, Maggie Geuens and Joeri van den Bergh, *Marketing Communications: A European Perspective* (Hemel Hempstead: FT Prentice Hall, 2004).

References

Baird, Thomas R., Wahlers, Russel G. and Cooper, Crystal K. (2007) Non-recognition of print advertising: emotional arousal and gender effects. *Journal of Marketing Communication*, 13 (1): 39–57.

Biel, A. (1989) Love the advertisement, buy the product? *ADMAP*, October.

Borremans T. (1998) Integrated (Marketing). *Communications in Practice: Survey Among Communication, Public Relations and Advertising Agencies in Belgium*. Proceedings of the 3rd Annual Conference of the Global Institute for Corporate and Marketing Communications.

Broadbent, Simon (1989) *The Advertising Budget*. Henley-on-Thames: NTC Publications for the Institute of Practitioners in Advertising.

Brown, G. (1991) Modelling advertising awareness. *ADMAP*, April.

Bruhn, M. (1995) *Intergrierte Unternehmenskommunikation: Ansatz punkte fur eine strategische und operative umsetzung intergrieter Kommunikationsarbeit*. Stuttgart: Schaffer–Poeschel.

Colley, Russell H. (1961) *Defining Advertising Goals*. New York: Association of National Advertisers.

Costa, Jamneen Arnold and Pavia, Teresa M. (1992) What it all adds up to: culture and alpha-numeric brand names. In John F. Sherry, Jr and Brian Sternthal (eds), *Advances in Consumer Research*, vol. 19. Provo, UT: Association for Consumer Research. p. 40.

Deetz, S.A. (1992) *Democracy in an Age of Corporate Colonization: Developments in Communication and the Politics of Everyday Life*. Albany, NY: State University of New York Press.

Duncan, T. and Caywood, C. (1996) The concept, process and evolution of integrated marketing communication. In E. Thorson and J. Moore (eds), *Integrated Communication: Synergy of Persuasive Voices*. Mahwah, NJ: Lawrence Erlbaum. pp. 13–34.

Eagle, L., Hyde, K. and Kitchen, P. (1998) *Advertising Effectiveness Measurement: A Review of Industry Research Practices*. Proceedings of the Third Annual Conference of the Global Institute for Corporate and Marketing Communications. Glasgow: Strathclyde University.

Engel, James F., Warshaw, Martin R. and Kinnear, Thomas C. (1994) *Promotional Strategy*. Chicago, IL: Irwin.

Flesch, R. (1979) *How to Write in Plain English: A Book for Lawyers and Consumers*. New York: Harpers.

Hartley, B. and Pickton, D. (1997) *Integrated Marketing Communication – A New Language for a New Era*. Proceedings of the Second International Conference on Marketing and Corporate Communication, Antwerp.

Hofstede, G. (1984) *Culture's Consequences: International Differences in Work-Related Values*. Beverly Hills, CA: Sage.

Institute of Public Relations (1984) *Public Relations Practice: Its roles and parameters*. London: The Institute of Public Realtions.

Katz, E. and Lazarsfield, P. (1955) *Personal Influence: The Part Played by People in the Flow of Mass Communications*. New York: Free Press.

Keegan, W. (1984) *Multinational Marketing Management*, 3rd edn. Englewood Cliffs, NJ: Prentice Hall International.

Majaro, S. (1982) *International Marketing*. London: Allen and Unwin.

Marketing News (1982) 21 ad agencies endorse copy testing principles. 19 February.

Mantovani, G. (1996) *New Communications Environments: From Everyday to Virtual*. London: Taylor and Francis.

McCracken, Grant (1986) Culture and consumption: a theoretical account of the structure and movement of the cultural meaning of consumer goods. *Journal of Consumer Research*, 13 (June): 71–81.

Nowak, G. and Phelps, J. (1994) Conceptualizing the integrated marketing communications phenomenon. *Journal of Current Issues and Research in Advertising*, 16 (1): 49–66.

O'Sullivan, T., Hartley, J., Saunders, D. and Fiske, J. (1983) *Key Concepts in Communication*. London: Methuen.

Peirce C.S., quoted in Mick, David G. (1986) Consumer research and semiotics: exploring the morphology of signs, symbols and significance. *Journal of Consumer Research*, 13 (Sept): 196–213.

Petrison, L.A. and Wang, P. (1996) Integrated marketing communication: an organisational perspective. In E. Thorson and J. Moore (eds), *Integrated Communication: Synergy of Persuasive Voices*. Mahwah, NJ: Lawrence Erlbaum. pp. 167–84.

Rosengren, Sara and Dahlen, Michael (2006) Brand-slogan matching in a cluttered environment. *Journal of Marketing Communications*, 12 (4): 263–9.

Schramm, W.A. (1948) *Mass Communication*. Urbana, IL: University of Illinois Press.

Schramm, W.A. (1971) The nature of communication between humans. In W.A. Schramm and D.F. Roberts (eds), *The Process and Effects of Mass Communication*. Urbana, IL: Illinois University Press.

Shimp, T. and Sharma, S. (1987) Consumer ethnocentrism: construction and validation of CETSCALE. *Journal of Marketing Research*, August: 280–9.

Stapel, J. (1990) Monitoring advertising performance. *ADMAP*, July/August.

Stapel, J. (1991) Like the advertisement but does it interest me? *ADMAP*, April.

Steen, J (1995) 'Now they're using suicide to sell jeans'. *Sunday Express*, 26 March.

Varey, R. (2000) A critical review of conceptions of communication evident in contemporary business and management literature. *Journal of Communication Management*, 4 (4): 328–40.

Vlasic, Goran and Kesic, Tanja (2007) Analysis of consumers' attitudes towards interactivity and relationship personalisation as contemporary developments in interactive marketing communication. *Journal of Marketing Communication*, 13 (2): 109–29.

More online

To gain free access to additional online resources to support this chapter please visit:
www.sagepub.co.uk/blythe3e

CHAPTER (8)
International marketing

Globalisation The view of the
world as a single market and
single source of supply.

LEARNING OBJECTIVES

After reading this chapter, you should be able to:

- Explain different theoretical approaches to internationalisation.

- Describe the factors involved in choosing and entering markets.

- Explain how to calculate the profit potential of a national market.

- Understand some of the difficulties involved in international marketing research.

- Explain the relationship between product and promotion strategies in
  international markets.

- Explain the main difficulties in setting up overseas branches.

Introduction

It has become almost impossible to escape from the effects of **globalisation**. Even companies that do not themselves sell their goods and services outside their national borders have found they are competing with firms entering from overseas. Additionally, firms are finding that their home markets are changing as a result of foreign travel, mass migrations and other factors.

The Internet has also opened up global markets for even the smallest of firms – and has equally opened up global markets to consumers, so that competition truly crosses borders. The biggest change that the Internet has brought to business is that any company, no matter how small, can establish a presence on the global stage.

An understanding of the international nature of business is therefore at least as essential for marketers as it is for anyone else in business.

Preview case study: Father's Day, Mother's Day and gifts

In the 16th century people were given a day off to visit their mother church (the main cathedral in the area) as part of the Lent festival. By the 19th century, this had evolved into Mothering Sunday, a day on which servants were given the day off to visit their families. For many, this was the only opportunity they would have to be reunited with their entire families – people's working lives involved much less time off than is the case in modern times. Later, the custom fell out of favour, but was revived in the United States during the 1920s (by Anna Jarvis) and eventually became the modern version of Mother's Day as a result of commercial organisations seeing the possibilities for extra sales at a quiet time of year.

Of course, fathers would not be left out. In 1910, Sonora Smart Dodd decided to establish a day to celebrate fatherhood: she organised a celebratory day at the YMCA in honour of her war-veteran father. The idea caught on, again driven by commercial interests: although progress was slow at first, it gained impetus during the 1930s when the Great Depression was hurting business and now Father's Day is celebrated worldwide.

Grandparents' Day was first proposed in the United States in the 1970s but didn't reach Britain until the 1990s. So far it has had limited success – commercial organisations have tended to merge it with Mother's Day and Father's Day, since the public appetite for gifts and cards has proved limited.

Traditionally, people give gifts on these celebratory days: in the United States and the UK, it is traditional to send a greetings card and flowers to one's mother, and a greetings card and a small gift to one's father. However, as commercialisation has increased, almost every type of firm has jumped on the bandwagon offering 'the perfect Mother's Day gift', whether it is perfume or a trip to the theatre. Fathers are offered power tools, alcoholic drinks, clothing, seats at football matches and even credit for on-line gambling.

For companies in a globalised world, the problem is manifold – apart from cultural differences, the celebrations fall on different days in different countries. This generates both difficulties and opportunities.

Globalisation of trade

International trade goes back a long way. In about 4000BC a stone axe factory was established in the Langdale Pikes, in the English Lake District. This factory was so successful that axes from it have been found as far away as the South of France – evidence that international trade occurred even before there were true nation-states.

The thrust towards globalisation comes from the following factors (see Figure 8.1):

Comparative advantage The degree to which one country is better at producing certain goods rather than another.

- **Comparative advantage.** Some countries are better placed to produce certain products than are others. Minerals such as oil and aluminium are obvious examples, but some countries develop expertise in service fields. For example, Holland has expertise in building dams and in handling large bodies of water, developed through the construction of its famous dykes.
- Economies of scale. For some goods the costs of development are so high that they can only be realistically amortised over very large production runs. For example, electronic products such as cellular telephones represent a huge cost in terms of research and development – only sales in the millions can justify the

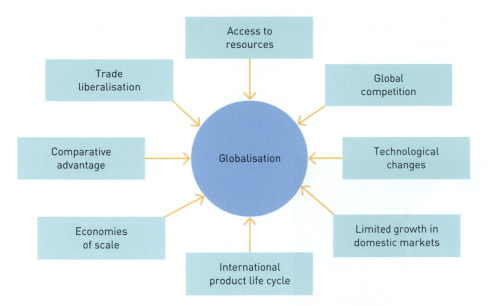

Figure 8.1   Forces for globalisation

outlay, so a world market is essential. Also, modern automated production lines mean that manufacturing capacity has increased by orders of magnitude – few modern consumer-goods factories can function efficiently if only serving a domestic market.

- Trade liberalisation. The realisation that free trade creates wealth is not a new one – it was British government policy for most of the 19th century. In recent years the idea has received a new boost with the creation of trading blocs such as the European Union, and the reduction of barriers to trade worldwide as a result of the World Trade Organisation agreements.

- International product life cycle. As a product reaches the decline phase in one country, it can be introduced into a new country in order to prolong its life. In fact, products cross borders even without the originating company trying to arrange this to happen – because of rapid world communications, ideas become disseminated and production of similar products in other countries will happen anyway.

- Limited growth in domestic markets. Most companies aim to grow, but clearly there will come a point at which the home market is saturated. Many firms become international because they cannot grow any more in their home markets.

- Technological changes. Improvements in air transport and telecommunications have made it much easier for firms to trade in other countries. Satellite TV has enabled firms to advertise internationally much more easily than they could before, and cheap airfreight has enabled firms to export small quantities of product relatively easily.

- Global competition. As foreign companies make inroads into a company's home markets, the company concerned might naturally decide that opportunities exist in the overseas markets. For example, an office-furniture supply company in the UK, faced with competition from Italy, might reasonably conclude that opportunities would exist in the Italian market.

- Access to resources. Companies that operate internationally not only sell goods overseas, they also access resources overseas. The ease with which manufacture can be relocated to low-wage countries, or components sourced from overseas suppliers, leads firms to realise that they can easily sell finished product in those markets.

As globalisation increases, new market segments appear, and marketers seek to meet their needs.

Think outside this box!

If globalisation is such a great idea, why is it that so many people protest about it? The anti-globalisation movement has tried to disrupt trade talks, has attacked global companies such as McDonald's and has protested to the point of rioting in all parts of the globe. Paradoxically, the anti-globalisation movement is itself global. So what's the problem?

Anti-globalists say that having everybody use the same products, watch the same TV shows and wear the same clothes is destroying the world's cultural diversity and reducing everything to the same grey goo. Also, they argue that globalised companies are too powerful – they are more powerful than national governments, in fact, and can literally ignore democratically elected representatives. Eventually, the argument runs, we will all be controlled by big business – if we aren't already.

On the other hand, if people didn't want the goods they wouldn't buy them. We know that McDonald's is an American corporation – that's part of the fun. And isn't sharing ideas a positive thing for the world, rather than keeping to some dogmatic principle that our own culture is better than anyone else's?

International business perspectives

The philosophy behind the company's internationalisation effort is an important starting-point for understanding the possible strategic and tactical approaches to internationalisation. One classification of business perspectives is the EPRG classification (Muhlbacher et al. 1999). This is shown in Table 8.1.

There are two main schools of thought on the internationalisation of the firm. The first is the Uppsala, or stages of development, approach in which it is believed that firms go through a series of stages in becoming international and (eventually) global firms. The stages are as follows:

1. Exporting. This implies the smallest level of commitment to the foreign market. The firm produces goods in its own country, and sells them in one or more foreign markets. The sales are made to a foreign importer, who then handles all the marketing in the foreign country. In some cases the exporting firm has acquired the business without actually seeking out an importer – the firm may have been approached at an exhibition stand, for example, or one of its own customers (a wholesaler or retailer) might have opened up a branch in the overseas market. The advantage of exporting is that it is cheap and relatively simple – the drawback is that the firm loses all control over the marketing of the product once it enters the foreign market.

Table 8.1   Classification of international perspectives

Ethnocentric perspective	An ethnocentric manager sees the domestic market as the most important, and the overseas markets as inferior. Often such managers do not perceive foreign imports as representing a serious threat at all.
Polycentric perspective	Polycentric managers look at each overseas market as if it were a separate domestic market. Each country is seen as a separate entity, and the firm seeks to be seen as a 'local' firm within that country. Each market has its own manufacturing and marketing facilities, and there is only limited overlap.
Regional perspective	Regional orientation means grouping countries together, usually on a geographical basis, and providing for the specific needs of consumers within those countries. National boundaries are respected, but do not have the same importance as cultural differences.
Geocentric perspective	The truly global marketer thinks of the world as a single market, with opportunities for procurement, production and sales in whichever market segments are the most appropriate. Global marketers look for global segments (for example the global youth market), and for global opportunities to rationalise communications, production and product development.

2. Establish a sales office in the foreign market. Once export sales are becoming established, the exporting firm might consider it worthwhile to take an interest in the marketing of its goods in the overseas market. This involves increased financial commitment, but also offers greater control and tends to engender confidence among overseas buyers.

3. Overseas distribution. This would involve establishing a warehouse and distribution network in the overseas market. This gives even more control, and also shortens the lines of supply so that foreign buyers' needs can be met more quickly.

4. Overseas manufacture. The company sets up subsidiary factories in the countries in which it does business, to shorten lines of supply and to adapt the product to local market conditions.

5. Global marketing. At this stage the firm sources raw materials and components from the most cost-effective countries, and markets its products to the most appropriate market segments. Company ownership may be spread across stock markets in several countries, and the company may well employ far more foreigners than nationals from its country of origin.

Polycentrism Viewing corporate activities as emanating from centres in a number of countries.

Geocentrism Viewing corporate activities in a global manner.

An alternative view of the internationalisation process has been proposed by Dunning (1993). Dunning's **Eclectic** Theory says that firms enter foreign markets by whatever means are most appropriate to the firm. The decision will be based on the firm's specific advantage over its competitors, both at home and overseas, and the entry method decided upon without necessarily going through any intermediate stages. For example, a firm with a strength in franchising will enter overseas markets on a franchise basis rather than begin by exporting. The eclectic paradigm also has implications for manufacture, since a firm will produce in whichever country is most appropriate or convenient. In recent years, due to the Internet, even small firms can trade easily in overseas markets – distance has become of little importance for many small and medium-sized enterprises (SMEs) (Brock et al. 2011).

Eclectic All-encompassing, taking account of all factors.

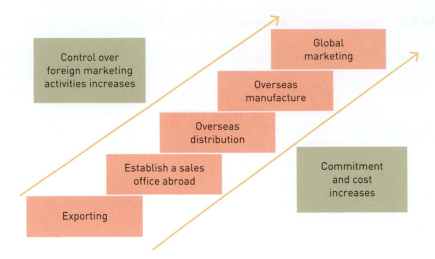

Figure 8.2   Stages of development approach

Some research indicates that there may be only small differences between firms that are 'born global' and those that take a traditional approach (Chetty and Campbell-Hunt 2004).

Globalisation occurs when managers concentrate on groups of customers with similar needs, regardless of country of residence. From a marketing viewpoint, this is obviously a customer-orientated approach, since country of residence actually says very little about a consumer's needs. The need for mobile telephones is the same whether the customer lives in Sweden or Zambia: only local systems and prices will change. Some cultural elements will, of course, need to be adapted: language and use of the product might be factors which would change as the product moves into different markets.

Assessing market attractiveness

Different markets have different levels of attractiveness. In some cases the overseas market may be less lucrative than the domestic market, but expansion may no longer be possible at home.

Choosing which countries to target is a crucial part of the globalisation process. It will involve screening countries against a number of factors, some of which are more relevant to some companies than to others.

- Market size. In general, the bigger the country's population the better, since (all else being equal) there will be more customers.
- Structure of the population (demographics). Some countries have ageing populations (Japan, most of Europe, the United States) whereas others have generally younger populations (Indonesia, most African countries, Central America and some Middle Eastern countries). Also, the lower the population density, the greater the distances goods need to be transported – Australia is a prime example.
- Economic development. City dwellers tend to be better-educated than those from remote rural areas, and are often also more cosmopolitan in outlook, and therefore more likely to appreciate foreign goods.

- Income and wealth. It is easy to assume that people from a poor country do not have the money to buy much, but in fact many poorer countries have a high wealth concentration, so that the country as a whole may have a substantial number of wealthy people. This means there may be a good market for upmarket goods such as luxury cars. A low concentration of wealth and income is probably better for marketing fast-moving consumer goods.
- Business environment. The existence of high tariff barriers, local product regulations, or a high level of local competition might well result in a country being struck off the list. Local availability of advertising agencies, PR consultants, and a media infrastructure might also affect the decision to enter a specific market.
- Storage and transport facilities. Warehousing must be suitable for the product class, and available in the necessary volume. There needs to be a suitable transportation infrastructure for the distribution of goods.
- Political considerations. Political instability increases the risk of not being paid for goods, or of having assets confiscated or nationalised. Disputes between the host country and the country of origin could cause business sanctions to be imposed.
- Local competition. The fact that competition exists does at least show that there is a market. However, local competitors already know the market, understand the rules, and are likely to be backed by their own government, so unless you have something very good to offer they will represent a real threat.
- Psychological proximity. Firms often approach markets in countries where they feel there are similarities with the home country. For example, British companies often seek to do business in the United States, because there is a perceived cultural similarity springing from using the same language and having a great deal of history in common. Likewise, French companies often target former colonies in Africa and the Caribbean, and Spanish companies try to do business in Latin America.

Assessing the attractiveness of the overseas market is not simply an issue of potential sales or potential profitability: it is also an issue of deciding the company's strategic direction. A firm might therefore enter one market in order to establish a position from which it can enter a more lucrative market. For example, when Honda entered the UK motorcycle market it began by selling small, low-powered motorcycles. This enabled the firm to become established, and eventually market large, high-powered bikes, which are much more profitable.

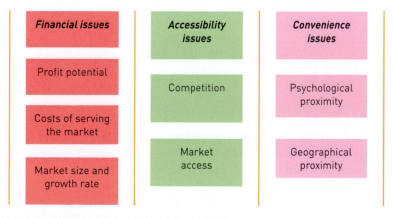

Figure 8.3   Assessing markets

Target markets might be chosen for any of the following reasons:

1. Geographical proximity.
2. Psychological proximity.
3. Market size and growth rate.
4. Costs of serving the market.
5. Profit potential.
6. Market access.
7. Competition.

Geographical proximity The closeness of the market in physical terms.

Geographical proximity refers to the closeness of the market in physical terms. For example, trade within the European Union is based on the physical proximity of the markets – moving goods from Dortmund to Maastricht is easier in practice than moving goods from Dortmund to Munich, since Dortmund and Maastricht are much closer together. The German–Dutch border presents no real barrier to the movement of goods. However, there may be a psychological barrier, based partly on language and partly on history.

Psychological proximity The degree to which countries are culturally close to each other.

Psychological proximity refers to the cultural similarities that exist between some countries. For example, many UK firms regard the United States as an attractive market, simply because the US and UK are similar culturally. This can overcome the obvious advantages of trading with, say, France or Holland which are much closer and which have virtually no border restrictions with the UK. Psychological proximity is often based on language – the UK feels closer to Australia, Canada, the United States, New Zealand and even India because these countries share a language. Likewise, Spanish companies often feel closer to Latin America than they do to Germany, and Portuguese companies feel closer to Brazil, Mozambique and Angola than they do to Italy or Greece.

Think outside this box!

Most English speakers get fairly lazy about learning foreign languages – after all, everybody speaks English nowadays, so why bother? This means, of course, that the English-speaking countries tend to trade with each other rather than with their nearest neighbours.

But if the neighbours speak English as well, because it is the world business language, where does that leave the argument? Why is it that British firms think first of trading with the United States, and second of trading with fellow EU members? Why do Americans trade only 10% of their gross national product, and rarely venture out to other countries at all? If trade is always good, why are we so reluctant to do it?

Maybe it's more than language. Maybe we are just afraid of the unknown – and American films and TV make the United States seem very familiar!

Market size and growth rate can be important factors. A large market is likely to be more attractive than a small market, since there will be more niches available for the foreign company. Markets with high growth rates tend to offer less competitive pressure than stable or shrinking markets since all the companies in the market can grow without having to compete for market share with the other firms in the market. There is evidence that growth is a more important consideration than size (Whitelock and Jobber 1994).

The level and quality of the competition already in the market is an important factor because a market with a heavily entrenched, strong group of competitors is unlikely to respond favourably to a foreign entrant. Defining the competition is of course important here – a foreign entrant may enter at a different position in the market from the one occupied in the domestic market. Also, foreign goods sometimes gain (or lose) from country-of-origin effects, whereby some of the country's image attaches itself to the brand. For example, Germany has a reputation for good engineering, so German products are often assumed to be well-engineered. This is, of course, a ridiculous assumption to make since there may well be many German manufacturers who employ poor engineers, but nonetheless the view is widely held. Likewise, China has a long way to go to overcome its image of producing shoddy goods and yet many high-quality products carry the 'Made in China' label.

Sometimes the country of origin causes 'symbolic' consumption: people buy the product simply because of its country of origin. This has been especially noticeable in transition economies (former Communist countries of Eastern Europe) where the consumption of Western products is symbolic of a desire for a Western lifestyle, and is even seen when individuals have no real knowledge of the products themselves (Clark et al. 2002). A particularly interesting example is the tortilla in Mexico. This is a culturally significant product, symbolising what it is to be Mexican, yet there is a strong belief that American-made tortillas are better than Mexican-made ones, simply because Mexicans tend to believe that anything American is better than anything Mexican (Gabel and Boller 2003).

The cost of serving the market can vary greatly between countries. For example, physical distribution costs can be extremely high in a country such as Australia, where distances are large between settlements: equally, in some countries (such as Japan) the distribution chains are long, with a large number of wholesalers and other middlemen involved in the process. Transportation costs in some developing countries vary with the seasons, as roads become flooded in the wet season or impassable deserts in the dry season. Advertising costs can vary dramatically: TV advertising in the United States is in general much cheaper than in the UK, for example. Some countries may lack a marketing infrastructure that would allow for cheap entry – for example, Germany has a well-developed system of manufacturers' agents, who are able to sell imported goods on a commission-only basis. This allows even the smallest firms to enter the German market (provided they can interest a good agent). Countries such as Zambia have no comparable system, so foreign companies need to set up their own sales organisation to do business there. Since salaries are generally low, this may not present the same problems it would in (say) Denmark, but the costs would undoubtedly be too high for a small firm.

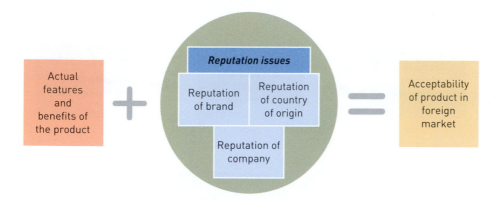

Figure 8.4   Country of origin effects

Think outside this box!

Country of origin is commonly used as an advertising theme. Audi uses the strap line 'Vorsprung durch Technik' in its world advertising, despite the fact that most non-German speakers would have no idea what this means (it means 'progress through technology' if you're curious).

So why put out an incomprehensible advertisement? Doesn't this fly in the face of everything we know about communication? Or is it that we are communicating the German-ness of Audi cars, in the hope that the German reputation for engineering will rub off on the Audi?

Does country of origin actually mean anything? On the one hand, one might expect that good engineers breed more good engineers, through training and education and by good example: on the other hand, why should a factory on one side of the Alps turn out better products than one a few miles away on the other side of the border?

Profit potential of the market is a function of the number of potential customers and the profit margin the product might command. In some cases the number of potential customers is so large that the market is worth approaching even though profit margins are small – an example is India. In other cases the margins are large but the number of customers is small, as in Denmark. Powerful buying groups, low per capita income, and strong competition are all factors which tend to reduce profit margins. High incomes, inefficient competition and good positioning within the market all help to raise profit margins (as of course is true in domestic markets).

Market access can be limited by the local industry structure, by government restrictions on imports, or by local competition rules. For example, in Japan there is no legal problem with importing goods, but the monolithic structure of industry, with the giant *sogo sosha* general trading companies controlling everything, means that there are few openings for foreign companies. On the other hand, the Caricom countries in the Caribbean have high external tariffs on many goods in order to protect their fledgling manufacturing industries from cheap foreign imports.

Some firms use market attractiveness indexes to compare different potential markets. Managers decide which are the factors that make a market attractive from

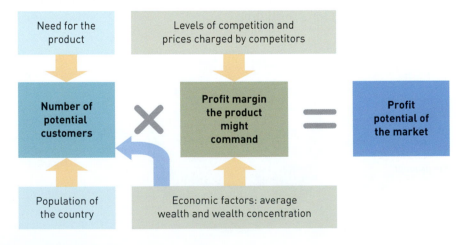

Figure 8.5   Assessing profit potential

Table 8.2 Stages of developing a market attractiveness index

Stage	Explanation
Establish the criteria to be used for selecting countries.	Criteria might include a significant proportion of the population wealthy enough to afford the product, a safe country to do business in, a country where the market should be easy to enter, or any of a dozen possible criteria.
Relate the selected criteria to appropriate variables.	Wealth of the citizens might be linked to gross domestic product of the country, but might also be related to wealth concentration – there are more millionaires in India than there are in the UK, simply because the wealth is more concentrated. Relating criteria to variables that can be measured (or gleaned from published research) will involve assessing market potential, entry and operating costs, and the competitive environment.
Determine the relative importance of each variable.	This may involve obtaining advice from local contacts in the target market, considering which variables are most important for reaching corporate objectives, and considering the entry barriers to various national markets. Weightings are applied accordingly.
Evaluate each country and establish a rank order.	Calculating the scores for each target market against the set of variables offered is straightforward, provided the weightings have been correctly evaluated and applied.
Conduct in-depth studies on highest-ranking countries.	Having calculated the relative scores of the countries based on published records, managers can assess which countries appear to be the most promising and can act accordingly by carrying out further, first-hand, investigations.

the firm's viewpoint, and apply weightings to the factors, then assess each potential market against those factors. The stages of developing such an index are shown in Table 8.2. As a result of the exercise, target countries can be classified as probables, possibles and 'no-hopers'. The last are discarded. Further information on the 'possibles' might be collected, and some of these might be promoted to 'probables', but the remainder will be discarded also.

The main problems with international marketing research also apply to market screening. These include:

- The high cost of gathering information, both in terms of money and in terms of time.
- The vast number of potentially relevant factors, and the difficulty of deciding which ones are truly relevant.
- The extent and frequency of changes in foreign market conditions. Often changes that are widely expected by local people (because they can read the clues well) are not apparent to foreigners, so that competitors in the foreign market are almost always better informed than foreign firms.
- The fact that the initial screening process relies on information that is published in the exporting firm's home country. Data for some countries are unreliable, and for most countries will be seriously out of date: the basis on which statistics have been collected will differ, with different factors being included for each country, so that 'educated guesses' will often need to be applied. For example, population age categories might vary: 'young' people might be defined as being aged under 15, or from 13 to 18, or from 10 to 20, and so forth. This makes comparisons extremely difficult.

A mitigating factor has been the Internet, and in particular, sites such as the American CIA website which contains standardised information on each country. Unfortunately the data available are relatively limited, and not likely to be very relevant to specific industries.

Far and away the biggest problem with market screening techniques is that they require a great deal of arbitrary judgement on the part of managers. Selection of factors, and the weighting of factors, is purely speculative: the fact that the final outcome is presented numerically makes it appear to be a credible, scientific approach but since the data going in are based on judgements by managers, the results are also simply based on managerial judgements. Having said that, market screening techniques can be a useful tool for clarifying management thinking and ensuring that all factors are taken into account, particularly if several people are involved in the process of deciding on the factors and their weightings.

A growing factor in globalisation is the existence of transnational market segments. These are groups of consumers with similar needs who inhabit different countries. This may occur because of migration (for example the substantial Malaysian and Chinese communities in Australia and British Columbia) or because of similarities of age (as in the world youth market) or because of similarities in lifestyle (the international executive market). There is some debate about whether these segments exist in a real sense: some commentators say that they only exist because the members have no choice (Kjelgaard and Askegaard 2004). Perhaps surprisingly in view of the cultural connotations of food, transnational segments have been identified in food products (Moskowitz et al. 2008). Specifically, researchers found that the market for dairy products could be segmented as health seekers and taste/fruit seekers, whether the consumers lived in France, the UK, or Germany.

Marketing in a changing world: Global homogeneity

Global marketing has its challenges because it seeks to supply similar products to disparate cultures. However, once the products have been supplied, there is each time a tiny dilution of the target country's culture. Over time, cultures become gradually more homogeneous.

Today it seems that we can travel more easily, but actually there is nowhere to go because everybody is wearing the same clothes, eating the same food and listening to the same music. Standards of living are converging as well, so that we can no longer be sure that (for example) wage rates will continue to be low in China or India. Globalisation may therefore carry the seeds of its own destruction, in that local manufacture becomes as cheap as overseas manufacture, and markets for local goods are as good as markets overseas. Coupled with increasing costs of transportation due to rising fuel costs, and we have a perfect storm for going back to local manufacture and marketing.

Detailed information on global market segments is, of course, difficult to collect because each country operates as a separate entity for the collection of statistics. From a conceptual viewpoint, the truly marketing-orientated company that wishes to go international should be looking for global segments rather than dividing up its customers according to country of residence. Country of residence is becoming less and less relevant as time goes by – mass migrations and foreign travel are having profound effects on the tastes and needs of consumers throughout the world, with ethnic segmentation growing steadily less easy to apply (Jamal 2003). Furthermore,

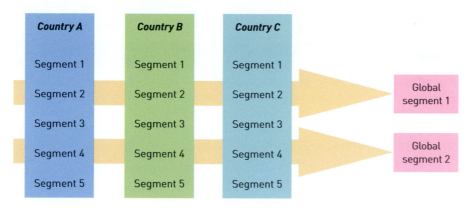

Figure 8.6 Global segmentation

people's desire for novelty is also driving the adoption of products from different cultures, so that items that are rooted in one ethnic context often sell well in other countries (Grier et al. 2006).

Global strategy

Strategy is about developing competitive capabilities and finding a competitive position within the marketplace. In international markets, the competitive capabilities that the firm has in one country may not be the same as those it has in another country: equally, the competitive position a firm adopts in one country may be different from that held in another. For example, Stella Artois beer is regarded as a standard, generic brand in its native Belgium, but in the UK it is marketed as a premium brand. Interestingly, the television advertisements for the beer are made predominantly in French, presumably as a way of increasing the apparent sophistication of the beer, but the brewery is in fact in Leuven, a predominantly Flemish-speaking city.

Firms wishing to enter a given overseas market will need to consider the same environmental issues as they would consider periodically within their home markets, but a key issue in global marketing is the degree to which the company is prepared to standardise its products and marketing approach. There are five basic strategic stances available, as shown in Table 8.3.

Firms might decide on a globalisation strategy by which the company's products, attitudes, brands and promotion are standardised throughout the world, with global segments being identified, or conversely might decide on a customisation strategy whereby the company adapts its thinking (and marketing) to each new market. The companies that are most likely to seek a globalisation policy are those whose products are not culturally specific, and whose promotions can be readily understood throughout the world.

Research shows that relatively few companies standardise their advertising (Harris 1996). Of the 38 multinational companies surveyed, 26 said they used standard advertisements, but only four of these were completely standardised. The others varied from limited standardisation (with perhaps only the corporate logo remaining the same) through limited standardisation of key elements, through to standard execution with some minor adaptations.

Table 8.4 shows the factors that contribute to standardisation of the marketing programme (Cavusgil and Kirpalani 1993).

Table 8.3   International marketing strategies

Strategy	Explanation
Keep product and promotion the same	This strategy minimises entry costs, but relatively few firms have achieved success this way. Coca-Cola uses this approach, selling the same core product worldwide and using broadly the same promotional campaigns. This is possible for US companies because Hollywood has made the world aware of American icons and cultural norms, so that the promotions are comprehensible worldwide.
Adapt promotion only	The product remains the same, but the promotion is adapted to local cultural norms. Provided the product is acceptable in the local market, this approach works well and is commonly used.
Adapt product only	Some detergent manufacturers use this approach. The product itself is reformulated to take account of local water supply, local washing habits, and local washing machine designs. The promotion can remain broadly the same, because the brand values remain the same.
Adapt both product and promotion	Sometimes the product and the promotion need to be adapted. This was the case with the Procter and Gamble brand, Cheer, which had to be adapted for the Japanese market to allow for the extra fabric softeners the Japanese use. The promotion emphasised that the product works well in cold water, since most Japanese wash their clothes in cold water.
Invent new products	If existing products cannot meet the conditions in the target market, a new product must be invented. For example, the clockwork radio was invented for use in countries where a mains power supply is not universal, and batteries are expensive or hard to obtain.

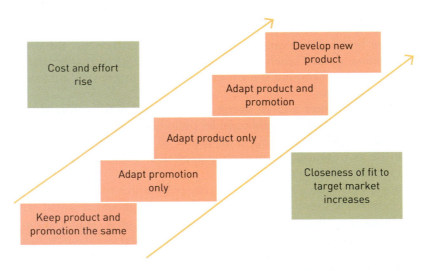

Figure 8.7   Product/promotion strategy

Political and legal environmental factors are important because they are likely to be different from those obtaining in the home market. For example, because alcohol is illegal in Saudi Arabia, hotels need to be designed and equipped differently. Also, the pricing structure of the hotels needs to different, since there will be no bar receipts but there will be increased sales of coffee and soft drinks.

Technical and social norms differ according to culture and infrastructure. For example, in Zambia credit card transactions are routinely conducted using machines that

Table 8.4   Factors in standardisation

Macro environmental factors	Similarity of legal requirements
	Political sensitivity
	Technical and social norms
	Geographical similarity
Product	Nature of the product
	Product uniqueness
	Cultural specificity
Market	Stage of the lifecycle
	Degree of urbanisation
	Structure of distribution system
	Degree of technical orientation
	Price sensitivity
Internal environment	International experience
	Attitude of corporate management
	Goals of internationalisation
	Costs of research and development

take a carbon-copy impression of the card. This technology was largely superseded in the UK several years ago, but because of the poorer telecommunications infrastructure in Zambia the system continues to be used. Technological norms sometimes persist due to cultural differences – for example, in Spain washing machines are often kept in outside areas because that is where the clothes are pegged out, so plastic covers are widely available to protect the machines from occasional rainfall. For Spaniards having the washing machine in the kitchen would be somewhat unusual, whereas in the UK that would be the logical place to have the washing machine, since it makes the plumbing task a great deal easier.

Geographical similarity between countries contributes to standardisation for many products. For example, car manufacturers sometimes provide gearboxes with different gear ratios according to whether the car is to be sold in mountainous areas or flat country: also, cars intended for hot climates might typically be supplied with air conditioning, but not heaters (this is common practice in Brazil).

Culture

Culture is obviously a major consideration when crossing national boundaries: managers typically underestimate the possible impact of cultural differences, causing a 'shock' effect (Pedersen and Pedersen 2004). Culture is easier to recognise than define, but a nation's culture represents a collective frame of reference through which a wide range of issues and problems is interpreted. It determines how symbols, sounds, pictures and behaviour are perceived and interpreted by individuals and affects socialisation, friendship patterns, social institutions, aesthetics and language (Delener 1990; Ferraro and Briody 2012; Usunier 1993). Culture consists of the following main elements:

- Religion. Even if the bulk of the population is non-practising, the prevailing religion permeates the culture: this is the case with Christianity in Britain, and with Islam in Turkey.
- Language. The language shapes the nation's thought, because some concepts are difficult (or impossible) to express in some languages, while others are easily expressed. For example, the Greek word for 'foreigner' (*xenos*) is also the word for 'guest'. When Greeks needed a word for 'foreigner' which did not imply guest status, they had to adapt a word from English – *touristikos*.
- Social structure. This may range from the rigid caste structure of India through to the so-called 'classless society' of Australia. Social structure also includes gender roles and family patterns: the Indian practice of giving and lending family gold to a new bride purifies her, and also binds her to the new family (Fernandez and Veer 2004).
- Shared beliefs and ethics. Beliefs about what is and is not acceptable behaviour are largely cultural. Most (but not all) of these beliefs derive from religious principles.
- Non-verbal language. This includes gesture and body language: while some gestures are universal (for example, smiling) most are not. Even nodding the head changes its meaning across national boundaries: in most of Europe an up-and-down nod means agreement, but in Greece a toss of the head accompanied by a click of the tongue means 'no'. Even smiling varies: Japanese people smile less in public than they do in private, whereas Americans smile more in public than they do in private.

Culture helps individuals to define concepts. A concept is a conscious linking together of images, objects, stimuli or events. Individuals receive huge numbers of messages, so the brain needs a system for classifying them into groups, which can then be dealt with efficiently. For instance, apples, oranges and bananas are all separate and unique items, but the brain can categorise them into a single concept of 'fruit'. Conceptualisations help the individual to manage data, identify relations among events and objects, and discover similarities and differences that enable a comparison of items of information. This is vitally important for the design of advertising images because culturally-based conceptualisations can determine how a

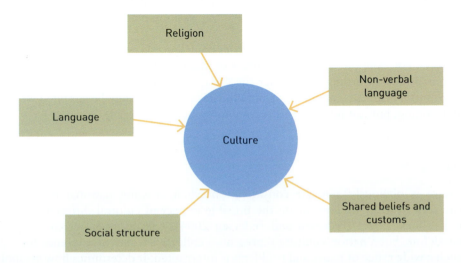

Figure 8.8 Elements of culture

message is interpreted, and also how the message recipient responds to its contents. A particular example is the gender of brands. In languages where all nouns are either masculine or feminine (e.g. Spanish) a brand name can acquire gender (Coca-Cola is feminine, for example). This can affect consumer perception of the brand quite dramatically (Yorkston and deMello 2004).

National media that carry advertisements are themselves influenced by a country's culture. This can manifest itself in the following aspects of the national culture:

- The spoken and written language used. Even within a single country, these can vary according to social class or region.
- Whether a country has a tabloid press. The existence of a cheap, downmarket newspaper affects the targeting of the message, and also the content of the message.
- The editorial content of magazines, newspapers and broadcast media.
- Attitudes adopted by the media towards national issues (manifest in the non-coverage of 'taboo' subjects, adoption of ideological lines, etc.).

Culture affects what people buy (taboos, local tastes, historical traditions, etc.), when they buy (e.g. the spending boom around Christmas in most Christian countries), who does the purchasing (men or women) and the overall pattern of consumer buying behaviour. Culture can also affect consumer behaviour in relation to:

- Which consumer needs are felt more intensively.
- Which family members take which purchasing decisions.
- Attitudes towards foreign-supplied products.
- The number of people who will purchase an item during the introductory phase of its life cycle.
- The segmentation of national markets.

On a wider level, cultural influences are evident in some aspects of a country's demographic make-up. For example, household size is culturally determined. In Western Europe it is common for young single people to set up home independent of their parents, whereas in many other cultures young people (especially women) will only leave their parents' homes when they marry. Also, in Northern European countries the family is usually defined as the parents and their children, whereas in many countries unmarried aunts, uncles, cousins and so forth would live in the same house as part of the nuclear family. Kinship patterns, social mobility and social stratification are all culturally based, and all have an effect on purchasing behaviour as well as on responses to marketing communications.

Real-life marketing: Cultural gaffes

We all grow up in our own cultures, and absorb its rules without conscious thought. So if you're travelling for business, you will find yourself with people who grew up with a different set of rules for polite behaviour – but it's you who have become the funny foreigner. Because the rules are subconscious, it's easy to offend people, and they won't always remember that you have a different set of rules, so they will just think you're rude. Ask yourself – how often have you thought that a foreigner was acting rudely?

(Continued)

(Continued)

When you're on a business trip abroad, follow these rules:

- Read up on local behaviour and customs beforehand – especially things such as body language.
- Talk to people from that culture beforehand.
- You will make mistakes: be ready to apologise if people look startled or upset.
- If in doubt, ask! And thank people for setting you straight.
- Be aware of other people's reactions.
- Watch what other people do, and do likewise.
- If the boot is on the other foot, and you are dealing with a foreign visitor who makes a cultural gaffe, be a nice person – explain to them (politely) where they have gone wrong.

At the same time, it is important to realise that culture only represents one aspect of the environment within which the firm operates. Political considerations and/or economic laws of supply and demand often outweigh cultural effects (Bangeman 1992), and some research indicates that in business-to-business markets cultural effects are far less important than language barriers, political barriers, geographic distance, technological differences and many other factors (Pressey and Selassie 2002).

MODELS OF CULTURE

Three main approaches to the analysis of culture have been developed:

1. Taxonomies of culture. Dividing cultures into different levels and/or into high-context or low-context cultures.
2. Lifestyle analysis.
3. Identification of cultural universals. These are the aspects of culture found in all societies. Examples of cultural universals include bodily adornment, courtship, household hygiene, sexual taboos, gift giving and status differentiation (Murdock 1945).

High-context culture A culture that is homogeneous and has rigid rules.

A **high-context culture** is one in which the norms and values are deeply embedded within its members and not expressed in any explicit manner (Hofstede 1980). People sharing the same high-context culture do not feel any need to explain their thoughts and behaviour to each other, so they can rely heavily on non-verbal communication. Characteristics of high-context culture are as follows:

- Communication within the high-context group is fast and efficient, but can break down in relation to outsiders who may not be able to understand what the group believes or is talking about.
- Behaviour within a high-context group is stable and predictable.
- The nature of a particular high-context group is likely to be understood by outsiders only by stereotyping the group as a whole.
- For effective communication to occur, all parties need to share the same perceptual field.

High-context cultures are orthodox, conservative and totalitarian: there is little room for personal expression within high-context groups, but on the plus side everyone has a clear understanding of what their role is and what they can expect from others within the group.

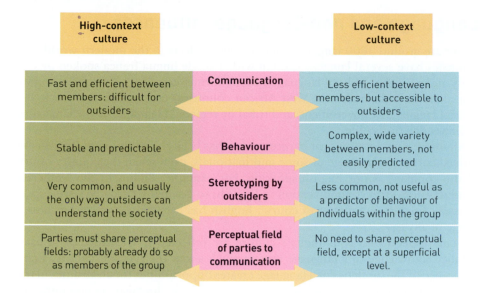

Figure 8.9   High-context and low-context cultures

Low-context cultures, on the other hand, are characterised by the following features:

Low-context culture A culture that is heterogenous and has tolerant rules.

- They are individualistic rather than collectivistic.
- Members communicate using clearly coded messages.
- Members' values, attitudes, perceptions and patterns of behaviour are diverse and liable to change quickly.

The United States and most of Western Europe have low-context cultures. Because of mass migrations and world travel, citizens of these countries have been exposed to many cultural differences and tend not to assume that their own culture is the only way things can be done. Inhabitants of countries such as Japan, which has very few foreigners living there, tend to have high-context cultures.

Think outside this box!

The whole point of globalisation is that it makes us all more like each other: at the same time, world travel has given us a taste for the exotic. So why should we pander to local cultures? Having something very foreign on offer might be exciting for them!

After all, American firms have done extremely well by being as American as possible. Likewise, Dutch people enjoy Indonesian food, Americans have literally millions of Mexican restaurants, the most popular restaurants in Britain are Indian or Bangladeshi, and even in France Chinese restaurants are springing up throughout the country. After all, nothing is as culturally specific as food!

On the other hand, the Mexican food served in Idaho or Wisconsin is far removed from the Mexican food served in Yucatan or Mexico City; the Indonesian food served in Haarlem is not the same as the Indonesian food served in Jakarta, nor is the Indian food served in Brixton the same as that served in Mumbai. So perhaps it isn't so much that we like foreign food, but more that we like the idea of eating foreign food!

Language and non-language influences

There are around 3000 languages and 10,000 dialects in the modern world. Many countries have several languages, often with a single lingua franca spoken by everybody and a number of local languages. Many former colonies of European countries (for example India and most West African countries) use English or French as the official language of government, and tribal or regional languages as the languages of ordinary day-to-day life.

An interesting development in recent years has been the adoption of English as the official corporate language of some multinationals, even when the country of origin of the company is not English-speaking. For example, Philips in the Netherlands conducts intra-firm communication in English, so company executives are expected to speak English as a matter of course. English has become the world business language in any case.

Many aspects of a community's culture are reflected in the language it uses. A detailed knowledge of a language reveals much about the relevant culture. Equally, ignorance of the subtleties of a language creates opportunities for absurdities in translation, mistaken messages and ambiguity. For example, linguistic communities have extensive vocabularies to describe activities and surroundings that are important to them (weather and agriculture in some societies, industry and commerce in others). Concepts of time, whether people approach issues analytically or intuitively, degrees of fatalism or of being organised and methodical, are all reflected in language.

Non-linguistic communication occurs not only through body language and gesture, but also through people's use of space. For example, standing close to someone is regarded as polite behaviour in the Middle East, but not in the United States, where it is regarded as a violation of personal space. Handholding and other forms of physical contact have different meanings in different cultures – in much of Africa it is normal to see friends walking in the street holding hands, but not lovers: the reverse would apply in most of Europe. These factors have very clear implications for advertising, and even for product adaptation.

The product itself will not need to be adapted if it is not culturally specific. Obviously a manufacturer of Buddhist prayer-wheels is unlikely to find a large market in a Muslim

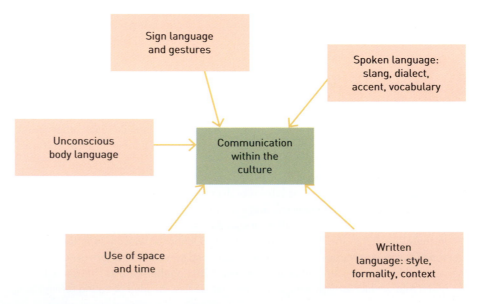

Figure 8.10   Language in context

country, but there are more subtle examples: for instance, French people tend to spend more of their time outdoors than do British people, and therefore expect to find a wide range of high-quality garden furniture in their hypermarkets. French people are more prepared to spend large sums on products used outside the home. On the other hand, personal stereos and mobile telephones are not especially culturally specific, apart from the need to translate instructions into the language of the target country.

If the product is unique, it can remain standardised for all countries. If it has close competitors this is less likely to be possible: in order to offer something different to consumers in the target country, the product may need to be adapted substantially.

If a product is in the same stage of its life cycle in two countries (for example, if it is growing rapidly in sales) the firm might be tempted to use a standardised promotional campaign. This could be a mistake if the product's growth is technology-driven in one market (for example it represents a major improvement over other products in the same market) and culture-driven in the other market (for example it has become the fashionable product to own).

The structure of the market itself contributes to the possibilities for standardisation. A highly urbanised country such as The Netherlands or Singapore has very different characteristics from an essentially rural country like India, where more than half the population lives in villages or small towns. In the urbanised environment, a campaign can reach a large number of people relatively easily: rural countries require different techniques in order to reach enough people to make the campaign worth while.

Marketing in a changing world: Global e-tailing

Global marketing is apparently simple through the Internet, and many specialist stores have set up websites in the hopes of doing business worldwide. After all, if you have a website, people can access your products from anywhere in the world. Software firms have found this particularly useful: many of them operate their helplines, and even their sales, on-line (although few have succeeded in eliminating the salesforce) (Moen et al. 2003).

In practice it is not that straightforward, as Amazon have found. Amazon began in the United States, and found that people from elsewhere in the world were accessing the site and ordering books – which was fine, except that the shipping costs often outweighed the savings made by on-line ordering. So Amazon established a presence in their major markets: there are separate websites for the UK, Germany, Japan, Canada, Austria, Spain, France, Italy, Brazil and China, and the capability to supply other countries, with books being shipped internationally. These physical presences in other markets have been expensive to establish, and since people cannot easily browse through the books (as they would in a bricks-and-mortar bookshop) they tend only to buy books with which they are already familiar.

Many people visit the Amazon sites simply to research what is available, with no intention of buying. The sites are expensive to maintain, with constant updating being necessary, and the end result is that Amazon lost money for the first five years it was in business, and has only recently recouped those early losses.

Amazon are not alone in finding that cultural differences get in the way of e-tailing. Websites are usually firmly rooted in the country of origin, and even when companies develop country-specific websites they do not adapt them much (Singh et al. 2005). For services, it is easier to adapt the site and so firms are more able to do this, but most still retain the main features of their home sites (Okazaki 2005).

The structure of the distribution system affects the degree to which products can be made available in specific markets. This applies both to the physical distribution of goods and to the structure of the retail and wholesale markets. For example, Spain has a large number of small grocery shops located in villages. The villages themselves often have extremely narrow streets, so physical delivery has to be made using small trucks that are able to negotiate winding alleyways. Order quantities are also much lower than is the case in countries like the UK, where food distribution is dominated by major supermarket chains such as Tesco and Sainsbury's. For manufacturers, this has implications in terms of packaging and shipping goods.

The degree to which the market is technologically orientated has a greater or lesser effect depending on the technology of the product. Markets such as the United States, which is heavily technology-orientated, are more accepting of technologically advanced products. This is particularly apparent in fields such as computers, where the United States has overtaken the UK as the most computer-literate country in the world. For less technology-orientated markets computers need to be made simpler, and fewer accessories can be sold until the market becomes more used to the technology.

The internal environment of the company includes such factors as degree of international experience, attitude of management and goals of internationalisation. The international experience of the management needs to go beyond simply having travelled extensively. Managers need to have direct experience of doing business in the target countries. Inexperienced managers are more likely to believe that they can standardise the product or the promotion or both. The company's reasons for internationalising in the first place may affect standardisation: companies that are internationalising simply to dump excess production will not adapt the product, and may well not adapt their promotion either. Finally, some companies face high research and development costs – drug companies are unlikely to adapt products for overseas markets simply because of the cost of reformulating, testing and obtaining government approval for new drugs.

Making the decision as to whether to standardise or not requires an evaluation of the overall situation in the market. One technique for doing this is the use–need model (Keegan 1969). This model evaluates the market need that is met by a given product against the way the product is used. Five combinations of use and need determine the degree of product and communication standardisation that is desirable, including consideration of their relative costs.

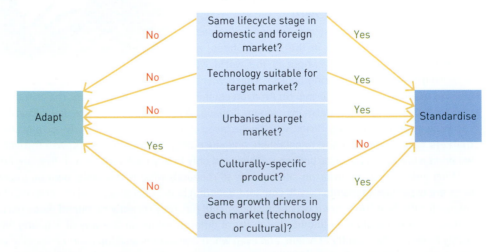

Figure 8.11   Adapt or standardise?

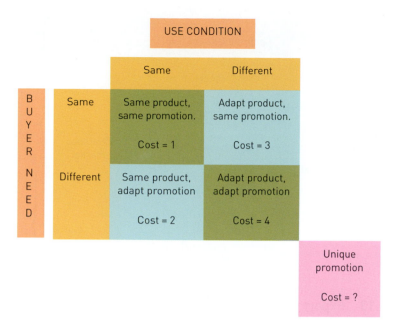

Figure 8.12   The use-need model

If a product is to be used differently in each market, but fulfils the same basic need, adapting the product and standardising the communication would be an appropriate decision. On the other hand, if the use is the same but the need is different, a different communications programme should be put in place, although the product might be standardised. For example, mobile telephones in the UK are often used as a social tool, keeping friends in touch with each other. In some other countries the mobile telephone is seen as being essentially a business tool, with little use in a social context.

After a corporate policy has been developed and the products and markets have been identified, the managers need to decide which countries are to be targeted. This will require the same type of environmental audit as was described in Chapter 2: an assessment of the micro and macro environments within the target countries. The basic strategic decision to be made is whether the company can find a competitive position within the target markets, in other words whether the firm can marshal the capability to compete effectively against firms that are already established in the market.

Having established that there is a competitive position which can be filled, the company can examine the tactics and marketing mix decisions that need to be implemented.

Market entry tactics

Exporting is the practice of manufacturing a product in one country and selling it in another. Exporting is generally favoured by governments, because it is helpful for the balance of payments: Governments need foreign currency coming into the country in order to fund essential imports such as raw materials and essential components, otherwise they need to raise interest rates in order to attract deposits of foreign currency into UK banks. The mechanisms for this are somewhat complex and outside the scope of this book, but suffice it to say that governments in most countries offer a great deal of help to exporters.

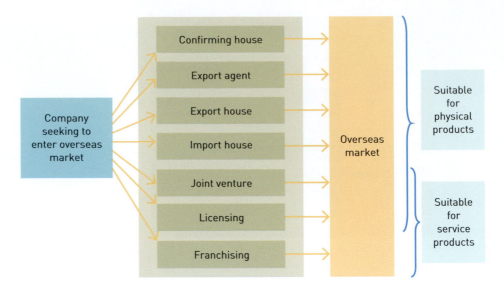

Figure 8.13   Export routes

The problem with exporting is that the company loses control over the marketing of the goods. This can lead to problems later on as the company's reputation may be badly affected by inappropriate (or even unethical) marketing practices. The main advantage of exporting is that it is relatively simple once the company has found an importer in the target country. This is because the importer knows the local market, understands local consumers, understands the legal position on doing business in the country, and is unlikely to make the kind of mistakes a foreign company might make when starting out in a new country. There are several different ways in which export deals can be set up, as follows:

Export agent A person or company that takes responsibility for organising the export of goods without taking title to the goods.

- **Export agents** bring together buyers and sellers, and are paid on commission: they do not actually buy the goods themselves. There is a wide variety of types of agent, and the use of agents is governed by different laws in each target country: some care needs to be exercised when using an agent. For example, in France agents are protected by employment law and cannot be arbitrarily dismissed, whereas in the UK an agent is regarded as self-employed and is subject only to the terms of any contract agreed between the agent and the manufacturer. In some countries agents are salaried, particularly in cases where they are dealing with major capital goods such as machine tools or agricultural machinery.

Export house An organisation that buys goods for sale abroad.

- **Export houses** buy goods for export to foreign countries. These are companies with contacts abroad, and with knowledge of the foreign markets in which they do business. In some cases export houses will buy on the instructions of a foreign customer – for example, they may have been contacted by a foreign firm looking for a components supplier. In other cases they will simply buy on their own account and find buyers in the foreign country.

Import house An organisation that buys goods in from abroad.

Confirming houses An organisation that handles the mechanics of exporting and importing on behalf of manufacturers or buyers.

- **Import houses** seek products in other countries and buy them for resale in their own countries. Sometimes importers will visit exhibitions and trade fairs in other countries looking for products to import (see Chapter 17). In some cases, overseas retailers will maintain buying offices in other countries (for example Sears of the United States maintains a buying office in London).
- **Confirming houses** arrange the details of credit and shipping on behalf of importers and exporters. The confirming house can arrange for the exporter

to be paid, and will collect payment from the importer: one of the major barriers to exporting is the problem of credit. Many firms are reluctant to trust a foreign firm about whom they know nothing, and to risk the problems of having to sue in a foreign court for their money. Confirming houses remove this problem.

- Joint ventures or export clubs. Sometimes it is possible to agree to share the risks with other firms in a similar or complementary business. A joint venture might involve getting together with a foreign firm – perhaps with reciprocal agreements to market each others' products – or with a same-nationality firm that is already established in the foreign market. Sometimes these deals involve piggy-backing, which is the practice of selling a complementary product to the same customers through the same salesforce. For example, an office-equipment supplier might join with an interior design firm to offer a complete service in fitting out new offices. Joint ventures are more likely to succeed if the partners are willing to learn (Farrell et al. 2011) and they value trust, communication, social bonding and co-operation (Yen and Barnes 2011).

- **Licensing** agreements. A manufacturer of goods that do not travel well (for example glass or some food products) might allow a foreign producer to use the firm's patents in exchange for a royalty fee. For example, Pilkington Glass now earn more money from licensing the float-glass technique abroad than they do from actually making glass. Licensing relies on the firm having good patents or other protection for its intellectual property.

Licensing An agreement to use a firm's intellectual property in exchange for a royalty.

- **Franchising** is similar to licensing, but is used for service industries. The franchisor allows the franchisee to use its branding and business systems in exchange for royalties. McDonald's, Holiday Inn and Dyno-Rod are all examples of successful franchises.

Franchising An agreement to use a firm's business methods and intellectual property in return for a fee and a royalty.

Rather than exporting, a firm might decide to set up a branch or a subsidiary in the target country. The difference between the two is that a branch is a direct extension of the parent firm into the foreign territory, whereas a subsidiary is legally a separate business. For example, Disneyland Paris is a separate company from the Disney Corporation, even though it is part-owned by Disney and pays the bulk of its profits to Disney in the form of royalties and licence fees.

Branches are easy to set up (and easy to remove) but complex tax situations can arise because some countries (for example Spain and the United States) relate the amount of tax payable by the branch to the worldwide profits of the parent company. Normally branches are concerned with the transport and storage of goods, marketing, providing after-sales service and liaising with local banks about credit for customers. Local assembly or manufacture would normally be carried out elsewhere.

Since branches are considered as part of the parent company, the profits and losses of the branch are treated as part of those of the parent company and are shown in the latter's accounts. Subsidiaries prepare separate accounts, even when the parent company owns a large part (or even all) of the subsidiary's shares. A comparison of branches and subsidiaries is shown in Table 8.5. The biggest advantage of setting up a subsidiary is that it acquires a local character and demonstrates to competitors and customers that the firm has a real commitment to the market. This can be especially important in a business-to-business context, where the company needs to be credible in the eyes of its customers.

Figure 8.14 compares the situation between a German branch and a French subsidiary. The German branch is actually part of the parent company, and is under direct control, whereas the French subsidiary is a separate entity with its own shareholders, banking arrangement and marketing.

Table 8.5 Branches versus subsidiaries

Branches	Subsidiaries
Parent liable for all debts.	Subsidiary is liable for its own debts.
Does not require its own capital or directors.	Can raise capital in its own name.
Special tax rules apply, depending on the country concerned.	Taxed as if it were a separate local business.
No company formation or winding-up procedures involved.	Usually incorporated as a limited company.
Accounts are incorporated into those of the parent company.	Maintains its own accounts independent of the parent company.
Losses can be offset against the parent's profits.	Accounts must be independently audited.
Branch employees can be (but need not be) regarded as employees of the parent corporation.	Employees are only employed by the subsidiary, with the rights and obligations of local employment law.
Assets can be transferred between the parent and the branch without incurring tax liabilities.	Shares in the company can be sold to outsiders.
Often there are low rates of tax on the repatriation of profits.	Carries a local identity.
Branch profits may be taxed in the parent company's country even if they have not been repatriated.	Internal reorganisations can occur without having to report this to the foreign authorities.

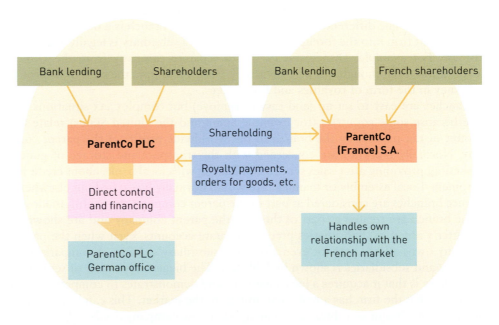

Figure 8.14 Branches and subsidiaries

In some major equipment contracts such as the construction of power stations or dockyards a firm is unlikely to want (or need) to establish a permanent base in a foreign country. In some cases these contracts are handled by agreeing a **turnkey contract**, in which the supplying firm builds the facility and operates it for a fixed period of time, eventually handing it over to local control. For example, during the 1970s the Fiat car company set up factories all over Eastern Europe as turnkey projects, selling off obsolete stamp mills and designs to Communist countries. This proved lucrative for Fiat, and allowed the client countries to develop their own car industries, which eventually became export industries for them.

Turnkey contract An agreement whereby one firm establishes an entire business in a foreign country and subsequently hands over the business to another firm, in exchange for a fee and occasionally royalties.

Think outside this box!

Setting up factories for somebody seems like a fast way to create some extra competition. Why would a company help a low-wage economy establish itself with a modern manufacturing facility? Surely this is the road to ruin!

Or maybe the idea is *not* to establish a modern facility, but merely to provide some obsolete technology which will never succeed against the parent company's facilities. If so, isn't this a little bit unethical? Deliberately charging the foreign company a huge sum of money, and then setting them up to fail?

Perhaps the truth lies somewhere in between. Technology which is obsolete in one market may be just the latest thing in another – yet still not be able to compete outside its own area. In which case everyone is happy – at least for a while!

Turnkey contracts enable the client country to have a new system installed to a predetermined specification, acquiring new technologies quickly and relatively painlessly, and with a lower risk of failure. However, the contractor might be slow in handing over the facility to local workers, so that the client firm becomes totally dependent on the supplier.

Overseas manufacturing may be an option if there are high transportation costs, high external **tariff barriers**, import quotas, or national rules on 'local content' (the percentage of the product which must be produced in the target country) which make exporting difficult. In a global context, overseas manufacture is likely to be based on costs of production: if it is cheaper to produce goods in a particular country, then that is where they will be produced regardless of the end market. Two main options are available: the firm can set up its own factory in the target country, as either a branch or a subsidiary, or it can contract the manufacture to a local firm. The latter option is more likely to generate economies of scale, but has the drawback that the company can lose control of its designs and technology. Often these are the only distinguishing features the firm has to bring to the new country, so their loss could be disastrous.

Tariff barriers Customs duties that make a product less competitive in an overseas market.

Another drawback to overseas manufacturing is the lack of economies of scale. Transportation costs are, in general, relatively low and tariff barriers are falling throughout the world, so the loss of economies of scale which come from large, automated production runs cannot be compensated for by lower transport costs and the avoidance of tariffs. Many countries have come to realise that establishing high tariff barriers is usually counterproductive in the long run – Brazil's long-standing tariff against computer imports simply resulted in the country being left behind in the technological revolution.

'Screwdriver' establishments can sometimes overcome these problems. A 'screwdriver' factory is one that assembles components which have been manufactured overseas.

Such an operation allows the company to label the product as manufactured in the destination country: it is difficult for national governments to define the point at which they are dealing with a foreign-made product. Japanese companies operating in Britain were accused of using screwdriver establishments to get round the European Union tariff barriers on imports of Japanese cars: the content of such products must now be 65% European to qualify as 'Made in the EU'. So contentious are these issues that the EU has set up a Committee on Origin to assess where the major part of the added value has come from.

Setting up and running a foreign presence is likely at some stage to involve sending staff from the home country to work in the foreign country for a substantial period of time. The number of expatriate staff has been in decline for some time now, however, at least in part because of the high cost of sending people to another country. An expatriate member of staff is likely to cost four times as much to employ as an equivalent member of staff in the home country (Boyacigiller 1991) and has limited effectiveness due to problems of language and culture. Failure of

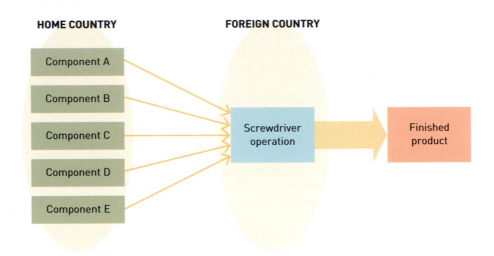

Figure 8.15   Screwdriver establishments

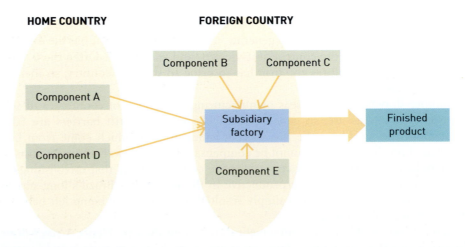

Figure 8.16   Overseas manufacturing subsidiary

expatriates to settle effectively in the foreign country is common, due to the following factors:

- Children not making progress at school, either because they are studying in a foreign language, or because they are in a special school for expatriates, or because they have been left at home at boarding school.
- Concerns for family safety.
- Spouse not adjusting to the local physical and cultural environment (McEnery and Desharnais 1990). Many executives possessing qualifications suitable for expatriate assignments will have professionally qualified spouses whose own career aspirations might make it difficult for them to move to a foreign country. In some cases the employing company needs to find a job for the expatriate's spouse as well as for the expatriate.

A further problem with employing expatriates in senior roles is that this blocks promotion prospects for local staff, who will then move to other companies, taking their new knowledge with them.

Getting employees to work well together in an international context involves two behavioural competencies (Vallaster and DeChernatony 2005). These are a clear brand vision, and facilitating both verbal and non-verbal social interactions.

Payment for goods

An issue that is related to market entry decisions is that of payment for the goods. In most cases payment can be made in a mutually agreed currency: the astute marketer will accept payment in the currency of the customer's country, because this presents the minimum difficulty for the customer. Sometimes, however, the economy of the target country is such that the local currency is not acceptable. If the target country has a high inflation rate, for example, the currency can devalue quite dramatically between delivery of the goods and receipt of payment, so the exporting company may reasonably ask to be paid in a hard currency such as pounds, Euros or US dollars.

In other cases, the country's government may not have sufficient foreign exchange to allow importers to have access to hard currencies. In such cases the exporting firm may need to be creative. **Countertrading** is one way of overcoming the problem. In a countertrade deal no money changes hands. The exporter accepts payment in goods instead, then sells the goods for hard currency in another market.

Countertrading Bartering of goods in international markets.

The system has many advantages for firms which are prepared to deal with the extra transaction costs. The value of the goods traded is often very much higher than their cash value, so that both parties gain: also, sale of the goods sometimes opens up contacts in third markets. Finally, many firms will shy away from countertrade dealings, so there will be less competition in the markets concerned.

Countertrade can be used by exporters to offer favourable prices to potential customers in countries where there is fierce local competition. It may well be the case that a customer in a country where there are no foreign exchange problems would still prefer to countertrade, perhaps because of having access to a supply of local export items.

Because countertrade typically involves dealing in goods that are unfamiliar to the exporter, intermediaries are crucial to the process. In some cases the intermediaries are able to offer complex deals involving several countertrade transactions. A variation of countertrade is **buyback**, which occurs when a firm supplies plant and equipment in exchange for a share of the future output of the equipment. For example, mining equipment might be supplied in exchange for payment in ore, to be supplied

Buyback An agreement on the part of a supplier to accept payment in finished products.

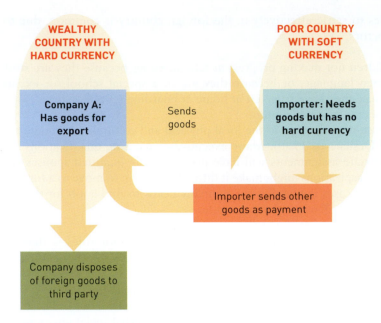

Figure 8.17   Countertrade in action

Counterpurchase An agreement on the part of a supplier to accept payment in kind, or to spend the proceeds of the sale in the country in which the sale is made.

over a number of years. The exporter can sell the ore contract for immediate cash on the futures market, and thus recoup the investment immediately.

Counterpurchase deals are sometimes required by governments of the target countries. In a **counterpurchase** deal, the company is paid in the currency of the target country, but must agree to spend the money on goods for export.

Real-life marketing: Payment in kind

During the late 1980s British coal mines were closing down almost on a daily basis. This meant that a great deal of mining equipment was available at scrap prices to anyone who could arrange for it to be taken away. The equipment still had years of life in it – but how to sell it on?

Step forward a very enterprising Chinese entrepreneur living in Britain. He arranged an option to buy the equipment with a view to shipping it to China (which was expanding and modernising its mining industry). He then flew to China, agreed to be paid for the equipment in coal (which would be mined by the new equipment) over a number of years. The next move was to fly to Hong Kong and sell the future stream of coal on the Hong Kong futures market. He then flew back to the UK, finalised the purchase contract, and paid for the equipment and its shipping. No capital needed – and everybody's happy.

To do this in practice, you have to be very organised, of course. Here are the rules.

- Don't buy anything until you have a contract to sell it. It's easier to back out of a contract to sell something than it is to back out of a contract to buy something.
- Know your market thoroughly (and have the skills you need to operate in it) – in this case, being a native Chinese speaker was essential.
- Be very, very flexible in your thinking. If someone plans to pay you in coal five years from now rather than pay cash, don't reject the deal – coal can be sold as well.

Countertrade and similar arrangements have been criticised for the following reasons, however:

- There is little evidence that countertrade actually improves the foreign exchange positions of the countries in which it is common. Often the goods supplied would have sold for much higher prices on the world market, which would have brought in more hard currency than is needed to pay for the imports.
- Foreign customers might be more interested in gaining unpaid distributors for their substandard export items than in buying the goods on offer.
- The system distorts the normal supply-and-demand mechanism, so it is damaging to competition.
- Disputes often arise over the quality of the goods supplied. There is considerable difficulty in agreeing a precise specification for the goods, and the exporter could be landed with shoddy goods that are difficult to sell. Slow-moving goods might impose a warehousing cost.

Countertrade has tended to decrease since the collapse of Communism in Europe, and the increase in world trade which has meant that most countries do not wish to find themselves outside the mainstream.

Advantages and disadvantages of globalising

Targeting a global market has the obvious advantage that the company's potential market will be a great deal larger, a particularly important consideration if the company's products appeal to a small market segment. Finding a segment that crosses borders can be an effective way of generating economies of scale for even a small firm, and the Internet makes it easy to do this. Another advantage is that the company can spread its risk – the periodical fluctuation in the world economy (the boom and bust cycle) happens at different times in different countries, so that the market might be booming in one country while it is declining in another. The same applies to the product life cycle – a product that is beginning to become obsolete in one country might be the latest must-have in another.

Governments usually offer incentives and help to exporting companies, but this in itself should not be a reason to globalise. If a global market for the product exists, then government help is a good thing to have; if there is actually little or no market for the product, then no amount of government help will save it.

For some firms, the domestic market has become saturated, or is too small to support the product. In those circumstances, globalising might be a way of continuing to grow. On the supply side, globalisation of component supply and raw material supply means that the firm can meet its needs from the cheapest or most secure source, and thus be less susceptible to supply disruptions.

There are, of course, disadvantages to globalisation. The obvious drawback is that the firm will have to commit resources to a market that may or may not respond well to the product offering. Another drawback is that the firm's products become exposed to competitors in other countries who may retaliate in kind once they see that the product does well in the domestic market. There is also the major problem of overcoming the many cultural, legal and logistical problems of dealing in an unfamiliar country.

Chapter summary

International marketing presents specific problems to marketers, but in fact the problems are no different from those faced by any company in a start-up mode. Managers need to understand that, in approaching a foreign market, they are in many ways starting with a clean slate – the environment, customers and competitors will probably all be different from the home situation. For most practical marketers this will be in itself a new situation, since they are unlikely to have been in at the start of the parent company, and will therefore have inherited most of the established customs and practice of the organisation. Also, most firms do not plan their growth – they simply solve problems as they arise, and eventually develop a way of functioning and an internal culture. International marketing enables marketers to plan from the outset – an opportunity not to be missed.

Key points

- Firms may go through a series of stages in developing their international marketing programme, or they may simply move straight to the most effective means of doing business in the foreign country.
- Markets might be selected for financial reasons, ease of access, or convenience, or a combination of all three.
- Profit potential is a function of the number of people who have a need for the product, their spending power, and the level of competitive pressure.
- Cross-border comparisons in market research are likely to be badly flawed, especially in secondary research.
- Marketers can adapt the product, adapt the promotion, adapt both, or invent an entirely new product. It is rare that a product and its promotion can cross a border intact.
- Branches are easy to set up and easy to dismantle, but create problems in running efficiently because they do not demonstrate commitment to the market.

Review questions

1. How does international marketing differ from domestic marketing?
2. What market entry methods are available?
3. How can overseas markets be assessed?
4. What are the cultural problems of marketing abroad?
5. What is globalisation?
6. How are marketing communications affected by crossing borders?
7. What is the difference between the Uppsala model and the stages of development model?
8. How is profit potential calculated?
9. What are the potential problems in sending expatriate managers to run foreign branches?
10. What are the advantages and disadvantages of countertrade?

Case study revisited: Father's Day

Although Father's Day generally falls on the same day throughout most of the world, Mother's Day has many different dates depending on country. In the UK in 2013, for example, it fell on 10 March, but in the United States it was 12 May. In Australia it was also 12 May, but in France it was 26 May.

Father's Day fell on the 16 June in the UK and USA, but in Australia it fell on 1 September. In Brazil it was 11 August, in Bulgaria 20 June, and so forth. For people who have emigrated to these countries there is a considerable problem because they do not have the convenient reminders from marketers that Mother's Day is imminent in their home countries – they have to rely either on memory, or on friends and family back homes sending them reminders.

In Australia, some people celebrate Mother's Day by carrying out a charity fundraising walk, or by taking their mother to a place of interest like the zoo or the botanical gardens. In the UK the weather is usually against doing anything outdoors, so taking one's mother out for Sunday lunch is a popular option. In Portugal and Spain the Virgin Mary is also honoured with a special church service. In France the day is treated much as one would treat a family birthday – the family gather for a special meal, with a Mother's Day cake.

Greetings card manufacturers obviously need to consider the design of the cards as well as the language of the greeting and the time of year: flowers might differ in each country as might gifts, and some cultural differences may be evident in terms of the icons associated with the day. For example, chrysanthemums are the traditional flower in Australia, and some men even wear them in their buttonholes on the day, whereas in the United States carnations are traditional – white ones if the mother is deceased. Mother's Day cards featuring white carnations might therefore not be a big seller in Kansas, whereas in the UK they might be perfectly acceptable.

Mother's Day has become predominantly a commercial exercise, and may well have simply died out if it were not for relentless pressure from manufacturers, printers, florists and restaurateurs. Anna Jarvis herself campaigned against its commercialisation (she was arrested in 1948 for disturbing the peace while protesting against the celebration of Mother's Day), but despite everything people continue to give gifts to their mothers and fathers on the appropriate days, so global marketers need to understand what happens in each country.

Case study: The 2013 horsemeat scandal

There are many countries in which eating horsemeat is perfectly acceptable – but not the UK or Ireland, and not in any European country where the meat is sold as beef.

In 2013, the shocking news broke that some ready meals sold in major supermarkets contained horsemeat, rather than the beef that was supposed to be in them. Most major supermarkets were affected, as were some restaurant chains and even some institutional caterers such as schools and hospitals. DNA testing had found substantial quantities of horse. Apart from the fact that most British people do not, and would not, eat horses since they are regarded as pets in Britain, some of the horses

may have been treated with painkillers that are illegal in animals intended for food. Perhaps worse, at the same time some supposedly halal meat was found to have been contaminated with pork, which of course would be a serious breach of religious dietary laws for any Muslims.

The products involved were typically minced meat or ready-meal products. In some cases beefburgers were found to contain 29% horsemeat. The discovery was first made by the Irish Food Standards Authority, which then alerted the equivalent organisations elsewhere. At first it appeared that one or two rogue abbatoirs were responsible. Owing to EU regulations dating back thirty years, abbatoirs tend to be very large and centralised in Europe and deal with all kinds of animals, so that cattle will be slaughtered in the same abbatoirs as horses. Horsemeat is consequently easily available, and is very much cheaper than beef, so the temptation to mince it up and mix it with the beef is very strong. However, as the investigations continued it turned out that abbatoirs throughout Europe were involved.

Silvercrest Foods of Ireland were identified first, then Dalepak in North Yorkshire, England; the French authorities followed on shortly, suspending the licence of A la Table de Spanghero, a meat supplier that has been accused of knowingly supplying horsemeat labelled as beef. Spanghero imported the meat from Romania and sold it on to Comigel, a French company manufacturing ready meals for French supermarkets and others in its factory based, not in France, but in Luxembourg.

Comigel also supplied Findus, the frozen-food company, and Findus ready meal lasagnes were found to contain between 60% and 100% horsemeat. The French authorities claim that Comigel knew exactly what was going on.

Meanwhile, elsewhere in the international food chain, H.J. Schypke, the German subsidiary of a Belgian-based company, was accused by its customer Nestlé (a Swiss company) of supplying horsemeat-contaminated beef to its French factories, where it was used to make catering lasagnes. Even the American company Birdseye got caught up in the scandal: their Belgian subsidiary found horsemeat in chilli con carne produced by Belgian firm Frigilunch. This is somewhat ironic, since horsemeat is commonly eaten in Belgium (and France) and is regarded as something of a delicacy.

Of course the scandal produced a flood of jokes: people made photo montages of horses galloping away from supermarket delivery vans, they told each other that the doctor had advised them to watch what they eat so they had bought tickets for the horse races, and when asked 'Would you like anything on your burger?' they would answer 'Five pounds each way'. Tesco supermarkets issued lengthy apologies, and even put up billboard posters and took out newspaper advertisements to say what they were going to do in future to ensure that the problem would not happen again, but that did not prevent two young men in Wales dressing up as a pantomime horse and cantering round their local Tesco shouting 'It's murder! You're killing me!' hotly pursued by security guards.

Getting to the bottom of the scandal is likely to prove difficult. Adulterating beef with cheaper horsemeat seems to have been practised in many places – some suppliers are claiming that the meat was clearly labelled as horse, but was re-labelled by the customers, some manufacturers and supermarkets have denied all knowledge and claim to have been innocent dupes, but the suspicion remains that the drive by supermarkets to force prices as low as possible may have driven some suppliers to look for cheap expedients, without asking too many questions. If Rumanian horsemeat was cheap enough, perhaps the factories simply turned a blind eye – equally, if a meat supplier was being forced to accept a ridiculously low price, the temptation to divert some horsemeat into the beef-packing line must have been very strong.

In any event, the fact that so many firms in so many countries are involved in the production of ready meals, burgers and meat products such as sausage would inevitably mean that the end retailer would have little or no ability to control the food chain. The propensity of consumers to want to pay as little as possible for ready meals is another driver – however, although consumers would have realised that the meat used would hardly be the finest cuts, they could scarcely have expected to find Dobbin in the lasagne.

Questions

1. How might the supermarkets have taken better control of the supply chain?
2. Why is this type of problem more likely in a global marketplace?
3. What is the role of price competition in this scandal?
4. Why might people object to eating horsemeat?
5. What cultural issues were involved in the scandal?

Further reading

There are many books on international business, most of them using the term 'global' rather than 'international'. Here is a selection.

H.D. Hennessey and Jean-Paul Jeannet, *Global Account Management: Creating Value* (New York, John Wiley, 2003). This is a very comprehensive guide to global marketing, providing a well-structured, in-depth textbook on the topic.

Warren J. Keegan and Bodo Schlegelmilch, *Global Marketing Management: A European Perspective* (Hemel Hempstead: FT Prentice Hall, 2000) is a Europeanised version of Keegan's American text. As is often the case with European versions, the text has very high production values and is readable, with a great many useful features to help the learning process.

For a more practitioner-orientated account of global marketing, N. Speare, K. Wilson and S.J. Reese's *Successful Global Account Management* (London: Kogan Page, 2001) is a book that, although it intends to concentrate mainly on the personal selling and account management part of global marketing, actually gives many practical ideas on managing in a global market.

References

Bangeman, M. (1992) *Meeting the Global Challenge*. London: Kogan Page.

Boyacigiller, N. (1991) The role of expatriates in the management of interdependence, complexity and risk in multinational corporations. *Journal of International Business Studies*, 21: 357–81.

Brock, Jurgen Kai-Uwe, Johnson, Jeffrey E. and Zhou, Josephine Yu (2011) Does distance matter for internationally-oriented small firms? *Industrial Marketing Management*, 40 (2): 384–94.

Cavusgil, S.T. and Kirpalani, V.H. (1993) Introducing products into export markets: success factors. *Journal of Business Research*, 27: 1–15.

Chetty, C. and Campbell-Hunt, Colin (2004) A strategic approach to internationalisation: a traditional vs. a 'born global' approach. *Journal of International Marketing*, 12 (1): 57–81.

Clark, Irvine III, Micken, Kathleen S. and Hart, H. Stanley (2002) Symbols for sale – at least for now. Symbolic consumption in transition economies. *Advances in Consumer Research*, 29: 25.

Delener, N. (1990) The effects of religious factors on durable goods purchase decisions. *Journal of Consumer Marketing*, 7 (3): 27–38.

Dunning, John H. (1993) *The Globalisation of Business.* London: Routledge.

Farrell, Mark Anthony, Oczkowski, Edward and Kharabsheh, Radwan (2011) Antecedents and performance consequences of learning success in international joint ventures. *Industrial Marketing Management*, 40 (3): 479–88.

Fernandez, Karen V. and Veer, Ekant (2004) The gold that binds: the ritualistic use of jewellery in an Indian wedding. *Advances in Consumer Research*, 31 (1): 53.

Ferraro, G. and Briody, E. (2012) *The Cultural Dimension of Global Business*, 7th edn. Harlow: Pearson.

Gabel, Terrance G. and Boller, Gregory W. (2003) A preliminary look into the globalisation of the tortilla in Mexico. *Advances in Consumer Research*, 30: 135–41.

Grier, Sonya A., Brumbaugh, Anne M. and Thornton, Corliss G. (2006) Crossover dreams: consumer responses to ethnic-oriented products. *Journal of Marketing*, 70 (2): 35–51.

Harris, Greg (1996) International advertising: developmental and implementational issues. *Journal of Marketing Management*, 12: 551–60.

Hofstede, Geert (1980) *Culture's Consequences: International Differences in Work-Related Values.* Beverly Hills, CA: Sage.

Jamal, Ahmed (2003) Marketing in a multicultural world: the interplay of marketing, ethnicity and consumption. *European Journal of Marketing*, 37 (11): 1599–620.

Keegan, W.J. (1989) *Multinational Marketing Management.* New York: Prentice Hall.

Kjelgaard, Dannie and Askegaard, Soren (2004) Consuming modernities: the global youth segment as a site of consumption. *Advances in Consumer Research*, 31 (1): 104–5.

McEnery, J. and Desharnais, G. (1990) Culture shock. *Training and Development Journal*, 44 (4): 43.

Moen, Oystein, Endresen, Iver and Gavlen, Morten (2003) Executive insights into the use of the Internet in international marketing: a case study of small computer firms. *Journal of International Marketing*, 11 (4): 129–49.

Moskowitz, Howard R., Beckley, Jacqueline H., Luckow, Tracy and Paulus, Klaus O. (2008) Cross-national segments for a food product: defining them and a strategy for finding them in the absence of 'mineable' databases. *Journal of Database Marketing and Customer Strategy Management*, 15 (3): 191–206.

Muhlbacker, Hans, Dahringer, Lee and Leihs, Helmuth (1999) *International Marketing: A Global Perspective.* London: Thomson.

Murdock, G.P. (1945) The common denominator of cultures. In R. Linton (ed.), *The Science of Man.* New York: Columbia University Press.

Okazaki, Shintaro (2005) Searching the Web for global brands: how American brands standardise their websites in Europe. *European Journal of Marketing*, 39 (1/2): 87–109.

Pedersen, Torbin and Pedersen, Bent (2004) Learning about foreign markets: are entrant firms exposed to a 'shock effect?' *Journal of International Marketing*, 12 (1): 103–23.

Pressey, Andrew D. and Selassie, Habte G. (2002) Are cultural differences over-rated? Examining the influence of national culture on international buyer–seller relationships. *Journal of Consumer Behaviour*, 2 (4): 354–68.

Singh, Nitish, Kumar, Vikas and Baack, Daniel (2005) Adaptation of cultural content: evidence from B2C e-commerce firms. *European Journal of Marketing*, 39 (1/2): 71–86.

Usunier, J.C. (1993) *International Marketing: A Cultural Approach.* Harlow: Prentice Hall.

Vallaster, Christine and DeChernatony, Leslie (2005) Internationalisation of service brands: the role of leadership during the international brand-building process. *Journal of Marketing Management*, 21 (1/2): 181–203.

Whitelock, J. and Jobber, D. (1994) The impact of competitor environment on initial market entry in a new, non-domestic market. *Proceedings of the Marketing Education Group Conference*, Coleraine, July, pp. 1008–17.

Yen, Dorothy and Barnes, Bradley R. (2011) Analyzing stage and duration of Anglo-Chinese business-to-business relationships. *Industrial Marketing Management*, 40 (3): 346–57.

Yorkston, Eric and deMello, Gustavo (2004) Sex sells? The effects of gender marking on consumers' evaluations of branded products across languages. *Advances in Consumer Research*, 31: 148–51.

More online

To gain free access to additional online resources to support this chapter please visit:
www.sagepub.co.uk/blythe3e

Part Three

Strategy and stakeholders

This section is concerned with formulating appropriate strategies. The purpose of strategic planning is to put the firm in the best position possible to exploit the opportunities presented by the marketplace, while avoiding the threats presented by competitors and changes in the business environment.

Chapter 9 looks at creating competitive advantage through strategic planning. The chapter looks at strategy theory in general and marketing strategy in particular. It includes a discussion of the relationship between corporate strategy and marketing strategy, and selecting the appropriate market stance and competitive moves. It also considers the issues surrounding problem-solving in complex environments, and outlines some current thinking on the role of marketing in creating shareholder value.

Chapter 10 looks at the ethics of marketing and at being socially responsible marketers in a global environment. In considers the impact of a firm's behaviour on stakeholders and how ethical behaviour is based around the prevailing view within a culture, meaning there can be no absolute definition.

Chapter 11 is concerned with establishing worthwhile relationships with customers. It looks at the value chain and value networks, customer retention and winback strategies, relationship marketing, the relationship between quality, service and value, and the relationship between all these issues and achieving strategic objectives.

Chapter 12 is about managing the firm's range of products. Achieving a balanced portfolio of products is no small task: marketers need to consider the profitability of each market segment they approach, the effect each produce has on sales of other products and the likely future sales of individual brands in the range. This chapter provides a set of approaches for making these decisions.

CHAPTER (9)

Marketing strategy, planning and creating competitive advantage

LEARNING OBJECTIVES

After reading this chapter, you should be able to:

- Explain the strategic planning process.

- Describe the relationship between marketing strategy and corporate strategy.

- Explain how strategic plans change when put into practice.

- Explain the difference between aims and objectives.

- Describe the three basic winning strategies.

- Describe the implementation strategies for the three basic strategic positions.

- Understand the role of collaboration with competitors.

- Explain the role of shareholder value in strategic planning.

Introduction

Strategy is not necessarily easy to define, and in particular the distinction between marketing strategy and corporate strategy is difficult to draw. This is especially true for organisations that consider themselves to be marketing-orientated, since one would reasonably expect that the marketing strategy would actually be the corporate strategy.

Because of the rapidly changing nature of business life, strategy cannot be reduced to a simple set of rules, so managers need to consider the possibilities of creating new approaches. For marketers, the idea of differentiation is well-understood, so the idea of adopting a different strategy from that of the organisation's competitors is straightforward and even obvious.

In most cases, marketing strategy is concerned with creating competitive advantage – in other words, improving the organisation's chances of surviving and prospering in the face of outside competition. All organisations compete for resources, customers, support from other organisations, employees and any of many possible factors that will enable the organisation to achieve its strategic objectives.

Preview case study: Las Vegas

Las Vegas used to have very little to recommend it. It is surrounded by desert, there are few if any natural resources anywhere near, there is very little water and not much chance of any agriculture in the barren landscape. To add to the problems, the area is subject to devastating flash floods. During the 19th century it was a stopping-off point for wagon trains heading to California: there was at least the Colorado River to supply enough water for the mules and horses of the wagon trains. The Union Pacific Railroad found Las Vegas to be in about the right place for a stopover, even though there was little to stop for.

Given the poor hand of cards the local authorities had been dealt, they had to resort to fairly desperate measures to maintain any kind of local economy. The first move was to legalise gambling, which occurred in 1931. The first casinos were small affairs, since there was such a small population in the surrounding areas, but the Second World War brought an influx of scientists and soldiers who were working on the Manhattan Project (building the first atomic bombs) and Las Vegas became a good place for some recreation when these people went on leave.

After the war Las Vegas might have slipped back into obscurity, but gangsters such as Bugsy Siegal and Meyer Lansky saw the possibilities of having a gambling resort with a railroad station within easy distance of the burgeoning cities of Los Angeles and San Francisco. Air travel was beginning to come into its own as well – the war had given civilian air transport a major boost, even though at that time it was still the prerogative of the rich.

The local authorities began to see the possibilities – provided they could position the city strategically.

Defining strategy

Perhaps surprisingly, there is some disagreement among academics and practitioners about what strategy actually is. There are almost as many definitions as there are academics. Here are some examples:

> *Strategies are means to ends, and these ends concern the purpose and objectives of the organisation. They are the things that businesses do, the paths they follow, and the decisions they take, in order to reach certain points and levels of success. (Thompson 1997)*

> *The positioning and relating of the firm/organisation to its environment in a way which will assure its continued success and make it secure from surprises. (Ansoff 1984)*

> *Strategy is making trade-offs in competing. The essence of strategy is choosing what not to do. Without trade-offs, there would be no need for choice and thus no need for strategy. (Porter 1998)*

An alternative approach is to define what strategy is and is not, by listing its features. This is commonly done by describing what are tactics and what is strategy. Steiner and Miner (1977) drew up a list of the differences between strategy and tactics, as follows:

1. Importance. Strategic decisions are significantly more important than tactical ones.
2. Level at which conducted. Strategic decisions are usually made by top management.
3. Time horizon. Strategies are long term: tactics are short term.
4. Regularity. The formulation of strategy is continuous and irregular: tactics are periodic and fixed time, for example annual budget/plan.
5. Nature of problem. Strategic problems are usually unstructured and unique and so involve considerable risk and uncertainty. Tactical problems are more structured and repetitive and the risks easier to assess.
6. Information needed. Strategies require large amounts of external information, much of which relates to the future and is subjective. Tactical decisions depend much more on internally generated accounting or market research information.
7. Detail. Strategic decisions are broad, tactical decisions are detailed.
8. Ease of evaluation. Strategic decisions are much more difficult to make.

In fact, all of the above features require further judgement to evaluate them. For example, how does one define importance? How does one define long term or short term? A year would be a long period in the fashion industry, but extremely short in the electricity generating industry.

Much of the conflict in the literature is actually the result of differing angles on the problem rather than fundamental conceptual difficulties. Strategic decisions are formulated at differing levels of the organisation, and certainly almost all decisions, at whatever level, may have strategic implications. Thus it may be argued that theoreticians offer differing theories because they are examining different parts of a complex structure.

There is an underlying assumption that the whole process is rational – that managers act by reasoning through the situation and the possibilities, and then come to a logical conclusion. This is often not the case at all. Managers act emotionally, decisions are made on an ad hoc basis as crises arise and must be dealt with, and in any case good strategic thinking is creative and therefore not linear. The process is often messy: planners return to previous decisions and revise them in the light of experience, and may even go back to the analysis stage of the process as environmental changes appear. This is, of course, a sensible approach: carrying on blindly with an inappropriate strategy, ignoring all changes around the organisation, will certainly lead to disaster. Strategy formation is therefore an iterative process, with the strategy growing incrementally in response to each new situation or each new idea from management.

Think outside this box!

If strategy has to be continually revised in the light of experience, what is the point of planning at all? Would it not be better simply to meet each problem as it arises, and hope for the best?

Or perhaps we need a plan so that we have something to deviate from? General Eisenhower said that plans are nothing, but planning is everything – which may be fine in a war situation, but is it appropriate for business?

Marketing strategy and corporate strategy

If marketing strategy is regarded as residing at the functional level, marketers will only be concerned with manipulating the 7Ps (Booms and Bitner 1981). In this scenario, corporate strategy will stand above marketing strategy and will inform (or even dictate) the marketing strategy. If the firm is truly customer-orientated, the marketing strategy will in fact be the corporate strategy since the company's whole approach is dictated by the marketplace, particularly customer needs (Brady and Davis 1993; Webster 1992). Some writers state that the market-orientated organisation is concerned not only with the interface between the firm and its customers, but also with the relationships within the organisation (i.e. with employees) and with the relationships between the organisation and other organisations (Piercy and Cravens 1999).

There are, in general, four main measures of corporate success (although some firms will have subsidiary measures in place). These are:

1. Profitability.
2. Growth.
3. Shareholder value.
4. Customer satisfaction.

Profitability ranks high in corporate thinking because it is how shareholders and lenders judge the company. Marketing contributes to profitability by identifying profitable customer groups (and of course unprofitable groups) and ensuring that the organisation's offerings can be supplied for a price that generates profit. Unfortunately, profitability suffers from a number of drawbacks as a measure: first, managers can easily manipulate the figures (at least in the short term) to create a paper profit. Second, if the company is funded through borrowing, profitability can rise dramatically in the short term but the firm is exposed to more risk. Cutting investment will raise profitability in the short term, but cause long-term damage to the firm. Finally, profitability looks at past performance, not at potential, so it encourages a short-term view on the part of management.

Growth of sales turnover is a main objective for around 80% of companies (Collins and Porras 1994). The reasons are obscure, but may relate to the idea that 'being the biggest' equates to 'being the most secure'. It may simply be that senior managers like to run big companies rather than small ones. In any event, marketers are expected to contribute to growth by recruiting more customers, and by extracting more business from existing customers. The problem with growth is that the current emphasis on sustainability precludes overall growth in the economy, at least in the long term, which means that growth can only be achieved by taking business away from competitors. Competitors will, not unnaturally, do whatever they can to prevent this happening. Some research has shown that a very rapid growth in sales often leads to an equally rapid death of the organisation, since there are too many challenges, changes and unforeseen threats involved in growing too fast.

There are four generic routes to growth, as shown in Table 9.1 (Ansoff 1968).

Growth in growing markets is likely to happen in any case, even without any formal strategic attempts to encourage it: the key to success here lies in measuring whether the company is growing faster than the market, slower than the market, or at the same pace as the market. Often firms that couch their growth objectives in financial terms fail to notice that they are growing more slowly than the market, and are thus (in effect) losing ground to competitors. Couching growth targets in terms of market share will avoid this pitfall, although obviously a reliable measure of the overall size of the market needs to be available.

Table 9.1   Growth strategies

Strategy	Explanation
Market penetration	This is the most common method of growing the business. The firm expands sales of its existing products in its existing markets, usually by taking business away from competitors.
Product development	Here the firm introduces new products within the existing market, either selling extra products to existing customers, or offering a slightly different product to people who are not entirely satisfied with the existing products.
Market development	If a firm has saturated its existing markets, growth is still possible by introducing the existing products into new markets. This is a common reason for exporting.
Diversification	Taking new products into new markets appears to be a risky growth strategy, but firms sometimes do this because the new product has production synergies. A safer route would be to expand through acquisition, buying out a firm in the target market.

Shareholder value depends on three factors: dividends paid, a rise in the share value and cash payments in respect of assets sold on to other firms. Some marketers believe that this should be the aim of all marketing efforts, since it is probably the key issue in corporate survival – if the shares fall in value enough, the company becomes a target for a takeover. **Value-based marketing** seeks to focus marketers on shareholder value (Doyle 2000). There is more on this later in the chapter.

Customer satisfaction is the measure that probably fits the marketing concept best, since that is what marketers view as the ultimate goal. However, there are various ways of applying the concept in practice. Ambler and Roberts (2008) suggest that the use of discounted cash flow analysis (in which sales are predicted into the future, and the potential cash flow is calculated from this) is useful for marketing planning purposes because it includes the idea of customer lifetime value (the value a customer will have throughout his or her time as a customer of the firm) and customer equity (the amount a customer or customers are worth in terms of overall profitability). The authors caution against using measures such as return on investment, which is beloved by finance directors, but instead use measures such as return on customer.

Using the appropriate measure for success is a subject of considerable debate: it is important because it focuses the minds of all managers, not just marketers.

> **Value-based marketing** Marketing whose end goal is raising the share value of the company.

STRATEGIC MARKETING MANAGEMENT

Marketing management comprises the following elements:

1. Identifying needs among those on whom the organisation depends.
2. Developing methods of meeting those needs – providing products or services that do so.
3. Promoting those products to customers in order to demonstrate how their needs will be met.
4. Handling the exchange processes that result.
5. Monitoring the overall process to ensure that changes in customer needs or competitive activity have not made the solutions inappropriate.

Piercy and Cravens (1999) offer a model which illustrates the level and focus of organisational analysis in marketing (Table 9.2).

Table 9.2   Levels and focus of organisational analysis in marketing

Strategic level	Unit of analysis	Examples of major issues	Examples of new organisational forms
Functional	Marketing subsystems	Organising and coordinating sub-functions of marketing such as advertising, marketing research, sales operations.	Channel management. Logistics/services specialists.
Business	Marketing department	The department of marketing and internal structure of the marketing department. The integration of marketing sub-functions. Relationships with other functions.	Sector/segment management. Trade marketing. Investment specialists. Venture/new product departments.
Corporate	Divisional marketing responsibilities and group-wide marketing issues	Centralisation/decentralisation of marketing decision-making and relationship between central and peripheral marketing units.	Marketing exchange and coalition companies. Network organisations.
Enterprise	Strategic alliances and networks.	External relationships and boundary-spanning with strategic marketing partners. Marketing 'make or buy' choices.	Partnerships. Alliances.

One of the complexities inherent in this model is that there is a trade-off between forming competitive alliances and competing to meet customer needs. Marketing academics have consistently emphasised the need to generate competitive advantage by meeting customer needs better than the competition, but the Piercy and Cravens model seems to suggest that forming coalitions and partnerships at the corporate and enterprise levels will improve the prospects for survival. This has a certain logic to it: companies that do not compete with each other cannot lose out to each other. On the other hand, competition almost always leads to the best outcomes for consumers – so perhaps collaboration will reduce customer satisfaction rather than increase it.

Real-life marketing: Co-operating with competitors

It's easy to lose sight of the real competition when you're battling for market share. There was a time when national flag-carrying airlines such as British Airways and Alitalia carved up the flying business between them, controlling landing rights at airports and deciding who could fly where. When low-cost airlines began operating (following a freeing-up of airspace in the 1980s) there was suddenly some serious new competition around, and the flag carriers had to start fighting back.

One of the key benefits the low-cost airlines had at the time was that flights could be booked easily on-line. The major airlines set up their own websites, but soon realised that they would be better off if they co-operated against the common enemy. Nine of the European flag-carriers set up their own on-line booking service,

Opodo. Opodo acts as an on-line travel agent, enabling people to book flights from anywhere to anywhere using a wide range of carriers. Unlike the low-cost carriers, Opodo can book you on a flight to and from anywhere in the world, all on one site: it isn't even limited to the founding airlines' flights, but can select from over 400 airlines worldwide. It can book the entire route, even if it means switching airlines.

In practice, you should do the following:

- Identify the key competitive advantage – it isn't necessarily price.
- Identify competitors who will benefit from, and can contribute to, the project.
- If necessary, sell other people's services as well, if it will create benefits for your customers. Benefiting the customer can always be made to pay somehow.
- Learn from competitors, but don't copy them exactly, or you will lose your unique selling proposition.

Much depends on the breadth of definition of competition. A narrow definition (e.g. 'we are in the restaurant business') might mean entering into competition with other restaurants. A broad definition ('we are in the leisure industry') might mean forming strategic alliances with other restaurateurs to compete against the cinema industry or the sports-centre industry.

Such arrangements are sometimes called 'co-opetition' because they combine elements of competition with elements of co-operation. An effective co-opetition arrangement between firms will generate the drive to innovate in some areas (to compete) and also will give access to new resources (through co-operation). The critical success factors in co-opetition are strong leadership from management, and trust between the parties (Osarenkhoe 2010). There is more on co-operating with competitors later in the chapter.

STRATEGIC PLANNING

Strategic planning is intended to generate a 'road map' for achieving the organisation's objectives. In most cases, this means obtaining some kind of competitive advantage: it may or may not be linked to profitability, since non-profit organisations also have strategies and also compete. The ultimate objectives may be linked to growth in market share, or growth in shareholder value, or achieving stability in an unstable market, or developing a particular reputation in the industry, or any one of a large number of possible outcomes.

Planning implies that managers intend to change something in the organisation, presumably in order to change the future outcomes of what the organisation is and does. There is an implied assumption that, without the new plan, the organisation would end up somewhere else entirely. The difference between what the planners expect to happen as a result of the new plan, and what would happen if no changes were made, is called the planning gap.

Good planning therefore begins with an assessment of what would happen if no changes are made. This is called a reference projection, and is the baseline by which

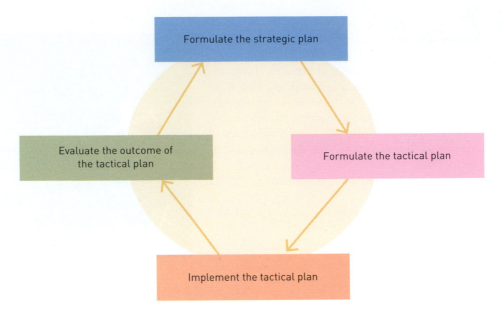

Figure 9.1   The cyclical nature of planning

all subsequent planning will be judged. The intention of planning, and indeed tactics, is to close the gap. If the planning gap is large, the firm obviously has a problem – identifying the problem correctly may not be straightforward. For example, a company might perceive a competitor's surprise entry into the market as the problem, whereas the real problem is the company's information systems which failed to predict the competitor's entry.

Figure 9.1 shows the traditional view of planning as being cyclical in nature. The cycle continues indefinitely as the evaluation of the outcomes of previous plans and activities is used to inform the new strategic plans. The process may not always be as tidy as this, of course, particularly when firms are operating in conditions of continuous change.

There is no single rule for creating strategic plans. All managers will carry out some planning, simply because they must ensure that resources are available in the right place, at the right time and in the right quantities to ensure that objectives are reached. Equally, almost all managers are in the position of needing to manage change, since organisations must respond to changes in the environment. Managers will therefore seek out opportunities to exploit, and threats to avoid, playing to the strengths of the organisation and minimising the effects of its weaknesses.

Having said that, there are three approaches to planning: first, the fully planned approach in which the organisation's future activities are detailed down to the finest level. At the opposite extreme, the adaptive model suggests that organisations change the strategy rapidly in the face of environmental changes, and by implication do not plan in detail or very far ahead. The third alternative approach is the incremental approach, in which an overall plan is in place but changes are made as circumstances change.

In the case of the fully planned approach, planning may be formal, with many of the decisions already made or with established decision-making rules in place, or it may be informal and therefore carried out on an ad hoc basis. Formal strategic planning works best in conditions of stability, where change is slow and where environmental conditions can be predicted fairly accurately. For example, the petroleum industry is fairly stable: the rules are laid down by the Organisation of Petroleum Exporting Countries (OPEC), and by the seven largest oil companies. The number of producers is limited, and the oil companies control the process from extraction right through to delivery at the petrol pump. Demand is unlikely to vary very quickly, major

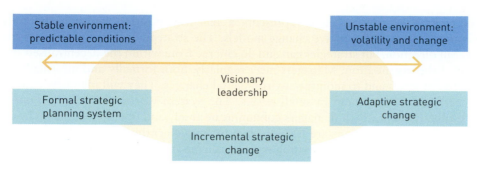

Figure 9.2 Planning and change

competition is unlikely to enter the market unexpectedly, governments are unlikely to make major changes in legislation and the companies themselves are powerful enough to control most of the potential changes that do exist. Oil companies are therefore able to plan years or even decades ahead with a fair degree of confidence.

On the other hand, the entertainment industry is extremely volatile. Consumer tastes are fickle, new competitors enter the market, fashions shift whether for night-clubs or for entertainers. Chaos theory (Stacey 1993) implies that intentional strategies are too inflexible for dealing with an inherently chaotic world, and therefore reliance on a tightly structured plan will lead to stagnation. Planning systems (rather than plans themselves) are useful in such circumstances, but are usually kept fairly loose and contain a lot of 'what-if' scenarios. This is more typical of adaptive strategic change, in which the firm adapts to changing circumstances rather than follows a rigid path.

Some organisations will be characterised by adaptive strategic change, in which managers throughout the organisation are empowered and encouraged to seek out new opportunities. The result of this is an increase in innovation at the business level, so that strategy develops from the bottom up: the rationale is that managers who are nearer to the customers (and other stakeholders) can respond much more quickly to changes in stakeholder needs. Adaptation to change will occur much more quickly in such organisations.

Many companies operating in an unstable environment rely on visionary leadership. The visionary leader (for example Sir Richard Branson of Virgin) has a clear idea of where the organisation is going and what it stands for, and is able to communicate this to employees. Such leaders have a clear grasp of the products, services and activities which will be acceptable to the organisation's customers, suppliers, shareholders and other stakeholders.

 Think outside this box!

Visionaries are often self-made, rising from poverty to huge wealth in a matter of a few years. Obviously visionary leadership works – so why don't all firms operate that way? After all, somebody sometime founded the firm, and presumably had dreams and the energy to turn them into reality!

Is it because there is a shortage of visionaries? Probably not – we all know people who have burning ambitions. Is it because visionaries can be hard to work with? Maybe. Or maybe we are losing sight of all the hundreds of people who start their businesses enthusiastically, energetically and single-mindedly, and yet fail anyway. Maybe visionary leadership only works in one in a thousand (or one in ten thousand) cases.

Incremental strategic change represents a half-way position between the fully planned system and adaptive change models. The strategic leadership provides the overall direction, but strategies can and do emerge from within the decentralised system of the organisation. Managers meet regularly, both formally and informally, to discuss progress and to monitor environmental changes. They will plan new courses of action, and test them in small stages. The system works best in **organismic organisations** in which managers communicate freely and operate on a team basis: hierarchical organisations are less effective for implementing change. There is also an implication that the organisation must be tolerant of mistakes, which is of course not always the case.

The systems described above are not necessarily mutually exclusive: different divisions within the same organisation may be using different approaches. The management style of the people involved will also affect strategic planning: junior managers may well decide to ignore or pervert the overall strategic plan that has been handed down from the Board, perhaps on the grounds that what looks realistic in the boardroom is unworkable in the field. A rapid change in circumstances (for example, a major accident at a corporate factory) may result in the implementation of a predetermined crisis strategy, whereas another sudden crisis (entry of a foreign competitor into the market) may result in the scrapping of a detailed plan. Whatever happens, it is useful to remember that strategic planning does not happen in isolation: no battle plan ever survives first contact with the enemy, and no strategic plan is ever set in concrete. Planning may be a linear process, but implementing plans is not.

Organismic organisations Organisations that do not have a fixed structure: they adapt according to the task facing the organisation.

THE MARKETING AUDIT

The starting-point for planning should be the marketing audit. This provides the firm with a snapshot of the current position, covering all aspects of the firm's marketing. Table 9.3 shows the basic audit.

Table 9.3 The marketing audit

Main areas	Subsections	Issues to be addressed
Marketing environment audit	Economic–demographic	Inflation, materials supply and shortages, unemployment, credit availability, forecast trends in population structure.
Macro-environment	Technological	Changes in product and process technology, generic substitutes to replace products.
	Political–legal	Proposed laws, national and local government actions.
	Cultural	Attitude changes in the population as a whole, changes in lifestyles and values.
	Ecological	Cost and availability of natural resources, public concerns about pollution and conservation.
Task environment	Markets	Market size, growth, geographical distribution, profits; changes in market segment sizes and opportunities.
	Customers	Attitudes towards the company and competitors, decision-making processes, evolving needs and wants.
	Competitors	Objectives and strategies of competitors, identifying competitors, trends in future competition.

Main areas	Subsections	Issues to be addressed
	Distribution and dealers	Main trade channels, efficiency levels of trade channels.
	Suppliers	Availability of key resources, trends in patterns of selling.
	Facilitators and marketing firms	Cost and availability of transport, finance and warehousing; effectiveness of advertising (and other) agencies.
	Publics	Opportunity areas, effectiveness of PR activities.
Marketing strategy audit	Business mission	Clear focus, attainability.
	Marketing objectives and goals	Corporate and marketing objectives clearly stated, appropriateness of marketing objectives.
	Strategy	Core marketing strategy, budgeting of resources, allocation of resources.
Marketing organisation audit	Formal structure	Seniority of marketing management, structure of responsibilities.
	Functional efficiency	Communications systems, product management systems, training of personnel.
	Interface efficiency	Connections between marketing and other business functions.
Marketing systems audit	Marketing information system	Accuracy and sufficiency of information, generation and use of market research.
	Marketing planning system	Effectiveness, forecasting, setting of targets.
	Marketing control system	Control procedures, periodic analysis of profitability and costs.
	New product development system	Gathering and screening of ideas, business analysis, pre-launch product and market testing.
Marketing productivity audits	Profitability analysis	Profitability of each product, market, territory and distribution channel. Entry and exit of segments.
	Cost-effectiveness analysis	Costs and benefits of marketing activities.
Marketing function audits	Products	Product portfolio; what to keep, what to drop, what to add, what to improve.
	Price	Pricing objectives, policies and strategies. Customer attitudes. Price promotions.
	Distribution	Adequacy of market coverage. Effectiveness of channel members. Switching channels.
	Advertising, sales promotion, PR	Suitability of objectives. Effectiveness of execution format. Method of determining the budget. Media selection. Staffing levels and abilities.
	Salesforce	Adequate size to achieve objectives. Territory organisation. Remuneration methods and levels. Morale. Setting quotas and targets.

Source: Adapted from Kotler, P. (2003) *Marketing Management,* 11th edn. © 2003. Reprinted by permission of Pearson Education Inc., Upper Saddle River, NJ.

The audit is obviously a very useful tool, but it suffers from several drawbacks. First, it only provides a snapshot of the current position, and since it takes some considerable time to compile it will in fact show a somewhat historical view. Second, since it is unlikely that all the elements will be analysed at the same time, the audit is likely to show a distorted view as well. Third, those given the job of reporting on their aspect of the audit may well distort the information in order to make themselves look good. Fourth, a lot of the factors in the audit require judgement on the part of the person reporting, so the result is unlikely to be objective. Finally, the process is time-consuming, and may be resented by busy people.

Perhaps the most valuable aspect of the audit is that it helps planners to focus on the issues, and causes people to think through what they are doing.

Setting objectives

Following on from the audit, setting the corporate objectives is the next stage for planning, since the planners should now have a clear idea of what the organisation is capable of doing. Objectives are derived from the overall strategy, and enable the planners to check progress towards the ultimate goal.

Objectives should meet the SMART criteria. These are:

- Specific. The objective needs to address a clear issue.
- Measurable. If an objective cannot be expressed in a measurable way, we have no way of knowing whether it has been achieved.
- Achievable. Setting an objective that cannot be achieved is not only pointless, it is also counter-productive because it will demoralise those tasked with its achievement.
- Realistic. If the objective is unrealistic, either because it is unattainable or because it is irrelevant, there is no point in setting it.
- Time-sensitive. Planners need to provide a timescale for the achievement of the objective, or nothing will happen.

Traditionally, marketing objectives tended to fall into three main areas: increasing market share, enlarging the overall market and improving profitability. Enlarging the overall market is probably only appropriate for firms that already have a large share of the market: increasing market share will risk retaliation from competitors, therefore many firms will go down the route of seeking to improve profitability. Techniques for doing this will vary from one firm to another and from one industry to another – they are very much in the realm of tactical decisions.

Market strategies

Market-scope strategies deal with coverage of the market. There are three main alternative strategies, as shown in Table 9.4.

Market scope can change as the market changes, or as the firm grows, so (like any other marketing strategy) the firm will need to reconsider the market scope as circumstances dictate. For example, an ethnic grocery shop might consider creating ready-meals or hot takeaway food, or even open a restaurant section to provide food from the same culture. A larger firm such as a ferry company might start offering package holidays or holiday-home rental. In either case the firm is moving from one type of business to another, even though there is a clear relationship in terms of providing the service. Equally, a company pursuing a multi-market strategy might fall on hard times and decide to concentrate on its core business – the ferry company

Table 9.4   Market scope strategies

Strategy alternative	Explanation and examples
Single-market strategy	The firm devotes all its efforts to one market segment. This is also known as niche marketing. In some cases the niche marketer seeks out a market that is too small or specialised for large firms to bother with (typically the route taken by small firms or those with limited resources), but in other cases there may be specialised capabilities which the firm can supply. For example, large washing-powder manufacturers specialise because of the prohibitive cost of the plant and equipment needed to manufacture washing powders.
Multi-market strategy	Here the firm seeks to serve several segments. For example, a glass bottle manufacturer may serve the food industry, the brewing industry, the soft drinks industry and even the gift and novelty industry. Each has different requirements, and each will need to be approached with a different tactical package.
Total-market strategy	Companies following a total-market strategy seek to serve every segment of their chosen markets. Motor manufacturers such as Ford seek to supply vehicles for every purpose, from compact cars through to heavy lorries.

might find that interest in the package holidays is waning as more people travel independently, and might revert to the simple transportation of vehicles and passengers.

MARKET-GEOGRAPHY STRATEGY

Market-geography strategy takes geographic segmentation into the strategy area by concentrating the firm's resources in a key geographical area. In some cases this is an approach typical of very small businesses: local take-away food outlets operate within extremely small geographical areas, for example. On the other hand, some very substantial businesses also operate a market-geography strategy. The London Underground carries three million passengers daily over 235 miles of railway track, and operates 257 stations. The Underground uses capital assets valued in the billions, but only operates within a relatively small geographical area, no larger than that covered by some taxi companies.

Regional-market strategy means that the firm operates within distinct geographical boundaries that go beyond the local area. For example, a brewery might have strong local ties but sell its beer nationally. The advantage of regional-market strategy is that it is easier to handle cultural characteristics of a region than to handle the different cultures that might be found across the country as a whole. The advertising campaigns of the SA Brain brewery, for example, might well be incomprehensible outside the company's native Wales – and in some cases, the advertising would not have much effect outside Cardiff.

National-market strategy is commonly adopted as the firm exhausts the possibilities within its own region. National-market strategy is relatively straightforward in small countries, but can prove difficult in large, diverse countries such as the United States or Brazil. Cultural differences between regions within one country can be substantial: residents of Munich have more in common with their Austrian neighbours in Salzburg than they do with their fellow-Germans in Kiel or Rostock, for example. The main advantage of a national strategy is economies of scale in production, but there may also be some benefits in terms of spreading risk across the whole economy rather than relying on a regional economy which might be affected by (say) the closure of a major employer.

MARKET ENTRY STRATEGIES

Another way of categorising market strategies is to consider the timing of market entry. Market entry strategies fall into three categories: first-in strategy, early-entry strategy and laggard-entry strategy.

First-in strategy means being the first to enter a given market. It has the major advantage of creating a lead that others then have to follow, but it carries the greatest risk in terms of possible failure in the market. This risk is high, since the market will be virtually unknown in the early stages. On the other hand, the first-to-market advantage means that a first-in strategist can cream off a large market share before competitors enter, and can maintain high profitability by price **skimming** in the early stages of the market's development. In general, first-in strategy is a high risk, high return approach.

Early-entry strategy means entering just after the first-in company. In most cases, the early-entry strategists have been developing products for the market, but were beaten by the other firm. In some cases the early-entry strategist deliberately holds back to allow another firm to test the market and make the early mistakes. Early-entry strategy works best for firms with a marketing advantage and the ability to learn from others – such firms also need sufficient resources to be able to take on the first-in strategist.

Laggard-entry strategy means entering the market towards the end of the growth phase of the product life cycle, or when the market is mature. **Imitators** entering the market have the opportunity to learn from the market leaders' mistakes without the heavy research expenditure the first-in and early-entry strategists have incurred. Research shows that the chances of failure are very much reduced for laggards. A laggard may enter the market with a new idea that enables the firm to capture a large part of the market – Amazon.com has made a considerable dent in the book-selling business, for example, although this market was extremely well established.

Figure 9.3 shows the relationship between these entry strategies.

Profitability will depend on the problems the first-in company encounters. For example, Philips of Holland introduced videodiscs as far back as the 1980s, shortly

Skimming Pricing products highly at first, but reducing the price steadily as the product moves through its life cycle.

Imitator A company that makes somewhat differentiated products which are similar to those produced by the market leader.

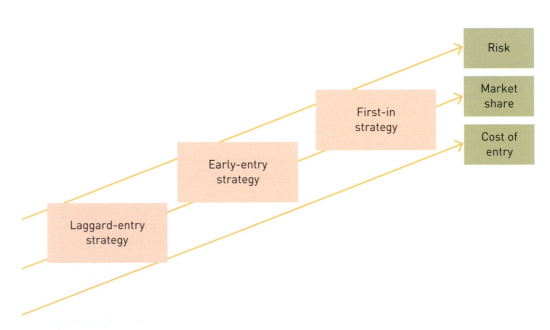

Figure 9.3 Entry strategies

Table 9.5   Market-commitment strategies

Level of commitment	Explanation and examples
Strong commitment	These firms devote much greater resources to the market than they do to other segments. In some cases (particularly niche marketers) the firm commits all its resources to one market. Most managers are aware that the bulk of the firm's sales come from a relatively small group of customers, so the strong-commitment strategy means devoting most or all of the firm's resources to those customers.
Average-commitment strategy	This is typical of firms that lack the resources to commit fully to a given market, perhaps because the firm's resources are already committed elsewhere. Such firms can afford to make mistakes in the average-commitment market because they are able to make up losses elsewhere, so in some respects the average-commitment firm is able to take more risks than the strong-commitment firm. The downside is that the average-commitment firm is likely to meet with strong opposition from high-commitment firms, as has been the case in the UK with the Direct Line insurance company. Direct Line is fully committed to telephone-based selling: other insurance companies which have tried to establish their own telesales operations have been unable to dent Direct Line's market. This is because telephone selling is the firm's entire *raison d'être*: for other firms it is merely a sideline.
Light-commitment strategy	This strategy is typical of firms with resources to spare from other activities. These firms may become market followers in a given market simply to shut out the competition, or to 'test the water'. Sometimes the firm's managers have a belief that the firm 'ought' to be in a given market.

after the introduction of video recorders. The project flopped completely, because the market was not yet ready – at the time, it was not possible to record onto videodiscs using equipment at home, whereas tape-based equipment could record from the television. However, in the early 21st century the DVD system was introduced, using Philips' original technology, and became a runaway success. This demonstrates that the first-in companies must stay ahead of the competition throughout, or risk simply paving the way for competitors.

COMMITMENT LEVEL

A further way of categorising strategies is to look at the level of commitment the firm has to the market. Firms might have strong, average or light commitment, as shown in Table 9.5.

Market-dilution strategies are ways of removing the firm from markets that are no longer profitable, or of divesting the firm of unprofitable customers. There are four basic strategies in this category: demarketing, pruning, key-market strategy and harvesting.

Demarketing is about reducing demand for a product or category of product. It comes in various types, as follows (Bradley and Blythe 2013):

1. Counter-marketing. This is typified by government anti-smoking or anti-drug use campaigns, which are intended to counter marketing activities by other organisations.
2. Selective demarketing. This is the process of discouraging certain groups of customers in order to reduce the costs of servicing unprofitable segments.

Firms may decide to give preferential treatment to 'key' customers, or they may ration supplies, or they may even recommend a competitor's product if the customer is really not worth keeping.

3. Synchromarketing. This is intended to even out peaks and troughs in demand, and may involve discouraging demand at peak times or encouraging demand during less popular times.

4. General demarketing. This is intended to create a reduction in demand across the board. For example, an exclusive restaurant may prefer to demarket in order to prevent large numbers of people turning up without reservations in the hope of a cancellation.

5. Ostensible demarketing. Here the marketer pretends to demarket a product (for example, threatening to withdraw it) in order to create publicity and stimulate demand.

6. Accidental demarketing. Sometimes marketers act with the best of intentions, hoping to increase business, but instead the campaign fails dramatically and actually reduces demand.

In terms of strategy, ostensible demarketing and accidental demarketing do not figure. Ostensible demarketing is clearly a tactic, whereas accidental demarketing (by definition) is something that is unplanned.

Pruning of marginal markets means pulling out of some segments altogether. Typically, firms will divest themselves of their low-commitment markets in order to concentrate on the core business, particularly if business is going through a downturn at the time. Firms may also prune in order to divert resources into new projects that might pay better.

Key-market strategy is the corollary of pruning strategy in that the firm makes a conscious effort to concentrate on key markets at the expense of marginal markets. A key-market strategy requires a strong focus, a reputation for quality and a strong position within the market.

Harvesting strategy is one in which the company deliberately cuts investment in a given market (or for a given brand) and allows the sales to slide downwards, grabbing the profit from it without further investment in the market. This is a common strategy when a product is reaching the end of its life cycle, and is also common if the market is disappearing. Harvesting is not always possible due to the existence of exit barriers. The company may have an investment in heavy equipment for which there is no resale market, or there may be customer goodwill issues, or there may even be a reluctance on the part of management to let go of a brand that has historical significance.

Competitive positions

Porter (1985) suggests four basic competitive strategies, of which three are winning strategies and one is a losing strategy:

1. Overall cost leadership. A company that is able to minimise its costs can obtain a competitive advantage over other companies either by reducing its prices or by increasing its profitability. Minimising costs may be an exercise in developing efficient systems or it may mean moving production to developing countries.

2. Differentiation. Companies that are able to show their customers that their products are significantly different from competing products are able to charge premium prices (provided, of course, that the customers believe that

the differences make the products better). Differentiation comes from two sources: first, real differences in the features and benefits which the brand has to offer, and second, strong promotional activities to make the differences apparent (and important) to potential buyers. Both these sources of differentiation cost money to implement, so the firm needs to be confident that the premium which customers are prepared to pay for the differentiated product more than covers the extra costs.

3. Focus. Here the company concentrates on a few market segments rather than trying to compete in the whole market. Often these will be exclusive markets: the market for luxury yachts falls into this category. In the industrial context, Novo Nordisk of Denmark specialises in producing industrial enzymes, and has become highly profitable by being the best in its chosen specialism.

The losing strategy is to try to achieve more than one of the above, and thus fail to achieve any of them. Combining low costs with differentiation is impossible, because a differentiation strategy requires higher expenditure on R&D and promotion if it is to be effective. Combining low cost with focus is also unlikely to work, because low cost depends on achieving economies of scale in production, which in turn means achieving high sales volumes across a very broad market. Focus and differentiation combine fairly well, but there are cost implications. The essence of the problem is to pursue a clear strategy which customers can identify with, so that the firm has a clear competitive position in the minds of the customers. If customers are unable to decide whether a firm is cheap, or is best at serving its market segment, or is offering the highest specifications, the firm's products will not stand out from the competition and are thus likely to be relegated to a lower status in the decision-making framework.

Think outside this box!

The theory seems to show that only one firm can be the cost leader in any given market. So how do low-cost airlines fit into this equation? Many of them fly to the same destinations (Malaga, Prague, Alicante etc.) and they often do so from regional airports which are sufficiently close to each other to be realistic alternatives for many passengers.

Is the theory wrong? If so, where is it wrong? How can all these companies apparently compete on price without causing each other any major problems?

Firms will occasionally try to carry out more than one strategy at a time because of a lack of consensus among managers. This can happen at all levels in the organisation, and is likely to be a result of poor communication of the corporate mission statement, vision, or corporate objectives statement. Consensus among managers improves performance at the strategic business unit (SBU) level, especially for differentiation strategies (Homburg et al. 1999), but appears unnecessary if the firm is pursuing a low-cost strategy. This may be because a low-cost strategy is easy to understand and relate to, even if disagreements occur elsewhere.

In practice managers may not consciously decide to categorise the strategy according to the model. In most cases, senior managers will decide what the organisation should and should not be doing and the strategy will develop from there: the categories are the result of observing reality, and are not necessarily intended to be prescriptive.

Competitive moves

Retaining a position in the market, or carving out a new one, requires firms to attack competitors or defend themselves from attack. The moves that are available to each firm will depend on its position in the marketplace relative to its competitors. Figure 9.4 illustrates the four basic market positions.

In Figure 9.4, the size of the circles represents the relative market share of each firm. The market leader has by far the largest market share, and drags the **market followers** behind it. The **niche marketer** occupies a position that does not represent a threat to any of the other firms, while the **market challenger** seeks to steal the market share from the market leader, with the aim of becoming market leader in turn. Market challengers may have been market followers in the past, or may be entering from outside the market, for example a foreign company entering the market for the first time.

For market leaders, both market-orientated and relationship-orientated strategies are important. For challengers, market-orientated strategies work best, and for followers and nichers relationship-orientated strategies work best (Tse et al. 2004).

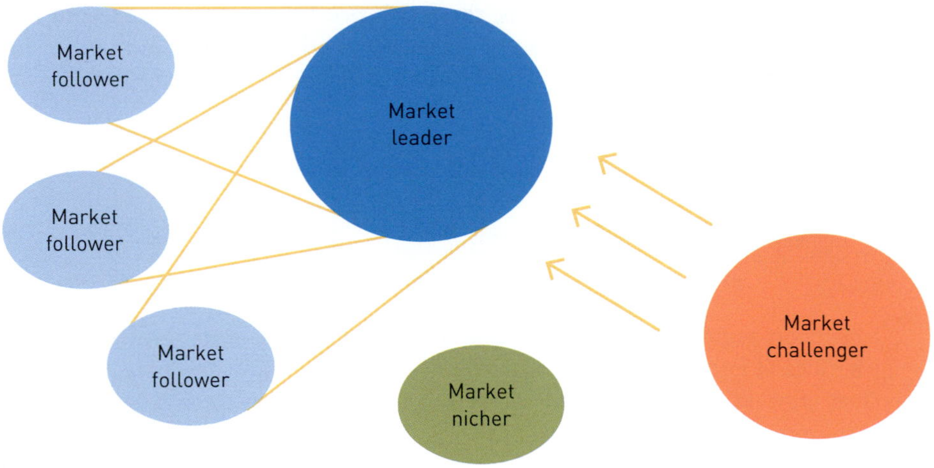

Market follower A company that follows the lead of the main company in the market.

Niche marketer A firm that is content with a small segment of the market.

Market challenger A company that seeks to grow at the expense of the market leader.

Figure 9.4   Basic market positions

Market leader strategies

Market leaders usually have the power to control the market to a large extent, but exercising this power too frequently might lead to the unwanted attentions of government monopoly regulators. Market leaders therefore have two basic growth strategies: they can try to continue to win a greater market share from their smaller rivals, or they can try to expand the total market.

Expanding the total market may well prove to be a viable option for a market leader, for two reasons. First, it may be easier to attract more customers into the market than it would be to try to steal customers from competitors, who are likely to defend their positions fiercely. Second, expanding the total market will not attract the attention of monopoly regulators since the overall market share is likely to remain much the same. Expanding the total market will, of course, benefit the firm's competitors as well, but this is not an important consideration for a firm that already has the largest market share: in any case, the object of the exercise is to run a successful business, not merely to bankrupt one's competitors. Expanding the total market can be achieved by expanding the total number of users, by finding new uses for the product, or by encouraging greater usage among existing users.

Expanding market share is achieved at the expense of the weaker competitors. Monopoly regulators may investigate this activity, but for most firms this is not a serious threat since regulators come in only when the market share is very substantial and where abuses can be proved. Basic routes to expanding market share are to win customers, to buy out competitors, or to increase the loyalty of existing customers.

Market leaders can also improve productivity, squeezing more profit out of the same sales volume. This strategy is easy for market leaders because their relative size gives them a bargaining advantage with suppliers and distributors, and also generates economies of scale. More commonly, market leaders need to maintain their defences against attacks from market challengers. The basic defence strategies are shown in Table 9.6.

Market leaders need to be constantly vigilant: the most effective strategy for all the other companies in the market is likely to be to take market share from the leader. Once this process starts, it is all too easy for the market leader to continue to lose share until it ceases to be the market leader, or even goes bankrupt.

Table 9.6   Defence strategies

Defence strategy	Explanation
Position defence	A position defence involves building barriers that prevent, or restrict, competitors from entering the market. This may mean, for example, incorporating features into the product which require a large capital investment (and consequently a large production run) to make them economically viable.
Flanking defence	Market leaders can sometimes ignore parts of the market that offer an opening to competitors. For example, Japanese car manufacturers were extremely successful in entering the US small car market, which had been left almost untouched by the American giants such as General Motors and Ford (www.gm.com; www.ford.com).
Pre-emptive defence	Here the market leader begins by attacking the other companies before they can move against the leader. A threat of entry might be pre-empted by a large price cut, for example.
Counter-offensive defence	When attacked, the market leader launches an instant counter-attack. This can take the form of a promotion campaign, a price war, or a new product development exercise to produce an improved version of the competitor's offering.
Mobile defence	The company is proactive in defending its current market position, by expanding into new markets ahead of the competition.
Contraction defence	If the company can no longer defend all its markets, it might decide to withdraw from some or all of those markets. In military terms, this is called a strategic withdrawal: however, the next part of the phrase used by the Army is 'to previously-prepared positions'. Sadly, some companies have managed the withdrawal part easily enough, but have not consolidated the positions they can hold, and consequently have simply continued to retreat until there is nowhere left to go.

Market challenger strategies

Market challengers seek to increase their share of the market, usually by aggressive competitive tactics. Market challengers are in a different position from market leaders in that they have two choices of competitor to attack: they can attack the market leader, which is risky but potentially has the highest rewards, or they can attack the smaller market followers either by out-competing them or by taking them over. Attacking the market leader almost always means attacking a larger opponent that is well-established in the market: the market leader almost certainly therefore has the resources and the experience to mount a vigorous defence. Smaller firms may not be so well placed to defend themselves, but on the other hand defeating the market leader usually means becoming market leader in turn, which has obvious advantages.

Real-life marketing: Find the USP

If you're going to challenge the leader, you need a good USP (unique selling proposition). This means you have to have something no one else has, and it has to be something that customers value.

K Shoes is a small shoe manufacturer (owned by Clarks Shoes) based in the English Lake District. The company produces good-quality, sensible footwear rather than fashion shoes, but it has a unique selling proposition – the K range of shoes don't squeak. Consumers see this as an indicator of the quality of the shoes, and it is indeed a real advantage. K Shoes decided to use this USP in their advertising, producing ads that showed the USP in a humorous way. For example, one ad showed a woman sneaking up behind her husband while he was dining with another woman, and dumping a bowl of noodles on his head. She couldn't have done that in squeaky shoes!

To make this work for you in practice:

- Don't try to guess what your USP is – find out what it is from the customer's viewpoint.
- Use the USP in all your promotional activities.
- If you can't find a USP, you need to develop one – otherwise you won't survive long against the big firms.

Attacking the market leader means having a clear competitive advantage: a cost advantage, or the ability to provide better value for money by offering a better product. Attacking smaller competitors may only require an aggressive promotional campaign, a short price war, or a takeover policy. The strategies open to a market challenger are shown in Table 9.7.

Guerrilla actions work best for small firms that are able to respond quickly and have the flexibility to move on as soon as their larger, perhaps more bureaucratic competitors try to retaliate.

Market follower strategies

Most firms operate with the view that competitors are 'the enemy' and will therefore try to attack them in order to seize market share. However, challenging the market leader or competing aggressively may not be the most effective strategy, since attack naturally leads to defence, followed by counter-attack. The primary task of any organisation is to survive, and an attack from a larger, better-resourced competitor may lead to the demise of the smaller firm.

Table 9.7 Market challenger strategies

Strategy	Explanation
Frontal attack	The challenger matches the competitor's marketing efforts across the board. It attacks the competitor's strengths, not its weaknesses, and in effect enters into a war of attrition. The company with the greater resources usually wins in these circumstances.
Flanking attack	Here the challenger concentrates on the competitor's weaknesses rather than its strengths. The challenger tries to find some portion of the competitor's business which is being poorly-served or which it feels able to serve better, and attacks that. Sometimes the competitor will withdraw without much of a fight: a lot depends on the relative resources of the two firms.
Encirclement attack	This strategy involves attacking from several directions at once. This approach works best when the attacker has more resources than the defender.
Bypass attack	Here the challenger bypasses the market leader completely and targets new markets. This might involve entering new geographic markets, or using new technology to tap into new groups of customers. This has the advantage of not offering a direct threat to the competitor, and thus minimising the risk of retaliation.
Guerrilla attack	The challenger makes occasional attacks on the larger competitor, using different tactics each time in order to demoralise and confuse the market leader. For example, a challenger might run a cut-price offer for one month only, followed the next month by a sales promotion, followed the next month by a promotional campaign. This constant switching of tactics does not allow the market leader time to organise a retaliatory strike, and instead forces the leader to become a follower, retaliating after the challenger has moved on to the next tactic.

Market followers typically allow the market leader to make most of the investment in developing new markets, then follow on to pick up any spare segments that might have been bypassed by the leader. The follower gains in terms of reduced costs and reduced risk, and although followers will never become market leaders they are often as profitable as leaders (Haines et al. 1989). Market followers fall into three types, as shown in Table 9.8.

Cloner A company that produces copies of products sold by the market leader.

Adapter A company that produces new products, superior to those produced by the market leader.

Table 9.8 Market follower categories

Category	Explanation
Cloner	These firms make almost exact copies of the leader's products, distribution, promotion and other marketing strategies. They can often do this at much lower cost, because they do not have the development costs or risks of the market leaders. Firms making exact copies of products are relatively rare, due to patenting and other intellectual property defences, but in some markets (particularly agricultural markets) cloning is perfectly feasible.
Imitator	Here the follower copies most of the leader's strategies, but retains some differentiation. This approach is more common than cloning, because it often avoids direct competition with the market leader, and can even help the leader to avoid charges of monopolistic behaviour. Typical imitator strategies would be supermarkets selling own brands that look like the market leader brands, or a new budget airline copying the online booking system of easyJet.
Adapter	Adapters go one step further than the market leader, producing improved versions of products or marketing programmes. Adapters can become industry leaders, and are really only one step short of being challengers.

Since the vast majority of new products on the market fail, the market leader position is invariably risky. Successful products have to cover the costs of all the unsuccessful ones. Followers can be more confident that their products will succeed, because they are able to learn from the mistakes of the market leader and copy only those products that are already successful. The same applies to promotional activities and distribution strategies: even though the bulk of the market is likely to go to the innovators, the costs of innovation are often large, so the profits may go to the followers.

Think outside this box!

If the safest way of running the business is to be a follower, why are so many firms so keen to be leaders? Why is it that firms spend millions on research and development, when it would be so much easier simply to sit back and wait for the competitors to do all the hard work and take all the risks?

Or maybe there's more to it than this? After all, what happens if someone develops a product that completely destroys our market – and we have no way of copying it? What happens if another follower produces a better copy than ours? And presumably we need to bring in the occasional new product, or the competitors will cream off the best of the market first!

Niche marketer strategies

Niche marketers are firms that concentrate on small segments of the market, seeking to meet the needs of those customers as closely as possible. Nichers usually operate on a low-volume, high-margin basis, so this is often a suitable strategic position for medium-sized companies (Clifford and Cavanaugh 1985).

Competitors are often closed out of the niche because the niche strategist develops an intimate knowledge of customer needs which is difficult for a new entrant to acquire. Furthermore, the niche is often too small to support more than one company. Niche marketers run the risk of their chosen market declining or even disappearing altogether: the key to success in niche marketing is specialisation, but this can mean that the company lacks the flexibility to move on if the niche shrinks. Table 9.9 shows the ways in which niche marketers can specialise.

Marketing in a changing world: Hypercompetition

In markets where change is rapid, hypercompetition may become the norm. Hypercompetition exists when companies can obtain short-term gains by acting in very aggressive or unexpected ways: the intention is to destabilise the market for a short-term gain, knowing that competitive gains cannot be sustained in the longer term.

The existence of hypercompetition has been called into question: there is no doubt that some companies enter markets with a somewhat Wild West approach, yelling and firing their guns in the air, but whether this approach is calculated or whether it arises simply from a lack of understanding of how the market operates is debatable. There have certainly been some high-profile entries and departures in the field of e-commerce (boo.com being one of the more spectacular examples) but these may have been more accidental than deliberate.

Whichever view one takes as an academic, the fact remains that competitors can appear suddenly, do something startling that disrupts the market, and perhaps grab a substantial market share while the established firms are still trying to formulate a response.

Table 9.9   Niche rôles

Role	Explanation
End-use specialist	The firm specialises in meeting all the needs of one type of end user. For example, Maplins aims to supply all the needs of amateur electronics hobbyists.
Vertical-level specialist	The firm specialises in one level of the production-distribution cycle. For example, Pickford's specialises in moving heavy equipment and abnormal loads.
Customer-size specialist	Here the firm concentrates on marketing to firms of a particular size. Often smaller firms are neglected by the industry majors, allowing a foot in the door for nichers.
Specific-customer specialist	The firm specialises in supplying one or two very large firms. This is typical of small engineering firms: they offer specialist manufacturing expertise to larger firms who find it cheaper to outsource than to manufacture in-house. Weber carburettors are an example: the firm supplies high-quality carburettors to most car manufacturers for their high-performance cars.
Geographical specialist	Here the firm stays within a small geographical area. For example, Welsh-language book publishers do not operate outside Wales and southern Argentina, where the Welsh language is spoken.
Product or feature specialist	The firm specialises in producing a particular product, or one with unique features. This type of specialisation is often based on a patented system or process.
Quality-price specialist	The firm operates within a niche at the top or bottom of the market. For example, the market for executive jet planes is dominated by Lear and Cessna.
Service specialist	The firm offers a service which is unavailable elsewhere. Only NASA offers a recovery and repair service for satellites, and only the Russian space agency offers space tourist flights (albeit at an extremely high price). However, competitors such as Virgin Galactic are proposing to enter the space tourism market at a much more reasonable price in the near future.

End-use specialist A firm that specialises in supplying all the needs of a specific group of customers, who use a product in a specific way.

Customer size specialist A company that specialises in dealing with customers of a specific size.

Specific-customer specialist A company that specialises in dealing with a narrow range of customers.

Collaborating with competitors

Most strategy authors tend to think of business strategy in terms of warfare. The aim is to beat the competitors into submission in some way, to capture markets, to conduct campaigns, to attack competitors. Hamel, Doz and Prahalad (1989) move away from this approach, and consider the possibilities for co-operating with competitors in order to ensure success for all. Strategic alliances generated through joint ventures, product licensing, or co-operative research strengthen firms against competitors from outside the partnership by increasing market coverage, reducing costs, generating greater efficiency and raising the profile of both companies. Many Japanese firms have used this approach to enter European markets.

Hamel et al.'s research showed that collaboration between Japanese firms and Western firms often left the Western company worse off in the long run. This has been seen as the 'Trojan horse' effect, whereby the Japanese firm has entered into the collaboration only for the purpose of learning as much as possible from the Western firm before abandoning the partnership and setting up in competition. Hamel et al. contradict this to an extent, attributing the failure of Western firms to gain from the alliance to poor negotiating skills, poor fit between strategic goals, and poor protection of sensitive information. On the other hand, more recent research from Hennart et al. (1999) shows that, provided the partnership is well-managed, the benefits of collaboration outweigh the risks. Firms that benefit most from competitive collaboration tend to follow the principles outlined in Table 9.10.

Companies often enter into alliances in order to avoid making investments, either in developing new products or in entering new markets. Unfortunately this often allows the partner firm to control the situation to their own advantage.

Table 9.10   Principles for successful collaboration

Principle	Explanation
Collaboration is competition in a different form	Successful collaborators remember that their partner may well try to take over the whole market later on, and become a major competitor. The collaboration may not last forever!
Harmony is not the most important measure of success	Occasional conflict may well lead to creative solutions for problems: like a marriage, if the partnership is a sincere commitment, arguments will happen now and then. Harmony usually only prevails where neither party really cares about the outcome, or indeed about the relationship.
Co-operation has limits	Strategic alliances often result in substantial transfers of information, perhaps well beyond that originally envisaged by senior management when they hammered out the deal. Successful collaborators will ensure that employees are well aware of what information can and cannot be passed on.
Learning from partners is paramount	Successful collaborators ensure that the new knowledge gained from the partner is diffused throughout their own organisation. This knowledge will remain even if the partnership dissolves.

Mutual gain is certainly possible, but firms should conform to the following conditions:

- The partners' strategic goals converge while their competitive goals diverge. Each partner must allow the other to prosper in the shared venture, and should avoid competing directly.
- The size and power of both partners is modest compared with the industry leaders. This ensures that the mutual need to attack the market leader, or defend the partners against retaliation by the industry leader, keeps the partnership on track.
- The partners should be of a similar size to each other. This helps to ensure that neither partner can develop a controlling interest in the venture.
- Each partner can learn from the other, but is able to restrict access to critically sensitive information.

Collaboration offers a good way forward for many small companies, and indeed some larger ones. Highly successful ventures include Iveco, the European alliance of truck manufacturers, and Transmanche Link, the consortium of civil engineering companies that built the Channel Tunnel.

Value-based marketing

Value-based marketing begins from the premise that the central task of management is to maximise shareholder value (Doyle 2000). This does not necessarily mean maximising profitability: shareholder value is more often related to capital growth, i.e. a rise in the value of the firm's shares, which is linked to many other factors than profit.

Maximising profit is often a short-term, tactical process involving cutting costs, reducing investment, downsizing, increasing sales at the expense of long-term customer loyalty and making short-term gains at the expense of long-term security. At the extreme, a profit focus can even lead to massaging the accounts to show a profit where there was not one before. Increased sophistication among shareholders has led to a realisation that long-term growth is likely to be more rewarding than immediate dividends: the spectacular collapse of firms such as Enron has led investors to avoid firms with spectacular short-term profits but little underlying substance. Therefore City analysts look more and more towards measures such as customer loyalty and brand awareness to judge whether stocks are likely to rise in value.

Unfortunately for investors, the marketplace is changing so rapidly that companies tend not to survive very long. The life expectancy of a company is now less than 20 years (De Geus 1997). Maintaining a profitable competitive advantage is likely to be even more elusive: as soon as it becomes apparent that a firm has found a profitable niche, competitors enter the market and profits are rapidly eroded until they reach the point where the company is unable to maintain an adequate return on its original capital investment (Black et al. 1998).

Obviously some companies are exceptions to this general trend. Large, well-established firms are able to retain shareholder value, using profits to increase the value of the firm rather than pay dividends. These blue-chip companies are regarded as safe investments because they maintain steady growth, although their dividend payouts are typically relatively low.

For marketers, the idea that the company should focus on maximising shareholder value rather than maximising consumer benefit may seem almost heretical. For the past fifty years, marketing academics have emphasised the centrality of consumer needs in all strategic planning. Value-based marketing implies that customer satisfaction is not an end in itself: rather it is the route to maximising shareholder value.

In fact, because marketers have concentrated on customer satisfaction, while other (often more senior) managers have been concerned with the value of the shares, marketing has often been relegated to a function rather than a strategic driver. The result of this is that marketing thinking has not fulfilled its early promise, and will not do so until marketers accept that the customers and consumers are the means to an end.

Doyle (2000: 70) has offered an alternative definition of marketing which encompasses this view:

Marketing is the management process that seeks to maximise returns to shareholders by developing and implementing strategies to build relationships of trust with high-value customers and to create a sustainable differential advantage.

This definition has the advantage of removing profitability from the equation and substituting shareholder value. It also includes a reference to the relationship marketing perspective: however, not all firms seek to build long-term relationships with customers, and in many cases it would be extremely unlikely that a long-term relationship would develop. Plastic surgeons, funeral directors and estate agents spring readily to mind. Also, many firms do extremely well dealing with a large number of low-value customers. From the viewpoint of value-based marketing, however, loyalty is important for building shareholder value since a solid group of loyal customers is part of what ensures the long-term viability of a firm. Low-value customers are frequently not loyal.

The difference in orientation between aiming for an increase in shareholder value and aiming for an increase in customer satisfaction is a small one. It is really a difference in focus rather than a new philosophy altogether: a key focus for marketers is the twofold problem of how to increase the brand value and how to cash in on the increased value in the long term. Simply harvesting profits is not the way forward – re-investing in further building of the brand, or in other ventures, is realistic and will increase shareholder value.

Chapter summary

Strategy and strategy planning are complex areas, mainly because it is difficult for firms to know where they are going and even harder to formulate a route for getting there. The conventional 'road map' analogy does not stand up well to close scrutiny: using a road map to go from one city to another works well because the cities are fixed geographically, the roads already exist and everything stays pretty much where it is while the planner moves from one place to another. This is not the case in the business world, where the goals shift, the road is frequently replaced or disappears, and in most cases the planner actually has to build the road in any case. Business strategy has little in common with motorway driving: it is much more like white-water rafting, where rocks may suddenly appear, water is pouring into the boat, everybody on board is screaming at once and the paddle is less than adequate to steer the boat.

Key points

- Strategic planning is an iterative process, not a linear one.
- There is no single rule for creating strategic plans.
- Formal planning is only typical of firms in stable industries: firms operating in conditions of change are more likely to use adaptive strategic change.
- Aims are general: objectives are specific and measurable.
- There are three basic winning strategies: overall cost leadership, differentiation and focus. They are mutually exclusive.
- Leaders defend, challengers attack, followers avoid conflict.
- Most new products fail, so safety lies in being a follower – and profitability may also be greater as a follower.
- Collaboration may be better than competition.
- Management's key objective may be increasing shareholder value rather than creating profits.

Review questions

1. Under what circumstances would a company not bother with developing a strategic plan?
2. What is the role of the marketing audit?
3. Why might a laggard strategy be a safe alternative?
4. What are the key differences between market leader strategies and market follower strategies?
5. In terms of Porter's categories of strategic position, why would a combination strategy be a failing strategy?
6. Under what circumstances would a collaboration with competitors be dangerous?
7. What is the connection between increasing shareholder value and customer centrality?
8. How might a company quantify an aim such as 'provide the best service in the industry?'
9. What is the role of commitment level in deciding strategy?
10. Explain the key elements of value-based marketing.

Case study revisited: Las Vegas

During the 1950s and 1960s prosperity in the United States rose dramatically: lacking any natural resources apart from 3800 hours of sunshine a year, the city authorities in Las Vegas realised that their only real hope lay in attracting tourists.

The city (and the State of Nevada) therefore prioritised attracting leisure businesses. This meant that the city had to have very relaxed rules about drinking, gambling and (to an extent) public decency. While they drew the line at legalising prostitution (it is illegal in Las Vegas and Reno, despite being legal in the rest of Nevada), gambling is legal, there is no State income tax or corporation tax, and the drinking laws are very liberal – alcohol is cheaper in Las Vegas than almost anywhere else. Glittering variety shows featuring scantily-clad showgirls are commonplace, and entry is often free provided the customer gambles. Even the railroad station was housed in a casino until Amtrak closed down the service.

As gambling has proved to be less popular, and competition has arisen from other sources (perhaps surprisingly, from Native American reservations, which are self-governing and therefore can run casinos), Las Vegas has had to adapt. Marriage and divorce are extremely easy in Las Vegas, and the city hosts an average 115,000 weddings a year – around 5% of all weddings in the United States. Divorce statistics are harder to come by, because the state does not record who has travelled to Las Vegas (or Reno) specifically for a divorce and who is normally resident in the state: state law requires prospective divorcees to live for at least six weeks in the state. This, of course, boosts Las Vegas' income even more: it still works out cheaper to spend six weeks in Las Vegas and have a quickie divorce than to get divorced in California.

In recent years a major development to the south of the city has made the Las Vegas Strip less popular, and it has become somewhat run-down. The city council therefore offered incentives to businesses to relocate to the area. The first to move was the Internal Revenue Service, which now has offices within walking distance of some of the world's most famous casinos. The city council has seen the writing on the wall, though – tourism is in decline as people travel outside the United States, and so the council is encouraging other businesses into the city. The council bought 61 acres of land from the Union Pacific Railroad in order to build the biggest furniture retail park in the United States, and has plans for a similar jewellery park; the site also will have apartment buildings and office buildings, a medical research facility and concert halls.

Las Vegas has always been more of a pick-up truck destination than a limousine destination, but the city council sees the future in mainstream businesses and retirement homes rather than in tacky shows and casinos. This strategic repositioning of Las Vegas will take time – but the city has a long history of creating something from nothing, so success is definitely on the cards.

Case study: Brittany Ferries

Brittany is a fairly remote part of France, on the far northwestern tip of the country. Many Bretons regard themselves as being entirely separate from France: their Celtic heritage and separate language (which is closer to Welsh and Gaelic than to French) means that they are virtually a separate nation.

Brittany itself is rugged, and relies on tourism and agriculture to earn its living. Apart from the big naval base at Brest, there is little else – and certainly in the days before mass foreign tourism the region relied on growing artichokes and onions. In 1973 local farmers got together and decided to establish a freight ferry link between Roscoff (which had opened up as a deep-water port) and Plymouth, in the south-west of England. The new ferry service would open up the UK market for Breton produce – Plymouth is much nearer to Roscoff than is Paris, so the new market should prove successful. Britain had joined what was then the European Common Market on 1 January 1973, so there were few trade barriers for Breton produce.

Such was the success of the new route that the company introduced a passenger and freight ship the following year, and began to look for new routes: the *Cornouaille* entered service in 1977, and new routes were opened to St Malo, Santander and Cork. Brittany Ferries collaborated with Swansea–Cork Ferries to operate routes between Cork and Roscoff.

During the 1980s and 1990s the company established routes to Normandy, via Cherbourg and Caen. On these routes they were in direct competition with P&O ferries running from Portsmouth to Le Havre, and from Newhaven to Dieppe. Brittany Ferries decided not to compete on price, but instead to compete on quality of service: by this time the company was doing far more business ferrying holidaymakers than it was carrying artichokes, so it aimed to have exceptional ships. The vessels were fitted out to a very high standard, much like cruise ships, with original artworks in the public areas, well-equipped cabins, on-board entertainment and (on the Santander route) marine biologists to help passengers identify the whales and dolphins they would see in the Bay of Biscay. The restaurants on board were, of course, French and therefore excellent. The à la carte restaurant produced food that would not disgrace a Michelin-starred restaurant, but each ship also had a self-service restaurant for those with more modest budgets.

During the early 21st century P&O withdrew from the Western Channel routes, selling some to LD Lines, a French company that operated mainly freight ferries. LD aimed to compete on price, but again Brittany Ferries kept to its strategy and remained the upmarket alternative, offering value for money rather than cheapness. In 2004 the *Pont-Aven* was introduced to the fleet, running to Santander and Cork. This vessel was faster and bigger than anything then in use. Only slightly smaller than the Titanic, *Pont-Aven* can carry 2400 passengers and 650 cars. There are 600 cabins on board, ranging from two-berth cabins up to Commodore suites with their own private balcony. The ship has a swimming pool, two cinemas, three restaurants, three bars and a nightclub. The crossing to Santander from Plymouth takes only 20 hours, much less than it would take to drive the same distance (taking account of an overnight stop) so the growing group of British people with holiday homes in Spain can shuttle between the UK and Spain without getting absolutely exhausted.

In 2012 the company suffered a damaging labour dispute: following a series of wildcat strikes, the company cancelled all sailings until an agreement could be reached with crew members. However, Brittany Ferries made arrangements with other carriers to honour tickets, and also recompensed those whose crossings had been cancelled. In this way they maintained the goodwill of passengers – most people were very impressed with the way the company had dealt with the crisis, and were happy to book again.

Brittany Ferries relies heavily on repeat custom, and operates a 'Travel Club'. Travel Club members pay an annual fee that entitles them to discounts on crossings, free breakfast on overnight crossings and rewards for recommendations (cleverly, Brittany Ferries gives a discount to any friends of Club members, so that Club members can enjoy doing a friend a favour as well as gaining a small reward). The Travel Club especially appeals to people with holiday homes, since they use the ferries frequently on the same routes: Brittany Ferries therefore also operates a holiday home letting service, which again increases potential business since the company can bundle the ferry crossing in with the booking.

Given the exceptional loyalty shown by Brittany Ferries customers, the company has a secure future. The customers are not especially price-sensitive, so provided the on-board service continues to be of the same high standard, the company is likely to go from strength to strength.

Questions

1. How has Brittany Ferries used collaboration with other ferry companies?
2. How has strategy evolved at Brittany Ferries?
3. What are the key strategic factors in Brittany Ferries' success?
4. What were the drivers for establishing a passenger car ferry service?
5. What is the company's strategic position against LD Lines, and against the Channel Tunnel?

Further reading

For general reading on management strategy, John L. Thompson's *Strategic Management* (London: Thomson Business Press, 1997) provides a very good, comprehensive overview.

For greater depth on marketing strategy, *Marketing Strategy* by Jim Blythe (Maidenhead: McGraw Hill, 2003) is a concise and reader-friendly text. For even greater detail, *Marketing: Planning and Strategy* by Subhash Jain (Cincinatti, OH: South-Western, 2000) covers the subject admirably.

References

Ambler, Tim and Roberts, John H. (2008) Assessing marketing performance: don't settle for a silver metric. *Journal of Marketing Management*, 24 (7/8): 733–50.

Ansoff, H.I. (1968) *Corporate Strategy*. Harmondsworth: Penguin.

Ansoff, H.I. (1984) *Implementing Strategic Management*. Harlow: Prentice Hall.

Ansoff, H. Igor (1984) *Implementing Strategic Management.* Harlow: Prentice Hall.

Black, Andrew, Wright, Philip and Bachman, John E. (1998) *In Search of Shareholder Value*. London: Pitman.

Booms, B.H. and Bitner, M.J. (1981) Marketing strategies and organisation structures for service firms. In J. Donnelly and W.R. George (eds), *Marketing of Services*. Chicago, IL: American Marketing Association.

Bradley, N. and Blythe, J. (eds) (2013) *Demarketing*. Abingdon: Routledge.

Brady, J. and Davis, I. (1993) Marketing's mid-life crisis. *The McKinsey Quarterly*, No. 2.

Clifford, D.K. and Cavanagh, R.E. (1985) *The Winning Performance: How America's High- and Mid-size Growth Companies Succeed.* New York: Bantam.

Collins, J. and Porras, J.I. (1994) *Built to Last: Successful Habits of Visionary Companies*. New York: Harper Business.

De Geus, Arie (1997) *The Living Company*. Boston, MA: Harvard Business School Press.

Doyle, P. (2000) *Value-Based Marketing: Marketing Strategies for Corporate Growth and Shareholder Value*. London: Wiley.

Haines, D.W., Chandran, R. and Parkhe, A. (1989) Winning by being first to market ... Or last? *Journal of Consumer Marketing*, Winter: 63–9.

Hamel, G., Doz, Y. and Prahalad, C.K. (1989) Collaborate with your competitors – and win. *Harvard Business Review*, 67 (1): 135–9.

Hennart, J.F., Roehl, T. and Zeitlow, D.S. (1999) Trojan horse or workhorse? The evolution of US–Japanese joint ventures in the United States. *Strategic Management Journal*, 20: 15–29.

Homburg, C., Krohmer, H. and Workman J.P. Jr (1999) Strategic consensus and performance: the role of strategy type and market related dynamism. *Strategic Management Journal*, 20 (4): 339–57.

Osarenkhoe, Aihie (2010) A study of inter-firm dynamics between competition and co-operation – a coopetition strategy. *Journal of Database Marketing and Customer Strategy Management*, 17 (3–4): 201–21.

Piercy, N. and Cravens, D.W. (1999) Marketing organisation and management. In *Encyclopaedia of Marketing.* London: International Thomson Business Press. pp. 186–207.

Porter, M.E. (1985) *Competitive Advantage.* New York: Free Press.

Porter, M.E. (1998) *Competitive Strategy: Techniques for Analysing Industries and Competitors.* New York: Free Press.

Stacey, R.D. (1993) Strategy as order emerging from chaos. *Long Range Planning*, 26 (1): 10–17.

Steiner, G. and Miner, J. (1977) *Management Policy and Strategy: Text, Readings and Cases.* New York: Macmillan.

Thompson, John L. (1997) *Strategic Management: Awareness and Change.* London: Thomson.

Tse, Alan C.B., Sin, Leo Y.M., Yau, Oliver H.M., Lee, Jenny S.Y. and Chow, Raymond (2004) A firm's role in the marketplace and the relative importance of market orientation and relationship marketing orientation. *European Journal of Marketing*, 38 (9/10): 1158–72.

Webster, E. (1992) The changing role of marketing in the corporation. *Journal of Marketing*, 56 (4): 1–17.

More online

To gain free access to additional online resources to support this chapter please visit:
www.sagepub.co.uk/blythe3e

CHAPTER ⑩
Marketing ethics and corporate social responsibility

LEARNING OBJECTIVES

After reading this chapter, you should be able to:

- Explain the elements of corporate responsibility.

- Describe the basis of ethical behaviour.

- Compare different philosophies of ethical behaviour.

- Apply ethical considerations to specific circumstances.

- Develop an ethics policy.

- Explain some of the ethical problems faced by marketers.

Companies are under considerable pressure to act in an ethical and socially responsible manner. The proliferation of the Internet and greater levels of education among the general population mean that bad behaviour is quickly exposed and disseminated; also, the Internet makes it very easy for pressure groups to organise themselves. Corporations that avoid their rightful tax obligations, or employ child labour, or use bribery to win orders will soon be exposed and punished by consumers, even if legal sanctions are avoided.

Apart from the fear of getting caught, companies try to be socially responsible and act ethically because that is what the people working for the companies would prefer. Companies are made up of people, most of whom like to act honestly and ethically. Whatever pressures employees are under to meet targets or win new business they still prefer to be able to sleep at night – not to mention that those who act unethically are likely to be under pressure from colleagues.

Social responsibility and ethics

Social responsibility is about ensuring that the company acts within the accepted morals of the society in which it operates, as well as within the moral code of the employees and managers. The view that companies should exercise a responsible approach and consider their relationships

Preview case study: Bhopal

On 2 December 1984 over 40 tons of lethal chemical gas was released into the air from the Union Carbide chemical factory in Bhopal, India. The accident was caused by water entering a tank containing chemicals: the resulting chemical reaction generated great heat and vented the poisonous gases into the atmosphere. As a result, thousands of people in the area were killed – estimates vary between 3800 and 8000 – and hundreds of thousands have suffered ill health ever since.

Union Carbide was held accountable by the world's press and the company was widely criticised by environmental groups. Union Carbide was seen as being slow to pay compensation, slow to make reparations at the plant and slow to implement a clean-up operation. Often the American parent company was accused of not caring simply because the victims were Indian.

Union Carbide has pointed out that only 51% of the plant was owned by the company, the rest being owned by the Indian government (26%) and private shareholders (23%). The Bhopal plant was staffed and managed entirely by Indians. In 1989 an Indian court ordered Union Carbide to pay US$470m in damages, in full and final settlement, and the company did so, but the trouble has not gone away. Campaigners say that birth defects in the area are caused by chemicals from the plant. This is denied by Union Carbide, who say that soil contamination is caused by chemicals that were never used at the plant, and that close interbreeding (a feature of marriages in the Bhopal area) is what is causing the birth defects. The US company denies any liability whatsoever, and has the backing of the Second Circuit Court of Appeals in Manhattan, which ruled in 1987 that the case belongs solely in India and the US company has no liability whatsoever. The Indian government was held partly liable and has bought health insurance for the 100,000 people who are thought to have been affected – but this health cover is woefully inadequate, considering the scale and nature of people's illnesses.

with society at large is part of the societal marketing philosophy (see Chapter 1) but is also an important part of maintaining good public relations.

Ethics are the principles that define right and wrong. Ethical thinking divides into the **teleological** (the belief that acts should be defined as ethical or otherwise according to the outcome of the acts) and the **deontological** (that acts can be defined as ethical or unethical regardless of the outcome). The teleological approach implies that the end can justify the means, in other words that an act that has a good outcome for most people can be justified, even when the act itself is damaging to some people. Teleology is concerned with the greatest good of the greatest number, which apparently seems reasonable but can lead to the oppression of minorities. For example, a firm that uses child labour in developing countries to manufacture its products might argue that the good of its other employees, its shareholders and its customers is best served by exploiting the poverty of a few hundred children, and within the teleological philosophy this argument would hold water, yet few people would regard such behaviour as moral or ethical.

The deontological approach is best summarised by Kant's Categorical Imperative, which states that each act should be based on reasons that everyone could act on, and that actions must be based on reasons that the decision-maker would accept for others to use. The problem with deontology is that it involves considerable practical

Ethics A set of rules for good behaviour.

Teleology The belief that acts can be judged by their outcomes.

Deontology The belief that actions can be judged independent of the outcome.

difficulties. For example, it implies that a company whose directors are able to gain a competitive advantage by misleading a competitor should also accept that their financial manager should be able to gain a personal advantage by misleading the company's auditors.

In most cases marketers do not become enmeshed in the philosophical arguments about ethics, but rely instead on the moral rules that are part of the corporate culture. Most business people have separate sets of ethics for their behaviour in work and at home (Fraedrich 1988) and corporations develop their own cultures and schemes of ethics. Where these accord broadly with the personal ethical values of the employees there will be less tension in the workplace – most employees would prefer to work for firms they consider to be ethical.

Many firms adopt codes of ethics. These lay down the rules by which the company operates, and these may be enshrined in a mission statement or corporate guidelines, intended to guide employees and to flag up to outsiders what the company's core values are. Carrying out good deeds does not guarantee customer acceptance, however: sometimes consumers become suspicious of companies, especially if there is a poor fit between the company's image and the cause it promotes (Becker-Olsen and Cudmore 2004). In some cases, a socially responsible initiative carried out in one country backfires when the firm tries to act in the same way in another country, as happened when McDonald's tried to establish a Ronald McDonald House in Norway. Although these houses are established to benefit sick children, the action met with resistance from politicians, academics and the general public, to the extent that McDonald's abandoned the exercise (Bronn 2006).

In Figure 10.1 the firm's ethical environment is broken down into five basic components. Terpstra and David (1991) describe the corporate structure as being the lines of command, the formal administrative structures such as the organisation chart, and the assignment of authority, responsibility and information flow. The ways in which the structure is created and adapted are also relevant here: for example, Richer Sounds is a firm that finds new employees through word of mouth from existing employees. If a vacancy arises, it will be filled by someone who is a friend or relative of an existing employee. Within the firm, this is seen as a highly commendable and very effective way of ensuring that everyone works well together, within a pleasant social environment. However, if this practice were to be adopted in a local authority or a government office

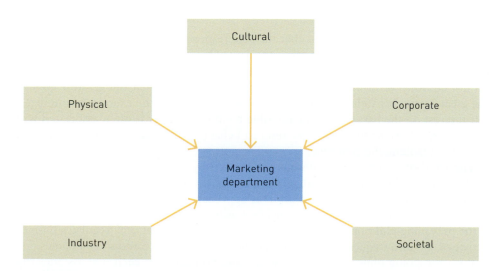

Figure 10.1   The ethical environment (adapted from Terpstra and David 1991)

it would be regarded as highly unethical. Government jobs are supposed to be open to all applicants, and giving jobs to relatives would go against the government's Equal Opportunities rules.

The societal environment includes social relationships as well as the broader responsibilities towards society at large. Within the societal environment the firm would need to consider its near neighbours to ensure that its activities did not impact adversely on them (for example creating noise pollution near an office complex), the ecology and its employment practices.

Industry considerations would include industry-wide codes of practice, fair competition, fair dealing with supply chain members such as suppliers and customers, and so forth. In some industries there are trade associations which lay down these rules, whereas in others the systems of behaviour develop as industry norms.

Corporate culture has been described as 'the way we do things round here'. The corporate culture often develops over time, but can be directed by a charismatic founder or head of the company. Entrepreneurs such as Richard Branson or Alan Sugar have stamped their personalities on their organisations: in an earlier era, the Quaker Rowntree family set up their chocolate-making firm around Quaker religious principles that still colour the corporate culture to this day.

The physical environment is largely concerned with ecological issues, but also includes issues such as the exploitation of limited resources. For example, the world diamond trade is controlled by a very few companies, since diamonds are found in any quantities only in South Africa and Russia. These companies maintain the price of diamonds on the market by controlling the supply, in much the same way as the major oil-producing nations fix the price of oil. On the other hand, opals (which virtually all come from Australia) are free-mined, in other words no restrictions are allowed on their mining and supply. Maintaining the value of diamonds means that there is stability of supply, and the end customers know that they have bought something of lasting value: the price of opals, on the other hand, fluctuates wildly according to whether the miners happen to have had a lucky strike. This means that opal mining is actually a high-risk business, unlike diamond mining which is stable.

Three basic views of corporate ethical stances have been identified (Goodpaster and Matthews 1982). These are as follows:

1. The invisible hand.
2. The hand of government.
3. The hand of management.

The invisible hand philosophy is that the sole responsibility of businesses is to make profits for their shareholders, within the law. This philosophy, often expressed by economists such as Milton Friedman, says that the marketplace will punish firms that do not conform or do not behave in acceptable ways, and that the greatest good of the greatest number (teleological approach) will result from the exercise of intelligent self-interest on the part of all. The invisible hand philosophy is often associated with right-wing governments, since they tend to believe in free-market forces as the best way of controlling the economy.

The hand of government philosophy, expressed by such people as economist John Galbraith, describes a system in which firms pursue economic objectives within a system of control developed by government. This approach has become more prominent in the early 21st century, with governments exercising more controls over corporations. It is the prevailing philosophy in Sweden, where government not only regulates business activities, but also frequently has large shareholdings in major Swedish companies.

Both foregoing philosophies have some common ground: each one assumes that morality and ethics have to be imposed on businesses from the outside, either by market forces or by government intervention. The third approach described by Goodpaster and Matthew is one by which corporations set their own morality, in a formalised structure that lays down the ethical stance of the company. In other words, executives (and indeed other employees) are not expected to work out their own ethical stances, but are shown the way by management. The hand of management approach therefore states that ethical and moral rules are generated from within the firm.

In some cases, of course, companies are founded because of ethical principles. These are not necessarily charities – Rowntree's has already been mentioned, and The Body Shop was started as an ethical response to large cosmetics companies. The John Lewis Partnership was founded as a response to the oppressive employment practices then in place. The aim of John Lewis (which operates 39 John Lewis department stores and 290 Waitrose supermarkets) is to ensure the happiness and wellbeing of the 85,000 partners who own and work in the stores – yet despite this staff-centred business model, the firm is hugely successful and very popular with customers.

In practice, managements need to strike a balance between the three approaches. Quite clearly government regulation plays a part in every business decision, but so does the imperative to make money for the shareholders. For marketers, the customer's interests come high up the list of priorities, so marketers are well aware that the market will punish unethical behaviour.

For marketers, there are specific customer-based issues that will impinge on ethical principles. Some examples are shown in Table 10.1.

Firms often establish ethical statements to guide employees. Figure 10.2 shows the Johnson & Johnson Credo.

ECOLOGICAL ENVIRONMENT

One of the key issues in social responsibility in recent years has been concern for the environment. Consumers consider the origins, content and manufacturing processes of the products they buy much more than they did in previous years, and therefore producers are concerned to be seen as being environmentally friendly. While adherence to the principles of environmentalism might be patchy and at times contradictory, there is little doubt that marketers need to take account of the feelings of consumers on this issue.

There are several sources of pressure for environmentalism. These are as follows:

1. Customers. The majority of customers in developed countries use some environmental criteria in making purchase decisions. These range from concern about the energy efficiency of appliances through to requiring assurances about the manufacturing processes involved in producing goods.
2. Green pressure groups. Pressure groups are organisations that conduct campaigns to influence policy and public opinion. In the environmentalist area, such groups carry out three main activities: first, they aim to provide information about environmental issues and bring these to the attention of the public and the policy-making bodies. Second, some groups (notably Greenpeace) take direct action against organisations they perceive as being environmentally damaging. Such action ranges from peaceful protests through to driving steel spikes into trees to damage chainsaws, or hindering the progress of a vessel at sea by sailing across its course. Third, environmentalist groups offer consultation and consultancy about the environmental impact of proposed developments. Using these services can be a useful way for firms to avoid the negative consequences of (perhaps innocently) implementing a new development that impacts the environment negatively.

Table 10.1 Examples of ethical problems for marketers

Problem	Explanation
Products	These should be honestly made and described. Commercial pressures may encourage firms to use cheaper materials or to use inappropriate additives, but customers should be informed of these changes – the horsemeat scandal in Europe (in which horsemeat was found in ready meals and beef burgers) during the early part of 2013 demonstrated this graphically.
Promotion	Advertising is often accused of being misleading, and firms should obviously try to avoid this. Within the UK the advertising industry is policed by the Advertising Standards Authority, which is an example of an industry-based regulatory authority. The ASA is independent of government, and polices the industry using the criteria 'legal, decent, honest and truthful'. In practice the ASA operates by responding to complaints from the public: it does not usually intervene unless the marketplace responds unfavourably to an advert. While a certain amount of advertising 'puff' is acceptable, it is clearly not acceptable to tell outright lies or even to use misleading phrases.
Pricing	Price fixing and predatory pricing (pricing below the cost of production in order to bankrupt competitors) are the two main areas where pricing practices fall foul of ethical standards. Price fixing, whereby the main firms in the industry agree to maintain prices at an artificially high level, is illegal in most countries when it happens through a formal agreement. However, it often happens through tacit agreements, whereby firms are extremely careful not to provoke a price war by undercutting their competitors. Another example of unethical pricing is situations where the full price is not disclosed – for example when prices are quoted without including VAT or another sales tax. Under EU law, all restaurants must display a menu with VAT-inclusive prices outside the premises so that customers can see what they are committing themselves to before they sit down. Even so, small print sometimes includes service charges which are not made apparent when the food is ordered. Similarly, some opticians fail to mention that the prices displayed are for the frames only – lenses cost extra.
Distribution	Abuse of power in managing distribution channels and failing to pay for goods within the specified credit terms of the supplier are both regarded as unethical, but frequently occur anyway. For example, several retailers operate no-quibble sale-or-return contracts that require suppliers to take back damaged goods even when there is no fault in the manufacture. This has been seen as unethical by some small manufacturers who have little bargaining power and few outlets for their products, even though it is seen as only fair and right by consumers.

3. Employees. Increasingly, employees are acting to improve the environmental credentials of the firms they work for. In some cases (for example research and development staff and production engineers) they are able to act directly. In other cases employees have lobbied management or have even become 'whistle-blowers' and taken their concerns to the news media.

4. Legislation. Politicians respond to the views of their constituents, and therefore will enact legislation concerning the environment. In some countries environmentalist political parties are powerful parliamentary groups in their own right (notably in The Netherlands and Germany). Pressure for legislation and regulation can also come from the industries themselves. This is because firms that wish to be environmentally friendly recognise that there are costs attached, and they do not want to be placed in an uncompetitive position against firms that ignore environmental issues. Legislation helps to ensure a level playing field.

5. Media. Most news media will report issues of environmental concern. Major oil spills and forest fires have always made the headlines, but in recent years

Our Credo

We believe that our first responsibility is to the doctors, nurses and patients, to mothers and fathers and to all others who use our products and services. In meeting their needs everything we do must be of high quality. We must constantly strive to reduce our costs in order to maintain reasonable prices. Customers' orders must be serviced promptly and accurately. Our suppliers and distributors must have an opportunity to make a fair profit.

We are responsible to our employees, the men and women who work with us throughout the world. Everyone must be considered as an individual. We must respect their dignity and recognise their merit. They must have a sense of security in their jobs. Compensation must be fair and adequate, and working conditions clean, orderly and safe. We must be mindful of ways to help our employees fulfil their family responsibilities. Employees must feel free to make suggestions and complaints. There must be equal opportunity for employment, development and advancement for those qualified. We must provide competent management and their actions must be just and ethical.

We are responsible for the communities in which we live and work and to the world community as well. We must be good citizens – support good works and charities and bear our fair share of taxes. We must encourage civic improvements and better health and education. We must maintain in good order the property we are privileged to use, protecting the environment and natural resources.

Our final responsibility is to our stockholders. Business must make a sound profit. We must experiment with new ideas. Research must be carried on, innovative programs developed and mistakes paid for. New equipment must be purchased, new facilities provided and new products launched. Reserves must be created to provide for adverse times. When we operate according to these principles, the stockholders should realize a fair return.

Figure 10.2   Johnson & Johnson Credo

stories about species extinction, wetlands draining and development, and other somewhat more obscure and less dramatic issues have also been reported widely. This means that firms can easily find themselves the subject of unwanted media attention.

6. Ethical investment. Some banks and unit trust funds now offer ethical investment packages, allowing their customers to specify that they want their money to be invested only in projects with impeccable environmental and ethical credentials. Environmentally active investors are thus able to influence the funding of 'green' projects, making it marginally easier for firms to raise the necessary finance for environmentally friendly projects.

Green customers can be segmented according to their degree of involvement in environmentalism. First, '**green activists**' are those who are members of, or supporters of, environmental pressure groups. These people are the most environmentally active, and are the most likely to make purchasing decisions on the basis of environmental issues. The second group are the '**green thinkers**'. These customers seek out environmentally friendly products and try to live in an environmentally friendly way. Again, this group will base their purchasing decisions on the environmental credentials of the firm and its products. The third group is the '**green customers**'. These people have changed their behaviour in some way to be more environmentally

Green activist One who is proactive in espousing an environmentally friendly lifestyle.

Green thinker One who believes in being environmentally friendly.

Green customer One whose purchases are influenced by environmental concerns.

friendly, for example by recycling, but have not made a radical change in their life-styles. Some decisions will be based on environmental concerns, but these consumers are as likely to override their environmental concerns when other considerations (such as price) intervene. Extroversion (the degree to which people want to be seen to be doing good), agreeableness (the degree to which people want to get on with other people) and conscientiousness (the degree to which someone wants to 'do the right thing') are the key variables in environmentally friendly consumption (Fraj and Martinez 2006).

Generally concerned One who believes that the environment is important, but does little to change his or her behaviour accordingly.

The final group is the '**generally concerned**' group. Currently, this group is thought to be the largest segment of the market. These people claim to concerned about the environment, but have made few if any concessions to it in terms of their purchasing behaviour. In general, this group will not act in an environmentally friendly manner unless they are forced to by legislation, or it becomes cheaper to do so. For example, when unleaded petrol was first introduced sales were extremely low, and motor manufacturers were unwilling to adapt cars to run on unleaded fuel when availability throughout the country was so low. Equally, oil companies were unwilling to invest in increased distribution when relatively few cars could run on the new fuel. The UK government, in common with many other governments worldwide, broke the impasse by giving a substantial tax break on the fuel, making it an average 5p a litre cheaper. This kick-started the move to unleaded, and now all petrol-driven cars throughout Europe use it. Leaded fuel is no longer available except through special outlets.

There is of course a group of people who are alienated by the environmental movement. These people see environmentalism as a passing fad, are pessimistic about the solutions, and are unlikely to be swayed by environmentalist claims on products. In general, this group are less educated, tend to be young families or elderly people, and also tend to lean to the left politically (Bennett and Williams, 2011).

The response of marketers to environmental issues has occurred on several levels. At the lowest level, marketers have implied that their products have environmentalist credentials without actually making any changes to the products themselves. The use of words like 'recyclable' on packaging may be truthful in a strict sense, but this places the responsibility on the consumer to send the packaging for recycling, which is unlikely to happen since most consumers fall within the 'generally concerned' group. The problem with operating at this superficial level is that many consumers have become aware of this approach and suspicious of it. In general, people resent being manipulated, and the use of misleading wording is likely to be counterproductive.

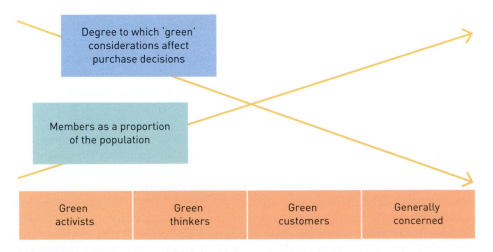

Figure 10.3   Degrees of environmental involvement

At the next level, marketers have made real changes to the product, its packaging or its manufacture in order to accommodate environmentalist principles. These changes can range from using recycled paper to package the product through to a fundamental redesign of the product.

At the highest level the firm will examine all its activities throughout the supply chain from raw materials to finished product, and will conduct an environmental impact study. Currently, relatively few firms do this, but some (notably The Body Shop) have managed to make a virtue of this approach and have become extremely successful by positioning themselves as ethical marketers. This approach will only work if consumers are prepared to support it, since there are likely to be substantial cost implications.

Some issues have been prominent in the environmentalist movement. Figure 10.4 shows some of these.

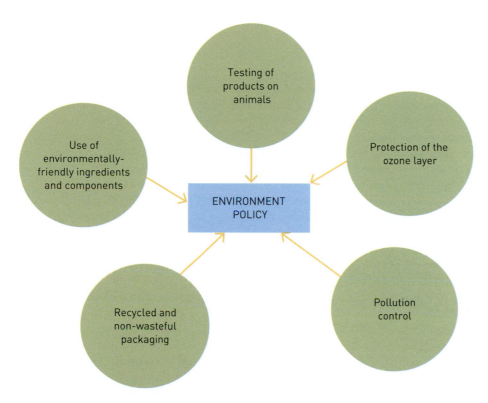

Figure 10.4   Issues in environmentalism

Use of environmentally friendly components and ingredients

In general, environmentalists encourage manufacturers to use ingredients and components that are environmentally friendly. This means the sources of the ingredients should be sustainable, should be recycled, recyclable or bio-degradable, and the manufacturing processes involved should not in themselves be polluting or otherwise damaging.

Sustainable sourcing means, for example, that wood and paper should come from managed forests, not from virgin forest. Many magazine and newspaper publishers tell their readers that two trees are planted for each tree cut to make newsprint, and furniture manufacturers typically label wooden furniture to explain that the wood comes from sustainable forests.

Cosmetics companies also emphasise the use of naturally occurring products such as aloe vera and vegetable oils rather than animal products.

Think outside this box!

Saying that wood comes from managed forests is all very well, but is this really environmentally friendly? Should we be planting millions of acres of forest simply to make yet another magazine, when people are starving? Or should we be using irreplaceable oil to make unleaded petrol? Or even biodegradable plastics?

Or maybe there is more to life than just feeding ourselves. Maybe it's important for us to have cosmetics, and cheap transportation, and news about our world, and entertainment. But is it environmentally friendly?

In recent years, the European Union has encouraged projects that reduce the EU's dependence on oil for fuel. This is largely because most EU countries do not have their own oil reserves: apart from Britain's North Sea holdings, there are few sources within the EU. One of the results of this has been the development of bio-fuel, which is diesel fuel produced from oilseed. While this fuel burns more cleanly than mineral oil, it requires a large acreage of land for its growth, and experiments have resulted in large areas of land becoming bright yellow as the oilseeds flower. Producing one ton of this biofuel requires 0.77 hectares of land (European Biomass Industry Association 2012). This is enough land to feed a family for a year, but one ton of biodiesel fuel is not enough to run a large lorry for a week. The EU's target was for biofuel to account for 5% of total fuel consumption by 2010 (Commission of the European Communities 2002) but this target was missed by a small margin, and in 2012 the EU Commission announced plans to cap the use of biofuel in order to protect food stocks. In 2008, the UK government's chief scientist warned that producing biofuel on a large scale would adversely affect world food supplies, creating more famines.

Meanwhile, in the United States 1.1 billion gallons of biodiesel was produced in 2011, comfortably exceeding the Environmental Protection Agency's targets. Biodiesel production created 39,000 jobs and $2.1 billion in household expenditures (National Biodiesel Board 2013). This demonstrates that environmentalism brings solid economic advantages as well as improvements in the quality of people's lives.

RECYCLED, RECYCLABLE AND NON-WASTEFUL PACKAGING

Marketers have come in for much criticism about the quantity and type of packaging used for products. Packaging is intended to keep the contents safe from the external environment, and vice versa, but marketers also use packaging as a promotional tool, making products stand out on retailers' shelves. Because modern packaging often uses several different types of material (plastics, paper and metal might all be used in a single package) recycling can be problematical. One-way bottles (bottles that are not returned to the bottling company for refilling) were introduced in the late 1960s and have contributed greatly to the quantity of packaging which finds its way into landfill sites rather than being recycled. The reason for using one-way bottles is that it is cheaper and less time-consuming to make a new bottle than it is to collect, wash and refill existing bottles. Interestingly, in the 1950s almost all bottles were returned because customers paid a substantial deposit on the bottle, refunded by the retailer when the bottle was returned.

Real-life marketing: Use the packaging!

Most of the time marketers think of packaging as a way of protecting the contents from damage, and protecting the environment from the contents. More astute marketers will use the packaging as a promotional device, perhaps to plug other products or to carry ideas on how to use the product, but mostly that's as far as it goes.

With a bit of thought, though, you can often find something really good to do with the packaging. Two examples come from French marketers. First, Amora brand Dijon mustard is packaged in drinking glasses – there are wine glasses, tumblers and shot glasses, all filled with bright-yellow mustard, and with plastic snap-on caps to keep the mustard fresh once opened. The result is that people use the glasses either to drink from or as containers for left-overs and sauces in their fridges. The glasses are, of course, very basic and made from cheap glass, but they are fine for everyday use, and nobody cares much if one gets broken. It doesn't add to the cost of the mustard, either – a big glass of mustard still costs around a euro.

The other example comes from Evian, the mineral-water producer. This one was more accidental – the company decided to package its water in crushable plastic bottles, to reduce the volume in recycling containers. The unexpected consequence was that people enjoyed crushing the bottles – rather like popping bubble wrap, the crushing process was somehow intensely satisfying – and sales of the product increased as a result.

Note that in both cases the companies have the moral high ground as far as their green credentials are concerned – it is obviously much more environmentally friendly to use the mustard pack as it is, rather than melt it down and use the glass to make something else.

To do this in the real world, you should do the following:

- Watch what people do with the packaging. Do they use it in some way (as a container, as a plant pot, whatever) or do they simply dump it?
- Think of ways the packaging can add value, without making it too difficult to fit onto a retailer's shelf.
- Try to create a USP with the packaging – it might be the only USP you have!

Almost all packaging has the potential for recycling, either by using recycled materials in the packaging or by recycling the packaging after use. This would reduce the need for importing raw materials, and would also reduce the need for landfill sites for dumping rubbish.

Recycling of packaging is likely to become of even greater importance in the future as raw materials become rarer. The cost of using landfill sites is likely to rise as suitable sites are filled, and at the same time recycling technology can be expected to improve. In the meantime, marketers are faced with the problem of continuing to make products interesting and appealing without creating an excessive amount of wasteful packaging. The degree to which people can be persuaded to recycle when they dispose of their possessions depends largely on their personalities – packrats (people who tend to hang on to their possessions) attach more meaning to their possessions than do purgers (people who dispose of goods regularly). Packrats think that purgers are wasteful, and see themselves as thrifty, whereas purgers see packrats as being messy and disorganised (Coulter and Ligas 2003).

Protecting the ozone layer

The ozone layer is a protective layer of ozone gas which encircles the Earth and protects it from excessive radiation from the sun. Chlorofluorocarbons (CFCs) are a group of gases formerly used in aerosols and the manufacture of insulating materials. CFCs have the effect of combining with ozone and thus destroying it. World agreement was reached in Montreal in 1990 to phase out production of CFCs by 2000, but this target was not achieved: additionally, foam insulation which has CFC trapped in it is still in existence throughout the world in products that were made before the ban came into effect. It is likely to be many years before the situation is rectified and CFCs are finally removed from the environment.

The lesson to be learned is that companies need to be prepared for the possibility that a product that appears innocuous may have a hidden danger. Marketers need to be prepared for this possibility, since changes to products and their promotion may become necessary at any time.

Testing products on animals

Testing products on animals has been seen as a way of minimising the risk to humans. This has been particularly the case with products such as shampoos and cosmetics which come into prolonged contact with the skin or may even be swallowed. Animal rights activists have protested at what they see as the unnecessary deaths of animals in these experiments, especially the notorious LD50 test in which a group of animals is fed the product until half of them are dead.

In 1998 the European Coalition to End Animal Experiments drew up an International Standard on 'Not tested on animals.' This international standard has been accepted by the world's animal protection pressure groups. For marketers, the standard presented an opportunity to establish the firm's animal-friendly credentials by enabling them to use the claim that their products are not tested on animals. This approach has been remarkably successful for some firms, especially in the absence of legislation: proposed European legislation banning all animal experiments has been postponed indefinitely.

Think outside this box!

Obviously nobody wants cute little animals to have shampoo put in their eyes. But isn't this better than having a damaging shampoo getting into a child's eyes? If we aren't going to test on animals, what *are* we going to test on?

Or should we maybe accept that we have enough shampoos and cosmetics, and call a halt to the 'arms race' of new products coming onto the market every day? Would it be realistic to try to prevent new product development in the cosmetics industry? Could our top models and actors manage without new cosmetics?

Maybe the little animals aren't safe just yet …

Pollution control

Preventing the escape of dangerous by-products into the environment has become a major concern in recent years. In many cases, firms have adopted **end-of-pipe solutions**, in other words they have not made substantial changes in their production processes but have instead tried to ensure that pollutants do not escape into the environment. Much of this effort has come about due to government legislation rather than through a desire to protect the environment.

A better approach, in the longer term, is likely to be a change in the process so that the polluting by-products are not produced in the first place. However, in most Western countries manufacturing industry is in the decline, and much manufacturing is carried out in developing countries where pollution is lower on the political agenda than is poverty, or job creation. This is, in itself, an ethical question for Western companies to address: on the one hand, moving production (and thus pollution) abroad solves the problem neatly. On the other hand, knowingly damaging the health of people in other countries would appear to be morally reprehensible.

End-of-pipe solution Cleaning up pollution after it has been created rather than re-engineering the process so that pollution is not produced.

Marketing in a changing world: Cleaning up

Pollution is, of course, nothing new. The problem is that most people don't want to stop what they're doing, they want somebody else to stop. The financial crisis and consequent global downturn in the economy has caused governments to backpedal on environmental commitments, due to a fear that falling living standards will lead to falling support from the electorate.

Despite the fact that the world could, without too much pain, revert to the living standards of fifty years ago and still be perfectly fine, governments are removing incentives to recycle, cutting back on environmental policing, and are reducing investment in

clean-up projects. This, then, leads to the heart of the problem: people do not vote for lower standards of living any more than turkeys vote for Christmas, and therefore pollution levels are likely to increase every time there is a business downturn, in other words about every seven years.

The next one is due around 2020. It will be interesting to see whether the next financial crisis is any different from any of the others – but at least as far as environmentalism goes, it seems unlikely.

Even service businesses create some pollution. Fast-food outlets create localised problems due to the amount of packaging they generate, but also create problems due to the amount of uneaten food that is discarded, creating a huge increase in the rat population of many cities. Cooking smells might also be considered a pollutant by many, and the smoke from frying is often greasy and unpleasant. Some fast-food chains employ people to collect discarded wrappers etc. from the immediate vicinity of the outlet, but this is an end-of-pipe solution. Other firms use biodegradable packaging, but again this introduces nutrients into the environment, resulting in problems from bacteria and rats.

From a marketing viewpoint, having a reputation for creating pollution is not good public relations: pollution damages brand values as well as the environment. Most people want to behave ethically – staff would rather work for a firm that does not pollute (especially as many of them are likely to live near their place of work) and most managers would rather not cause environmental problems. The difficulty lies in striking a balance between environmentalism and commercial considerations – in an ideal world this conflict would not exist, of course.

Ethical considerations in research

By its nature, marketing research seeks to elicit people's private thoughts and behaviour, and therefore depends heavily on establishing an atmosphere of trust and honesty between the researcher and the respondent. Unfortunately, abuse of this trust does occur, either deliberately or accidentally: Table 10.2 shows some of the possible ethical issues raised in marketing research.

As explained in Chapter 5, respondents should be made aware of the true purpose of the research, and should know that they are co-operating with a research process. This means that people who are the subjects of an experiment should be told exactly

Sugging Selling under the guise of market research.

Table 10.2   Ethical issues in marketing research

Ethical issue	Explanation
Intrusions on privacy	Most market researchers will need to know some private information about the respondents. Income, marital status, and job status are commonly asked for, but sometimes researchers need to ask intimate questions about lifestyle and attitudes. Under no circumstances should this information be divulged to anyone: no information which could be used to identify respondents should ever be disclosed under any circumstances.
Misuse of research findings	If the findings are to be used in a promotional campaign, there is an obvious temptation to bias the results in order to support the advertiser's claims. This is a problem even when an agency is used to conduct the research: the agency often realises that a failure to produce the 'right' answer will jeopardise future business relations.
Competitive information gathering	Although competitors are naturally reticent in providing information about their plans, some methods of finding out what they have in mind are clearly unethical. Industrial espionage (where, for example, an employee of the company takes a job at a competing company in order to find out what their plans are) is not illegal in the UK, but is considered to be unethical. Bribing competitors' employees to pass on sensitive information is illegal, and is certainly unethical.
Sugging (selling under the guise of marketing research)	This practice is still fairly common, and is practised by sales-orientated companies. The company representative may begin by pretending to be conducting a survey, but quickly moves into a selling mode once he or she has found out about the respondent's personal circumstances. Sugging is very damaging to genuine marketing research because it makes people less likely to trust researchers in future. Unfortunately, it is difficult to prevent – despite the fact that it rarely works effectively since people are unlikely to buy from an organisation that has demonstrated its dishonesty already.

what is going to happen and why, so that they can give their informed consent. This can, of course, affect the research adversely since it is sometimes useful if people give an unconsidered response: telling them ahead of time what they are going to be asked about is likely to bias their answers.

Individuals should never be identified in any research project. Confidentiality is an essential part of research: if people do not feel confident that their privacy will be maintained, they will either refuse to participate or (worse) will be untruthful in their answers.

As with any other ethical issue in business, managers need to consider the long-term effects of their actions. Apart from the obvious unease most people feel when being dishonest, there is the practical aspect of the potential effect on the company's reputation. Having a reputation for underhand dealing is not good for business.

Ethics and personal selling

There are several ethical problems in personal selling: an obvious one is bribery. In some countries, bribery is practically non-existent and is legally and culturally frowned upon, but in others payments ranging from small 'dash' or 'grease' payments to large special commissions have been the norm. The cost of bribery can be a major expense. According to the World Economic Forum and the World Bank, bribery costs around 5% of global GDP annually, adds 10% to the cost of doing business worldwide, and as much as 25% to procurement contracts in developing countries (Bannerman and Roberts 2012). A salesperson confronted with this has an ethical decision to make depending upon home country and host country laws and customs.

According to Terpstra and David (1991), both frontstage and backstage culture exist in every country. Frontstage culture includes the standard, normal, proper ways of doing things that insiders are willing to share with outsiders. It is relatively easy for a visiting salesperson to determine what frontstage culture is all about. This includes the question of formality versus informality in addressing new acquaintances, gift-giving traditions, the relationship between social engagement and business negotiations and so on. Backstage culture, defined as knowledge that insiders see as standard ways of doing things that they are not willing to share with outsiders, is much harder to deal with. Insiders may not want to share knowledge because the activities may be illegal or because the special knowledge gained gives the insider a competitive advantage – and very often, the most carefully guarded backstage cultural activity is the bribe or so-called 'commission'. The difficulty is always that, in many countries, officials are expected to accept bribes in order to supplement their meagre salaries: in effect, supplier companies are being asked to pay the wages bill. Thus a major cultural and economic change has to be made if the practice is to stop.

For many years, the United States was alone in enforcing strict anti-bribery regulations. The Foreign Corrupt Practices Act, which took effect in 1977, provides for fines of up to $2 million for corporations and up to $100,000 for officers, directors, stockholders, employees and agents in addition to a prison term of up to five years for those who bribe government officials to gain an advantage in securing contracts in countries outside the United States. The immediate effect was a steep drop in US business in several developing countries, so naturally some companies began to look for ways round the legislation.

In 1997, the Organization for Economic Cooperation and Development (OECD) adopted the Convention on Combating Bribery of Foreign Public Officials in International Business Transactions. The Convention recommended that OECD members enact laws to criminalise bribery activity. As of 2003, all 35 countries who signed the convention did enact the recommended laws (Report to the Senate and House of Representatives 2003). It should be noted that both the OECD Convention and the FCPA do not relieve a firm from responsibility when managers use a third party such as an agent to deliver the 'commission' to a government official. The OECD Convention also includes the proviso that legislation be adopted to eliminate the tax deductibility of bribes paid to public officials. This has been accomplished by the 35 original participant countries. Even though many Islamic countries are not OECD members, managers from those nations are prohibited from engaging in bribery or other forms of 'marketing dishonesty' by religious principles (Saeed et al. 2001).

A distinction is made between 'dash' or 'grease' payments and large-scale bribery. The former are small payments such as those made to customs officials in airports. This kind of traditional payment is not a violation of the laws in some countries, but still represents a corrupt practice and is, of course, a business cost.

In the case of bribery, laws in developed countries may obviate the ethical issues. What is illegal is almost certainly unethical and this makes the manager's decision an easy one. Nevertheless, there have been examples of questionable activity in many industries. For example, according to *The Economist* (14 June 2003), the fraud squad descended on Airbus headquarters in Toulouse, France, to 'check whether there was possible falsification of documents, bribery or other infractions as part of a [1997] sale of Airbus aircraft to Sabena' (the Belgian Airline). Sabena had purchased 34 A320s which it did not need and which 'helped trigger the airline's collapse four years later'. Until France ratified the OECD Convention in 2000, Airbus would have been permitted a tax deduction for any bribery (if it is proven they had done so). Airbus's major competitor, Boeing, has repeatedly felt it was the subject of unfair competition from Airbus but Boeing has not been immune to questions of impropriety. In November 2003, Boeing dismissed its chief financial officer and a vice president for discussions they had about a possible job offer for the latter while she was a US government official negotiating a contract with the firm (Wayne 2003).

The aircraft industry appears particularly prone to bribery accusations. Lockheed was involved in a major scandal in which bribes were paid to very high-ranking individuals, including royalty. Such bribes have a long history – even Howard Hughes admitted bribing US Air Force officers in order to sell military aircraft.

Other ethical issues arise in personal selling. Perhaps a customer has misunderstood something crucial about the products, but correcting the mistake would mean losing the sale – should the salesperson simply keep quiet, thus saving the sale and perhaps safeguarding the jobs of employees at the company, or should he or she correct the mistake and lose the sale? In practical terms it would probably be sensible to correct the mistake – the customer will find out sooner or later, and that will be the death knell for any future sales. The practical aspects do not affect the ethical dilemma though, and a teleologist would probably say that the sale should go through, because only one person will be hurt by this and many will be protected.

Salespeople have a natural tendency to tell customers what they want to hear, but this should not cross the line to being outright lying. Selling something that the salesperson knows will not meet the customer's needs, omitting facts about safety issues, being less than truthful about payment terms, are all examples of ways in which salespeople might gain a sale, but ultimately lose a customer and certainly be acting unethically.

Ethics in advertising

As we saw in Chapter 2, there are regulations about what can and cannot be said in advertising. In the UK, the industry is self-regulating via the Advertising Standards

Table 10.3 Main provisions of the Radio Authority Code of Practice

Provision	Explanation
Prohibition of some products entirely	Cigarettes, pornography and escort agencies are banned completely.
Endorsement by presenters	Station presenters may not recommend advertisers' goods, so advertisers cannot employ them to do voice-overs on their advertisements.
Advertisements must not offend against taste or decency	No racist, sexist or obscene language is allowed (even as a joke). Obviously standards of what is acceptable change over time: the Code of Practice applies the standards of the 'reasonable person', or relies on complaints from listeners.
Advertisements must not use knocking copy	Advertisers are not allowed to make derogatory comments about rivals' products, even if they are true: they may not make comparisons between their own products and those of competitors.
Advertisements must not use sound effects that might endanger drivers	Sounds of police sirens, tyres squealing, or sounds of crashes might distract drivers. This restriction only applies to radio – there is no problem with using such sound effects on television, since drivers cannot watch TV while driving.
Advertisements must not mislead the audience	Although a certain amount of 'puff' is expected, advertisements must not deliberately set out to deceive the listeners. This means that advertisements are expected to be reasonably truthful – and this especially applies to medicines, financial services and environmental (green) claims.

Authority, which seeks to ensure that advertising is 'legal, decent, honest and truthful'. The Authority has powers to ask the media not to carry offending advertisements, but it relies entirely on complaints from the public: in that way, the Authority cannot be accused of making arbitrary decisions, because it uses public opinion as the yardstick for what is morally acceptable and what is not.

In the UK, radio advertising is regulated by the Radio Authority Code of Practice, in addition to the Advertising Standards Authority. The main provisions of the Code are shown in Table 10.3

Television advertising has a similar code of ethics, but is regulated by the ASA (by authority delegated from the Office of Communications, or OfCom). The regulations are such that advertisements are much more closely-regulated than the programming.

Regulation aside, marketers may have ethical problems in advertising. In some cultures, comparison advertising is allowed, in which the company can compare its products with a rival company's products, to the rival's disadvantage. This is permitted in the UK provided the advertising is truthful, but relatively few firms do it. The reason is twofold: on the one hand, comparison advertising serves to publicise the rival's brand name as well as the company's own brand, and on the other hand people often feel that such advertising is unethical and they therefore feel sorry for the maligned competitor. In other cultures people may have no such ethical stance.

Ethics in public relations

No aspect of corporate responsibility has attracted as much negative attention as public relations. PR is often seen as an exercise in spin doctoring – in other words, using half-statements, emotive language and even outright lying to put a good face on something that is fundamentally unacceptable.

PR is often seen as a set of techniques for concealing the truth in a crisis, but in fact good PR seeks to be proactive in ensuring that a crisis never occurs. Even when events happen outside the company's control, public relations officers try to ensure that the corporate behaviour enhances its reputation.

There will always be a temptation to emphasise the firm's positive behaviour and play down the negatives, and it is extremely difficult to see where a line is to be drawn between reasonable celebration of a firm's successes and outright lying about its failures. The key question is whether a stakeholder would be misled by a PR activity to the extent of suffering a potential loss. One way of limiting the risk of this happening is to engage in dialogic rather than monologic communications (Botan 1997). A dialogue is more likely to ensure that the stakeholder's doubts are dealt with fully and the truth is arrived at.

Non-profit marketing

Not all marketing activities take place in a profit context. As we saw in Chapter 1, the definition of marketing as being entirely profit-led is misleading, since many activities that we would normally define as marketing take place within a non-profit context. Charitable organisations spend considerable time and effort in finding better ways of persuading people to donate, or to change their behaviour in ways that fulfil the aims of the organisation.

Non-profit marketing falls into two main categories: charitable donations and cause-related marketing. Charities may simply be seeking donations to fund their work, or may be seeking to change public attitudes concerning an issue. For example, Oxfam frequently runs TV advertising asking for donations so that they can build wells or provide food aid, both of which are expensive things to do. On the other hand, the National Society for the Prevention of Cruelty to Children runs campaigns encouraging people to report cases of child abuse, and the Samaritans run advertising encouraging depressed or suicidal people to call the Samaritans for help. The NSPCC campaign raised over £100 million in the biggest-ever campaign by a charity, breaking new ground in its sector (Pegram et al. 2003). Non-profit organisations are often more brand-oriented than are commercial, profit-making organisations (Napoli 2006).

In non-profit-marketing, the question for many marketers is what is the exchange? What do the contributors to charities gain from their donation? In the case of government advertising, what do people gain from responding? In most cases, the donors obtain a sense of having done the right thing by giving to charities. The warm glow of generosity that results from a donation recompenses the donor. In the case of business contributions, socially responsible behaviour on the part of corporations actually boosts sales: also, charities supported by a corporation with a previous poor record of social responsibility often receive higher donations from the public at large (Lichtenstein et al. 2004).

In one study of high-earning young professionals in the City of London, researchers found that these people tended to support charities with well-established reputations, and also liked to be rewarded with 'social' events such as invitations to gala benefit dinners. 'Planned giving' where the donors receive tax breaks was not highly regarded by this group, who evidently enjoy the high profile aspects of being seen to support the charity (Kottasz 2004).

Charities are not always good at marketing, however. Relatively few of them have people on the streets with collecting tins any more, since the amount of money raised is usually so small it would be better for the person wielding the tin to get a job for the same number of hours and pay their wages to the charity. Charities tend to ask people to commit to regular sums by direct debit, to respond to TV advertising and make a credit card donation over the telephone, or to make donations via websites. Recent research shows that charitable websites are often not very effective (Wenham et al. 2003) because they ignore the customer's needs and concentrate on the needs of the organisation. Wenham et al.'s research was conducted with environmental organisations, whose websites were mainly promoting their causes: the researchers found that, although the websites scored well on information provision and even on design, they evidently had not made any attempt to identify customers' needs.

In recent years, not-for-profit marketers have been prepared to take bigger risks with advertising, making it more hard-hitting than in previous years: their remit does not fit the same paradigms as profit-based organisations, so they can afford to take greater risks (West and Sargeant 2004).

The exchange is not always made in financial terms. Charities frequently use volunteers, whose needs must also be met. Volunteers give up their time in order to help the charity, and will need to feel compensated in some way. Sometimes the compensation comes in the form of social contact, because many volunteers are either retired or unemployed and welcome the opportunity to return to a work environment where they can enjoy the company of other people, while at the same time remaining in control of the hours they work and the degree of commitment they give. Women tend to volunteer much more often than do men (Rohrs 1986), although this trend may be reducing as more women have careers outside the home. Although some researchers have found that volunteers are motivated by the desire to help others, such self-reports may not be reliable. Other authors suggest that all volunteers are actually motivated by self-interest. In fact, the truth is likely to lie somewhere in between: as might be expected, different volunteers act for different reasons (Wymer 2003).

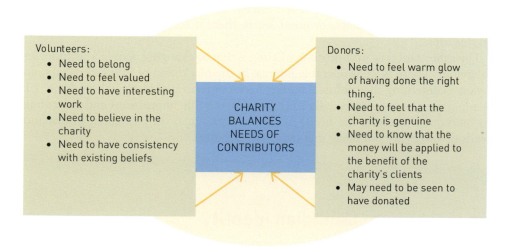

Figure 10.5 Contributors to charities

Think outside this box!

If people volunteer to help a charity only because there is something in it for themselves, is this really volunteering at all? Shouldn't we be helping out simply because it's the right thing to do – not expecting a ticket of admission to the Kingdom of Heaven for our efforts?

Or perhaps we should give people credit for being the kind of person who derives pleasure from helping others – in contrast to some people who apparently derive pleasure from harming others!

This means that volunteers can be grouped according to the type of motivation that will attract them, and treated accordingly (Kotler 1982). Since many charities assume that their volunteers come forward because they support the aims of the charity, their recruitment campaigns tend to operate in the same way as their fund-raising campaigns, which may well not be the correct focus. (Kotler 1982). Presumably it would be more realistic to consider how volunteers differ from each other, and try to meet the needs of a group of volunteers who have similar needs (Yavas and Reicken 1985). In a survey of volunteers for a literacy programme, volunteers obtained one or more of the following benefits from volunteering (Wymer 2003):

- Volunteers experienced personal satisfaction from making a difference to someone's life.
- Retired people, especially former teachers and librarians, derived a sense of feeling useful and needed.
- Volunteers derived social benefits from interacting with the students and with each other.
- A few volunteers reported that volunteering was consistent with their Christian or other religious beliefs.

In terms of demography, this study found that volunteers tended to come from wealthier households with small families. Gender, age and income were all significant, but personality traits such as self-esteem and empathy do not appear to affect whether someone volunteers or not. Clearly, there is scope for much more research on this topic.

The other aspect of non-profit marketing is that of changing people's attitudes and behaviour. There is a considerable interest in the marketing of political parties, and a view is emerging that political parties have concentrated too much on 'spin' (the manipulation of the news media to create a favourable impression) and not enough on marketing (meeting the needs of their constituents). In particular, information needs of voters are not being met (Mortimore 2003).

Real-life marketing: Canadian identity

Canada is now the largest country in the world, stretching over 3000 miles from the Atlantic coast to the Pacific, and from the Arctic Circle to the United States. It contains a wide diversity of terrain, people and cultures – everything from the sophisticated French city of Montreal to the Inuit igloos of the north-west. In the

west, Vancouver has become a new Hong Kong, with thousands of immigrants (many extremely wealthy) coming in from the former British colony. In the east, Toronto is a busy, modern city with a European feel.

Developing a sense of unity among all this diversity is a major task for the Canadian government. For almost 100 years campaigns have been run to develop a sense of 'Canadian-ness' among the population, and to foster a view of Canada that goes beyond its former status as part of the British Empire, or its occasional status as a kind of poor relation of the United States. This has led to the creation of certain myths (beliefs unfounded in experience) about what it is to be Canadian (Rose 2003).

Starting from early campaigns to orientate new immigrants in the early 20th century, the Canadian government has run campaigns to answer the complaints of minority groups (notably the French-speaking Quebecois community, who at one time were vocal in seeking independence for Quebec) and the Inuit, and more recently the Olympic Games campaign in 1998, aimed at hosting the 2008 Olympic Games (the bid failed). There is therefore a long history of government advertising in Canada, and even (recently) government sponsorship of events.

These advertisements have not always been uniformly successful. In 1989 the Canadian government ran a series of advertisements promoting a change in the sales tax system. This change was extremely unpopular with voters, but the government saw a need to reform the system in order to ensure that Canadian goods remained competitive. The government used the Maple Leaf symbol to appeal to Canadians' patriotism, and this was widely seen to be manipulative: one respondent in a research programme described it as a 'snow job', meaning that it was a way of fooling the public.

Eventually, consumer research showed that, although Canadian opinion had moved somewhat towards the view that the tax reform was necessary, a much higher proportion of the public had moved towards the view that the government should pay more attention to wasteful spending in its own departments. In some respects, therefore, the Canadian government's campaign had backfired. Of course, taxation is always a difficult thing to 'sell' to the taxpayer; campaigns designed to encourage Canadians to see themselves as a distinct nation, separate from either the UK or the United States, have been a resounding success.

As far as changing public opinion on issues of concern goes, various options are available. For example, campaigns encouraging 'safe sex' as a way of combating AIDS have been attempted using three general approaches, as follows:

1. The rational approach. The advertisement explains what causes AIDS, what the risks are and what steps might be taken to minimise risk.
2. Emotional strategy based on a negative message. Here the advertisements use frightening or shocking imagery to make the audience afraid of the possibility of catching AIDS.
3. Emotional strategy based on a positive message. These advertisements use imagery showing how good behaviour is rewarded.

Research shows that the rational strategy created more concern about AIDS, but the emotional strategy based on negative outcomes had the greatest impact on the behaviour intentions of the audience (Marchand and Filiatrault 2002). An experiment in changing adolescents' views about smoking showed that 'cosmetic' appeals (statements that smoking makes you smell bad, etc.) had more effect on adolescent males than long-term health fears: the reverse was the case in adolescent females (Smith and Stutts 2003). One of the problems of dealing with adolescents is that

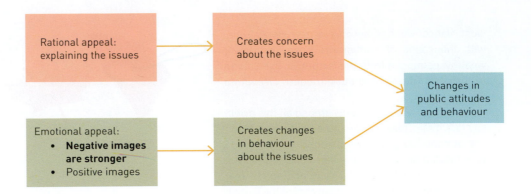

Figure 10.6   Creating changes through cause-related advertising

they often think they know all the answers, which makes them less likely to accept the marketing communications they are faced with. Sadly, even those who think they are streetwise are often lacking in accurate knowledge, even when they are exposed to social problems such as AIDS and drug abuse within their local area (Parker et al. 2006).

Cause-related marketing also manifests itself in the use of some credit cards. Banks issue the cards as normal cards, but make a contribution to a specific charity whenever the card is used. For the cardholder, this is a painless way of contributing to a charity: for the bank, it offers an added value to the cardholder at very little cost to the bank – not to mention that the cardholders are, by definition, socially responsible people who are unlikely to default on the credit given. However, it transpires that cardholders are most strongly swayed by the cognitive benefits of the card, and secondly by the feelings they have towards the organisation that benefits from the card. The bank itself ranks third in the equation (Fock et al. 2005).

Some people adopt ethical positions regarding advertising itself, and can find themselves in a difficult dilemma when faced with advertising aimed at promoting a specific issue. Beliefs about the ethicality of issue advertising depend on their beliefs about the economic effects of advertising and on the degree to which they already support the issue being advertised (Sego 2002).

Chapter summary

Ethical behaviour is not an absolute. It relies on the views of the majority of people living within a culture, and can therefore change over time (although such changes are slow). Problems arise when companies deal globally, because the business crosses value systems and can therefore easily do things that are regarded as unethical in one or other of the cultures. This is especially the case when dealing with issues such as child labour or bribery, each of which is viewed very differently in different cultures.

Corporate social responsibility is a slightly different matter: it involves acting in a responsible and caring manner towards all stakeholders, whatever their circumstances, and is in part a public relations exercise. Employees like to work for socially responsible companies, and indeed people prefer doing business with a company that cares – after all, if the company is known for taking a responsible attitude to its stakeholders, it is unlikely to cheat its customers.

Key points

- Corporate responsibility is about considering the impact of the firm's behaviour on stakeholders.
- Ethical behaviour is based around the prevailing view held within the culture, not on any absolute definitions.
- Teleology judges actions by outcomes: deontology seeks absolutes in moral behaviour.
- The specific circumstances of a company will inform decisions about creating an ethics policy.
- Ethics policies should be created with staff involvement at all levels.
- Marketing activities almost all involve ethical problems, because marketing is concerned with people's needs and wants.

Review questions

1. Why would a company worry about corporate responsibility?
2. How might a firm resolve ethical conflicts between the needs of shareholders and the needs of customers?
3. How might a pharmaceutical company develop an ethical policy?
4. Why is bribery regarded as unethical?
5. Why is cause-related marketing a popular route for companies?
6. What disciplinary measures might need to be in place to enforce ethical behaviour among employees?
7. Why do people who give to charity need to feel rewarded?
8. How might charities improve their chances of obtaining support from corporations?
9. What are the key drivers for ethical behaviour?
10. Why do people volunteer to help with charitable work?

Case study revisited: Bhopal

The case has further been complicated: in 2001 Dow Chemical bought Union Carbide. Dow, understandably, does not feel any responsibility whatever for Bhopal and is refusing to consider any further claims. Meanwhile, campaigners have persuaded an Indian court to issue a warrant for the arrest of Union Carbide's former CEO, Warren Anderson, on charges of culpable homicide. Anderson is unlikely to be extradited from the United States, but probably should not visit India any time soon.

Union Carbide commissioned an independent engineering report which found that the incident had been caused by deliberate sabotage caused by an employee removing a gauge and deliberately squirting water into the chemical tank. Employees at the plant claimed that cleaning water had got into the tank due to faulty pipework, but the engineering report said that attempts to duplicate this event had demonstrated that water could not have entered in this way.

US courts have consistently rejected claims emanating from Bhopal: in 2005, Indian architects were invited to bid for the job of designing a memorial complex to commemorate the victims, which was to be erected at the site of the disaster. This came to nothing, but in 2011 a group of European academics were invited to a conference at the site, with the aim of achieving the same outcome. Part of the problem is that the site had been used for dumping toxic chemicals during the years following the disaster, so that the levels of pollution have reached epic proportions. In 2009, an investigation for the BBC found levels of carbon tetrachloride at 1000 times the World Health Organisation's maximum permitted level in a pump used to collect drinking water for local families.

In 2010, seven former employees of Union Carbide (India) were convicted of causing death by negligence, and sentenced to two years imprisonment. As soon as the sentence was passed, all were released on bail – since some of them were in their seventies there perhaps did not seem to be much point in making them serve their sentences.

Meanwhile, the survivors of Bhopal wait. The case has dragged on for more than 30 years: the compensation worked out to only $500 each, which may be a lot of money to someone who only earns $2 a day, but still won't cover the medical bills. Union Carbide (India) is now owned by an entirely different company, which (like Dow in the United States) feels no responsibility for the disaster. The campaigning continues, however, presumably until the last of the survivors has died.

Case study: Comic Relief

Following on from the hugely successful Band Aid project, which raised funds for famine relief in north-east Africa, Comic Relief was founded in the UK in 1985 by comedy scriptwriter Richard Curtis and comedian Lenny Henry. The charity aimed to raise funds for famine relief by two main avenues: the first was a telethon in which comedy performers gave their services free in exchange for donations from the viewing public, and the second was organising Red Nose Day, a day on which people were encouraged to carry out humorous fund-raising stunts.

Unlike Band Aid, Comic Relief has survived and prospered in the intervening years. The aim of the charity is to create 'a just world free from poverty' – somewhat ambitious as an aim, but it does give everyone something to aim for. A later addition to the charity was Sport Relief, which follows the same general approach, but through sports people and sports activities.

Red Nose Day has become something of an institution in the UK. Every two years people buy themselves a comedy plastic red nose (the exact design changes each time, so noses cannot be kept from one year to the next) and do 'something funny for money'. Stunts have ranged from sitting in a bath full of baked beans to having one's head shaved. The streets, stores and supermarkets are filled with people in fancy dress, collecting money. Apart from collecting a very large amount of cash (the 2013 event raised over £75 million) people have a lot of fun participating. In the alternate years, Sport Relief carries out similar activities, but sport-related.

The telethon intersperses comedy acts with film footage showing some of the work the charity has funded. The TV coverage naturally helps publicise the problems the world faces, which should help to mould opinions: it also helps in providing credibility to Comic Relief by showing that money contributed really does do some good in the world.

Naturally, commercial organisations have joined in the fun. British Airways set a Guinness World Record for the highest comedy gig in the world during the 2011 Red Nose Day; Walker's Crisps created four new flavours for the 2011 event, named after comedians

(Frank Skinner's Roast Dinner and Stephen Fry-Up being two of them) and Sainsbury's sells merchandise on behalf of the charity. All proceeds go to the charity – British Airways alone raised over £800,000 – but of course there is a PR pay-off. Being seen to support such a popular charity does these companies no harm, although they do have many other possible ways of raising their already-high profiles.

Red Nose Day has become such a national institution that it has almost achieved the status of a holiday. Children are allowed to wear what they like to school, employees are given time off work for fundraising, and there is a general air of jollity in the country (much needed, since the event usually takes place during a rainy and wind-swept March). The concept has even crossed the Atlantic, with such comedy stars as Robin Williams and Whoopi Goldberg organising and contributing to the events. The US version has yet to be as successful as the UK one – perhaps because there is no participation from the public except to contribute to the telethon – but it has still raised over $50 million since its inception in 1986.

Comic Relief, on the other hand, has raised around £800 million during its lifetime. To raise over three-quarters of a billion pounds is remarkable for any charity – but to do it simply by making people laugh is truly exceptional.

Questions

1. Why would a company become a partner for Comic Relief?
2. What is the significance of Red Nose Day in terms of meeting stakeholders' needs?
3. How might the US version of Comic Relief improve its success rate?
4. Why would someone give to Comic Relief rather than to a longer-established charity such as Oxfam?
5. Why has Comic Relief survived and prospered, where Band Aid did not?

References

Bannerman, Doug and Roberts, David (2012) Why eliminating corruption is crucial to stability. *The Guardian*, 17 January.

Becker-Olsen, Karen and Cudmore, B. Andrew (2004) When good deeds dilute your equity. *Advances in Consumer Research* 31 (1): 78–9.

Bennett, Graceann and Williams, Freya (2011) *Mainstream Green: Moving Sustainability from Niche to Normal*. The Red Papers. Chicago: Ogilvy & Mather. https://assets.ogilvy.com/truffles_email/ogilvyearth/Mainstream_Green.pdf (accessed June 2013).

Botan, C. (1997) Ethics in strategic communications campaigns: the case for a new approach in public relations. *Journal of Business Communications*, 34 (2): 188–202.

Bronn, Peggy Simcic (2006) Building corporate brands through community involvement: is it exportable? The case of the Ronald McDonald House in Norway. *Journal of Marketing Communications*, 12 (4): 309–20,

Commission of the European Communities (2002) Communication from the Commission to the European Parliament concerning the common position of the Council on the adoption of a Directive of the European Parliament and the Council on the promotion of biofuels for transport. Brussels: CEC.

Coulter, Robert A. and Ligas, Mark (2003) To retain or relinquish: exploring the disposition practices of packrats and purgers. *Advances in Consumer Research*, 30 (1): 38.

Economist (2003) Airbus's secret past. *The Economist*, 367 (iss. 8328), 14 June, pp. 55–8.

European Biomass Industry Association (2012) Biodiesel. www.eubia.org/index.php/about-biomass/biofuels-for-transport/biodiesel (accessed May 2013).

Fock, Henry K.Y., Woo, Ka-Shing and Hui, Michael K. (2005) The impact of a prestigious partner on affinity card marketing. *European Journal of Marketing*, 39 (1/2): 33–53.

Fraedrich, J. (1988) Philosophy type interaction in the ethical decision making process of retailers. PhD dissertation, A&M University, Texas.

Fraj, Elena and Martinez, Eva (2006) Influence of personality on ecological consumer behaviour. *Journal of Consumer Behaviour*, 5 (3): 167–81.

Goodpaster, K.E. and Matthews, John B., Jr (1982) Can a corporation have a conscience? *Harvard Business Review*, 60 (1): 132–41.

Kotler, P (1982) *Marketing for Non-Profit Organisations*. Englewood Cliffs, NJ: Prentice Hall.

Kottasz, R. (2004) How should charitable organisations motivate young professionals to give philanthropically? *International Journal of Nonprofit and Voluntary Sector Marketing*, 9 (1): 9–28.

Lichtenstein, Donald R., Drumright, Minette E. and Braig, Bridgette M. (2004) The effects of corporate social responsibility on customer donations to corporate-supported non-profits. *Journal of Marketing*, 68 (4): 16–32.

Marchand, June and Filiatrault, Pierre (2002) AIDS prevention advertising: different message strategies for different communication objectives. *International Journal of Nonprofit and Voluntary Sector Marketing*, 7 (3): 271–87.

Mortimore, R. (2003) Why politics needs marketing. *International Journal of Nonprofit and Voluntary Sector Marketing*, 8 (2): 107–21.

Napoli, J. (2006) The impact of non-profit brand orientation on organisational performance. *Journal of Marketing Management*, 22 (7/8): 673–94.

National Biodiesel Board (2013) www.biodiesel.org/production/production-statistics (accessed March 2013).

Parker, Andrew M., Fischoff, Baruch and de Bruine, Wandi (2006) Who thinks they know more – but actually knows less? Adolescent confidence in their HIV/AIDS and general knowledge. *Advances in Consumer Research*, 33 (1): 12–13.

Pegram, G., Booth, N. and McBurney, C. (2003) Full stop: an extraordinary appeal for an extraordinary aspiration – putting leadership theory into practice? *International Journal of Nonprofit and Voluntary Sector Marketing*, 8 (3): 207–12.

Report to the Senate and House of Representatives mandated by IAFCA (2003). www.tcc. mac.doc.gov/pdf/Bribery2003_text.pdf (accessed 21 November 2003).

Rohrs, F.R. (1986) Social background, personality and attitudinal factors influencing the decision to volunteer and level of involvement among adult 4-H leaders. *Journal of Voluntary Action Research*, 15 (1): 87–99.

Rose, Jonathan (2003) Government advertising and the creation of national myths. *International Journal of Nonprofit and Voluntary Sector Marketing*, 8 (2): 153–5.

Saeed, Mohammad, Ahmed, Zafar U. and Mukhtar, Syeda-Masooda (2001) International marketing ethics from an Islamic perspective: a value-maximization approach. *Journal of Business Ethics*, 32: 127–42.

Sego, Trina (2002) Consumers' ethical judgement of issue advertising. *Advances in Consumer Research*, 29 (1): 80–5.

Smith, Karen H. and Stutts, Mary Ann (2003) Effects of short-term cosmetic versus long-term health fear appeals in anti-smoking advertisements on the smoking behaviour of adolescents. *Journal of Consumer Behaviour*, 3 (2): 155–77.

Terpstra, V. and David, K. (1991) *The Cultural Environment of International Business*. Cincinnati, OH: South-Western.

Wayne, Leslie (2003) Boeing dismisses 2 in hiring of official who left Pentagon. *New York Times*, 25 November: A1, C2.

Wenham, K., Stephens, D. and Hardy, R. (2003) The marketing effectiveness of UK environmental charity websites compared to best practice. *International Journal of Nonprofit and Voluntary Sector Marketing*, 8 (3): 213–23.

West, Douglas C. and Sargeant, Adrian (2004) Taking risks with advertising: the not-for-profit sector. *Journal of Marketing Management*, 20 (9/10): 1027–45.

Wymer, Walter W. (2003) Differentiating literacy volunteers: a segmentation analysis for target marketing. *International Journal of Nonprofit and Voluntary Sector Marketing*, 8 (3): 267–85.

Yavas, U. and Reicken, G. (1985) Can volunteers be targeted? *Journal of the Academy of Marketing Science*, 13 (2): 218–28.

More online

To gain free access to additional online resources to support this chapter please visit:
www.sagepub.co.uk/blythe3e

CHAPTER (11)

Building customer relationships

LEARNING OBJECTIVES

After reading this chapter, you should be able to:

- Explain how the salesforce's activities affect the quality of the buyer–seller relationship.

- Explain what is meant by quality.

- Describe how service quality helps to differentiate suppliers.

- Explain how to resolve customer complaints.

- Describe the stages in customer defection.

- Describe how customer win-back operates.

Introduction

In the early days of marketing, the emphasis was on encouraging people to buy products and services from a specific producer. Advertising and other promotional activities were intended to bring in new customers, but once the customers had made their purchases companies tended to lose interest in them, assuming that they would remain loyal provided the products were satisfactory.

Recently this view has been challenged. Increased competition lures customers away: customers are, in any case, less loyal than they might have been in the days when there were few choices of product. A dwindling number of potential customers (as a result of falling populations) and a reduction in the effectiveness of advertising (as a result of an increase in clutter from excessive competition) means that there is a greater emphasis on retaining existing customers rather than attracting new ones. Various estimates have been put forward as to the relative costs of attracting new customers as opposed to retaining existing ones, but it is almost certainly cheaper to retain an existing customer than to recruit a new one.

Preview case study: Accor

Accor is a French hotel chain, operating hotels throughout the world in every price range and quality range. Accor operates everything from the most basic overnight rooms through to five-star resort hotels. At the lower end, Formule I hotels have basic rooms with shared bathroom and shower facilities. These are popular with young people on a night out, tired drivers who won't make it all the way home tonight and people on a road trip who simply need somewhere basic to sleep before moving on in the morning. These hotels have few staff, automated systems for paying for rooms and almost no facilities other than a clean room.

At the other end of the scale, MGallery boutique hotels are located in the most upmarket, exotic locations, Sofitel luxury hotels provide five-star comfort in locations worldwide, and Ibis and Mercure hotels provide practical, business-class hotels with conference facilities and good-quality catering.

Of course, there are very many hotels in the world and very many hotel chains. For Accor to maintain loyalty across the wide range of offerings they have available takes some doing. After all, their customer base is as diverse as the hotel range, and the tired driver who just wants to have a clean bed for the night may, tomorrow, be the business executive who needs somewhere upmarket for their next meeting. At the weekend the same person may want to treat their partner to a romantic stay in a boutique hotel for their birthday. In other words, the same customers may expect different things from their hotels at different times.

This is where Accor needed to find a new approach to its customer retention scheme. Where other hotel chains have separate schemes for each brand, Accor designed a scheme that would work across the whole chain – rewarding people for remaining loyal to Accor, not just to the individual brands in the chain.

Building relationships

Building long-term relationships with customers has long been practised in business-to-business marketing. This is because there are relatively few customers in business markets, so that the loss of even one customer can have serious consequences. For example, there are only nine major High Street banks in Britain: a company specialising in computer software for ATMs would be ill-advised to create a bad relationship with even one of them. **Relationship marketing** has met with rather less success in consumer markets, perhaps because consumers do not see any advantage in establishing a close relationship with the firms that supply the goods they use.

Relationship marketing The practice of concentrating on the lifetime value of customers rather than their value in the single transaction.

There is, in fact, little research evidence to show that long-term customers are always more profitable than short-term ones, and also little evidence to show that satisfaction leads to loyalty (although it does lead to recommendations, which of course are likely to lead to the acquisition of new customers) (East et al. 2006). Other researchers claim that there is a relationship between customer loyalty and profitability (Helgesen 2006), so it seems likely that other factors (for example, industry and product types) affect the relationship.

The history of relationship marketing goes back to the Japanese *keiretsu* system, in which the companies in the value chain become extremely closely linked through a system of agreements, often for exclusive supply of components and raw materials. The *keiretsu* operate mainly on verbal agreements: Japanese businesses rarely worry too much about written contracts, since the Japanese legal system is not geared to enforcing such contracts. The result is a system that involves high degrees of trust and loyalty, and apparently functions extremely efficiently.

The lesson was not lost on Western organisations. Companies such as Bose, Compaq and Motorola began to send their engineering personnel to their suppliers in order to liaise on new product development and to consider ways of making the supply process more efficient, and they also stationed their salesforce in the retailers' offices to help in merchandising the products (Leenders and Blenkhorn 1988). Upstream and downstream involvement by the major companies in running the value chain made everything work more efficiently, and therefore more profitably for all concerned. Another driver for relationship marketing may be that companies are often unskilled at managing customer acquisition: few companies have a co-ordinated system for acquiring new customers (Ang and Buttle 2006).

Think outside this box!

Are business relationships really that close? Do firms readily join together and fall in love with each other? Or are such relationships mere marriages of convenience?

After all, a firm has many people it has a much closer responsibility to – its customers, its employees, its neighbours, and not forgetting the poor old shareholders who put up the money in the first place! So is it right that the managers should try to create close relationships elsewhere? Aren't they being disloyal – some might even say unfaithful – in contracting relationships with other firms?

Or is it more the case that those close to the firm – customers, employees, etc. – are more like family, and they should encourage the firm to 'date' other firms?

A turning point in the thinking on relationship marketing came with the publication of research by consultants Bain & Co. in which they found that **cross-selling** to an existing customer costs one-sixth as much as selling to a new customer. What is more, they found that a 5% increase in customer retention would increase the value of each customer by between 25 and 100% (Reed 1999). Later research has supported this view of relationship marketing: firms that adopt relationship marketing have been shown to be more successful than firms that do not (Chaston et al. 2003), and the relationship between companies has been shown to be more important than either service quality (Roberts et al. 2003) or even price (Oederkerken-Schroeder et al. 2003). Even in consumer markets, loyalty is initially the result of perceived value, but later on affection for the company mediates the loyalty of customers (Johnson et al. 2006).

How good the buyer–seller relationship remains is determined by how well the seller manages it (Weitz and Bradford 1999). Managing the relationship, in the business-to-business arena, is largely the responsibility of the salesforce because it is the salespeople who regularly see the customers, but in a truly relationship-orientated company the whole firm should be involved in maintaining good relationships with customers. This means that the firm's engineers should be in contact with the other firm's engineers,

Cross-selling Selling new product lines to an existing customer.

the administrators should be seeking ways of making their interactions run more efficiently, the delivery drivers should be considerate of the customer's warehouse staff, and so forth. Establishing such a broad range of contacts may not be simple, and it may not happen overnight, but such arrangements can only be beneficial for all parties: in business relationships, interactions range from the single exchange through to a full relationship portfolio of exchanges at every level (Holmlund 2004). The evidence is that empowering employees to manage problems between themselves will significantly increase customer satisfaction, loyalty and perceived quality (Evans and Laskin 1994: Dunleavy and Olivieri 2001).

Having established the relationship, both parties need to keep in mind that relationships depend on reciprocity: neither party should harm the other, but if harm does occur the injured party should not retaliate, and the party that caused the harm should make ample reparations (Pervan et al. 2009).

Real-life marketing: Love what your customers love

If you're really close to your customers, you'll love your own products as much as they do. Salespeople are often told to buy and use the company's products themselves – where appropriate, of course – because this conveys a sense of trust in the company's products. After all, if the sales guy doesn't use the product, why should the customer?

Waterstones bookshop chain is an example. When Tim Waterstone founded the company in 1982 he really needed a job – having just been fired by newsagent WH Smith. He decided from the start to share his love of books – he even provided comfortable seating so that people could sit and read the books before (or even instead of) buying. In other bookshops, people who spent too long dipping into books would be told 'This isn't a public library, you know!' By contrast, senior management appear on the corporate website reading the books that have shaped their lives – they are shown almost hidden by the books.

Staff are chosen for their love of books, as well as expert knowledge about specific types of book – travel guides, poetry, cookery, fiction or whatever customers might want to know more about. The staff are always helpful and knowledgeable, not because they have been through a 'customer relations training course' but because they genuinely love what the customers love.

To make this work in practice, you need to:

- Remember why you wanted to work in the industry in the first place.
- Think about your customers. Do you share the same love of the product?
- Work out what you can do to encourage their enthusiasm and help them enjoy your mutual interest.
- Make sure your staff and colleagues feel the same.

Ultimately, good relationships depend on commitment and trust (Morgan and Hunt 1994). Trust moderates the effects of interdependence by enhancing the perception of the relational orientation of both manufacturer and supplier (Izquierdo and Cillan 2004).

Quality, value and service

Quality is determined by the relationship between what customers expect, and what they get. If a customer's expectations of a product are low, then he or she will not be disappointed: if, however, the customer has been led to expect a high-quality product and is in fact given a poor-quality one, he or she has the right to feel aggrieved. If the product exceeds expectations, the quality of the product will be perceived to be high.

Perception of quality is closely-related to the customer's views on what constitutes value for money. For example, a hotel room might cost anything between £50 a night and £500 a night – or more. The person staying in the £500 room clearly considers this to be value for money, as does the person staying in the £50 room: the difference lies in their relative perceptions of the value of money, and the level of comfort and service they expect for their money.

It follows from this that quality is not an absolute. Quality is in the eye of the beholder – or at least in the perception of the consumer, because each individual is starting with a different set of expectations. Service support is critical to relationship marketing, because it is during the pre-sale and after-sale support that customers are approached as individuals. It is at this time that customers' perceptions of quality will become apparent – and the front-line staff (salespeople, etc.) who deal directly with customers are able either to adjust the customers' expectations (pre-sale) or correct any problems with the product (after-sale).

In the past, quality was seen as the province of the production department, which led to the product concept mentioned in Chapter 1. Under a relationship marketing ethos, quality has become the integrating concept between production orientation and marketing orientation (Gummeson 1988). Marketing has the role of managing the customers' expectations – either by adjusting the expectations or by fine-tuning the product: concentration on the product alone is not enough.

If we subscribe to this philosophy, then service quality can be defined as the ability of the organisation to meet or exceed customer expectations. The relationship marketer therefore needs to monitor the quality of the firm's output against two criteria: the customers' expectations, and the firm's actual output. A well-known model for assessing service quality is Parasuraman et al.'s Servqual model (Parasuraman et al. 1985), shown in Figure 11.1.

The model shows various gaps that might develop, and need to be addressed. These are as follows:

- Gap One: The difference between actual customer expectations, and management perceptions of customer expectations.
- Gap Two: The difference between management perceptions of customer expectations and service quality specifications.
- Gap Three: The difference between service quality specifications and the service actually delivered.
- Gap Four: The difference between service delivery and what is communicated about the service to customers.
- Gap Five: The difference between customer expectations and the perceptions of what is actually received. This gap is influenced by the other four.

In order to close the gaps, marketers may need to adopt a series of quality control procedures. Some of these may already be well known to the production department, others are more specific to marketers.

TOTAL QUALITY MANAGEMENT

The intention behind total quality management is to ensure that the firm and its associates do the right things at the right time at every stage of the value chain. The

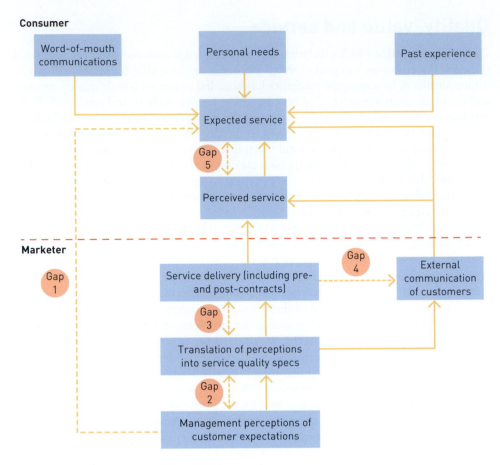

Figure 11.1   Servqual model

theory is that if every stage of the process is carried to the highest standards, or at least the appropriate standards, the outcome will be a product or service of the appropriate quality. The problem with this is that it does not take account of the customer's expectations, but instead relies on the firm's view of what constitutes a high-quality process. This means that the company will have difficulty in deciding at what level to pitch the quality assurance at each stage of the process.

The main contribution total quality management has is in the reduction of waste, and consequently a reduction in costs, because finished products will not need to be rejected due to component failures. The concept of zero-defect manufacture has led to dramatic cost savings in some industries, but apart from the cost savings has relatively little effect on marketing issues.

BENCHMARKING

Benchmarking Setting performance parameters by comparing performance with that of the best of the competing firms.

Benchmarking is the process of comparing each element of the value chain, including company departments, with the most successful equivalent element in equivalent value chains. If each element in the value chain operates to a level equivalent to the best example from all other value chains, the result should be a value chain that is the best of the best. The value chains chosen are not necessarily those in the same business: for example, someone who is assessing the efficiency of the check-in procedures of an airline may well compare them with the

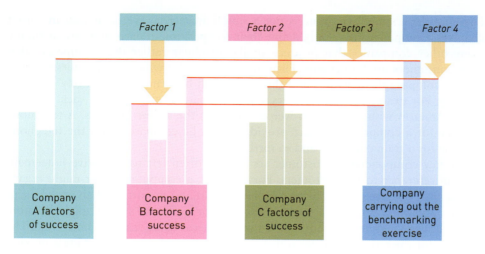

Figure 11.2   Benchmarking

queue-handling systems at his or her usual supermarket. Telephone call centres are compared with other call centres, not with other firms in the same industry.

In practice, benchmarking generates considerable difficulties. First, it is often very difficult to obtain truly accurate data on the functioning of other companies. Second, even when data are available, it may be difficult to decide which are the critical factors in the competitors' success. Third, at a conceptual level it would seem strange to allow the firm's quality control to be dictated by other companies. Fourth, if benchmarking is adopted by everybody, it will stifle innovation. Finally, the costs incurred in bringing all departments up to the best standards of all other companies are likely to be high, which will inevitably have an effect on prices.

Benchmarking is likely to lead companies back into the fallacious product orientation approach. Consumers do not necessarily want the highest quality at all times – they do want the highest quality they can get for the money they have available to spend, in other words best value for money.

Service quality is often a major competitive differentiator for firms. For example, in the lubricating oil industry the specifications for the oil are laid down by engine manufacturers: the oil companies have to supply oil of a particular type, and this is the same across the industry with little opportunity to differentiate the physical product. Where the companies can differentiate themselves is in the service they offer: this may be concerned with delivery times, after-sales service, advice lines and so forth.

Christopher et al. (1991) have drawn up a five-stage approach to services benchmarking. This is as follows:

Stage 1: Define the competitive arena, i.e. with whom are we compared by customers, and with whom do we want to be compared?

Stage 2: Identify the key components of customer service as seen by customers themselves.

Stage 3: Establish the relative importance of those service components to customers.

Stage 4: Identify the customer position on the key service components relative to the competition.

Stage 5: Analyse the data to see if service performance matches customers' service needs.

Defining the competitive arena is not a simple matter, as we have seen in earlier chapters. Companies frequently define their competition in narrow terms, as simply being other companies that produce similar products rather than companies that offer consumers similar benefits. Firms need to consider which competitors the consumers compare them with – and these may well be firms in an entirely different industry. For example, Internet users might compare a retail website such as booksellers Amazon with other retail websites in (say) the airline business. A telephone helpline for a computer software provider might be compared with the telephone helpline for a train company, and so forth.

The key components of customer service are often left to executive judgement without reference to the customers. For example, a computer owner might regard on-site maintenance calls as being far more useful and important than on-line support for software. A car owner whose car is in for its annual service might be more appreciative of a lift to the train station than of the car being ready by lunchtime. The problem for the service provider is that different people have different ideas of what is important – someone unfamiliar with computer software might set great store by a free helpline service, whereas someone who is very computer-literate but who lives a long way from a computer store might prefer on-site maintenance engineers to fix hardware faults.

Think outside this box!

There seems to be a growing view among companies that people want ever-better service and choice. This seems to have become the key to differentiating the product – but is it really the case?

Anyone who has visited the United States knows what restaurants are like there. The bewildering range of options for salad dressing, the many different options for how the food is to be cooked (low salt, low sugar, low fat, well-done, over easy, etc. etc.) and even the choice of bread rolls means that ordering a simple meal becomes a marathon task, not to mention the problem of remembering who ordered what. Compare this with the simplicity of ordering a meal in France, where the chef (as the acknowledged expert on food) *knows* what will taste good and what goes together well, and makes sure you get it.

So do we really need all this service and choice all the time? Aren't there times when we just want to be told to sit down, shut up and eat the dinner? After all, which country has the better reputation for its food?

Once the key components are established, their relative importance needs to be assessed. This will vary from one person to the next, so it is helpful to segment the market: in the example given above, a computer retailer might deliberately aim for a 'beginners' market, or offer a beginners package, which would include a lot of on-line or telephone 'hand-holding.' An alternative package of after-sales service might be offered to the more computer-literate, perhaps offering free upgrades or more advanced software.

Identifying where we are in customers' minds relative to the competition is a basic marketing function in any case. In the case of service provision, we should be doing this across a range of firms who offer similar types of after-sales and before-sales service, rather than simply firms that offer the same core product.

Having gone through the previous four stages, examining what we do in order to decide whether it fits with what the customers actually want us to do is relatively straightforward.

Customer relationship management

Although relationship marketing appears to have flourished better in business-to-business markets, it has had some impact on consumer markets. The purpose of establishing a long-term relationship with the end consumers is to ensure that they come back, and keep coming back. This is in part a function of involvement (see Chapter 4). A loyal customer of a car manufacturer might easily spend £200,000 on cars over a lifetime, yet few manufacturers trouble to contact their end consumers regularly to check that the car is working well. Importantly, companies need to recognise that people do not respond well to the idea of being managed; consumers will seek to control the relationship if they can. In some cases people have a fear of getting too close to a company or brand in case they are 'sold to'; in other cases people might have a fear of loss, abandonment or rejection. People who are either low on both these dimensions, or high on both, report high satisfaction with brands: those who are high on one and low on the other report low satisfaction (Thompson and Johnson 2002).

In Figure 11.3, the cost of acquiring a new customer for each transaction is estimated at five times the cost of retaining an existing customer. Over the course of five transactions, the cost of finding new customers each time comes out at 10% of the revenue obtained. Retaining the existing customer costs less than 4% of the revenue. Over a longer period, the figures become even more favourable – for each transaction, the existing customer costs only 2% of the revenue obtained, whereas a new customer will still cost 10%.

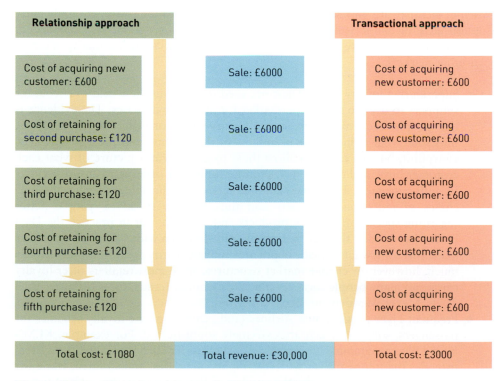

Figure 11.3   Relationship marketing in action

Marketing in a changing world: Savvy consumers

Companies seem to have found out that it's cheaper to keep an existing customer than find a new one, so they go to considerable efforts to stop people defecting to the competition. This includes giving people free product, extra discounts, free gifts and so forth if they threaten to leave. The problem with this is that people quickly understand what's going on and act accordingly, threatening to leave whenever they fancy a new phone or a better price.

People now are much better-educated than in the past: in the 1960s only 2% of school leavers went to university, compared with 50% now. Also, people talk, and can access information very quickly, so word gets round fast. Marketing in particular is discussed a great deal, and a lot of people have completed a marketing course (since there are many business studies classes in school, and even people who work for McDonald's get some training in marketing). Marketers therefore should assume that everyone knows exactly what's going on and can think of ways of turning it to their advantage.

Perhaps in the future, marketers will be relying on people's goodwill not to take advantage of the poor old company. For sure, consumers really do have the upper hand now.

Part of the problem for marketers is that many consumers prefer not to establish relationships with the people who provide them with products and services. From a consumer's viewpoint, being telephoned or mailed regularly by everyone from whom they buy anything would be an imposition rather than a pleasure, and only in cases where the consumer feels heavily involved, or where there is some immediate material benefit, will they want to be troubled. Far too many companies use the 'courtesy call' approach when in fact they are only seeking to sell something else to the customer – only fairly sophisticated relationship marketers put the relationship first, and the sales call second.

Having said that, there are some good examples of relationship management in consumer markets.

- Supermarket loyalty cards. These are used throughout the world to encourage shoppers to use the same supermarket for all their purchases. The evidence is that people frequently carry several loyalty cards for different supermarkets, thus somewhat reducing the usefulness of the system from the supermarkets' viewpoint, but the cards do allow them to get a clearer picture of what each customer buys, and enables stores to fine-tune their offering to ensure a closer fit with customers. In theory, supermarkets should be able to predict the purchases of individual customers and thus be able to advise people better regarding special offers, new products and so forth, but in practice the Data Protection Act and the fact that people still shop in a wide variety of stores has made this somewhat difficult in practice. Loyalty cards no longer affect loyalty much, however, or change market structures, since most retailers offer loyalty cards and many people carry several cards from different stores (Allaway et al. 2006; Meyer-Waarden and Benavent 2006).
- Frequent Flyer programmes. Airlines (and others) operate loyalty schemes for passengers, some of which are extremely sophisticated. For example, KLM's Flying Blue programme has two parallel systems for earning points: one system provides the frequent flyer with free flights, upgrades, and so forth, while the other system (which includes the number of flights taken within a given period as well as the distance flown) provides frequent flyers with extra baggage allowances, use of executive lounges at airports, rapid check-in, and so forth.

- 'Friends' schemes for the Arts. The Friends of Sadler's Wells Opera obtain 20% discounts on tickets, get buy-one-get-one-free ticket deals, discounts on programmes, and many other benefits. All these benefits are obtained in exchange for a £40 membership fee. Such schemes ensure loyalty at least until the initial fee has been recouped, and probably for some time afterwards.
- Establishing a presence on social media sites such as Facebook and Twitter. This has the advantage of giving a measure of control to the customer, who is able to interact via social media or not as he or she wishes. There is more on social media in Chapter 18.

In each of these cases the sponsoring company gains access to a list of names and addresses of people who have shown an interest in the firm, its products and its way of doing business. This is an essential stepping-stone in developing direct marketing.

An important point to remember about relationship marketing is that many of the techniques used to generate loyalty are expensive and require considerable commitment: in the long run, the effort will pay off, but relationships are not built overnight and firms that try to cash in on the relationship too early are likely to do a great deal of damage to future business. The Internet has been helpful, as has electronic communication generally, especially for small firms (Harrigan et al. 2011). Corporate blogs have also proved to be extremely useful in maintaining good relationships with customers (Halliburton and Ziegfeld 2009).

Loyalty and retention do not always come from satisfaction, however: barriers to switching are also important (Patterson 2004). If it is difficult or expensive to switch from one supplier to another, people will apparently remain loyal – but of course, if it becomes easier to switch, or if the situation becomes intolerable, they may switch and will be difficult to win back. People who switch suppliers as the result of a recommendation from a friend or family member (referral switchers) are likely to become more loyal and have higher satisfaction ratings than switchers in general, and also are more likely to pass on the recommendation to others (Wangenheim and Bayón 2003). Switchers also tend to be more price-sensitive, whereas stayers are more sensitive to service quality (Leong and Qing 2006).

Loyalty sometimes comes about simply because the customer has little or no choice, or the switching costs are high: for example, even on the Internet (where the assumption has always been that there is very little to prevent people using different sites) research shows that people get bored with clicking through multiple sites to find bargains, and instead tend to stick to their usual supplier, where they know how to navigate the site and feel confident in what they are doing (Murray and Haubl 2002). People prefer not to spend a lot of time searching for information, another reason for staying with a familiar site (Zauberman 2002).

Customer retention strategies

Customer retention has become increasingly recognised as the key to long-term survival. In the past, most companies have operated on a 'leaky bucket' basis, seeking to refill the bucket with new customers while ignoring the ones leaking away through the bottom of the bucket. According to research by Gupta et al. (2004), a 1% improvement in customer retention will lead to a 5% improvement in the firm's value. A 1% improvement in marginal cost or in customer acquisition cost only makes a 1% increase in firm value respectively. In other words, according to Gupta et al. customer retention is five times as effective as cutting costs.

A study performed by the Cumberland Bank in the United States showed that the top 5% of the customer base accounted for 40% of total deposits, that a 5% increase

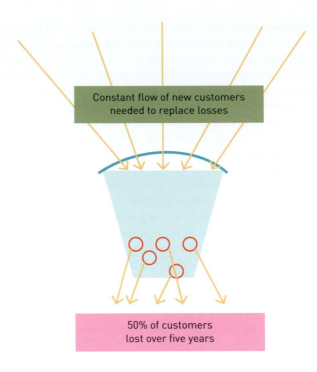

Figure 11.4   The leaky bucket

in retention of top customers added 4% to the bank's profitability, and the minimum balance of the top 20% of customers is $20,000. Reichheld (1996) found that, in US corporations, 50% of customers are lost over five years, 50% of employees are lost in four years and 50% of investors are lost in less than a year. Firms therefore need to recognise and reward loyal customers and ensure (as far as possible) that they remain as customers of the company's products.

Think outside this box!

Obviously it makes sense to retain customers if at all possible rather than have to go through the rigmarole of acquiring new ones. On the other hand, what are the implications?

Presumably a customer defected because he or she did not like what was on offer. In order to regain that lost customer, then, the firm has to offer something different and perhaps better. So what effect does that have on the thinking of other customers? Presumably the best way to get some extras is to defect, then sit back and wait for the phone call! Is this the message we want our loyal customers to have?

Maybe we should think of a better way to regain lost customers!

Customers who remain with the firm are said to be loyal, but there are different types of loyalty. Table 11.1 shows the basic types of loyalty exhibited by customers. Loyalty programmes that offer real economic benefits to customers affect both retention and customer share development positively (Verhoef 2003). Having said

Table 11.1 Customer loyalty

Type of loyalty	Explanation
Price loyalty	Provided the organisation remains the price leader, these customers will remain loyal. If they do desert, it is more likely to be a result of a change of lifestyle (for example increased earnings) than a result of being lured away by a lower price elsewhere. Some businesses can make use of this fact: for example Tesco supermarket's own-brands cater for the wealthier customers (Tesco's *Finest*) and for the less wealthy (Tesco's *Value*).
Monopoly loyalty	The few firms who can exercise a monopoly have a captive customer base. However, as soon as an alternative becomes available they will defect.
Inertia loyalty	Most people are surrounded by different decisions that need to be made every day. This means that most of us remain loyal to most of the products we buy simply because it saves us the trouble of finding a new product. Even though there might be major benefits attached to the new product, inertia prevents us from moving on. This is particularly true in banking: the vast majority of people stay with the same bank for most or all of their lives. Companies should beware of complacency, however – once defection starts, it will grow.
Emotional loyalty	Emotional loyalty is a function of involvement (see Chapter 3). Customers who are prepared to pay extra for the product, who are loyal to it whatever happens, and who recommend the product to their friends are emotionally loyal.
Disloyalty	Dissatisfied customers will tell other customers of the same organisation about their experiences, and will often persuade the other customers to defect as well. This type of behaviour can be extremely damaging, because the experience of the disloyal customer is given great credence by other people.

that, loyalty to on-line supermarkets is related more to speed of delivery and promotions rather than price *per se*: in common with other supermarkets, people tend to be more loyal to the supermarket than to the brand of the products they are buying (Cui and Wang 2010).

The starting-point for building trust is to keep promises, and the first set of promises any firm must keep is the promises surrounding the product and its performance. On the whole, customers understand that things do not always go perfectly, but a failure on the part of the firm to correct any faults in the product or the service means that the firm has broken its promises – a sure way to lose a customer. After a failure on the part of a supplying company, people adopt various coping strategies – re-evaluation of the brand's trustworthiness, apportioning blame, or re-interpreting the brand into stereotypes. Sometimes the relationship actual strengthens if the problem is resolved, but the relationship may be renegotiated, or the customer may exit or avoid the brand in future. Forgiveness of the brand will involve a release of negative emotions (Chung and Beverland 2006). The possibility that the violation of trust might be repeated in future is more important in generating a negative word of mouth and defection to the competition than is the magnitude of the violation (Wang and Huff 2007). In other words, people are more likely to forgive a major failure if they believe it is a one-off mistake rather than one of a series of even small failures.

The second area that any firm must get right is the interface with the customers. This is quite clearly the responsibility of the marketing people, but it is also the responsibility of everyone who comes into contact with customers in the course of the working day. Customer loyalty is positively related to technical service quality, functional service quality and customer education (Bell and Eisengrich 2007). The key to ensuring that customers are satisfied (better still, delighted) is to empower these front-line employees to make redress appropriately and on the spot.

The relevance of the brand to the consumer is also relevant to defection – if the values expressed through the brand are salient, defection is less likely (Romaniuk and Sharp 2003). Customer satisfaction not only relates to greater return rates and word-of-mouth recommendations, it also makes advertising more effective and increases staff performance (dealing with satisfied customers is a great deal more pleasant than dealing with complaints) (Luo and Homburg 2007).

If a problem arises, there are three main elements in resolving the problem for the customer (Tax and Brown 1998). These are:

1. Offer a fair outcome. Refunds, replacements, credits, repairs and corrections of charges are typical forms of redress expected by customers. Most customers would also expect an apology as partial recompense for being treated unfairly or rudely, but Tax and Brown found that the majority of customers did not feel that their complaints had been met fairly. On the other hand, customers who felt that they had been treated fairly reported that they had received compensation for the inconvenience suffered as well as the basic exchange or repair. These customers also reported that they liked being offered a choice of compensation (for example a restaurant might offer a choice of vouchers against future meals, or a free liqueur with a customer's coffee).
2. Offer a fair procedure. Customers who thought that the procedure had been unfair had typically been frustrated by a prolonged procedure, often having to repeat their complaint to a number of different people, or being asked to deal with most of the problem themselves.
3. Offer fair treatment. Customers responded well to being treated honestly, politely and with concern. Making a genuine effort to resolve the problem was seen as a positive factor in remaining with the firm.

Perception of fairness depends on surrounding factors and social interactions, in other words people will take account of mitigating circumstances, and are also affected by the way they are treated by staff (Carlson and Sally 2002).

Typically, people go through three distinct phases before finally terminating the relationship with a company that is giving unsatisfactory service (Griffin and Lowenstein 2001). These are:

Value breakdown A situation in which the service offered by a producer does not materialise.

1. **Value breakdown**. The service promise offered by the producer does not materialise. This may be a temporary failure, but much depends on how it is handled: for example, if a hotel has a breakdown in its hot water system, guests might be offered free drinks in the bar as a partial compensation while the system is repaired. If the failure is not addressed, the customer may simply accept the situation, and continue to buy, but with doubts.
2. The season of discontent. After a series of value breakdown experiences, the customer will begin to look elsewhere, but may not actually defect yet. The warning signs for the firm are a reduced level of activity from this customer, and (in the case of business-to-business relationships) signs such as a reduced level of access to senior managers, a reduction in approvals for new proposals, and negative feedback in the form of complaint letters or lowered performance ratings. Left unaddressed, the initial discontent will eventually lead the customer to defect to a competitor.
3. Termination. At this stage the customer either tells the firm that their relationship is over, or the customer simply takes his or her business elsewhere.

It seems that developing customer loyalty is not so much a matter of providing excellent service as it is of minimising service breakdowns. For example, people who are upgraded by an airline (perhaps due to the overbooking of economy class seats) become marginally more loyal, whereas customers who are downgraded or refused boarding because the aircraft is full become extremely dissatisfied and usually defect to a competing airline in future (Wangenheim and Bayón 2007).

In fact, if a customer does decide to go elsewhere, all is not lost. Studies show that the most lucrative source of new business prospects is customers who have defected: after all, they already know the company and its products, and provided the problems which drove them away can be resolved, there is no reason why they should not return (Bogomolova and Romaniuk 2010). Even so, some customers will defect anyway, even when they are satisfied with the company's efforts, simply because they get a better offer elsewhere or they feel like a change. Under those circumstances, they may be reluctant to admit their real reason for going (Naumann et al. 2010).

Customer winback

Customers do not always give companies a formal warning that they are about to defect. In many cases, they leave informally. For the manager, this can create a problem: do we in fact have a lost customer, or is this simply a seasonal downturn, or a temporary loss of business?

The second decision point for the managers is to decide whether they actually want the customer back anyway. In some cases, the customer defects because they simply have no real need for the product, and have never bought in any substantial quantities. In these circumstances, there is little point in going to much effort to win back the customer, since the resulting business is not worthwhile.

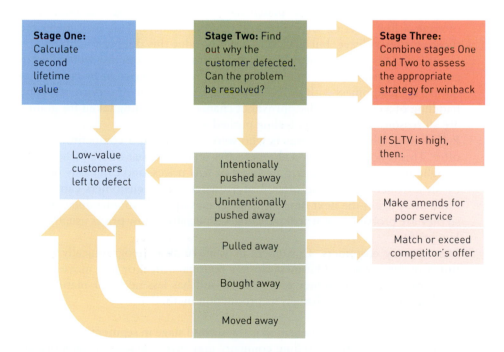

Figure 11.5   Segmenting the defectors

Second lifetime value The value of a former customer who has been won back to the firm's products.

Deciding on whether to win back the customer is a process of segmentation. The first stage in calculating this is to look at the customer's **second lifetime value** (Stauss and Friege 1999). Second lifetime value (SLTV) may differ from the same customer's first lifetime value for the following reasons:

1. The defected customer is familiar with the company, and also with its competitors. Either of these factors might be positive or negative in terms of winback.
2. The company knows more about the defected customer than about any new customer – in particular the company should be able to work out what the customer does not like.
3. Recognition of the customer's needs expressed during the winback process might well lead to a sales performance better than that obtained first time round, because the customer appreciates the extra attention.
4. The length of the **sales cycle** will be shorter because the customer and the company know each other better.

Sales cycle The series of activities undertaken by salespeople.

Calculating the actual SLTV for a given customer will depend greatly on the industry, and on what the individual customer's behaviour was previously. In business-to-business markets, firms may well be able to calculate the figures for individual customers, but in consumer markets the marketers will need to calculate on the basis of market segments instead.

Stauss and Friege (1999) identified five defector categories:

1. Intentionally pushed away. These are customers who are really not worth keeping: the costs of serving them outweigh the value the firm gains from them. The customer is sometimes wrong: sometimes people can be rude, unpleasant, or expensive to do business with. Some companies even write to such customers and tell them to take their business elsewhere (Freiberg and Freiberg 1996). In other cases, companies might match the service level to the customer value, offering a low level of service to low value customers. This may mean that those customers leave, but since they are low value this does not matter.
2. Unintentionally pushed away. These are customers whom we would like to continue serving, but who were pushed away by poor service or by mistakes on our part. Unhappiness with a product delivery, installation or service; improper handling of a complaint; disapproval of changes; and feeling taken for granted are all reasons for customers feeling pushed away.
3. Pulled away. These are customers who were attracted by a competitors' better offer. This is not necessarily a cheaper offer – just one that offers better value.
4. Bought away. These customers are lured by low prices, and can easily be lured by an introductory pricing offer. Unfortunately, these customers can also be lured away again the next time someone comes up with an introductory offer, so they are probably not worth pursuing – especially as low prices usually mean low profits.
5. Moved away customers. Customers may move away geographically (a consumer moves house or a business closes a regional office) or may move away in terms of needs (a consumer gets married and has less need for mating-game products, or a business changes its production methods).

Finding out the reasons for the defection is the second stage in segmenting the defectors. Asking people within the selling company may give one side of the story, but ultimately the company must ask the customers themselves. When asking members of the company their side of the story, the following procedures might help:

1. Review the customer's history with the people who actually dealt with the customer.
2. Read through the customer's file.
3. Look for possible causes for defection in letters, salespeople's reports and so forth.
4. Look at the pattern of the customer's orders, and relate this to any changes in the company's business practices or the customer's situation.

Customers who have defected should be interviewed to find out their reasons for leaving. Managers should bear in mind that customers may not always want to give the true reason, or may decide to embroider their reasons in the hope of gaining more concessions from the supplying company. It is important that the company does not try to re-sell the customer when conducting an exit interview – the purpose of the exercise is to learn for the future, and this will not happen if the customer is suspicious that the interview is simply a sales pitch.

Think outside this box!

Presumably when people decide to defect, they do so because they do not like the company or its products. Imagine their delight when they are telephoned a few days later by someone trying to find out why they left. Is it likely that the customer is going to tell the truth about why they left? Either they will not want to appear rude, or they will want to make a point, or they will want to 'get their own back' on the person telephoning. In any case, it is likely to be an embarrassing or painful experience for all concerned. So why put ourselves through it? Is it because we need to get some kind of feedback? Perhaps, at the least, we might get some idea of what annoys people about what we're doing – and in some cases maybe we can put the problem right for the defector!

The third stage in segmenting the defectors is to combine the SLTV with the reasons for defection. The most attractive segment will be the ones with the highest SLTV who are also in the unintentionally pushed away, or pulled away categories. This is because bought-away customers are likely to be fickle, moved-away customers are unlikely to be persuaded to move back, and the intentionally-pushed customers are undesirable anyway. These customers all left for reasons that would jeopardise any future relationship.

Real-life marketing: Lost customers may not be lost!

It's easy to assume that a customer who has defected is gone forever. In any case, part of you won't want to call up a disaffected customer in case they give your ear a hammering over what a rotten company you are. But think about this – there must have been something they liked about you, and they already know you – so if you can put right what went wrong, maybe you can win them back.

(Continued)

(Continued)

BellSouth Mobility is a major mobile telephone company operating in the southern United States. Mobile phones have a high churn rate (customers come and go regularly) but BellSouth realised that its own churn rate was exceptionally high. Research showed that there were four key reasons why customers left: (1) BellSouth did something that upset the customer. (2) BellSouth wouldn't issue a credit for a failed call. (3) BellSouth gave free phones to new subscribers, but not to existing customers. (4) BellSouth wouldn't give current promotions to existing customers.

At first, the company contacted 3500 defected customers and offered them a free phone and free calls if they would come back, but the response was very disappointing: overall this campaign cost $800 for each customer who returned, which is clearly not economic. Some thought on the part of BellSouth's marketers revealed the problem – defectors were tied into new contracts which they couldn't break. Next time, the company contacted people 11 months after they had defected, about the time when their new contracts would be expiring, and followed up the mailing with a telephone call. This time the campaign cost only $325 per re-recruited customer, which may sound like a lot but is still a lot cheaper than finding a new customer.

To do this in practice, you should:

- Plan around the real customer defection issues. Don't guess – research it. It should be easy enough to do this!
- Let them know that you know why they left, and you are prepared to do something about it.
- Test your approach. If you get it wrong, the customers will REALLY be lost!
- Time your win-back effort with the customer's ability to return.

Obviously these rather long-drawn-out procedures are unlikely to be used in the case of a consumer who has decided to switch from one mobile-telephone network to another, but in business-to-business markets the returns are potentially extremely high.

Customer retention and customer winback are both sides of the same coin: establishing and maintaining long-term relationships. Although relationship marketing has met with its main successes in business-to-business marketing, the future of consumer marketing is thought to lie with those firms that are able to retain customers and establish relationships with them. The most fertile ground for this approach is likely to be in services marketing environments, since the transactions always involve dealing with people. In some service industries (hairdressing, banking, restaurants, even hotels) people do establish relationships of trust, which may last for many years.

Chapter summary

Developing closer relationships with customers is a crucial part of business success. Given that the number of customers is shrinking in both consumer markets (due to falling birth-rates in the developed world) and in business markets (due to increasing mergers and acquisitions), the importance of keeping the ones that remain is even greater than before.

Even when the relationship strategy fails, however, it is still possible to regain lost customers. Often these customers will be easier to win back than a new customer would be to gain: provided the company is careful in its approach, old customers can be persuaded to return to the fold.

Key points

- The value chain (and value network) concepts take a holistic view of supplying customer needs.
- Cutting out the middleman is likely to increase costs, not reduce them.
- There are four core activities in the value chain: procurement, human resource management, technical development and infrastructure.
- The quality of the buyer–seller relationship depends on how well the seller manages it.
- Quality is the relationship between expectation and reality.
- Service quality is often a major differentiator – sometimes it is the only differentiator.
- Solving customer complaints is a matter of offering a fair outcome, a fair procedure and fair treatment.
- There are three stages in customer defection: value breakdown, season of discontent and termination.
- Not all customers are valuable: not all should be encouraged to return.

Review questions

1. What is the difference between the value chain and the value network?
2. Why do some firms concentrate on service quality?
3. How would you choose which customers were worth keeping or winning back if you were marketing manager for a bank?
4. Why is the onus on the seller to manage the buyer–seller relationship?
5. What are the key elements in building trust?
6. What are the differences between the way a customer views benchmarking and the way a comparing might view it?
7. How does quality affect people's loyalty to the product and to the firm? How might firms manage quality?
8. Why might someone regard a £50,000 car as value for money?
9. Why might there be a difference between customer expectations and management's perception of customer expectations?
10. Explain the Leaky Bucket theory.

Case study revisited: Accor

Accor's loyalty scheme is actually three separate schemes. Le Club Accor is a free card that builds points whenever the holder stays in any Accor hotel. Points are based on the amount spent, so someone staying in a Sofitel or MGallery would build points faster than someone staying in an Ibis or Novotel. The more the person stays, the better the card gets because those who stay more frequently or who spend a lot will be upgraded: after ten stays or 2500 points the member moves to Silver status, which means that more points are awarded for every pound spent. After 30 nights or 10,000 points the customer moves to Gold status, and after 60 nights or 25,000 points the customer moves to Platinum status. Not only does this reward the more frequent guests and the biggest spenders, it also acts as a disincentive to cash in one's points. Two thousand points is equivalent to €40 towards a stay in an Accor hotel.

The second loyalty scheme is aimed at business travellers and other frequent travellers. Called the Accor Favourite Guest, this card costs €170 but it provides discounts on room rates and also discounts on car hire. This is very much aimed at companies who would buy the cards for their travelling employees – Accor even have a special scheme for companies that buy more than five cards.

Finally, there is a dedicated loyalty scheme for Ibis hotels. Again, this card is paid for – €160 – but it provides substantial discounts at Ibis hotels and also reward points that are valid at all other Accor hotels. Cardholders have a guarantee of a room provided they book more than three days in advance – a useful guarantee for someone who is, for example, a sales rep.

Accor's schemes may seem complex, but what they provide is flexibility, and a recognition of the realities of the hotel business. People who hold Accor cards are unlikely to stay anywhere else: after all, the choice is wide enough to suit any pocket, and any set of circumstances.

Case study: Netflix

Netflix is an American company, founded in 1997 by Marc Randolph and Reed Hastings. The idea for the business model came when Hastings was charged $40 for the late return of a video he had rented (he was *very* late with it!). Netflix operated on-line, but (in those early days of the Internet) had to mail out videos and DVDs. The company operated on a basis of not charging late fees and not charging for postage, in exchange for which subscribers pay a monthly membership fee.

The concept proved to be a great success. People certainly liked the convenience of being able to rent movies from their own homes, and in a country as large as the United States Netflix filled a gap in the market – not everyone was able to get to a video store to rent a movie, and certainly for people in rural areas collecting and returning movies was a major headache. In common with many early dot.com companies, Netflix lost money at first, but was still able to launch on the stock market in 2002 with a market value of almost $80m. The company showed its first profit in 2003 and seemed set to do very well: by 2005, Netflix was sending out almost a million movies a day and had 5.6 million subscribers. By 2007, DVDs were in decline (and tape-based videos were almost dead in the water), so Netflix began offering direct downloads to subscribers, which at the time were delivered as video on demand as opposed to streaming downloads.

Netflix became one of the world's leading distributors of movies, as well as an important player as an independent film distributor. This was previously the realm of tiny, artsy companies who delivered films made by little-known producers and directors: the Netflix model made such distribution cheap and easy, and for the company the marginal cost of distributing a film which would appeal to only a small audience was so tiny it was irrelevant. Netflix was revolutionising film distribution, with its loyal subscriber base and film-makers clamouring to place their movies through Netflix.

In 2010 the company decided to phase out its 'friends' feature, which allowed subscribers to communicate with each other (presumably about movies which they had liked or disliked). This created protests on Facebook and Twitter, but the company continued to phase out the service, pointing out that only 2% of users actually made use of it.

Unfortunately, the attempt by Netflix to enter the digital streaming market in 2011 was handled less than effectively – corporate decision-makers appeared not to have learned from the 'friends' protests. At this point, the company's business was turning over $16bn a year, and they saw that the future lay in the new technology of streaming downloads. The advantages were obvious: people with the appropriate technology could download a movie to watch at any time, rather than wait for the physical delivery of a DVD; the whole process could be conducted automatically, with almost no human intervention, which of course created an enormous cost benefit to the company.

Netflix launched their Qwikster download service as an easy alternative to mail order. Unfortunately, having both systems in place made the system more complex, and also more expensive for subscribers – the company failed to give existing subscribers the new system for free, and thus lost 800,000 subscribers and 77% of the company's share value in only four months. This was an impressive example of unintentional demarketing (the process of losing your market by mistake) – the company even failed to notice that the name Qwikster already belonged to a Twitter account holder, which effectively barred Netflix from using Twitter. In October of that year, Netflix reversed its decision and brought the two halves of the company back together under one subscription, following a spate of negative comments on Facebook and Twitter.

The company bounced back – it actually increased profits (probably due to the cost reductions of streaming) and added 610,000 subscribers during the following year. The company has first-run rights with several major studios (meaning that Netflix can distribute movies at the same time as they appear in cinemas, unlike TV companies which have to wait for anything up to two years).

Netflix entered the UK market in 2012, with a TV campaign and (in 2013) a door-to-door sales campaign. It remains to be seen whether they can develop the business to the point it has reached in the United States: the UK is a very different market.

Questions

1. Why would people protest about losing the 'friends' feature?
2. How might Netflix have avoided the Qwikster debacle?
3. How might customer winback operate in these circumstances?
4. Why might a further 610,000 subscribers have signed up for Netflix?
5. What might be the advantage of using a door-to-door campaign to recruit new subscribers?

Further reading

J. Bank, *The Essence of Total Quality Management* (Hemel Hempstead, Prentice Hall, 1992). Although it is now quite old, this book offers a clearly written and concise overview of total quality management.

John Egan, *Relationship Marketing: Exploring Relational Strategies in Marketing*, 3rd edn (Hemel Hempstead: FT Prentice Hall, 2008). This very readable book shows how relationship marketing has a major role to play in strategy.

Gerhard Plenert, *The eManager: Value Chain Management in an E-Commerce World* (Dublin: Blackhall, 2001). Although e-commerce is a dynamic field, this text manages to give the reader a view that is sufficiently conceptual to be slow to age. Managing the value chain is often driven by IT, so this text is well worth reading by anyone who has an interest in managing suppliers and customers

References

Allaway, Arthur W., Goover, Richard M., Berkowitz, David and Davis, Lenita (2006) Deriving and exploring behaviour segments within a retail loyalty card programme. *European Journal of Marketing*, 4 (11/12): 1317–339.

Ang, Lawrence and Buttle, Francis (2006) Managing for successful customer acquisition: an exploration. *Journal of Marketing Management*, 22 (3/4): 295–17.

Bell, Simon and Eisengrich, Andreas B. (2007) The paradox of customer education: customer expertise and loyalty in the financial services industry. *European Journal of Marketing*, 41 (5/6): 466–86.

Bogovoloma, S. and Romaniuk, J. (2010) Brand equity of defectors and never boughts in a business financial market, *Industrial Marketing Management*, 39 (8): 1262–1268.

Carlson, Kurt A. and Sally, David (2002) Thoughts that count: fairness and possibilities, intentions and reactions. *Advances in Consumer Research*, 29 (1): 79–89.

Chaston, I., Badger, B., Mangles, T. and Sadler-Smith, E. (2003) Relationship marketing, knowledge management systems and e-commerce operations in small UK accounting practices. *Journal of Marketing Management*, 19: 109–29.

Christopher, M., Ballantyne, D. and Payne, A. (1991) *Relationship Marketing.* Oxford: Butterworth–Heinemann.

Chung, Emily and Beverland, Michael (2006) An exploration of consumer forgiveness following marketer transgressions. *Advances in Consumer Research*, 33: 98–9.

Cui, G. and Wang, Y. (2010) Consumers' SKU choices in an online supermarket: a latent class approach. *Journal of Marketing Management*, 26 (5/6): 495–514.

Dunleavy, June and Olivieri, Colin (2001) Relationship marketing: satisfaction, loyalty and perceived quality. *Journal of Selling and Major Account Management*, 3 (3).

East, Robert, Hammond, Kathy and Gendall, Philip (2006) Fact and fallacy in retention marketing. *Journal of Marketing Management*, 22 (1): 5–23.

Evans, J. and Laskin, R. (1994) The relationship marketing process: a conceptualisation and application. *Industrial Marketing Management*, 23: 439–52.

Freiberg, K. and Freiberg, J. (1996) *Nuts: Southwest Airlines Crazy Recipe for Business and Personal Success.* Austin, TX: Bard Books.

Griffin, J. and Lowenstein, M. (2001) *Customer Winback.* San Francisco: Jossey-Bass.

Gummeson, E. (1988) Service quality and product quality combined. *Review of Business*, 9 (3).

Gupta, Sunil, Lehmann, Donald R. and Stuart, Jennifer Ames (2004) Valuing customers. *Journal of Marketing Research*, 41 (1): 7–18.

Halliburton, Chris and Ziegfeld, Alice (2009) How do major European companies communicate their corporate identity across countries? An empirical investigation of corporate internet communications. *Journal of Marketing Management*, 25 (9/10): 909–25.

Harrigan, Paul, Ramsey, Elaine and Ibbotson, Patrick (2011) Critical factors underpinning the e-CRM activities of SMEs. *Journal of Marketing Management*, 27 (5/6): 503–29.

Helgesen, Oyvind (2006) Are loyal customers profitable? Customer satisfaction, customer (action) loyalty and customer profitability at the individual level. *Journal of Marketing Management*, 22 (3/4): 245–66.

Holmlund, Maria (2004) Analysing business relationships and distinguishing different interaction levels. *Industrial Marketing Management*, 33 (4): 279–87.

Izquierdo, Carmen Camarero, Cillan, Jesus Gutierrez (2004) The interaction of dependence and trust in long-term industrial relationships. *European Journal of Marketing*, 38 (8): 974–84.

Johnson, Michael D., Herrmann, Andreas and Huber, Frank (2006) The evolution of loyalty intentions. *Journal of Marketing*, 70 (2): 122–32.

Leenders, Michael R. and Blenkhorn, David L. (1988) *Reverse Marketing: The New Buyer–Seller Relationship.* New York: Free Press.

Leong, Yow Peng and Qing Wang (2006) Impact of relationship marketing tactics (RMTs) on switchers and stayers in a competitive service industry. *Journal of Marketing Management*, 22 (1): 25–59.

Luo, Xueming and Homburg, Christian (2007) Neglected outcomes of customer satisfaction. *Journal of Marketing*, 71 (2): 133–49.

Meyer-Waarden, Lars and Benavent, Christophe (2006) The impact of loyalty programmes on repeat purchase behaviour. *Journal of Marketing Management*, 22 (1/2): 61–88.

Morgan, Robert M. and Hunt, Shelby D. (1994) The commitment–trust theory of relationship marketing. *Journal of Marketing*, 58 (July): 20–38.

Murray, Kyle B. and Haubl, Gerald (2002) The fiction of no friction: a user skills approach to cognitive lock-in. *Advances in Consumer Research*, 29: 11–18.

Naumann, E., Haverila, M., Khan, S. and Williams, P. (2010) Understanding the causes of defection among satisfied B2B service customers. *Journal of Marketing Management*, 26 (9/10): 878–900.

Oederkerken-Schroeder, Gaby, Ouwersloot, Hans, Lemmink, Jos and Semeijn, Janjaap (2003) Consumers' trade-off between relationship, service, package and price: an empirical study in the car industry. *European Journal of Marketing*, 37 (1): 219–42.

Parasuraman, A., Zeithaml, V.A. and Berry, L.L. (1985) A conceptual model of service quality and its implications for future research. *Journal of Marketing*, 49 (Fall): 41–50.

Patterson, Paul G. (2004) A contingency model of behavioural intentions in a service context. *European Journal of Marketing*, 8 (9/10): 1304–5.

Pervan, Simon J., Bove, Liliana L. and Johnson, Lester W. (2009) Reciprocity as a key stabilizing norm of interpersonal marketing relationships: scale development and validation. *Industrial Marketing Management*, 38 (1): 60–70.

Reed, David (1999) Great expectations. *Marketing Week*, 29 April, pp. 57–8.

Reichheld, F. (1996) *The Loyalty Effect.* Boston, MA: Harvard Business School Press.

Roberts, Keith, Varki, Sajeev, and Brodie, Rod (2003) Measuring the quality of relationships in consumer services: an empirical study. *European Journal of Marketing*, 37 (1): 169–96.

Romaniuk, Jenni and Sharp, Byron (2003) Brand salience and customer defection in subscription markets. *Journal of Marketing*, 19: 25–44.

Stauss, B. and Friege, C. (1999) Regaining service customers. *Journal of Service Research*, May: 347–61.

Tax, S. and Brown, S. (1998) Recovering and learning from eservice failures. *Sloan Management Review*, 40 (1): 78.

Thompson, Matthew and Johnson, Allison R. (2002) Investigating the role of attachment dimensions as predictors of satisfaction in consumer-brand relationships. *Advances in Consumer Research*, 29 (1): 42.

Verhoef, Peter C. (2003) Understanding the effect of customer relationship management efforts on customer retention and customer share development. *Journal of Marketing*, 67 (4): 30–45.

Wang, Sijun and Huff, Lenard C. (2007) Explaining buyers' response to sellers' violation of trust. *European Journal of Marketing*, 41 (9/10): 1033–52.

Wangenheim, Florian von and Bayón, Tomás (2003) Satisfaction, loyalty and word-of-mouth within the customer base of a utility provider: differences between stayers, switchers and referral switchers. *Journal of Consumer Behaviour*, 3 (3): 211–20.

Wangenheim, Florian von and Bayón, Tomás (2007) Behavioural consequences of overbooking service capacity. *Journal of Marketing*, 71 (4): 36–47.

Weitz, Barton A. and Bradford, Kevin D. (1999) Personal selling and sales management: a relationship marketing perspective. *Journal of the Academy of Marketing Science*, 27 (Spring): 241–54.

Zauberman, Gul (2002) Lock-in over time: time references, prediction accuracy, and the information cost structure. *Advances in Consumer Research*, 29: 9–10.

More online

To gain free access to additional online resources to support this chapter please visit:
www.sagepub.co.uk/blythe3e

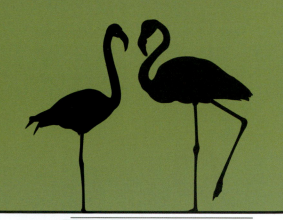

CHAPTER ⑫
Product portfolio and strategic branding

LEARNING OBJECTIVES

After reading this chapter you should be able to:

- Describe the stages a product goes through between launch and obsolescence.

- Explain how to manage a portfolio of products.

- Describe the role of executive judgement in managing the product portfolio, and show how theoretical models can help.

- Explain the advantages and disadvantages of matrix models.

- Describe the relationship between services and physical products.

- Explain the transition from product orientation to service orientation in business markets.

- Explain the role of packaging in marketing.

Introduction

Products, or bundles of benefits, are the main things that companies offer to their customers as their part of the exchange. A product provides benefits to its consumers, which is why they are prepared to part with their hard-earned cash to buy it: products might be anything that is put together by someone for the purposes of selling it. This includes services, of course – a haircut is as much a product as is a loaf of bread.

It is common to speak of 'the product', as if the company offered only one product, but in fact the vast majority of companies offer several, even many, products to their customers. Handling a portfolio of products is another aspect of the marketer's role.

In the nature of things, products become obsolete or unfashionable, and competitors come up with new ideas: it would be an unwise company that hoped its products would be saleable forever, so companies need to manage the portfolio of products in such a way as to ensure that it still meets the needs of the customers, dropping products that no longer meet customer needs effectively and introducing new ones that fit the market better.

Product portfolio The range
of goods offered by a firm.

This chapter looks at the management of the **product portfolio**, and explores some of the problems of managing products in the real world.

Preview case study: HJ Heinz

It has been many years since Heinz had only 57 varieties. In fact, the number 57 was chosen by the company's founder, Henry J. Heinz, simply because he liked the sound of it – it had no other significance.

HJ Heinz produce almost 6000 varieties, spread across 200 brands worldwide. Food is produced and sold in eight different categories: Convenience Meals, Condiments and Sauces, Infant Feeding, Weight Control, Frozen Food, Pet Food, Foodservice and Seafood. Although the parent company is American, the British part of the company is the biggest overseas subsidiary, and many British consumers think of the company as British.

Managing such a huge range of products is by no means simple. In the UK, the Jones Knowles Ritchie packaging design company took over the account in 1997, and found a wide range of different packaging designs in place. The situation had grown up because each product had its own particular packaging problems and needs – but the situation had got out of hand, with no clear brand image being presented and a confusing message being presented to consumers.

Meanwhile, Heinz USA had decided to follow the example of its Weightwatchers brand and lose some weight. The company sold off its pet food business in 2002, and a number of its other marginal brands over the next few years. In the UK, sales of salad cream were falling – salad cream is an entirely British product, with virtually no market outside the UK. Also, healthy eating was becoming the latest fad – demand for organic food, low-fat food and even low-carb food as a result of the popularity of the Atkins Diet, meant that Heinz had to make a number of tough decisions.

The product life cycle

A key concept in product portfolio management is the product life cycle (see Figure 12.1). The basis of the product life cycle (PLC) is that products move through a series of stages from their introduction to their final withdrawal from the market. Products tend to lose money when they are first introduced (because sales are low initially, and the costs of producing tend to be high because there are no economies of scale). Eventually, if all goes well, the product's sales improve and it begins to return a profit, but sooner or later the growth in sales will peak out, because the product reaches the limit of the number of people who want to buy it. As alternative products enter the market (perhaps because competitors seize an opportunity to bring out their own version, or perhaps because fashions and tastes change) the product will go into a decline and will eventually cease to have any market.

In fact, the situation is often much more complex than this, so the basic product life cycle (as shown in Figure 12.1) does not always describe what actually happens in practice.

Figure 12.1   The product life cycle

The product life cycle is a useful concept for explaining what happens to products, but it suffers from a number of weaknesses. First, the model cannot predict with any accuracy what will happen, because there is no good way of knowing what the length of the maturity phase will be: for a fashion item, the maturity phase might last only a few months, whereas for a product such as pitta bread the maturity phase has already lasted several thousand years and shows no sign of changing.

Second, the model ignores the effects of marketing activities. If a product's sales are declining, marketers might decide to reposition the product in another market, or might run a major promotional campaign, or might decide to drop the product altogether and concentrate resources on another product in the portfolio. These alternatives are shown in Figures 12.2 and 12.3.

Third, the model does not account for those products that come back into fashion after a few years in the doldrums. Recent examples include the Mini Cooper, the Volkswagen Beetle, and the yo-yo (which seems to undergo revivals every ten to fifteen years).

Fourth, the model does not take account of the fact that the vast majority of new products fail. This would give a life cycle such as that shown in Figure 12.4, where the product never moves into profit.

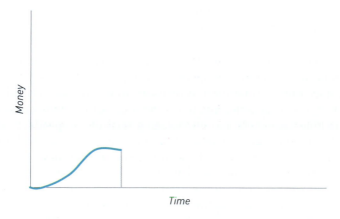

Figure 12.2   Product dropped shortly after introduction

Think outside this box!

It is not unusual for products to disappear almost as soon as they are launched: test marketing sometimes shows disappointing results, so the product is taken off the shelves. But the product life cycle tells us that products often lose money at first – and some products are 'sleepers', which do nothing for several years and then suddenly take off for no apparent reason.

There are also products that appear to be eminently sensible and yet do not find a market, possibly through a lack of professionalism on the part of the marketers. So should there be a marketer's life cycle instead? If the product doesn't perform, should we keep the product and fire the managers?

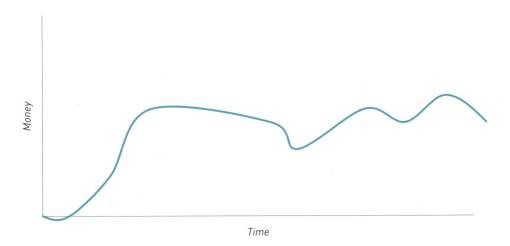

Figure 12.3   Effects of marketing activities on the product life cycle

Finally, the PLC looks at only one product, whereas most marketing managers have to balance the demands of many different products, and decide which of them is likely to yield the best return on investment (or perhaps which one will take the company nearest to achieving its strategic objectives).

Despite these weaknesses, the PLC is widely quoted and used in making decisions about marketing tactics. The type of decisions to be made might be as follows.

Introduction phase: The strategic objective will be to build the market as quickly as possible in order to shut out the competition. The product itself is likely to be a fairly basic model, since there has been no feedback from the market yet and therefore no opportunity to refine it or differentiate it. The focus of the firm's promotion effort will be on creating awareness and encouraging trial of the product: advertising is more effective in the introduction phase than it is later (Vakratsas and Ambler 1999). The price is likely to be high, since the firm needs to recoup development costs and (at least for the time being) does not have to compete, since competitors have yet to introduce their own versions of the product. Distribution of the product is likely to be patchy at this stage, since many distributors will not want to risk carrying an unknown product.

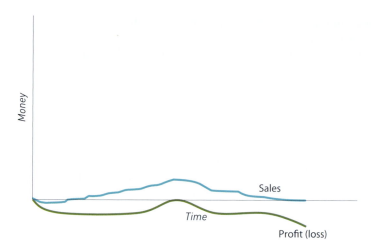

Figure 12.4 Failed product

Growth: The strategic thrust will still be on building the market as quickly as possible, but there will be a shift in promotional emphasis from creating awareness towards encouraging repeat purchases and brand preference. The product itself is likely to be available in several different versions by now, and the price will be lower as competitors enter the market: since their development costs will have been considerably lower (because they have an existing product to copy) they can still show a profit on a lower price. Distribution will be much wider in the growth phase as distributors become more confident of selling the product.

Maturity: At this stage the strategy shifts to one of maintaining market share in the face of increased competition. The promotional thrust is concerned with maintaining brand loyalty, and with maintaining awareness. The price will be at its lowest, and there will be several versions of the product available in order to meet the needs of several market segments. Competition will also be at its peak, especially as some competitors will be trying to increase market share by using aggressive marketing tactics. Distribution will be intensive.

Decline: The strategy in the decline phase is likely to be one of harvesting, in which very little money is spent on promoting or developing the product further, and it is allowed to decline, with the company reaping a profit from the remaining sales. The product will not be available in all its variants at this stage, since the company will be rationalising the range to reduce production costs. Promotional expenditure will be at a minimum, or cut out altogether, but the price will be rising in order to make as much as possible from the remaining sales. Distribution will shrink as some distributors find that they can no longer carry the product profitably. Eventually, the product will be eliminated as it will no longer be viable. It should be noted that most decisions to eliminate products are made on the basis of intuition and judgement rather than any formal analysis (Greenley and Barus 1994), which is not surprising since there is always the option to try to revive the product's fortunes by investing in the brand.

For some companies there are serious doubts as to whether it is worth investing in new products at all, and in fact there are companies that have produced essentially the same product for many years. These companies do not innovate at all, but as a result they run the risk of their product being superseded by a superior competitive product. Also, research shows that new products are more successful than sales promotions in producing the following results (Pawels et al. 2004):

1. Long-term financial performance and firm value.
2. Investor reaction (which grows over time).
3. Yielding top-line, bottom-line and stock market benefits.

This in itself means that new products are worth pursuing.

Managing product portfolios

The main lesson the PLC teaches us is that all products will, eventually, decline. This means that managers need to look at a regular introduction of new products into the range (the portfolio) offered by the firm. At any moment in the company's existence it will have some products that have only just been introduced and are therefore losing money, some of which are mature and are making at least some money, some of which are doing extremely well, some of which are weakening and dying, and so forth. Since any company has only limited resources at its disposal, marketing managers need to make decisions about which products need the most support, and which ones can either manage with less support, or need no support because they will shortly drop out anyway.

Real-life marketing: Give the product away

Giving products away might be the only way to establish a new market. Not everybody wants to be the first to try a new product – so charging for it might simply create a barrier to adoption. If the product is one that links to other products further down the line, it may be worth giving it away and taking the profit from the spares and peripherals you will sell later.

When King C. Gillette invented the safety razor he was working as a salesman for a manufacturer of bottle caps. He knew that he would have to make the disposable razor blades in very large numbers if the price was to work out – but there was no market for the blades unless men already owned the razors. He needed a quick way of getting men to switch from cut-throat razors to safety razors – so he gave the razors away free, with some free blades. Once men tried the safety razor, they would never go back to the cut-throat razor (they don't call it a cut-throat for nothing, you understand).

Once the product was established, Gillette could start charging for the razors themselves: word of mouth took care of that. Yet Gillette continued to sell the razors at or below the cost of production: he made his money on the blades.

There are some necessary conditions if this is to work in practice, though.

- The product must involve a long-term commitment to buy spares or peripherals – for example, printers need ink and mobile phones need telephone calls to be made from them.
- The target market needs to be clear. Giving the product out to everybody is no use unless they will tell other people about it.
- The product (and more importantly the peripherals) must have good intellectual property protection. If it isn't patented, competitors can sell the peripherals much cheaper than you can, because they don't have to recover the cost of producing the main product.

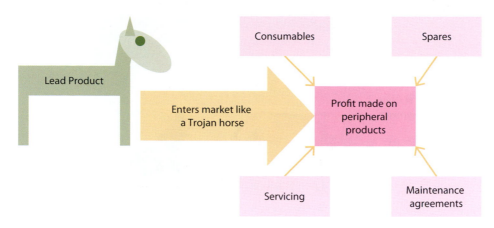

Figure 12.5 Linked products

The decision is not necessarily a simple one: some products may be unprofitable in themselves, but may stimulate sales of other products. For example, a power-tool manufacturer may make very little profit from sales of a power saw (due to competition from low-cost imports, or perhaps due to the strong negotiating power of retailers) but may make much healthier profits from sales of replacement blades. Because many managers have specific, small ranges of product to look after they will often lose sight of the big picture, so that the company's product portfolio is not a coherent, well-balanced mix but is instead an ill-matched assortment of products that do not have very much relationship to each other.

Portfolio planning is therefore a strategic issue, since it dictates the overall direction the company will go in. Portfolio planning is complex, but needs to be carried out if the firm is to direct its marketing resources in the most effective direction.

The Boston Consulting Group matrix

It is possible to superimpose the PLC diagrams for each product onto the graph to give a composite view of what is happening to the firm's product portfolio. Apart from making the graph extremely complex, this will give a long-term overview, but the problems of prediction still remain. For many managers, a 'snapshot' of what is happening now is more useful. The Boston Consulting Group (BCG) developed a matrix for decision-making in these circumstances. The original BCG matrix is as shown in Figure 12.6.

Stars are products with rapid growth and a dominant share of the market. Often the costs of fighting off the competition and maintaining growth mean that the product is actually absorbing more money than it is generating, but eventually it is hoped that it will be the market leader and the profits will begin to come back in. The problem lies in judging whether the market is going to continue to grow, or whether it will go down as quickly as it went up. Even the most successful Star will eventually decline as it moves through the life cycle.

Stars Products with a large share of a growing market.

Cash Cows are the former Stars. They have a dominant share of the market, but are now in the maturity phase of the life cycle and consequently have low growth. A Cash Cow is generating cash, and can be 'milked' of it to finance the Stars. These are the products that have steady year-in year-out sales and are generating much of the firm's profits; examples might be the Big Mac hamburger, Coca-Cola and the Ford Mondeo.

Cash Cow A product with large share of a mature market.

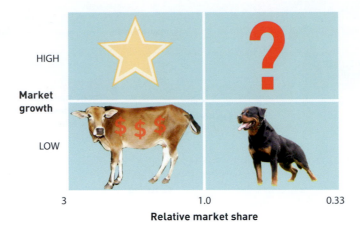

Figure 12.6   Boston Consulting Group matrix (© The Boston Consulting Group)

Dog A product with a small share of a mature market.

Dogs have a low market share and low growth prospects. The argument here is not whether the product is profitable; it almost always is. The argument is about whether the firm could use its production facilities to make something that would be more profitable, and this is also almost always the case.

Problem Child A product with a small share of a growing market.

The **Problem Child** has a small share of a growth market, and causes the marketer the most headaches since it is necessary to work out a way of building market share so as to turn the product into a Star. This means finding out why the share is so low, and developing strategies to increase market share rapidly. The Problem Child (or question mark) could be backed with an even bigger promotion campaign, or it could possibly be adapted in some way to fit the market better. Market research plays a crucial role in making these decisions; finding out how to adapt a product is a difficult area of research, but the potential rewards are huge and adapting the product to meet people's needs better is almost always cheaper than increasing the advertising spend.

The policy decisions that arise from this view of the firm's product portfolio lie in the following areas:

- Which products should be dropped from the range entirely? This question not only hinges on how profitable the product itself is; sales of one product, will also often indirectly generate sales of another more profitable product.
- Which products should be backed with promotion campaigns? Backing the wrong product can be extremely expensive; advertising campaigns have no second-hand value, so if these do not work the money is just lost.
- Which products could be adapted to fit the market better, and in what ways? This very much hinges on the market research findings, and on customer feedback.
- Which new products could be introduced, and at what cost?

Like the product life cycle, the BCG matrix is a simple model that helps marketers to approach strategic product decisions. Again, like the PLC, it has a number of flaws. It is based on the following assumptions:

- Market share can be gained by an investment in marketing. This is not always the case; some products will have lost their markets altogether (perhaps through environmental changes) and cannot be revived, no matter how much is invested.

- Market share gains will always generate cash surpluses. Again, if the market share is gained by drastic price cutting, cash may actually be lost.
- Cash surpluses will be generated when the product is in the maturity stage of the life cycle. Not necessarily so; mature products may well be operating on such small margins (due to competitive pressure) that the profit generated is low.
- The best opportunity to build a dominant market position is during the growth phase. In most cases this would be true, but this does not take account of competition; a competitor's product might be growing even faster.

Because of these limitations, the BCG matrix has been widely criticised (even though it has proved popular with planners for many years). Here are some of the criticisms levelled at the BCG matrix:

- Assuming that cash flow is determined by the product's position in the matrix is incorrect. Some Stars can show strong positive cashflows, and so can some Dogs, especially if there is little competition in the market.
- Focusing on market share and growth rates can be misleading because it ignores competitive advantage. Although the market share might derive from a competitive advantage, it is by no means certain, and a competitor might develop a new competency which could be missed by a manager who is concentrating on market growth rates. A competitive advantage might come from cost advantages, the ownership of key assets, and so forth.
- Market growth rate is not the same as market attractiveness. A small, stable market might be more attractive for a number of reasons than a rapidly growing, volatile market that is attracting large numbers of competitors.
- Building a market share is not always a good idea. Attempts to do so may provoke retaliation from a strong competitor, thus wiping out any gains made.
- Some products are interdependent (as in the example of the power saw mentioned earlier). More subtly, some distributors may want to be provided with a full range of products, or some customers might feel aggrieved if a favourite product were to be dropped from the range, and boycott other products.
- Some products have a very short life cycle, so instead of being groomed to become Cash Cows they should be heavily exploited while still in the Star stage. The matrix does not allow for this.
- The matrix does not consider a potential competitive response. Whatever the firm does this is likely to be met with retaliation of some sort.
- The matrix assumes that resources are limited, whereas in fact products that show a positive return can be funded from borrowed money or the capital markets relatively easily. Thus the kind of choice the matrix implies does not in fact always have to be made.
- The dividing lines between the boxes are vague and arbitrary. How is high growth defined? How is a large market share defined? Indeed, how is the market defined?
- The matrix is based on cash flow (revenue) whereas profitability might be a better criterion.
- The Problem Child remains a problem – the matrix offers no guidance.
- The matrix does not take account of the possibility of shrinking markets, which are of course a reality, especially during periodic recessions when most markets are shrinking.

In 1982 Barksdale and Harris proposed two additions to the BCG matrix, as shown in Figure 12.7. **War Horses** have a high market share, but the market has negative growth; the problem for management is to decide whether the product is

War Horse A product with a large share of a shrinking market.

		Relative Market Share	
		HIGH	LOW
Market Growth	HIGH	Star	Problem Child
	LOW	Cash Cow	Dog
	NEGATIVE	War Horse	Dodo

Figure 12.7 Expanded BCG matrix

Dodo A product with a small share of a shrinking market.

in an irreversible decline, or whether it can be revived, perhaps by repositioning it in another market. **Dodos** have a low share of a negative growth market, and are probably best discontinued.

The BCG matrix has proved a useful tool for analysing product portfolio decisions, but is really only a snapshot of the current position with the products it describes. Since most markets are to a greater or lesser extent dynamic, the matrix should be used with a certain degree of caution.

The size of the product portfolio and the complexity of the products within it can have further effects on the firm's management. For example it has been shown that manufacturing a wide range of products with many options makes it difficult for the firm to use just-in-time purchasing techniques and complicates its supply activities.

The General Electric Market Attractiveness–Competitive Position model

The GE matrix, developed by management consultants McKinsey, is wider ranging than the BCG matrix. It is really a tool for deciding the strategic direction, because it compares market attractiveness and competitive strength and can therefore be used to consider all aspects of the company's activities, not just its products. However, it can be used for product portfolio management, since the company is able to look at the competitive strengths of each product in the portfolio, measured against competing products in the same market.

The criteria for judging competitive strength were as follows:

- Market size.
- Market growth rate.
- Strength of competition.
- Profit potential.
- Social, political and legal factors.

The criteria for judging competitive strength were:

- Market share.
- Potential to develop a differential advantage.
- Opportunities to develop a cost advantage.

- Reputation.
- Distribution capabilities.

Management should be able to decide which criteria are most important for the specific products under consideration. This makes the GE matrix more flexible than the BCG matrix, since it can be tailored to specific circumstances. Managers should then agree on a weighting system for each criterion to reflect its importance in the product's potential success.

Managers then score each market attractiveness factor and each competitive strength factor on a scale of one to ten: each score is then multiplied by the weighting to obtain an overall score for both market attractiveness and competitive strength. These scores can be plotted on the matrix to give an overall picture of the firm's competitive position for each product.

In Figure 12.8, the yellow circle represents a strong product in a medium to highly attractive market. The green circle represents a product that is in a highly attractive market, but weak compared with competing products; this product is unlikely to succeed in this market, and managers should consider withdrawing it or repositioning it in another market. The blue circle represents a product in an unattractive segment, but with medium-to-strong capabilities. Managers have two choices here: either they can build up the market in some way, or they can seek a more attractive segment. Finally, the white circle represents a product with weak capabilities in an unattractive segment. There is a clear case here for pulling out and investing elsewhere.

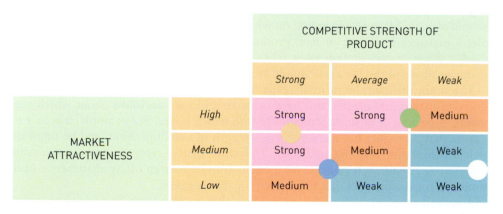

Figure 12.8 GE matrix

Think outside this box!

Snapshots are all very well, but by the time the information has been collected and analysed, the world has moved on. Taking a photograph halfway through a race will not tell you who won – and by the time the picture is developed, the result is known anyway.

So what use are snapshots? Perhaps what we need is a video camera, giving us a constant view of the changes that are happening, with constantly updated projections of what is about to happen next.

The GE matrix is more detailed than the BCG matrix because more factors are taken into account, the weightings provide a finer discrimination between products and it is more flexible so it can be tailored better to specific situations. The drawback is, of course, that it is more complex to use and it requires considerable judgement on the part of managers, so there is a strong possibility of bias creeping in as managers try to secure more resources for their products, or simply try to champion their own products through the system.

Positives and problems with grid analysis

Grid analyses such as GE and BCG matrices provide a useful tool for thinking about the problem. They clarify the issues, and in particular they stress that different products should be treated differently because they are at different stages in the life cycle, and they have different roles in the company's product strategy. For example, many companies act as if all products should return the same profit margin (this is especially the case in companies where cost-plus pricing is in evidence – there is more on this in Chapter 14). This is potentially damaging, because it would be unreasonable to expect a newly launched product to show a profit immediately, and an attempt to do so might result in cutting the promotional budget associated with the product in order to increase the returns. Equally, a Cash Cow might be capable of returning a much larger profit margin than that set by a manager wedded to the idea of equal profits across all products.

As a consequence, there is an implication that products in different categories should be handled by different managers, and the reward systems for managers should also be different depending on which type of product they handle. For example, a manager in charge of new product launches might be targeted in terms of market share or sales growth rates, whereas a manager in charge of a product in the maturity phase of the life cycle should be rewarded on a profitability basis.

The main difficulty with matrices is that they provide a spurious credibility in decision-making. Managers still have to make arbitrary decisions about which segments, products, or business strengths fit into which boxes. For example, it is easy to decide that a product has a competitive strength in one dimension, and be unaware that a competitor is about to launch a product that is even stronger in the same dimension. Equally, it is possible for a segment to be written off as unattractive until someone finds a product that fills a need for that segment.

A second problem with matrix planning is that it often leads firms to concentrate on growth, either through growing the firm's share of an existing market or through expanding into a growing market. While most firms do look for growth, an over-emphasis on entering growing markets can lead to the firm entering a market about which it knows very little, and abandoning or milking dry the stable, core products on which its success was founded. Going for high growth is a risky strategy, but is one that may well please the capital markets and is thus often seen as a good way to go.

Matrix models should therefore be treated with a degree of caution: having said that, they do have the advantage of simplifying the problem and clarifying the issues, which is likely to help the planning process.

Industrial product strategy

Although there are many similarities between the marketing of consumer products and the marketing of industrial products, industrial (business-to-business) products differ from consumer products in a number of ways, as follows:

- First, consumer product strategies focus much more on brand identity and product appearance than do industrial products.
- Second, many industrial products are sold alongside related services such as installation, training, maintenance packages and so forth, so that industrial products need to be offered as a total package.
- Third, business buyers try to minimise the emotional content of the decisions they make, so they tend to be concerned with specific, tangible, measurable benefits of the products.
- Fourth, the marketing and design of a business-to-business product usually requires a full understanding of the customer's value-creating activities in order to understand how the product on offer can contribute to the customer's value chain (see Chapter 11).

Within the global context, firms will tend to produce a proliferation of different versions of the product, because each market will demand something different. In some industrial markets this will also happen, because each buyer is big enough to be able to negotiate changes to the product. For example, a supplier of components to car manufacturers (e.g. wiring harnesses) not only has to supply a slightly different version of the product to each manufacturer, but also has to supply different versions for each model of car.

In such circumstances, the company is producing customer-specified products, in which it is the customer that specifies exactly what is to be produced. The company is then in a position whereby its marketing activities revolve around demonstrating competency in being able to manufacture to the required specifications.

A recent trend in business-to-business markets has been the transition from product to service orientation. For firms based in the wealthy countries of Western Europe and the United States, manufacturing is often no longer viable: production of physical goods is handled better by firms in the developing world, where costs (especially labour costs) are much lower. Western firms therefore need to differentiate themselves by providing services (which have to be provided locally), leaving the production of the physical products to lower-cost providers who can then ship the products in.

Think outside this box!

Ultimately, every country in the world is likely to become industrialised, and presumably will then move towards a post-industrial society in which more companies will want to transit from production to services. How is it possible for everyone to become service providers? Can we all make a living opening doors for each other? Or should there still be some manufacturers around?

Or maybe the economies of scale in manufacturing are such that a very tiny number of highly automated factories will be able to produce all the manufactured goods we need. From a marketer's viewpoint this appears very risky – such a system would put too much power in the hands of a few members of the value chain. Perhaps the balance of power will shift away from retailers and back to manufacturers!

Greenberg (2000) suggests that, instead of firms being 'solutions providers' whereby they add a range of services to their traditional product ranges, they should become customer value providers. A customer value provider seeks to provide value

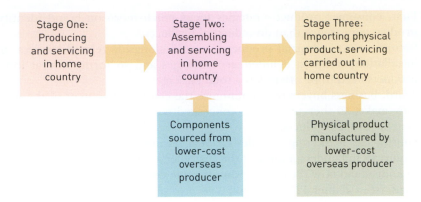

Figure 12.9   Transition from product to service orientation

further down the value chain, helping its clients to provide value to their customers. Majewski and Srinivas (2002) point out that managers often underestimate the true cost of shifting the company's orientation: they offer five business models for professional services, a shown in Table 12.1.

Table 12.1   Business models for professional services

	Product-centric	Professional services	Outsourcing	Information services	Financial services
Service value proposition	After-sales support Warranty services Maintenance offerings	Installation and support services Consulting services Other professional services	Lower fixed and/ or variable costs Access to enhanced capabilities Increased flexibility Reduced head-count	Information base for: Maintenance Inventory management Supply chain Trading Remote monitoring Data aggregation	Financing for product purchases May include other value-added financial services Move assets from balance sheet to income statement
Operating model	Network or depot repair In-bound call centre Field service force Integrated sales force	Traditional leveraged engagement model Separate services organisation New channels to market	Headcount transfer of client Technology transfer or updating Scale economies Service level tracking	Solutions selling skills Installed base of networked products Technology platforms and integration	Separate financial services organisation Financial operational processes (risk management, billing, etc.) Internal balance sheet

Packaging

Packaging is intended primarily to protect the product from the environment, and vice versa. For marketers, the packaging goes far beyond this, to the point where it conveys extra benefits to the customer, and thus becomes part of the product itself. Packaging carries out the following additional functions:

- Informs customers. This includes using the packaging to promote the company and its other products, for example by including recipe instructions, and also joint promotions with partner companies. Interestingly, though, corporate branding on the packaging seems to have little impact on customers, whereas brand category dominance has a significant effect (Laforet 2011).
- Meets legal information requirements.
- In some cases, packaging aids use of the product (for example, ring pulls on cans of fish make it easier to open the can without spilling the contents or making the can opener smell of fish).

Packaging decisions might include such factors as tamper resistance (paper strips around caps to prevent bottles being opened in supermarkets), and customer usage (for example the development of beer packaging from bottles to cans to ring pulls to non-waste ring pulls to draught beer systems). In recent years, environmental considerations have resulted in packaging that is either recyclable (or even recycled) or is biodegradable. Customer acceptability is clearly a factor: packaging must be hygienic and convenient for the customer, and it must look right as well: The ratio of the sides of the package affect people's perception of the product, but this depends also on the seriousness of the context – if the product is not important to the consumer, the shape of the packaging becomes less important as well (Raghubir and Greenleaf 2006).

Think outside this box!

Do people really care about the packaging of a product? Most of us just rip the packaging open as fast as possible to get our hands on the goodies – unless, of course, the product is packed in a shrink-wrap plastic shell!

Some packaging seems to have been designed for the maximum inconvenience to the customer. Unless you have a dog with strong teeth it's almost impossible to get into some packaging – so why do producers do this? Presumably it's to reduce pilfering – after all, if the customer can't get the packaging open without using bolt cutters, it's unlikely that the average shoplifter can sneak something out of its package in the store. So if the packaging is for the store's convenience, where does that leave customer centrality?

Some packaging has been designed in such a way that it can be protected by law: in the UK this is covered by the 1994 Trade Marks Act, which enables producers to prevent competitors from selling their products in similar packaging. In some cases the packaging has been rendered expensive to copy, requiring special machine tools to produce complex shapes, or expensive printing processes. 'Me-too' packaging has become common among supermarket own-brand products, and there has been some debate about the ethics of this. In some countries these imitators contravene copyright or patent laws (Davies 1995).

Packaging can raise ethical issues: oversized packs can give the impression that the consumer is buying more than is in fact the case, for example. This is called slack packaging (Smith 1995). Manufacturers of products such as powder detergents and breakfast cereals usually print a statement to the effect that the contents of the box may settle in transit (which is of course true) in order to avoid claims of slack packaging. Misleading labelling is another area in which packaging can be deceptive – packaging is commonly labelled 'recyclable', which is true but not very helpful, since virtually everything is recyclable, at a price. The implication is that the packaging is somehow more environmentally friendly than other packaging, which is unlikely to be the case. Foreign imports can be labelled as originating in the home country provided they have been packaged there, and there is a great deal of latitude in food labelling. Smoked bacon may well have had smoke flavour added, 'farm-fresh' eggs are likely to be from battery hens, and 'farmhouse' cheese may be from industrial cheese factories (Young 1999). To counter these problems, the UK's Food Standards Agency has drawn up a list of commonly used words, and has made recommendations as to when those words can be used. They have also recommended that phrases such as 'natural goodness' and 'country style' should be avoided, since they have no definite meaning (Benady 2001).

Marketing in a changing world: One-way packages

Up until the 1970s most glass bottles were recycled. Liquids were sold in bottles that had a substantial deposit on them, often more than the value of the liquid inside, and bottles were returned to the retailer in exchange for the deposit. Any bottles that were carelessly lost were usually picked up by children who supplemented their pocket money by collecting the deposits.

Then some clever person figured out that it would be cheaper to make a new bottle every time rather than return and clean the used ones. Energy costs were low, glass is made from cheap raw materials, what's the problem? Unfortunately we are now, forty years later, running out of holes in the ground into which to put the packaging.

Protests about the amount of packaging used for food are escalating, with activists removing packaging from products and leaving it at the checkouts in supermarkets. Moving from glass to plastic bottles hasn't helped, either – glass eventually recycles itself as it gets ground away to sand, but plastics are made from irreplaceable oil and do not return to nature. Manufacturers, food packers and retailers are all likely to find that the pressure is on to use properly biodegradable packaging or none at all – which presents a challenge for designers who have to come up with something that is eye-catching, protects the product, is cheap, can carry printed instructions and ingredients lists, and is also environmentally friendly. Recycling by putting things in the right bins is a stop-gap. It will not be long before packaging will have to disappear back into the natural world without having to be processed and without causing any damage.

Branding

The main vehicle by which marketers focus their activities is the brand. For marketing practitioners, the brand is the main area of responsibility – it is the one part of the business that is unquestionably their territory, and acts as the measure of the marketer's success. A brand that has a large market share, or occupies a prestigious position in the market, demonstrates the marketer's skill in the profession. Some products are unbranded – building materials such as bricks and sand, for example. These products have virtually no input from marketing, whereas all the activities needed to establish a brand are contributed by marketers.

Adding value to the product by branding involves a great deal more than merely giving the product a catchy name. Branding is the culmination of a range of activities across the whole marketing mix, leading to a brand image that conveys a whole set of messages to the consumer (and, more importantly, to the consumer's friends and family) about quality, price, expected performance and status. For example, the Porsche brand name conveys an image of engineering excellence, reliability, sporty styling, high speed and high prices, and of wealth and success on the part of the owner. People do not buy Porsches simply as a means of transport; for that purpose a basic Ford is perfectly adequate. Even children are affected – research shows that they need to have the right brand of snack in their lunch boxes if they are to maintain credibility in school (Roper and La Niece 2009).

Because branding involves all the elements of the marketing mix it cannot be regarded simply as a tactical tool designed to differentiate the product on the supermarket shelves. Instead, it must be regarded as the focus for the marketing effort, as a way of directing the thought processes of the management towards producing consumer satisfaction. The brand acts as a common point of contact between the producer and the consumer, as shown in Figure 12.10.

In Figure 12.10, the consumer benefits from the brand in terms of knowing what the quality will be, knowing what the expected performance will be, and gaining some self-image values (for example, a prestigious product conveys prestige to the consumer by association – conversely, a low-price product might enhance a consumer's sense of frugality and ability to find good value for money).

In many cases the core product will have very little to differentiate it from other products, and the brand is really the only differentiating feature. Despite the apparently artificial nature of differentiation by branding, the benefits to the consumer are

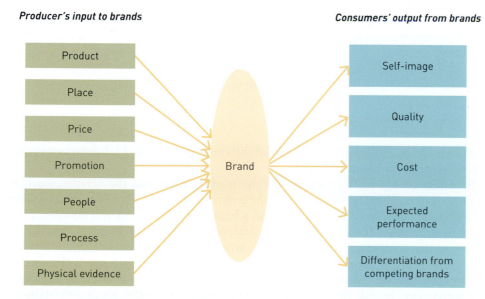

Figure 12.10   Brands as a contact point

very real; experiments show that branded analgesics work better than generic analgesics at relieving pain, even though the chemical formula is identical. This is because of the psychosomatic power of the brand. Someone driving a prestige car gains very real benefits in terms of the respect and envy of others, even if the performance of the car is no better than that of its cheaper rival.

Brands begin to exert influence early on in people's lives: an analysis of 422 letters to Santa Claus showed that most children are brand-orientated and are able to use sophisticated request strategies to get what they want (O'Cass and Clarke 2002). Also, children from poorer homes in the UK are acutely aware of the need to wear the right trainers, not only to appear 'cool' but also to avoid being bullied (Elliott and Leonard 2003). This effect was so strong that children actually said they preferred to talk to someone wearing branded trainers.

Real-life marketing: The Pepsi Challenge

For many years in towns and seaside resorts around Britain Pepsi-Cola used to set up a roadshow. Passers-by were asked to try two different cola drinks and say which they preferred. One of the drinks was Pepsi, the other was (of course) arch-rival Coca-Cola. Often to people's surprise, the majority said they preferred the Pepsi. However, when the same experiment is conducted with the brand names clearly displayed, most people prefer the Coke. Coke outsells Pepsi in almost every market in the world – and the only explanation for this is the power of the brand!

If your brand is second, but people like yours better when they try it, you might want to copy Pepsi's approach. However, the following conditions will have to apply:

- Both products need to be easy to try.
- You will need access to quite a large number of people who will be prepared to try the test.
- The product should be a fast-moving consumer product rather than a capital good such as a car or a washing-machine.
- It needs to be fun – calling it a 'challenge' is a great way to encourage people to try it.
- Use the competing product – don't be tempted to use a cheap substitute!

Brands can be looked at in a number of different ways. Table 12.2 shows eight different strategic functions of brands.

Branding clearly has advantages for the manufacturer and the retailer, since it helps to differentiate the product from the competitor's product. Economies of scale and scope are attributed to branding, and a brand with high sales will generate production economies (Demsetz 1973). A successful brand also creates a **barrier to entry**, so that competitors find it harder to enter the market (Demsetz 1982). Brands also allow firms to compete other than on price (Mercer 1996), which clearly has advantages since the firm does not have to cut its profit margins in order to compete.

Furthermore, brands that are held in high esteem tend to be more consistent in their sales, riding over the ups and downs of the marketplace (Png and Reitman

Barrier to entry A factor that prevents a firm from entering a specific market.

Table 12.2   Strategic functions of brands

Function	Explanation
Brand as a sign of ownership	Brands were at one time a way of showing who had instigated the marketing activities for the brand. This was an attempt to protect the formulation of the product in cases where intellectual property protection is insufficient, and also to ensure that customers knew whether they were buying a manufacturer's brand or a retailer's brand.
Brand as a differentiating device	A strong brand undoubtedly does differentiate the product from similar products, but having a strong brand name is not enough. The product itself also needs to be different in some way; the brand image is the communicating device that conveys the difference to the consumer.
Brand as a functional device	Branding can be used to communicate functional capability. In other words, the brand conveys an image of its quality and expected performance to the consumer.
Brand as a symbolic device	The symbolism of some brands enables the consumer to say something about themselves. This is particularly apparent in the 'designer' clothes industry – a very ordinary T-shirt acquires added value because the name of the designer is printed on the front. If the consumers believe that the brand's value lies in its communication ability they will spend considerable time and effort in choosing the brand that conveys the appropriate image.
Brand as a risk reducer	Every purchase involves a degree of risk; the product might not perform as expected, and if it fails to do so then the vendor might not be prepared to make restitution. Buying a strongly branded product offers the consumer a degree of reassurance about both the product and the producer. Astute marketers find out what types of risk are of most concern to the customers or consumers and develop a brand presentation which addresses those risks.
Brand as a shorthand device	Brands are used as a way of 'tagging' information about a product in the consumers' memories. This is particularly relevant when the brand is extended to other product categories, since the consumer's view of the parent brand is transferred to the new brand; for example, Virgin have successfully extended the brand image from records to retailing to airlines to financial services, all offering the same innovative approach and serving similar market segments.
Brand as a legal device	Brands give a certain amount of legal protection to the producer, since pack design and name can be protected whereas (often) the formulation of the product cannot. Strong branding offers some protection for the firm's intellectual property.
Brand as a strategic device	The assets constituting the brand can be identified and managed so that the brand maintains and builds on the added value which it represents.

1995). Not all brands are priced at a premium; many are competitively priced in order to take advantage of consistent sales.

Branding has advantages for the consumer: it is easy to recognise the product, and easy to identify with it. Messages about the formulation and benefits are clearly conveyed, and in most cases the use of a particular brand says something about the consumer (for example, wearing designer clothes) (Bagwell and Bernheim 1996). Because most purchases only involve limited problem-solving behaviour, branding helps to reduce the decision-making time and also the effort of evaluating competing products. Consumers who either don't want to spend time on an extended information search, or who don't have the expertise to do so, can use the brand as an implicit guarantee of quality (Png and Reitman 1995). This is especially important when buying an unfamiliar product – the evidence is that new products benefit greatly from being associated with an existing, tried-and-trusted brand (Besharat 2010). If a product is unbranded, people will often seek out other ways of confirming the quality of the product, and may even pay a premium for doing so (for example, buying from a reputable retailer) (Ubilava et al. 2011).

Chunking The mental process whereby information is stored alongside connected information.

Information storage and retrieval in humans is carried out by a process of **chunking** or collecting information in substantial quantities and storing them under a single 'file name' (Buschke 1976). In effect, the brand name provides an informational chunk: the individual is able to summon up a huge amount of information from memory using the brand name as the trigger.

Metaphor A sign that relates to an object.

From a strategic viewpoint, the brand image provides a focus for the creative energies of the marketing team. Koestler suggests that creativity involves the bringing together of hitherto unrelated, yet familiar, objects to generate a creative insight (Koestler 1964). The difficulty for marketers is that product and brand development is often a team process, and as such the team needs to keep a firm picture of what the product is intended to convey – the 'personality' of the product – if they are to maintain consistency in the creative activities. One way of doing this is to use a **metaphor** for the product. For example, the Honda Accord developers used the metaphor 'Rugby player in a dinner suit' to achieve product coherence across the team, even though the entire creative team consisted of hundreds of people, from automotive stylists through to ad designers (Clark and Fujimoto 1990).

Brand planning is important, but time-consuming; often the job is given to a brand manager, many of whom are young and inexperienced. Developing the brand is a process of integrating a number of strands of business activity, so a clear idea of the brand image is essential, as is a long-term view. To see branding as merely being about design or advertising or naming is inadequate and short-sighted; successful brands are those that act as a lens through which the consumer sees the corporation and the product. Constant evaluation of the image seen through the lens is essential if the brand is to retain its status.

The brand name is the usual starting-point for developing a brand. A brand name is a term, symbol or design that distinguishes one seller's product from its competitors. The strategic considerations for brand naming are as follows:

1. Marketing objectives. The brand name should fit the overall marketing objectives of the firm; for example, a firm intending to enter the youth market will need to develop brand names that appeal to a young audience.

Brand audit The process of determining whether a specific brand is being marketed effectively.

2. **Brand audit**. An estimate of the internal and external forces such as critical success factor (also known as the unique selling proposition).
3. Brand objectives. As with the marketing objectives, the overall intentions about the brand need to be specified.
4. Brand strategy alternatives. The other ways of achieving the brand's objectives, and the other factors involved in its success, have a bearing on the choice of brand name.

Registration A system for protecting brand names.

Brand names can be protected in most countries by **registration**, but there is some protection for brands in that it is illegal to try to 'pass off' a product as being a branded one when it isn't. For example, using a very similar brand name to a famous brand, or even using a similar package design, could be regarded as passing off. This is a civil offence, not a criminal one, so it is up to the offended brand owner to take legal action.

Ries (1995) suggests that brand names should have the following characteristics:

1. They should shock, i.e. catch the customer's attention.
2. They should be alliterative; this helps them to be memorable.
3. They should connect to the product's positioning in the consumer's perceptual map.
4. They should link to a visual image; again, this helps the memorability.
5. They should communicate something about the product, or be capable of being used to communicate about the product.
6. They should encourage the development of a nickname (for example, Bud for Budweiser Beer).
7. They should be telephone- and directory-friendly.

Real-life marketing: Startling brand names

Having a brand name that stands out from the crowd is really important – yet many small businesses miss the point. Calling yourself Church Street Cafe or ABC Plumbers is not very imaginative, after all. It's a classic wasted opportunity.

Controversial marketing is nothing new – many firms use shocking advertisements to promote their products (and better still, get themselves banned and enjoy the publicity). But few have a shocking brand name.

Enter French Connection UK. The initials are close to a somewhat crude Anglo-Saxon word, so the company used them on their T-shirts and other products. Seeing someone walking round wearing a T-shirt which says 'Hot as fcuk' (or in Australia, 'no fcukin' worries') certainly attracted attention. Of course the company's advertising was banned immediately, and the entire company was banned in Boston, Massachusetts – which did them no harm at all. When they opened in San Francisco, a much less strait-laced town, the company hung a poster on the store saying 'San Francisco's First fcuk'.

Being controversial carries risks – but in this case it worked very well for the company. If you want to try it yourself, remember these rules:

- Try to be funny as well as controversial – you are more likely to get away with it.
- Don't go too far – you don't want to be banned altogether.
- If you can link the controversial brand to your company's name you are less likely to find yourself in trouble.
- Controversial brand names appeal to young people, in the main. It won't work so well for an older audience, and may not be too effective for 'serious' products like financial services. Though you never know …

Developing the brand further will usually result in it acquiring a personality of its own. Marketers often speak of the brand's personality, and there is research evidence to show that consumers often think of brands as having personalities. For example, brands that are perceived as 'female' attract different responses from those that are perceived as 'male'. Men respond more favourably to brand extensions of 'female' brands than do women to 'female' brands (Jung and Lee 2006). When people are asked to consider the dimensions 'I understand the brand' and 'The brand understands me', women tend to distinguish 'close' and 'distant' brands using both dimensions, whereas men only judge 'close' and 'distant' by their own actions towards the brand (Monga 2002). This tendency to personify brands may be naturally occurring in people – many of us have pet names for possessions such as cars or favourite clothing. On the other hand, it may be marketer-induced, through linking personalities of actors in adverts to the brand, or possibly by the recent emphasis on relationship marketing (Bengtsson 2003). Sometimes people appear to associate with brands on a personal level. Research indicates that people tend to prefer brands containing letters from their own names (Brendl et al. 2003).

Brands and semiotics

Semiotics The study of meaning.

Semiotics is the study of meaning, and is concerned with the symbolism conveyed by objects and words. Semiotics refers to systems of signs; the most obvious system is words, but other systems exist. For example, a film would use the sign systems of the spoken word, the gestures of the actors, the music of the soundtrack and the conventions of movie direction and production to generate an overall meaning. The overall meaning is generated as a result of an interaction between the sign system and the observer or reader: the viewer interprets the information in the light of existing knowledge and attitudes, later including it in an overall perceptual map of reality (see Chapter 4 for more on consumer behaviour).

Brands are important symbols, often using more than one sign system to create meaning; the brand name, the logo, the colour and the design of the packaging all contribute.

In terms of semiotics, brands have four levels.

Utilitarian Appertaining to the practical aspects of ownership.

Socio-cultural Appertaining to the social effects of buying or not buying a product.
Myths Heroic stories about a product.

1. A **utilitarian** sign. This is about the practical aspects of the product, and includes meanings of reliability, effectiveness, fitness for purpose and so on.
2. A commercial sign. This about the exchange values of the product, perhaps conveying meanings about value for money or cost-effectiveness.
3. A **socio-cultural** sign. This is about the social effects of buying (or not buying) the product, with meanings about membership of aspirational groups or about the fitness of the product for filling social roles.
4. A sign about the mythical values of the product. **Myths** are heroic stories about the product, many of which have little basis in fact; for example the Harley–Davidson motorcycle brand has a strong mythical value due (in part) to its starring role in the film *Easy Rider*. The same is true of James Bond's Aston Martin, and several brands of beer.

Myths provide a conceptual framework through which the contradictions of life can be resolved, and brands can build on this. For example, modern industrial life is, presumably, the antithesis of frontier adventure. Yet the Harley–Davidson, a product of 20th century industry, was used to represent the (probably mythical) freedom and adventure of the American West. Most powerful brands have at least some mythical connotations: in the UK, the Hovis bread brand has mythical connotations centred around corner bakery shops at the turn of the century; in Malaysia and Singapore Tiger Balm carries mythical connotations about ancient Chinese apothecaries; in Australia Vegemite carries mythical connotations about Australian family life which its main competitor, Promite, has never tapped into.

The association of different values with the brand name can be extremely useful when researching the acceptability of a brand's image. The importance that consumers place on these values can be researched using focus groups, with a subsequent analysis of the key signs contained within the brand, and consumers can be segmented according to their responsiveness to the particular signs contained within the brand and their relevance to the consumer's own internal values.

Research carried out by Gordon and Valentin (1996) into retail buying behaviour showed that different retail outlets convey different meanings to consumers in terms of a continuum from planned, routine shopping through to impulse buying. Each store type met the needs differently and conveyed different meanings in terms of appropriateness of behaviour. **Convenience stores** conveyed an image of disorder and feelings of guilt and confusion (perhaps associated with having forgotten to buy some items in the course of the regular weekly shop). Supermarkets represented planned shopping and conveyed an image of efficient domestic management and functionality. Petrol stations carried a dual meaning of planned purchase (for petrol) and impulse buying (in the shop). Business travellers seeking a break from work and pleasure travellers seeking to enhance the 'holiday' feeling both indulged in impulsive behaviour motivated by the need for a treat. Finally, off-licences legitimated the purchase of alcohol, allowing shoppers to buy drinks without the uneasy feeling that other shoppers might disapprove. Off-licences also provided an environment in which people felt able to experiment with new purchases.

Convenience stores Stores located in residential areas which stock frequently purchased items.

These signs are relevant not only for the retailers themselves in terms of their own branding, but also for branded-goods manufacturers who need to decide which outlets are most appropriate for their brands and where in the store the brand should be located. For example, snack foods and chocolate are successfully sold in petrol stations, where the travellers are often looking for a treat to break up a boring journey.

According to research conducted by DeChernatony and Cottam, successful brand owners have the following characteristics:

1. They are holistic, consistent and integrated.
2. They focus on excellent customer service.
3. They have an ethos that challenges the norm.
4. They are responsive to change.
5. They have a high level of brand literacy.
6. There is synergy between the brand and the organisational culture.

Brands are not always liked, of course. Sometimes people will express their dislike of a particular brand, and this may or may not be based on product features. There are three possible reasons for disliking a brand (Dalli et al. 2006). First is dissatisfaction with the product itself; this may be as a result of poor performance, or simply a poor fit with the individual's needs. Second, the consumer might dislike what the brand symbolises – it could be a brand that has become associated with an undesirable group of people, or it may be that the brand symbolises something that the individual considers to be objectionable (for example, conspicuous consumption). Third, the individual may dislike the corporation that owns the brand, perhaps because of unethical business practices.

If a brand is disliked, the company may decide to rebrand, in other words change the name, the style, the packaging and everything else about the brand in order to re-launch it. However, rebranding in most cases is provoked by structural changes in the firm (for example merger or acquisition) since these affect the corporate identity and core strategy (Muzellec and Lambkin 2006).

Chapter summary

The product is what the marketer is offering for exchange with the consumers, so getting it right is of considerable importance. Having the right products on offer at the right time is obviously important, but marketers also need to consider their resources and seek to ensure that the products they offer constitute the best use of limited resources. This means that they must manage the portfolio with regard to each product's performance, and also with regard to the overall mix of products.

Packaging performs a number of functions for both the producer and the consumer, but a key point is that the packaging actually forms part of the product, because it can offer definite benefits to the consumer (not to mention the retailers and wholesalers).

Key points

- The product life cycle (PLC), though severely flawed, offers a model for understanding the stages a product goes through.
- Products do not sell in isolation – they are often linked, and should be considered as a portfolio.
- The Boston Consulting Group (BCG) matrix offers a snapshot of the product's current position, but executive judgement still needs to be applied.
- Matrix analysis offers a spurious credibility, but does help to clarify the issues.
- Most products involve elements of both service and physical product.
- Many business-to-business companies are experiencing a transition from product orientation to service orientation.
- Packaging is part of the product; because it is the first contact many people have with the product, ethical issues might be raised.

Review questions

1. What are the main drawbacks of the PLC?
2. What are the main drawbacks of the BCG matrix?
3. What strengths does the General Electric (GE) GE matrix have over the BCG matrix?
4. What are the key advantages of a strong brand, from a customer's viewpoint?
5. What are the main considerations when choosing a brand name?
6. Why might a company drop a product shortly after its introduction?
7. Why might a company retain a product that actually loses money?
8. How might a chain restaurant company manipulate the physical evidence aspect of its activities to increase profits?
9. Why might a company move from a manufacturing to a services orientation?
10. How might packaging of take-away foods help consumers enjoy the product better?

Case study revisited: HJ Heinz

Jones Knowles Ritchie began by linking all the different products through the Heinz Keystone design – the badge-shaped symbol which appears on all Heinz products. The agency realised that what consumers thought was important was the quality symbolised by the Heinz brand, rather than the actual product contained in the bottle or can. This still left plenty of scope for individualising the brands – the turquoise colour used for the baked beans (reputedly because it enhances the colour of the beans when the can is opened) could remain, as well as the individual graphics for the children's products such as Eazy Squirt.

Heinz's PR consultants issued a statement that salad cream might be withdrawn due to falling sales. This press release made the TV news, and amid a flurry of protests from millions of Britons who had grown up with salad cream, the threat was withdrawn. Sales rose sufficiently for Heinz to introduce an organic version of salad cream, to be sold alongside its existing traditional salad cream as well as the ever-expanding range of organic products. In February 2003 the Soil Association (Britain's leading promoters of organic food) gave Heinz an award for their organic range of foods.

In the United States Heinz introduced 'one-carb' sauces, low-carbohydrate sauces intended for Atkins dieters.

Managing the portfolio is, for Heinz, a constant, dynamic process. Introducing new products to meet consumer needs, cutting out products that no longer show sufficient profit, packaging products in an eye-catching manner and responding to the rapidly changing world of nutrition is a continual activity for Heinz managers. This may be why Heinz has such a solid place in the hearts and minds of consumers.

Case study: Smith & Nephew

In 1856, a pharmaceutical chemist named Thomas James Smith opened a shop in Hull, UK. Forty years later, his nephew Horatio Nelson Smith became his business partner, and the firm of Smith & Nephew was created. Horatio was interested in developing dressings for wounds, and the business moved towards the manufacture of bandages and other dressings.

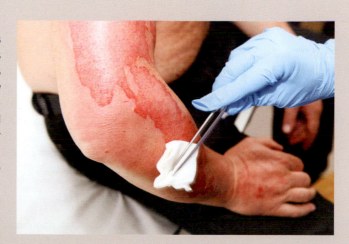

Massive expansion during the First World War (to meet the needs of wounded soldiers) took the company from 50 employees to 1200 in only four years. In 1928 the company began development of Elastoplast, the adhesive bandage designed to compete with Johnson & Johnson's recently introduced Band-Aid bandage. Band-Aid and Elastoplast were, at the time, revolutionary products: Band-Aid, introduced in 1920, sold only $3000 dollars' worth in its first year and was hand-made until 1924. Elastoplast was originally a cloth bandage with an antiseptic pad and adhesive edges; it was not until 1966 that the company introduced the Airstrip variant, which was a ventilated plastic adhesive strip with an antiseptic pad.

Smith & Nephew expanded by acquisition during the 1970s and 1980s, in the process of which the company acquired subsidiaries that produced medical equipment such as orthopaedic implants and continuous passive motion machines, which keep patients' joints moving after surgery in order to avoid stiffness. Smith & Nephew were thus beginning to move away from their concentration on wound management, and heading into general areas of patient recovery.

This in turn led to an interest in surgery. Smith & Nephew have been at the sharp end of developing endoscopy – the so-called keyhole surgery – which enables surgeons to use an extremely small incision when carrying out internal surgical procedures. Endoscopy used miniature cameras and remote surgical instruments, and is being used more and more widely as surgeons realise the benefits of causing the minimum wound. Patients can often leave hospital the same day as their surgery, and recovery times are markedly faster.

In 1999 Smith & Nephew bought out 3M's shoulder and hip implant business. The company also announced a new three-part Group Strategy, focused on orthopaedics, endoscopy and wound management. During 2000 this new strategy led the company to sell off its feminine hygiene and toiletries products in a management buy-out. Elastoplast was sold to Beiersdorf AG, who also took over the distribution of Nivea in the UK. Thus Smith & Nephew pulled out of the consumer products market entirely, concentrating solely of its products for healthcare professionals. The company now offers over 1000 products, and continually spends on research and development to increase the range and efficacy on its products. During 2003 the company spent £67 million in R&D – 6% of the company's total turnover. Research is concentrated in the company's three strategic areas.

Graphic proof of the efficacy of Smith & Nephew's products came in October 2002. The Bali bombing killed over 200 people, but the wounds suffered by other victims were truly horrific. One young mother of two suffered 85% burns: she was treated immediately with Smith & Nephew's Acticoat dressing, and in the Sydney hospital where she was taken she was treated with Transcyte temporary skin until skin grafts could be carried out. Even five years earlier, a patient with 85% burns would not have been expected to live – but this woman was discharged from hospital within a month, and was able to spend Christmas with her children.

Questions

1. Why would Smith & Nephew sell off its consumer products divisions?
2. Why does the company spend such a large portion of its turnover on research?
3. What stage of the PLC was Band-Aid in during 1924?
4. What stage of the PLC was Elastoplast in when Smith & Nephew sold it?
5. To what extent are Smith & Nephew's products customer-specified?

Further reading

There is a great deal written about new product development, but relatively little about product management. Here is one of the few books on the topic:

Linda Gorchels, *The Product Manager's Handbook*, 4th edn (New York: McGraw Hill, 2012). This is a readable, practitioner-orientated American text. It uses interesting cases and examples to illustrate points, and concentrates strongly on the product manager's role.

References

Bagwell, L.S. and Bernheim, B.D. (1996) Veblen effects in a theory of conspicuous consumption. *American Economic Review*, 86: 349–73.

Barksdale, H.C. and Harris, C.E. (1982) Portfolio analysis and the PLC. *Long Range Planning*, 15 (6): 74–83.

Benady, D. (2001) Will they eat their words? *Marketing Week*, 2 August, pp. 24–6.

Bengtsson, Anders (2003) Towards a critique of brand relationships. *Advances in Consumer Research*, 30: 154–8.

Besharat, Ali (2010) How co-branding versus brand extensions drive consumers' evaluations of new products: a brand equity approach. *Industrial Marketing Management*, 39 (8): 1240–9.

Brendl, C. Miguel, Chattopadhyay, Amitava, Pelham, Brett W., Carvalho, Mauricio and Pritchard, Evan T. (2003) Are brands containing name letters preferred? *Advances in Consumer Behaviour*, 30: 151–3.

Buschke, H. (1976) Learning is organised by chunking. *Journal of Verbal Learning and Verbal Behaviour*, 15: 313–24.

Clark, K. and Fujimoto, T. (1990) The power of product integrity. *Business Review*, Nov/Dec: 107–18.

Dalli, Danielle, Romani, Simona and Gistri, Giacomo (2006) Brand dislike: representing the negative side of consumer preferences. *Advances in Consumer Research*, 33: 87–95.

Davies, I. (1995) Look-alikes: fair or unfair competition? *Journal of Brand Management*, Oct: 104–20.

DeChernatony, Leslie and Cottam, Susan (2006) Internal brand factors driving successful financial services brands. *European Journal of Marketing*, 40 (5/6): 611–33.

Demsetz, H. (1973) Industry structure, market rivalry and public policy. *Journal of Law and Economics*, 16 (1): 1–9.

Demsetz, H. (1982) Barriers to entry. *American Economic Review*, 72: 47–57.

Elliott, Richard and Leonard, Clare (2003) Peer pressure and poverty: exploring fashion brands and consumption symbolism among children of the 'British poor'. *Journal of Consumer Behaviour*, 3 (4): 347–59.

Gordon, W. and Valentin, V. (1996) Buying the brand at point of choice. *Journal of Brand Management*, 4 (1): 35–44.

Greenberg, D. (2000) *Product Provider to Customer Value Provider: Escaping the Services Maze.* Somers, NY: IBM Institute for Business Value, IBM Global Services.

Greenley, G.E. and Barus, B.L. (1994) A comparative study of product launch and elimination decisions in UK and US companies. *European Journal of Marketing*, 28 (2): 5–29.

Jung, Kwon and Lee, Winston (2006) Cross-gender brand extensions: effects of gender of the brand, gender of the consumer, and product type on cross-gender extensions. *Advances in Consumer Research*, 33 (1): 67–74.

Koestler, A. (1964) *The Act of Creation.* London: Pan Books.

Laforet, Sylvie (2011) Brand names on packaging and their impact on purchase preference. *Journal of Consumer Behaviour*, 10 (1): 18–30.

Majewski, B.M. and Srinavas, S. (2002) *The Services Challenge: Operationalising your Services Strategy.* Somers, NY: IBM Global Services.

Mercer, D. (1996) *Marketing*, 2nd edn. Oxford: Blackwell.

Monga, Alokparna Basu (2002) Brand as a relationship partner. *Advances in Consumer Research*, 29: 41.

Muzellec, Laurent and Lambkin, Mary (2006) Corporate rebranding: destroying, transferring or creating brand equity? *European Journal of Marketing*, 40 (7/8): 825–45.

O'Cass, Aron and Clarke, Peter (2002) Dear Santa, do you have my brand? A study of brand requests, awareness and request styles at Christmas time. *Journal of Consumer Behaviour*, 2 (1): 37–53.

Pawels, Koen, Silva-Risso, Jorge, Srinavasan, Shuba and Hanssens, Dominique M. (2004) New products, sales promotions and firm value: the case of the automobile industry. *Journal of Marketing*, 68 (4): 142–56.

Png, J.P. and Reitman, D. (1995) Why are some products branded and others not? *Journal of Law and Economics*, 38: 207–24.

Rhagubir, Priya and Greenleaf, Eric A. (2006) Ratios in proportion: what should the shape of the package be? *Journal of Marketing*, 70 (2): 95–107.

Ries, A. (1995) What's in a name? *Sales and Marketing Management*, Oct: 36–7.

Roper, Stuart and La Niece, Caroline (2009) The importance of brands in the lunch-box choices of low-income British school children. *Journal of Consumer Behaviour*, 8 (2/3): 84–99.

Smith, N.C. (1995) Marketing strategies for the ethics era. *Sloan Management Review*, Summer: 85–97.

Ubilava, D., Foster, K.A., Lusk, J.L. and Nilsson, T. (2011) Differences in consumer preferences when facing branded versus non-branded choices. *Journal of Consumer Behaviour*, 10 (2): 61–70.

Vakratsas, D. and Ambler, T. (1999) How advertising works: what do we really know? *Journal of Marketing*, 63: 26–43.

Young, R. (1999) First read the label, then add a pinch of salt. *The Times*, 30 November, pp. 2–4.

More online

To gain free access to additional online resources to support this chapter please visit:
www.sagepub.co.uk/blythe3e

Part Four

Marketing in practice

The second half of the book is devoted to practical aspects of day-to-day marketing. Having covered the theoretical groundwork, the book now moves on to practicalities, describing the tools and techniques marketers use in their daily lives. This is linked throughout (and supported by) academic research in the field.

Chapter 13 looks at developing new products. Eventually, all products become obsolete, but in any case a firm that intends to expand needs to update its product range continually by adding new products to the portfolio. This chapter explains the process of new product development and the theoretical basis for adoption of innovation.

Chapter 14 is about pricing. Price can be used as a promotional device, as a communication tool, as a surrogate for judging quality and for many other things. This chapter outlines the various bases for pricing and the rationale behind pricing to meeting consumer demand profitability.

Advertising is probably the most prominent of all marketing activities. Chapter 15 discusses various forms of advertising, and looks at media buying, budgeting, creative issues and choosing an agency. Planning for advertising and the use of new media are also covered.

Public relations and sponsorship are somewhat neglected in the academic literature, but have an important role to play in establishing both the credibility of the firm and the quality of its brands.

Chapter 16 looks at practical aspects of PR and sponsorship, crisis management, choosing sponsorship targets and proactive public relations.

Chapter 17 is about selling and key-account management. Personal selling is a very common first job in marketing, and for many it becomes a lifetime career: selling is marketing at the individual, personal level. Key-account management is about handling customers who are of strategic importance to the firm, either because they represent a major part of the firm's turnover or because they represent a way into an attractive market. Managing key accounts is an extremely responsible job, because the future fate of the company may hang on how well the key-account managers perform – but at the end of the day, it is still marketing.

CHAPTER (13)

New product innovation and development

LEARNING OBJECTIVES

After reading this chapter, you should be able to:

- Outline ways of generating ideas for new products.

- Explain the differences and similarities between project champions and project teams.

- Describe the factors in new-product success.

- Explain how innovations are diffused through the population.

- Explain the factors that make up new product acceptability.

- Describe the different characteristics of innovative consumers.

- Show how marketers can affect the rate at which innovations are diffused.

Introduction

As we saw in Chapter 12, products pass through a life cycle and eventually cease to generate sales. For companies to remain in business, therefore, a constant stream of new products needs to be developed in order to replace those that have reached the end of their useful lives. Additionally, firms need to add new products to the range if they are to grow: new markets demand new products.

For marketers, there is likely to be a conflict arising from this. On the one hand, marketers need to look towards creating new products for their existing and potential customers, but on the other hand the products customers might need may not be ones that can easily be produced by the company. For example, a company that produces guitars is unlikely to have the capacity or expertise to produce guitar strings, or amplifiers, or even plectrums. In most cases the production of such items would have to be undertaken by another firm.

Changing customer tastes, competitive pressures, technological advances and changing corporate strategy all contribute to the pressure to create new products. The rate of change differs between industries, but change itself is inevitable: firms that do not innovate will eventually disappear, along with their obsolete products. Firms that do innovate are likely to dominate global markets in the future, provided they have the imagination to dominate fundamentally new markets (Hamel and Prahalad 1991).

Preview case study: Boeing Dreamliner

Boeing Commercial Airplanes is a company that goes back a long way – William Boeing built his first seaplane in 1916, in his Seattle shipyard. He crashed it a few months later, and had to design and build another one. When the United States entered the First World War in 1917, Boeing won a contract to supply seaplanes to the Navy, but after the war the company had a setback when the aircraft market was flooded with war-surplus aircraft. Boeing produced furniture and cabinets for a few years until in 1919 it produced a seaplane which could carry a pilot, two passengers and a quantity of mail: this aircraft went into service flying mail from Seattle to Vancouver. In 1923, the company won a contract to supply fighter aircraft to the Army Air Service, and the rest is history.

Boeing is now one of the largest aircraft manufacturers in the world. During the late 1990s the company began considering ideas for an aircraft to replace the 767 and 747–400, which were losing ground against Airbus products manufactured in Europe. At the time, the industry was looking for ever-greater speed: the supersonic Concorde had failed to fulfil its early promise, due to high operating costs and small carrying capacity, but clearly the main selling point of flying somewhere is that it is quicker than surface transport. Boeing began work on an aircraft that would fly just below the speed of sound, 15% faster than competing aircraft.

Unfortunately, rising fuel prices killed the project, so Boeing switched its attention to designing an aircraft that would be more fuel-efficient than anything else in the air. The company could use some of the technology developed for their Sonic Cruiser, mainly carbon composites which are stronger than steel but weigh much less than aluminium, and some other weight-saving technologies including lithium-ion batteries. Much of the work of building the airliner was subcontracted out internationally, with two converted 747s used to transport components to the assembly plant in Washington State. Japanese co-operation in building the aircraft was crucial: Japanese companies were responsible for co-designing and building around 35% of the aircraft. The result of subcontracting was a dramatic improvement in the time it took to assemble the aircraft – final assembly in Washington took only three days.

So far, the future was looking pretty good for the Dreamliner, with an advance order for 50 aircraft signed by All Nippon Airways for delivery in late 2008.

Types of new product

Various attempts have been made to define what is a new product. Products are not either new or old: there are degrees of newness, but in most cases the measurement of these degrees of newness is subjective.

One categorisation comes from Booz-Allen and Hamilton (1982). This is as follows:

1. Product replacement. This is essentially an improvement or redesign of an existing product. The new model of a car, the replacement of one formulation of shampoo for another, or the repositioning of an existing product into a new market are examples of product replacements. These account for around 45% of new product launches.
2. Additions to existing lines. Brand extensions, complementary products such as coffee whitener, and products that make existing products easier to use or more effective come into this category. These are thought to account for about 25% of new product launches. The fit between the parent brand and the extension product is crucial to the success of brand extensions (Volckner and Sattler 2006).
3. New product lines. Around 20% of new product launches, these products are launched for the purpose of moving into new markets. Building on existing brand values, the products have only a small connection with the original product lines, and really constitute a new departure for the firm.
4. New-to-the-world products. These are products that create entirely new markets, and change the way people behave in a fundamental manner. Mobile telephones and the Internet are recent examples, but in the past radical inventions such as the car, the communications satellite, and the aeroplane have achieved the same radical changes.

The boundaries between these categories are by no means rigid, and sometimes the effects of a new product cannot be recognised until much later. A further drawback of these categories is that they tend to view the product from the producer's viewpoint: customers may not think that the new product line is really new at all.

An alternative, and more comprehensive, categorisation of products was developed by Calentone and Cooper (1981). These researchers also calculated the success rates for the new product clusters. The evidence from Calentone and Cooper's study is that less radical products are more likely to succeed than radical, new-to-the-world

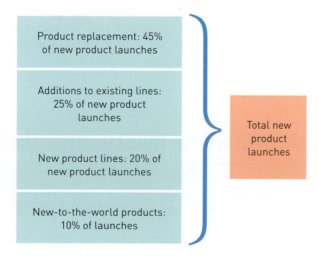

Figure 13.1 Categories of new product

Table 13.1   New product clusters

Clusters	Description
Cluster 1: The Better Mousetrap with No Synergy (36% succeeded)	This is a product that, while being an improvement over existing offerings, does not fit in with the firm's existing product lines.
Cluster 2: The Innovative Mousetrap that Really Wasn't Better (No successes at all)	This might be a product that, while being technically excellent, has no real advantage for the consumer over existing products.
Cluster 3: The Close to Home Me-Too Product (56% succeeded)	A copy of a competitor's offering. Not likely to be perceived as new by consumers.
Cluster 4: The Innovative High-tech Product (64% succeeded)	A truly new-to-the-world product.
Cluster 5: The Me-Too Product with No Technical/Production Synergy (14% succeeded)	A copy of a competitor's product, but with no real connection with existing product lines.
Cluster 6: The Old But Simple Money-Saver (70% succeeded)	Not a new product at all, except to the firm producing it.
Cluster 7: The Synergistic Product that was New to the Firm (67% succeeded)	A product that fits the product line, but is new.
Cluster 8: The Innovative Superior Product with No Synergy (70% succeeded)	A product that does not fit the existing product line, but is new.
Cluster 9: The Synergistic Close-to-Home Product (72% succeeded)	A product line extension; perhaps a minor improvement over the firm's existing products.

ones. Of course, the authors do not outline the extent to which a product succeeded – there is little doubt that a radical product such as the Sony Walkman made the company a great deal of money, more than compensating for the many other radical products launched by Sony which apparently sank without trace. On the other hand, products that have no synergy (either in production or in marketing) with the firm's existing products appeared to have no successes at all.

Marketing in a changing world: Globalisation and NPD

Globalisation has its pluses and minuses – greater choice, greater economies of scale, bigger markets for producers on the one hand, and on the other a cultural imperialism that many people find abhorrent.

One big problem for manufacturers is the rapid increase in technological change. Because so many countries have advanced research and development facilities (either at manufacturing plants or in universities) new techniques appear on a daily basis. Because of globalisation, these new developments are disseminated extremely rapidly. Sixty years ago the first transistor radio appeared, some seven years after the invention of the transistor:

the lithium-polymer battery, developed in 1997, was in commercial use within two years. Early in 2013 scientists announced that they could store data by growing artificial DNA: how long will it be before that comes to market, rendering all other storage methods obsolete?

There has always been global competition in research and development, but the speed of disseminating information creates a real threat to firms' R&D efforts. A firm could spend millions on developing something that is rendered obsolete by something that has been developed 7000 miles away, so it pays to be fast to market with new ideas.

There is a problem with measuring the success (or otherwise) of a product, since success might be considered in terms of profit, of market share, of strategic outcomes, or of long-term sustainability. The most commonly used measures in consumer markets are as follows (Huang et al. 2004):

1. Customer acceptance.
2. Customer satisfaction.
3. Product performance.
4. Customer perception of quality.

Innovation can be looked at from two viewpoints. Innovation on the part of a producer is the development of an idea that offers a new solution to an old problem, or a new solution to a new problem. Innovation on the part of a consumer is the degree to which new solutions are adopted.

Think outside this box!

It would appear from the Calentone and Cooper research that innovation is not a good idea after all. The most innovative products on the scale seem to be the ones most prone to failure, and the most successful ones seem to be those that are merely copies of competitors' products or minor alterations to existing products.

Or are we perhaps seeing only part of the picture? Maybe the definition of success is at fault – after all, a new product might have strategic importance, taking the company into a new market. Or the new product might simply take a very, very long time to take off. Or maybe the new products that succeed, succeed spectacularly, while the me-too products barely break even. Either way, companies continue to innovate!

A classification that is often quoted is that of Robertson (1967). Robertson classified products according to their effects on consumers' lives. The classification is as follows:

- **Continuous innovation.** An innovation that follows on incrementally from previous solutions, and offers only minor new benefits. It has been defined as the modification of the taste, appearance, performance or reliability of an existing product rather than the creation of a new one (Blackwell et al. 2001).

Continuous innovation Incremental improvements in an existing product.

Dynamically continuous innovation A product that is a substantial shift in technology but does not change people's lives.

Discontinuous innovation A new product that significantly changes consumers' lifestyles.

Examples might include adding fluoride to toothpaste, 'lite' versions of beer brands, or 'heavy-duty' batteries.

- **Dynamically continuous innovation**. This may involve the creation of a new product or the substantial modification of an existing product, but it does not lead to a change in people's shopping or usage patterns. DVD players do not significantly alter people's television viewing patterns in the same way that video recorders did: they simply replaced video recorders. Likewise, the electric toothbrush does not change the number of times people clean their teeth.
- **Discontinuous innovation**. This involves the creation of an entirely new product that significantly alters consumers' behaviours and lifestyles. Mobile telephones, video recorders, television and (in their day) cars and radio all changed the way people lived.

Calentone and Cooper's research was borne out by research published in 2006, in which the authors found that incremental innovations carry the least risk for firms which are the first to bring them to market (Min et al. 2006). The same research found that discontinuous innovation carried the greatest risk for firms who are first to market, and also those who follow later.

Firms wishing to be innovative need to establish a culture of innovation. Marketing orientation certainly tends to create an innovation culture, since products need to be developed to meet new customer need, or to meet existing needs more effectively (Tajeddini et al. 2006). New product development works best if the research and development (R&D) people get on well with the marketing people, in other words have a good working relationship (Rodriguez et al. 2007).

Creating an innovative culture within the firm is not easy. Innovators run the risk of failure, and many firms are less than tolerant of failure. Some common methods of encouraging innovation are as follows:

1. Reward success, but tolerate failure.
2. Give a clear message that innovation is essential to the organisation.
3. Allow people time to develop their ideas.
4. Try to avoid the 'not invented here' syndrome in which ideas are discouraged simply because the manager did not think of the idea first.
5. Provide adequate resources for ideas to develop.
6. Be available to staff to discuss their ideas in a positive way.

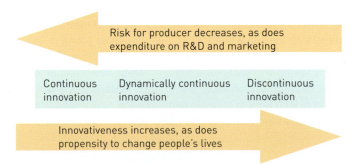

Figure 13.2   Degrees of innovation

The NPD process

Cooper and Kleinschmidt (1986) developed the following model for the new product development (NPD) process:

- New product strategy. The firm needs to decide what its overall NPD process is expected to achieve in strategic terms: which markets should the firm be entering, which competitors should it be attacking and which ones should not be confronted, which customer needs is the firm best placed to serve, and so forth.
- Idea generation. Ideas might be generated by any member of staff, or might be generated by teams set up for the purpose. There is more on this later.
- **Screening**. Ideas need to be considered in terms of the firm's strategic intent, and also in terms of feasibility. Feasibility includes production as well as marketing issues.
- **Concept testing**. Having selected from the ideas, concept testing with customers and production people can take place. At this stage, no prototype is necessary: a mock-up and description of what the final product is intended to do will be sufficient.
- Business analysis. The products that survive concept testing will need to be considered in terms of their profitability, their effect on sales of other products, their strategic worth in terms of building the business, and so forth.
- Product development. At this stage the research and development engineers take over. The final design of the product needs to reflect the results of the concept testing, and also needs to fit within the cost structures dictated by the business analysis.
- Market testing. The final product needs to be tested in the market. This could be carried out through focus group analysis of a prototype, or by test marketing (see Chapter 5). This is the final stage of the process before the company commits to mass production and mass marketing.
- Commercialisation. This is the point at which the company launches the final product onto the market and commits to major expenditure.

Screening Selecting new product ideas for further development.
Concept testing A market research exercise in which feedback is obtained on the basic idea for a new product.

Products might be dropped at almost any point in the proceedings, but obviously the earlier the product is dropped, the lower the cost implications. Products that do not meet the strategic intent of the company should really never even be considered at the idea generation stage – people's thinking can be directed in other directions. The model is useful in the sense that most products pass through most of the stages: however, some products will be rushed through some stages and will spend longer in others, and sometimes stages are omitted altogether.

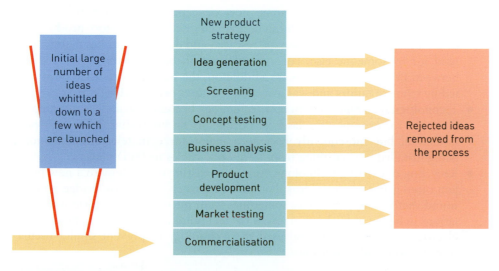

Figure 13.3 NPD process

Product champion An individual who has or is given the role of guiding a new product through the development process.

Furthermore, in the real world many products are launched that are simply the brainchild of an influential person in the company. Such products are carried through by the determination (or power) of the **product champion**. One famous example is the Sony Walkman, which was invented by Akio Morita, the founder of Sony. As a former Navy electronics engineer, Morita built the first Walkman at home, in his spare time, using a reporter's Dictaphone as the basis. Morita was able to force the product through into production over the protests of his marketing people, and of course it went on to be a worldwide success.

Think outside this box!

The Walkman is only one example among many radical inventions that appeared to fly in the face of conventional marketing wisdom. The Dyson vacuum cleaner, the clockwork radio, even the personal computer all started out as the ideas of engineers. They were products looking for a market – a concept that is anathema to marketers!

Yet these are products that have been phenomenally successful. So are the marketers wrong? Should we listen more to the engineers – who are, after all, consumers themselves and also know all about the art of the possible? Or perhaps the frame of the picture is too small to show the products which engineers loved, but the public hated – the products that clutter up the patent office and provide endless amusement for industrial historians!

Sources of ideas

Ideas might come from any of the following sources:

- Market feedback. Salespeople might bring back ideas from customers, or market research might generate some new concepts. Also, competitors might produce something new which can be adapted or copied: 'me-too' products are often highly successful, because the research and development has mainly been paid for by someone else. For example, within hours of the royal wedding between Prince William and Kate Middleton, the wedding dress had been copied by Chinese tailors and was available for other brides (Moore 2011).
- Technological advance. Often new technology becomes available through pure research: for example, the laser was originally an interesting laboratory phenomenon, but subsequently became a major force in telecommunications, being installed in everything from fibre-optic cables to DVD players.
- Recycling of existing technology. Applying existing technology to a new problem often generates new ideas. For example, when suspension bridge builders found that the support cables sometimes went into dangerous harmonic oscillations in high winds, they borrowed the technology of vibration dampers from electrical engineers, who had used the technology to prevent similar oscillations in overhead power lines.

- Generation by employees and managers within the organisation. To an extent, these ideas should be treated with a degree of suspicion because they are often based on what the company is capable of doing rather than on what a suitable market segment would be prepared to buy. In terms of the Calentone and Cooper classifications, these products would be Synergistic Products New to the Firm, but could also be Innovative Mousetraps – i.e. technically exciting products that actually do not offer the consumers anything new. These products showed no successes at all, because the market had no need for them.

- **Brainstorming**. Brainstorming involves getting a group of interested parties together and briefing them to generate new ideas, often around a strategic theme. Brainstorming teams are often interdisciplinary: marketers, designers, engineers and even delivery personnel might become involved on the team, so that ideas can be pre-screened for practicality. In general, brainstorming sessions can be extremely productive if the team approach it in a positive spirit.

  > **Brainstorming** Generating new product ideas by group discussion.

- **Customer-specified innovation**. In many business-to-business markets, innovation is forced by major customers. For example, if a motor manufacturer redesigns a vehicle, many (or all) of the components will need to be redesigned to a greater or lesser extent. In some cases, the component suppliers will need to expend substantial time and effort on research and development in order to meet the specification. In such circumstances, the engineers from the customer company are likely to become involved in the process, so a close relationship between supplier and customer is essential.

  > **Customer-specified innovation** New product ideas that are generated by customers.

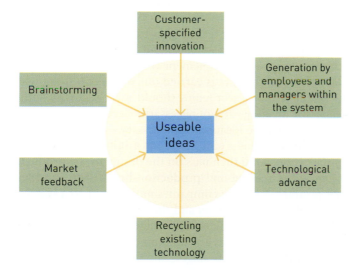

Figure 13.4   Sources of ideas

Organising for NPD

In too many firms, innovation is stifled by the corporate culture or by the corporate structure. New ideas are easily discouraged – failure often brings criticism or even ridicule, so retaining the status quo is often seen as the low-risk option. Innovative firms therefore go to considerable efforts to be proactive in encouraging innovation, and adopt many different structures for encouraging and developing new product

Figure 13.5   Project team structure

Project teams Groups of people with the responsibility for guiding products through the development process.

ideas. **Project teams** are interdisciplinary groups composed of individuals from different departments. A project team might be formed from people from marketing, finance, engineering, even administration and shipping (depending on the product). They operate in a similar way to the brainstorming groups mentioned earlier, but the project team work together to carry the product right through the NPD process until it is launched. Such groups are also sometimes called venture teams.

The advantage of using a project team is that each member can carry the thoughts of the group back to their own departments and disseminate the ideas. The departments can then work on ways to implement their own part of the overall plan, so that the final launch of the product is carried out with the full knowledge and commitment of the whole firm. Project teams should meet regularly, although Internet technology means that meetings do not necessarily need to be physical: members can video conference from remote locations as necessary.

Simultaneous engineering Carrying out development processes in parallel rather than sequentially in order to reduce time to market.

An extension of project teams is **simultaneous engineering**. In the past, designers would develop the product and then pass on the design to the production engineers, who would organise the tooling and production-line design in order to manufacture the finished product. Japanese companies moved over to a system of simultaneous engineering in which the designers and the production engineers work together throughout the process, thus cutting out one stage and speeding up the launch.

In some firms, product champions are appointed. A product champion has the role of taking the product through all its stages, and ensuring that colleagues contribute their part of the work at the appropriate time in the process. Product champions perform a useful task in that they ensure that the product actually comes into existence, rather than being sidelined by the routine tasks of making existing products. However, some researchers see product champions as a sign of a failed management: management, it can be argued, should be the ones who take responsibility for keeping the firm up to date (Johne and Snelson 1990).

There are six broad types of innovation strategy:

1. Offensive. Firms adopting an offensive strategy take pride in being the first to market. There are undoubtedly advantages in being the first with a new product: the firm can capture a substantial portion of the market before the

competitors are off the starting-blocks, and (provided the firm continues to innovate) can maintain the lead. This is the strategy adopted by Sony and 3M, both highly innovative firms.

2. Defensive. This strategy involves producing slightly improved copies of leaders' products. The defensive company only innovates in response to competitive challenges, either from leaders or from market challengers. As we saw earlier, incremental innovations reduce the risk for first movers in a market: early followers into a new market have some survival risks, but discontinuous innovation carries the greatest risks, so in fact there is only a disadvantage in being a first mover with a new product (Min et al. 2006). This means that a defensive strategy is probably the safest, even though the rewards may not be high.

3. Imitative. Imitative companies simply produce copies of other firms' products, with few (if any) adaptations. These firms have the advantage of generating minimal R&D costs, and of being sure that there is a market for the product. The main drawback is, of course, that the company which first developed the product has first-to-market advantages and will already have captured much of the market, which means that the imitative company needs to put in a greater effort on promoting the product in order to poach customers, and probably has to sell at a lower price as well.

4. Dependent. The companies produce customer-specified innovations. For example, a component supplier to a major car manufacturer is not in a position to develop new products independent of the customer: the firm can only produce new components that are compatible with the car manufacturer's models.

5. Traditional. These firms are not really innovative at all: they resurrect old-fashioned designs or produce products that have been around for many years. In the UK, brands such as Hovis and Bovril have been manufactured in much the same way for over a hundred years – in Singapore, Tiger Balm is in this category, and in Australia Vegemite is a traditional product.

6. Opportunist. The opportunist company produces and markets inventions. The Dyson vacuum cleaner, and the BayGen clockwork radio (invented by Trevor Bayliss), are examples of inventions that have succeeded. It should be pointed out that the vast majority of inventions actually fail to find a market, mainly because they tend to be technically-driven rather than market-driven.

Within the Traditional category, recent years have seen many 'new' products launched which are in fact reproductions of old designs. The Chrysler PT, the Volkswagen Beetle and the Mini Cooper are all examples of 'retro' designs that have been revived. There are also many household appliances such as fridges, toasters and the like which have been designed in 1950s' styles. The desire for tradition extends to services as well – people prefer 'the real thing' when going to pubs, but often have trouble distinguishing them from 'replica' products (Lego et al. 2002). These products rely on the following factors for their success (Brown et al. 2003):

- Allegory. This is the mythology and story surrounding the original brand and its design. Allegorical impact is created when the original product has a well-known history: the original Beetle was so well-loved it starred in a series of movies, and the Mini is remembered for its starring role in the original film of *The Italian Job*. Fifties-style toasters evoke memories of childhood, and myths grow up around products.

- Aura. This is the essence of the brand, the mystique surrounding it. The Chrysler PT evokes imagery of 1940s America, and other retro products evoke similar auras.

● Arcadia. This is the idealised community in which such products might be used. Arcadia is based on nostalgia, but generally evokes a non-existent past: the 1950s is often seen as a golden age, for example, whereas in fact it was a decade filled with war, the fear of war and a general atmosphere of paranoia.

● Antinomy. This is brand paradox. New technology is viewed as unstoppable and overpowering, but at the same time is responsible for people's desire to return to a simpler, less high-tech past. People buy the retro products because they evoke the past, but at the same time expect the products to perform to modern standards: the original Mini Cooper was leaky, unreliable and uncomfortable both to drive and to ride in, but people liked the style. The new version is comfortable, reliable and efficient, but retains the style (albeit on a somewhat larger scale).

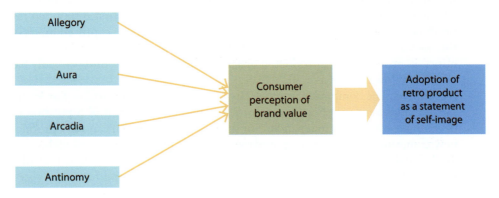

Figure 13.6   The four As of retro design

Real-life marketing: Make the product easy to demonstrate

When typewriters were first invented by Remington, the company knew that getting such a revolutionary product accepted would be difficult. After all, a typewriter was an expensive item compared with a pen or pencil, which appeared to do the same job. The typewriter's main advantage was that it was much faster to type than to write by hand, so this had to be demonstrated to potential buyers.

Remington laid out the keyboard so that it would be easy to type the word 'typewriter', since this would be the word everyone would want to see in a demonstration. As you have no doubt noticed, the top line of a keyboard says QWERTYUIOP – so 'typewriter' can be written using only letters from the top line.

Despite the fact that a QWERTY keyboard is slow to use for everyday typing, the layout stuck because everyone got trained to use it and it's difficult to switch (as you'll know if you ever tried to use a French or German keyboard, where the letters are in different places). Of course, the alternative might have been that the typewriter would have remained an interesting novelty, a product that was never adopted.

If you like this idea, keep the following in mind:

● The idea works best for complex products.
● Don't be afraid to redesign the product if this will make the demonstration more striking.
● The easier to operate something looks, the more likely people will adopt it.

Whether or not to go ahead with a new product is a decision that revolves around five dimensions (Carbonell-Foulquie et al. 2004). These are as follows:

1. Strategic fit. This is the degree to which the new product fits in with the company's overall marketing and corporate strategy. The questions the company will ask are: Does this product take us nearer to where we want to be in the market? Does this product detract from our existing marketing plan? Does this product hurt our other products, and cannibalise sales?

2. Technical feasibility. This is not just about whether the product can be made, or even whether it can be made economically: it is also about whether the product can be made economically within the product management portfolio (see Chapter 12).

3. Customer acceptance. Obviously no marketer should be launching a product the customers do not like or would have difficulty accepting. Sadly, many products are launched every year that do not find a market – sometimes for no apparent reason.

4. Market opportunity. This is the level of competition the firm might have to face, and the current state of the external environment. The market opportunity takes account of all the elements that make up the market – the customers, the competitors, the macro- and micro-environment, and so forth.

5. Financial performance. Firms do not necessarily aim to show a profit on every product they sell, but financial return is obviously important, and in the long run a product must be viable financially. If the product can never be profitable, the firm will have to make a decision as to whether there is any point in launching it at all.

Although all of the above factors are important, it is customer acceptance that decides the product's fate. If customers will not buy the product in sufficient numbers, all the other considerations are futile: if, on the other hand, customers have indicated that they will buy the product in large quantities, all the other problems can be overcome in time.

Think outside this box!

Retro products appear to be all the rage at present. Design styles from the sixties and fifties, re-vamped and updated models of traditional products, and even clothing fashions are being re-issued to an eager public.

At the same time marketers are still using the word 'new' on almost everything from washing powder to cars. So which is the bigger selling point? New, or old? Modern/futuristic, or traditional/old-fashioned?

Diffusion of innovation

New products are not immediately adopted by all consumers. Some consumers are driven to buy new products almost as soon as they become available, whereas others prefer to wait until the product has been around for a while before risking their hard-earned money on it. Innovations therefore take time to filter through the population:

Figure 13.7   Factors in the launch decision

this process is called diffusion, and is partly determined by the nature of consumers and partly by the nature of the innovation itself.

Everett M. Rogers (1962) classified customers as follows:

- Innovators: those who like to be first to own the latest products. These consumers predominate at the beginning of the product life cycle (PLC).
- Early adopters: those who are open to new ideas, but like to wait a while after the initial launch. These consumers predominate during the growth phase of the PLC.
- Early majority: those who buy once the product is thoroughly tried and tested. These consumers predominate in the early part of the maturity phase of the PLC.
- Late majority: those who are suspicious of new things, and wait until most other people already have one. These consumers predominate in the later part of the maturity phase of the PLC.
- Laggards: those who adopt new products only when it becomes absolutely necessary to do so. These consumers predominate in the decline phase of the PLC.

The process of diffusion of innovation is carried out through reference-group influence (see Chapter 3). Groups and individuals obviously have a strong influence on people's attitudes and behaviour; the history of the theory is not so much one of advancing knowledge about the mechanisms involved, but is rather a history of the way society has changed in the period in which the theories were evolving.

Three main theories concerning the mechanisms for diffusion of innovation have been proposed: trickle-down theory, two-step flow theory and multistage interaction theory.

Trickle-down theory says that the wealthy classes obtain information about new products, and the poorer classes then imitate their 'betters' (Veblen 1899). This

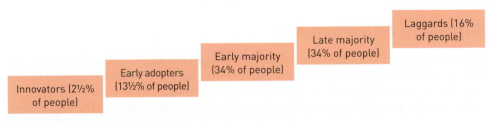

Figure 13.8   Adopter categories

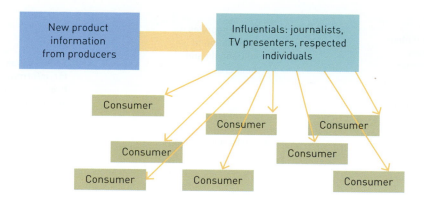

Figure 13.9 Two-step flow theory

theory probably held true in the late 19th century, when class distinctions were much stronger than they are in the early 21st century, and also mass communication was not as widespread. Nowadays, the theory has been largely discredited in wealthy countries because new ideas are disseminated overnight by the mass media and copied by chain stores within days. It is common for the designer dresses worn by film stars at movie premieres to be copied almost overnight by chain stores and sold to the general public within weeks or even days. The dress worn by Princess Diana at her wedding was available to the 'ordinary' bride within less than a week as chain-store tailors copied every detail of the dress from the TV coverage. What is replacing trickle-down theory is **homophilous influence**, which refers to transmission between those of a similar age, education, social class, etc., in other words those who already have a lot in common.

Homophilous influence The love of being like everyone else.

Two-step flow theory is similar, but this time it is 'influentials' rather than wealthy people who are the start of the adoption process (Lazarsfield et al. 1948). This has considerable basis in truth, but may be less true now than it was in the 1940s when the theory was first developed; access to TV and other information media has proliferated and information about innovation is disseminated much faster. Certainly in the diffusion of innovative high-tech products there is strong evidence for the theory: however, there is a weakening of this mechanism due to the preponderance of mass media. In the 1940s most homes did not have TV and there was no commercial radio in the UK; the availability of commercial information was therefore more restricted to the wealthy. Also, the two-step flow assumes that the audience is passively waiting for the information to be presented, whereas in fact people actively seek out information about new things by asking friends and relatives and by looking for published information.

Influentials might include TV programmes (for example, the BBC's *Tomorrow's World* programme disseminated information about products using new technologies, and programmes like *Top Gear* and *Fifth Gear* present information about new cars) or journalists (for example, there are several magazines devoted to new developments in IT).

The Multistage Interaction model (Engel et al. 1995) agrees that some people do exercise more influence than others, but also recognises that the mass media affect both influential and seeker. The influential doesn't mediate the information flow, as the two-step model suggests, but rather acts as a mechanism for emphasising or facilitating the information flow. Within the model, there is a continuous dialogue between marketers, seekers and influentials with many stages of influence before the new idea is adopted or rejected.

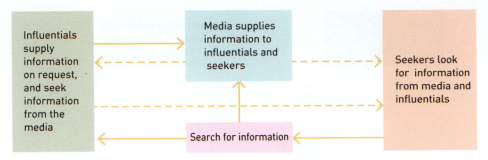

Figure 13.10   Multistage interaction model

Table 13.2   Characteristics of influentials

Characteristic	Description of influential
Demographics	Wide differences according to product category. For fashions and film-going, young women dominate. For self-medication, women with children are most influential. Generally, demography shows low correlation and is not a good predictor.
Social activity	Influencers and opinion leaders are usually gregarious.
General attitudes	Generally innovative and positive towards new products.
Personality and lifestyle	Low correlation of personality with opinion leadership. Lifestyle tends to be more fashion conscious, more socially active and more independent.
Product related	Influencers are more interested in the specific product area than are others. They are active searchers and information-gatherers, especially from the mass media.

Source: Adapted from Engel et al. 1995

Clearly it is important for marketers to identify who the influential people are likely to be, and much research has been carried out into this area. Table 13.2 shows the main characteristics of influentials which have been identified so far; but this is probably not an exhaustive list, nor will it be generally applicable to all cases.

Influencers (and others) like to pass on their knowledge, and there are several reasons for doing this, as follows:

- Involvement is a major force. The influencer is actually interested in the subject area, and wants to share the excitement with others. A hi-fi enthusiast who buys a new Arcam stereo at the weekend will want to tell friends and colleagues all about it on Monday morning. Telling other people acts as an outlet for the pleasure of owning the new product (Venkatraman 1990).
- Self-enhancement is about airing one's superior knowledge. Appearing to be a connoisseur, whether of fine wines or works of art or classic cars, is something many influencers strive for. Partly this goes to a need for the esteem of others, and partly it is a function of self-esteem.

- Concern for others often precipitates influence. The genuine desire to help a friend to reach a good decision often prompts the expert to say 'OK, I'll come with you when you go to the shop.' This factor works most strongly when there is a strong link between the individuals concerned, and when the influencer has been very satisfied with the product or service concerned (Bone 1992).
- **Message intrigue** is the factor concerned with comments about advertising messages. If an advertisement is particularly intriguing or humorous, people will discuss it; this enhances the message by repetition.
- **Dissonance** reduction is about reducing doubts after making a major purchase (Robertson and Gatignon 1986). As word-of-mouth influence this can be good or bad; sometimes the influencer will try to reassure him- or herself by telling everybody about the good points of the product; more often, though, disappointed customers will use word-of-mouth to complain bitterly and explain how the wicked manufacturer has cheated them. This is sometimes a way of passing the responsibility over to the supplier rather than admitting that the influencer has made a bad decision or a bad choice.

Message intrigue The increased interest developed by ambiguous communications.

Dissonance The emotional state created when expectations do not match with outcomes.

People often need considerable persuasion to change from their old product to a new one. This is because there is always a cost of some sort. For example, somebody buying a new car will lose money on trading in the old car (a switching cost), or perhaps somebody buying a new computer will also have to spend money on new software, and spend time learning how to operate the new equipment (an **innovation cost**).

Innovation cost The expenditure of money and effort resulting from adopting a new product.

Real-life marketing: Tailor the product

When the PC revolution started in the 1980s people began to buy computers for home use. Each of those individuals would have had slightly different needs – selling standardised machines to a large company was relatively straightforward, but meeting the disparate needs of many people was not so easy.

However, computers are in fact composed of a lot of separate modules, so although the product is complex it should be possible to bolt together a custom-made machine, provided the systems for specifying and assembling the computer were in place. A 19-year-old student figured out the way to do it, and began a mail order company that could custom-build computers in a subcontracted factory. The student's name was Michael Dell.

Dell computers are now sold on-line, in retail stores, and by mail order. The company is one of the world's largest computer manufacturers, and Michael Dell is a wealthy man.

If you want to be like Michael Dell, you need to follow these rules:

- Technical support is essential for this to work. People will need advice on what can and cannot be added to their machine, and will need help in understanding how their needs in using the machine relate to the finished product.
- Quick turnround of manufacture is important. People want the product now, not weeks from now, and may be prepared to accept a less tailored, standard product from someone else rather than wait.
- People will pay more for a tailored product – but probably not a lot more. You have to be sure that the extra cost of tailoring the product is more than covered by the premium people are prepared to pay.

On the other hand there is some evidence that newness as such is an important factor in the consumer's decision-making process (Haines 1966). This is why companies often use the word 'new' in advertising. In other words, people like new things, but

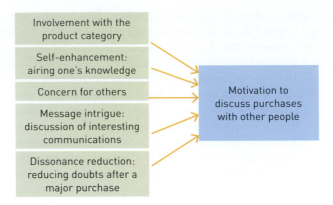

Figure 13.11   Motivation for Influencers

there is a cost attached. Provided the new product offers real additional benefits over the old one (i.e. fits the consumer's needs better than the old product), the product will be adopted.

Think outside this box!

Don't we have enough new stuff already? It seems as if we have only just learned to use our mobile telephones when somebody comes out with a new one, with all those must-have features (games, video capability, turns on the central heating and puts the cat out, etc., etc.)

Why not call a halt now? Everything works just fine, we have had enough of transferring all our friends' numbers from one phone to the other, and for sure we have had enough of puzzling over the 40,000 word manual (printed in teensy-weensy writing) just to find out how to send a text. Do our hearts sink when we see the word 'new' or 'latest'? Or do we get excited at the prospect of having something our friends don't have yet?

Consumers must first become aware of the new product, then become persuaded that there is a real advantage in switching from their existing solution. A useful model of this adoption process is as follows:

- Awareness. This will often come about as a result of promotional activities by the firm.
- Trial. For a low-price item (e.g. a packet of biscuits) this may mean that the consumer will actually buy the product before trying it; for a major purchase, such as a car, the consumer will usually need to have a test-drive. Increasingly, supermarkets hold tasting sessions to allow customers to try new products.
- Adoption. This is the point at which the consumer decides to buy the product, or make it part of the weekly shopping list.

Obviously, not all products are successful. Many apparently promising new ideas sink without trace: others are popular for a while, then disappear. Successful products

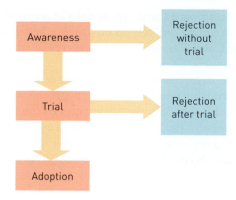

Figure 13.12   Adoption/rejection process

become culturally anchored, in other words become an integral part of people's lives in such a way that the person–product interface is a part of the individual's self-concept (Latour and Roberts 1991).

Rogers (1962) identified the following perceived attributes of innovative products, by which consumers apparently judge the product during the decision-making process:

- **Relative advantage**. The degree to which the innovation is perceived as better than the idea it supersedes. If the innovation does not offer something different from the solutions currently available, there is no reason to risk adopting it. Relative advantage is very much linked to cognition – it implies a rational calculation on the part of the prospective adopter of the product. Sometimes just the newness of the solution will create some sales, but these will tend to die out if the product really is not better (in terms of Calentone and Cooper, this would be designated as the Innovative Mousetrap That Really Wasn't Better).

  > **Relative advantage** The degree to which a new product is better than the one it replaces.

- **Compatibility**. Consistency with existing values, past experiences and needs of potential adopters. If the product is compatible with existing knowledge and consumption practices, it is more likely to be adopted quickly: a new toothpaste does not involve any new learning or changed behaviour in brushing one's teeth, whereas a new diet requires changes in lifestyle.

  > **Compatibility** The degree to which a product fits into the adopter's life.

- **Complexity**. Ideas that are easily understood are adopted more quickly. DVD players are actually a straightforward concept for someone who already owns a computer and a video recorder, but a digital camera presents the new owner with a great deal of learning if his or her previous camera used film. Software producers go to great effort to make their software user-friendly, with the least possible new learning necessary for users. Obviously someone who is using a computer for the first time is likely to find the software dazzlingly complex to use, compared with someone who has a few years' experience, so complexity is a subjective concept.

  > **Complexity** The degree to which the product is difficult to understand.

- **Trialability**. Degree to which a product can be experimented with. Some products (notably service products) cannot be tested before purchase. Others can be tried out (for example cars can be test-driven). If the product is very innovative, lack of trialability can kill sales from the outset. Trialability is also a function of overall cost – if the cost of testing the product (whether financial or in terms of risk) is low, people will be more prepared to try it. For example, a new brand of biscuits is relatively cheap and easy to try out – if the biscuits are no good, the financial loss is only a few pence. On the other hand, trying

  > **Trialability** The degree to which the product can be tried out before adoption.

out a new type of surfboard carries great risks in terms of finance and physical risk, so a surfer would be unlikely to buy such a board simply for the opportunity to try it out. Retailers and manufacturers need to address these issues when offering products.

Observability The degree to which the product can be seen by others.

- **Observability.** The degree to which the results of an innovation are visible to others. This has two main components: the degree to which the adopter is able to show friends and neighbours the advantages of the new product is likely to affect adoption, and also the degree to which prospective adopters can see the product being used by others will affect their decision to adopt (or not). Observability is largely an affective component of adoption: opinion leaders and influentials like to show off their new products, and (for the observer) there is an opportunity to see the product in action.

The five characteristics described above can be a guide as to the potential success of the product in the marketplace. Products that score high on several characteristics are likely to succeed; those that score low, or score on only one or two characteristics, are likely to fail. This is not, of course, an infallible guide, but in the long run successful products tend to conform to the characteristics outlined above.

Innovation is also a characteristic of consumers. Apart from the issue of adopting a new product as it stands, there is the concept of re-invention of existing products by the consumers. Sometimes users find new ways to use the product (not envisaged by the designers) and sometimes this leads to the creation of whole new markets. For example, in the 1930s it was discovered that baking soda is good for removing stale smells from refrigerators, a fact that was quickly seized on by baking soda manufacturers. Deodorising fridges is now a major part of the market for baking soda.

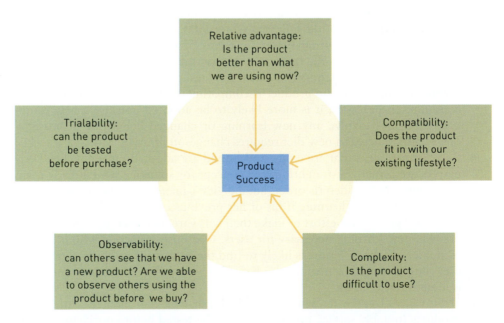

Figure 13.13 Characteristics of successful new products

Influences on the diffusion process

The diffusion process is influenced by many factors. The first of these is innovation, both on the part of the producer and on the part of the consumer. The more

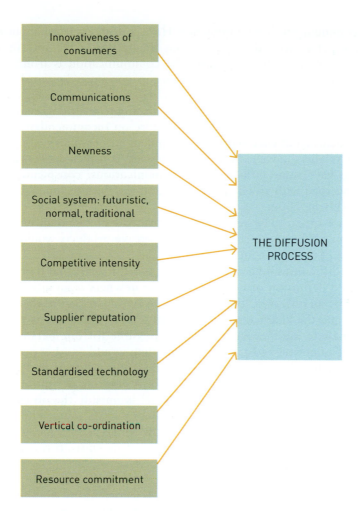

Figure 13.14 Influences on diffusion

innovative the consumer, the faster the product is adopted. Innovativeness is the degree to which an individual makes innovative decisions independent of the communicated experiences of others (Midgely 1977).

Innovativeness among consumers is somewhat difficult to assess, because innovativeness for one category of product does not necessarily equate to innovativeness for all categories. In other words, someone who is eager to buy the latest hi-fi equipment might have no interest at all in buying the latest digital camera. Innovativeness is linked to involvement (see Chapter 3), so people become innovators only for the product groups they are involved with. Having said that, there is evidence that some people like gadgets and new technology generally – these are called **technophones**. **Technophobes**, on the other hand, exhibit a reluctance to use new technology and are wary of it (Mitchell 1994). Innovation has both a cognitive element and an affective element. Research using the Kirton Adaptive-Innovative Index (Kirton 1976) shows that there is a correlation between innovativeness and KAI scores (Foxall 1989). However, it transpires that involvement is a much more important factor (Foxall and Bhate 1993). The actual usefulness of the product, as opposed to its visibility or exciting technical features, is largely governed by factors that are internal to the consumer, with little reference to social factors (Munnukka and Järvi 2011).

Technophone Someone who has an interest in new technology.

Technophobe Someone who does not like new products.

Second, communication is an influence. How consumers learn about new products, and the perceptions they form about them, affects the way they respond to the product offering. In some cases the communication is from producer to consumer, in other cases it is from consumer to consumer by word of mouth or by demonstration (see Observability above). There is some evidence that people rely on different forms of communication according to their degree of innovativeness (Blythe 2002). Innovators tend to rely more on recommendations by friends and on hands-on experience with the equipment rather than on manufacturers' brochures or retailers' advice. Whether people are conspicuous consumers or not also seems to have some influence on communications: conspicuous consumers are more concerned with visual appearance, and less with technical brochures and descriptions (Blythe 2002).

Price does not appear to be significantly correlated with rate of diffusion, although it might reasonably be expected that more expensive products would diffuse more slowly because of the higher financial risk.

One of the difficulties inherent in studying innovation is that there is no generally recognised definition of newness. Because newness is an attribute accorded to a product by an observer, it is derived from two factors: the characteristics of the product, and the characteristics of the observer. What is new to one person may not be new to another, and it may be possible for one person to accord a greater degree of newness to a given product than would another person. Equally, the same person may be able to observe two different products and ascribe different degrees of newness to each (Blythe 1999). A working definition for newness might be 'the degree to which a given product is outside the observer's experience'. Because newness is often used as a benefit in its own right in marketing communications, it would be useful to know what people mean by newness: unfortunately, because of the subjective nature of newness, this is unlikely to be possible.

The social system to which individuals belong will affect the adoption of innovation. The rate of diffusion will be affected according to whether the society is futuristic, normal or traditionalist (Wills et al. 1991). Some societies (such as that of the United States) tend to be futuristic, to welcome new inventions and ideas, whereas others (such as many European countries) are traditionalist and avoid new ideas. For example, in Andalucía (southern Spain) grants are available for the installation of solar power, yet the vast majority of people in Andalucía have not installed the systems as yet, despite the obvious advantage of having free electricity as a result of innovating. Many Northern European immigrants to the area have solar power, on the other hand, and the region has a large number of solar-power farms where arrays of solar collectors generate electricity for the national grid.

Some of the factors that affect diffusion are under the control of marketers (Robertson and Gatignon 1986). These are as follows:

- Competitive intensity. Highly competitive firms who adopt aggressive marketing strategies and often price competitively will speed up the process of adoption. Intense competition might lead to price wars: also, the more innovative a product is, the more likely a competitor is to retaliate with a similar product innovation (Kuester et al. 1999).
- Supplier reputation. The better the reputation of the supplier, the faster the diffusion. This is because potential customers will perceive the source as being more credible, which reduces uncertainty and risk in the decision.

- Standardised technology. If there are several competing systems on offer, consumers are likely to be more cautious about adopting the product. For example, video recorders took a long time to be adopted because (initially) there were three competing systems. Once it became clear that the industry was standardising around the VHS system, adoption moved much more rapidly. The lesson was not lost on the industry: when DVDs were introduced the system was standardised from the outset, although it was later superseded by Blu-Ray.
- Vertical co-ordination. If the relationships between the distribution channel members are close and interlocking, diffusion will be faster. Because the information flow between members of the distribution chain is faster, the flow from supplier to end customer (the consumer) is also likely to be faster. There is also less uncertainty between channel members and (ultimately) the end consumer.
- Resource commitment. If the firm has committed substantial resources to the product and to innovation generally, diffusion is likely to be faster. This is partly because the company will make efforts to ensure that it gets a quick return on its investment, and partly because the company has more experience of promoting innovation. Also, as the company's reputation for innovation grows, customers who are themselves innovative will be attracted to products from that company. Research indicates that a more rapid adoption of innovations tends to shorten the product life cycle, which in turn forces managers to move faster in approving new projects (Rosenau 1988).

The speed at which innovation is adopted, and the success of innovation, appear also to be affected by the degree of marketing orientation of the firm. Some research suggests that market orientation facilitates technology-based innovation, but inhibits innovation aimed at emerging market segments (Zheng Zhou et al. 2005). Knowledge of the market, knowledge change and sharing knowledge about the market all contribute to increased innovative effort (Marinova 2004), and (perhaps not surprisingly) firms that provide greater marketing support for radical new products are likely to gain higher rewards in the long run (Sorescu et al. 2003). Interestingly, acquiring another company also seems to stimulate innovation (at least in the pharmaceutical industry) (Prabhu et al. 2005).

It is therefore no surprise that firms with a strong market orientation are more likely to be successful in launching new-to-the-world products (Augusto and Coelho 2009), nor that firms with strong customer relationship management also find it easier to innovate (Battor and Battor 2010).

Chapter summary

Innovation is the lifeblood of any company, and indeed this is so for most individuals as well: life would grow extremely tedious if nothing ever changed. The constant search for novelty on the part of consumers leads to a similar search on the part of companies. Organising for innovation is by no means straightforward: often there is resistance within the firm, and there are many influences on the new-product development process, as well as on the new-product diffusion process in the market.

Innovation can happen at many different levels, from the simple copying of a competitor's product through to the development of a radical new solution to a problem that people did not realise they had.

Key points

- Products can be replacements, additions, new lines or new-to-the-world.
- Less radical products are more likely to succeed than radical products, but may not succeed to the same extent.
- Creating an innovative culture within the firm is a useful, but difficult, step to take.
- Ideas can come from brainstorming, technological advances, recycling existing technology, market feedback, generation by employees, or by customer specification.
- Project teams and project champions are both powerful in guiding new products through from idea to launch.
- There are six broad categories of NPD strategy: offensive, defensive, imitative, dependent, traditional, and opportunistic.
- There are five necessary factors for a successful product launch: strategic fit, technical feasibility, customer acceptance, market opportunity and financial performance.
- Innovation diffuses gradually through the population: innovators for one product category are not necessarily innovators for another.
- Newness is a factor in product acceptability.
- The level of acceptability of a product depends on the following factors: relative advantage, complexity, compatibility, trialability and observability.
- People have different communication styles according to their level of innovativeness.
- Some, though by no means all, of the factors that affect the diffusion of innovation can be controlled by marketers.

Review questions

1. What are the main problems in establishing an innovative corporate culture?
2. How might a firm identify innovators for its product category?
3. What is the role of a product champion?
4. What is the role of a project team?
5. How does the role of a project team differ from that of a brainstorming group?
6. What is the difference between an imitative strategy and a defensive strategy?
7. If newness is a factor in product acceptability, why does relative advantage matter?
8. What is the role of involvement in innovativeness?
9. How might a firm hasten the adoption of products?
10. What is the difference between a technophone and a technophobe?

Case study revisited: Boeing Dreamliner

Perhaps not surprisingly when dealing with such a radical new design (and production system), the aircraft began to suffer from delays. First, the prototypes turned out to be over two tons overweight, despite everyone's best efforts to cut weight. Weight is crucial in aircraft – every pound has to be lifted from ground level to seven miles above the surface and kept there, so every pound costs fuel. Two tons makes a very big difference.

Second, there were delays with the supply chain. Components did not arrive on time, paperwork did not show up and software problems meant that the aircraft's maiden flight had to be delayed. Boeing announced a fifteen-month delay in delivery, to the third quarter of 2009. Third, a strike at the Boeing plant, coupled with further component delays, meant that the maiden flight would be put back until the second quarter of 2009, which meant deliveries would not start until 2010. By now, the airlines who had ordered the aircraft were beginning to talk about suing for compensation.

Further delays followed – testing found faults in the airframe, the weight could still not be reduced to the target level, there was an engine blowout, test flights were delayed due to bad weather, and many other hold-ups meant that the first aircraft was delivered to All-Nippon Airlines in September 2011. On the plus side, ANA reported that the aircraft exceeded fuel economy targets, costing 20% less in fuel than previous airliners.

Unfortunately the problems did not end there. Part of the Dreamliner's energy efficiency came from using electrical power for on-board systems – previous aircraft had bled off air directly from the engines to run pneumatics and hydraulics on board. The Dreamliner's system extracts 35% less engine power, but relies on lithium-ion batteries, which have been known to catch fire since they produce their own oxygen. Despite Boeing's best efforts, on 13 January 2013 a Dreamliner's batteries caught fire at Logan International Airport in Boston: luckily the aircraft was empty at the time. Three days later, another Dreamliner had to make an emergency landing when the system reported a fire in a compartment. Although ANA reported that this was a false alarm, they (and Japan Airlines) voluntarily grounded their Dreamliner fleets. Later the same day, 16 January, the Federal Aviation Authority grounded all Dreamliners until the systems had been checked over.

All new airliners suffer from teething problems, and the Dreamliner uses so much that is new it is not surprising that there have been difficulties. So far the aircraft has responded well: no one has been endangered, let alone killed, and the company seems to be on top of fixing the problems, allowing the Dreamliner to be cleared for flying again. Previous aircraft have not been so fortunate: the DeHavilland Comet, the world's first jet airliner, had a habit of breaking up in mid-air. Three Comets crashed in this way before the aircraft was grounded for modifications. The Douglas DC-10 also suffered from early design flaws: altogether the aircraft has been responsible for over 1200 deaths, but it is still in service following extensive modifications.

Case study: Innovations catalogue

The Innovations catalogue has almost become a UK institution. Launched in 1985, the catalogue offered gadgets and inventions of all descriptions to an unsuspecting public – pioneer of the radio-controlled clock, the recharger for ordinary carbon-zinc batteries, the treeless hammock and the extendable window-cleaning device. The company also offered some less immediately useful devices: the fun-fur-lined golf club cover, the portable paper shredder and the one-size-fits-all galoshes.

In 2003, the catalogue appeared to be heading into the decline stage of the product life cycle. Its owners, Great Universal Stores, said that the catalogue was underperforming and had to be closed down. The Spring 2003 catalogue was the last – but the brand continued, shifting itself (inevitably) to that most modern of media, the Internet. Now part of Shop Direct Group, the Innovations mail order service continues unchecked, offering lip-shaped pillows, patented oyster-openers and Toastabags (which allow people to make toasted sandwiches in an ordinary toaster).

Gadget lovers are attracted by the catalogue – a glance at the section that says 'customers who bought this also bought ...' reveals that customers for a novel folding bed also bought Toastabags and festive rubber gloves (washing-up gloves with Christmas tinsel on them). Not to mention Wormie, the colour-coded terracotta worm that tells you when to water your plants.

In fact, a trawl through the Innovations website is a real adventure for anyone who loves gadgets. Some are eminently sensible, some are incomprehensible, some are clearly useful but somehow unappealing: most are novel, relatively few are traditional or resurrected designs. Innovations claim to have only one goal: to seek out the world's latest innovations and market them first. Innovations is an admirer of the lone inventor, toiling away in the garden shed, and are happy to advise inventors about how to bring their products to market.

The appeal of the catalogue to consumers has never really been clear. Because of its eclectic approach, Innovations offered products for everyone from gardeners to hi-fi enthusiasts: alongside products intended to make housework easier were products for the office, and on the next page to the electric coin-sorting machine were the advertisements for dog-hair removing equipment. Even the seafood-eating kit (obviously aimed at the gourmet market) appeared alongside the Air-Flow Mouse, a computer mouse with a built-in fan to keep the hands cool while surfing the Web.

This lack of a market segment may have been what killed the paper catalogue, but it does not appear to be a problem for the on-line version. Products are arranged by category – gadgets, health and fitness, car and travel, home and garden, sound and vision, and what's new. This still begs the question of how the catalogue is targeted.

Throughout its life, Innovations has provided a talking-point for people. Because of the novelty of its products, people have actually read the catalogue and often told friends about products – often in a sense of poking fun at some of the more outlandish gadgets, but nonetheless talking. Almost everybody in the UK has heard of the Innovations catalogue and knows what it has to offer (at least in a broad sense), and most people will have browsed through it at one time or another. Obviously enough people stop and buy items for the catalogue to have remained viable for twenty years – and equally obviously there is no shortage of ideas for new products to fill its pages.

Questions

1. How might Innovations seek to overcome the segmentation problem?
2. What type of innovation strategy is Innovations pursuing?
3. What might be the appeal of Innovations to the average person?
4. What factors have enabled Innovations to maintain its success?
5. Why would somebody buy fun-fur-lined golf club covers?

Further reading

Johne, A. and Snelson, P. (1990) *Successful New Product Development.* London: Blackwell. This book is written by two of the foremost experts on innovation, and describes research carried out into new product successes in 40 British and American firms.

Markides, C. and Geroski, P. (2004) *Fast Second: How Successful Companies Bypass Radical Innovation to Enter and Dominate New Markets.* New York: Jossey–Bass/Wiley. This book extols the virtues of being a follower rather than a leader in innovation.

References

Augusto, Mario and Coelho, Filipe (2009) Market orientation and new-to-the-world products: exploring the moderating effects of innovativeness, competitive strength, and environmental forces. *Industrial Marketing Management*, 38 (1): 94–108.

Battor, Mustafa and Battor, Mohamed (2010) The impact of customer relationship management capability on innovation and performance advantages: testing a mediated model. *Journal of Marketing Management*, 26 (9/10): 842–57.

Blackwell, R.D., Miniard, Paul W. and Engel, James F. (2001) *Consumer Behaviour*, 9th edn. Cincinnati, OH: South-Western.

Blythe, Jim (1999) Innovativeness and newness in high-tech consumer durables. *Journal of Product and Brand Management*, 8 (5): 415–29.

Blythe, Jim (2002) Communications and innovation: the case of hi-fi systems. *Corporate Communications: An International Journal*, 7 (1): 9–16.

Bone, Paula F. (1992) Determinants of word-of-mouth communications during product consumption. In John F. Sherry and Brian Strenthal (eds), *Advances in Consumer Research*, 19: 579–83.

Booz-Allen and Hamilton (1982) *New Products Management for the 1980s*. New York: Booz-Allen and Hamilton Inc.

Brown, Stephen, Sherry, John F. and Kozinetts, Robert V. (2003) Teaching old brands new tricks: retro branding and the revival of brand meaning. *Journal of Marketing*, 67 (3): 19–33.

Calentone, Roger J. and Cooper, Robert G. (1981) 'New product scenarios; prospects for success', *American Journal of Marketing*, 45: 48–60.

Carbonell-Foulquie, Pilar, Munuera-Aleman, Jose L. and Rodriguez-Escudero, Ana I. (2004) Criteria employed for go/no-go decisions when developing successful highly-innovative products. *Industrial Marketing Management*, 33 (4): 307–16.

Cooper, R.G. and Kleinschmidt, E.J. (1986) An investigation into the new product process: steps, deficiencies and impact. *Journal of Product Innovation Management*, June: 71–85.

Engel, James F., Blackwell, Roger D. and Miniard, Paul W. (1995) *Consumer Behaviour*, 8th edn. Fort Worth, TX: Dryden Press.

Foxall, G.R. (1989) Marketing, innovation and customers. *Quarterly Review of Marketing*, Autumn: pp. 14–22.

Foxall, G.R. and Bhate, S. (1993) Cognitive style and personal involvement as explicators of innovative purchasing of 'healthy' brands. *European Journal of Marketing*, 27: 5–16.

Haines, George H. (1966) 'A study of why people purchase new products', *Proceedings of the American Marketing Association*, pp. 685–97.

Hamel, G. and Prahalad, C.K. (1991) Corporate imagination and expeditionary marketing. *Harvard Business Review*, 69 (4): 81–92.

Huang, Xueli, Soutar, Geoffrey N. and Brown, Alan (2004) Measuring new product success: an empirical investigation of Australian SMEs. *Industrial Marketing Management*, 33 (2): 101–123.

Johne, A. and Snelson, P. (1990) *Successful Product Development; Management Practices in American and British Firms*. Oxford: Blackwell.

Kirton, Michael (1976) Adaptors and innovators: a description and measure. *Journal of Applied Psychology*, 61 (5): 622–9.

Kuester, Sabine, Homburg, Christian and Robertson, Thomas S. (1999) Retaliatory behaviour to new product entry. *Journal of Marketing*, 63: 90–106.

Latour, Michael S. and Roberts, Scott D. (1991) Cultural anchoring and product diffusion. *Journal of Consumer Marketing*, 9 (Fall): 29–34.

Lazarsfield, Paul F., Bertelson, Bernard R. and Gaudet, Hazel (1948) *The People's Choice*. New York, Columbia University Press.

Lego, Caroline, Solomon, Michael R., Turley, Darach, O'Neill, Martin and Engels, Basil (2002) Real or replica? Deciphering authenticity in Irish pubs. *Advances in Consumer Behaviour*, 29 (1): 45.

Marinova, Detelina (2004) Actualising innovation effort: the impact of market knowledge diffusion in a dynamic system of competition. *Journal of Marketing*, 68 (3): 1–19.

Midgley, David F. (1977) *Innovation and New Product Marketing.* London: Croom Helm.

Min, Sungwook, Kalwani, Manohar U. and Robinson, William T. (2006) Market pioneer and early follower survival risks: a contingency analysis of really new vs. incrementally new products. *Journal of Marketing*, 70 (1): 15–33.

Mitchell, Susan (1994) Technophiles and technophobes. *American Demographics*, 16 (Feb): 36.

Moore, Malcolm (2011) Royal wedding: Chinese tailors rush to copy Kate Middleton's dress. *Daily Telegraph* (London). Retrieved from www.telegraph.co.uk/news/uknews/royal-wedding/8485272/Royal-wedding-Chinese-tailors-rush-to-copy-Kate-Middletons-dress.html (30 April 2011).

Munnukka, J. and Järvi, P. (2011) The value drivers of high-tech consumer products. *Journal of Marketing Management*, 27 (5/6): 582–601.

Prabhu, Jaideep C., Chandy, Rajesh K. and Ellis, Mark E. (2005) The impact of acquisitions on innovation: poison pill, placebo or tonic? *Journal of Marketing*, 69 (1): 114–30.

Robertson, Thomas S. (1967) The process of innovation and the diffusion of innovation. *Journal of Marketing*, 31 (1): 14–19.

Robertson, Thomas S. and Gatignon, H. (1986) Competitive effects on technology diffusion. *Journal of Marketing*, 50 (July): 1–12.

Rodriguez, Nuria Garcia, Perez, Ma Jose Sanzo and Gutierrez, Juan A. Trespalacios (2007) Interfunctional trust as a determining factor in new-product performance. *European Journal of Marketing*, 41 (5/6): 678–702.

Rogers, Everett M. (1962) *Diffusion of Innovations.* New York: Macmillan.

Rosenau, Milton D. Jr. (1988) Speeding your new product to market. *Journal of Consumer Marketing*, 5 (Spring): 23–35.

Sorescu, Alan B., Chandy, Rajesh K. and Prabhu, Jaideep C. (2003) Sources and financial consequences of radical innovation: insights from pharmaceuticals. *Journal of Marketing*, 67 (4): 82–102.

Tajeddini, Kayhan, Trueman, Myfanwy and Larsen, Gretchen (2006) Examining the effect of marketing orientation on innovativeness. *Journal of Marketing Management*, 22 (5/6): 529–51.

Veblen, T. (1899) *The Theory of the Leisure Class.* New York: Macmillan.

Venkatraman, Meera P. (1990) Opinion leadership: enduring involvement and characteristics of opinion leaders: a moderating or mediating relationship. In Marvin E. Goldberg, Gerald Gorn and Richard W. Pollay (eds), *Advances in Consumer Research*, 17: 60–7.

Volckner, Franzisca and Sattler, Henrik (2006) Drivers of brand extension success. *Journal of Marketing*, 70 (2): 18–34.

Wills, James, Samli, A.C. and Jacobs, Laurence (1991) Developing global products and marketing strategies: a construct and research agenda. *Journal of the Academy of Marketing Science*, 19 (1): 1–10.

Zheng Zhou, Kevin, Chi Kin, Yim and Tse, David K. (2005) The effects of strategic orientations on technology and market-based breakthrough innovations. *Journal of Marketing*, 69 (2): 42–60.

More online

To gain free access to additional online resources to support this chapter please visit:
www.sagepub.co.uk/blythe3e

CHAPTER (14)
Pricing and Strategic Decision-Making

LEARNING OBJECTIVES

After reading this chapter, you should be able to:

- Explain the relationship price has with the other elements of the marketing mix.

- Explain the importance of price in the marketing mix.

- Show the important elements in the calculation of price.

- Explain consumer perception of price.

- Explain the relationship of price to the total cost to the consumer.

- Understand which is the most customer-orientated pricing method.

- Compare business-to-business pricing with business-to-consumer pricing.

- Explain the role of competition laws on pricing.

Introduction

Pricing is often regarded as the least exciting element of the marketing mix. However, it is the only element that directly relates to income, and it is also an element that crosses over dramatically to the other elements. Promotional campaigns frequently carry messages about price, sales promotions are often based on price reductions and discounts, price conveys messages about the quality of the products, and it can even control the features and benefits of the products – after all, if customers are not prepared to pay the stated prices, the product needs to be built for a price customers will pay, which may mean cutting some corners on features and benefits.

Price also has a strategic element, since it is commonly how products become positioned against other products in the market: undercutting competitors on price is a common way of competing. Although several areas of marketing activity, including managing the supply chain, can lead indirectly to cutting costs, price is the only area where marketers can directly improve the profits of the firm. Even a small increase in the price can generate a very large increase in profits: for marketers, the problem often lies in finding ways to justify a price rise to consumers.

Preview case study: International software market

Computer software is an unusual product. It is entirely intangible, and the costs of supplying it can also be negligible – it is the cost of writing it in the first place which is the main expense. Once the software exists, the costs of putting it onto CDs and packaging it are tiny in comparison. Still cheaper is distribution over the Internet – which is why there is so much free software available on-line.

Software is also easily copied by pirates, which makes life difficult for major software companies, and also each company seeks to make its own software the industry standard, so that they can sell upgrades and add-ons. The switching costs for someone who has adopted a particular company's software can be high, so there is a considerable advantage in being the first software a customer commits to.

The situation is further complicated by international marketing. Obviously the software company needs to make an overall profit, and therefore generate a substantial turnover from worldwide sales of the software, but at the same time customers in the wealthy countries of Western Europe, the United States and Australia can afford to pay much more than customers in the developing world such as India, parts of Asia and Africa. At the same time, computers are a global phenomenon, so it pays for companies to ensure that each country uses the same systems. In other words, it is worthwhile to subsidise poorer countries, because it helps adoptions in wealthier countries.

This creates a nightmarish problem for software marketers. Setting a price that people will pay is one thing, but ensuring that people in the wealthier countries do not feel that they are being cheated is another. For major players such as Sun Microsystems and Microsoft, the stakes are high – customers in the developing world are numbered in the billions, and in the software industry the plans for world domination are constantly on the agenda. Companies that do not dominate will go to the wall – there is no room for second-best. Microsoft always operated on a one-price basis – everybody paid the same, whatever country they were in. This ensured that customers in the developed world did not feel cheated, and also prevented software from being bought in one country for use in another. However, as the 21st century began, it became obvious that this position would not be tenable in the long run. Something would have to change in Microsoft's pricing!

Price and the bottom line

As has been pointed out above, price is the only place where marketers can directly improve the bottom line. They do this by pricing products for maximum profitability. Figure 14.1 illustrates the mechanism by which this happens.

At the original price of £10 the firm sells one million units for a total revenue of £10 million. The direct cost for manufacturing the product (including all of the variable

	Original Price	**New Price**
		(increase price 5%)
Sales Revenue (1 million units @ £10)	£10,000,000	£10,500,000
Direct Costs (Labour, materials, etc) (@ £6.00 per unit)	£ 6,000,000	£ 6,000,000

Figure 14.1 Price and profitability

costs) at £6 per unit adds up to £6 million. Administrative costs are £3 million. In this case, as can be seen from our simple example, the profit to the firm is £1 million. Now let us assume that the marketing director decides to raise the price 5%. Therefore, the product will now be sold at £10.50. If one million units are sold, the total revenue would be £10.5 million. The direct cost for making one million units remains £6 per unit for a total of £6 million and the administrative costs also remain the same at £3 million. This example shows how a 5% increase in price results in a 50% increase in profit from £1 million to £1.5 million.

This example shows how a small movement in price can result in very large benefits to the firm. However, this example has some obvious flaws. First, it assumes that the firm will still sell one million units, even though the price is now higher. Basic economics teaches us that demand curves slope downward toward the right, as we saw in Chapter 1: that is to say, the higher the price, the lower the sales tend to be (depending on how elastic the demand curve is).

This demand curve certainly holds true for commodity products where all the offerings are exactly the same, such as sand or milk. However, in some consumer markets and in almost all business-to-business markets, the demand curve actually looks more like the one shown in Figure 14.2. This is a 'stepped' demand curve. The stepped demand curve implies that there are price ranges within which the demand will not change. If our marketing director is clever enough to determine that customers are not price sensitive to a difference between £10 and £10.50, he or she would realise the increased revenue from changing the price.

Figure 14.2 Stepped demand curve

A second possible criticism of the example is that the increased price may require increases in expenses in order to justify the price rise. This may range from increased expenditure on advertising, through to changing the product in some way to offer better value. Provided the extra costs are substantially less than the extra price that can be obtained, the changes should be made.

The pricing process

Figure 14.3 shows an overview of the pricing process. First, managers must set pricing objectives in line with the firm's corporate objectives. Second, the managers should develop the pricing strategy to be used in each market segment. In some cases, the prices charged for the same product will differ in different market segments: for example, the price charged to professional garages for spare parts for cars may differ from the prices charged to the general public. Likewise, prices often differ in international markets.

Managers should then try to determine what the demand will be at various pricing levels. This is by no means simple, because markets are dynamic: a prediction about demand in a given market may be completely overtaken by changes in consumer taste, by competitive activity, by a poorly executed (or well-executed) promotional campaign, or by any one of hundreds of possible eventualities. Having calculated an estimate of the demand, he or she will estimate costs. This estimate will include manufacturing costs as well as marketing costs, and is intended to provide a profitability forecast.

Real-life marketing: Charge what it's worth

Many managers, especially in small firms, seem to think that competing on price is the way to go. The problem with that approach is that it cuts profit margins very seriously – and also, there will always be someone who will undercut you, even if they go broke doing it.

In most cases customers are prepared to pay a premium price for a quality product or service, especially if you can show them that it will save them money in the longer term. For example, in 1969 three Californians (Adrian Dalsey, Larry Hillblom, and Robert Lynn) noticed that ships entering and leaving San Francisco and Honolulu were often held up because paperwork had not arrived in time for customs clearance. A merchant ship represents a very large investment, and having one sitting idle in harbour while the cargoes rot and the port fees build up is seriously bad business.

Dalsey, Hillblom and Lynn set up a business whereby they would fly on a passenger airline to the port where the ship was berthed or due to arrive, carrying all the necessary documentation in their hand luggage. OK, this was an expensive thing to do, but it was cheap for the shipping companies compared with even one day's port fees. Frequently cargoes could be cleared by customs before the ships even arrived.

And thus the international courier company DHL was born. If you think you have seen a similar opportunity, keep the following in mind:

- Always think about what the customer is getting from you, not what your competitors are charging for a worse product.
- Don't worry about what it costs you to provide the service, think about what it is worth to the customers.
- Ensure that what you provide matches (or exceeds, preferably) customer expectations.
- Don't be afraid to look expensive (and therefore high quality) rather than cheap (and therefore low quality).

The next stage is to review the competition. Competing offerings might offer better value for money, in which case the price will need to be adjusted: competitors may be planning a major promotional campaign, which might be countered by a price cut, or may be forced to raise their own prices, offering an opportunity to raise prices generally. Obviously, managers will not always know what their competitors are planning, and in most countries it is illegal for competitors to collude in fixing prices, since this always results in a worse deal for the consumers.

The final stage is to select a pricing method and policy, and determine the exact prices to be assigned to each individual product and product.

Often, this somewhat complex approach to calculating the price will not happen, simply because the manager has inherited the pricing structure from a previous manager. This means that, in most cases, managers are not calculating prices from scratch, but are instead adjusting prices incrementally to meet changing market conditions.

Figure 14.3 The pricing process

Think outside this box!

If you ask most people, they will tell you that they always look for the cheapest product. 'Why pay more?' is a very common slogan used in advertising, and indeed what's wrong with that proposition? Presumably, then, everybody buys the cheapest version they can get their hands on, right?

Er, actually, no. Look at the motor industry. If everybody bought the cheapest, we'd all be driving round in basic Eastern European cars, or cars with dubious Oriental origins. In India, Tata manufactures a car (the Nano) that costs less than £2000 – why aren't we driving one of those each?

And another thing – if demand increases as the price falls, why don't we each have two or three of Tata's cars instead of one small Japanese car? Or 50 of them instead of a Rolls–Royce? It seems there's more to this than meets the eye!

Pricing objectives

Generally speaking, pricing objectives can be divided into three major types as follows (McCarthy and Perrault 2002):

- Profit-orientated. Profit-orientated objectives include pricing to realise a target return on the investment or to maximise profits. This is popularly supposed to be the commonest (or even the most intelligent) approach to pricing, but in fact firms frequently have other objectives.
- Sales-orientated. Sales-orientated objectives aim to increase sales either in currency or unit terms, or to penetrate markets and increase share. Firms will often aim for a sales-orientated approach when entering a new market, in order to maximise share and shut out competition: in the early stages of the product life cycle, this can be an effective strategy, with the ultimate aim of moving to a profit-orientated approach when the market matures.
- Status quo-oriented. Status quo-oriented pricing includes meeting the competition or choosing to compete on a non-price basis. Many firms in well-established markets operate in this way in order to avoid triggering price wars, which would be to the detriment of all firms in the industry. Also, small firms will avoid direct attacks on market leaders, since it is too easy for those market leaders to retaliate.

In some cases a firm will not have the luxury of pricing to maximise its profits: pricing is geared to survival in the face of an industry with very strong competition and overcapacity.

Some firms will set an internal rate of return for particular product lines and then set prices with this in mind, while other firms will seek a particular margin on sales. The choice depends upon the nature of the industry. In a business where few sales are made per year, the target return on investment is most likely the best approach: in a high volume business, the margin on sales becomes more important. These accepted versions of pricing strategies do not include the most favourable approach, which is to establish pricing based on the value customers place on the product. This requires an in-depth knowledge of the customer's business and the ways in which the product is put to use by that customer.

Pricing strategy

An overview of pricing strategy development can be seen in Figure 14.4.

Considerations within the firm are (first) the corporate objectives that the firm has established. Pricing needs to fit within the overall corporate vision: is the firm aiming to be at the cheap end, or at the exclusive end of the market? Second, costs are critical. This not only means costs of the product but also the costs of marketing, including the market entry costs of foreign locations. An important factor in the cost of production is where the production facility is located – a location in a high-labour-cost region such as the United States, Western Europe or Japan will impact on the final cost of the product. On the other hand, the firm needs to take account of the shipping costs inherent in an overseas location, and the degree to which the firm can invest in automation.

Finally, the marketing programme in the firm is critical since price must match up with the rest of the marketing. For instance, if a firm decides to offer a laptop computer that will withstand the rigours of a building site, it should charge accordingly. If the firm designs the product to be the most durable available, then advertises it as such and aims for the salesforce and distributors to place the product in the most

Figure 14.4   Pricing strategy development (adapted from Hollensen 1998 and Cavusgil 1996)

difficult environments, it would hardly make sense to price the product below ordinary competing laptops.

Another consideration is the relationship of the price of the product to the pricing of other products in the line (and to other product lines). Often sales of one product are dependent on another – for instance, a firm may choose to price inkjet printers at low prices because they will make money on sales of ink cartridges over a significant period of time. Sometimes prices are set by customary practice: for example, the price of electric motors may be established by long tradition in the industry of pricing according to horsepower. Prices must be set to match these customer expectations even though they are not based on costs.

Think outside this box!

If price is a competitive tool, and relates to the company's strategy, why would anyone want to follow a customary pricing approach? Shouldn't we be differentiating ourselves by offering something that the customer *isn't* expecting? Maybe something even better?

It's possible that too many companies just go along with what customers expect, instead of offering something new – after all, change is life!

The environment impacts on the pricing strategy in many ways: government regulations, including price controls, import duties and quotas as well as taxes, will restrict pricing possibilities. In countries where governments do not allow rapid price increases, perhaps in an attempt to control inflation, managers can avoid the restrictions by assigning the highest possible price to any product that is new or modified. The value of a currency and the stability of that value will again impact on whether a firm can feel comfortable with a particular price level or whether the firm needs to adjust the price frequently to meet changing market conditions. Finally, the relative growth or decline in a particular economy will have an obvious effect

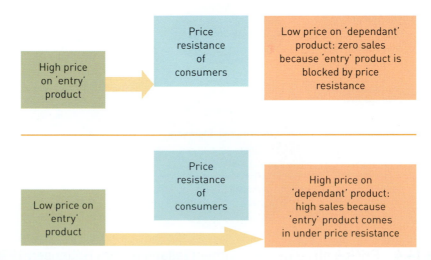

Figure 14.5   Co-dependent products

on pricing: declining economies are likely to exhibit greater downward pressure on prices as local competitors struggle to keep afloat.

Distribution channels also have an impact on the pricing strategy. The costs associated with the services performed by distributors will have a major effect upon the final price paid by the customer. Marketing managers need to be sure that the value added by the distributor exceeds the additional costs imposed by the distributor's profit margin. A further problem for marketing managers is that some distributors may see an opportunity for **grey market** re-export. This occurs when marketers offer the product at different prices in different markets in order to meet local competition. Some distributors in the low-price market overbuy and sell the excess in the high-price market, beating the latter market's much higher prices and turning a neat profit. Dealing with these 'grey market' products is an ongoing problem for many international marketing managers.

Grey market (1) Re-import of brands from markets where the prices are lower. (2) Older consumers.

Competitors also have an influence on pricing strategy. First, one must examine their offerings in detail to understand the benefits and drawbacks of their products versus the firm's products. In some cases, especially when dealing with government departments, bidding is not required to be made public and sales are infrequent so it may be difficult to obtain competitors' pricing. Nevertheless, an effort should be made. Finally, competitors' costs are a very important factor in pricing strategy, since a competitor with a high cost base will have difficulty in the event of a price war. Here again it may be difficult to obtain these costs, but the manager should attempt at the very least to estimate.

Think outside this box!

If we really have no idea what our competitors' costs are, or what their plans are, why are we even trying to guess? Why not just give our salespeople and distributors the power to negotiate prices and make adjustments as they go along?

Or would this just lead to anarchy? Would it be better to sit down with our competitors and discuss things like civilised people? On the other hand, that would be collusion – which is illegal. So maybe we are doomed to continue with an inefficient system!

The most important factor in the pricing strategy is obviously the customer. Understanding how consumers use the product, and knowing what value they get from it, enables the marketing manager to establish true value-in-use prices. The perceptions customers have of the product and the manufacturer are also important: the ability to pay for the product is sometimes a problem, but astute marketers will find ways for potential customers to pay for the product on credit or through trade-in.

Determining demand – customer perceptions of price

As we have seen in Chapter 3, people perceive a total product including core benefits, product attributes and support services yielding a package of benefits they need. These benefits must be balanced against the various costs customers will incur. Usually, the most obvious cost is the net outlay of funds required from the customer firm to gain these benefits. This outlay includes not only the initial price, but also the

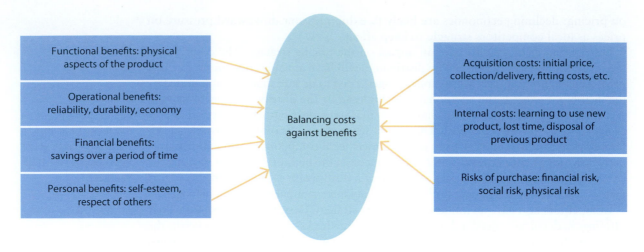

Figure 14.6   Cost–benefit trade-offs

servicing and running costs over the useful life of the product. Customer perceptions of costs and benefits are shown in Figure 14.6.

As can be seen in Figure 14.6, customer benefits fall into functional, operational, financial and personal categories. The functional are those that come to mind most readily, related to the physical aspects of the product – these often relate closely to the individual's cognition of the product. In the longer term, operational benefits such as reliability and durability, financial aspects such as savings made over the period of ownership and personal benefits such as feelings of well-being and of ownership will assume greater importance.

Customer costs include acquisition costs such as the initial price plus delivery, fitting, internal costs such as learning to use the product, lost time in buying it and getting it to work properly, and disposal: and finally, costs related to risk. Not all of these costs are financial, and the price charged by the supplier is not always expressed financially, either. Suppliers might expect customers to accept a higher level of risk as part of the price of obtaining the product – for example, a hotel might charge a lower price for an Internet booking, but specify that there will be no refund in the event of a cancellation. This passes on the risk to the customer

Provided the benefits exceed the costs, the customer will be happy with the outcome: if the costs exceed the benefits, the customer will not be happy with the outcome. In the long term, marketers should seek to ensure that benefits always outweigh costs, but either side of the equation can be adjusted: if the marketer can offer greater benefits without increasing the cost to the customer, this is a valid way of achieving value for money. If benefits cannot be improved, then the only way to improve value for money is to reduce the overall cost to the customer – not necessarily the initial acquisition price, but (possibly) the other costs.

Research shows that a perception of loss of quality is more important to most people than a price loss – in other words, it is better to raise prices than to reduce quality (Hankuk and Agarwal 2003). The same researchers found that perceptions of loss are more important to consumers than comparable gains, which makes maintaining quality even more important.

PRICE SENSITIVITY

Establishing the needs of each segment is a precursor to developing appropriate pricing for each segment. In some cases, a product can be customised to meet the

Table 14.1   Factors affecting customer price sensitivity

Economics

- Percentage of total expense
- Type of consumer
- Level of involvement

Search and usage

- Cost of information search
- Ease of comparing competitive alternatives
- Switching costs

Competition

- Differentiation
- Perception of price

specific needs of a segment and priced at a premium because of the customisation. In setting prices for specific segments, the marketing director must estimate the price sensitivity of that particular market segment. Dolan (1995) listed factors that affect customer price sensitivity: these are listed in Table 14.1.

Customers will be more sensitive if the percentage of the particular item is large in comparison to the total outlay that the customer is making to achieve a particular end. Should the item be of extreme importance to the customer, price sensitivity will tend to decline because reliability becomes paramount.

Marketing in a changing world: Deciding the price

Setting prices used to be easy – manufacturers were allowed to set the retail price for their products, and retailers had to accept that price. This protected both the manufacturer and the retailer: retailers could not be undercut by other retailers, so prices were the same everywhere for the same goods. Fair enough, you might say, but what about consumers?

In 1964 the UK government passed the Resale Prices Act, which abolished resale price maintenance and opened the door for price competition between retailers. Supermarkets could discount prices and negotiate better deals with suppliers for the first time, so consumers got a better deal.

Now, though, perhaps the price competition has got out of hand. Internet providers, having extremely low overheads, can cut prices even further, and some may have cut the price too far. Competing on price cuts profits, so undoubtedly some will go bankrupt and some already have. Consumers, on the other hand, can shop around very easily on-line for the lowest prices, and are likely to do so.

At the same time, governments are interfering more and more in the pricing process for some products. In the UK, there is a proposal that there should be a minimum price per unit for alcoholic drinks, in an attempt to curb binge drinking: there is pressure to raise fuel prices in order to reduce consumption and thus reduce carbon emissions: there is pressure to increase air ticket prices for the same reason.

All these factors mean that producers are no longer in a position to set prices, and since price is a major factor in determining demand producers are likely to find it increasingly difficult to predict, still less control, the markets they are entering.

Reviewing the search and usage category, customers will be more price-sensitive if the information search is easy and cheap, and competitive offerings are easily compared. In addition, the customer's price-sensitivity is increased substantially where switching costs are low. Switching costs are all the costs associated with changing from one particular product or service to another. For example, someone might become persuaded that Apple Mac software is better than Microsoft's, but would find it difficult to change because of the time needed to learn the new system, and the time needed to convert existing files. These (admittedly short-term) costs may outweigh the benefits seen from a potential new system. Finally, price sensitivity is decreased where the manufacturer's offering is clearly differentiated from its competition and where price perception gives an aura of quality to a particular product.

COSTS

For marketing managers, developing reliable costs to use in pricing decisions may be a frustrating process. It is often the case that the same resources are used to produce several different things, so the allocation of costs by the finance department is often arbitrary. In manufacturing, products that are easy to manufacture and have low material costs often assume too much of the overhead of a facility, making the marketing manager's task in pricing to meet market conditions quite difficult. In this regard, marketing people are advised to study the costing process used at a particular facility in-depth so they can argue the case for a proper costing of particular product lines.

Activity based costing (ABC) is a relatively new approach to establishing cost which may provide a more accurate estimate of which costs should be assigned to particular product lines and customers. According to Narayanan and Sarkar (2002), under ABC managers keep separate accounts of the expenses required to produce individual units and batches, to design, maintain and produce, and to keep the manufacturing facility running. ABC requires that costs be allocated not only to products but also to customers so that a manager can determine the cost to serve a particular customer. In Narayanan and Sarkar's study, Insteel Corporation tracked the overhead needed to serve special customer needs including packing and loading, order processing and invoicing, after-sales service and the cost of offering credit. These costs were attributed to each customer and allocated to products based on the volume of each product purchased by a particular customer. Through the ABC approach, Insteel discovered that, at one factory studied, freight represented 16% of the total people and physical resources cost. After detailed analysis, management decided to increase the weight shipped per truck load, resulting in a 20% reduction in freight expense. The transparency of the ABC system also allowed Insteel to change the product line and increase prices for less profitable products.

Think outside this box!

ABC certainly sounds like a wonderful way to increase efficiency – provided the forms are filled in properly! What happens when managers are too busy to work the figures? What happens if the forms are too complicated?

In short, what happens when a manager is overworked, has a crisis to handle and simply scribbles down any figures that come to mind? How can the system be made to cope?

Although the high risks associated with it have been well-established, the idea of 'pricing down the learning curve' is one that has persisted for at least three decades. Learning curve (or experience curve) theory simply states that costs decline rapidly with each doubling of output of a particular product. Experience curve effects come from three major sources (Day and Montgomery, 1983):

- Learning: increased efficiency because of practice and skill or finding new and better ways to do things.
- Technological improvements: new production processes and product changes that improve yield.
- Economies of scale: increased efficiency resulting from larger operations.

These improvements are especially relevant to investment and operating costs. Day and Montgomery found significant limitations of the strategic relevance for experience curve approaches and they warned against an all-out dedication to this approach. While it may give some advantages in some markets, it also introduces a rigidity that may make the firm slower and less flexible in its ability to respond to customer or competitive changes. The experience curve will only be strategically relevant when the three major effects identified above are important in the strategic environment of a particular firm. Ames and Hlavacek (1984) point out that slavishly following the experience curve approach has yielded disastrous results, especially for established or mature products where gains through experience diminish rapidly.

COMPETITION

Understanding competitive offerings, including their prices, is critical. To begin with, a firm must be careful about setting its prices higher than those of the competition. This obviously depends upon the strategic position the firm finds itself in. Should the company be a leader in its market, it probably will price higher than competitors. In monopolistic competition situations, smaller firms would realise no benefit by attempting to price lower than the dominant competitor since the large firm could easily match the smaller firm's prices or even retaliate by lowering prices further, putting a much larger financial strain on the smaller firm than it would realise itself. In high growth or hyper-competitive markets, some firms may attempt to disturb the status quo (see Chapter 2 for more on hypercompetition). An important tool in these markets is the race to the next price point, equivalent to the next step in the stepped demand curve (see Figure 14.2). While this is more common in consumer markets, there is a strong effect in B2B markets as well. Moore (1995) points out that when workstation prices were lowered to under £50,000 and then under £10,000 the result was 'huge boosts in sales volumes'. As the firm drops to the next price point, a new market segment will be in a position to buy the products, and competitors will need to follow suit. This is true even in the case where these smaller competitors have to sell below their costs.

Understanding your competitors' current position obviously affects pricing decisions, but an equally important aspect is competitor reaction. A correct assessment of competitors' potential reaction to increasing or decreasing price may determine whether the strategy chosen by the company is the correct one. Sophisticated companies are able to include in their records information about past competitive reactions to pricing moves. This knowledge can help the managers make more informed decisions about potential competitive actions.

Pricing methods

Pricing methods are closely related to pricing objectives. The three basic methods are cost-based pricing, customer-based pricing and competition-based pricing. Cost-based pricing usually follows one of two methods: **cost-plus** pricing and **mark-up** pricing. Cost-plus pricing is often advocated by accountants and engineers because it is simple to use and appears to guarantee that the firm will reach a pre-determined profit level. Cost-plus pricing works by calculating the cost of producing the product, then adding on a fixed percentage profit to the total. An example of this type of calculation is shown in Table 14.2.

Although this pricing method appears logical and straightforward, it is actually fairly dangerous because it takes no account of the marketplace. If customers feel that the price is too high, they will not buy the product: on the other hand, if the price is much lower than customers would be prepared to pay, the company is losing out on potential profit.

Cost-plus pricing Setting prices by calculating the outlay on producing the items, and adding on a profit margin.

Mark-up Gross profit calculated as a proportion of the price paid for an item.

Figure 14.7   Pricing methods

Table 14.2   Cost-plus pricing

Item	Cost per unit
Labour costs	£2.74
Raw materials	£4.80
Electricity	£0.08
Tooling costs (assuming a production run of 50,000 units)	£2.71
Overheads (factory, office etc.)	£1.17
Total production cost per unit	£11.15
PLUS profit margin of 20%	£2.30
Total price, ex-factory	**£13.45**

Some government contracts are awarded on a cost-plus basis, but experience in the United States has shown that allowing cost-plus contracts to be granted will often result in the supplier inflating the costs to make an extra profit.

MARK-UP PRICING

Mark-up pricing is similar to cost-plus pricing, and is the method used by most retailers. Typically, a retailer will buy in stock and add on a fixed percentage to the bought-in price (a mark-up) in order to arrive at the **shelf price**. The level will vary from retailer to retailer, depending on the type of product; in some cases the mark-up will be 100% or more, in others it will be near zero (if the retailer feels that stocking the product will stimulate other sales). Usually there is a standard mark-up for each product category.

Profit margins can be expressed either in terms of a mark-up, or a **margin**. Mark-up is calculated on the price the retailer pays for the product; margin is calculated on the price the retailer sells for. This means that a 100% mark-up equals a 50% margin; a 25% mark-up equals a 20% margin (Table 14.3).

Shelf price The cost of a product when it is on the shelf, not including delivery costs etc.

Margin Gross profit calculated as a proportion of the price a product is sold for.

Table 14.3   Mark-up versus margin

Bought-in price	£4.00
Mark-up at 25% of £4.00	£1.00
Price on the shelf	£5.00
Margin of 20% of £5.00	£1.00
Bought-in price	£4.00

Retailers use this method because of the number of lines the shop may be carrying. For a hypermarket, this could be up to 20,000 separate lines, and it would clearly be impossible to carry out market research with the customers for every line. The buyers therefore use their training and knowledge of their customer base to determine which lines to stock, and (to some extent) rely on the manufacturers to carry out the formal market research and determine the recommended retail prices.

Think outside this box!

Retailers nowadays usually hold the whip-hand in the distribution chain. They are closest to the consumers, they are the final customers in the chain and they have a wide range of possible suppliers. Manufacturers are in the unhappy position of having to meet the retailers' terms, or have no market.

So how might a manufacturer counteract this? Can a manufacturer be a price setter? Is there a case for manufacturers getting together to fight the power of the retailers – or would this simply mean that they would fall foul of the law on collusion? Retailers do not seem to have any difficulty in controlling the situation, whether by collusion or by consensus – so why have manufacturers allowed the initiative to be lost?

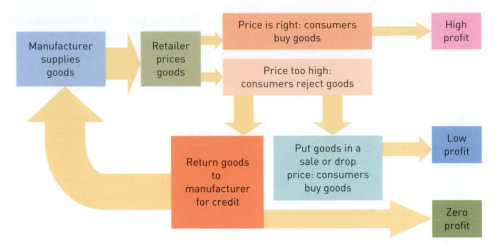

Figure 14.8 Alternative price adjustment strategies

This method is identical to the cost-plus method except for two factors: first, the retailer is usually in close contact with the customers, and can therefore develop a good 'feel' for what customers will be prepared to pay, and second, retailers have ways of disposing of unsold stock. In some cases this will mean discounting the stock back to cost and selling it in the January sales; in other cases, the retailer will have a sale-or-return agreement with the manufacturer, so that unsold stock can be returned for credit. This is becoming increasingly common with major retailers such as Toys R Us who have sufficient 'clout' in the market to enforce such agreements. In a sense, therefore, the retailer is carrying out market research by test-marketing the product; if the customers do not accept the product at the price offered, the retailer can either drop the price to a point that will represent value for money, or return it to the manufacturer for credit.

Figure 14.8 shows the retailer's alternatives. Putting the goods into the annual sale, or selling them off at a discounted price, usually means that profit is small but it is still preferable to returning the goods to the manufacturer for credit, because that option means that the retailer makes no profit at all (and of course damages the relationship with the manufacturer).

Customer-based pricing methods

The various approaches to customer-based pricing do not necessarily mean offering products at the lowest possible price, but they do take account of customer needs and wants, and also of psychological factors in perception of price.

CUSTOMARY PRICING

Customary pricing The price a product has always been sold for.

Customary pricing is customer-orientated in that it provides the customer with the product for the same price at which it has always been offered. An example is the price of a call from a coin-operated telephone box. Telephone companies need only reduce the time allowed for the call as costs rise. For some countries (e.g. Australia) this is problematical since local calls are allowed unlimited time, but for most European countries this is not the case.

The reason for using customary pricing is to avoid having to reset the call-boxes too often. Similar methods exist for taxis, some children's sweets and gas or electricity pre-payment meters. If this method were to be used for most products there would be a steady reduction in the firm's profits as the costs catch up with the selling price, so the method is not practical for every firm.

DEMAND PRICING

Demand pricing is the most market-orientated method of pricing. Here, the marketer begins by assessing what the demand will be for the product at different price levels. This is usually done by asking the customers what they might expect to pay for the product, and seeing how many choose each price level. This will lead to the development of the kind of chart shown in Table 14.4. As the price rises, fewer customers are prepared to buy the product, as fewer will continue to see the product as good value for money. In the example given in Table 14.4 the fall-off is not linear, i.e. the number of units sold falls dramatically once the price goes above £5. This kind of calculation could be used to determine the stages of a skimming policy (see below), or it could be used to calculate the appropriate launch price of a product.

For demand pricing, the next stage is to calculate the costs of producing the product in the above quantities. Usually the cost of producing each item falls as more are made (i.e. if we make 50,000 units, each unit costs less than would be the case if we only make 1000 units). Given the costs of production it is possible to select the price that will lead to a maximisation of profits. This is because there is a trade-off between quantity produced and quantity sold; as the firm lowers the selling price, the amount sold increases but the income generated decreases.

The calculations can become complex, but the end result is that the product is sold at a price that customers will accept, and that will meet the company's profit targets. Table 14.5 shows an example of costings that match up with the above figures. The

Demand pricing Calculating the price according to what consumers are prepared to pay.

Table 14.4 Demand pricing

Price per unit	Number of customers who said they would buy at this price
£3 to £4	30,000
£4 to £5	25,000
£5 to £6	15,000
£6 to £7	5,000

Table 14.5 Costings for demand pricing

Number of units	Unit cost (labour and materials)	Tooling-up and fixed costs	Net cost per unit
30,000	£1.20	£4000	£1.33
25,000	£1.32	£4000	£1.48
15,000	£1.54	£4000	£1.81
5,000	£1.97	£4000	£2.77

Table 14.6   Profitability at different price bands

Number of units sold	Net profit per unit	Total profit for production run	Percentage profit per unit
30,000	£2.17	£65,100	62
25,000	£3.02	£75,500	67
15,000	£3.61	£54,150	66
5,000	£3.73	£18,650	57

tooling-up cost is the amount it will cost the company to prepare for producing the item. This will be the same whether 1,000 or 30,000 units are made.

Table 14.6 shows how much profit could be made at each price level. The price at which the product is sold will depend on the firm's overall objectives; these may not necessarily be to maximise profit on this one product, since the firm may have other products in the range or other long-term objectives that may preclude maximising profits at present.

Based on these figures, *the most profitable* price will be £4.50. Other ways of calculating the price could easily lead to making a lower profit from this product. For instance, the price that would generate *the highest profit per unit* would be £6.50, but at this price they would sell only 5,000 units and make £18,650. The price that would generate *the highest sales* would be £3.50, but this would (in effect) lose the firm more than £10,000 in terms of foregone profit.

A further useful concept is that of contribution. Contribution is calculated as the difference between the cost of manufacture and the price for which the product is sold – in other words it does not take account of overheads. Sometimes a product is worth producing because it makes a significant extra contribution to the firm's profits, without actually adding to the overheads. It is not difficult to imagine a situation where a product carries a low profit margin, and is therefore unable to support a share of the overheads. A calculation that included an overall share of the overheads might not give a fair picture, since the contribution would be additional to existing turnover.

Demand pricing works by knowing what the customers are prepared to pay, and what they will see as value for money.

PRODUCT-LINE PRICING

Product-line pricing In circumstances where sales of one product are dependent on sales of another, calculating both prices to take account of the price of each product.

Product-line pricing means setting prices within linked product groups. Often sales of one product will be directly linked to the sales of another, so that it is possible to sell one item at a low price in order to make a greater profit on the other one. Printer manufacturers use this approach for pricing to computer owners: the printers are extremely cheap, and are often given away free with a home computer purchase, but the replacement ink cartridges are expensive. In the long run, this is a good strategy because it overcomes the initial resistance of consumers towards buying something untried, but allows the firm to show high profits for years to come.

Polaroid chose to sell its instant cameras very cheaply (almost for cost price) for the US market and to take their profit from selling the films for a much higher price. For Europe, the firm chose to sell both films and cameras for a medium-level price and profit from sales of both. Eventually this led Kodak to enter the market with its own instant camera, but this was withdrawn from sale in the face of lawsuits from Polaroid for patent infringement.

SKIMMING

Skimming is the practice of starting out with a high price for a product, then reducing it progressively as sales level off. It relies on two main factors: first, that not all customers have the same perception of value for money, and second that the company has a technological lead over the opposition which can be maintained for long enough to satisfy the market.

Skimming is usually carried out by firms who have developed a technically advanced product. Initially the firm will charge a high price for the product, and at this point only those who are prepared to pay a premium price for it will buy. Profit may not be high, because the number of units sold will be low and therefore the cost of production per unit will be high. Once the most innovative customers have bought, and competitors begin to enter the market, the firm can drop the price and 'skim' the next layer of the market, at which point profits will begin to rise. Eventually the product will be sold at a price that allows the firm only a minimum profit, at which point only replacement sales or sales to late adopters will be made.

Figure 14.9 shows how skimming works. At each price level the product shows a standard product life cycle curve: as the curve tops out and begins to fall back, the company lowers the price and the cycle starts again with a new group of consumers. The process continues until either the market is saturated or the company decides that it cannot make any further price reductions.

The advantage of this method is that the cost of developing the product is returned fairly quickly, so that the product can later be sold near the marginal cost of production. This means that the competitors have difficulty entering the market at all, since their own development costs will have to be recovered in some other way.

Skimming is commonly used in consumer electronics markets. This is because firms frequently establish a technological lead over the competitors, and can sometimes even protect their products by taking out patents, which take some time for competitors to overcome. An example of this was the Sony Walkman, which cost over £70 when it was first introduced in the early 1980s – at the time, this was more than half a week's pay for the average person. Allowing for inflation, the price is now around one-tenth of what it was then. Recent research shows that customers are aware of skimming in the electronics markets, and are delaying purchases of new electronic devices until the prices drop. This may affect the way firms view skimming in the future.

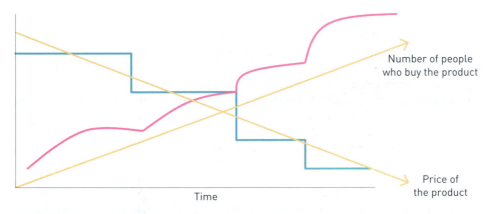

Figure 14.9 *Skimming*

Skimming requires careful judgement of what is happening in the marketplace, both in terms of observing customer behaviour and of observing competitive response. Market research is therefore basic to the success of a skimming policy, and very careful monitoring of sales to know when to cut the price again.

PSYCHOLOGICAL PRICING

Psychological pricing relies on emotional responses from the consumer. Higher prices are often used as an indicator of quality, so some firms will use prestige pricing. This applies in many service industries, because consumers are often buying a promise; a service that does not have a high enough quality cannot be exchanged afterwards. Consumers' expectations of high-priced restaurants and hairdressers are clearly higher in terms of the quality of service provision; cutting prices in those industries does not necessarily lead to an increase in business. **Odd–even pricing** (sometimes also called odd-ending pricing) is the practice of ending prices with an odd number, for example £3.99 or $5.95 rather than £4 or $6. It appears that consumers tend to categorise these prices as '£3 and a bit' or '$5 and change' and thus perceive the price as being lower. The effect may also be due to an association with discounted or sale prices; researchers report that '99' endings on prices increase sales by around 8% (Schindler and Kirby 1997). However, there is some evidence to suggest that, in the case of first-time trial of products, rounding the price up to the nearest whole number can increase trials (Bray and Harris 2006). Note that odd–even pricing can be used in conjunction with any other pricing method.

Recent research has shown that odd–even pricing does not necessarily work in all cultures (Suri et al. 2004). In Poland, for example, the effects are negligible. Odd–even pricing also has effects on perceptions of discounts during sales. Rounding the price to (say) £5 from £4.99 leads people to overvalue the size of the discount, which increases the perception of value for money (Gueguen and Legoherel 2004). Thus the positive effect on sales of using a 99-ending can be negated by the effect when the product is on offer in a sale.

In China, there is evidence to suggest that prices ending in 8 are more effective than prices ending in 4, because 8 is a lucky number and 4 is unlucky (Simmons and Schindler 2003).

There are many other psychological effects in pricing – offering a high-priced product increases sales of lower-priced products (Krishna et al. 2002), and bundling other services with the product (such as free shipping and handling) is a good purchase incentive (Roggeveen et al. 2006). The same researchers found that separating the price from the delivery charges led to more favourable memories of the transaction and fewer product returns, however.

One particularly interesting piece of research showed that the introduction of the Euro in Germany (where it replaced the lower-value Deutschmark) resulted in higher perceptions of quality when the price was expressed in Deutschmarks than when it was expressed in Euros. Presumably this is because the DM price was a higher number than the Euro price (Molz and Gielnik 2006).

Discounting can have different effects on consumers if the retailer sets an upper or lower limit on the number of people who can benefit from it. If a retailer offers a discount for buying more of a product (10% off for buying three or more items, for example) people will tend to buy more of the product than they had intended, whereas an upper limit (10% off, limited to two items per customer) tends to make people want to buy less than they had intended (Yoon and Vargas 2011). Therefore this type of special offer is probably counter-productive from the retailer's viewpoint, even though it might seem that limiting the offer would make it more desirable.

Odd–even pricing Using '99p' or '95c' endings on prices.

Real-life marketing: Prices on freebies

An interesting facet of human nature is that we don't value anything we get for nothing. Many organisations give us freebies, for whatever reason, and it's easy to assume that the item is therefore worthless. Maybe you should consider putting a price on the item – even if you're giving it away.

For example, the Chartered Institute of Marketing has a members' journal, *The Marketer,* which goes out free to all members of the Institute. It is not available in newsagents, and although there is a mechanism by which non-members can subscribe very few would do so. In fact, the total circulation of the magazine is slightly less than the worldwide membership of CIM.

However, the magazine does have a cover price of £10 on it, which is expensive for a magazine, even a glossy one like *The Marketer.* This signals the quality of the magazine, and also gives the impression that membership of CIM confers a real, tangible benefit.

If you're sending out a free magazine like this, or indeed giving away anything else, the following might be helpful.

- Don't set the price too high – if it isn't realistic, people will discount it.
- The price should look natural – it should be about the right level for the quality and size of the magazine, and it should be in no more obtrusive a position than would be the case for a paid-for publication.
- It's worth including a telephone number for subscribers. Apart from the (faint) possibility that someone might actually want to subscribe, it increases the credibility of the cover price.
- Any free gift should have a price tag – it doesn't just apply to magazines.

Second-market discounting

Second-market discounting is common in some service industries and in international markets. The brand is sold at one price in one market, and at a lower price in another; for example, museums offer discounts to students, some restaurants offer discounts to elderly people on week-nights, and so forth. Often these discounts are offered to even out the loading on the firm; week-night discounts fill the restaurant on what would otherwise be a quiet night, so making more efficient use of the premises and staff.

Figure 14.10 shows how second-market discounting works. At the bottom of each column is the amount of full-price business a retailer does on each day. Friday and

Second-market discounting Charging lower prices in some markets or some market segments than in others.

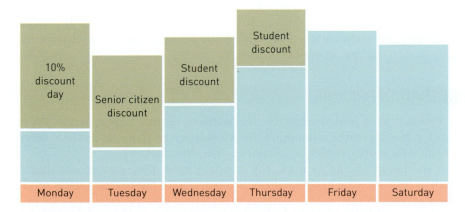

Figure 14.10   Second-market discounting

Saturday are the busiest days, so on the other four days of the week the firm offers various discounts. On Monday the retailer offers 10% off to all customers, which boosts business that day to a level higher than that of the weekend trade. Tuesday is senior citizen day, and Wednesday and Thursday are student discount days. These days are aimed at people who are able to shop mid-week.

Obviously these discounts may cannibalise sales on other days: a senior citizen might have been willing to shop on a Saturday and pay the full price (or might even have shopped on a Tuesday anyway, simply because the shop is quieter).

In international markets products might be discounted to meet local competition. For example, Honda motorcycles are up against strong local competition in India from Royal Enfield, so the price of their basic 150cc motorcycle is around Rs71,000 (about £850). A similar Honda motorcycle in the UK costs around £3000. The specifications of the motorcycles do differ somewhat, and of course taxation makes a difference – but it is difficult to see any difference that would account for a £2000 price differential.

Competitor-based pricing

Competitor-based pricing recognises the influence of competition in the marketplace. Strategically, the marketer must decide how close the competition is in providing for the consumers' needs; if the products are close, then prices will need to be similar to those of the competition. A meet-the-competition strategy has the advantage of avoiding price wars and stimulating competition in other areas of marketing, thus maintaining profitability. An undercut-the-competition strategy is often the main plank in the firm's marketing strategy; it is particularly common among retailers, who have relatively little control over product features and benefits and often have little control over the promotion of the products they stock. Some multinational firms (particularly in electronics) have the capacity to undercut rivals since they are able to manufacture in low-wage areas of the world, or are large enough to use widespread automation. There is a danger of starting price wars when using an undercutting policy (see penetration pricing below). Undercutting (and consequent price wars) may be becoming more common.

Firms with large market shares often have enough control over their distribution systems and production capacity within their industries to become price leaders. Typically, such firms can make price adjustments without starting price wars, and can raise prices without losing a substantial market share (see Chapter 2 for an explanation of monopolistic competition) (Rich 1982). Sometimes these price leaders become sensitive to the price and profit needs of their competitors, in effect supporting them, because they do not wish to attract the attention of monopoly regulators by destroying the competition. Deliberate price fixing (managers colluding to set industry prices) is illegal in most countries.

PENETRATION PRICING

Penetration pricing Setting low prices in an attempt to capture a large market share.

Penetration pricing is used when the firm wants to capture a large part of the market quickly. It relies on the assumption that a lower price will be perceived as offering better value for money (which is, of course, often the case).

For penetration pricing to work, the company must have carried out thorough research to find out what its competitors are charging for the nearest similar product. The new product is then sold at a substantially lower price, even if this cuts profits below an acceptable level; the intention is to capture the market quickly before the competitors can react with even lower prices. The danger with this pricing method is that competitors may be able to sustain a price war for a long period and will eventually bankrupt the incoming firm. It is usually safer to compete on some other aspect of the offering, such as quality or delivery.

PREDATORY PRICING

In some cases, prices are pitched below the cost of production. The purpose of this is to bankrupt the competition so that the new entrant can take over entirely; this practice is called **predatory pricing**, and (at least in international markets) is illegal. Predatory pricing was successfully used by Japanese car manufacturers when entering the European markets in the 1970s, and is commonly used by large firms who are entering new markets. For the strategy to be successful, it is necessary for the market to be dominated by firms that cannot sustain a long price war. It is worth doing if the company has no other competitive edge, but does have sufficient financial reserves to hold out for a long time. Naturally, this method is customer-orientated since it can work only by providing the customers with very much better value for money than they have been used to. The company will eventually raise prices again, however, in order to recoup the lost profits once the market presence has been established.

In Figure 14.11 the firm entering the market has a choice (basically) of three price levels. At the highest level, the firms are competing 'fairly': each is making a normal profit and covering the overheads. However, the foreign firm has a lower overall cost base – the manufacturing costs are lower, as are the overheads. At the second, lower, price level the foreign firm is still covering its overheads, but is now causing the domestic firm some difficulties because the domestic firm cannot cover its overheads if it meets the price. The lowest price is the predatory price – here the foreign firm relies on other markets to cover its overheads and profit margins, and sells into the new market at the marginal cost of production, which is actually below the price that the other firm can make the product for. At this level, it would be cheaper for the domestic firm to buy product from the foreign firm and resell it rather than manufacture itself. At this level, the domestic firm will lose money (and in fact will lose more money if sales increase), whereas the foreign firm can maintain this position indefinitely.

The ultimate in predatory pricing is **dumping**. This is the practice of selling goods at prices below the cost of manufacture, and was at one time commonly practised by communist countries desperate for hard currency. Dumping is illegal under international trade rules, but is difficult to prove, and by the time the victim countries have been able to establish their case and have the practice stopped, it is usually too late.

> **Predatory pricing** Pricing at extremely low levels (sometimes below the cost of production) with the intention of damaging competitors or forcing them to leave the market.

> **Dumping** Disposing of products in a foreign market at prices below the cost of production.

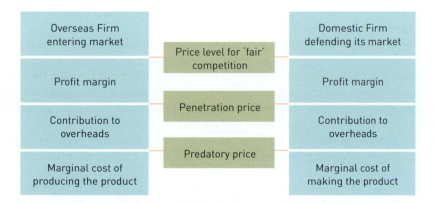

Figure 14.11   Predatory pricing

Competitor-based pricing is still customer-orientated to an extent, since it takes as its starting-point the prices that customers are currently prepared to pay.

Pricing in international markets

International exporters use three basic methods (Cavusgil 1996):

- Rigid cost-plus pricing: where the price is set simply by adding all the costs incurred for serving an international customer to the costs of manufacturing the product plus a margin.
- Flexible cost-plus pricing: is similar to rigid cost-plus pricing but allows for some price variation, such as discounts for large orders or to meet local competition.
- Dynamic incremental pricing: assumes that fixed costs are incurred whether the firm sells outside its home market or not so that the exporter seeks only to recover the international variable costs.

Stottinger (2001) showed that most exporters use either the rigid cost-plus or flexible cost-plus approach, focusing on costs and competition rather than customer value in their pricing method.

More sophisticated firms analyse cost and demand, and develop prices for a target return on investment. This method generally assumes demand at a certain level and does not sufficiently take into account the changes in demand resulting from changes in price or potential competitive moves.

Firms using sales-orientated objectives attempt to set prices which will grow their sales in units or currency or increase market share. These approaches have been discussed in some depth above. Those with status quo objectives generally set prices to meet those of the competition. Finally, firms that attempt to use value-in-use pricing base their pricing decision upon extensive work with customers. While it would be naïve to say that they should ignore costs entirely, marketing managers who wish to be successful must price from the market in, knowing customer needs and willingness to pay as well as competitors' offerings, current and future possible pricing. Should market prices in a particular country fall below the costs to serve customers in that country, management must re-examine the entire marketing strategy for that particular market and take steps to lower costs or decide not to serve customers in that particular market at that particular time.

A special consideration for exporters is the escalation of price that can take place because of the additional costs of exporting, the import duties and value added taxes (VAT) applied in various markets.

As can be seen from Table 14.7, a domestic product that is sold at the factory for £5 and is subject to the normal mark-ups by distributors and retailers might be sold to consumers for £9.38. This same product sent to an export market may be subject to the various costs escalations shown in Table 14.7, resulting in a consumer price 72% higher than that of the domestic price. (This table makes the assumption that the domestic market has no VAT.) Even adding VAT for the domestic market, export pricing can often be much higher. Firms can take several actions to reduce this price escalation. As recommended by Czinkota and Ronkainen (2004), first the firm may attempt to eliminate some steps in distribution. In the example shown in Table 14.7, for simplicity, a number of wholesale steps were eliminated, but in some markets multiple steps in wholesaling are the norm, and are desirable for the good reason that they increase efficiency in those markets.

Table 14.7 Escalation in export markets

Cost factors	Domestic	Export markets
Manufacturer's price at factory	5.00	5.00
+ Insurance, shipping (15%) (CIF)	–	0.75
Landed costs (CIF value)	–	5.75
+ Tariff (20% of CIF value)	–	1.15
Importer/distributor's cost	–	6.90
+ Importer/distributor's margin (25% of cost)	1.25	1.72
Subject to VAT (full cost + margin)	–	8.62
+ VAT (18% on cost + margin)	–	1.55
Retailer's cost	6.25	10.17
+ Retailer's margin (50% on cost)	3.13	5.08
+ VAT (18% on margin)	–	0.91
Consumer price (retailer's cost + margin + VAT)	9.38	16.16
% Escalation over domestic price	–	72%

CIF, cost, insurance and freight.

Source: Adapted from Becker, H. (1980) Pricing: an international marketing challenge. In H. Thorelli and H. Becker, *International Marketing Strategy.* New York: Pergamon Press.

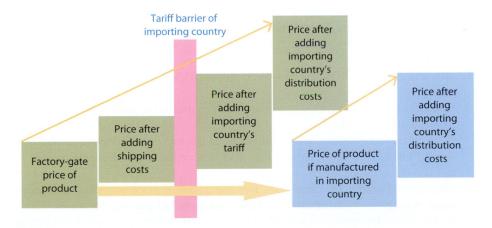

Figure 14.12 Effects of manufacturing in the target country

A second method to reduce a final price in exporting is to adapt the product using lower cost components or ingredients and taking out costly additional features that can be made optional in particular markets. A third way to reduce escalation is to change tariff or tax classifications. This may require local lobbying of the taxing or importing authorities. A final method would be to assemble or produce overseas.

Once foreign sourcing is established with lower cost components, all costs applied to the product will be reduced. Shipping components to the local market for assembly is often a good cost-cutting approach, because local tariffs may be much lower for components than for finished products; countries often prefer foreign firms to assemble locally, because it provides employment for local people.

Pricing policies in business-to-business markets

In business markets, pricing has a somewhat different role because the purchasing process tends to be more rational, and is often much more price-sensitive. Pricing policies include deciding upon list price and discount levels, allowances, rebates and geographic differences (standardisation vs differentiation).

The question of list price varies by industry. In some industries, list prices are set in such a way that no customer ever pays that price. The list prices for a product line are set in order to provide various levels of discounts. Discounts can be given for volume purchases, whether cumulative or based on an individual order, or based on time of order.

Allowances and rebates are simply price reductions given to dealers or distributors to help them promote a particular manufacturer's product. Some firms give advertising allowances to their distributors in order to encourage them to promote their particular product or even for identifying their facilities such as showrooms or service vehicles with a particular brand name. A firm may choose to offer a trade-in allowance for older products in order to replace them with newer versions. A rebate is a fee paid to a purchaser once the product is bought and installed.

A firm must decide on its geographic policies. First and foremost will be whether one standard price will be established in all markets with the final local price determined by varying import duties, currency and local laws. Differentiated pricing allows local distributors or sales agents to set prices. In Stottinger's study of 45 industrial firms heavily involved in exporting, all but three made pricing decisions centrally and the largest firms were more likely to have centralised pricing decisions. Firms that used a company salesforce internationally tended to standardise price while those with independent distributors tended to allow differentiation.

Keegan and Green (2003) describe three global pricing policy alternatives:

- Ethnocentric (extension), where the price per unit is the same no matter where in the world it is sold.
- Polycentric (adaptation), which allows local managers or independent distributors to establish whatever price they feel is acceptable. In this case, prices are not co-ordinated between countries.
- Geocentric, where the firm does not use a single price worldwide or allow local managers or distributors to make independent pricing decisions. This is an intermediate approach which recognises that there are unique local market factors that impact the pricing decision, and that price must be integrated with all elements of the marketing programme across the world. In this case, headquarters may decide to use a market penetration approach for a particular market in order to gain a short-term market share and a skimming approach elsewhere to reap profits used to offset low margins in markets where penetration is used.

Keegan and Green (2003) point out that in global marketing, 'there is no such thing as a normal margin'. The geocentric approach is one that allows a true global competitive strategy in which a firm can take into account competitors and markets on a worldwide basis.

Legality of pricing policies

Many nations regulate pricing in various ways. The most obvious controls relate to anticompetitive actions. In the EU and the United States, firms cannot collude to set prices and this type of law is widely enacted (although intermittently enforced) in various other markets throughout the world. In the United States, a manufacturer must generally treat each class of customer equally. That is, the customer who buys a particular quantity of product should receive the same discount as another customer buying the same quantity. However, some exceptions to this rule are allowed. Manufacturers can use discriminatory pricing to meet a competitive threat in a particular market or if it can be proved that their costs to serve one customer are lower than another.

In setting international prices, companies can sometimes be suspected of dumping. Dumping simply means that a product is sold at a level less than its cost of production. Anti-dumping penalties have increased in the United States, the EU, Canada and Australia and this will continue to be a key issue in international marketing. Managers must be careful that their pricing decisions can be defended against anti-dumping accusations.

TRANSFER PRICING

Transfer pricing can have an important effect on pricing decisions. Transfer prices are those set for goods or services that are bought by one division of a firm from another division. These are inside or intra-corporate prices. As might be expected,

Transfer pricing Internal pricing in a multinational company.

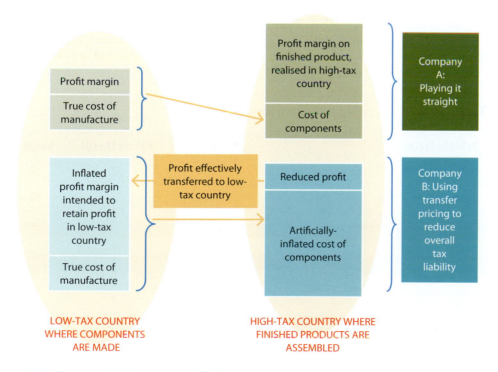

Figure 14.13   Transfer pricing

local tax authorities are quite interested in the transfer prices set inside corporations, since a firm can charge a high transfer price for components it produces in a low-tax country, thus reducing the profits of its divisions in high-tax countries and effectively transferring the profits to a country where taxation is low.

Transfer pricing can also have a significant effect upon the motivation of local partners. If for tax reasons prices are set in such a way as to reduce the profits of a local subsidiary or joint venture, managers of this entity may become de-motivated. This 'softer' portion of the pricing decision between entities of a particular firm must also be taken into account.

COMPETITIVE BIDDING

B2B sales are often completed through competitive bids. This is especially true for government institutions and non-profit organisations such as hospitals. Some non-governmental firms also use competitive bids. In some cases, a firm may require a bid to a particular specification and then reserve the right to negotiate further with the winning bidder. Firms use specification buying especially for large projects. These firms develop detailed specifications based either on the performance or description of a particular product, service or a combination of both. Firms supplying military products, large power stations or other major projects need to develop expertise not only in the bidding process, but also in the specification process. 'Specmanship' means a firm's salesforce is expert at helping a customer develop specifications that will limit the bidders. The most successful salespeople can develop specifications with requirements that can be met only by their firm. When faced with a potential competitive bidding situation that will be based on specifications to be developed by a large customer, it is necessary to spend the required time to gain the most favourable specifications possible before bidding documents are released.

The development of a competitive bid should be viewed as equal in effort to developing a total business plan. In some cases a firm might spend several thousand pounds to complete the analysis required to provide responsive bids to a particular customer. Before a firm decides to take on this major effort, a screening procedure should be completed. Table 14.8 shows a procedure for evaluating bid opportunities.

Table 14.8   Evaluating bid opportunities

Pre-bid factor	Weight (%)	Rating (1–10)	Value
Firm's capacity to deliver on the contract	20	10	200
Competition	10	8	80
Follow-up opportunities	10	7	70
Quantity	10	7	70
Delivery	10	5	50
Profit	20	9	180
Experience	10	9	90
Bid capability	10	8	80
Total	**100%**	**N/A**	**820**

An analysis tool such as this can be used to assign a weight to each factor and then rate the firm's capability for this particular bid. Multiplying the weights by the ratings gives a value for each factor and adding all of the values together gives the firm some idea of whether they should pursue this particular bid. Of course if there are other opportunities, these can be compared using this same tool.

The factors include (first) the firm's capacity to deliver on the contract. The firm must consider whether winning this bid will place an unusual strain on its resources, or whether the firm is running at a low level and has spare capacity. Competition must be considered as well, both in terms of the number of competitors and their possible bids. Past experience with competitors will serve as a guide here. A third and most important area is the possibility for follow-up opportunities. In some cases, a firm winning a bid will be placed on a preferred supplier list (such as with a government) and many additional orders may follow. In addition, a firm may receive orders for associated product. Here, the marketer must be careful because many sophisticated purchasers will indicate a large follow-up to a particular order with the goal of pushing the supplier to reduce the initial price.

Order size is another issue. Obviously, a very large order is more attractive than a smaller one, and a large order for a standard product is more attractive than an order for a mix of products. If the quantity can create economies of scale for a supplier, it will be more attractive than one that simply pushes a supplier past the point of diminishing returns.

In some cases, a large quantity of product is required to be delivered all at once, which may put an undue strain on the producer's facilities. For example, a restaurant that can easily cope with eighty or a hundred diners over the course of an evening might have trouble serving a party of twelve who arrive all at once and each order something different. Marketers also need to consider the effect on customers of accepting a large order, both from a delivery and capacity point of view. If a large order has the potential of reducing the company's capability to satisfy loyal customers in the future, it may not be as attractive. While this analysis must take place before final prices are determined, a general idea of the prices required to gain this order should be employed so that the firm can make an estimate of the possible profit to be realised. In some cases, a firm may decide that profit is not the overriding

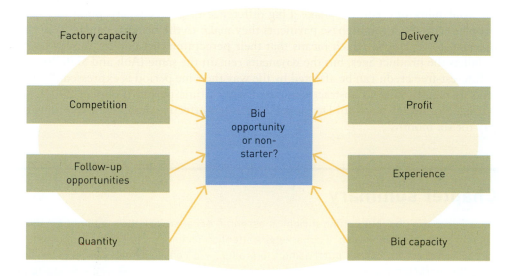

Figure 14.14 Factors in bidding

concern and that in order to use its resources effectively it will move ahead with a relatively unprofitable bid. This is the basis of second-market discounting, which was discussed earlier.

Developing a winning bid for a particular project may take as much effort as an entire business plan for a new venture. If the firm has experience in developing bids of this kind, bidding will be easier and quicker. Finally, bid capability means the availability of people and financial resources to complete the work. There may be times when the firm simply does not have the capability to do the required work and therefore the project becomes less attractive.

Table 14.8 shows a hypothetical bid situation where the firm has assigned weights to each of these factors and then rated the attractiveness of this bid along each one of the factors. The total value is then added and for this particular bid opportunity the number is 820. The firm may have set a minimum hurdle for proceeding with a bid: if we assume a hurdle of 700 for this firm, it would proceed with the bidding process, but if the hurdle was set at 900, the bidding would not go ahead.

Once a firm has decided to move ahead, must develop a pricing strategy: the strategy for bids is the same as the general pricing strategy discussed earlier. In some cases, a firm may price simply for survival in order to get some business to keep the factory running. In most cases, the firm will decide whether it wishes to gain a market share, increase profitability or use any of the other strategies described above.

Internationally, insisting on competitive bidding can be a problem in a high-context culture, where the project will probably be given to the firm the buyers feel is best positioned to do it based on the past establishment of trust. However, in a low-context culture a firm would develop specifications and push the supplier to meet the specifications as written.

CREDIT

In B2B markets, credit is expected as a standard term of business. In some cases, firms will stretch out the actual period of credit – if the contract says 30 days' credit, they will pay in 90 days. This is especially prevalent when a large firm is dealing with a small supplier: in the UK there is legislation which allows the small supplier to charge interest on late payments, but in practice few small firms are prepared to invoke this law, since they are afraid of losing the customer. In consumer markets, the availability of credit can make a big difference to people's perception of price: people relate the hire purchase payments they make to the benefits gained from the product, for example, which means that their perception of value for money tends to fall as the product ages, but the payments remain the same (Auh and Shih 2006).

Interest-free credit can be affected by the way the time period is expressed. People tend to regard dates as abstract compared with a time period (LeBoeuf 2006), so stating 'Nothing to pay until December 31st' is less effective than saying 'Nothing to pay for six months'.

Chapter summary

Price is not exciting, but getting it right is essential because it is the customer's half of the exchange. Although much of a marketer's attention focuses on the offer, the customer focuses on the total cost of purchasing the product – a consideration that includes the price the marketer is asking for the item. Price colours expectations as well – people tend to assume that a high-priced item is a high-quality item.

Key points

- Price affects all the elements of the marketing mix.
- Price is the only element of the mix that generates revenue.
- Price should relate to the market, not to the firm's costs of production.
- Consumer perception of price is functional, operational, financial and personal.
- Price is only one element in the total cost to the consumer.
- Demand pricing is the most customer-orientated method.
- Business-to-business markets tend to be more price-sensitive than consumer markets.
- Competition laws may affect pricing, whether prices are pitched excessively high (through collusion) or excessively low (in dumping).

Review questions

1. List the factors in the pricing process.
2. What are the three major types of pricing objectives firms may use?
3. In developing a pricing strategy, what factors should a manager consider?
4. How does the customer perceive costs and benefits in weighing whether a price seems fair?
5. Explain the concept of switching cost.
6. When should the experience curve be used as a basis for pricing and when not?
7. What are the most common pricing methods used by international exporters? What are the drawbacks to these methods?
8. In developing pricing policies, what should an international firm consider?
9. How can transfer pricing affect the results realised by local partners?
10. When a firm enters a competitive bidding situation, how might it analyse the attractiveness of entering a particular bid?

Case study revisited: International software market

Companies in the software business have been forced to use differential pricing in developing countries, simply because a price tag of $90 seems very expensive in countries where most people earn an average of $2 a day. Even though people who can afford a computer are in much higher income brackets, the temptation to buy pirated software is high.

Microsoft's answer to this was to introduce cut-down versions of Windows XP specifically adapted for the developing world. In December 2004 the company began offering versions of XP in the local language, with some features removed, in India, Russia, Malaysia and Indonesia. The product had already been piloted in Thailand, and had been greeted with great enthusiasm. Microsoft's Kenneth Lundin said that the move was intended to give more people access to software, and also reduce the incidence of pirating of software. Because the cut-down XP systems were only available in the local language, grey-market copies were unlikely to be shipped out to the wealthier Western markets, and also the software was only being made available to computer manufacturers – not to the general public. This meant that the software would come either ready-installed on the computer, or would be protected so that it could only be installed once. Microsoft agreed this as part of a deal with the Malaysian government, intended to increase the use of computers in the country from 15% of the population to 35%. The company is understandably coy about exactly how much it is charging for the software, but since the simplified computers sell for around £350, the software has to be a lot cheaper than the £100-plus price tag of the UK version. Microsoft continued with this policy as far as the Vista version was concerned, but as yet have not produced separate versions of later editions of Windows – presumably this is so that mainstream customers in developed countries still maintain a lead over those in developing countries.

At the same time, Sun Microsystems is entering the business sector with a version of its Java software. Sun is using a unique pricing system, based on the number of people in the country and the country's state of development as verified by the United Nations. John Loiacano, executive vice-president of software at Sun, said: 'With our new per citizen pricing model, governments of developing nations can now reallocate punitive software licensing fees to critical tasks such as health care and education. And the expanded platform support allows these nations to deliver network services to citizens and customers on the architecture of their choice.'

Both companies are suggesting that their actions are at least partly philanthropic: Microsoft talks about extending the benefits of computer ownership to the poorer nations, and Loiacano of Sun talks about allowing countries to spend their money on hospitals and schools rather than on education. Seeking the moral high ground is, of course, fine and what the company spokesmen say is quite true – but the fact remains that both companies have now won a captive market for their software, probably for the next twenty years at least. In Malaysia alone, Microsoft is likely to pick up around three million new customers – and Malaysia has a population of only 26 million.

Case study: Internet auctions

The Internet has opened up many opportunities for increasing consumer power, and nowhere has this been more apparent than in the proliferation of Internet auction sites. Sellers are able to post goods for sale on sites such as eBay or eBid, with or without a reserve price, and buyers are able to place their bids from (theoretically) anywhere in the world. The price rises as more people bid, until there is only one buyer left, who then buys the product at the final bid price. Buyers can pay by credit card through an escrow company (which holds the funds until the goods are delivered), or can make arrangements directly with the seller for payment.

In recent years the process has moved a step further with the advent of reverse auctions. Firms such as Letsbuyit.com bring buyers together to bid for products. The philosophy is simple: rather than bidding against other purchasers, and forcing the price up, the reverse auction arranges for buyers to join together and force the price down. For example a manufacturer may offer an LCD TV for £800. If, however, 100 people are prepared to place a single order, the price might drop to £600. If 200 people are prepared to buy, the price might drop to £500. The price paid to the supplier will be dictated by the number of buyers, so Letsbuyit. com begins by negotiating a series of steps at which the price will fall. The prices are posted on the website for a set period, but once the product is sold out it will not be available to later bidders. If the number of people wishing to buy the product does not meet a pre-set minimum, the purchase does not go ahead, and the bidders pay nothing. Those who bid therefore run the risk of getting nothing: on the other hand, if the deal goes through they will undoubtedly walk away with a real bargain.

The implications of this for traditional High Street retailers are potentially extremely damaging. Although they might argue that consumers will still prefer to come to a store where they are able to examine the products, get advice from the staff, and even try out products, there is obviously nothing to stop consumers doing this and then making the actual purchase via a reverse auction. The implications for manufacturers are equally far-reaching: although the power of retailers will be curtailed, which for many manufacturers would be a godsend, the power of consumers is likely to increase dramatically.

On the one hand, reverse auctions offer manufacturers a kind of instant marketing research: on the other hand, the process may mean the end of price skimming, psychological pricing and all the other tried-and-tested techniques for maximising the profitability of innovative products.

In some cases consumers have gone even further by cutting out the Internet service provider altogether. They have taken to sending tenders to car dealers and other retailers asking them to bid for supplying the product. On a new-car purchase an astute logged-on consumer might save hundreds or even thousands of pounds in this way – a saving that more than compensates for a few minutes spent sending out e-mails.

If these consumer-led techniques catch on, the outcomes are by no means entirely bad for manufacturers, but the overall effect is a major change in the way pricing is carried out. Prices are much more directly controlled by the end consumer than ever before – and marketers need to adjust to that fact.

Questions

1. How might a manufacturer retain a skimming policy when dealing with a reverse auction?
2. How might a car dealer encourage a prospective customer to increase the tender price?
3. What advantages might there be for manufacturers in participating in reverse auctions?
4. How might a manufacturer calculate the appropriate price bands for a reverse auction?
5. What might retailers do to counteract the effects of reverse auctions?

Further reading

Robert J. Dolan and Herrmann Simon's *Power Pricing: How Managing Price Transforms the Bottom Line* (New York: Simon and Schuster, 1997) is aimed at practitioners, but has a wide range of genuine examples from major companies. The book is written in a lively and compelling way, and covers segmentation, promotional pricing, customary pricing and indeed everything you need to know about pricing.

Another practitioner book is Michael V. Marn, Eric V. Roegner and Craig C. Zawada, *The Price Advantage* (New York: John Wiley, 2004). This is written by three McKinsey consultants and based on experience with hundreds of companies. It provides a comprehensive and practical overview of pricing policies and methods, with some interesting case studies and examples.

References

Ames, B. Charles and Hlavacek, James D. (1984). *Managerial Marketing for Industrial Firms*. New York: Random House.

Auh, Seigyung and Shih, Chuang-fong (2006) Balancing giving-up vs. taking-in: does the pattern of payments and benefits matter to customers in a financing decision context? *Advances in Consumer Research*, 33 (1): 139–44.

Bray, Jeffrey Paul and Harris, Christine (2006) The effect of 9-ending prices on retail sales: a quantitative UK-based field study. *Journal of Marketing Management*, 22 (5/6): 601–7.

Cavusgil, Tamer S. (1996) Pricing for global markets, *Columbia Journal of World Business*, 31 (4): 66–78.

Czinkota, Michael and Ronkainen, Ilkka A. (2004) *International Marketing*, 7th edn. New York: Harcourt.

Day, George S. and Montgomery, David B. (1983) Diagnosing the experience curve. *Journal of Marketing*, 47 (Spring): 44–58.

Dolan, Robert J. (1995) How do you know when the price is right? *Harvard Business Review*, 73 (5): 174–83.

Gueguen, Nicolas and Legoherel, Patrick (2004) Numerical encoding and odd-ending prices: the effect of a contrast in discount perception. *European Journal of Marketing*, 38 (1): 194–208.

Hankuk, Taihoon Cha and Agarwal, Praveen (2003) When gains exceed losses: attribution trade-offs and prospect theory. *Advances in Consumer Research*, 30 (1): 118–24.

Hollensen, Svend (1998) *Global Marketing: A Market Responsive Approach*. Hemel Hempstead: Prentice Hall Europe.

Keegan, Warren J. and Green, Mark C. (2003) *Global Marketing*. Upper Saddle River, NJ: Prentice Hall.

Krishna, Aradnha, Wagner, Mary and Yoon, Carolyn (2002) Effects of extreme-priced products on consumer reservation prices. *Advances in Consumer Research*, 29: 86–8.

LeBoeuf, Robyn A. (2006) Discount rates for time versus dates: the sensitivity of discounting to time-interval description. *Advances in Consumer Research*, 33: 138–9.

McCarthy, E. Jerome and Perrault, William D. Jr (2002) *Basic Marketing: A Global Managerial Approach*, New York: McGraw–Hill.

Molz, Gunter and Gielnik, Michael (2006) Does the introduction of the Euro have an effect on subjective hypotheses about the price-quality relationship? *Journal of Consumer Behaviour*, 5 (3): 204–10.

Moore, Geoffrey A. (1995) *Inside the Tornado*. New York: Harper Collins.

Narayanan, V.G. and Sarkar, Ratna G. (2002) The impact of activity-based costing on managerial decisions at Insteel Industries – a field study. *Journal of Economics and Management Strategy*, 11 (2): 257–88.

Rich, Stuart A. (1982) Price leaders: large, strong, but cautious about conspiracy. *Marketing News*, 25 June, p 11.

Roggeveen, Anne L., Xia, Lan and Monroe, Kent B. (2006) How attributions and the product's price impact the effectiveness of price partitioning. *Advances in Consumer Research*, 33 (1): 181.

Schindler, R.M. and Kirby, P.N. (1997) Patterns of right-most digits used in advertised prices: implications for nine-ending effects. *Journal of Consumer Research*, 24 (2): 192–201.

Simmons, C. Lee and Schindler, Robert M. (2003) Cultural superstitions and the price endings used in Chinese advertising. *Journal of International Marketing*, 11 (2): 101–11.

Stottinger, Barbara (2001) Strategic export pricing: a long and winding road, *Journal of International Marketing*, 9 (1): 40–63.

Suri, Rajneesh, Anderson, Rolph E. and Kotlov, Vassili (2004) The use of 9-ending prices: contrasting the USA with Poland. *European Journal of Marketing*, 38 (1): 56–72.

Yoon, Sukki and Vargas, Patrick (2011) 'No More' leads to 'Want More,' but 'No Less' leads to 'Want Less': Consumers' counterfactual thinking when faced with quantity restriction discounts. *Journal of Consumer Behaviour*, 10 (2): 93–101.

More online

To gain free access to additional online resources to support this chapter please visit:
www.sagepub.co.uk/blythe3e

CHAPTER (15)
Advertising across different media

LEARNING OBJECTIVES

After reading this chapter, you should be able to:

- Explain the difference between the weak theory and the strong theory of advertising.

- Understand the relationship between advertising, the marketing strategy and the corporate strategy.

- Explain the relationship between adverting objectives and marketing objectives.

- Explain the advantages and disadvantages of various media.

- Explain how the theory of sought and unsought communication is applied in advertising.

- Explain how people relate to television advertising.

- Understand the role of music in advertising.

- Explain the use of questions in advertising.

Introduction

To the lay person, advertising is often thought of as being the main activity of marketers. This is largely because it is far and away the most obvious of marketing activities: like the tip of an iceberg, it is the part of marketing that is most visible, although nine-tenths of marketing activities go on 'below the surface' and are not visible to the outside observer.

Advertising has been defined as a paid insertion of a message in a medium. This means that advertising is not messages on T-shirts, it is not messages contained in newspaper articles and it is not messages passed on by word of mouth. It has a very specific and narrow meaning, in other words.

Advertising should be seen as part of an integrated communications strategy: there are things that advertising will do, and things it will not do. In general, it can create awareness and move people closer to a purchase: it can help in positioning brands, and it can help in informing people about product attributes. It will not substitute for good product offerings, it will not persuade people to buy things they have little or no need for, and it will not cover up errors in other marketing areas.

Preview case study: John West Foods

John West is a UK-based canned fish company. It was originally formed as Pelling Stanley and Company in 1857, specialising in importing what was then something of a novelty product – canned seafood. Perhaps because the company name was less than memorable, or perhaps because their main source of products was the John West Company in Oregon, Pelling Stanley bought the rights to the name in 1888. The first cans of John West Salmon appeared on the UK market in 1892.

The company is now owned by Thai Union Group, but is still regarded as quintessentially British, and the company's advertising reflects that. John West is the only fish canner to own and operate its own fleet of fishing vessels, which means that the company can be absolutely sure that all its fish are sourced sustainably, and that other marine wildlife such as turtles and dolphins are not harmed by the company's fishing.

For many years the company's advertising used the strap line 'It's the fish John West rejects that makes John West the best'. In the TV version of the ad, this line was accompanied by an image of cans of fish being swept off a table, leaving just the John West can in place. This ad was two-edged, however – on the one hand it gave an undoubted impression of high quality, but on the other hand it implied that a large amount of food was being discarded, i.e. wasted. This image did not sit well with audiences in the 1990s and beyond, so the company needed to find a new approach to its advertising.

How advertising works

How advertising works (and occasionally whether advertising works) has been a topic for debate in marketing academia for a number of years now. Part of the problem is that there is no way of telling whether something works unless one first defines what it is that one is trying to achieve. Since there are many possible objectives for an advertising campaign, ranging from increasing purchases through to reinforcing attitudes, there can be no single explanation for whether advertising works (Wright and Crimp 2000).

Two general theories about advertising have emerged from the debate. The strong theory suggests that advertising is a powerful force that can change attitudes and make a significant contribution to people's knowledge and understanding. The weak theory of advertising suggests that advertising can only 'nudge' people in the direction in which they are already moving, in other words it reinforces rather than persuades (Ehrenberg 1992).

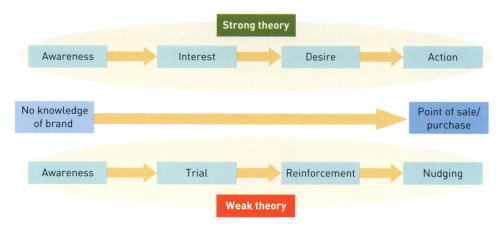

Figure 15.1   Strong and weak theories of advertising

The main criticisms of the strong theory of advertising are (first) that there is little evidence to show that consumers develop a strong desire for the brand before trying it, and second, the model only considers non-buyers who become buyers. In most markets, advertising is intended to affect people who have already tried the product, either with a view to informing them about changes in the product, or to remind them about the product, or to encourage increased purchases of the product. The strong theory tends to be more prevalent in the United States, and it is of course possible that American experience is different from European experience: the weak theory tends to have more adherents in Europe. Research in FMCG (fast-moving consumer goods) markets shows that people are not usually loyal to one brand, and it is extremely difficult for a new brand to become established in the portfolio of brands that people buy. In these circumstances, most advertising is intended to improve brand loyalty and therefore defend the brand: this would tend to support the weak theory, because it implies that the main people to be affected by the advertising are existing customers for the brand.

Think outside this box!

If advertising is only a weak force, and doesn't persuade anybody, why is so much money spent on it by companies? Surely they wouldn't pay out billions of pounds, dollars, yen and Euros every year just on the chance that it might work?

On the other hand, when was the last time you saw an advert and then went rushing out to buy a product? Have you *ever* been persuaded by an advertisement? Are advertisements like the bumble bee – in theory too aerodynamically unsound to fly, but in practice it still flies?

Level of involvement has a role to play in determining the effects of advertising, and may also have a bearing on when the strong theory applies, and when the weak theory predominates (Jones 1991). In the case of a high-involvement purchase, consumers are more likely to access sought communications (Blythe 2005; see also Chapter 3) and are likely to be more affected by advertising since they will be actively seeking out advertising messages. In the case of low-involvement purchases, consumers are less likely to seek out advertising and are therefore only likely to be moved slightly by the unsought communications around them.

One way in which advertising almost certainly does work is in reinforcing the value of companies' shares. Investors are affected by advertising as much as consumers (obviously, since they are all people) and research shows that advertising expenditures reduce the risk of stock falling in value (McAlister et al. 2007). This factor alone would justify a great deal of advertising expenditure, even without the potential effects on consumer attitudes and behaviour.

Developing an advertising strategy

The starting-point for planning the advertising strategy is, of course, the marketing strategy. Knowing where the firm is planning to be in relation to its customers and the marketplace is an essential first step in deciding advertising's role in the process. It is clearly not reasonable to take decisions about advertising without considering all the other elements of the marketing mix: advertising can be a crucial element in positioning the product, for example, but positioning also relies on pricing and product design.

Having developed a clear understanding of the overall marketing strategy, the advertising manager is in a position to identify the target audience. This is the group towards which the advertising is to be aimed, and usually corresponds to the market segment (although there are cases where the advertising will be aimed towards people who influence the members of the market segment. For example, the market segment for textbooks is students, but promotional material is usually aimed at lecturers.)

The next stage is to define the advertising objectives, or in other words decide how we would like the target audience to respond. The received wisdom is that advertising is intended to stimulate sales, but in fact this outcome cannot be guaranteed: advertising might be able to stimulate demand for a product category, but this does not necessarily translate into sales for the advertiser. It can just as easily translate into sales for competitors. A famous example of this was a series of advertisements for Cinzano vermouth, starring Leonard Rossiter and Joan Collins. Many viewers thought that the advertisements were actually for Cinzano's arch-rival, Martini. Consequently, sales of Martini increased while sales of Cinzano remained little changed: as a result, the campaign was withdrawn. In general, managers should aim to set communications objectives rather than marketing objectives: raising awareness of the brand, repositioning the brand, or correcting misconceptions about the brand are all reasonable objectives for advertising. Generating sales, increasing profits, or improving customer loyalty may result from these communications outcomes, but cannot be guaranteed or measured realistically. There is more on measuring advertising effectiveness later.

The next stage in the process is to set the budget. Budget-setting has already been covered in Chapter 7. To recap, there are five basic approaches to budget-setting, as follows:

1. Objective and task method: the budget is set according to the tasks to be accomplished.
2. Percentage of sales method: the budget is set as a proportion of the company turnover.

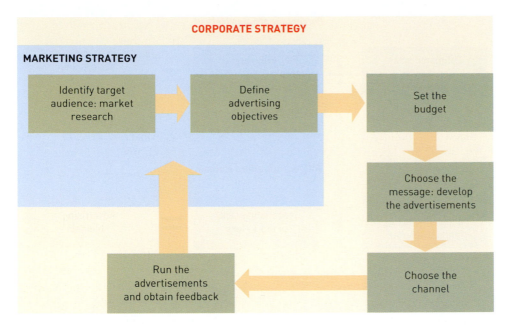

Figure 15.2 Stages in planning advertising

3. Comparative parity: competitors' spending is matched in proportion to relative market share.
4. Marginal approach: spending continues up to the point where further spending will not generate extra sales.
5. All you can afford: the budget is set through a process of negotiation with finance directors and colleagues from other departments.

These approaches are not necessarily mutually exclusive, and sometimes marketers will switch (or be forced to switch) from one to the other.

The budget has to reach a certain minimum level, because there is a great deal of advertising clutter around: no matter how creative the copywriters and artists are, a certain amount of money has to be spent in order to be heard at all.

Choosing the message is the next stage. Writing appropriate copy, or selecting an appropriate image, means selecting a communication platform that will appeal to the target audience as well as selecting a message that will result in the response the firm is hoping for. Producing an appropriate advertisement is a creative exercise, but cannot be carried out without regard for the characteristics of the target audience as well as the characteristics and needs of the firm and its brands. The starting point is to decide on the advertising platform: this is the basic selling proposition which is to be used in the advertising. For example, a car manufacturer may decide to sell on a platform of reliability (as Volkswagen does) or on a platform of style (as Ferrari does). The platform should be something that is important to the target audience, and also should communicate competitive advantages. For example, research shows that some types of appeal work better than others for specific audiences: cosmetic appeals (statements about the effects on appearance and smell) work better in discouraging young men from smoking than do appeals about health risks. The reverse is true for young women (Smith and Stutts 2003).

The message itself is likely to be focused through the brand (see Chapter 12). The brand personality will be a key element in this: the personality is used to focus the brand attributes and allow for self-expression on the part of consumers.

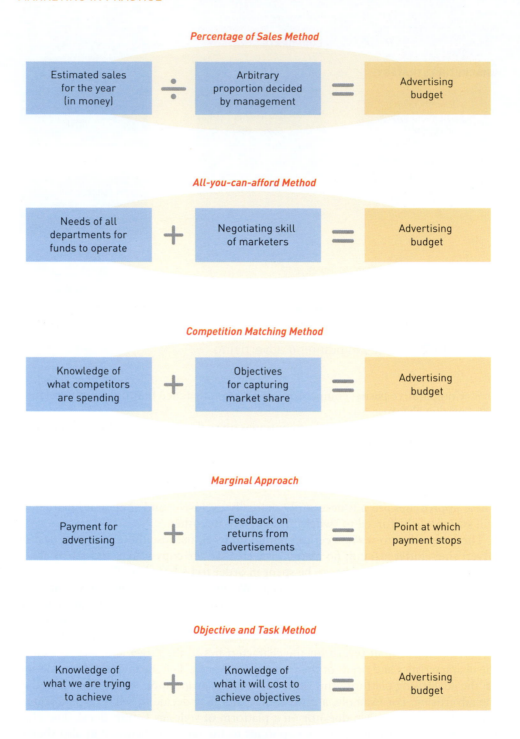

Figure 15.3   Setting advertising budgets

Choosing the channel is an extension of developing the message, because the channel is itself part of the message. The newspaper, TV programme, radio station or billboard location each convey their own image, which reflects on the products. For example, the French station Canal 5 (which was once owned by former Italian Prime Minister Silvio Berlusconi) faced falling audiences. The station owners decided to

Real-life marketing: David Ogilvy

Ogilvy's advertising career was meteoric – despite the fact that he had been thrown out of Oxford University for 'indifference' and had tried various careers including tobacco farming, door-to-door selling and even a spell in British Intelligence. As a founder and senior partner in Ogilvy & Mather he became a multimillionaire, with clients such as Rolls–Royce and Nestlé to work for. With such famous statements as 'People do not buy from bad-mannered liars', and 'The consumer's not a moron, she's your wife. Don't insult her intelligence', he trained several generations of advertising executives and changed the shape of advertising.

Ogilvy & Mather became the world's largest advertising agency. When Ogilvy died in 1999 he left behind him three excellent books on advertising and some of the biggest ideas in marketing – among them the concept of brand positioning and of using consumer research in advertising design.

He gave the following guidelines for press advertising – you would be well advised to use them!

1. The message appeal should be of benefit to the target audience.
2. The appeal should be specific: evidence to support it should be provided.
3. The message should be couched in the customer's language, not the language of the advertiser.
4. The advertisement should have a headline that might:

   i. Promise a benefit.
   ii. Deliver news.
   iii. Offer a service.
   iv. Tell a significant story.
   v. Identify a problem.
   vi. Quote a satisfied customer.

5. If body copy (additional copy following on from the headline) is to be used:

   i. Long copy is acceptable if it is relevant to the needs of the target audience.
   ii. Long paragraphs and sentences should be avoided.
   iii. The copy should be broken up, using plenty of white space to avoid it looking heavy to read.
   iv. If the advertiser is after enquiries, use a coupon and put the company address and telephone number at the end of the body copy. This is particularly important for industrial advertisements where more than one member of the decision-making unit (perhaps from different departments) may wish to send off for further details.

increase the audience numbers by showing soft-porn movies and sleazy game shows: audience figures improved dramatically, but advertising revenues fell because advertisers did not want to be associated with that type of programming. Canal 5 eventually went bankrupt, which is a considerable achievement for a TV station.

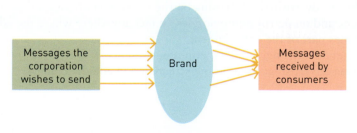

Figure 15.4   Focusing the effect of the brand

Think outside this box!

Looking at many advertisements, especially those for personal grooming, one might imagine that all advertisers ever think about is sex! Perfumes, after-shave lotions, hair gels, skin creams and even shampoo are all sold with a preponderance of semi-nudity and sexual innuendo. So what's the problem with booking these advertisements into shows with similar themes? Where do advertisers draw the line between what is shown in TV programmes and what they do themselves?

Looked at from the other direction, are regulators using double standards when they put prudish restrictions on advertising, while apparently allowing 'anything goes' in the programming?

Finally, the advertisement should run and the company should collect feedback. Collecting feedback might involve carrying out formal market research, or it might involve checking coupon returns. Increases in sales are an unreliable method of judging advertising because too many other factors might come into play.

Types of media

Advertising takes place through a number of media. More and more organisations are realising that advertising revenue can help to defray costs, so more and more media are being created. One of the criticisms levelled against advertising is that it adds to the cost of goods, because the advertising budget has to come from the prices consumers pay. However, advertising revenue subsidises public transport, virtually pays for our newspapers and commercial TV and radio, subsidises our theatres and cinemas, and even contributes to our litter bins and bus shelters. The main media are as follows:

- Print advertising: newspapers, magazines, directories, freesheet newspapers.
- Broadcast advertising: radio, television, cable and even some pre-recorded DVD and video releases.
- Outdoor advertising: street furniture, billboards, posters.
- Transport advertising: adverts inside buses, trains, bus and train stations, and on the outsides of buses, taxis and (in some areas) trains.
- Ambient advertising: advertising on the risers of staircases, on the backs of bus tickets, and on petrol-pump nozzles, in fact anywhere where the advertisement becomes part of the environment.
- Internet advertising: banners, pop-ups, presence websites.
- Cinema advertising: both on the screen and inside the cinema.

PRINT ADVERTISING

Print advertising covers newspapers, magazines, the technical press, directories and even leaflets handed out in the streets. It accounts for more than half of all advertising

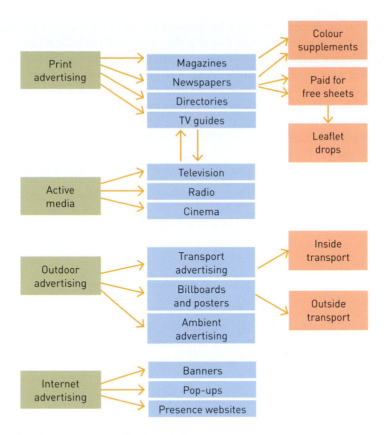

Figure 15.5   A taxonomy of advertising

expenditure in the UK: several million advertisers use print media every day, and there are more than 12,000 publications in the UK alone. These figures do not necessarily relate to other countries, however: the World Association of Newspapers published a report in 2013 which showed that newspaper circulation was increasing in Asia, while dropping dramatically in Europe and the United States (WAN 2013).

Print advertising has the following characteristics:

- Permanence: the print is permanent (unlike TV or radio) so the advertisement can be clipped and saved, or re-read. Newspapers tend to be thrown away soon after purchase, but magazines tend to be kept for long periods. In particular, magazines are often kept for months in doctors' waiting-rooms, hairdressing salons and even second-hand bookshops. Directories are often kept for years.
- Variety of approaches. This is particularly true of magazines. Magazines often target very tight segments of the market, so advertisers are able to reach very specific groups of people. In some cases, the market segment is actually defined by the medium: for example, *Cosmopolitan* readers are a very distinctive group that would be difficult to define except by saying that they are *Cosmopolitan* readers. Even newspapers attract specific types of reader, so that specific segments can be targeted easily.
- Print media can be read on trains, in buses or on aeroplanes: people rarely carry radios on public transport. In these circumstances, the medium has the full attention of the reader.

- Advertising success can often be assessed by checking coupon returns, particularly if the coupons are coded so that the individual periodical can be identified.
- Statistics are usually available on sales, circulation and readership figures (these are not necessarily the same thing – sometimes magazines are passed on to other readers, or placed in libraries and archives). This makes media planning easier. Also, many magazines collect data on the characteristics of their readers, and are able to tell potential advertisers what the demographic breakdown of the readers is, and even what kind of purchases they make.

The advantages and disadvantages of print advertising are shown in Table 15.1.

Table 15.1   Advantages and disadvantages of press advertising

Advantage	Explanation
Cheapness	Small advertisements can be placed very cheaply, and even a large campaign can be carried out relatively cheaply.
Ads can be inserted quickly	TV stations normally need considerable notice before inserting advertisements. In Germany it can be over a year between booking a slot and the ad actually being aired, and in the UK it would typically be approximately two months. Newspapers are able to accept advertising a day or two ahead of publication day.
Direct response is easy	Print advertising can carry coupons or order forms, unlike broadcast media. This makes mail-order purchase easier for consumers, and also provides instant feedback for the advertiser.
Targeting is easy	Because many magazines are aimed at specialist markets and hobbies, readers are likely to be interested in the advertising as well as in the editorial. Besides the ability to reach the exact audience who will be receptive to the product category, therefore, the advertiser is also reaching an involved audience who will read the advertising.
The press can always accept more advertising	Most European countries apply restrictions to the amount of advertising allowed on TV, and in any case air time is limited because space must be left for programmes and there are only so many minutes in a day. The press need only add some extra pages to the publication.
Products are often grouped together	Classified sections in newspapers or specific trade sections in directories group products together. This means that consumers who are on an information search are likely to read all the advertisements, which means that advertisements can be smaller and cheaper without losing much impact.
Disadvantages	**Explanation**
Short life	This only really applies to newspapers. Apart from Sunday papers, which are often kept all week, most newspapers are thrown away within a few hours of purchase.
Poor print quality	Again, this applies to newspapers and to most directories. Magazines usually have a high print quality, and can therefore carry high-resolution photographs and so forth.
Passive medium	The advertisements do not reach out to the reader in the way that a TV or radio advertisement would, and the medium is not interactive like the Internet.
Static medium	Because the advertisements are fixed, they are less eye-catching and engaging than moving advertisements would be.
Poorer literacy levels	In most of Western Europe and the USA, functional literacy levels are falling, and many people are not in the habit of reading. Many people watch TV news rather than read a newspaper, so circulation (and readership) levels have been falling for some time.

Creative issues

Print advertising contains both sought and unsought communications (Blythe 2005). Sought communications are the classified advertisements, which are categorised according to product type or consumer need: these are the advertisements that people seek out. Unsought advertisements are the display advertisements, which are usually intended to be eye-catching. From a creative viewpoint, the approach to each advertisement type is very different.

Sought communications need to contain all the salient information needed by the reader to make a decision, including information about the firm's USP (unique selling proposition). This means that the advertisement can contain a relatively large amount of copy: the same is not true of unsought communications, i.e. display advertising.

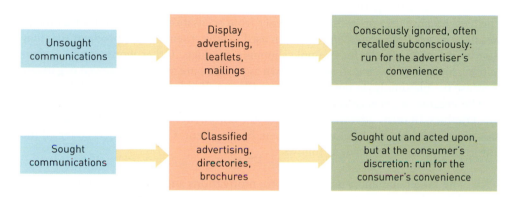

Figure 15.6   Sought and unsought communications in print advertising

 ## Marketing in a changing world: The demise of print?

There is a popular view that the Internet will take over from printed media. This seems logical – why would someone buy a newspaper when everything is available on-line? Why would someone buy a magazine when it's easy to download articles about almost anything that might interest us? Logic would tell us that print media will eventually disappear.

However, the print media are fighting back. It's hard to access the Internet when you're on public transport on your way to work – smartphone screens are small, tablets are too big and too easy to drop when you're standing up on a train, and if you commute using an underground railway (as in London or Glasgow) you can't get a signal. Hence the *Metro* newspaper, which is given out free to commuters. *Metro* is short (so that it can be read in about 25 minutes, the length of an average commute), and designed to appeal to young commuters (the people who do not buy newspapers). It's been so successful that the *London Evening Standard* has to be given away free as well now.

Research shows that doctors often prefer to read paper versions of their professional journals because it's easier to flip back and forth between pages and easier to file back issues.

Print media will probably survive for quite some time yet, but media owners need to be aware that the threat is still there, and perhaps marketers need to think about how people will replace current printed materials – it may not be with the current formats available on-line.

When someone buys a newspaper, he or she has bought it for the news content, and is likely to flip past the display advertisements in the search for hard news. This means that the display advertisement will need to be eye-catching, and will also need to get the main point across in a very few words, since the reader will almost certainly retain only a brief impression of the advertisement and will remember only the hook line (or strap line) at most. In terms of capturing the audience's attention, there are three key elements (Pieters and Wedel 2004), as follows:

1. The brand. If the brand is well known already, it will tend to attract attention and direct it to the other two elements.
2. The pictorial element. Graphics are superior to everything else in capturing attention, regardless of the size of the picture.
3. Text. Text captures attention in a manner proportional to its size.

People are generally negative about the use of words such as 'probably', 'may' or 'could' in advertising (Berney-Reddish and Areni 2005). These words, known as 'hedges' because they protect the advertiser from accusations of inaccuracy that might result from a definite statement, are often used in advertisements for products that may not work on everybody, for example slimming products. Other words, such as 'definitely', 'undoubtedly' and so forth (known as pledges) are also often viewed negatively because people simply do not believe them (Berney-Reddish and Areni 2005).

The creative aspects of the advertisement consist of two elements: the copy and the graphics. In many advertising agencies, the copywriter and the graphic artist work as a team on a creative brief given to them by the client. Creative briefs cover all the information the team need, as follows:

- The target audience, its perceptions, motivations and buying criteria.
- What the advertisement is supposed to communicate, in other words the creative platform.
- Choice of media.
- The objectives of the advertisement, in other words the response expected from the target audience.

The creative brief is a contract between the client and the agency, so it merits careful reading before signing.

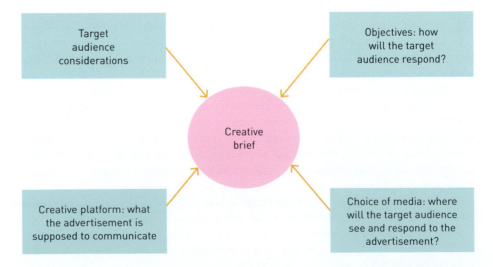

Figure 15.7   The creative brief

Copywriters are among the most creative writers in the world, because they need to get the message across in a very few words: some classic strap lines are as follows:

'At 60 miles per hour, the loudest sound in this new Rolls–Royce comes from the electric clock.' (Rolls–Royce cars: 1960s)

'Heineken refreshes the parts other beers cannot reach.' (Heineken beer: 1970s until now)

'I can't believe I ate the whole thing!' (Alka-Seltzer)

'Freshly Squeezed Glaciers.' (Canadian mineral water)

'We're number two. We try harder.' (Avis car hire)

All these slogans are clear, memorable and straight to the point, referring directly to the product's USP. However, in order to condense the message copywriters often have to make cultural references: for example, a copywriter might use part of a well-known quotation, or may make a reference to a popular TV show in order to get the point across. These cultural referents may not cross borders very effectively, and indeed may not be understood even outside a specific region of the country.

Graphic artists have less of a problem in this area. Of course, what looks like a friendly smile to one person might look like a threatening grimace to another, and images of local places or buildings might not be recognisable elsewhere, but in general pictures are less of a problem than words.

If the client is a major one, the creative team will produce **roughs** or **scamps** for the client's approval. Sometimes these will be pre-tested with potential consumers (see Chapter 7). The agency will also produce a conceptual rationale that will explain how the advertisements are supposed to work, and what the advantages of the approach are. Creatives in advertising see their managers and clients as being unprepared to take risks (El-Murad and West 2003). This undoubtedly affects the relationships, but is understandable: creative people are likely to want to produce eye-catching, innovative advertising, whereas clients are likely to prefer something that will not cause offence to anyone.

> **Roughs** Draft advertising materials produced for a client's approval.
> **Scamps** See Roughs.

In the UK, advertisers will often seek the approval of regulatory bodies such as the Committee of Advertising Practice, which acts as a watchdog for the industry. The Advertising Standards Authority is linked to the CAP and handles complaints from the public: it does not pre-approve advertising, but it does follow up on public complaints. If an advertisement causes offence, the ASA can ask for it to be withdrawn. Since the ASA has no statutory powers, advertisers can refuse to comply with the suggestion, but the ASA would then issue a media warning to its members, including newspaper and magazine publishers, which would effectively ban the advertisement from running. The vast majority of publications would not want to run advertisements that may offend their hard-won readership.

Misleading advertisements can be forcibly withdrawn under the Control of Misleading Advertisements Regulations 1988, although this is rarely necessary since the ASA and CAP between them maintain effective control over offenders.

ACTIVE MEDIA: TV, RADIO AND CINEMA

Radio, TV and cinema are powerful media because they are active – they actually do something. TV and radio are probably the most pervasive media in most countries – in Western Europe, TV ownership is almost 100%, and many homes have several television sets. Radio ownership is at least as widespread.

Television advertising

People watch TV while eating, doing housework, relaxing, or even while entertaining friends. In some homes the set is rarely switched off. Significantly, the biggest-selling

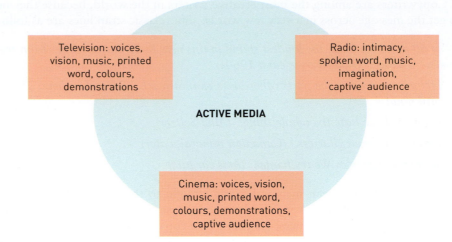

Figure 15.8   Active media

consumer magazines in most Western European countries and in the United States are the TV programme guides.

Because television advertising is an unsought communication (people will rarely, if ever, switch on the TV in order to see a favourite advertisement) it works best for activating needs or providing information for the internal search. In most case advertisers are aiming to build the image of their product or firm, and to a large extent these aims can be met by television (McKechnie and Leather 1998).

TV advertising has the advantages shown in Table 15.2 (Jefkins 1994). There are, of course, disadvantages to television as a medium, and these are shown in Table 15.3.

Table 15.2   Advantages of TV advertising

Advantage	Explanation
Realism	It is possible to show the product in use in a typical and realistic way. Because the audience can see how to use the product, and can also see the kind of person who is using it, advertisers can position the brand appropriately. Often viewers are able to identify the social class of the person in the advertisement by their accent and clothing, which helps position the brand.
Receptive audiences	TV advertisements are often seen as entertainment: many are produced to high standards, by world-class directors. Many advertisements tell a story, with surprising or amusing twists at the end.
Repetition	Advertisements can be repeated until sufficient of the audience have had an opportunity to see it. Agencies monitor this using published audience figures for each programme the advertisement appears in.
Appeal to retailers	Most retailers have a strong belief in the power of television, and are more likely to give the product prominence on their shelves if they know a TV campaign is planned. Of course, the fact that the product has more shelf space might in itself increase sales, so there is no way of being sure that the advertisement actually increased consumers' propensity to buy.
Zoning and networking	In the UK and most other countries it is possible to localise advertising to the immediate TV region, or to 'go national' with advertisements which are broadcast throughout the network.
Links with other media	Further information, coupons and order forms can be printed in other media and the TV advertisement can direct people to look for them. Printing such items in TV guides is a useful ploy: this combines the strengths of both media.

Table 15.3 Disadvantages of television

Disadvantage	Explanation
Lack of selectivity	Television is a mass medium: it is hard to segment, even though some programmes appeal more to some people than to others. This means that advertisers are probably wasting the majority of their expenditure in talking to people who have no need for the product.
Impermanent medium	Once the advertisement has been aired, it has gone forever (barring repeat airings). It is difficult for viewers to take note of where products are available, or to note down telephone numbers and so forth.
Zapping and **zipping**	Remote controls allow audiences to 'zap' advertisements, either by muting the sound or by switching channels when watching programmes in real time. If programmes have been recorded, the viewers can 'zip' past the ads using fast forward. Indeed, some systems automatically remove all advertising. Zapping has been called 'The greatest threat to capitalism since Karl Marx' (Kneale 1988). It may also be a threat to television itself, since TV is largely funded by advertising revenues.
Clutter	In some countries TV advertising rates are so low that frequent, and lengthy, advertising spots are sold: the USA and Italy are examples of this. Viewers become bored with the sheer volume of advertising, and frequently leave the room.
Audience fade-out	Audiences often leave the room while the advertisements are on, so although the ratings for the show might be high, the advertisements may not actually have been seen.
Cost	TV can be very expensive. Although it reaches a large audience, and therefore the cost-per-thousand-viewers might be low, the audience may not be composed of the right target group. The entry threshold is high: in the UK, which is admittedly one of the most expensive countries in the world for TV advertising, a nationally-networked advertisement can easily cost £300,000 for one 30-second exposure.
Long lead times	Booking air time can be a lengthy process, taking weeks or even months. Additionally, production times for a commercial are likely to be long.
Restrictions on content	Most broadcast regulatory authorities take a conservative view on what can be shown in TV advertising. Sexual imagery, swearing and some categories of product (tobacco and condoms being two examples) are absolutely banned (despite being common in programmes). Restrictions vary from one country to another – for example, in France it is illegal for retailers to advertise on TV, and in Germany toys cannot be advertised during children's TV programmes.
Dilution of audiences	As the number of available channels increases due to satellite and cable provision, plus the use of recording and on-demand technology, the number of available viewers for any one programme has fallen. Also, high-quality programmes are spread across more channels so that the average quality of programming has fallen. This has led to a reduction in time spent watching TV and an increase in other activities. This trend may be peaking out – there have been instances recently of cable TV channels going bankrupt, which indicates that there may be a limit to the number of channels audiences are prepared to support.

Zapping Using the TV remote control to avoid advertising messages.

Zipping Using the fast-forward function to skip past TV advertising in a recorded programme.

Audience fade-out The tendency for TV viewers to leave the room or lose concentration when the commercial breaks occur.

Table 15.4   Behaviours in commercial breaks

Behaviour	Explanation
Social interaction	People often talk about their day, discuss household problems, or gossip while the commercial break runs.
Reading	Many people watch TV with a book or magazine at hand, to read during the breaks. Sometimes the reading will be a TV guide.
Tasking	The commercial break often affords an opportunity to load the dishwasher, do some house cleaning, do some ironing, pay bills, or make telephone calls.
Flicking	Jumping from one channel to another appears to be mainly a male activity. Flicking falls into two categories: almost random surfing across a number of other channels while waiting for the programme to restart, or alternatively going to a 'visit channel' such as a news channel for a specific length of time before returning to the programme.
Watching an advertisement	In many cases, the advertisements are actually watched, and often commented on by the family members.
Advertising interaction	The advertisements are not only watched, but commented on; researchers recorded viewers singing along with the jingles, and even playing a game in which family members scored 'points' by being the first to recognise the brand.

Source: Ritson 2003

Research at the London Business School shows that people do not necessarily watch the advertisements even if they are still in the room when the advertisement airs (Ritson 2003). The researchers identified a total of six behaviours that occur while the advertisement is on-screen: these are shown in Table 15.4. The first three activities are interesting in that the standard method of measuring advertising on TV, which is the people meter, would have shown that people were in the room and would therefore have assumed that they were watching the advertisement. In fact, in each of these three cases, presence in the room does not mean observation of the advertising.

Interestingly, there is research evidence that advertisements that are zapped are more likely to have a positive effect on brand purchase than those that are not (Zufryden et al. 1993). This is presumably because the viewer has to watch at least part of the advertisement and process the content before knowing that it is a candidate for zapping.

Fast-paced advertisements appear to have a positive effect on involuntary attention, in other words they are more eye-catching, but have little effect on involuntary attention (they are no more likely to be watched actively) (Bolls et al. 2003). Furthermore, fast-paced advertisements tend to focus people on the style of the advertisement, not on its content: people remember the advertisement, but not the brand. Mood affects people's response to advertisements, so placing the advertisement in an appropriate programme may have a critical effect on its success or otherwise (Bakamitsios and Siomkos 2003).

There is a clear relationship between liking the advertisement and subsequent sales, but this is not always a positive relationship. Liking the advertisement seems to be related to whether the product is meaningful and relevant to the person at the time (Biel 1990), and there is evidence that advertisements relating to food and drink are more likely to be liked than are non-food advertisements (Biel and Bridgewater 1990). Liking is usually linked to a positive view of the product, which in turn is likely to lead to sales (Biel 1990: Stapel 1991).

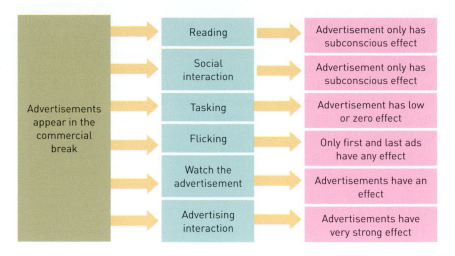

Figure 15.9 Activities in commercial breaks

This situation is sometimes reversed when dealing with (for example) insurance products and the like, where the advertisement might contain shocking imagery as a 'cautionary tale' to show people what can go wrong if they do not have insurance. Messages that emphasise positive outcomes are more effective than those that emphasise negatives, however (Guangzhi and Pechmann 2006). Humour can be very important in advertising – but it is vital to distinguish between remembering the advertisement and remembering the product. Humour frequently results in people remembering the advertisement, but being unable to remember the brand name (Hansen et al. 2009).

Real-life marketing: Relevant communication

Sometimes the product's actual features and benefits are not all that exciting. Putting the excitement back in through your advertising might be a good way forward in those circumstances.

Grolsch is a Dutch lager aimed at mature males who prefer premium brands. It tastes pretty much like most other premium lagers, and it was losing ground to the more aggressively promoted Stella Artois and Kronenbourg 1664 brands. Grolsch's distinctive feature is that it is brewed more slowly than other beers, which allegedly gives it a fuller flavour: but that's a pretty boring explanation, right? So the company produced a series of TV advertisements which showed a 'typically' laid-back, easy-going Dutchman in various situations in which he showed that things go better when you don't rush. For example, one advertisement showed bank robbers attacking a bank that had only been partly-built: 'Schtop!' shouted our hero, and the strap line 'We only let you drink it when it's ready', flashed up on the screen.

Grolsch sales increased by 58.4% as a result of the campaign, beating the company's projection by a handsome margin.

In practice, you should:

- Check your existing strap lines. Have they become boring? Have they always been boring?
- Find a humorous or startling way to convey the USP.
- See which other features and benefits of your product could be linked to the USP – country of origin, production methods, age of the firm, and so forth.

It may be difficult to deconstruct all the factors involved, since a truly unpleasant advertisement is likely to be ignored, so that the viewer is less likely to process the information cognitively. Such 'cautionary tale' advertisements are difficult to produce because the affective element is likely to repel the customer, whereas the cognitive element is likely to attract. Products can be placed on an approach-avoidance continuum, with products that are inherently attractive (food and beverages) at one end, and products that are inherently unattractive and are bought only out of dire necessity (pensions, life insurance) at the other (Wells 1980).

Think outside this box!

If people tend to 'switch off' from unpleasant advertisements, why produce them at all? Why show people scenes of crashed cars and devastated homes in order to frighten them into buying insurance? Maybe the school bully could frighten children into handing over their pocket money – but we're all grown-ups now!

Or maybe people have to be terrorised into buying insurance – otherwise they will just keep putting it off until after they have been burgled or crashed the car! After all, in most countries it is a legal requirement to have car insurance – so doesn't this prove that people won't buy it unless they are threatened with jail?

Off-the-screen commercials (direct response television) appear to be a type of television advertising that breaks all the rules. These advertisements have a high copy content, are extremely informative and they aim to obtain a direct response from viewers by getting them to call an order line and buy the product directly. In the United States, off-the-screen selling has gone a step further with the **infomercial**, a (typically) half-hour programme consisting of entertainment and news about a specific product. For example, an infomercial about a new type of fishing lure might show anglers using the device, show people catching fish, give tips about the most effective locations for using the lure, and so forth. Infomercials were illegal on TV in the UK until 2009, but OFCOM now allows up to three hours per day of infomercials on any one channel. Infomercials provide advertisers with enough time to inform and persuade people about the product's benefits: from the cable TV company's perspective, infomercials fill up air time that would otherwise have to be filled with paid-for programmes.

Infomercial A feature-length TV programme about a product.

Radio advertising

Radio is the Cinderella of advertising, often ignored in favour of the higher profile of television. And yet, according to research conducted for Red Dragon Radio, commercial radio has a strong impact on people's lives. According to Red Dragon:

- 44% of radio listeners wake up to a radio alarm.
- 27% of people listen to the radio in the bathroom, and 43% of the 15–24 age group do so.
- 72% of adult listeners listen to the radio in the kitchen.
- 44% of car drivers listen to the radio while driving.
- 44% of employees listen to the radio in the workplace.
- 53% of adults aged 15–24 listen to their radios in the garden.

Most commercial radio is broadcast on the FM (frequency modulated) system, which gives a short range but high sound quality. There are some commercial AM

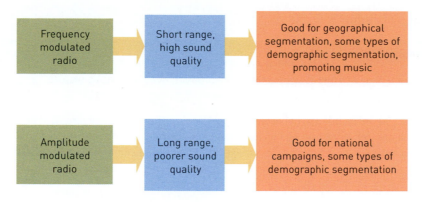

Figure 15.10   FM versus AM radio

(amplitude modulated) stations which have a greater range but give a poorer sound quality. This means that the bulk of commercial radio is localised, and can therefore offer good geographical targeting. In the UK, independently audited listener figures are compiled by the Radio Joint Advertising Research organisation (RAJAR) organisation, which is jointly owned by the BBC and the independent radio stations.

The advantages of radio as an advertising medium are shown in Table 15.5. There are, of course, disadvantages with radio advertising, and these are outlined in Table 15.6.

Narrowcast Accurate targeting of audiences in broadcast media.

Table 15.5   Advantages of radio

Advantage	Explanation
Radios are cheap and portable	Most people own a radio, and most households own several: they are often taken on outings, or to work, so advertisements can be heard in most locations.
There is no need to be literate to enjoy radio	The spoken word is understood by everyone who is native to the country. In many developing countries, literacy rates are so low that radio is the main means of communication, especially in remote areas.
Live medium	Like TV, radio is active, so it commands attention better than newspapers or billboards.
Does not require the listener's sole attention	Radio is often listened to while driving, working, doing housework, or engaging in leisure pursuits.
Hard to zap advertisements	Unlike TV, radios are not usually fitted with remote controls, so listeners are unlikely to zap the advertisements. Frequently, changing stations is also harder than is the case for TV, so surfing is less likely to happen.
Can be localised	Because much, if not most, radio is FM, advertising can be targeted on a small geographical area.
Can be targeted on different segments at different times of day	Workers listen for time-checks at around breakfast-time; drivers listen for traffic news on the way to and from work; people at home and factory workers listen during the day. The ability to target accurately has been called **narrowcasting**.
Cheapness and flexibility	Radio has much of the immediacy of TV, but at a fraction of the cost: in particular, the production costs of radio advertisements are tiny compared with TV production costs.
Intimacy of the medium	People listen to the radio in a relaxed and often private location. Radio is more like a friend than an advertising medium – it is listened to in bed, in the bathroom, while driving, or while relaxing at home.

Table 15.6   Disadvantages of radio

Disadvantage	Explanation
Audio medium only	This means that it is impossible to show the product, even as a static picture.
Relies heavily on audience imagination	Because audiences need to contribute a great deal to the joint development of knowledge, there is a greater emphasis on individual perception and consequently the advertiser has less control over outcomes. This makes it difficult to position the brand, because the listener has a greater influence than the advertiser.
Transient, impermanent medium	Like television, radio is impermanent: listeners would need to be ready with a pen and paper to take down telephone numbers or addresses, and this is unlikely to happen given the circumstances under which most radio listening takes place.
Inattention of listeners	Radio is often used as a background noise to make tedious tasks more tolerable – the listener is rarely giving the radio his or her full attention.
Low number of listeners	The number of listeners to any given programme is normally low compared with the number of people within range of the station, which is itself a relatively low figure compared with television or even the national press.
Difficult to measure	Much of the effect of radio advertising occurs below a conscious level: the lack of coupon responses or telephone calls as a result of radio advertising means that advertisers find it hard to measure the effects.

Radio advertising is often seen as a back-up medium for television, although in many countries it is a mainstream medium: for example, in much of Africa television coverage is sporadic, and television ownership is low, whereas radio reaches everywhere.

Scripting radio advertisements is much like scripting TV advertisements, except that everything must be conveyed in the script. Sound effects become important as triggers for listeners' perception: the sound of waves on a beach and children playing signifies holidays, the sound of a champagne cork popping signifies a celebration, and so forth. These triggers are culturally based: Muslims are unlikely to associate alcohol with celebrations, and many Australians have rarely visited the seaside. Radio requires imagination on the part of the listeners: in some cases this may actually be advantageous because it means that the advertisement is, in effect, more interactive (Ritson and Elliott 1995).

Music has a powerful role to play in radio advertising. It attracts listeners' attention and also helps position the brand by providing linking value – in other words, it helps the listener to make sense of the world (Cova 1997). It has been argued that pop music is most effective in adverts where the brand being promoted also provides linking value (Shankar 1998). For example, clothing provides linking value, so presumably music would work well in advertisements for clothes retailers.

Table 15.7 shows some ideas for writing slogans that will stick in the mind.

Questions are powerful in scriptwriting: a question tends to force the listener to think, in an attempt to find the answer. Questions can also contain assumptions that the listener does not query because he or she is distracted by the question itself. For example, asking listeners 'How can you remove those stale smells from clothing?' assumes that the listener's clothing smells stale, and the listener can

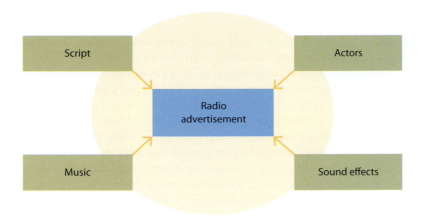

Figure 15.11   Creating radio advertisements

Foregrounding Bringing an advertising slogan to the forefront of a customer's mind.
Alliteration Using similar sounds in a slogan to aid memory.
Assonance Repetition of vowels in a slogan to aid memory.

Table 15.7   Making slogans stick

Device	Explanation
Rhythm	Using a slogan with a natural beat aids memory. In the UK, Kwik-Fit car repairers used the phrase 'You can't get better than a Kwik-Fit Fitter' which has a natural rhythm: the phrase is almost instantly memorable.
Foregrounding	Bringing the slogan to the forefront of the mind can be achieved either by parallelism (an unexpected regularity, as in the Kwik-Fit slogan) or by an unexpected irregularity.
Alliteration	Using the same sound repeatedly creates a resonance. This does not necessarily mean using the same initial letter: 'ph' and 'f' have the same sound, so 'Fred Philips' Pharmacy' will resonate nicely.
Assonance	The repetition of vowel sounds, as in 'Gillette – the best a man can get!' The assonance of 'Gillette' and 'get' make the slogan more memorable.
Rhyme	Some languages have more rhymes than others. Welsh, Spanish and Italian are particularly rich in rhymes: these languages also have a natural rhythm because the emphasis in the words tends to fall in the same place. German and Greek are less rhythmic, and have fewer rhymes.
Intonation	Stressing different syllables from those expected in ordinary speech can add to the deviation effect.
Puns	Homophones are words that sound similar but have different meanings. Carefully used, these can have a high impact: foreign languages are a rich source of possibilities. Homophones work better in print than on radio, however.

easily accept this idea unquestioningly while still trying to think how to remove the smells.

Most questions asked in radio scripts are rhetorical: asking listeners 'Would you like to save money on car insurance?' does not really invite a 'No' answer. Listeners can easily assume that what follows (the advertisement for an insurance broker) will solve the problem for them.

Cinema advertising

For many years the cinema was the only visual advertising medium. Television meant that cinema audiences declined dramatically in the 1950s and 1960s, but in recent years the trend has reversed. A combination of 'blockbuster' movies that have attracted audiences and the emergence of comfortable, well-equipped cinemas in entertainment complexes has led to a resurgence of cinema attendance as part of a night out.

From the advertiser's viewpoint, cinema has all the advantages of television plus one other: it is impossible to zip, zap or leave the room while the advertisements are on. Consequently, cinemas provide an unrivalled opportunity to speak to a captive audience. UK Film Council statistics show that cinema attendances have risen from 34 million per annum in 1988, to 174 million visits in 2009 – no small audience for advertising (UK Film Council 2010). Another factor in rising cinema attendance is the relatively poorer quality of television programming.

Typical cinema audiences are young people in their teens and early twenties: 81% of people aged 15– 24 visit the cinema at least once a year, and 40% visit at least once a month: this compares with 60% and 18% respectively for the population as a whole. The audience is also strongly ABC1 in socio-economic profile (UK Film Council 2010). In some developing countries (notably India) cinema attendance is widespread because of the relatively low level of television ownership.

The medium is extremely flexible – cheap packages are available for local firms, using stock film to which a voice-over is added, while at the same time major corporations can screen their TV commercials on the big screen. In most countries cinema advertising is less regulated than TV advertising: in the UK, advertisements have to be passed by the British Board of Film Censors, but the restrictions are much less stringent than those for television, since the cinema audience has already been pre-screened.

Cinema is probably under-used as a medium. It accounts for a very small proportion of overall advertising expenditure in the UK, yet it offers a relatively cheap way of reaching a key target audience – also, it is an audience which has little choice but to watch the advertisements.

BILLBOARD ADVERTISING

Outdoor displays are the oldest form of advertising: such displays have been in use for thousands of years. Outdoor signs have been found in the ruins of Pompeii and in mediaeval towns throughout Europe. Probably the most ubiquitous and obtrusive of outdoor advertising media is the billboard. Most vacant sites in cities have billboards on them, and they appear on the sides of buildings, beside major roads, beside railway lines, and even mounted on trailers and towed through the streets.

Billboards have the following advantages:

- Low cost. A billboard poster is relatively cheap to design and print, and the site rentals are also low.
- Can be targeted geographically. If the company wishes to reach a specific geographical market segment, billboards in that area can be booked. One site can be booked to promote a local retail outlet, for example.
- Can be used seasonally for short periods. Posters can easily be changed, so that the products advertised can be adjusted according to the season, or to other changing circumstances.

Billboards are exceptionally useful for teaser campaigns. A teaser campaign is one in which an apparently meaningless advertisement is run for a few weeks, then another advertisement is run which explains the original one. Teaser campaigns work by

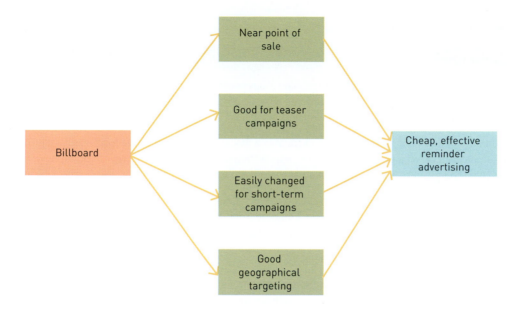

Figure 15.12   Billboard advertising

using message intrigue: the observer becomes intrigued as to what the advertisement actually means, and is thus sensitised to look out for the answer when it finally arrives. Billboard advertising is also widely used during political campaigns, because the posters can be changed quickly as different issues come to the fore.

Because of their public nature, billboards can often be used to generate controversy. This has been the case (famously) with Benetton, but in Zambia the Harveytiles company has used controversial billboards to advertise its roofing tiles. In many cases, the religious references in Harveytiles billboards have caused considerable offence to local Christian groups, and the company has attracted a great deal of criticism, but the posters remain and the result is that everyone has heard of Harveytiles in Southern Africa. However, in most countries billboards are among the least regulated of advertising media – in the UK, the only regulation is the Advertising Standards Authority, which of course only acts after complaints have been received (i.e. after the billboards have appeared).

Think outside this box!

We are often told that some advertising is offensive, or is offensive to some religious group or ethnic minority. Yet advertising has to cut through the clutter and be noticed – what better way than to be shocking? And anyway, in a pluralist society it is really very difficult to produce advertising that offends no one: if we were really strict about this, there would be no advertising for alcoholic drinks, no advertising for cosmetics, no advertising for many movies, and no advertising even for tea or coffee, because all of these products are prohibited by one religious sect or another.

So why not go the whole hog, and produce *really* offensive advertisements? Why not have everyone reeling in horror at what is on the billboard? In short, why not produce advertisements that shock people all the time?

Table 15.8   Disadvantages of billboards

Disadvantage	Explanation
Limited capacity	Since billboards are read literally in passing, copy must be extremely brief and to the point. Often billboards can only be used as a reminder, or to direct potential customers to another information source (e.g. a website).
Difficult to evaluate	Audience figures are extremely hard to measure, because they may be walking or driving past, or even be on a bus. Traffic counts help somewhat, but there is no way of telling how many of the passers-by actually looked at the advertisement.
Difficult to target	Segmentation by ethnic group might be possible in cities where ghettoes have sprung up, but segmentation by (for example) age would be impossible. A billboard on a main road is likely to be passed by people from all backgrounds and income levels.
Vulnerability	Billboards are often vandalised or defaced.
Noise	Passing traffic, crowded pavements, or the problems of driving in a city centre will often prevent people from paying attention to the billboards. Sometimes this can work to the advertiser's advantage, though: an advertisement for car air-conditioning might work well on a hot, dusty day.
Environmental restrictions	In many countries there are strict restrictions on the design, location and number of billboards. This is in response to the proliferation of outdoor advertising in some areas, where it has become an environmental problem, inasmuch as it obscures views of the countryside.

Advertising folklore has it that two-thirds of consumer decision-making takes place immediately before the purchase, at the point of sale (Brierley 1995). Billboards are often used as a last reminder before purchasing, which is why they are widely used to advertise frequently purchased items such as soft drinks and snacks.

The disadvantages of billboard advertising are as shown in Table 15.8.

Billboards can be extremely effective as a support medium for other advertising. They can be used as reminders for other advertising such as TV or radio, and can also be used to direct people to websites: because billboards are a more or less permanent medium, a commuter (for example) can take note of a Web address when returning home or going to work the next day (or next week).

TRANSPORT ADVERTISING

Transport advertising falls into two categories: inside transport, and outside transport. Inside transport advertising is carried out inside trains, buses, railway stations and bus stations. It provides travellers with something to look at, and is unusual in that it can use a great deal more copy than any other form of unsought communication.

Advertising on stations and inside trains is more tightly targeted than advertising in the street because it will be seen predominantly by commuters and tourists (at least in London, Paris, Athens or other major cities). As with billboards, zoning is possible to an extent, but specific campaigns can be aimed at a commuter audience. For example, the UK charity the Samaritans, which has an emergency helpline for people who are depressed or suicidal, ran a highly successful campaign aimed at commuters. Posters on bus stops and stations in the suburbs read, 'Can't face going to work? Call the Samaritans'. Posters in city-centre locations read, 'Can't face going home? Call the Samaritans'.

On public transport, people often try to avoid eye contact with their fellow passengers: this means that advertisements are likely to be read several times in each journey, especially when the trains are crowded and people are forced to stand, since reading a book or newspaper is much harder in these circumstances.

Advertising on the outsides of buses, taxis and trains has much the same advantages as billboard advertising, except that this time it is the medium that moves, while the audience may or may not be static. Advertisements low down on the backs of buses are at eye level for any motorists following the bus, so this is a good location for advertising anything to do with cars, from tyre fitting to insurance. In some cities it is possible to have whole buses painted with the company's design: this is called **livery**. Taxis often carry advertising, and a recent development in some UK cities is the bicycle rickshaw, which gives free rides to passengers, but carries advertising. The advertising fees are enough to cover provision of the service.

Livery Painting a public-transport vehicle in corporate colours or advertising.

DESIGNING OUTDOOR ADVERTISING

With the exception of inside transport advertising, outdoor advertising must use a minimum of copy and a maximum of imagery, because observers will see it only very briefly in most cases. Icons, symbols and indices play a large part in this (see Chapter 7), but there is a strong tendency to use stereotypes because this is the quickest way to get the message across. Whereas in most writing authors try to avoid being gender-specific, copywriters have little choice, because gender-neutral words are less appealing (DeVoe 1956). 'He' or 'she' would be interpreted as someone known to the reader, and 'you' of course means the reader. The famous First World War recruiting poster showing General Kitchener apparently pointing at the reader and saying, 'Your country needs YOU!' needed to be interpreted by the observer – clearly an 85-year-old woman would know that the poster did not mean her, but a man of military age would know it meant him (Myers 1994). This poster was highly successful, and was later copied by the Americans, using Uncle Sam instead of Kitchener.

Language can also be used as a sign. Using French words in an English-speaking country can convey an image of chicness and sophistication that goes beyond the meaning of the slogan itself. Phrases such as '*je ne sais quoi*' or '*savoir-faire*' are in common use, at least in Britain, so most people would understand them. In Australia, Aboriginal words such as '*corroboree*' would convey an Australian image: some Australian terms (such as 'the barbie') would convey an Australian image to British people, whereas the equivalent South African word for a barbecue ('*braai*') would not be understood. Americans, on the other hand, would probably associate a 'barbie' with Mattel's Barbie doll.

Use of accent (different pronunciation) or dialect (different words) can also convey impressions of wealth, of solid down-to-earth character, of traditional values, of youth, and of modern go-getting attitudes. Accent can be conveyed by different spellings for common words, and in some cases standard spelling for dialect words already exists. This foregrounds the information and makes the communication more noticeable as well as more memorable. Advertisements using accent are common in the UK, perhaps because of the wide range of accents and dialects.

Airborne media

Airships, blimps, banner-towing, hot-air balloons and even skywriting are all eye-catching methods of advertising outdoors. Airborne advertisements have the advantage of being visible over many miles, although the message is liable to be limited because of legibility from a long distance: in most cases only the brand name, and perhaps a logo, can be used.

Probably the best-known airship is Goodyear's. In itself, the airship conveys a message of unhurried freedom from care (Bounds 1994), but airships attract attention, so the brand name is seen by anyone the airship flies over. The Goodyear airship is often used as a camera platform at sporting events and major concerts: in these circumstances, it gives triple value, because it is filmed as part of the coverage of the event, it is in constant sight of the audience at the event, and it is mentioned by the commentators every time the view switches to the camera on the airship. The cost of operating an airship is high – around £250,000 a month – but the impact is also high.

A cheaper alternative is the unmanned blimp. These inflatables cost around £20,000 and can be tethered above business premises. Unfortunately, they have become commonplace, and as a result have lost most of their impact: any advertising method which relies on novelty will lose its impact if it is over-used.

Towing a banner behind a light aircraft (or underneath a helicopter) is another high-impact method of advertising. It tends to work best at locations where people are congregated in a long line (for example a beach) but the signs can be hard to read unless the aircraft flies too low for safety. As with any other outdoor advertising, the copy needs to be as brief as possible: confining it to the logo and a slogan is usually sufficient. Helicopters were widely used by the Conservative party during the UK's 2005 General Election.

In 1919 a former Royal Flying Corps major called Jack Savage bought a war-surplus fighter aircraft and fitted smoke canisters to it. He then sold his services to major companies as a skywriter: he would fly in patterns which spelled out messages. The messages were sometimes a mile or more long, written in smoke against the sky. Skywriting became popular because it is extremely eye-catching: Savage wrote 'Persil', 'Castrol' and 'Daily Mail' over the skies of London, and wrote 'Hello USA' on a visit to New York in 1922.

Skywriting has fallen out of fashion in recent years, and has been banned in several countries (including the UK) because of the risk of collisions between aircraft. The medium is not, of course, permanent: Savage's message to New York only lasted ten minutes. On the other hand, the message can be read by a very large number of people – skywriting over cities such as London or New York would reach millions of people, and would certainly be eye-catching.

Hot-air balloons have proved to be extraordinarily effective in corporate advertising. The balloons can be made in the shape of the product (provided the product is a suitable shape, of course) and the balloons are often seen at displays or competitive events that draw large crowds. The main drawback of hot-air balloons is that they are extremely affected by adverse weather conditions, so that their use is seasonal at best, and unreliable at worst.

At present, there is little or no academic research into flying media. The only regulation on flying media is that imposed by air traffic control regulations and Civil Aviation inspectors, whose concern is safety not advertising appropriateness – for example, aircraft are not allowed to fly within 500 feet of the ground or of any group of people, which naturally affects the legibility of the copy. The effectiveness of flying media is therefore highly debatable, although such an eye-catching medium is likely to be effective.

AMBIENT ADVERTISING

Traditional marketing communications techniques are becoming less effective as markets fragment, costs increase, audiences diminish and clutter worsens (Evans et al. 1996). Therefore, new routes for communicating with customers and consumers are being sought.

Ambient advertising is somewhat difficult to define, although plenty of examples of it are around: in general, it is advertising that becomes part of the environment, where the message becomes the medium. For example, for one campaign an underarm deodorant manufacturer arranged to replace the hanging straps in London Underground carriages with empty bottles of the deodorant. Strap-hanging commuters are acutely aware of underarm odours, and holding onto the bottles instead of the usual straps meant that they had already assumed the position one uses when applying the deodorant. Another development is the invention of a device that converts shop windows into loudspeakers so that the window can 'talk' about the products on display (Grapentine 2003).

Ambient advertising offers the following advantages:

- It is often cheaper than sales promotions, and when used near the point of purchase gives a good incentive without the loss of profit associated with sales promotion discounts.
- Well-executed ambient campaigns enhance brand image and cut through clutter.
- Novel ambient campaigns often create press coverage: some ambient campaigns are designed with this in mind.
- They are very effective for activating needs.

Ambient advertisers need to consider the relationship between the medium being used, the advertised product or service and the proximity to the point of sale as well as the basic objectives of the campaign. Ambient advertising works best when it is either close to the location of the problem or close to the point of purchase. For example, Kellogg's Nutrigrain bar was promoted as a snack for commuters who had missed breakfast, so Kellogg's arranged for advertisements for the product to be printed on bus and train tickets. Many travellers were reported to have bought the bars as a result, buying them from station news-stands or kiosks near bus stops.

Real-life marketing: Ads on cars

Marketers are always looking for ways to cut through advertising clutter. People are very adept at avoiding advertisements – so marketers try to be ever more startling, ever more interesting and ever more amusing in an attempt to get people to look at the advertising. Many of the techniques used however just irritate the potential customers – not a great idea.

There are now several firms that can arrange for advertising messages to appear on private cars. Car owners are paid a small amount for having their cars liveried (which helps with running costs) and they are allowed to choose which companies they are happy to promote. From your viewpoint, the advantage is that the cars are seen – stopped at traffic lights, in supermarket car parks, at the golf club and so on. Ads are applied as a plastic wrap, so they can be changed easily.

If you think this might work for you, remember the following:

- As always, the adverts need to be brief. People may have only seconds to read the message.
- Choose your drivers carefully: a golfer will take your message right to the golf club, a supermarket worker will take your message to the supermarket car park.
- If you can find people who already like your product, these make the best recruits as drivers – it gives them an excuse to talk about your firm.
- Consider paying people in product, if appropriate – cheaper for you, better for them.

Placing the advertisement near the point of sale might involve, for example, using petrol nozzles to promote goods that are available from the petrol station shop. Equally, nozzle advertising was used by Volkswagen to publicise the fuel efficiency of the Volkswagen Golf TDI, thus using a medium close to the problem.

Advertisements printed on eggs cause an impact at breakfast-time, adverts printed on the rising barriers at car parks are guaranteed to make an impact, and art installations in city centres often attract audiences. Ambient media can be classified according to campaign objectives and proximity to the point of sale, as shown in Table 15.9 (Shankar and Horton 1999).

Table 15.9   Classification of ambient media

Objectives of the campaign	High proximity to the point of sale	Low proximity to the point of sale
Strategic: designed to create long-term effects.	Toilet walls (e.g. anti drink–driving campaigns).	Stunt ambient media designed to gain publicity: sky banners, skywriting, art installations, painted aeroplanes, risers on staircases.
Tactical: designed to create an immediate response.	Petrol pump nozzles, toilet walls, in-store floor advertising, supermarket till rolls, credit card vouchers, stair risers, supermarket trolleys.	Ticket advertising, supermarket till rolls, credit card vouchers, betting slips.

Consumers tend to exhibit little pre-purchase decision-making for low-involvement purchases (Foxall and Goldsmith 1994), and some studies have shown that 70% of all decisions to purchase specific brands are made inside the store (POPAI [1994]1997). Trolley advertising makes around 19% difference to the purchase of specific brands (Shankar 1999a), which demonstrates the power of ambient advertising to nudge consumers. Table 15.10 maps ambient advertising against Ehrenberg's ATRN model of advertising effects (the weak theory) (Barnard and Ehrenberg1997; Ehrenberg 1997).

Ambient advertising is difficult to measure. First, the creativity of some campaigns is such that no advance predictions can be made. Second, research into the effects of ambient advertising has been relatively small as yet, so suitable test instruments have not been devised. Third, there is no industry-wide evaluation system: there is no estimating system to find out how many people picked up a particular petrol nozzle and therefore saw the advertisement, for example (Shankar 1999b).

In the future, it seems likely that ambient advertising will grow. Although greater creativity is involved in developing a campaign, the impact is high and the cost is relatively low, especially considering the potential spin-off in terms of news coverage. Ambient advertising fits well within an integrated marketing communications approach because it both supports, and is supported by, other communications tools.

INTERNET ADVERTISING

Internet advertising is distinct from Internet marketing, which also includes on-line purchasing, on-line market research, social media and many other interactive processes. Internet marketing is covered more fully in Chapter 18.

Advertising on the Internet is usually seen as complementing other media, and even now advertisers are still struggling to learn how to use the Internet as an effective

Table 15.10   Mapping of ambient advertising against the ATRN model

Stage	Explanation	Role of ambient advertising
Awareness	Consciousness of a new brand is followed by interest.	Consciousness is developed by a high-impact, innovative campaign, e.g. replacing straps with deodorant bottles.
Trial	Trial purchase of the brand may occur, perhaps with the consumer in a sceptical frame of mind.	Ambient advertising close to the point of sale may be enough to nudge the consumer towards one brand rather than another.
Reinforcement	Satisfactory use of the brand will encourage further purchase, or even establish a habitual propensity to buy the brand.	Ambient advertising has only a reminder role to play at this stage, and may be no more effective than other advertising.
Nudging	Propensity to buy may be enhanced or decreased by the nudging effect of advertising – either the firm's own or that of competitors.	Ambient advertising is thought to be better than other advertising for nudging consumers, since it has a greater proximity both to the problem and the point of purchase.

element in the marketing mix (McLuhan 2000). There is some evidence that people who visit a firm's website are more likely to visit its premises, and that a good website improves brand image (Muller and Chandon 2004).

Internet advertising breaks down into the following elements:

- **Banners**. These are small advertisements placed on host websites. The host website is often a free site, in other words it offers something attractive (such as stock market information) at no cost to the Internet user, but the site is paid for by banner advertisers. A banner advertisement usually carries a hyperlink to take the surfer to the advertiser's website, where more information (and often an order form) will be available.

  Banners Advertising messages on websites.

- **Pop-ups**. A pop-up is an advertisement that automatically appears on screen when the Internet user accesses a site. Pop-ups are widely regarded as a nuisance, and software is available to block pop-ups, but advertisers continue to use them because people do occasionally respond.

  Pop-ups Advertising messages that appear on websites.

- **Presence websites**. Although these are growing rarer, presence websites are sites that do not contain any interactive features. A presence website usually explains what the company does, and directs visitors to a telephone number, e-mail address or 'snail mail' address to find out more. Such sites really do not take advantage of the possibilities of the Internet.

  Presence website A website that is not interactive but directs customers to another medium.

- E-mail advertising. This can take the form of **spam** (unsolicited e-mails about products or services) or can be opt-in newsletters. Spam, like pop-ups, is regarded as one of the less desirable features of the Internet, and in the past spammers have experienced retaliation from disgruntled recipients of spam. Retaliation has taken the form of flaming (sending insulting messages by e-mail), mail-bombing (sending large files such as telephone directories, book manuscripts, or picture files to the spammer) or complaints to the spammer's Internet service provider (ISP). Opt-in newsletters are commonly used by firms with whom the Internet user already has a relationship – for example, a low-cost airline might send out special offers to people who fly with them regularly.

  Spam Unwanted commercial e-mails.

In the UK, spam was made illegal in 2003, but this only applies to UK companies: since most spam originates in the United States, the anti-spam legislation has had little effect. It has been estimated that spam accounts for 87% of all e-mails (Harnet 2009). Spam creates problems for companies because it clogs e-mail systems and wastes the time of employees – very little of it is relevant, but it takes time to delete the files.

Think outside this box!

There seems to be a great deal of interest in the ethics of Internet advertising, especially spam and pop-ups. OK, these forms of advertising are a nuisance to many people – but are they really more of a nuisance than, say, mailings through the letterbox? Or billboards that obscure the view?

The bottom line, surely, is that advertisers would not use these methods if people did not respond – so somebody obviously likes the adverts! After all, they must occasionally have something to offer – so what's the problem?

A particularly pernicious development in Internet advertising has been the use of viral spam programs. Spammers hire virus writers to develop viruses that will propagate spam messages through the address books of infected computers. In late 2004, for example, such a viral spam program was used to promote a database of American medical institutions. Infected computers spread the spam around the world, with some users receiving five to ten copies of the advertisement per day. Clearly such tactics are unethical, and will almost certainly be banned: the difficulty is that the Internet is largely unregulated, messages can originate anywhere in the world and therefore legislation would need to be ratified by virtually every nation on earth if unethical practices are to be stamped out entirely. It may be possible in the future for ISPs to be forced to develop ways of filtering spam from unregulated countries, but in the current state of the art this is extremely difficult, and many ISPs would regard such measures as being counterproductive since the whole point of the Internet is that it offers worldwide access.

CONSUMER RESPONSES TO ADVERTISING

People respond to advertising on both an emotional and a cognitive level. If advertisements are more emotionally based, people tend to remember them better (Williams 2003), but of course this does not necessarily mean that they are more likely to buy as a result. When people pay conscious attention to advertising at all, which may not be often, they will seek to process the information in some way. The more the person already knows about the subject, the less likely he or she is to rely on the advertisement for information, and therefore the less likely he or she is to make a purchase (Wang 2006).

Sometimes people become activists, and complain about advertising on a regular basis. According to research conducted by Volkov et al. (2006), people can be categorised according to their responses to advertising as follows:

1. Advertising aficionados. These people tend to believe that advertising is in general a good thing, providing valuable information, and that it paints a reasonably fair picture and is essential for decision-making.

2. Consumer activists. These people are regular complainers, who complain to suppliers or via the media in an attempt to improve the lot of the consumer. They are campaigners, on a crusade to make things better for everyone. People who counter-argue against an advertisement show increased strengths in their attitudes afterwards (Rucker and Petty 2004), probably because they persuade themselves more than they persuade others.
3. Advertising moral guardians. Moral guardians believe that advertising is creating a materialist society, in which people's baser needs are encouraged and this erodes the values of a decent society.
4. Advertising seekers. These people watch a lot of advertisements on TV, and become expert on their content – for them, the advertisements are a form of entertainment.

The implication of this research is that people always respond in some way to advertising: the responses are not always positive, and do not always result in a sale, but people do process the information and it does have an effect. Even when advertisements have apparently failed to persuade, they often reduce certainty levels (Tormala et al. 2004).

Chapter summary

Advertising is the most visible of marketing activities, and yet often the most misunderstood, even by marketers themselves. Advertising is, at the end of the day, a communications medium, with all that that entails. It can only be judged for its effectiveness in communicating, not in terms of its effects on sales, yet discussions of advertising (and evaluation of it) often centre around real or imaginary increases in sales as a result of the campaigns undertaken.

Advertising is essentially a creative exercise – at the same time, marketers need to consider the effects of the advertising on the population at large, as well as on the target consumers and customers. The many media that are available, and the new media that are emerging on an almost daily basis, place a premium on maintaining that creative thrust.

Key points

- Opinion is divided as to whether advertising is a strong force or a weak force, but it quite clearly is not able to persuade people against their will.
- Advertising fits within the marketing strategy, but also relates to the corporate strategy.
- Print advertising is cheap and durable, but is a passive medium.
- Display advertising should be concise: classified advertising should be detailed.
- People do not necessarily watch television advertisements even when they are in the room.
- Radio offers good geographical targeting.
- Pop music is most effective in advertising when the brand also provides linking value.
- Questions are powerful in communications because they force people to think.
- Billboards are cheap, are good for geographical targeting and can be changed easily.
- Inside transport advertising is often read in its entirety.
- Airships often gain extra coverage because they are newsworthy.
- Ambient advertising works best close to the point of purchase.

Review questions

1. What is the difference between the strong theory of advertising and the weak theory?
2. Why might a company switch from the objective-and-task method of budgeting to the all-you-can-afford method?
3. What is the main drawback of the proportion-of-sales method of budgeting?
4. What type of advertising would you expect a small service business such as a plumber to use?
5. How might television advertisers increase the number of people who actually watch the advertisements?
6. What advantages does radio advertising have over billboards?
7. Why do advertisements often use questions?
8. What are the main differences between inside transport advertising and outside transport advertising?
9. Why does ambient advertising work best when it is close to the problem?
10. Why might a firm use pop-ups, despite the fact that many people now block them?

Case study revisited: John West Foods

John West's advertising needed to be revamped if the company was to be taken seriously in the new century. The company was already under a certain amount of fire for its tuna sourcing – in 2008 Greenpeace named and shamed John West as being the least sustainable tuna fishing company – and clearly this needed to be turned round.

In 2000 the company produced an advertisement that went viral on YouTube. The ad shows a group of bears catching fish in a river, with a voiceover by a David Attenborough sound-alike, apparently explaining the scene in terms of animal behaviour. Suddenly a man dressed as a fisherman runs out and starts fighting one of the bears for its fish: the man wins the fight and runs off with the salmon, leaving the bear bereft. This ad proved so popular on YouTube it has been seen 300 million times, making it the sixth most viewed advert ever on YouTube.

The humorous approach worked well for John West, so CheethamBell JWT were brought in to develop a whole new campaign for the company. The creatives came up with a campaign called 'Story in Every Can'. The adverts featured a weathered old fisherman holding up a can of tuna and explaining exactly how and when it was caught. Viewers were invited to enter the code number from the top of the can into the company's website, where they would be able to see the place and date on which the fish was caught, and even the name of the fishing boat responsible. Each story was humorous – how Lucky Pete wins the lottery, but his ticket blows overboard so now he is just called Pete; how a crewmember's comb-over is trimmed by his disgruntled shipmates; and how two fishermen almost kiss accidentally (as in *Lady and the Tramp*) during a brief power cut on board.

The ads succeeded in part because they were funny, in part because they engaged the audience and encouraged them to buy a can in order to see where the fish had been caught, and in part because they emphasised John West's environmental credentials. Knowing exactly where each can of fish had come from is important for many consumers – responsible and sustainable fishing practices can only be guaranteed with John West, since no other canner has its own fleet.

In the long run, it is possible that catching wild fish will prove to be unsustainable. Fish farming is becoming much more common, and although it brings environmental problems of its own John West will no doubt manage to overcome these as well. Meanwhile, the company's advertising does an excellent job of conveying John West's brand values.

Case study: Bangkok Insurance

Insurance is not the most exciting product in the world to advertise. Most people only buy insurance because they really have to – if they have a loan or a mortgage, or if they are travelling, or if they are key executives in their companies. Probably because most of us prefer not to think about potential disasters, and hope they won't happen to us, most of us keep our money in our pockets when it comes to insurance.

Bangkok Insurance was founded in 1947, shortly after the Japanese were defeated in the Second World War. The Japanese occupation had left Thailand in a poor state economically, and post-war reparations demanded by the Allies (Thailand's position during the war had been ambivalent at best – they had in fact officially been on the Japanese side, but had also had a strong resistance movement which was anti-Japanese) left the country in an even worse state. Bangkok Insurance therefore had something of a struggle to get started, but the company overcame its early difficulties and became well established.

The company is essentially a family business, largely belonging to the Sophonpanich family, despite being listed on the Bangkok Stock Exchange. The company operates on a customer-orientated basis, and achieved ISO 9002 status for all its insurance products in 2002. The company prides itself on its integrity, and on the solidity of its asset base – it has registered capital of 700 million baht (approximately £15 million).

Conveying these values to customers is tricky. Most insurance company advertising is a serious matter – companies emphasising the length of time they have been established, or how willing they are to pay out on claims, or how they can help quickly in a crisis. Almost all tend to be somewhat gloomy, showing how disaster might strike at any time, almost making people paranoid, thinking that a tree might fall through the roof or the car might crash at any moment. Bangkok Insurance decided to take a very different tack.

The company's advertising is humorous, and shows some extremely unlikely sets of circumstances. In one ad, a bank robber is shown brandishing a pistol and firing it in the air to frighten bank staff. The bullet ricochets around the room several times, finally hitting the robber in the foot: he promptly hops out of the bank, screaming. The strap line shows the odds on this actually happening – several million to one against – but the implication is obvious. Another ad shows a car shedding a front wheel, which then bounces off several other vehicles before miraculously re-attaching itself to the car. Again, millions to one against this happening – but of course it just might, so insurance is a good idea.

The ads have proved extremely popular, and have gone viral on YouTube with over a million viewings. The company continues to have a humorous approach to its advertising, even when promoting such products as life insurance and serious illness insurance – it's an unusual approach, but in a culture that lives by the concept of *sanuk* (having fun) the ads have a strong resonance.

Questions

1. Why would humour sell insurance better than an emphasis on settling claims?
2. What brand values is Bangkok Insurance conveying?
3. How has YouTube featured in the company's success?
4. Why do people avoid buying insurance?
5. How might Bangkok Insurance integrate its advertising efforts?

References

Advertising Association (1998) *Advertising Association Yearbook.* Henley on Thames: Advertising Association.

Bakamitsos, George and Siomkos, George J. (2003) Context effects in marketing practice: the case of mood. *Journal of Consumer Behaviour*, 3 (4): 304–14.

Barnard, N. and Ehrenberg, A. (1997) Advertising: strongly persuasive or nudging? *Journal of Advertising Research*, 37 (1): 21–31.

Berney-Reddish, Ilona A. and Areni, Charles S. (2005) Effects of probability markers on advertising claim acceptance. *Journal of Marketing Communications*, 11 (1): 41–54.

Biel, A.L. (1990) Love the ad. Buy the product? *ADMAP*, 299: 21–5.

Biel, A.L. and Bridgewater, C.A. (1990) Attributes of likeable television commercials. *Journal of Advertising Research*, 30 (3): 38–44.

Blythe, Jim (2006) *Essentials of Marketing Communications*, 3rd edn. Harlow: FT Prentice Hall.

Bolls, Paul D., Muehling, Darrel D. and Yoon, Kak (2003) The effects of television commercial pacing on viewers' attention and memory. *Journal of Marketing Communications*, 9 (1): 17–28.

Bounds, W. (1994) Fuji's spirits soar as its blimp is winner of a World Cup contest. *The Wall Street Journal*, 21 June.

Brierley, S. (1995) *The Advertising Handbook*. London: Routledge.

Cova, B. (1997) Community and consumption: towards a definition of the linking value of products and services. *European Journal of Marketing*, 31 (3/4): 297–316.

DeVoe, M. (1956) *Effective Advertising Copy*. New York: Macmillan.

Ehrenberg, A. (1997) How do consumers buy a new brand? *ADMAP*, March.

Ehrenberg, A. (1992) Comments on how advertising works. *Marketing and Research Today*, August: 167–9.

El-Murad, Jaafar and West, Douglas C. (2003) Risk and creativity in advertising. *Journal of Marketing*, 19: 657–73.

Evans, M., O'Malley, L. and Patterson, M. (1996) Direct marketing communications in the UK: a study of growth, past present and future. *Journal of Marketing Communications*, 2 (March): 51–65.

Foxall, G. and Goldsmith, R.E. (1994) *Consumer Psychology for Marketing*. London: Routledge.

Grapentine, Terry (2003) Window shopping. *Marketing Research*, 15 (4): 5.

Guangzhi, Zhao and Pechmann, Connie (2006) Regulatory focus, feature positive effect, and message framing. *Advances in Consumer Research*, 33: 100.

Hansen, Jochim, Strick, Madelijn, van Baaren, Rick B., Hooghuis, Mirjam J. and Wigboldus, Daniel H. (2009) Exploring memory for product names advertised with humour. *Journal of Consumer Behaviour*, 8 (2/3): 135–48.

Harnet, Dermot (2009) Spam and phishing landscape 2009. Symantec. www.symantec.com/connect/blogs/spam-and-phishing-landscape-december-2009 (accessed June 2013).

Jefkins, F. (1994) *Advertising*. London: M&E Handbooks.

Jones J.P. (1991) Over-promise and under-delivery. *Marketing and Research Today*, November: 195–203.

Kneale, D. (1988) Zapping of TV ads appears pervasive. *The Wall Street Journal*, 25 April.

McAlister, Leigh, Srinavasan, Raji and Kim, Minchung (2007) Advertising, research and development, and systematic risk of the firm. *Journal of Marketing*, 71 (1): 35–48.

McKechnie, S. and Leather, P. (1998) Likeability as a measure of advertising effectiveness: the case of financial services. *Journal of Marketing Communications*, 4: 63–85.

McLuhan, R. (2000) A lesson in on-line brand promotion. *Marketing*, 23 March, pp. 31–32.

Muller, Brigitte and Chandon, Jean-Louis (2004) The impact of World Wide Web site visits on brand image in the motor vehicle and mobile telephone industries. *Journal of Marketing Communications*, 10 (2): 153–65.

Myers, G. (1994) *Words in Ads*. London: Edward Arnold.

Pieters, R. and Wedel, M. (2004) Attention capture and transfer in advertising: brand, pictorial and text size effects. *Journal of Marketing*, 68 (2): 36–50.

POPAI ([1994]1997) Point of purchase consumer buying habits study. In T.A. Shimp (ed.), *Advertising, Promotion and Supplemental Aspects of Integrated Marketing Communications*, 4th edn. Fort Worth, TX: Dryden Press.

Ritson, M. (2003) *Assessing the Value of Advertising*. London: London Business School.

Ritson, M. and Elliott, R. (1995) A model of advertising literacy: the praxology and co-creation of meaning. *Proceedings of the European Marketing Association Conference*. Paris: ESSEC.

Rucker, Derek D. and Petty, Richard E. (2004) When counter arguing fails: effects on attitude strength. *Advances in Consumer Research*, 31: 87.

Shankar, A. (1998) Adding value to the ads? On the increasing use of pop music in advertising. *Proceedings of the Academy of Marketing Conference*, Sheffield.

Shankar, A. (1999a) Ambient media: advertising's new opportunity? *International Journal of Advertising*, 18 (3): 305–22.

Shankar, A. (1999b) Advertising's imbroglio. *Journal of Marketing Communications*, 5 (1): 1–17.

Shankar, A. and Horton, B. (1999) Ambient media: advertising's new media opportunity. *International Journal of Advertising*, 18 (3): 305–22.

Smith, Karen H. and Stutts, Mary Ann (2003) Effects of short-term cosmetic versus long-term health fear appeals in anti-smoking advertisements on the smoking behaviour of adolescents. *Journal of Consumer Behaviour*, 3 (2): 155–77.

Stapel, J. (1991) Like the advertisement, but does it interest me? *ADMAP*, April.

Steenhuysen, J. (1994) Adland's new billion-dollar baby. *Advertising Age*, 11 April.

Tormala, Zakary L., Brinol, Pablo and Petty, Richard E. (2004) Hidden effects of persuasion. *Advances in Consumer Research*, 31 (1): 81.

UK Film Council (2010) *Statistical Yearbook*. London: UKFC. http://industry.bfi.org.uk/statsyb2010.

Volkov, Michael, Harker, Michael and Harker, Debra (2006) People who complain about advertising: the aficionados, guardians, activists and seekers. *Journal of Marketing Management*, 22: 379–405.

World Association of Newspapers (2013) *World Press Trends*. Darmstadt: WAN.

Wang, Shih-Lung Alex (2006) The effects of audience knowledge on message processing of editorial content. *Journal of Marketing Communications*, 12 (4): 281–96.

Wells, W.D. (1980) Liking and sales effectiveness: a hypothesis. *Topline*, 2 (1).

Williams, Patti (2003) The impact of emotional advertising appeals on consumer implicit and explicit memory: an accessibility/diagnosticity perspective. *Advances in Consumer Research*, 30 (1): 88.

Wright, L.T. and Crimp, M. (2000) *The Marketing Research Process*. London: Prentice Hall.

Zufryden, F.S., Pedrick, J.H. and Sankaralingam, A. (1993) Zapping and its impact on brand purchase behaviour. *Journal of Advertising Research*, 33: 58–66.

More online

To gain free access to additional online resources to support this chapter please visit:
www.sagepub.co.uk/blythe3e

CHAPTER (16)
Public relations and sponsorship

LEARNING OBJECTIVES

After reading this chapter, you should be able to:

- Explain the difference between PR and spin-doctoring.

- Explain how corporate reputation affects stock market valuations.

- Demonstrate the internal role of public relations.

- Describe how to organise a crisis team.

- Explain the role of outside agencies in public relations.

- Explain the relationship between sponsorship and advertising.

Introduction

Public relations is about making the world feel good about the organisation and its products. This is partly about establishing a corporate reputation, and partly about establishing the firm's activities in a positive way in people's minds. Changing people's attitudes about the company can be a long-drawn-out process (see Chapter 3), but well-managed public relations lead to very real benefits to the firm. PR should not be confused with spin-doctoring: spin-doctoring is about covering up bad news, and twisting the truth in a crisis. PR is about ensuring that the company does the right things at the right times, and ensures that its publics know what it is doing.

Sometimes PR is seen as being solely the responsibility of the public relations department, but in fact everyone in the firm has a role in public relations: many of the firm's employees have direct contact with people outside the organisation during their working day, but in any case everybody goes home, and talks to friends and family about the company's activities.

Corporate reputation management goes a step beyond PR in that it involves a web of interactions between members of the corporation's publics as well as simply dealing with outbound communication from the firm itself.

Preview case Study: Chapter Arts Centre

Arts centres have been established in all sorts of places in the UK, and many have disappeared without trace or have only survived through heavy subsidies from local councils or government bodies. Many have acquired a reputation for being too rarified – only hosting arts events that are so far out of the mainstream that no one else will give them space – and many have become fringe venues, only held together through the commitment and vision of a few dedicated artists.

Chapter is something of an exception. Founded in 1971 in a disused school in Cardiff, it has always aimed to host an eclectic mix of arts events. Located to the west of the city centre, in a mainly working-class residential area, Chapter was also within easy reach of the BBC and HTV television studios and therefore had a certain number of 'media' people living within close proximity. The building is also close to a major secondary shopping area, so there are plenty of people passing close by.

From the outset, Chapter sought to avoid catering solely to the weird and wonderful. The Centre hosted local bands playing everything from Bach to Willy Nelson (many bands got their start at Chapter), and in amongst the foreign 'art' films the Chapter cinema shows mainstream movies (during 2013 Chapter screened *Les Misérables*, *Lincoln* and *Django Unchained* as well as movies made by the inmates of a maximum security jail in Italy, and a Japanese film about two brothers who make a wish as two bullet trains pass). Chapter is innovative in its approach: each Friday morning the cinema hosts a session for mothers and babies. Called 'Carry On Screaming', the session provides an opportunity for mothers to see a movie without worrying about the baby disturbing anyone else – admission without a baby is not permitted.

Chapter has a bar and a restaurant, and despite being one of the more expensive places to go for a drink locally the bar is always busy – no small feat in a period when pubs are closing down at the rate of several per day in Britain. The reason is that there is always something to see at Chapter – much of what happens is free (music in the bar, the art gallery, occasional performances) and also the Centre operates as a meeting place for the arts community. There are meeting rooms that can be booked, and also anyone who is involved in the arts is likely to bump into a friend or colleague at pretty much any time. In addition, Chapter hosts special events: in March 2013 the Centre hosted the Perrantide Festival, a special week of Cornish-inspired activities – the bar served Cornish beers and the restaurant served authentic pasties, while the Centre featured Cornish artworks and music.

Chapter is undoubtedly one of the most dynamic and successful arts centres in Europe, and is a real asset to Cardiff, but not everybody is delighted with it. Like any organisation, Chapter has its public relations problems.

PR and external communication

Public relations or PR is the management of corporate image through the management of relationships with the organisation's publics. Roger Hayward (1998) offered an alternative definition, as follows:

> *Those efforts used by management to identify and close any gap between how the organisation is seen by its key publics and how it would like to be seen.*

PR has more than just a role in defending the company from attack and publicising its successes. It has a key role in relationship marketing, since it is concerned with building a long-term image rather than gaining a quick sale. There is a strategic

Figure 16.1   Publicity, PR and press relations

relationship between publicity, PR and press relations. PR occupies the overall strategic role in the relationship.

Many firms use PR solely for crisis management, seeing it either as a tool for complaint handling (usually by employing somebody with a nice smile and a friendly voice to handle complaints), or as a tactical tool, whereby the firm formulates a plan for handling problems only after things have gone wrong. This is a fire-fighting or reactive approach to public relations, and is generally regarded as being far less effective than a proactive approach, which seeks to avoid problems arising.

PR managers have the task of co-ordinating all those activities that make up the public face of the organisation, and will have some or all of the following tasks to handle:

- Organising press conferences.
- Running staff training workshops.
- Organising social events.
- Handling incoming complaints or criticism.
- Grooming senior management for TV or press interviews.
- Moulding the internal culture of the organisation.

PR people talk about 'publics' rather than 'the public'. This is because they are dealing with a wide range of people, all with differing needs and preconceptions. The following publics might be part of the PR manager's remit:

1. Customers.
2. Suppliers.
3. Staff.
4. Government and government departments.
5. Local government.
6. Neighbours.
7. Local residents.
8. The general public.
9. Pressure groups such as environmentalists or trade unions.
10. Other industry members.

In each case the approach will be different, and the expected outcomes will also be different. The basic routes by which PR operates are word-of-mouth, press and TV news stories, and personal recommendation. The aim of good PR is to put the name of the firm and its products into people's minds in a positive way.

PR is not advertising, because it is not directly paid for. Advertising can also be both informative and persuasive, but PR can only be used for conveying information or for placing the company before the public eye in a positive way. PR does not generate business directly, but achieves the company's long-term objectives by creating positive feelings. The ideal outcome is to give the world the impression that this is 'a good firm to do business with'. In some cases this will result in more sales, in other cases it might result in reduced costs (for example less absenteeism, less time wasted dealing with complaints, and less money spent compensating disgruntled customers).

PR and marketing do not always fit together well: there is often a lack of fit between the information processing requirements of marketers and those of PR professionals (Cornelissen and Harris 2004).

Creating and managing a reputation

Corporate reputation The overall image of the organisation.

Corporate reputation has been defined as the aggregate perceptions of outsiders about the salient characteristics of firms (Fombrun and Rindova 2000). In other words, an organisation's reputation is composed of the overall view that people have about the organisation. Reputation is important for two reasons: first, it has a direct effect on the bottom line because organisations with good reputations are more likely to attract customers, and second, a good reputation acts as a buffer should a crisis occur.

A favourable reputation is a resource that increases performance (Deephouse 1997). One of the main advantages of a favourable reputation is that it cannot be copied by other organisations, so it becomes a differentiator for the firm (Roberts and Dowling 1997).

Of course, reputation is more than simply good or bad. In some cases the organisation's reputation will be good in some respects and bad in others, or it may be that the organisation has a reputation for a particular type of behaviour that is perceived as good by some people and bad by others. For the manager, therefore, the problem is not so much one of creating a good reputation rather than a bad one. It is rather a problem of creating the right reputation so that the organisation's publics are clear about what to expect. Attempts to create the wrong reputation (good or bad) will result in frustrated expectations.

Think outside this box!

For most individuals, reputation is something that just happens. We acquire a reputation for telling funny stories, or being tight with money, or being good to talk over problems with, without actually trying all that hard or being self-conscious about it. In fact, the worst reputation someone can have is one of being manipulative and self-obsessed – in other words, trying to create a particular reputation is frowned upon by most people.

So why should companies be any different? Why would we be prepared to trust a firm that is apparently out to establish a reputation for being trustworthy? Surely the words 'Just trust me' are the surest way to make anyone suspicious!

Managing reputation is more than just an exercise in **spin-doctoring**. Spin-doctoring is a process of putting a good face on unacceptable facts, whereas managing reputation is a process of ensuring that the facts themselves are acceptable. It is about ensuring that everyone's experience of the organisation is in keeping with the reputation the organisation has or hopes to build. This means that everyone within the organisation has a role to play: each member of staff has the power to work well or badly, each shareholder has the power to affect the share price, each customer has the power to buy or not to buy. More importantly, each stakeholder has the power to make or break the organisation's reputation simply by saying or doing the right things, or the wrong things, when dealing with those outside the organisation.

Spin-doctoring Attempts to cover up bad news by slanting it in a way that puts the organisation in a favourable light.

Corporate communications officers have responsibility for **boundary scanning**. This means that they should be aware of what is happening at the boundaries between the organisation and its stakeholders, and need also to be aware of what can be done to improve interactions at the boundaries. This is similar to the role of marketers: marketers are responsible for what is done at the boundaries, communications officers are responsible for what is said.

Boundary scanning The practice of monitoring the interfaces between the firm and its public.

The sources of knowledge that influence reputation are:

1. Direct experience of dealing with the organisation.
2. Hearsay evidence from friends, colleagues and acquaintances.
3. Third-party public sources such as newspaper articles, TV documentaries and published research.
4. Organisation-generated information such as brochures, annual reports and advertising.

The degree to which the corporate communications officer has influence over these sources is in inverse proportion to the influence on attitude. This is illustrated in Figure 16.2. A corporate communications officer has the role of seeking to influence communications about the company, whatever the source of those communications might be: this moves the role away from one of simply managing outgoing communications from the company, and towards one of seeking to create an atmosphere in which even word-of-mouth between people unconnected with the firm still conveys the desired image.

Reputation affects decision-making on the part of all stakeholders, so the reputation of an organisation is both created and consumed by its members. In other words, someone who is a customer or an employee of the firm has that role in part because of the corporate reputation, and in turn adds to the reputation by telling others about the firm and its products. There is an element of positive feedback involved – a particular reputation will attract people who feel positive about the organisation and will repel those who feel negative about it. Once inside the organisation, people will act in ways that reflect the reputation. For example, a company with a reputation for treating its staff well will attract managers who like to work in that type of managerial paradigm: these are likely to be managers who, in turn, try to treat their staff well. Figure 16.3 shows how these elements relate.

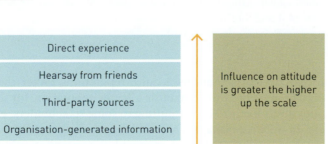

Figure 16.2 Hierarchy of information sources

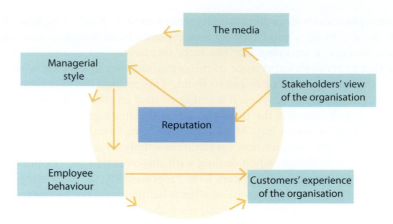

Figure 16.3   Creating a reputation

One of the problems with reputation management is that different reputations may be attractive to different stakeholders. Stakeholders are people or groups of people who are affected directly or indirectly by a firm's activities and decisions (Post et al. 2002). An employee may be attracted by an organisation's reputation for paying its staff generously, but this same attribute might repel a shareholder. Like-wise, customers might be attracted to a firm with a reputation for keeping its prices, staff costs and profits at rock-bottom, but this would hardly attract either staff or shareholders. Ultimately it is not possible to please everybody, so managers need to identify who are the key players, and should seek to establish a good reputation with those people.

Marketing in a changing world: Green credentials

Corporate reputation depends increasingly on having appropriate environmental credibility. Firms that pollute, firms that use up scarce resources, firms that cause environmental damage all risk being attacked not just by environmental activists but by almost everybody.

The problem for some firms is that it just isn't possible to do what they do without causing some damage. Mining companies, steel producers, aluminium smelters and airlines all cause environmental damage but point out that people still want to buy copper kettles, steel cars, aluminium drinks cans and holidays in the sun. No matter how hard those companies try not to cause damage, damage will occur.

The PR problem therefore becomes one of putting the best possible face on what is, in fact, an unacceptably ugly situation. This in itself causes ethical problems of its own – should the PR people spin the bad news, or should they be upfront about it and thus bring down the wrath of the population on themselves?

In practice, organisations acquire reputations rather than develop them. While it may be possible to re-establish a better reputation (or at least a more appropriate one) this is likely to be off-putting to some stakeholders, even if it is attractive to others. In practice managers are unlikely to create a reputation from scratch – they are much more likely to be tinkering with the organisation's existing reputation to make it more attractive to some people, or to make it more explicit to the stakeholders.

Maintaining a strong reputation pays direct dividends for the enterprise. Research shows that investors are prepared to pay higher prices for the shares of companies with good reputations, even when risks and returns are comparable with other firms in the same industry. Cordeiro and Sambharaya (1997) showed earnings forecasts made by financial analysts were heavily influenced by the non-financial component of the corporate reputation. Surveys of MBA students show that they are attracted to companies with good reputations, which means that companies that are larger and more visible are apparently better to work for. Part of this attraction is the reflected glory of working for a high-profile company, and part of it is about a perception that working for a major company is likely to be more secure and better rewarded.

The reputation of the organisation is important to all stakeholders, but there may be conflicts between the groups: this means that the board of directors often finds itself in the position of being a clearing house for pressures from different stakeholder groups. Even when stakeholders are in broad agreement as to where the company should be heading there will be differing opinions on how to get there.

For companies, there is a problem in meeting the differing needs of different market segments while still maintaining a consistent corporate reputation. For example, a major supermarket needs to meet the needs of many different income groups. This means that most major supermarket chains offer a budget range of products as well as the mainstream branded goods, but the quality of the budget range still needs to be of a reasonably good standard to avoid damaging the corporate reputation.

Real-life marketing: Building a corporate brand

Companies have brands on their products pretty much as a matter of course, to distinguish their offerings from those of their competitors. Larger companies often take this a stage further, by creating a corporate brand that expresses the overall status of the company, in other words its corporate personality.

The corporate brand often comes under the category of 'nice things we would like to have if only we could afford it', yet it is also one of the main things by which stakeholders judge you.

When Eddie Stobart took over the haulage part of his family's agricultural supplies business, he decided to make an impact. He was competing against hundreds of other hauliers, all offering the same basic business, so he began by giving all his lorries women's names (the first were named after female entertainers from the 1970s such as Dolly Parton and Susie Quatro). His drivers were told to dress smartly and be courteous to other road users, and to take a pride in their vehicles. From a customer viewpoint, taking a delivery from a Stobart driver makes a refreshing change from the 'service' given by some of the scruffy hooligans who turn up at the warehouse demanding a signature.

Eddie Stobart is now the best-known haulier in Britain, and even has a fan club and collectable models. If you want to aspire to Stobart's league, you will need to do the following:

- Be prepared to spend money on building your corporate image.
- Find something different to say about yourself – something the others aren't offering.
- Be passionate about your brand. If you don't feel passionate about it, why would anybody else?

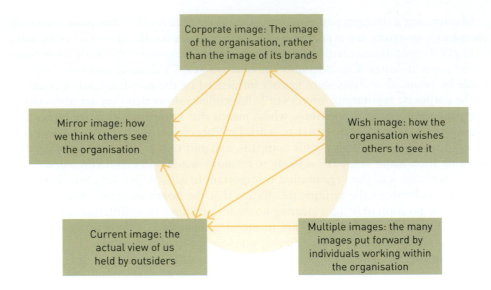

Figure 16.4   Types of image

Image The overall
impression a company or
brand has in the eyes of its
publics.

Image is the affective component of attitude towards the organisation. It is the gut feeling or overall impression that the organisation's name and brands generate in the minds of the organisation's publics. The overall image created is not necessarily the one that managers intended.

Corporate image is the image of the organisation, as opposed to the image of its products and services. Corporate image is composed of organisational history, financial stability, reputation as an employer, history of corporate citizenship and so forth. It is possible to have a good corporate image and a poor reputation for products and vice versa. For example, IBM has an exemplary corporate image although its products are not greatly different from those available elsewhere, whereas Rolls–Royce has an outstanding image for its products despite a somewhat chequered corporate history involving several bankruptcies and re-launches.

A multiple image occurs when separate branches of the business or even individuals within the business create their own image within that of the overall corporation. An obvious example is that of sales representatives, each of whom has a personal image and reputation with customers which may or may not accord with the overall corporate image. Organisations such as IBM try to overcome this by using very strict selection criteria when employing salespeople: at one time, IBM salespeople wore a company uniform of blue blazers and grey trousers, but this was discontinued after a 'revolution' by French IBM salespeople, who simply refused to wear the uniform. Even now, IBMers tend to have a similar appearance, conforming to the strong corporate culture.

Think outside this box!

Creating a standard corporate image is obviously desirable. Yet for most purchasing firms, the only real contact they have with the supplier is through the sales representatives – who are all individuals.

We are told that the strength of the sales function is the ability to provide a personalised, individual service. But if we insist on hiring a group of clones, how are we to individualise what we do? And even if the salespeople are very similar, the simple fact of tailoring the company's service to each customer is bound to lead to variations in the image.

So is it really possible *ever* to generate a consistent corporate image? Or are we left with the unpalatable truth that we cannot force our employees into neat little moulds?

Corporate image and added value

Corporate image is not a luxury. The image of a corporation translates into hard added value for shareholders. This is partly because of the effect that image has on the corporation's customers, but is also a function of the effects it has on staff, and is very much a result of the influence the image has on shareholders. High-profile companies are more attractive to shareholders, even if the firm's actual performance in terms of profits and dividends is no better than average. Since the central task of management is to maximise shareholder value, image must be central to management thinking and action.

Maximising shareholder value is not the same as maximising profits. Profit maximisation tends to be short-term, a matter of cutting costs, reducing investment, downsizing, increasing sales volumes at the expense of long-term customer loyalty, and so forth. Adding value to the shareholders' assets is about creating a secure, growing, long-term investment. Since the dot.com bubble burst investors have become painfully aware that investments in firms with spectacular profits but little underlying solidity are a quick way to lose money. City analysts look more and more towards using measures such as customer loyalty, brand awareness and investment levels in judging the long-term prospects for firms.

The counterargument for this is that the shifting global marketplace has reduced survival prospects for companies. The life expectancy of a firm is now less than twenty years (De Geus 1997). Maintaining a profitable competitive advantage is also problematical. If a firm finds a profitable market niche, competitors respond rapidly and profits fall to the point where it is almost impossible to maintain an adequate return on the original capital investment (Black et al. 1998).

The value that accrues from image management has always been accounted for under the heading of 'goodwill' on the firm's balance sheet. The goodwill element of the firm's value is the difference between the value of the firm's tangible assets and its value on the stock market. For some firms, the value of goodwill is actually the bulk of the firm's overall value. For example, Coca-Cola's goodwill value is more than

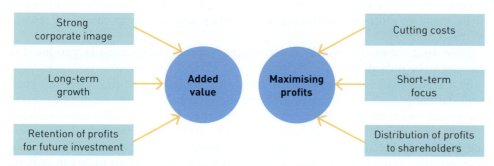

Figure 16.5 Comparison between adding value and maximising profits

80% of the firm's total value. Much of this goodwill value comes from the Coca-Cola brand itself. This approach to valuing the firm's reputation and image is now regarded as being somewhat crude, and new measures are being developed to take account of brand value, customer loyalty values and so forth to move away from the reliance on financial measures when assessing firms' successes.

Think outside this box!

Boards of directors often use the stock market valuation of the company's shares as a barometer of the company's success. Yet this is rarely reflected in the corporation's mission statement. Most of these talk about caring for staff and customers.

Does this mean that the mission statement is not strictly true? Or does it mean that staff and customers are mere instruments in attaining the goal of share value? And if a higher share value is independent of profit, does that mean that the wool is being pulled over shareholders' eyes? In short, are most boards of directors behaving in some Machiavellian way in order to shore up their own positions?

Or are they perhaps merely trying to balance the needs of a wide group of people?

TOOLS OF PUBLIC RELATIONS

Press releases News stories about the organisation.

Sponsorship Payment to a cause or event in exchange for publicity.

PR people use a number of different ways to achieve their aims. The list in Table 16.1 is by no means comprehensive, but does cover the main tools available to PR managers. Of these, the **press release** and **sponsorship** are probably the most important.

A press release is a favourable news story about the organisation, which originates from within the organisation itself. Newspapers and the trade press earn their money mainly through paid advertising, but they attract readers by having stimulating articles about topics of interest to the readership. Editors need to fill space, and are quite happy to use a press release to do so if the story is newsworthy and interesting to the readership. In a business-to-business context, the trade press relies heavily on press releases, since industry news would be difficult to collect in any other way, but even the popular press relies on individuals and companies to alert them to news stories. This is the essence of the press release.

The advantages of using press releases are that they are much more credible than an advertisement, they are much more likely to be read and the space within the publication is free. There are, of course, costs attached to producing press releases – someone has to be paid to write the story, and often some effort needs to be made to cultivate journalists so that they are alerted to the press release before it arrives.

Table 16.2 shows the criteria under which the press stories must be produced if they are to be published.

Increasing scepticism and resistance to advertising has meant that there has been a substantial growth in the use of press releases and publicity in recent years. Press stories are much more credible, and although they do not usually generate business directly, they do have a positive long-term effect in building brand awareness and loyalty. It should be said that advertising alone also does not usually generate business immediately: as outlined in Chapter 15, communications tools can only be judged by communications outcomes, not by marketing outcomes.

Table 16.1 Tools of PR

Tool	Description and examples
Press releases	A press release is a news story about the organisation, usually designed to put the firm in a good light but often intended just to keep the organisation in the public eye. For example, a community arts group might write to the local newspapers to tell them about a forthcoming performance or event. The newspaper might run this on its 'what's on' page, or might use it as a human-interest story about how community arts organisations benefit the community.
Sponsorship	Sponsorship of events, individuals or organisations is useful for creating favourable publicity. For example, many firms sponsor sporting events, putting the company name in the public eye.
Publicity stunts	Sometimes firms will stage an event specifically for the purpose of creating a news story, for example a publisher might arrange a book-signing session involving a famous author. Such events are often reported in local news media: if the author is famous enough the story might even make the national news. This is less common in business-to-business markets, since mass-media publicity is of less value.
Word-of-mouth	Generating favourable word-of-mouth is an important aim of PR. For example, a firm might book out seats at a sporting event such as the Wimbledon Tennis Championships in order to invite good clients. The clients are almost certain to talk to colleagues and friends about their day out, and will certainly recall the name of the company that provided them with the seat.
Corporate advertising	Corporate advertising is aimed at improving the corporate image, rather than selling products. Such advertising is very common in the trade press, but occasionally appears in the mass media. British Airways have successfully used television to promote the company's image, aiming specifically at business-class sales: this is a rare example of using mass-media advertising in a business-to-business market.
Lobbying	Lobbying is the process of making representations to members of Parliament, congressmen, or other politicians. For example, the tobacco industry has lobbied against plain packaging for cigarettes, and has been successful in the UK: their argument was that plain packaging would make life too easy for counterfeiters, thus causing a loss of revenue for the Government.
Product placement	Products can be introduced into TV shows and movies, usually in exchange for paying a fee to the film producers. In some cases, the product can be written into the script.

Table 16.2 Criteria for successful press releases

Criterion	Example
Stories must be newsworthy, i.e. of interest to the reader.	Articles about your new lower prices are not newsworthy; articles about opening a new factory creating 200 jobs are.
Stories must not be merely thinly disguised advertisements.	A story saying that your new processing equipment is a bargain at only £23,000 is not news. A story saying that you have concluded a partnership agreement with a machine tool manufacture in Poland probably is, at least in the trade press. A story that you are financing a new training initiative for underprivileged teenagers is probably news in the national press.
Stories must fit the editorial style of the magazine or paper to which they are being sent.	An article sent to *Cosmopolitan* about your new machine tools would not be published. An article about your new female marketing director probably would.

Real-life marketing: know your journalist

Journalists frequently complain about getting poorly written and poorly targeted press releases. If a journalist gets a press release that has obviously been sent out indiscriminately to everybody on the mailing list, he or she is unlikely to respond favourably – it's the PR equivalent of junk mail, really.

If you can, get hold of copies of the journalist's last five stories, read them through carefully and make some notes. This won't take long, but it will give you an idea of what your journalist is interested in, and also gives you the opportunity to open a conversation. All of us like it when someone notices something we have done, so calling up the journalist to say how much you enjoyed a specific article will go down well. You will be in a much better position to create something that will fit in with what your journalist (and the readers) will enjoy and find interesting.

To do this in practice, you will need to:

- Put some time and effort into researching your journalist.
- Get your facts straight before calling the person – know how to pronounce the journalist's name, and find out what they have written and when, and if possible where they worked previously. Social sites such as LinkedIn often have this kind of information.
- Once you have opened a dialogue, discuss what kind of press releases the journalist would like. This will avoid you sending something unsuitable – which is irritating and pointless.

Editors do not have to publish press releases exactly as they are received. They reserve the right to alter stories, add to them, comment on them or otherwise change them around to suit their own purposes. Editors will frequently cut stories in order to fill a specific space in the newspaper, so journalists are taught to write in an 'inverted pyramid' style, so that stories can be cut from the bottom. Figure 16.2 shows an example of this, using a story about a company's new initiative to help homeless people.

The story in Figure 16.6 could be cut at any point, starting from the bottom up, without losing the sense of a complete story. Each paragraph adds something else, but does not have to be there for the story to make sense: the reader would not be left with a feeling of needing more if the story were cut after the second or third paragraph, or even after the first paragraph. Obviously the company would prefer it if the story appeared in its entirety, but this will not always happen: editors need to make the stories fit the page.

Editors will occasionally change a story, or incorporate the press release into a story about something else, and of course stories are often simply scrapped if something more newsworthy comes in. There is nothing substantial that company press officers can do about this. Cultivating a good relationship with the media is therefore an important part of the press officer's job.

Sometimes this will involve business entertaining, but more often the press officer will simply try to see to it that the job of the press is made as easy as possible. This means supplying accurate and complete information, it means writing press releases so that they require a minimum of editing and rewriting, and it means making the appropriate corporate spokesperson available when required.

When business entertaining is appropriate, it will often come as part of a media event or press conference. This may be called to launch a new product, or to announce

Bellingham Industries offers new hope to the homeless	Headline: contains the main feature of the story
Bellingham Industries Ltd. today announced a new work-for-housing initiative which will enable homeless people to get off the streets. The company is offering training and housing for homeless people, in an effort to break the cycle of deprivation which keeps people on the streets.	First paragraph contains the essence of the story. The story could be cut at this point, and it would still make sense and give the reader the gist of what has happened.
The scheme will work by giving homeless people on-the-job training, and accommodation at Bellingham's own hostel, which is situated near the factory. Bellingham, which manufactures electrical appliances, will initially employ twelve people under the scheme, but hope to expand the scheme in future.	Second paragraph provides more detail of how the scheme works, but could still be cut at this point without any sense of loss.
James Whittle, Bellingham's personnel director, said, 'The tragedy of homelessness is that many of these people are unable to find work because they have no fixed address, and of course they cannot rent or buy a home because they have no jobs. We are delighted to be able to offer a way out of the cycle, at least for some homeless people.'	Third paragraph gives the company's viewpoint, and further raises the corporate reputation. It also explains the rationale behind the scheme.
Once established in the hostel, the new employees will be able to seek work and housing elsewhere, though it is anticipated that most of them will be in the scheme for at least a year.	Final paragraph gives more detail, and the prognosis for the future of the scheme.

Figure 16.6   Press release example

some major corporate development such as a merger or takeover or (less often) when there has been a corporate crisis. This will involve inviting journalists from the appropriate media, providing refreshments and supplying corporate spokespeople to answer questions and make statements. This kind of event only has a limited success, however, unless the groundwork for it has been very thoroughly laid: journalists are often suspicious of media events, sometimes feeling that the organisers are trying to buy them off with a buffet and a glass of wine. This means they may not respond positively to the message the PR people are trying to convey, and may write a critical article rather than the positive one that was hoped for.

To minimise the chance of this happening, media events should follow these basic rules:

1. Avoid calling a media event or press conference unless you are announcing something that the press will find interesting.
2. Check that there are no negative connotations in what you are announcing.
3. Ensure that you have some of the company's senior executives there to talk to the press, not just the PR people.
4. Invite only those journalists with whom you feel you have a good working relationship.
5. Avoid being too lavish with the refreshments.
6. Ensure that your senior executives, in fact anybody who is going to speak to the press, have had some training in doing this. This is particularly important for TV.
7. Be prepared to answer all questions truthfully. Journalists are trained to spot lies and evasions.
8. Take account of the fact that newspapers (and indeed broadcast media) have deadlines to adhere to. Call the conference at a time that will allow reporters enough time to file their stories.

It is always better from the press viewpoint to speak to the most senior managers available rather than to the PR people. Having said that, the senior managers will need some training in handling the press and answering questions, and also need to be fully briefed on anything the press might want to ask. In the case of a press conference called as a result of a crisis this can be a problem: there is more on crisis management later in the chapter. Press officers should be prepared to handle queries from journalists promptly, honestly and enthusiastically, and arrange interviews with senior personnel if necessary.

WORD OF MOUTH

Word of mouth is probably the most powerful PR tool available, but it is also the hardest to control. People often discuss products and services; most people like to pass on good advice about products they have bought (or avoided buying), and recent purchases are a common topic of conversation between friends.

The reasons for the effectiveness of word of mouth are as follows:

- It is interactive, because two or more parties discuss the product or the company. This forces both parties to think about the product or company and its features and benefits – which in turn helps to fix the brand in the individuals' memories. For marketers, the problem here lies with the fact that neither of the individuals concerned is under the control of the company.
- As a communication, word of mouth allows for confirmation of messages through feedback.
- A message from a friend or relative carries a great deal more credibility than a message from a corporation – after all, people know full well that the company is trying to sell its products.

People who switch brands as a result of a recommendation from a friend or family member are much more likely to stay loyal to the brand than are people who switch as a result of marketing activities (Wangenheim and Bayón 2003). People who switch brands are also much more likely to be big users of word of mouth, both in terms of relying on it when making decisions and in passing good advice along to others.

Positive word of mouth can be generated (or at least encouraged) by using press releases, but a more proactive way is to use 'bring a friend' schemes. This is often seen as a sales promotion device (see Chapter 17) but it also generates word of mouth if the scheme is handled well. It is usually better to offer a benefit to the 'friend' rather than to the existing customer – people often feel guilty at recommending something to a friend in exchange for a reward. Awards and certificates often form the basis for word of mouth: someone receiving a loyalty gift is likely to talk about it, particularly if it is conspicuous (for example a clock or a barometer). Promotional clothing can sometimes generate word of mouth: T-shirts or fleeces with logos on can provoke comment.

The richness of the message and the strength of its advocacy (i.e. the enthusiasm of the person talking about the brand) are the key factors in successful word of mouth (Mazzarol et al. 2007). In some cases word of mouth can be powerful even before the product has been tried out, provided the product is innovative enough: for example, when a blockbuster movie is about to be released, word of mouth is strongest before release, i.e. before anyone has seen the movie (Liu 2006).

PRODUCT PLACEMENT

Arranging to have a brand featured in a movie or TV show has a strong impact on people's impressions of the product. In some cases the product placement is subtle (for example most American movies are likely to feature Coca-Cola at some point, even if only as a background advertisement or a shot of a Coca-Cola vending machine) or the placement is more overt, as in the case of the Mini Coopers used in the remake of *The Italian Job*.

Because the products appear quite naturally, cinema audiences tend not to filter out the message: when the film's hero orders a Jim Beam on the rocks, the brand becomes associated with the hero without any overt effort. The same is true of James Bond's Aston Martin, which was replaced by a BMW in *Tomorrow Never Dies*, reputedly because Aston Martin could not afford the placement fee (Oakes 1997). From the viewpoint of a film producer, product placement and merchandise spin-offs can easily cover the entire cost of making the movie – films such as *Toy Story* and *Godzilla* could have been complete flops at the box office, and still made money simply on the placement and merchandise deals.

A major advantage of product placement from the marketer's viewpoint is the longevity of films. The film may be shown all over the world, then released on DVD, then be shown on TV perhaps for many years to come. Some products might not be permitted in TV advertising (cigarettes are an obvious example) but can appear in films that are screened on TV. Likewise, some TV stations such as the BBC are not allowed to carry advertising, but a product placed in a film will appear.

If products can be placed in TV soap operas, this also has a powerful effect, because soaps have a parasocial function for many people: in other words, they replace the real social life that such people lack (Russell and Stern 2006). This means that featured products have a greater importance, almost as great as they would have if they were used by friends.

The evidence is that people remember 'placed' products better than they do advertised products, but in some cases there can be a backlash because sometimes people feel that product placement is equivalent to manipulation. This in turn leads to mistrust of the brand (Bhatnagar and Aksoy 2004).

The most extreme example of placement is when the brand becomes an intrinsic part of the plot line. This is called branded entertainment, and was commonplace in the United States in the 1940s and 1950s. TV shows commonly plugged the sponsors' products, often in such a blatant way as to cause people to become confused about the actual storyline. To some extent branded entertainment still exists (although shows such as *The Kraft Theatre* no longer exist) in the form of films where a specific brand is the mainstay of the film. The popular *Herbie* films of the 1970s are an example, where the hero of the story is a Volkswagen car. More recently *The Italian Job* (2003) featured Mini Coopers as the stars. There may be moral and ethical issues attached to this extreme form of placement, however (Hudson and Hudson 2006).

Sponsorship

Sponsorship has been defined as 'An investment, in cash or kind, in an activity in return for access to the exploitable commercial potential associated with this activity' (Meenaghan 1991). Sponsorship of the arts or sporting events is an increasingly popular way of generating positive feelings about firms.

Sponsorship in the UK grew a hundredfold between 1970 and 1993, from £4m to £400m. It has continued to grow ever since, with estimates for 2009 ranging between £2000m and £3000m. However, a large part of this increase came from tobacco firms, due to global restrictions on tobacco advertising. Sponsorship of Formula One motor racing, horse racing, cricket, and many arts events such as the Brecon Jazz Festival by tobacco companies allowed tobacco companies to promote their products despite the Europe-wide ban on tobacco advertising on TV, but the UK government (responding to a European Union directive) banned any new tobacco sponsorship deals in 2003, and has required organisations to phase out tobacco sponsorship entirely. Some events, having been unable to find alternative sponsors, have disappeared altogether as a result of the ban on tobacco sponsorship, and the ban has certainly had a detrimental effect on the arts, whatever its effect on the nation's smokers. Withdrawal of sponsorship, for whatever reason, causes problems for the staff involved: they may try to continue with relationships established with staff of the sponsoring organisation even when senior management tries to stop these (Ryan and Blois 2010).

The value of sponsoring events is in little doubt: as a way of promoting a firm and its products, and in particular as a way of improving the corporate image, sponsorship has much to offer. Sponsorship has been shown to create a sustainable competitive advantage (Fahy et al. 2004). Companies sponsor for a variety of different reasons, as shown in Table 16.3 (Zafer Erdogan and Kitchen 1998).

The basis of sponsorship is to take the customers' beliefs about the sponsored event and link them to the company doing the sponsoring. Thus a firm wishing to appear middle-class and respectable might sponsor a theatre production or an opera, whereas a company wishing to appear to be 'one of the lads' might sponsor a football team. As far as possible, sponsorship should relate to the company's existing image.

Sponsoring sports teams has a degree of risk attached to it, since the fortunes of the sponsor are linked to the fortunes of the team: if the team performs badly, the team's supporters are less likely to buy the sponsor's products (Lings and Owen 2007). Some firms have tried to get round this problem by sponsoring rival teams – in the hope that if one fails, the other will succeed. This tends to alienate committed supporters of both teams, however, because they feel betrayed by the sponsoring company (Davies et al. 2006). Sponsorship of individuals can be even more risky – an individual such as a sports star might be involved in (say) a drug scandal or an incidence of cheating. Brand managers might respond in a number of different ways, depending on

Table 16.3 Reasons for sponsorship

Objectives	% Agreement	Rank
Press coverage/exposure/opportunity	84.6	1
TV coverage/exposure/opportunity	78.5	2
Promote brand awareness	78.4	3
Promote corporate image	77.0	4
Radio coverage/exposure/opportunity	72.3	5
Increase sales	63.1	6
Enhance community relations	55.4	7
Entertain clients	43.1	8
Benefit employees	36.9	9
Match competition	30.8	10
Fad/fashion	26.2	11

attribution of blame, societal norms, zone of tolerance and the public perception of the severity of the event (Westburg et al. 2011).

Sponsorship will work only if it is linked to other marketing activities, in particular to advertising. Hefler (1994) estimated that two to three times the cost of sponsorship needs to be spent on advertising if the exercise is to be effective. The advertising should tell customers why the firm has chosen this particular event to sponsor, so that the link between the firm's values and the sponsored event is clear. A bank that claims to be 'Proud to sponsor the Opera Festival' will not do as well as they would if they were to say 'We believe in helping you to enjoy the good things in life – that's why we sponsor the Opera Festival'. A recent development in sponsorship is to go beyond the mere exchange of money as the sole benefit to the sponsored organisation or event. If the sponsored organisation can gain something tangible in terms of extra business or extra publicity for their cause, then so much the better for both parties.

Real-life marketing: Lincoln Mercury

In 1996 sales of the upmarket Lincoln Mercury car were at an all-time low – and the company (a Ford subsidiary) had an even worse problem on its hands. Analysis of the ownership of Lincoln Mercury cars revealed that the average age of owners was 57 years. This meant that the lifetime value of Lincoln owners was low – these drivers were heading rapidly towards old age and would not be driving much longer, and in particular would not be changing their cars very frequently. It seemed highly likely that many Lincoln drivers would never buy another car, especially since the cars themselves are built to last.

Jim Rogers, Lincoln's new marketing manager, realised that drastic action would have to be taken. He moved production to California and introduced a new model (the Lincoln Navigator) which stopped the rot temporarily, but Rogers knew that he had to attract the 35- to 49-year-olds who were currently buying BMW and Lexus cars. 'Changing the product was not enough,' Rogers said. 'We needed to change what the brand stood for on an emotional basis. After all, nobody needs to pay $40,000–50,000 for a car.'

Rogers committed $90 million to the most integrated car publicity campaign ever undertaken. The campaign centred around another new model, the Lincoln LS, and was linked by the innovative Cirque du Soleil, a Montreal-based circus group. Lincoln arranged for three of the circus acts to conduct a mini-tour of eight major cities, ahead of the main tour of the circus (also sponsored by Lincoln). The mini-tour pulled in hundreds of potential buyers, identified by local Lincoln dealers in each city and invited specifically to the circus. These people in turn talked to friends and work colleagues about Cirque du Soleil, so that the main tour was a sell-out: of course, at each performance the Lincoln LS was available for circus-goers to inspect, and even to book test-drives.

The result of this sponsorship was that by August 1999 Lincoln had sold all the LS sedans they could make – 30,000 cars in all, representing $1.4 billion gross revenue. The company had been able to approach potential LS customers who would otherwise have been completely unavailable, a lucrative group of people who change their cars every two years or so. Cirque du Soleil also gained: apart from the sponsorship, the group now has a high profile in the United States as well as in its native Canada. Overall, the campaign was outstanding value all round for only $90 million.

(Continued)

(Continued)

If you want to try this yourself, here are the rules:

- Find a partner who is targeting the same segment.
- You should be looking either for a partner who needs something exciting and profile-raising (in the above example that would be Ford) or a partner who is exciting, but lacks the resources to get to a wider audience (in this case Cirque du Soleil).
- Find a scheme or project that will benefit both of you, and create a medium- to long-term partnership.

There is evidence that consumers feel gratitude towards the sponsors of their favourite events (Lacey et al. 2007), but there is no evidence regarding business buyers. Any feelings of gratitude may be an emotional linking between the sponsor and the event rather than a feeling of gratitude that the sponsor made the event possible. The difference between these emotions is merely academic in any case – if sponsorship leads to an improvement in the firm's standing with customers that should be sufficient. There are also spin-offs for the internal PR of the firm; most employees like to feel that they are working for a caring organisation, and sponsorship money often leads to free tickets or price reductions for staff of the sponsoring organisation.

The following criteria apply when considering sponsorship (Hefler 1994):

- The sponsorship must be economically viable; it should be cost-effective, in other words.
- The event or organisation being sponsored should be consistent with the brand image and overall marketing communications plans.
- It should offer a strong possibility of reaching the desired target audience.
- Care should be taken if the event has been sponsored before; the audience may confuse the sponsors, and you may be benefiting the earlier sponsor.

There is certainly a long-term effect from sponsorship: following the ending of a long-term relationship between a sponsor and an event, regular audiences of the event still demonstrate strong awareness of the sponsoring brand (Mason and Cochetel 2006).

In the business-to-business arena one of the main benefits of sponsorship of sports events and arts events is the availability of tickets or reserved seating for sponsors. This enables the sponsoring firms to offer seats as a relationship-builder or deal-sweetener to possible customers.

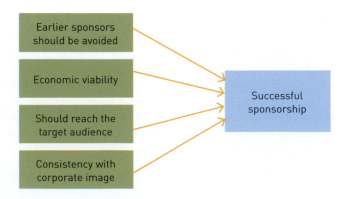

Figure 16.7   Considerations in sponsorship

Think outside this box!

Anyone watching a major sporting event such as the Wimbledon tennis championship or the 2012 Olympic Games will have noticed many empty seats. Anyone wanting to obtain tickets for such events finds them hard to get. So why does this happen?

Corporate sponsorship is the culprit. Corporations are given many free seats, which they are unable (or unwilling) to use on the days they are available; therefore seats are empty while real sports fans are unable to obtain tickets. This naturally causes a degree of resentment among fans – and a feeling that 'Big Business' is acting against the interests of ordinary people.

So how do corporations gain by this? What does this achieve in terms of enhancing the corporate reputation? Perhaps in the business-to-business environment there is no need to care about Joe Public, but isn't that attitude somewhat cynical?

Or perhaps there is an opportunity for someone. Could corporations make unwanted seats available to the public on a first-come-first-served basis?

RISK MANAGEMENT

No matter how carefully PR activities are planned and prepared for, crises will develop from time to time. Preparing for the unexpected is therefore a necessity. Some PR agencies specialise in crisis management, but a degree of advance preparation will certainly help if the worst should happen. Preparing for a crisis is similar to organising a fire drill. The fire may never happen, but it is as well to be prepared.

Crises may be very likely to happen, or extremely unlikely. For example, most manufacturing firms can expect to have a product-related problem sooner or later, and

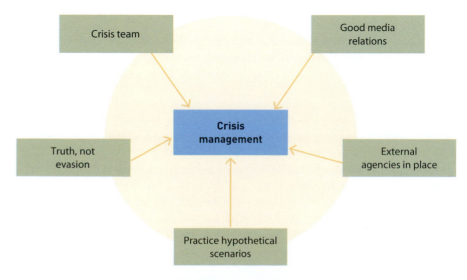

Figure 16.8   Elements of good crisis management

either need to recall products for safety reasons, or need to make adaptations to future versions of the product. On the other hand, some crises are extremely unlikely. Assassination or kidnapping of senior executives is not common in most parts of the world, nor are products rendered illegal without considerable warning beforehand.

Crises can also be defined as within the firm's control, or outside the firm's control. Many firms have been beset by problems that were really not of their making; however, very few problems are entirely outside the firm's control. In most cases events can at least be influenced, if not controlled. Sometimes, however, the cost of such influence is out of all proportion to the level of risk involved.

Establishing a crisis team

Ideally, the organisation should establish a permanent crisis management team of perhaps four or five individuals who are able to take decisions and act as spokespeople in the event of a crisis. Typical members might be the personnel manager, the safety officer, the factory manager, the PR officer and at least one member of the Board of Directors. Keeping the crisis team small means that communication between members is easy and fast.

Real-life marketing: Crisis teams

When a Eurolines bus bound for London from Warsaw was hit by a lorry in Germany, the company had a sudden crisis on its hands. Luckily, no one was killed, but the company's crisis team were ready – some passengers had to be hospitalised in Germany, some were given the option of returning to Warsaw, others were given the option of continuing to London.

At the London end, a large hotel was booked for passengers and relatives. Medical staff were brought in to check over any injured passengers (although they had received some treatment in Germany) and interpreters were available. Checks on the passenger list showed that there were people on the bus from Latvia, Lithuania, Estonia and even Russia as well as Poles, so several interpreters were needed. A buffet was provided for all those present, and the following day Eurolines staff issued new tickets for onward travel within the UK, recognising that many people would have missed their connections or relatives would have been unable to meet them. Eurolines' operational director was present, as was the PR officer, in case the news media turned up but specifically to prevent journalists from harassing the passengers.

The organisation was exemplary – smooth, efficient, and unruffled despite the obvious fact that this was not something that happens every day, or even every year. Eurolines clearly have an extremely effective crisis team, and have worked through this scenario (and others) many times in the office. If you need to set up your own crisis team, you need to do the following:

- Choose the right people for the team. You need some senior people on there, first because they will know what the company can and cannot do, but second because they will have the authority to act decisively in a crisis.
- Ensure that the team meet regularly to consider possible scenarios and map out what to do in each case. Obviously they need to keep records of those decisions.
- Practice. An occasional 'dummy run' will expose any weaknesses in the plan – for example, it's no good calling up your emergency doctor if he's gone golfing in the Algarve for a week.
- Train your team to deal with the news media. Saying 'No comment' to every question is a PR disaster in itself, without having a crisis to contend with too.

The team should meet regularly to review potential risks and formulate strategies for dealing with crises. It may even be possible to rehearse responses in the case of the most likely crises. Importantly, the team should be trained in presentation techniques for dealing with the media, especially in the event of a TV interview.

The team should be able to contact each other immediately in the event of a crisis, and should also be provided with deputies in case of being away on business, on holiday, off work sick, or otherwise unavailable. The essence of planning for crises is to have as many fall-back positions as possible. Having a Plan B is obvious, but it is wise to have a Plan C or even a Plan D as well.

DEALING WITH THE MEDIA IN A CRISIS

One of the main PR problems inherent in crisis management is the fact that many crises are newsworthy. This means that reporters will be attracted to the company and its officers in the hope of getting comments or newsworthy statements that will help to sell newspapers. The news media can greatly increase the negative impact on the firm's image, as compared with the effects that occur purely through consumers' direct experience (Yannopoulou et al. 2011).

Provided the groundwork has been laid in advance, the company should have a good relationship with the news media already. This will help in the event of a crisis. However, many managers still feel a degree of trepidation when facing the press at a crisis news conference. The journalists are not there to help the company out of a crisis, they are there to hunt down (or create) a story. Their objectives are probably not compatible with those of the company, but they are under an obligation to report the news reasonably accurately.

Preparation is important. As soon as the crisis breaks, the crisis team should be ready to organise a press conference, preferably on the company's own territory. The press conference should be held as soon as is reasonably possible, but it allows the spokespeople sufficient time to prepare themselves for the journalists and gives a reasonable excuse for not talking to reporters ahead of time. The crisis team should remember that they are in charge. It is their information, their crisis, and their story. They are not under an obligation to the news media, but they are under an obligation to the company's shareholders, customers, employees and other publics. The media may or may not be helpful in communicating with these publics in a crisis situation. Another important consideration is to ensure that the situation is not made worse by

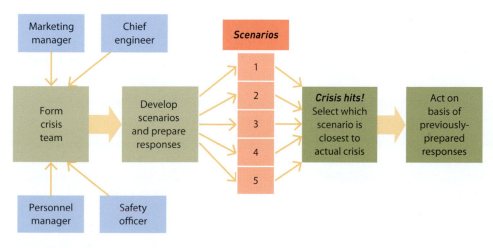

Figure 16.9 Crisis management

careless statements. Insurance and legal liability may be affected by what is said, so this should be checked beforehand.

Crisis teams need to have a special set of talents, as well as the training needed to perform their ordinary jobs. Rapid communication, and a rapid response, are essential when the crisis occurs. Good relationships with the news media will pay off in times of crisis.

Crisis management should not be left until the crisis happens. Everyone involved should be briefed beforehand on what the crisis policy is. This enables each person to respond appropriately, without committing the company to inappropriate actions – in simple terms, being prepared for a crisis will help to prevent panic reactions and over-hasty responses that might come back to haunt the company later.

The role of PR within the organisation

Organisations, just like people, have needs. Some of these needs are common to all organisations, and have different levels of importance according to the circumstances of the organisation, or the particular stage in its development. A hierarchy of organisational needs was developed by Pearson (1980). Table 16.4 shows how PR can help in satisfying those needs. Pearson's hierarchy is useful as a concept but less useful as a practical guide because so many firms deviate from the order in which the needs are met.

Internal communications are important because all of us go home after work. People talk to their friends and families about the organisation, and (perhaps unfortunately) what they say is not always complimentary. The intention behind internal PR is to foster a positive attitude towards the company which then spills over into positive statements about the firm, as well as a much more positive working environment.

Table 16.4   The hierarchy of organisational needs

Organisational need	Requirements	Typical PR activity
Output	Money, machines, manpower, materials	Staff programmes to attract the right people
Survival	Cash flow, profits, share performance, customers	Publicity aimed at customers; events publicising the firm and its products
Morale	Employee job satisfaction	Staff newsletters, morale-boosting activities, etc.
Acceptability	Approval by the external stakeholders (shareholders, government, customers, suppliers, society in general)	External PR, shareholder reports, lobbying of government departments and MPs, events for suppliers and customers, favourable press releases
Leadership	Having a respected position in the company's chosen field; this could be customer satisfaction, employee involvement, industry leadership in technology, or several of these	Corporate image-building exercises, customer care activities, publicity about new products and technological advances, sponsorship of research in universities, sponsorship of the arts

Source: Adapted from Pearson (1980)

Internal communications media

HOUSE JOURNAL

House journals are printed information books or sheets, which are made available to employees. Journals may be of any of the following types:

- Magazines. Containing feature articles and illustrations, these magazines are relatively expensive to produce but have a professional, credible feel about them.
- Newspapers. These can be produced to resemble a tabloid newspaper, which makes them more accessible to some groups of employees. Content consists of news articles about the firm, with some feature articles.
- Newsletter. Common in small firms, a newsletter would probably be A4 or foolscap size, and will contain brief items, usually without illustration. Newsletters are cheap and easy to produce, especially in small numbers.
- **Wall newspaper**. These look like posters, and are fixed to walls. They are useful for brief communications about events or changes in company policies.
- Electronic newsletter. Internal e-mail systems offer great potential for disseminating newsletters. The medium is cheap to use, effective and often increases the likelihood that the newsletter will be read. Furthermore, it is possible to tell who has opened the newsletter and who deleted it without reading it – although, of course, opening it is not the same as reading it. If the newsletter is part of the **Intranet**, this becomes much easier since each staff group can have its own page and people will be able to choose which pages to access.

House journal A medium for disseminating information within an organisation.

Wall newspaper A poster giving information to employees.

Intranet A computer-mediated system for internal communications within an organisation.

When planning a house journal, you need to consider the issues shown in Figure 16.10 and listed as follows:

- Readership. Different groups of staff may have different needs, so it may be necessary to produce different journals for each. Research workers are likely to have different needs from truck drivers, for instance.
- Quantity. The greater the number of copies, the lower the production cost per copy. If the number of employees is large, a better-quality journal can be produced; if numbers are small, the firm may need to produce newsletters or wall newspapers instead.
- Frequency. Frequent publication means that the journal is more likely to become part of the daily routine of staff. Some large firms even publish such journals daily.
- Policy. The journal should be more than simply a propaganda device for senior management. It should fit in with an overall PR programme, and should have a clear editorial policy to ensure the quality of content.
- Title. The title should be characteristic of the organisation. Changing the title is difficult once it has become established, just as with any other brand name.
- Printing process. To an extent the printing process will affect the content, since simple, cheap printing processes cannot reproduce some illustrations. Cost will also affect the choice of process, as will the desire for a good quality, credible journal.
- Style and format. Credibility is linked to the degree to which the journal resembles a commercial magazine. Style and format are part of the communication in the same way that packaging is part of a product.

- Price. Obviously the vast majority of house journals are free to staff, but it is feasible to make a charge if the journal is sufficiently interesting. There is no reason why a cover-price should not be put on the journal in any case, even if it is free. This conveys to the staff that the journal is valuable, and it is then more likely to be read.
- Advertisements. Carrying advertising may be a useful way to reduce costs. If the circulation is sufficiently large, outside organisations might be prepared to place advertising – this is particularly true if the firm is large and in a single location, since local shops, restaurants and entertainment venues might well wish to promote their products. Employees may well want to advertise items for sale or forthcoming social events, and this also increases the readability of the journal.
- Distribution. Journals can be delivered by hand, by post to the employee's home address, or at distribution points within the firm (for example mail pigeonholes). The decision rests on the frequency of the journal, the location of employees and the type of journal involved.

House journals are often edited independent of senior management in order to ensure that the focus is on the employees' need for information rather than on the management's need to control or manipulate: in large firms, the entire process might be contracted out. There is a view that hard copy journals will be replaced by on-line journals, perhaps as web pages on the staff-only part of the firm's website, but there is still a role for paper journals since people such as drivers or salespeople who work off-site can carry them around more easily and read them during breaks in the working day, whereas they may have difficulty accessing the Internet when away from the office.

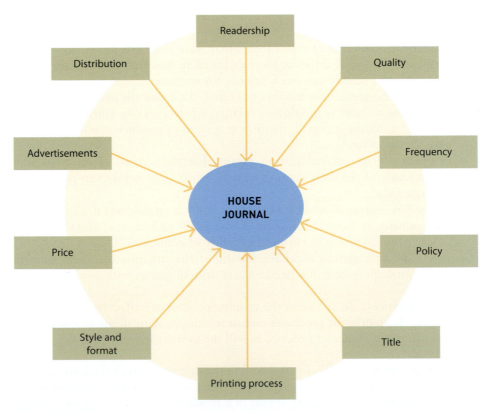

Figure 16.10   Issues in designing a house journal

WEBSITES

Most firms' websites are mainly geared towards external marketing. In many cases, firms operate internal websites aimed at employees. These sites are password protected so they are not accessible by outsiders, and they fulfil the same function as the house journal. The main advantage is that the costs are greatly reduced compared with producing a house journal. The disadvantage is that employees are unlikely to access the site except during working hours, and in some cases may not be able to access the site at all because the nature of their work does not involve using a computer (for example, a delivery driver may not access the site very often). This difficulty is reduced if people use computers at home, of course, but not everybody's broadband access is fast enough for large files, so the staff part of the website should not use graphics that require a lot of bandwidth (for example videos).

Internal websites are most useful in organisations in which virtually all employees are provided with computers, and in which there is no problem about allowing employees to scan the website during working hours. Website design is a specialist area, but some rules have been developed. Sites need to be simple to access and use, graphics should be kept simple to minimise download time and articles should fit onto one screen as far as possible.

INTERNAL BRIEFINGS AND OPEN MEETINGS

Some organisations give staff the opportunity to have access to senior management at open meetings or briefings. These briefings have the advantage of allowing senior management to gain direct access to grass-roots views from the workforce, as well as allowing the workforce the chance to question senior managers about company policies.

The overall effect is to increase openness within the firm, and break down barriers. Employees (in general) work better if they understand why things are being done the way they are being done. This also enables them to use their initiative better if the system breaks down for any reason.

Using outside agencies to build corporate image

Outside public relations agencies are frequently used for developing corporate image. The reasons for doing this might be as follows:

1. The firm is too small to warrant having a specialist PR department.
2. External agencies have expertise which the company lacks.
3. The external agency can provide an unbiased view of the firm's needs.
4. External agencies often carry greater credibility than internal departments or managers.
5. Economies of scale may make the external agency cheaper to use.
6. One-off events or campaigns are more efficiently run by outsiders, without deflecting attention away from core activities.

The Public Relations Consultants' Association lists the following activities as services that a consultancy might offer:

- Establishing channels of communication with the client's public or publics.
- Management communications.
- Marketing and sales promotion-related activity.
- Advice or services relating to political, governmental, or public affairs.

- Financial public relations, dealing with shareholders and investment tipsters.
- Personnel and industrial relations advice.
- Recruitment training and higher and technical education.

This list is not exhaustive. Since outside agencies often specialise, the firm might need to go to several different sources to access all the services listed above. Even firms with an in-house public relations department may prefer to subcontract some specialist or one-off activities. Some activities that might involve an outside agency may be as follows:

- Exhibitions. The infrequency of attendance at exhibitions (for many firms) means that in-house planning is likely to be disruptive and inefficient. Outside consultants might be setting up four or five exhibitions a week compared with the average firm's four or five a year, so they will quickly acquire strong expertise in exhibition management.
- Sponsorship. Outside consultants will have contacts and negotiating expertise which are unlikely to be available in-house. In particular, an outside firm will have up-to-date knowledge of what the 'going rate' is for sponsoring particular events and individuals.
- Production of house journals. Because of the economies of scale available in the printing and publishing industry, house journals can often be more cheaply produced by outsiders than by the firm itself.
- Corporate or financial PR. Corporate PR relies heavily on having a suitable network of contacts in the finance industry and the financial press. It is extremely unlikely that a firm's PR department would have a comprehensive list of such contacts, so the outside agency provides an instant network of useful contacts.
- Government liaison. Lobbying politicians is an extremely specialised area of public relations, requiring considerable insider knowledge and an understanding of current political issues. Professional lobbyists are far better able to carry out this work than a firm's public relations officer would be.
- Organising one-off events. Like exhibitions, one-off events are almost certainly better subcontracted to an outside agency.
- Overseas PR. Firms are extremely unlikely to have the specialist local knowledge needed when setting up public relations activities in a foreign country.

Figure 16.11   Example of task division between in-house staff and agency staff

Competence and Reputation	*Staff*
• Years in business. • Size – people and billings. • Full service or specialisms • Reach – local, national, international. • Growth pattern and financial stability. • Types of accounts. • Experience with accounts similar to yours, or conversely conflicts of interest with competitors' accounts. • Samples of work. • Sample list of suppliers used.	• List and qualifications of staff – full time, project clients, freelance/consultants. • Names of several former employees. • Staff to be assigned to your account – qualifications and length of time with the firm. • Percentage of their time to be devoted to your account – other accounts they will handle. • Staff or personnel backup available. • Staff turnover in the past two years.
Clients	**Results and measurement**
• Existing client list. • Past clients. • Average number of clients during the last five years – retainer clients, project clients. • Oldest clients and length of service. • Average length of client-firm relationship. • Clients lost in the last year.	• Does the firm understand your objectives and needs? • How will progress be reported? • How will results be measured? • What will it cost – billing process, hourly rate, expenses billed, approval process?

Figure 16.12 Checklist for choosing a PR consultancy (from Harley W. Warner, APR, Fellow Warner Communication Counselors Inc. Reprinted with permission of *Public Relations Review*)

Choosing an appropriate agency or consultancy begins with the agency's ability to carry out the specific tasks you need. Deciding which tasks the agency should do can be a process of elimination. Begin by deciding which tasks can be completed in-house, then whatever is left is the task of the agency. Figure 16.11 gives an example of in-house and agency task division.

Figure 16.12 gives a checklist for choosing a PR consultancy, which was developed by Warner Communication Counselors Inc.

Unless the outside agency has been called in as a result of a sudden crisis (which is possibly the worst way to handle both PR and consultants), the consultancy will be asked to present a proposal. This allows the consultancy time to research the client's situation, and its existing relationships with its publics. The proposal should contain comments on the following aspects of the problem:

- Analysis of the problems and opportunities facing the client company.
- Analysis of the potential harm or gain to the client.
- Analysis of the potential difficulties and opportunities presented by the case, and the various courses of action (or inaction) that would lead to those outcomes.
- The overall programme goals, and the objectives for each of the target publics.
- Analysis of any immediate action needed.
- Long-range planning for achieving the objectives.
- Monitoring systems for checking the outcomes.
- Staffing and budgets required for the programme.

Client firms will often ask several agencies to present, with the aim of choosing the best among them. This approach can cause problems, for several reasons. First, the best agencies may not want to enter into a competitive tendering situation. Second, some agencies will send their best people to present, but will actually give the work to their more junior staff. Third, agencies in this position may not want to present their best ideas, feeling (rightly in some cases) that the prospective client will steal their ideas. Finally, it is known that some clients will invite presentations from agencies in order to keep their existing agency on its toes.

Such practices are ethically dubious and do no good for the client organisation's reputation. Since the whole purpose of the exercise is to improve the firm's reputation, annoying the PR agencies is clearly not an intelligent move. To counter the possibility of potential clients stealing their ideas, some of the leading agencies now charge a fee for bidding. There is more on the ethics of PR in Chapter 10.

Relationships with external PR consultancies tend to last. Some major firms have used the same PR consultants for more than twenty years. Changing consultants frequently is not a good idea. Consultants need time to build up knowledge of the firm and its personnel, and the firm needs time to develop a suitable atmosphere of trust. Consultancies need to be aware of sensitive information if they are not to be taken by surprise in a crisis, and the firm is unlikely to feel comfortable with this unless the relationship has been established for some time.

DEVELOPING A BRIEF

The purpose of the brief is to bridge the gap between what the firm needs and what the consultant is able to supply. Without a clear brief, the consultant has no blueprint to follow, and neither party has any way of knowing whether the exercise has been successful or not.

Developing a brief begins with the firm's objectives. Objective setting is a strategic decision area, so it is likely to be the province of senior management. Each objective needs to meet SMARTT criteria, as follows.

1. Specific: in other words, it must relate to a narrow range of outcomes.
2. Measurable: if it is not measurable, it is merely an aim.
3. Achievable: there is no point in setting objectives that cannot be achieved, or are unlikely to be achieved.
4. Relevant to the firm's situation and resources.
5. Targeted accurately.
6. Timed: a deadline should be in place for its achievement.

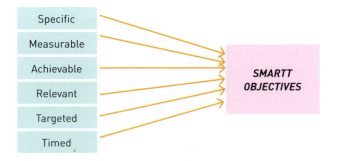

Figure 16.13   Criteria for objective setting

The objectives will dictate the budget if the firm is using the objective-and-task method of budgeting. This method means deciding what tasks need to be undertaken to achieve the final outcome, and working out how much it will cost to achieve each task. Most organisations tend to operate on the all-we-can-afford budgeting method, which involves agreeing a figure with the finance director. The SMARTT formula implies that, in these circumstances, the budget will dictate the objectives since the objectives must be achievable within the available resources.

Setting the objectives is, of course, only the starting point. Objectives need to be translated into tactical methods for their achievement, and these tactics also need to be considered in the light of what the company is trying to achieve.

The brief will be fine-tuned in consultation with the PR agency itself. From the position of their specialist knowledge, the agency will be able to say whether the budget is adequate for what needs to be achieved, or (conversely) say whether the objectives can be achieved within the budget on offer. The agency can also advise on what the appropriate objectives should be, given the firm's current situation.

MEASURING OUTCOMES

If the outcomes from the PR activities do not match up with the budgeted objectives, conflict between the client and the agency is likely to be the result. The most common reason for the relationship breaking down is conflict over the costs and hours billed, as compared with the outcomes achieved. From the agency's viewpoint, much of what happens is outside their direct control. Sponsored events might not attract sufficient audiences, press releases might be spiked as a result of major news stories breaking, and special events might be rained off. Many a carefully planned reputation-enhancing exercise has foundered when the celebrity athlete involved has been caught taking drugs, for example.

Measuring outcomes needs to be considered at the objective setting stage. A good PR agency will not offer any guarantees of outcomes, but it should be feasible to assign probabilities to the outcomes and to put systems in place for assessing whether the objectives were achieved.

Table 16.5 shows some possible evaluation methods.

Evaluating activities is never an easy task. It is difficult to be objective, and some activities are too difficult or expensive for the evaluation to be worthwhile, but without evaluation managers have no way of knowing what corrective action to take.

Table 16.5 Evaluating PR

Activity	Possible evaluation methods
Press campaign to raise awareness	Formal market research to determine public awareness of the brand/company.
Campaign to improve the public image	Formal market research. Focus groups for perceptual mapping of the firm against competitors. Measures of attitude change.
Exhibition or trade show	Records of contacts made, tracking of leads, formal research to determine improvements in image.
Sponsorship of a sporting event	Recall rates for the sponsorship activity.

Chapter summary

Corporate reputation goes beyond merely putting spin on the corporation's activities. It is a co-ordinated effort to influence communications to and from stakeholders, and also between stakeholders, in order to improve the corporation's position in the minds of its publics. In this sense, corporate reputation has a strategic role, because it involves positioning the corporation in the public consciousness: this has real pay-offs in terms of share values, employee satisfaction and behaviour, and customer perceptions of the firm.

Key points

- Corporate reputations are not built through spin-doctoring.
- Corporate reputation has a stock-market valuation.
- Public relations has an internal role.
- Crises will happen: having a crisis team in place is prudent.
- Outside agencies are often cheaper and more effective than carrying out PR tasks in-house.
- Between two and three times the cost of sponsorship should be devoted to other communications efforts in order to support the sponsorship expenditure.

Review questions

1. Why might a firm prefer to handle its corporate reputation activities in-house?
2. What are the key issues in building a crisis team?
3. If corporate reputation has such a strong effect on the firm's stock-market valuation, why bother with any other activities?
4. What are the main criteria for deciding to sponsor an event or organisation?
5. How might a company avoid PR disasters such as that resulting from the Bhopal tragedy discussed in Chapter 10?
6. What are the main advantages of publishing an in-house newsletter?
7. How should a firm handle internal PR when recruiting new staff?
8. How might a firm resolve conflicts between stakeholders?
9. Why might an individual's opinion about a firm change as a result of sponsorship?
10. Which components of attitude are likely to be most affected by PR activities?

Case study revisited: Chapter Arts Centre

One of Chapter's PR problems lies with its immediate neighbours. The Centre is in the middle of a residential area, which on the one hand creates a useful catchment for casual visitors and customers for films and theatre (not to mention the bar and restaurant), but on the other hand many local residents would prefer not to have cars and people coming and going from 8.30 in the morning through to 11.00 at night. Noise from some events (notably rock bands) led to Chapter being prevented from hosting loud music events, and the Centre is careful to ask people to be considerate when leaving at night. To be fair, the average theatre-goer is likely to be well-behaved when going home.

Of course, most of the people who live nearby have moved there after Chapter opened, so there is an argument to say that people who choose to live near a major arts venue should be prepared to accept that there will be some comings and goings, and a certain amount of noise from time to time. Unfortunately Cardiff City Council (who regulate noise pollution) have to accede to the complaints of voters, so some restrictions are in place. To help bring local residents 'on-side' Chapter issues them with Local Cards, which entitle them to discounts on tickets and even meals from the restaurant and drinks from the bar. Not all residents would use the card – but the fact that Chapter gives them out shows that the Centre's heart is in the right place.

Second, Chapter has to consider the needs of the organisations that support it through funding or other help. Many events at Chapter are sponsored by government or commercial organisations: recent events have been sponsored by the Arts Council for Wales, by the Henry Moore Foundation, and even the Queensland Government, Australia. Cardiff City Council provides some financial support, in recognition of the Centre's status as a tourist asset, and Chapter seeks sponsorship for special events from local corporate sources. The needs of all these disparate sponsors need to be balanced, without compromising Chapter's unique personality: although most of the Centre's revenue comes from the mainstream cinema screenings and from bar and restaurant takings, the more 'artsy' events would not happen without outside support.

Third, Chapter has to maintain its image with its customers, and do this largely without advertising. This means retaining its 'high art' image at the same time as generating revenue through mainstream cinema and running what is, in effect, a pub. This has proved surprisingly effective – Chapter continues to attract artists, audiences, arts administrators and people simply looking for a good night out.

Case study: Applebee's and the waitress

Applebee's is a restaurant chain that operates outlets throughout the United States. In the US, waiters and waitresses rely heavily on tips for their living, and it is normal practice to tip 20% or more to waiting staff in restaurants.

In common with other restaurants, Applebee's has a policy of adding an automatic tip to bills for large groups (six or more). The tip is a relatively modest 18%: restaurants do this because it simplifies the calculations for large groups who will be dividing up the bill, and saves arguments from group members over how much to tip. However, not everybody is happy with tipping, and not everybody agrees the amount. One Applebee's customer wrote on the bill: 'I give God 10%, why do you get 18?'

A fairly simple, mild protest – or so one would think. However, the waitress's co-worker, Chelsea Welch, thought it was either funny enough or annoying enough for her to post it on Reddit.com with the comment, 'My mistake, sir, I am sure Jesus will pay for my rent and my groceries'. Unfortunately the customer had signed the bill: it was a female pastor, Reverend Alois Bell, and she claimed that making her mild admonition public was a breach of her privacy. The situation escalated – the Reverend began receiving angry phone calls and e-mails from people who thought she was simply being a cheapskate, and so she complained to Applebee's who promptly fired Chelsea.

This, of course, led to a further escalation. Support groups began to form on the Internet, demanding that Chelsea be reinstated: at this point Applebee's PR people began to get involved, in particular their social media officers. The first response was to post a statement on the company's Facebook page, as follows:

We wish this situation hadn't happened. Our Guests' personal information – including their meal check – is private, and neither Applebee's nor its franchisees have a right to share this information publicly. We value our Guests' trust above all else. Our franchisee has apologized to the Guest and has taken disciplinary action with the Team Member for violating their Guest's right to privacy.

Facebook users (and supporters of Chelsea) quickly responded to this, pointing out that Applebee's had themselves posted a receipt a couple of weeks earlier, on which a customer had written a note complimenting the restaurant – complete with the customer's name. Apparently compliments are not private, whereas complaints are.

Applebee's social media officers came back with a counter-argument, pointing out that Pastor Bell had, in fact, been charged automatically for the 18% gratuity, and had also left $6 in cash, so the waitress had been tipped, and in any case it wasn't Chelsea who had served the Pastor's party. This was in fact another PR blunder: it simply sounded as if the company was arguing with the on-line posters and desperately trying to justify its position. Eventually, the company posted a comment that was critical of the customer:

Please note that we are also not excusing the Guest's behavior in this matter and the unacceptable comment she wrote on the receipt, which is offensive to us and all our hard working Team Members.

This comment was buried in a lot of other self-justification, which again poured petrol (or rather, gasoline) on the flames, because now the company appeared to be shifting the focus of the blame onto the customer. The company made several other major gaffes: they deleted negative comments from their Facebook page; they reported negative tweets on Twitter and had tweeters blocked; they tried to respond on Twitter, but again sounded desperate because they only responded to positive Tweets and ignored the negatives; they blocked negative posters from their Facebook page, which simply made the posters go elsewhere (in fact, usually to several elsewheres); and they responded to negative e-mails with a cut-and-paste of their standard press release rather than with a personalised response.

Pastor Bell was eventually interviewed on TV, where she apologised for her comment and pointed out that she had, in fact, tipped twice. Applebee's have remained relatively quiet, but continue to delete negative comments from their Facebook page. There are at least six Facebook groups dedicated to boycotting Applebee's, and there is little doubt that the whole debâcle will have cost the company hundreds of thousands of dollars in lost business. At the time of writing posts were still appearing on Applebee's Facebook page, but the company (perhaps wisely) seems to have given up on responding, and has not reinstated Chelsea Welch.

Eventually the whole affair will die down, no doubt, but meanwhile the company has suffered a major PR disaster. The loss of business is likely to be permanent – people who were once customers will stay away, and will tell others to do so, but in the scheme of things many major corporations have had similar PR problems and have survived. It's a shame that, in this case, the company had the opportunity to salvage the situation but instead spent considerable time and effort on making matters worse.

Questions

1. How might Applebee's have saved the situation by acting early?
2. What were the key factors in escalating the problem?
3. What should Applebee's do now, to put matters right?
4. What was wrong with the company's handling of e-mail complaints?
5. How might Applebee's prevent this from happening in future?

Further reading

Penn, Bill (2004) *Be Your Own PR Expert.* London: Thomson. This is a 'how-to' book with a direct style, written by an industry expert. Penn outlines the practical aspects of running one's own PR campaigns in a lively, engaging style. He also wrote *Market Yourself through the Media*, which explains how the news media operate and how to use the media to get your message across.

Regester, Michael and Larkin, Judy (2001) *Risk Issues and Crisis Management: A Casebook of Best Practice.* London: Kogan Page. This book covers crisis management, using case studies from famous companies to illustrate the points made. It is intended for students rather than practitioners, but has something to offer everyone.

References

Bhatnagar, Namita and Aksoy, Lerzan (2004) Et tu, brutus? A case for consumer scepticism and backlash against product placements. *Advances in Consumer Research*, 31: 77–9.

Black, Andrew, Wright, Philip and Bachman, John E. (1998) *In Search of Shareholder Value*. London: Pitman.

Cordeiro, J.J. and Sambharaya, R. (1997) Do corporate reputations influence security analyst earnings forecasts? *Corporate Reputation Review*, 1 (2): 94–8.

Cornelissen, Joep and Harris, Phil (2004) Interdependencies between marketing and public relations disciplines as correlates of communicative organisation. *Journal of Marketing*, 20 (1): 237–65.

Davies, Fiona, Veloutsou, Cleopatra and Costa, Andrew (2006) Investigating the influences of a joint sponsorship of rival teams on supporter attitudes and brand preferences. *Journal of Marketing Communications*, 12 (1): 31–48.

De Geus, Arie (1997) *The Living Company*. Boston, MA: Harvard Business School Press.

Deephouse, D.L. (1997) The effect of financial and media reputations on performance. *Corporate Reputation Review*, Summer/Fall, pp. 68–71.

Fahy, John, Farrelly, Francis and Quester, Pasquale (2004) Competitive advantage through sponsorship: a conceptual model and research propositions. *European Journal of Marketing*, 38 (8): 1013–30.

Fombrun, C.J. and Rindova, V. (2000) The road to transparency: reputation management at Royal Dutch Shell. In M. Schultz, M.J. Hatch and M.H. Larsen (eds), *The Expressive Organization: Linking Identity, Reputation, and the Corporate Brand*. Oxford: Oxford University Press.

Hayward, R. (1998) *All About PR*. London: McGraw–Hill.

Hefler, Mava (1994) Making sure sponsorship meets all the parameters. *Brandweek* (May).

Hudson, Simon and Hudson, David (2006) Branded entertainment: a new advertising technique or product placement in disguise? *Journal of Marketing Management*, 22 (5/6): 489–504.

Lacey, Russel, Sneath, Julie Z., Finney, Zachary R. and Close, Angeline G. (2007) The impact of repeat attendance on event sponsoring effects. *Journal of Marketing*, 13 (4): 243–55.

Lings, Ian N. and Owen, Kate M. (2007) Buying a sponsor's brand: the role of effective commitment to the sponsored team. *Journal of Marketing Management*, 23 (5/6): 483–96.

Liu, Yong (2006) Word of mouth for movies: its dynamics and impact on box office revenue. *Journal of Marketing*, 70 (3): 74–9.

Mason, Roger B. and Cochetel, Fabrice (2006) Residual brand awareness following the termination of a long-term event sponsorship and the appointment of a new sponsor. *Journal of Marketing Communication*, 12 (2): 125–44.

Mazzarol, Tim, Sweeney, Gillian C. and Soutar, Geoffrey N. (2007) Conceptualising word of mouth activities, triggers and conditions: an exploratory study. *European Journal of Marketing*, 41 (11/12): 1475–94.

Meenaghan, J.A. (1991) The role of sponsorship in the marketing communications mix. *International Journal of Advertising*, 10 (1): 35–47.

Oakes, P. (1997) Licensed to sell. *The Guardian*, 19 December.

Pearson, A.J. (1980) *Setting Corporate Objectives as a Basis for Action.* Johannesburg: National Development and Management Foundation of South Africa.

Post, James E., Lawrence, Anne T. and Weber, James (2002) *Business and Society: Corporate Strategy, Public Policy Ethics*. New York: McGraw–Hill.

Roberts, P.W. and Dowling, G.R. (1997) The value of a firm's corporate reputation: how reputation helps attain and sustain superior profitability. *Corporate Reputation Review*, Summer/Fall, 72–6.

Russell, Antonia and Stern, Barbara (2006) Aspirational consumption in US soap operas: the process of parasocial attachment to television soap characters. *Advances in Consumer Research*, 33: 136.

Ryan, Annmarie and Blois, Keith (2010) The emotional dimension of organisational work when cultural sponsorship relationships are dissolved. *Journal of Marketing Management*, 26 (7/8): 612–34.

Wangenheim, Florian von and Bayón, Tomás (2003) Satisfaction, loyalty and word-of-mouth within the customer base of a utility provider: differences between stayers, switchers and referral switchers. *Journal of Consumer Behaviour*, 3 (3): 211–20.

Westberg, Kate, Stavros, Constantino and Wilson, Bradley (2011) The impact of degenerative episodes on the sponsorship B2B relationship: implications for brand management. *Industrial Marketing Management*, 40 (4): 603–11.

Yannopoulou, Natalia, Koronis, Epaminondas and Elliott, Richard (2011) Media amplification of a brand crisis and its affect on brand trust. *Journal of Marketing Management*, 27 (5/6): 530–46.

Zafer Erdogan, B. and Kitchen, P.J. (1998) The interaction between advertising and sponsorship: uneasy alliance or strategic symbiosis? *Proceedings of the 3rd Annual Conference of the Global Institute for Corporate and Marketing Communications*, Strathclyde Business School.

More online

To gain free access to additional online resources to support this chapter please visit:
www.sagepub.co.uk/blythe3e

CHAPTER (17)

Promotion and sales

LEARNING OBJECTIVES

After reading this chapter, you should be able to:

- Explain the role of selling in communications.

- Understand the importance of after-sales activities.

- Describe the main differences between key-account selling and small-account selling.

- Understand some of the key issues in recruiting, training and motivating salespeople.

- Explain how to link sales promotions to exhibitions.

- Explain how to plan for an exhibition.

- Explain how sales promotions can be used by salespeople.

- Describe the difference between push strategies and pull strategies.

Introduction

Personal selling is often regarded with some suspicion because it is often associated with high-pressure techniques, and with the needs of the seller rather than the needs of the buyer. In fact, this view of selling is false: in practice, successful salespeople succeed because they are able to find solutions to customers' problems. The practice of selling has little or nothing to do with the selling concept described in Chapter 1, because customers are not generally willing to buy from someone who is pushy or who clearly does not have the customer's interests at heart.

Selling is frequently about personal relationships, especially in the business-to-business area. Even though business people often aim to be totally rational in their buying behaviour, the personality of the people they see conveys an image about the personality of the supplying corporation: for the buyer, the sales representative *is* the company. Personal selling has a special place in business-to-business transactions. Because of the higher order values and smaller number of buyers, suppliers feel the need to offer a personal service, supplied by the salesforce.

Equally, in many areas of consumer marketing personal selling has a strong role. For major purchases such as cars, houses, home improvements and even timeshare apartments the personality and professionalism of the salespeople will be the deciding factor in purchasing. For complex products such as consumer electronics, holidays and financial products such as insurance and pensions the salesperson can provide important guidance and help in tailoring the product to suit the individual's needs.

Preview case study: Jamie at Home

TV chef Jamie Oliver is famous for many things: his relaxed, fun attitude towards food, his campaign to improve school dinners, his very practical recipe books and his love of family, friends and good food. He was first discovered as a TV personality while working as a chef in Fulham, London: he appeared in a brief documentary about the restaurant at which he worked (the River Cafe) and was invited to appear in a TV series called *The Naked Chef* in which he cooked food for friends and family, describing what he was doing as he went along. He was then aged 22, and the combination of his enthusiastic personality and hands-on cooking style made food look both fun, and simple to prepare.

Now in his late thirties, Jamie Oliver has become something of a national institution. He has a chain of restaurants nationwide, has hosted several TV series about food, has written numerous recipe books and has been an outspoken crusader in favour of healthy, nutritious food: he was awarded an MBE for his support of young people from disadvantaged backgrounds (each year he trains 15 of them in the restaurant business, and has opened three restaurants to employ them) and he is a great advocate of making meals that are quick to prepare, healthy to eat and above all interesting to share with friends and family.

One of the many ways Jamie Oliver aims to change people's approach to cooking is to ensure that they have the right equipment. He has developed his own range of cooking utensils, ranging from knives through pans to salad spinners and items to improve the presentation of the food. Coupled with his recipe books and other merchandise, he has a wide range of items for sale – but relatively few places in which to sell them. Retailers' mark-ups tend to be high, and they also tend to impose conditions on suppliers – many retailers require suppliers to pay for shelf space, and no-quibble sale or return agreements are commonplace. This represents a risk for the supplier, one that a small supplier such as Jamie Oliver is unable to take.

The answer was obvious – sell direct to the public.

The role of personal selling

Sales presentation A structured interview in which a salesperson ascertains a customer's needs and offers a solution that will meet those needs.

Personal selling is probably the largest single budget item in most marketing departments. Salespeople earn high salaries and need expensive back-up: company cars, administration assistance, expensive brochures and sales materials, and so forth. Allowing for travelling time, preparation time and so forth salespeople spend only a fraction of their time actually making **sales presentations**. This therefore begs the question: why have we not been able to find a cheaper way to get business?

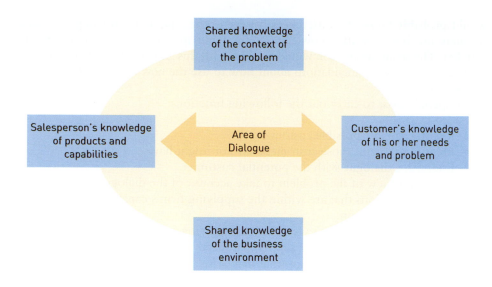

Figure 17.1 The function of selling

The reason is that salespeople help solve problems. A salesperson is able to meet a customer, discuss the customer's problems, and develop a creative solution. The customer understands his or her present situation and needs, the salesperson understands the capabilities of the supplier and their products, and (usually) the two share knowledge about the context of the problem and the solution. This relationship is illustrated in Figure 17.1.

Despite the great leaps forward in other areas of marketing, notably the Internet and other electronic communications methods, there is still a strong need for salespeople (Troilo et al. 2009; Wachner et al. 2009). Computers and communication alone cannot solve customer problems. The key point in this is that selling is about establishing a dialogue: it is not about persuading people to buy things they don't really want, it is not about fast-talking a buyer into making a rash decision and it is most definitely not about telling lies about the firm's products. Modern salespeople are concerned with establishing long-term relationships with customers (Singh and Koshy 2011).

Think outside this box!

There is a great deal of talk nowadays about establishing relationships, generating dialogues, asking people's opinions and even about choice. But is this really what customers want? Do people really want dialogue and choice – or would they be happier if they simply had a product that really worked and did the job for them? Would it, in fact, be better if companies simply said 'Here it is – take it or leave it.' Or would that seem too direct altogether?

For example, an amateur astronomer who intends to buy a new telescope would have knowledge of what types of astronomical body he or she is most interested in, and might have some knowledge of the telescopes on the market. An amateur astronomer would probably know the differences between reflecting and refracting telescopes, but may not have specific knowledge of the telescopes available from a particular supplier. The retail salesperson would be able to fill this gap, and would probably also be able to make recommendations about how to use the new telescope to make best use of its features.

Salespeople exist to carry out the following functions:

- Identify suitable possible customers.
- Identify problems those customers have or might have.
- Establish a dialogue with the potential customer.
- Refine the view of the problem to take account of the dialogue.
- Identify solutions that are within the supplying firm's capabilities.
- Explain the solution.
- Represent the customer's views to the supplying company.
- Ensure a smooth process of supply that meets the customer's needs.
- Solve any after-sales problems that may arise.

Marketers usually think of personal selling as part of the promotional mix, along with sales promotion, advertising and publicity. Personal selling is different from the other elements in that it always offers a two-way communication with the prospective customer, whereas each of the other elements is usually a one-way communication: the salesperson can clarify points, answer queries and concentrate on those issues that seem to be of greatest interest to the prospect. More importantly, the salesperson is able to conduct instant 'market research' with the prospect and determine which issues are of most relevance, often in an interactive way that allows the salesperson to highlight issues of which the prospect was not aware.

It is this problem-solving aspect of personal selling that marks it out as being less about communications *per se*, and more about marketing. In effect, salespeople are marketers who operate on a one-to-one basis rather than on a mass market.

As with other forms of marketing, selling works best as part of an integrated campaign. Salespeople find it a great deal easier to call on prospects who have already heard something about the company through advertising, publicity, or exhibition activities, and many salespeople regard it as the main duty of the marketing department to deliver warm leads (or even hot ones). Equally, marketers regard it as part of the salesperson's responsibility to 'sing the same song' by communicating the company's core message, in conjunction with the other communications methods.

Salespeople and marketers often have divergent views about the relationship between selling and marketing, and this is occasionally a source of conflict between them (Dewsnap and Jobber 1998).

Types of salesperson

Donaldson (1998) offers the following classification of selling types:

1. Consumer direct. These salespeople deal with consumers, they are order-getters who rely on selling skills, prepared presentations (canned presentations) and conditioned response techniques to close sales.
2. Industrial direct. These salespeople are also order-getters, but operate on a much larger scale. Usually these salespeople deal with one-off or infrequent purchases such as aircraft sales to airlines, machine tools, greenfield civil engineering projects and so forth. The emphasis for these salespeople is on negotiation skills.

3. Government institutional direct. Similar to industrial direct, these salespeople specialise in dealing with institutional buying. Because institutions typically operate by putting purchase contracts out to tender, these salespeople need special techniques: on the other hand, many of these organisations issue publications which explain how to sell to them, sometimes specifying the rules of business and acceptable profit levels. Often the salesperson's main hurdle is to become accepted as an approved supplier.

4. Consumer indirect. These salespeople call on retailers. Selling is normally on a repeat basis to established customers, but the main thrust of the salesperson's effort goes into understanding the consumer market. This means that the salesperson needs to help the retailer sell more of the product, by using creative merchandising, by advising on sales techniques, and (in the case of fast-moving consumer goods) negotiating with the retailer for extra shelf space for the products.

5. Industrial indirect. Most of the activity of these salespeople is in supporting distributors and agents. They need strong product knowledge, and will need to concentrate on defending existing business from incoming competition: this is because it is typically the case that product and price are similar between competitors. The service level the salesperson offers is therefore the main competitive tool.

6. **Missionary** sales. This type of selling is most effective when the selling cycle is long but the information needs of potential specifiers are immediate, when other forms of communication cannot convey the whole picture, and when the buying process is complex.

> **Missionary** A salesperson who does not sell directly, but who has the task of 'spreading the word' about a product to people who influence purchase.

7. Key-account salespeople. A **key account** is one that is of strategic importance, which represents a substantial proportion of the supplier's turnover, or which is likely to lead to a change in the way the firm does business. Key-account salespeople need very strong negotiating skills, a high degree of confidence, and the ability to relate to people at many different levels in the organisation (Cespedes 1996; Millman and Wilson 1995, 1996).

> **Key account** A customer or potential customer with strategic importance to the firm.

8. Agents. A manufacturer's agent represents many different suppliers, but does not take title to the goods. Agents typically call on the same regular group of customers, but offer a wide range of goods: the skills required are therefore the ability to understand a wide range of products, the administrative ability to keep track of the orders and to meet the differing order formats of client companies, and the ability to work efficiently, often on low margins. Good agents do not carry products that compete directly, although there are exceptions to this general rule.

9. **Merchandisers**. Merchandisers call on large and small retail outlets specifically for the purpose of maintaining in-store displays and point-of-sale materials. In some cases (for example Procter and Gamble) suppliers have their own employees stationed in supermarkets so as to improve the co-ordination of their supply operations. These salespeople are sometimes called customer account managers, which more accurately describes the breadth of their role.

> **Merchandiser** A type of salesperson who has the responsibility of establishing and maintaining in-store displays.

10. **Telesales**. Telesales staff operate from call centres, where calls can be either inbound or outbound. Inbound telesales involves responding to customer enquiries, often generated by advertising or exhibitions. Outbound telesales usually involves cold-calling prospects, but may replace a personal visit with a telephone call. The main advantage of telesales is that it is very much cheaper than personal calls: the main disadvantage is that it is considerably less effective on a call-for-call basis, and it is also regarded by many recipients as extremely irritating. Call centre staff need good communication skills, including a clear

> **Telesales** Selling over the telephone.

speaking voice. Often they have access to a lot of information about prospects because they are sitting in front of a computer screen.

11. **System selling**. This involves teams of salespeople, each of whom brings a different skill to bear on the problem. Missionary salespeople, new-business salespeople and technical salespeople may all be involved in selling to the same account.

12. Franchise selling. Franchising is much the same as licensing, but is much more extensive. The franchisor grants the franchisee the right to use its business system, and provides extensive support services and promotional input. In exchange, the franchisee pays a substantial royalty and an up-front franchise fee, and agrees to conduct the business exactly according to the instructions from the franchisor. An example of this in the business-to-business field is Snap-On Tools, which supplies tools to the light-engineering and motor trade.

There are, of course, many other ways of describing types of salesperson. Suggestions have included customer partner, buyer–seller team co-ordinator, customer service provider, buyer behaviour expert, information-gatherer, market analyst, forecaster and technologist (Rosenbloom and Anderson 1984; Wilson 1993). As personal selling develops in complexity, other classifications may well emerge.

Figure 17.2   System selling

The selling cycle

Figure 17.3 shows the selling cycle. The selling sequence is drawn as a circle to indicate that it is an ongoing process, although in practice each salesperson will divide up his or her day in such a way as to carry out several, or even all, of the separate processes at once.

Lead generation activities are sometimes also called prospecting, although in fact they differ considerably. Lead generation is a process of establishing first contact: leads are generated via advertising, cold-calling (making visits or telephone calls

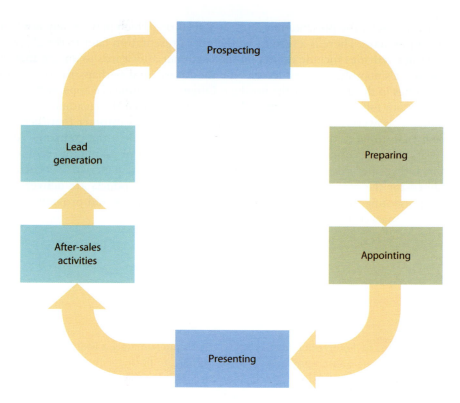

Figure 17.3 The selling cycle

without an appointment), by running exhibition stands, by sending out mail shots, or by personal recommendation.

Prospecting is about establishing that the potential customer has a need for the product, and also has the means to pay for it. In some cases these issues cannot be clearly determined in advance of meeting the potential customer, but a good salesperson will try to investigate a prospect as thoroughly as possible before wasting time on making a sales call.

Preparing for the sale involves preparing both physically and mentally: wearing the right clothes, having the right presentation materials to hand, having the right mental attitude and having appropriate knowledge of the prospect's circumstances. Physical appearance is especially important – looking the part is at least halfway to being the part, and there is even evidence that salespeople's appearance affects the way they are assessed by sales managers (Vilela et al. 2007). Preparing is likely to be complex in business-to-business sales, since in many cases the salesperson will be calling on several firms in one day, each with a separate set of data to remember, and each with a separate set of needs.

Appointing means making appointments to see the appropriate decision-maker. In consumer sales, this probably means ensuring that both husband and wife are present: salespeople are often advised to ensure that all the decision-makers are present, but in a business-to-business context this is unlikely to be possible. Therefore the salesperson may well go through a process of using one appointment to generate the next until all the decision-makers have been seen.

The sales presentation is a process of conducting a directed conversation in which the prospect's need is established and agreed, the supplier's solution is explained and the sale is closed. Closing the sale may mean that the order is placed or it may not: the purpose of the presentation is to get a decision, which may or may not be in favour of purchase. There is a section on the sales presentation later in the chapter.

After-sales activities include calling on the customer afterwards to ensure that the process went smoothly, to learn lessons for the future, and perhaps to correct any shortcomings in the delivery or the product. Often salespeople are apparently afraid of carrying out follow-up calls, perhaps because of a fear that the customer will have a complaint: however, it is far better to find out from the customer that there is a problem than to be told that the customer has complained to the company. After-sales visits also offer opportunities for making further sales or asking for recommendations. Other after-sales activities include ensuring that the paperwork is correctly completed for the company's systems, ensuring that the products are delivered on time, representing the customer's views back to the company and providing other appropriate market information.

Real-life marketing: Following up

The Futon Shop follows up on sales approximately a year later, offering add-on products such as drawers to fit under the futon, covers, cleaning, and so forth. After a year the customer is used to having the futon around, and has often recognised a need for some of the accessories that were available at the time of purchase. In general, people welcome the approach – they are often ready to buy, and are happy to hear about items that will improve their enjoyment of the product.

If you're going to try this in practice, you need to do the following:

- You must keep really good records, and diarise everything well.
- You have to offer customers something of real value, not just call them up with a generalised sales pitch.
- You need to calculate the appropriate time gap. For some products it will be a few weeks, or even days: for others, it might be several years.
- Try to avoid using the phrase 'courtesy call' – everybody knows you've called to try to sell something, and it's better to be honest about it.

THE SALES PRESENTATION

Figure 17.4 shows the sequence of events that leads to a decision on the part of the customer, and possibly a sale.

Particularly when first meeting a new customer, the salesperson needs to establish a personal rapport. This is established by showing a genuine interest in the customer and his or her problems; the traditional view of the salesperson as being a backslapping individual with a fund of good jokes is a long way from the truth.

Typically salespeople begin with an **icebreaker.** This is an opening remark or series of comments that tend to put the relationship on a human level; often the aim of the exercise is to create a perceived similarity between the salesperson and the prospect. If the prospect feels they have something in common, this will increase the level of trust in what the salesperson has to say (Dion et al. 1995). Salespeople seek to establish relationships with their prospects, because this is a

Icebreaker A statement or question used at the beginning of a sales presentation with the intention of establishing a rapport with the buyer.

Figure 17.4   The sales visit

more certain way of making sales (McKenna 1991); it is also a way of making the working day more pleasant.

During the presentation salespeople should be prepared to listen to what their customers have to say; selling is not about talking well, it is about listening to people's problems and finding solutions. Second, salespeople need to be very aware of the customer's sensibilities. The overall impression should be that the salesperson is a 'friend in the business' – and in fact most salespeople will agree that it easier to find another company to work for than it is to find new customers. Finally, telling lies to customers is counter-productive, since the lie will inevitably come to light once the customer takes delivery of the product. This leads to the cancellation of contracts, return of the goods and even lawsuits – which the customer will almost certainly win.

Although some customers regard salespeople with suspicion, the evidence is that salespeople actually seek to develop and maintain good relationships with their customers even when this conflicts with instructions from their marketing departments (Anderson and Robertson 1995). Many salespeople regard themselves as managers of the firm's relationship with its customers, which sometimes leads them to identify rather more strongly with the customer than with the firm, which in turn can cause problems for managers (Davies et al. 2010).

For the customer, the salesperson is a source of information, a source of help in problem-solving and is an advocate back to the supplying company. Good salespeople are also adept at helping their customers through the decision-making process; often this is the hardest part of making a sale.

The obvious way to find out the customer's needs is by asking questions. The traditional approach, which was developed by E.K. Strong in the 1920s, is to divide questions into two types: open questions and closed questions. An open question has a number of different possible answers, whereas a closed question can only be answered yes or no (Strong 1925). Here are some examples of open questions:

> *'What sort of maintenance bills are you paying at the moment on your equipment?'*
>
> *'Who is in charge of the budgets for maintenance?'*
>
> *'Where should the shipment be delivered?'*

And some examples of closed questions:

> *'Would you like me to show you how you can save on maintenance?'*
>
> *'Shall I put you down for the 24-hour call-out service?'*
>
> *'Should we deliver to the main warehouse?'*

Open questions are actually *opening* questions; they are the main tool the salesperson has for finding out about the customer's needs. Closed questions tend to be *closing* questions, used towards the end of the sales presentation to bring the customer to the decision point. Questions have a further important function in that they enable the salesperson to keep control of the direction in which the presentation is going. Questions are powerful in directing people's thoughts; anybody with small children knows that the constant stream of questions is both distracting and wearing because the child keeps triggering the adult's mind to think of a response. Questions demand attention in a way that statements do not.

Think outside this box!

If the sales presentation is a directed conversation, with the salesperson doing the directing, where is the consideration of the customer's needs? If the customer is being directed to say certain things, and answer certain questions in a particular way, and is (in short) being manipulated, how can we possibly then assert that his or her needs are being dealt with?

Or is it, perhaps, that the salesperson is somehow better-qualified to lead the customer through the decision-making process? Do salespeople have some kind of special talent in problem-solving?

Objections Questions raised by a prospect in the course of a sales presentation.

Objections are queries or negative statements raised by the prospect in the course of the presentation. The prospect may, for example, say that a particular feature of the product is not wanted, or is an expensive frill. In most industries the same objections tend to crop up over and over again; common ones are 'We can't afford it', and 'I need to consult someone else about this'. Although objections are often seen as being barriers to making the sale, good salespeople recognise them as requests for further information. Provided the objection is successfully answered, the negotiation can continue until a mutually acceptable solution is reached.

Conditions Situations that make a sale impossible.

Objections should be distinguished from **conditions:** a condition prevents the sale going ahead. The commonest ones are as shown in Table 17.1. Often, conditions do not really exist, and are being used to cover up another objection which the prospect would prefer not to raise.

Table 17.1 Common conditions

Condition	What the salesperson should do
The prospect has no authority to make the decision	Find out who does have the authority, and ask the prospect to make an appointment to see that person.
The firm has no money	If this is true, the sale cannot go ahead. In most cases it is not true; buyers will often say that the budget has run out as a way of getting rid of the salesperson. Astute salespeople will find out who has the authority to increase the budget, or will arrange for payment to be deferred into the next financial year.
No need for the product	Unless there is a need, no purchase will take place. This is a problem the salesperson has caused by not properly identifying the needs in the first place.

Think outside this box!

If a customer is claiming that there is a condition in order to avoid raising an objection, shouldn't we respect that? Where does the salesperson get off, making people feel uncomfortable in order to get a sale?

Or is it simply that people are afraid of making a wrong decision, so they try to avoid making any decision at all? Are salespeople really more in the role of therapists, getting people to stand up and be counted when hard decisions have to be made?

Objections can sometimes be used for a trial close: the salesperson says 'If we can overcome that problem for you, are we in business?' This can sometimes mean closing the sale early, but at the very least it brings out any other objections. As a general rule, it is advisable to deal with objections as they arise; leaving them all to the end of the presentation means that the prospect is sitting with negative feelings about the product for a long time. Objections must always be taken seriously; even if the salesperson feels that the problem is a small one, and the prospect is getting too concerned over a triviality, it may not seem that way to the prospect.

Once all the objections have been answered, the sale can be closed. **Closing techniques** are ways of helping the prospect over the decision-making hurdle. Perhaps surprisingly, most people are reluctant to make decisions, even more so if they are professional buyers. This is perhaps because of the risks attached to making a mistake, but whatever the reason buyers often need some help in agreeing to the order. Salespeople use a number of closing techniques to achieve this; Table 17.2 has some examples. There are, of course, many other closing techniques. Salespeople will typically use whichever one seems most appropriate to the situation.

Salespeople should avoid asking prospects to 'sign' the order. This has negative connotations because it implies a final commitment – people talk of 'signing your life away' or 'signing your death warrant'. It is better to ask people to 'OK that for me' or 'Autograph this for me'.

Closing techniques Those questions and behaviours that end the sales presentation and elicit a decision from the buyer.

Table 17.2   Examples of closing techniques

Technique	Explanation	Example
Alternative close	The prospect is offered two alternatives, each of which leads to the order.	'Would you like them in red, or in green?'
Order-book close	The salesperson writes down each feature in the order book as it is agreed during the presentation.	'OK, you want the green ones, you want four gross, and your best delivery date is Thursdays. If you'll just autograph this for me, we'll get it moving for you.'
Immediate gain close	The prospect is shown that the sooner he or she agrees to the deal, the sooner he or she will get the benefits of the product.	'Fine. So the sooner we get this paperwork sorted, the sooner you'll start making those savings, right?'

Think outside this box!

We are told that selling is about solving problems. All well and good, but what happens when the customer says that the solution being offered isn't good enough? Does the salesperson give up? No. Apparently he or she then goes into objection-handling mode, then rapidly into closing mode using all sorts of psychological gymnastics to get the buyer signed up.

Is this behaviour peculiar to salespeople, though? How about when we are persuading a friend to come out for the evening, or to go on a trip together? Even more so, when we are persuading our partner to lose weight or give up smoking? We know it would be good for them to do this, and they know it too, but can they make a firm commitment?

Could it be that we are all salespeople at heart, just some of us are not trained enough to do it well?

During the face-to-face part of the salesperson's job the prospect's needs always come first, followed by an acceptance of the needs, followed by the presentation of the solution to the need problem. Acceptance of the solution, or rejection of it, determines whether the sale goes ahead or not.

POST-PRESENTATION ACTIVITIES

Sometimes salespeople are afraid that, by leaving information and contact telephone numbers, the customer will be encouraged to cancel; they may also be nervous about going back to customers they have sold to, for fear of cancellations or for fear of having to deal with complaints. The reason for this is that salespeople need to maintain a positive outlook about the company, the products and themselves, and dealing with customer complaints may mean that the salesperson becomes infected with negativity.

In fact it is always worthwhile revisiting customers once the delivery of the product has been made. The reasons for this are as follows:

- If there is a problem, the visit offers an opportunity to rectify matters. Research shows that customers whose complaints are dealt with to their complete satisfaction become more loyal than those who didn't have a complaint in the first place (Coca-Cola Company 1981). Perhaps salespeople should actually encourage customers to complain, so that they can demonstrate how well they can handle complaints!

● If the customer is completely satisfied with the product (which is usually the case) this helps the salesperson feel even more positive about the firm and the products.
● Repeat sales often result, and a longer-term relationship can develop.

Salespeople usually find that only positive outcomes result from maintaining a good after-sales service.

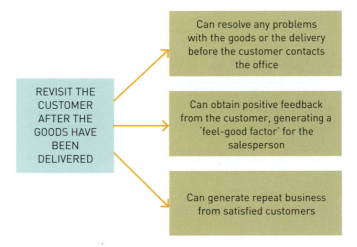

Figure 17.5 Benefits of revisiting customers

Key-account selling

A key account is one that possesses some or all of the following characteristics:

● It accounts for a significant proportion of the firm's overall sales. This means that the supplying firm is in a vulnerable position if the customer goes elsewhere. This in turn means that the supplier may be expected to negotiate significant changes in its methods, products and business practices in order to fit in with the customer's business practices and needs.
● There is co-operation between distribution channel members rather than conflict. This places the emphasis strongly on good, effective channels of communication, with the salesperson in the front line.
● The supplier works interdependently with the customer to lower costs and increase efficiency. This again implies lengthy negotiations and frequent contact between the firms.
● Supply involves servicing aspects such as technical support as well as the delivery of physical products. Servicing aspects will often fall to the salesperson, and because of the intangible nature of services, good communication is at a premium.

Key-account selling has the following features:

1. There will be many decision-makers involved, with very little likelihood of being able to meet all of them at one time.

2. It is frequently the case that the salesperson is not present when the final decision is made, and he or she may never meet the most senior decision-makers.
3. The problems the salesperson is expected to address are complex and often insoluble in any permanent sense.
4. The consequences of the problem are often much more important than the immediate problem would suggest.

Traditional selling emphasises objection handling, overcoming the sales resistance of the buyer and closing the sale. This naturally tends to lead to a focus on the single transaction rather than on the whole picture of the relationship between the supplier and the buyer.

Marketing in a changing world: Global key accounts

Globalisation has had a mixed press, but there isn't much doubt it's here to stay. Companies make things and sell things worldwide, and source materials and components worldwide, too – but how does this work out when both the supplier and the customer are global?

Increasingly we are seeing global corporations like Ford sourcing from global corporations like Tata. Although Ford seeks to standardise component purchases, regional differences in consumer tastes and local regulations will almost certainly mean that it will be unable to produce a single model for all markets. Key-account salespeople might therefore be talking to people from several different cultures in several different countries in order to get a decision, and at the same time will need to talk to people within their own organisation in several different countries and cultures.

This seems to be a tremendous opportunity to see the world and meet interesting people: it is certainly a major challenge for key-account selling.

In itself, this may not matter for many purchases. A firm selling photocopiers, for example, has many competitors who are supplying broadly similar products. This means that a quick sale is essential, since otherwise the buyer will be getting several quotes from other firms and will probably make the final decision based on the price alone. In addition, repeat business will be unlikely to materialise, and will be a long time coming if it does, so the salesperson is not looking to establish a long-term relationship with the buyer, nor is the buyer particularly interested in establishing a long-term relationship with the salesperson. Both parties are mainly interested in solving the customer's immediate problems, then moving on to other business.

Selling to major accounts cannot follow the simplistic approach of finding out needs and closing, which is used in traditional selling situations; it involves a much more drawn-out procedure. Buyers who are considering a major commitment to a supplier, either for a single large purchase or for a long-term stream of supplies, are unlikely to be impressed with a one-hour presentation. Also, the salesperson will need to sell the solution to his or her own firm, since major changes in products and practices are often needed.

From a sales management viewpoint this has major implications. In small-account sales, the one-call sale is the norm. Typically, sales managers operate on the basis that the more calls the salespeople make, the more sales will result. On the face of it, this is perfectly logical. If a salesperson has a closing rate of one in four (one sale for

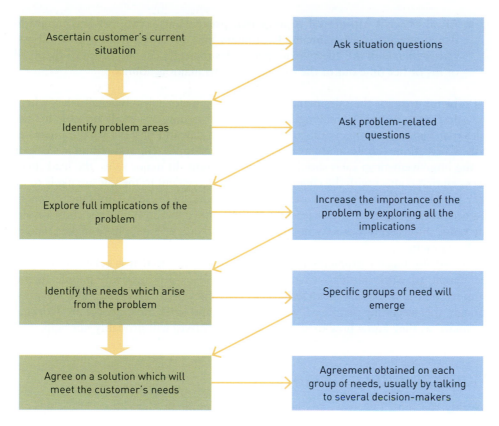

Figure 17.6 Sales process in major accounts

every four calls) then twenty calls will produce five sales, forty calls will produce ten sales, and twelve calls will only produce three sales. Therefore most sales managers will apply pressure to their salesforces to make more calls.

In major account selling this approach would be disastrous. Encouraged (or compelled) to call on more customers, the salesperson will inevitably begin to call on only those customers who can be sold to quickly and easily, in other words the smaller accounts.

Sales managers should follow these principles when becoming involved in major sales:

- Only become involved when your presence makes a unique difference. The salesperson involved on the account is probably very deeply immersed in it, and will know a lot about the customer and the state of the negotiation; you cannot possibly know as much.
- Do not make sales calls on a customer unless your salesperson is with you. You could upset a delicate stage of the negotiation, or at the very least introduce new factors.
- Before any joint call, agree on specific and clear selling roles with your salesperson. Again, control needs to be strongly with the salesperson who is responsible for the account, so it is essential to trust that person's judgement.
- Be an active internal seller for your salespeople. The solution arrived at for the client is likely to involve internal changes for the supplier, some of which will not be popular with the other people in the firm. They will need to be convinced, and the sales manager is the best person to do this.

- Always have a withdrawal strategy that prevents any customer becoming too dependent on you personally. Customers may prefer to deal with 'the boss' rather than with the salesperson, but a sales manager cannot afford to spend all of his or her time out of the office, selling to major accounts.

Problems arise for the sales manager in coaching major sales. In small sales, where the salesperson is perhaps making four or five calls a day, it is easily possible for the sales manager to accompany the salesperson for a day and observe what happens in calls. Corrections can be made to the salesperson's approach, and within a week or so the improvement in sales should become apparent. In major sales, the lead times between first contact with the client and the final agreement to the sale are likely to be very long indeed, often months and sometimes years; in those circumstances, coaching becomes difficult, to say the least. Improvements in methods may not show results for years, and therefore it may be difficult to motivate salespeople to make changes in their practices.

One of the biggest problems for the sales manager is that it is relatively easy to get people to work harder – extra incentives will usually motivate people to put in more hours, or otherwise increase sales efficiency. Increasing sales effectiveness, though, means getting people to 'work smarter', and since most people are working as 'smart' as they know how to already, extra incentives will probably not help.

Managing the salesforce

Possibly the most expensive marketing tool the company has, the salesforce, is in some ways the hardest to control. This is because it is composed of independently minded people who each have their own ideas on how the job should be done, and who are working away from the office and out of sight of the sales managers.

Sales managers are responsible for recruitment, training, motivation, controlling and evaluating salesforce activities and managing sales territories.

Recruitment is complicated by the fact that there is no generally applicable set of personality traits that go to make up the ideal salesperson. This is because the sales task varies greatly from one firm to another, and the sales manager will need to draw up a specific set of desirable traits for the task in hand. This will involve analysing the company's successful salespeople, and also the less successful ones, to find out what the differences are between them.

Some companies take the view that almost anybody can be trained to sell, and therefore the selection procedures are somewhat limited, or even non-existent; other companies are extremely selective and subject potential recruits to a rigorous selection procedure.

Sources of potential recruits are: advertising, employment agencies, recommendations from existing sales staff, colleges and universities, and internal appointments from other departments.

Training can be long or short, depending on the product and the market. Table 17.3 illustrates the dimensions of the problem. The role the salesperson is required to take on will also affect the length of training: missionary salespeople will take longer to train than order-takers, and closers will take longer than telesales operators. Traditional salesforces are under pressure from direct channels and from key-account sales approaches. The solution is to improve training so that people 'work smart', to manage interfaces between customer and salesperson better and to integrate processes better (Piercy and Lane 2003).

Typically, training falls into two sections: classroom training, in which the recruits are taught about the company and the products and may be given some grounding in

Table 17.3   Factors relating to length of training of sales staff

Factors indicating long training	Factors indicating short training
Complex, technical products	Simple products
Industrial markets with professional buyers	Household, consumer markets
High order values (from the customer's viewpoint)	Low order values
High recruitment costs	Low recruitment costs
Inexperienced recruits – for example, recruited direct from university	Experienced recruits from the same industry

sales techniques, and field training, which is an ongoing training programme carried out in front of real customers in the field. Field training is often the province of the sales managers, but classroom training can be carried out by other company personnel (in some cases, in larger firms, there will be specialists who do nothing else but train salespeople). Sales team learning is impacted by the salesforce's perception of the organisation's willingness to change, however: if salespeople feel that the organisation will still expect them to continue with the same processes and procedures, they are unlikely to want to study new methods (Rangajaran et al. 2004).

People tend to learn best by performing the task, so most sales training programmes involve substantial field training, either by sending out rookies (trainees) with experienced salespeople, or by the 'in-at-the-deep-end' approach of sending rookies out on their own fairly early in their careers. The latter method is indicated if there are plenty of possible customers for the product; the view is that a few mistakes (lost sales) won't matter. In business-to-business selling, though, it is often the case that there are fewer possible customers and therefore the loss of even one or two could be serious. In these circumstances it would be better to give rookies a long period of working alongside more experienced salespeople.

Ultimately, of course, salespeople will lose more sales than they get. In most industries, fewer than half the presentations given result in a sale; a typical proportion would be one in three.

Payment for salespeople traditionally has a **commission** element, but it is perfectly feasible to use a straight salary method, or a commission-only method. Although it is commonly supposed that a commission-only salesperson will be highly motivated to work hard, since otherwise he or she will not earn any money, this is not necessarily the case. Salespeople who are paid solely by commission will sometimes decide that they have earned enough for this month, and will give themselves a holiday; the company has very little moral power to compel them to work, since there is no basic salary being paid. Conversely, a salesperson who is paid salary only may feel obligated to work in order to justify the salary.

Herzberg (1960) says that the payment method must be seen to be fair if demotivation is to be avoided; the payment method is not in itself a good motivator. Salespeople are out on the road for most of their working lives and do not see what other salespeople are doing – whether they are competent at the job, whether they are getting some kind of unfair advantage, even whether they are working at all. In these circumstances a commission system does at least reassure the salesperson that extra effort brings extra rewards. There is evidence that salespeople also judge pay fairness on supervisory behaviour, trust and interactional fairness, i.e. negotiation and explanation (Ramaswamy and Singh 2003).

Commission Performance-related payments made to salespeople.

Table 17.4   Trade-offs in salesperson's pay packages

Mainly salary	Mainly commission
Where order values are high	Where order values are low
Where the sales cycle is long	Where the sales cycle is short
Where staff turnover is low	Where staff turnover is high
Where sales staff are carefully-selected against narrow criteria	Where the selection criteria for staff are broad
For new staff, or staff who have to develop new territories	For situations where aggressive selling is indicated (e.g. selling unsought goods)
Where sales territories are seriously unequal in terms of sales potential	Where sales territories are substantially the same

This may be part of the reason why salespeople perform better if they are allowed to manage themselves, within a team context. Control of teamwork improves performance at the team level: performance at the individual level is related much more to control of selling skills (Lambe et al. 2009).

The chart in Table 17.4 shows the trade-offs between commission-only and salary-only; of course, most firms have a mixture of salary and commission.

Motivation, perhaps surprisingly, tends to come from sources other than payment. The classic view of motivation was proposed by Abraham Maslow (1954). Maslow's Hierarchy of Need theory postulates that people will fulfil the needs at the lower end of a pyramid (survival needs and security needs) before they move on to addressing needs at the upper end (such as belonging needs, esteem needs and self-actualisation needs). Thus, once a salesperson has assured his or her basic survival needs, these cease to be motivators; the individual will then be moving onto esteem needs, or belonging needs. For this reason sales managers usually have a battery of motivational devices for salespeople to aim for (Figure 17.7 gives some examples).

Rookie A new sales recruit.

For **rookies**, the award of a company tie might address the need to belong; for more senior salespeople, membership of a Millionaire's Club (salespeople who have sold more than a million pounds' worth of product) might address esteem needs. Many sales managers offer prizes for salespeople's spouses or partners. This can be a powerful incentive since salespeople often work unusual hours, and thus have disrupted home lives; the spouse or partner is sometimes neglected in favour of the job, so a prize aimed at them can help assuage the salesperson's natural feelings of guilt.

Territory The geographical area or group of potential customers allocated to a salesperson.

Sales **territory** management involves ensuring that the salesforce have a reasonably equal chance of making sales. Clearly a garage tools salesperson in a major city will have an easier task than one in a rural area, simply because of the shorter distances between prospects; such a salesperson would spend more time in presentations and less time driving. On the other hand, the city salesperson would probably face more competition and might also have to spend more time caught in traffic during rush hour periods.

Territories can be divided geographically or by industry: IBM divide territories by industry, for example, so that salespeople get to know the problems and needs of the specific industry for which they have responsibility. IBM salespeople might be given responsibility for banks, or insurance companies, or local government departments. This sometimes means that salespeople have greater distances to travel in order to

Figure 17.7 Motivation tools

present IBM products, but are more able to make sensible recommendations and give useful advice. Geographical territories are more common, since they minimise travel time and maximise selling time.

It is virtually impossible to create exactly equal territories. Thus it is important to discuss decisions with salespeople in order to ensure that people feel they are being treated fairly. For example, some salespeople may be quite happy to accept a rural territory because they like to live and work in the country, even if it means earning less.

Exhibitions and trade fairs

Exhibitions and trade fairs represent a substantial commitment on the part of marketers. Total expenditure on exhibitions and trade fairs in the UK is consistently higher than the spend on magazine advertising, and is also higher than the combined expenditure on outdoor, cinema and radio advertising. Yet few exhibitors assess the effectiveness of this activity in any realistic way, and there is continuing academic debate about whether exhibitions are actually effective in communicating with target markets. Attitudes are polarised among exhibitors: some believe strongly that exhibitions are excellent promotional tools, whereas others believe exhibitions are marginal at best (Blythe and Rayner 1995).

One of the areas of dispute is the split between activities relating directly to making sales (generating leads, identifying prospects, even making sales pitches on the stand) and the non-sales benefits of exhibitions (public relations, enhancing corporate reputation, carrying out market research, etc.). Most exhibitors are concerned mainly with immediate sales (Blythe 1997; Kijewski et al. 1992; Shipley et al. 1993). Having said that, some exhibitors are more concerned with non-selling activities.

Exhibitions occupy a key role in business-to-business marketing, since they allow contact with buyers who otherwise might never meet due to geographical or time constraints. This is particularly the case with international trade fairs such as those held in Germany, where exhibitions occupy a more important role than in most other countries. Exhibitions such as these can bring together people who might otherwise not have known of each other's existence. Since contact at a fair takes place on neutral territory, both parties can feel more relaxed, so exhibitions offer an opportunity for the relationship between buying company and selling company to develop more

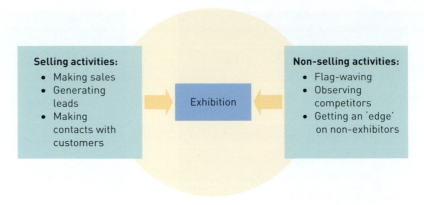

Figure 17.8   Selling and non-selling activities at exhibitions

fully, and perhaps develop in unexpected directions. Since many visitors are technical people or administrators rather than buyers, there are many opportunities for establishing contacts at all levels of the organisation.

Think outside this box!

It's interesting to note how people seem to separate marketing from selling. Of course, personal selling is a separate activity within marketing, but presumably the aim of *all* marketing is to increase the amount of business the firm does? Or at the very least, to persuade customers and others to behave in particular ways towards the firm and its products?

Let's not get too precious here – Alan Sugar once famously said, when asked what his corporate mission was, 'We want your money!' So how do we divide selling activities from non-selling activities? And does it matter?

As a public relations exercise, exhibitions have much to offer. Since buyers are only a tiny minority of visitors to exhibitions (less than 10% at most) (Blythe 2000; Gramman 1994), selling objectives are probably not the most important activities to be undertaken. Yet almost everybody who visits has some interest in the industry for which the exhibition is organised. This means that many of them will be influential in the buying decision, or at the very least might talk to people who are influential.

In terms of semiotics, trade fairs provide signs about the company and its products. For some firms, the sign is the main reason for exhibiting – being at the exhibition at all gives a signal that the company is at the forefront of the industry, or at least is not one of the laggards. In most cases, though, trade fairs are the vehicle by which signs are delivered. Sign systems of trade fairs are well-known – the stand, the suited personnel, the product samples, the free gifts, the product demonstrations and set-piece displays are typical of trade fairs. Each system has an accepted etiquette, so that visitors and exhibitors know what their role is when attending the show.

Syntactically, trade shows tend to be stylised. The meaning of a brochure offered at a trade show is not the same as the meaning of a brochure offered by a salesperson

Table 17.5 Ranking of exhibition aims

Reason for exhibiting	Ranking
Meeting new customers	1
Launching new products	2
Taking sales orders	3
Interacting with existing customers	4
Promoting existing products	5
Enhancing the company image	6
General market research	7
Meet new distributors	8
Keeping up with the competition	9
Getting information about the competition	10
Interacting with existing distributors	11
Getting an edge on non-exhibitors	12
Enhancing staff morale	13

at a customer's office. Because trade shows have a cultural context of their own, the resulting meanings differ from those encountered outside the exhibition hall.

Shipley et al. (1993) identified thirteen reasons for exhibiting, of which seven were directly related to selling while six represent non-selling activities. Research conducted by Blythe (1997) showed that the selling aims were ranked highest in importance by the majority of exhibitors (see Table 17.5).

Attempts to determine whether exhibitions are effective or not are also coloured by the assumption that they are primarily selling devices. Sharland and Balogh (1996) defined effectiveness as the number of sales leads generated, followed up and successfully closed, and efficiency as the comparison between the cost of participation in the trade show versus other sales and promotion activities.

VISITOR EXPECTATIONS

Research conducted among visitors to trade fairs shows that most of them are not directly involved in purchase decisions, and many of them have no role whatsoever in purchasing (Bello and Lohtia 1993; Gramman 1994; Munuera and Ruiz 1999; Skerlos and Blythe 2000).

Various categorisations of visitors have been proposed, many of them based on job titles: Blythe (2002) categorised visitors according to their aims in attending the exhibition, and came up with the following categories:

- Tyre kickers – have no purchasing intent or power, but pretend that they do
- Wheeler-dealers – have power and intention to buy, but go round all suppliers as they want the best deal
- Technocrats – engineers or technicians – mostly information-seekers

- Foxes – have their own agenda, for example spying on competitors or selling their own products to exhibitors
- Day trippers – students, retired people or just people generally having a day out of the office.

This categorisation was validated by Schwartz and Blythe (2003) in a study of German trade fair visitors, and again by Price and Blythe (2004) in a UK study. In this study, the following proportions of visitors were found at two exhibitions studied:

- Tyre kickers   6%
- Wheeler-dealers   8%
- Technocrats   20%
- Foxes   59%
- Day trippers   7%

If this finding is general to all exhibitions, it would appear that the vast majority of visitors have no buying power, and no intention to buy: in fact, most of them are there to sell to the exhibitors rather than to buy anything.

Real-life marketing: Making exhibitions work

Most exhibitors invest in shows with the aim of making sales. Maybe not on the stand itself – but at least they expect to generate leads, meet buyers, get the process going.

Unfortunately there is something missing from the picture – buyers. The research shows that only a small minority of visitors have a direct role in buying anything. If you want to sell at an exhibition, it looks as if you're on a wild goose chase – but if you use the exhibition wisely, all is not lost.

Since a large number of visitors are engineers and the like, why not put one or two of your own engineers on the stand? The visitors might be users of your product and would appreciate talking technical to someone, and may well provide you with the name of the person responsible for buying. In fact, almost anyone from your potential buying organisation could be an influencer or user, and would be happy to help you sell something they like the look of.

In practice, think about doing it this way:

- Keep the salespeople away from the exhibition. They have more important things to do – following up the leads you generate.
- Remember fewer than 10% of visitors are buyers. Go for the 90% you can get, not the 10% you can't.
- The purpose of your exhibition is to make contacts, not immediate sales.
- Keep the visitors' needs in mind – talk tech to engineers, systems to administrators, the old days with retired people. This way you will exchange something of value.

There is some evidence to show that even those people who are able to make recommendations or purchases are often not yet ready to make decisions – they attend the exhibition with the idea of collecting information for later use, perhaps several months or years later (Tanner and Chonko 1995). This means that tracking sales and attributing them to the exhibition is difficult at best, and in many cases is simply impossible.

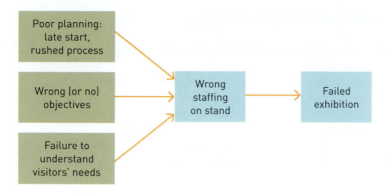

Figure 17.9 Why exhibitions fail

WHY EXHIBITIONS FAIL

Exhibitions frequently do not work for firms. In most cases, this is because exhibitors have not thought through their strategies clearly enough, have not set objectives and have not evaluated their activities sufficiently rigorously (or at all, in many cases) (Blythe 2000). As in any other area of marketing, failing to meet the needs of the customer (in this case the visitor) will result in a failure to communicate effectively and hence the failure of the exhibition.

In other cases, exhibitions fail because the exhibitors have inappropriate objectives. Although orders are sometimes placed at exhibitions or shortly afterwards, going to an exhibition with the sole objective of making sales is almost certainly unrealistic in most cases because so few buyers are present as a proportion of visitors. Even when buyers are present, they are likely to be in the information-gathering stage of the buying process and are unlikely to be in a position to place an order anyway. These reasons are shown in Figure 17.9.

As in other areas of business, much of the risk of failure can be reduced by planning ahead. Unfortunately, many exhibitors leave the planning of the exhibition to the last minute and do not prepare sufficiently in advance.

ALTERNATIVES TO EXHIBITIONS

Because of the cost and commitment attached to exhibiting, not least the disruption to the exhibitors' normal routine, firms are beginning to look for alternative routes for meeting buyers and promoting their products. Since one of the major advantages of exhibitions is the 'neutral territory' aspect, allowing buyers and sellers to discuss matters in a more relaxed way, many exhibitors are moving towards private exhibitions or roadshows to exhibit their products.

Private exhibitions

A private exhibition is one to which specific people are invited: it is organised by one firm, or sometimes by a group of firms, independent of an exhibition organiser. Private exhibitions are sometimes run at venues near to the public exhibition, and coinciding with the main event. Typically such events are held in hotels or small halls where the buyers are invited.

The main advantages are as follows:

- The atmosphere is usually more relaxed and less frenetic than that obtaining in the main exhibition.
- No competitors are present to distract the visitors.
- The exhibitor has much more control over the environment than would be the case at the public exhibition, where the organisers may impose irksome regulations.
- Superior refreshment and reception facilities are available.
- If the event is held in a hotel the staff will have access to their rooms and can easily take breaks.
- Sometimes the overall cost is less.

The main drawback of the private event is that visitors will come to it only if they are given advance warning, and even then may decide to visit just the main exhibition. The invitations need to be sent out early enough so that visitors can make allowance for the event, but not so early that they forget about it, and some incentive to make the necessary detour may also need to be in place. It is extremely unlikely that the list of desirable visitors will be complete – one of the main advantages of the public exhibition is that some of the visitors will be unknown to the exhibiting company, and a first contact can be made.

Private exhibitions work best in situations where the company has a limited market, where the costs of the main exhibition are high, and where a suitable venue is available close to the main site.

Roadshows

A roadshow is a travelling exhibition that takes the product to the buyer rather than the other way round. In some cases these are run in hotels, in other cases trailers or caravans are used. Roadshows are useful in cases where large numbers of buyers are concentrated in particular geographical areas, and where many of them would not make the journey to visit a national exhibition. In some countries industries may be geographically concentrated (in the United States, for example, the film industry is concentrated in California and the steel industry in Pennsylvania), making a roadshow more economical.

Like private exhibitions, roadshows allow the exhibitor to control the environment to a large extent. They can be run in conjunction with other firms, which reduces the cost and increases the interest level for the visitors; this can be particularly effective if the firms concerned are complementary rather than competing.

In common with private exhibitions, the roadshow's organiser is entirely responsible for all the publicity. In the case of a major public exhibition the exhibition organisers and even the firm's competitors will ensure that a certain minimum level of visitors will attend; in the case of a roadshow the exhibitor will need to produce considerable advance publicity and even send out specific invitations to individual buyers and prospects. This adds to the risk as well as the cost.

Sales promotion

Sales promotions are intended to create a short-term increase in sales. They can take many forms, from short-term discounts through to extra quantities, free packs and free gifts. Sales promotions are typical of push strategies: this is one in which the goods are heavily promoted to distributors rather than to the end customer. The

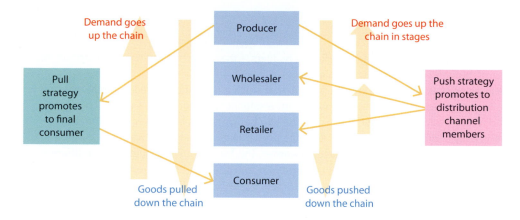

Figure 17.10   Push versus pull strategies

theory is that the distributor will, in turn, promote the product heavily, thus pushing the goods through the distribution chain. The converse of a push strategy is a pull strategy, in which the goods are promoted heavily to the final users in order to create a demand that will pull the goods through the distribution chain.

Expenditure on sales promotion has increased in recent years as producers find that push strategies can be more accurately targeted and are less prone to clutter (the effect of too much promotion vying for the customer's attention). One of the major benefits of sales promotion is that it deflects interest away from price as a competitive tool, particularly if the promotion is not of the 'extra discount' variety. Creating the campaign should be based on the 'who do I want to do what?' question (Cummins 1998). In other words, the objective of the campaign needs to be couched in precise terms – an aim 'to increase sales' is too vague, whereas an aim 'to encourage customers to recommend the product to their friends' is one that can be used as the basis for creative thinking.

Sales promotions can be used to encourage a trial, to **trade up** (buy the more expensive version of the product), or to expand usage: when aimed at distributors, they can encourage distributors to increase stock levels (load up). This may effectively only move sales from the future to the present: when the promotion is over, the distributor may de-stock and therefore reduce purchases for a period. This may not matter if the purpose of the promotion is to even out demand in order to schedule factory production better, or if the purpose is to lock out competitors from shelf space at the warehouse, but it is important to understand that sales promotions usually have a short-term effect.

Trade up Buying the more expensive model.

Real-life marketing: Promotional gifts that promote

Goldwell is a German hair cosmetics manufacturer, dealing exclusively with hairdressing salons. When the firm entered the UK market they found themselves facing an established market in which L'Oréal, Schwarzkopf, Wella, Clynol and Clairol had sewn up the bulk of the market between them. All of these companies were bigger

(Continued)

(Continued)

than Goldwell, and consequently had much bigger marketing budgets – they also had nationwide distribution, both directly to salons and through cash-and-carry wholesalers.

Goldwell began by equipping their salespeople with vans, so that stock could be delivered immediately – no waiting for the order to be processed and delivered. Although some salespeople thought this approach seemed unorthodox at best, and unprofessional at worst, it did give the company a slight edge over the others in the market. Where Goldwell really scored, though, was in its sales promotions. Salespeople were empowered to give away free samples of product – but if a salon placed an order, the free samples would be of a different product in the Goldwell range. Salon owners would use the products, and perhaps order them next time – thus obtaining free samples of yet another product. This approach meant that Goldwell gradually displaced other companies' products.

Sales promotion bought Goldwell a substantial share of the professional market in the UK, and coupled with its rapid delivery system made the company a major player within five years of entering the market.

To do this in practice, follow these rules:

- This works best in a business-to-business context because the vendor will have a good record of what each buyer has bought in the past.
- The free product needs to be given in enough quantity for the buyer to use it regularly for a while.
- This works best if the buyer is also the person using the product, in other words, it works best for small businesses.

In capital-goods markets such as cars, major household appliances and (in business-to-business markets) heavy machinery, reduced-interest or zero-interest deals can be powerful incentives, as can leasing deals. These incentives can overcome situations where the customer has little or no money, or where (in business markets) the finance director has declared a moratorium on expenditure. The problem for the supplier can lie in working out the cost of such deals, so many firms will involve an outside bank or finance company to handle the details. Finance companies will judge the supplier against the following criteria:

1. The goods need to be durable, identifiable and movable (in case of repossession).
2. The goods should have a value greater than the outstanding debt at all times, which means there should be a well-established second-hand market.
3. The supplier must itself be a reliable, well-established business.

Some suppliers are large enough to act as their own finance companies. This was notably the case for IBM, which from its foundation up until the mid-1980s did not sell any of its equipment outright – everything was leased. This meant that IBM retained ownership of all its equipment throughout the world, which gave the company a substantial measure of control over its customers, though at the cost of cash flow problems in the early years.

Many sales promotions involve the customer in doing something: filling in a form, scratching panels on a scratch card, collecting tokens towards a prize and so forth. The actions are called **mechanics**, and need to be carefully designed so as to maximise the effectiveness of the promotion. The following considerations apply to designing a mechanic:

Mechanics In sales promotion, the activities the customer must undertake.

- The mechanic should not involve a task that is too complex, or might be seen as too much trouble. A task that is too complex will result in people giving up

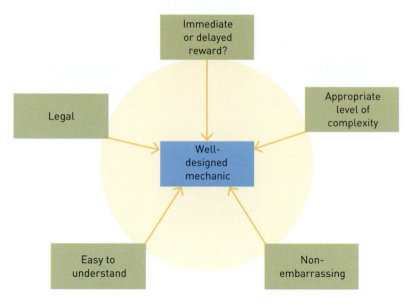

Figure 17.11   Issues in designing mechanics

or not attempting the mechanic: on the other hand, those who do carry out a complex task are likely to be the most highly motivated and therefore may be highly desirable customers.

- Embarrassing or personally intrusive mechanics should be avoided. The feelings of the person carrying out the mechanic need to be considered, and in particular notice needs to be taken of cultural issues.
- The mechanic should be comprehensible to the target group. There is no reason why a mechanic should not be made incomprehensible to an undesirable market segment – for example, a sales promotion for a company offering activity holidays in France might be written in French if the company wants to exclude non-French speakers.
- The mechanic might be immediate (a scratch card giving an instant prize) or delayed (a discount on a future purchase). Immediate rewards are often more appealing to the consumer, but may not result in future purchases.
- The mechanic must be legal. Mechanics that involve gambling may be illegal in some countries, and even in the UK a mechanic involving a game of chance cannot be dependent on a purchase. In other words, the consumer can demand a scratch card without actually buying anything – though few people would do so.

Categories of sales promotion

Sales promotions fall into three categories: promotions aimed at the sales team, promotions aimed further down the value chain at middlemen and promotions aimed at the consumer.

Promotions aimed at the salesforce are part of the motivational programme. Prizes, cash rewards and extra benefits such as 'salesman of the month' status all come under this category, and can be considered as sales promotions since they are aimed at gaining a short-term increase in sales. Such promotions work well in single-transaction type selling, but can be seriously counterproductive in key-account management, since salespeople are encouraged to go for quick results rather than build long-term relationships.

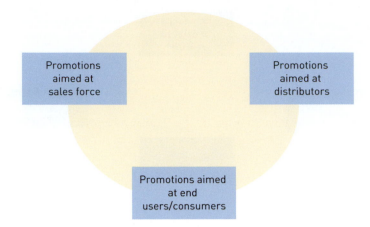

Figure 17.12   Categories of sales promotion

Sales promotions aimed at channel intermediaries form part of a push strategy. Early in the product life cycle, incentives to middlemen may be necessary to gain acceptance of new products by channel members. This can be an important consideration for the customer, since onward sales of the goods need to be assured. Incentives to encourage distributors to carry the product will also help in shutting out later competition. For example, a manufacturer of an artificial sweetener may want to encourage food manufacturers to incorporate the sweetener. In order to do this, a sales promotion encouraging retailers to stock products containing the sweetener would clearly help. Promotions aimed at customers might be used to shift the time of purchase, stimulate a trial, or encourage continued use of a product. These probably represent the mainstream of sales promotions.

Sales promotion is less widely used in business-to-business markets than it is in consumer markets. The reasons for this are obscure: it may be that business buyers are less likely to be swayed by temporary promotions, or it may be that a sales promotion is not conducive to building long-term relationships. There is, however, a role for sales promotion in the business-to-business arena, even if only in the form of 'deal sweeteners' which are available to salespeople to cement orders and build relationships.

Think outside this box!

Sales promotions to consumers often take the form of free gifts, and the same is true in business-to-business markets. Where, then, is the difference between this and a straight bribe? If we offer the business buyer (say) a 'training course' which just happens to take place in Tenerife or the Bahamas, why does this not constitute an arrestable offence?

In a sense, does it matter if we do this? Who loses out, after all? Sales promotions only shift sales – they don't necessarily increase sales over the year. Maybe gifts of this sort are just ways of smoothing the path of business, making things more flexible, and providing all of us with an easier life. But if so, where do we stop? How do we distinguish between giving reasonable business gifts, or the simple courtesy of picking up the bill for lunch, and the seduction of buyer into doing something that is not in their employers' best interests?

SALES PROMOTION TECHNIQUES

Sales promotions aimed at consumers come in many varieties, but some of the more common ones are as follows:

- Free tastings. New food products are often promoted in supermarkets by companies who offer free tastings to shoppers. This technique is expensive, because the demonstrators have to be paid to give away free product, but it is extremely effective in encouraging a trial. The consumer often feels under a small obligation to buy the product, having accepted the 'gift' of a taste.
- Money-off vouchers in press advertisements. The main advantage of this type of promotion is that the marketers can check the effectiveness of one print medium over another, i.e. the managers can see which newspaper or magazine generates the highest number of coupon redemptions. The main drawback is that it tends to lead to short-term brand switching: when the offer ends, consumers are likely to revert to their usual brand.
- Two-for-one. Customers pay for the product, but are given an extra one free. This is equivalent to a generous price discount, so it will appeal to price-sensitive consumers, who will typically switch brands to take advantage of the offers without demonstrating any subsequent brand loyalty. Two-for-one offers are useful for disposing of excess stock (especially perishable stock) and for shutting out competitors, but they are of course expensive.
- **Piggy-backing** or bundling. This promotion works by providing a free sample of a product, attached to a complementary product. For example, Amazon (the on-line book retailer) will frequently offer an extra book, on a complementary subject, to textbook purchasers.
- Instant lottery or scratch cards. This type of promotion is commonly used in petrol stations, with the intention of encouraging motorists to stop at the same petrol station. In many countries these promotions are illegal, because they involve gambling: in the UK the promoters cannot require customers to make a purchase, nor can the scratch cards be linked to purchases of a specific minimum amount. In other words, people can (in theory) demand a scratch card without buying anything, although in practice few people would have the courage to do this.
- Free gift with each purchase. Free gifts are often enclosed with children's breakfast cereals, but other promotions have ranged from a free Frisbee with suntan lotion to a free sunroof with a new car. Free gifts can encourage brand switching: this can be particularly effective when selling to children, because children are less likely to switch back again: children are not price-sensitive, and will tend to keep to their favourite brand.
- Loyalty cards. These cards offer rewards to customers for shopping at the same retailer, or (in the case of airlines or ferry companies) using the same company for travel. Usually the rewards are given as discounts or vouchers against future purchases, but sometimes (notably in hypermarkets in France and Spain) in-store discounts are available for loyalty cardholders, and sometimes points can be redeemed against goods that are available only to cardholders. Likewise, some airlines allow frequent flyers to use the Business Class lounges, or to bring a partner on a business flight.

Piggy-backing Attaching one product to another for the purposes of sales promotion.

In general, sales promotions involve giving something away. The gift should (ideally) be something that is not too expensive for the promoter to supply, offers extra added value for the consumer, and is relevant to the product being promoted. The offer should not look 'too good to be true' for two reasons: first, the company might find itself unable to fulfil the promotion, and second, consumers might suspect that there is a 'catch', which would certainly be counter-productive.

An interesting variation on the standard sales promotion (which benefits the purchaser only) is to offer something to a friend of the purchaser. This can be surprisingly powerful, especially if the product is regarded as a luxury or a treat – people often feel guilty about spending money on treating themselves, but if a friend will also benefit, this helps reduce the guilty feelings and makes the purchase more likely (Lee and Corfman 2004). For example, somebody who buys a week at a luxury hotel might be given a voucher for a friend to have a one-night stay during the week, or the purchaser of a new hairdo might be given a discount voucher to give to a friend. Promotions such as this also have the advantage of encouraging word of mouth.

Off-the-shelf promotions are provided by suppliers that specialise in sales promotions. For example, a common promotion is to offer free hotel accommodation to customers. The customers are usually required to take their evening meal and breakfast at the hotel, and pay for these, so the hotel is guaranteed some revenue. This makes the promotion relatively cheap for the promoter. Often the vouchers are valid for off-peak periods only, when the hotel rooms might be empty anyway: the hotelier would obviously rather have some income than none, and also the guests may like the hotel and return at a later date, paying the full price.

Off-the-shelf promotions do require a certain degree of trust on all sides, since the company offering the promotion has very little control over the quality of the service provided, or the terms on which other people are benefiting from the same offer. For example, a discount voucher for a meal at a posh restaurant will not seem like a bargain if it turns out that the restaurant offers the same discount to anyone who turns up on the same night. If run well, though, off-the-shelf promotions provide benefits to all parties – the promoter gains because customers want the discounts, the firm giving the discounts gains because of the extra business during an off-peak period, and the customer gains by obtaining a cheaper deal than would otherwise be the case.

Joint promotions are a way of reducing the costs of promotions by sharing them with another (related) firm. Entering into a joint-promotion agreement with another company allows the firm to gain in several ways: the cost of the promotion is reduced, the scope of the promotion is increased because the other firm will contact its own customer base and the customer's perception of value is often increased. Piggy-backing (bundling) promotions operate this way, but joint promotions can be linked to a charity or cause, or can link to products or companies with which the promoter might have a marketing synergy. For example, Kimberley-Clark (manufacturers of Kleenex) ran a highly successful promotion during the summer months, based on hay-fever sufferers. Kleenex sells best during the winter, when people have colds or 'flu: hay fever sufferers who could supply three proofs of

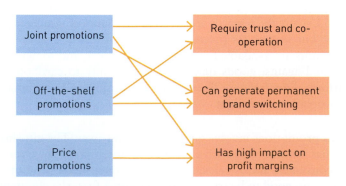

Figure 17.13   Strengths and weaknesses of sales promotions

Table 17.6   Immediate discounts

Type of discount	Example
Seasonal discount	January sales and summer sales are both ways of boosting business during times when consumer spending is often low. In recent years, however, many people in the UK have been deliberately delaying their purchases until the January sales, seriously affecting the pre-Christmas trade of many retailers.
Multibuys	Offering discounts for bulk purchase (two-for-one offers) is actually a price promotion. A study by the London Business School found that 95% of multibuys are bought by only 27% of households, who then promptly switch to a competitor's product when the multibuy promotion ends.
Banded packs	Banded packs are similar to multibuys, but in this case, the goods are wrapped together in an outer package, thus forcing the customer to buy two or more.
Reduced shelf price	Grocery retailers frequently reduce the price of goods that are approaching their sell-by dates. Such promotions can reduce the propensity of consumers to pay the full price: near to closing-time, groups of customers can often be seen hovering around the 'reduced items' shelves of supermarkets.
Extra-fill packs	Special extra-large packs are produced, labelled (for example) '25% Extra Free'. The main advantage of this type of promotion is that the cost of the extra product is relatively small: distribution, packaging, and marketing costs far outweigh the cost of the product.

purchase of Kleenex were sent a free 'hay fever kit' containing an Optrex eye-mask, Merethol lozenges, a travel pack of Kleenex and a batch of money-off coupons for hay fever-related products.

Price promotions are an obvious form of sales promotion, but are risky because they inevitably reduce profit margins. Price promotions might involve immediate discounts (see Table 17.6), or delayed discounts. A delayed discount might be a voucher valid against future purchases, or a coupon from a newspaper advertisement. There are three drawbacks to coupon-redemption schemes: first, it is difficult to estimate the redemption rate of coupons in advance, and therefore difficult to estimate the cost of the promotion. Second, coupons are sometimes cut from batches of newspapers and redeemed through a retailer who is an accomplice. Third, some retailers will accept coupons against any purchases, regardless of whether the customer is actually buying the product being promoted or not. Some retailers even honour vouchers from other retailers, as a way of sabotaging the rival firm's promotion.

Whatever type of sales promotion is used, marketers should be careful not to overuse the technique. Sales promotions work because they offer something unusual: if the product always has a 'special' price reduction consumers will come to expect it, and will switch away from the product when the promotion ends. This in turn forces the company to re-introduce the promotion, so that (in effect) the company has simply cut its profit margins, often by a substantial amount.

Multibuys A sales promotion in which customers are offered extra packs of product when they buy one or more packs.

INTEGRATING SALES PROMOTIONS WITH OTHER COMMUNICATIONS TOOLS

Sales promotions are often thought to be relatively ineffective because the temporary increase in sales is followed by a fall in sales, as customers have stocked up on the product. If the purpose of the promotion is to even out seasonal sales, this may not matter, but the view is based on the following assumptions:

1. Loyal customers will stock up on the product (where this is possible) and will therefore not need to buy any more of the product for some time.
2. Some consumers who switch brands will switch to another supplier as soon as the promotion ends (Krishna et al. 1991).
3. There are hard-core loyal consumers who will not switch brands, no matter what incentives are offered. These are likely to be the most valuable customers for the brand.

On the plus side, many people who stock up on the brand will give samples away to their friends (Wansink and Deshpande 1994). Second, some people will stay with the new brand – even habitual brand switchers will often stay with the brand until there is some reason to switch (competitors running a promotion, for example). Third, even hard-core loyal customers will eventually switch brands, if only because their own brand ceases production.

Integrating sales promotion with other communications is intended to create what is called the ratchet effect. This is the process whereby sales are sharply increased as a result of a sales promotion, and sustained at the new level by the judicious use of other promotional tools. A clever or controversial sales promotion can create publicity: a sales promotion with a good mechanic can create a database, and a good retailer promotion can support the salesforce in winning orders from retailers.

As with any other form of integration of communications, clarity of objectives, consistency of message and consideration of the synergy between the different tools will always benefit the campaign.

Chapter summary

The salesforce is a major part of business-to-business budgets. In many cases, salespeople spend relatively little time actually selling, and a great deal of time filling in paperwork, travelling between appointments and so forth. This means that much sales management effort is directed towards ensuring that the salespeople spend as little time on administration as possible, and are effective when they are in front of a customer. Sales promotions offer a valuable tool for creating temporary increases in sales, but may or may not lead to long-term increases in business. Like any other marketing tool, sales promotions need to be placed in a context: they should operate within an overall framework of marketing communications.

 Key points

- Selling is about solving problems for customers, it is not about persuasion.
- Salespeople often identify with customers.
- After-sales activities are essential, but are often neglected.
- Techniques used in small-scale accounts are counterproductive in key-account selling.
- Commission is a way of ensuring fairness: it is probably not a strong motivator.

- Buyers are very much in the minority at most, if not all, exhibitions.
- Most visitors are on an information search, not on a shopping trip.
- Most exhibitors are focused strongly on selling, whereas they should be focused on making useful contacts.
- Sales promotions can be useful as deal sweeteners or facilitators.
- Sales promotions often only result in shifting sales forward, rather than increasing sales in the long term.
- Sales promotions can be used for the salesforce, for intermediaries, for customers, or for the customers of customers.
- Promotions can backfire: although the best ones are highly innovative, so are the disastrous ones.

Review questions

1. What are the main differences between key-account selling and small-account selling?
2. Which remuneration system would you expect to be more highly motivating: a commission-only system, or a straight-salary system?
3. Why is ice-breaking important?
4. Why do salespeople tend to identify with customers more than with the firms they work for?
5. Why are after-sales activities often neglected?
6. What is the difference between an objection and a condition?
7. What would be the most appropriate staffing approach for an exhibitor seeking to relate to existing customers?
8. What type of sales promotion would be most effective for a firm entering a new market?
9. How might salespeople use sales promotions to close deals? What might be the dangers of doing this?
10. How might a sales promotion be linked to an exhibition?

Case study revisited: Jamie at Home

Using the title of one of his TV shows, Jamie Oliver set up a party-plan operation to sell his merchandise. The name was, of course, already well-known due to his TV appearances: all he (or rather his company) needed to do was to recruit party-plan organisers to run the parties.

Party plan operates by asking people (predominantly women) to invite their friends to their homes in order to try out (and buy) products. A party organiser from the supplier helps by demonstrating and selling the products, and expediting the orders: the hostess is expected to supply a venue and refreshments, and in exchange is given a gift and discount off her own purchases.

Jamie at Home recruits organisers via its website, and also from recommendations from existing organisers. Party hostesses win four points for every pound spent at their party, redeemable against Jamie Oliver products. Each party involves a video of Jamie Oliver creating one of his recipes, plus some quizzes and competitions. Hostesses can save the points: some hold several parties through the year, and redeem the points in one go, perhaps to buy Christmas presents.

The party organisers are self-employed and work on a commission-only basis. They have the responsibility for selling products at the parties, and for running the parties: they receive 20% commission on everything sold at the party and are given training in sales techniques and (of course) in product knowledge. Becoming a party organiser is a good way of earning extra cash, or even of making a full-time living, since it is flexible and can fit around family commitments (or even other work commitments). It is a popular way of life for women especially – the selling aspects are conducted in a friendly social atmosphere, and they effectively have no boss. There is no hard sell, and there are opportunities to advance – an organiser who recruits other organiser will gain a small override commission on their sales as well as her own.

For the company, party plan offers a way of remaining in complete control over how the products are presented. The target audience is self-selecting, since people invite their friends who are, presumably, much like themselves. The lack of retailers and wholesalers in the distribution chain frees up some margin for paying the organisers and hostesses without cutting margins, and although the products themselves are not cheap the party atmosphere makes it easy for people to buy. What's more, party plan fits extremely well with the Jamie Oliver persona – his down-to-earth, working-lad-made-good style makes him the kind of person most of us would feel comfortable inviting into our homes.

Case study: Whopper Face

Burger King is a Florida-based fast-food corporation that operates globally. The company was founded in 1953 after Keith Kramer and Matthew Burns had visited the original McDonald's restaurant in California. The company was not, at first, a great success and was bought out in 1954 by two of its franchisees.

The company has certainly had something of a rough ride since. It has changed hands four times, and in 2010 the majority of the shares were owned by a Brazilian investment company. In common with other fast-food outlets, Burger King has come in for criticism regarding the health risks of their products as well as the environmental impact of the restaurants: in addition, and perhaps not surprisingly considering the company's origins, Burger King has always operated in the shadow of McDonald's. The flagship product, the Whopper, is similar to the Big Mac except it has a more embarrassing name, and it is difficult to see what the company's USP (unique selling proposition) is. Differentiating itself from McDonald's is clearly difficult.

Having said that, Burger King continues to be profitable and popular. McDonald's aims itself firmly at the family market, offering sales promotions such as free toys for children and of course Ronald McDonald, whereas Burger King has aimed at a young adult market – the 18–34 demographic. The problem for the company is therefore developing sales promotions that will appeal to this audience.

Burger King's main claim to differentiation is that the burgers are not standardised. Each one is custom-made to the customer's specification – in other words, people can ask for the pickle to be left out, or have extra bacon, or no cheese, or whatever variations on the basic burger they might prefer. This sounds like an easy concept to get across, and also an attractive feature of Burger King as opposed to McDonald's, but in fact people don't always know (or care) that the burgers are made to order.

Burger King have therefore piloted a remarkable sales promotion in one of their outlets in São Paulo, Brazil. Using a camera and a printer, the company printed customers' photographs on the paper wrapper used to wrap the Whoppers. The campaign, dreamed up by Ogilvy Brazil, led to gasps of surprise from customers, some complaints that the pictures were unflattering, but for the most part general delight: more importantly, it led to a massive word-of-mouth response and a video that went viral on YouTube with more than three-quarters of a million hits. People flocked to Burger King to have their photographs taken buying a burger, and many of the wrappers found their way into people's homes and offices where they could be displayed for friends and family – people who are frequently in the same target demographic.

Comments varied on YouTube: some were still negative about fast food in general, but the majority were positive, referring to the promotion as 'cool' or (as one Brazilian poster put it) 'Uma das melhores ações de promo e direct que vi nos últimos anos' [One of the best direct promotion actions I have seen in recent years]. Whichever way people commented, the fact remained that Burger King was being talked about, and the main message – customisation – was getting across.

Whether the promotion needs to be repeated elsewhere is another question – the effect has been dramatic this time, but may not be quite so exciting another time.

Questions

1. How has this sales promotion linked into other promotions?
2. Why not roll this out internationally?
3. Why would some people still be negative about Burger King?
4. How can Burger King leverage the campaign further?
5. What might be the permanent effects of this promotion?

Further reading

The classic book on key-account selling is N. Rackham, *Spin Selling* (Aldershot: Gower, 2000). Although it is intended for practitioners and managers, it is based on sound research and offers exceptionally good, clear advice for salespeople.

One of the few academic textbooks on the sales process is Jim Blythe, *Sales and Key-Account Management* (London: Thomson Learning, 2005).

References

Anderson, Erin and Robertson, Thomas S. (1995) Inducing multi-line salespeople to adopt house brands. *Journal of Marketing*, 59 (2): 16–31.

Bello, D.C. and Lohtia, R. (1993) Improving trade show effectiveness by analyzing attendees. *Industrial Marketing Management*, 22: 311–18.

Blythe, Jim (1997) Does size matter? Objectives and measures at UK trade exhibitions. *Journal of Marketing Communications*, 3 (1).

Blythe, Jim (2000) Objectives and measures at UK trade exhibitions. *Journal of Marketing Management*, 16: 203–22.

Blythe, Jim (2002) Communications and innovation: the case of hi-fi systems. *Corporate Communications: An International Journal*, 7 (1).

Blythe, Jim and Rayner, Tony (1996) The evaluation of non-selling activities at British trade exhibitions – an exploratory study. *Proceedings of the Marketing Education Group Conference*, Bradford Business School, July.

Cespedes, F.V. (1996) *Managing Marketing Linkages: Texts, Cases and Readings.* Upper Saddle River, NJ: Prentice Hall.

Coca-Cola Company (1981) Measuring the Grapevine: Consumer Response and Word-of-Mouth. Coca-Cola Company Consumer Information Centre.

Cummins, J. (1998) *Sales Promotion: How to Create and Implement Campaigns That Really Work.* London: Kogan Page.

Davies, Iain A., Ryals, Lynette J. and Holt, Sue (2010) Relationship management: a sales role, or a state of mind? An investigation of functions and attitudes across a business-to-business sales force. *Industrial Marketing Management*, 39 (7): 1049–62.

Dewsnap, B. and Jobber, D. (1998) *The Sales and Marketing Interface: Is It Working?* Proceedings of the Academy of Marketing Conference, Sheffield.

Dion, P., Easterling, D. and Miller, S.J. (1995) What is really necessary in buyer–seller relationships? *Industrial Marketing Management*, 24: 1–9.

Donaldson, W. (1998) *Sales Management Theory and Practice.* London: Macmillan.

Gramann, J. (1994) *Independent Market Research.* Birmingham: Centre Exhibitions with National Exhibition Centre.

Herzberg, F. (1966) *Work and the Nature of Man.* London: William Collins.

Kijewski, V., Yoon, E. and Young, G. (1992) *Trade Shows: How Managers Pick Their Wnners.* University Park, PA: Institute for the Study of Business Markets.

Krishna, A., Currim, I.S. and Shoemaker, R.W. (1991) Consumer perceptions of promotional activity. *Journal of Marketing*, 55 (April): 4–16.

Lambe, C. Jay, Webb, Kevin L. and Ishida, Chiharu (2009) Self-managing selling teams and team performance: the complementary roles of empowerment and control. *Industrial Marketing Management*, 38 (1): 5–16.

Lee, S.N. and Corfman, K.P. (2004) A Little something for me, and maybe for you too. Promotions that relieve guilt. *Advances in Consumer Research*, 31 (1).

Maslow, Abraham (1954) *Motivation and Personality.* New York: Harper and Row.

McKenna, R. (1991) *Relationship Marketing.* London: Century Business.

Millman, A.F. and Wilson, K.J. (1996) Developing key account management competencies. *Journal of Marketing Practice*, 2 (2):7–22.

Millman, T. and Wilson, K.J. (1995) *Developing Key Account Managers.* IMP 12th International Conference Proceedings, Manchester Federal School of Business and Management, 1995.

Munuera, Jose L. and Ruiz, Salvador (1999) Trade fairs as services: a look at visitors' objectives in Spain. *Journal of Business Research*, 44 (1): 17–24.

Piercy, Nigel F. and Lane, Nikala (2003) Transformation of the traditional salesforce: imperatives for intelligence, interface and integration. *Journal of Marketing Management*, 19: 563–82.

Price, E. and Blythe, J. (2004) Information source usage by trade fair attendees. *Proceedings of the Academy of Marketing Conference*, Cheltenham, July.

Ramaswamy, Sridhar N. and Singh, Jagdip (2003) Antecedents and consequences of merit pay fairness for industrial salespeople. *Journal of Marketing*, 67 (4): 46–66.

Rangajaran, David, Chonko, Lawrence B., Jones, Eli and Roberts, James A. (2004) Organisational variables, salesforce perceptions of readiness for change, learning, and performance among boundary-spanning teams: a conceptual framework and propositions for research. *Industrial Marketing Management*, 33 (4): 289–305.

Rosenbloom, B. and Anderson, R.E. (1984) The sales manager: tomorrow's super marketer. *Business Horizons*, Mar/Apr: 50–6.

Schwartz, A. and Blythe, J. (2003) Visitor typology and the trade fair servicescape. Proceedings of the Academy of Marketing Conference, Aston Business School, July.

Sharland, A. and Balogh, P. (1996) The value of non-selling activities at international trade shows. *Industrial Marketing Management*, 25 (1): 59–66.

Shipley, D., Egan, C. and Wong, K.S. (1993) Dimensions of trade show exhibiting management. *Journal of Marketing Management*, 9 (1): 55–63.

Singh, Ramendra and Koshy, Abraham (2011) Does salesperson's customer orientation create value in B2B relationships? Empirical evidence from India. *Industrial Marketing Management*, 40 (1): 78–85.

Skerlos, K. and Blythe, J. (2000) *Ignoring the audience: exhibitors and visitors at a Greek trade fair*. Proceedings of the Fifth International Conference on Corporate and Marketing Communication, Erasmus University, Rotterdam, 22 and 23 May.

Strong, E.K. (1925) *The Psychology of Selling.* New York: McGraw–Hill.

Tanner, J.F. and Chonko, L.B. (1995) Trade show objectives, management and staffing practices. *Industrial Marketing Management*, 24: 257–64.

Troilo, Gabriele, De Luca, Luigi M. and Guenzi, Paolo (2009) Dispersion of influence between marketing and sales: its effects on superior customer value and market performance. *Industrial Marketing Management*, 38 (8): 872–82.

Vilela, Belen Bande, Gonzalez, Jose Antonio Varela, Ferrin, Pilar Fernandez and delRio Araujo, Luisa (2007) Impression management tactics and affective context: influence on sales performance appraisal. *European Journal of Marketing*, 41 (5/6): 624–39.

Wachner, Trent, Plouffe, Christopher R. and Grégoire, Yany (2009) SOCO's impact on individual sales performance: the integration of selling skills as a missing link. *Industrial Marketing Management*, 38 (1): 32–44.

Wansink, B. and Deshpande, R. (1994) Out of sight, out of mind: pantry stockpiling and brand-use frequency. *Marketing Letters*, 5(1): 91–100.

Wilson, K.J. (1993) Managing the industrial sales force of the 1990s. *Journal of Marketing Management*, 9 (2): 123–39.

More online

To gain free access to additional online resources to support this chapter please visit:
www.sagepub.co.uk/blythe3e

Part Five

Marketing in motion

Chapter 18 covers the vital topic of digital marketing, including the use of social media and Internet marketing. The future of electronic marketing is hard to predict, but some possible scenarios are discussed. There is little doubt that it will continue to grow in importance and this chapter provides a foundation for understanding the drivers for this growth.

Managing intermediaries effectively can make a very large difference to the bottom line for most firms. Chapter 19 looks at the practical aspects of controlling a distribution channel, whether from the viewpoint of a retailer, a wholesaler or a manufacturer. Database and direct marketing are covered. The chapter also looks at logistics and physical distribution methods.

Chapter 20 takes a more detailed look at the day-to-day activities of retailers, wholesalers and agents. The chapter covers the nature of retailing and wholesaling, types of retailer, non-stop retailing and retailer strategy.

Chapter 21 looks at the management of individuals involved in delivering marketing outcomes. Front-line staff are the people who deal with customers as part of their everyday jobs: they have specific responsibilities and pressures, and can be a crucial element in maintaining the corporate image. The chapter also looks at the process for delivering customer value, and at ways of improving the processes. Finally, the chapter covers physical evidence issues such as retail environment, decor and atmospherics, and such evidence as brochures and documentation.

CHAPTER ⟨18⟩
Digital marketing and social media

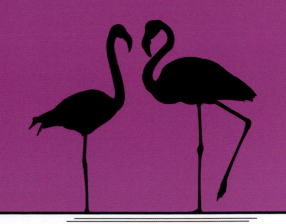

LEARNING OBJECTIVES

After reading this chapter, you should be able to:

- Explain the differences between digital marketing and traditional marketing.

- Describe the ways in which social media can be used to good effect by marketers.

- Explain the uses and abuses of SMS marketing.

- Describe the basics of good Web design.

- Explain the barriers to Internet-based marketing.

Introduction

Digital marketing refers to any exchange processes conducted via electronic means. It is the cutting edge of marketing – thirty years ago it did not exist at all, and development is so rapid that the field moves on faster than it can be written about or researched. For example, Twitter was only founded in 2006, yet it now has 500 million subscribers worldwide, and very few people will not have heard of it. Facebook was founded in 2004, and now has almost 15% of the world's population as subscribers. **SMS** (text messaging) was first launched in the early 1990s (the first ever message sent via SMS was 'Merry Christmas', sent by one of the developers of the system in 1992). SMS is now the most-used electronic communication system, with 3.6 billion users worldwide – more than half the world's population.

Marketing via the Internet has become one of the fastest-growing areas of marketing, in part because it can reach the wealthier and better-educated segments of the market. It is probably true to say that younger people are much more at ease with the Internet, in general, than older people, so those aiming for a younger market would be unwise to ignore the Internet; but older people are certainly catching up – the largest age group on Twitter is 35–49-year-olds, and the median age for residents of Second Life is 33. LinkedIn's average age is 41, perhaps not surprising for a website devoted to professionals.

SMS Short Message Service, or texting on cellular telephones.

Social media have become ubiquitous also, and since they are mainly funded by advertising they cannot be ignored by marketers. The ability to target very specific segments by using media such as LinkedIn and Facebook makes them a very attractive place to promote goods and services.

Preview case study: Manchester United and Facebook

Manchester United is one of the most popular football teams in the world, with fans spread throughout the globe – in fact, the vast majority of MUFC's fans have never seen the team play at their Old Trafford home ground, but have only followed them on TV. Like any other major team, Manchester United operates as a business, with much of its revenue coming from sources other than gate receipts – if there were no gate receipts at all, MUFC would hardly be affected since most of its income comes from TV and merchandising.

Maintaining its pole position as a club, therefore, goes far beyond what happens on the pitch. MUFC has its own TV channel, it has fan clubs worldwide (even in countries like the United States, where association football, or soccer, is a minority sport). The club has been quick to use any new opportunities that present themselves to maintain its status and encourage more people to become fans, and spend on products: since many fans feel closer to their football team than they do to their families, this is not especially difficult. Social media such as Facebook therefore present a perfect opportunity for keeping up with fans: making 'friends' with MUFC on Facebook is a natural development – but how popular is it?

Digital vs traditional marketing

Digital marketing should be a marketer's dream come true because it is controlled entirely by the participants, not by corporations. At the core of all digital media is the concept of interactivity – participants communicate with each other and with organisations, and expect to be treated as individuals. They therefore tend to resent blatant advertising, and will be looking for useful content in any communication with a company. In other words, digital media should not be regarded as a one-way proposition. Table 18.1 lists the differences between digital and traditional media.

Because digital marketing is almost always interactive, marketers need to offer an exchange simply to encourage people to visit their sites. This means providing hard information rather than a sales pitch – a point that many site owners seem to miss. It also means making the sites enjoyable and easy to navigate.

Social media

Social media grew from Web 2.0, the second generation of collaborative tools launched in the late 1990s. Social media refers to the collection of tools, websites and on-line platforms that enable people to share content: it includes blogs, podcasts, on-line video, photo-sharing sites, social networks, virtual worlds and social bookmarking sites.

Table 18.1   Differences between digital and traditional media

Traditional marketing	Digital marketing
Dominated by one-way communication	Dominated by dialogue
Marketers control the amount of information released	Information is widely available and few secrets can be kept
Communication and purchase behaviour happen in different places	Communication and purchase often happen in the same place
Segments are created by dividing up large groups into smaller ones with similar needs	Segments are created by individuals joining groups with similar needs
Research is time-consuming and expensive	Research is fast, accurate and cheap
Marketers control the process	Consumers control the process
Corporate reputation is the key to success	Individuals are the key to success

Most people tend to think of social media in terms of branded on-line services – Facebook, LinkedIn, MySpace, Twitter, Flickr, Second Life and so forth, but in fact the term covers all user-moderated on-line communications. Table 18.2 describes these sites.

Table 18.2   Social media companies

Company	Description of services
Facebook	A networking site that allows people to post news, photographs and links to interesting sites for their friends. Users are able to restrict circulation of their posts by using Facebook's privacy settings.
LinkedIn	A networking site for professional people to create links between each other for the purpose of networking, thus increasing opportunities for forging business relationships, finding new career opportunities, and so forth.
MySpace	This is a forerunner of Facebook, offering a platform for people to post messages to each other and to the world at large: it has declined in popularity in recent years, losing ground to Facebook.
Twitter	This communication platform allows users to post 'tweets' of a maximum of 140 characters. These tiny messages can be read by anybody, and are used to comment on the news, to tell the world what you happen to be doing, and to debate issues.
Flickr	Flickr is a photo-sharing site. Users can post pictures on the site, and can control who sees them (using various privacy settings). Photos can be distributed on Facebook and other social networking sites, so Flickr acts as an adjunct to these as well as operating independently.
Second Life	This is a virtual world in which members can lead a 'second life'. Members interact via their avatars (three-dimensional computer-generated entities) and can chat (and be overheard by nearby avatars) or send private messages. They can travel around the virtual world, and can trade with each other using virtual money: members can create items for sale, or perform services.
YouTube	YouTube allows users to upload video content of their own making. People post videos of their pets, of themselves doing interesting (or foolish) things, and put together compilations of video content such as aircraft crashes, accidents, and even advertisements. YouTube exists by selling advertising, so will only allow advertising compilations that it deems to be funny or interesting in general, but YouTube does not monitor what is uploaded, and instead relies on users to complain if anything offensive or copyrighted is posted.

Sometimes the boundary between cyberspace and the real world becomes blurred – Second Life has its own currency, the L$, which is traded on currency markets. Some Second Life residents have earned substantial sums of money on the site, for example Ailin Graef (Anshe Chung, as her avatar is named) reportedly grossed over $1m a year – and those are real United States dollars, not play money. Second Life has a GDP of around $567 million, larger than that of Dominica, Tonga or American Samoa – all of which are real countries.

From a marketing viewpoint, there are many ways of using these sites. On Facebook it is possible simply to place advertising, as one would in any other medium, but with the difference that the advertising can be targeted very accurately. Obviously this costs money, because that is how Facebook is funded – private members do not pay to join. Advertising can be very effective, even though the adverts appear in a small format as links to the advertiser's website, but it is probably more effective to establish a Facebook page for the company. This enables the company to disseminate news about its activities, to encourage customers to visit the site and to recommend it to friends (by clicking the 'Like' button) and to offer useful content.

The key to success in using Facebook is to use it as a social media site rather than as an advertising medium. This means, in the first instance, creating a personal page with a link to the business website. The next move is to join some Facebook groups that might be of interest: this allows the marketer to start building up a group of friends on the personal page. Marketers should resist the temptation to send out indiscriminate messages to all members of the group – this is a social website, not an advertising medium.

The core principles of using social media for marketing purposes were outlined by Reed (2011) as follows:

1. Be authentic, open and transparent. Marketers should not try to pass themselves off as something they are not, and should not try to conceal anything, but should behave in a professional way.
2. Don't go for the hard sell. Providing useful information for an on-line community is a good approach: sending an advertising message around the whole group is not.
3. Build social currency. Marketers should use the social medium for itself, and should have a regular presence that does not involve pitching for business. Establishing a regular presence on site provides 'permission' from the other members to talk business. (This has a parallel in personal selling – salespeople should always establish a human connection before discussing business.)
4. Don't view it as just another marketing channel. Social media demand a fundamentally different approach to marketing. Using such media is a commitment, not a tactic in a campaign.
5. Don't treat these as a one-way broadcast medium. It is possible to send out a press release on a blog, and it's possible to use Twitter as an automatic feed from a blog, but that would not use social media in the most effective way. Social media should be used to instigate a two-way conversation between the firm and its customers.
6. Be clear about responsibilities. Small businesses will have only one person running the social media programme, but in a larger firm it is essential to be clear about who is updating what, and when, so as to avoid duplication of effort and (worse) mixed messages.
7. Be patient. Social media need a long-term approach. A new blog takes a good six months to establish itself and build a following. Once established, the on-line presence will continue to build and will provide an essential source of potential customers.

Table 18.3   Tools of social media

Tool	Explanation
Content tools	These are the four main content types found on the Internet: text, images, audio and video. In social media sites, these translate into blogs, photo sharing, podcasts and online video (e.g. YouTube).
Outreach tools	Social networks such as Facebook, LinkedIn, Twitter and so forth. Content can be passed on via social bookmarking buttons which link the networks (share on Facebook, Tweet This, etc.). These tools are used to disseminate the content and raise awareness about it.
Listening tools	These are used to gain marketing intelligence: listen in on conversations about the firm and its products, find existing online communities and so forth. This may happen via Outreach tools, or through search tools such as Google Blog Search. It is possible to keep abreast of relevant blogs by subscribing to their RSS feeds, and by using Google Alerts to monitor websites by keyword.
Measurement tools	These include the metrics built into Facebook or YouTube by which researchers can check the profiles of groups of users, can find out how many people 'Like' a given post, and so forth. They also include tools such as Google Analytics, which can track and analyse visits to a website.

Reed goes on to categorise the tools used in social media, as shown in Table 18.3.

Measuring success is clearly an important issue here, since for many companies establishing a presence on social networking sites will be a new experience. Even for those already established, the world is moving on so quickly that monitoring the situation is essential: fortunately the sites themselves provide a powerful research tool for assessing people's needs and attitudes (Woodcock et al. 2011).

Real-life marketing: John Lewis

In 2011 the John Lewis department store produced a classic advertisement. It showed a young boy's impatience, waiting for Christmas morning – he was shown using his magic set to try to make the clock go faster, opening his advent calendar, anxiously tapping his foot (to the annoyance of his father), then on Christmas Eve gobbling down his food and getting to bed early, eager for Christmas morning. The surprise at the end came when he was shown going into his parents' bedroom with their gift – his impatience was about giving, not about what he was going to get.

This advertisement was charming, even moving, and encapsulated the Christmas spirit beautifully. It went out in standard 30-second format on TV, but the really clever bit was that John Lewis produced a longer, one and a half minute, version which went out on YouTube. It recorded over 5 million hits and 23,000 'Likes' (plus a few 'Dislikes', presumably from Ebenezer Scrooge) and was still being viewed two years later. People forwarded the

(Continued)

link to friends worldwide: comments eventually had to be disabled on YouTube due to the huge number of posts.

If you want to do this in practice, here are some rules:

- Make the video as slick as possible, preferably professionally produced. If you don't have the money to do this, at least use good equipment and a format that doesn't require you to be a great actor.
- Keep it humorous, or surprising, or entertaining in other ways.
- Don't patronise your audience or try for a hard sell – the audience won't like it, and nor will YouTube. After all, they charge firms for advertising, so if they let yours on for free it's only because people really like what you're doing.

Fortunately there are several ways of getting rapid feedback about the success (or otherwise) of the firm's Web activities. First, there are Web analytics, such as Google Analytics, which provide instant feedback about the number of visitors to the website and the sources of those visitors. Clicky Web Analytics provides information on social media sources of hits.

A simple count of the number of Facebook fans, Twitter followers and LinkedIn connections gives an idea of how successful the company has been in reaching people on those sites. Number of viewers of a YouTube video, numbers who have downloaded a podcast and numbers who have subscribed to the blog's RSS feed are also useful. Although these numbers can be misleading, since some people will have downloaded or subscribed by mistake and will cancel later, they will give some idea of the company's reach.

Rankings are calculated for blogs (on www.technorati.com) and for Twitter accounts (on www.wefollow.com). These sites are useful for seeing the effects of different activities on the blogs or Twitter sites: effective posts will send the firm up the rankings, unpopular ones will send the company down. Again, this is a somewhat blunt instrument, because other firms may have come up with something truly amazing which raises their rankings, but with so much movement these effects will probably cancel out.

Calls to action (for example, asking followers to 'Like' something, or asking them to apply for a discount) can be helpful in seeing how many people are serious about following the company's activities and how many are simply curious.

Surveys can be conducted fairly easily on-line. There are several survey sites which can provide a simple questionnaire and analysis, either free or for a small fee.

Conversational index applies to blogs. It is calculated by dividing the number of comments by the number of blog posts, and should always be above 1. It indicates the level of engagement people have with your content: if people are commenting on the blog, it indicates that they have found the content interesting.

Unique landing pages can be set up to monitor responses from specific sources. For example, notes on a YouTube video can direct viewers to a Web address that redirects automatically to the firm's normal address. Hits on the first website would only have come from YouTube: other addresses can be specified for other social media sites, so that the number of hits from each one can be seen and therefore the effectiveness of each site presence can be monitored.

A presence on social websites is rapidly becoming essential for any company expecting to be taken seriously, but it is easy to make mistakes – the sites are primarily intended for private individuals to communicate with friends and the world at large, and so the users will rapidly become annoyed with firms which break the trust that accrues from the sites.

SMS marketing

SMS (short message service) systems (commonly known as texting) have become a new tool in the hands of direct marketers. SMS has the advantage of reaching a predominantly young audience, who might be expected to have a high lifetime value: although often their overall incomes are relatively low, the lack of mortgages and other major outgoings often means that young people have relatively high disposable incomes.

The audience for SMS messages is likely to be interested in fast food, music, films, alcoholic drinks, magazines, books and mating-game products such as clothes, concerts and cosmetics. Typically the SMS recipients opt in to being contacted by the firms concerned, subscribing to newsletters about issues they might be interested in. Banks now use SMS to contact customers about their bank accounts, and some SMS systems exist to update people about stock exchange movements.

The main advantages of SMS marketing are as follows:

- Cost effectiveness. The cost per message is between 2p and 3p, compared with 50p to £2 for a direct mailing.
- Personalised messages. The messages can easily be addressed to individuals, or to subgroups within the database. This means that subscribers can opt to be informed about specific types of product.
- Targeting. SMS use is high among younger age groups. This means that SMS can target a relatively young audience fairly easily (although it should be noted that SMS use is rapidly spreading amongst older age groups). Because of the opt-in nature of SMS, the audience selects and segments itself, however.
- Interactive capability. The recipient of the message can easily text a reply, often to make a purchase or (for example) book a concert ticket.
- Customer relationships can be built. Because the SMS system is interactive, dialogues can become established.
- Time flexibility. The messages can be sent at any time of day, and of course can be read by the recipients whenever it is convenient to do so.
- Immediacy and measurability. Because replies can, and usually are, made very shortly after the messages have been sent out, the response rates can be measured fairly easily.
- Database building. The information that is sent back from subscribers can be used to improve the detail and accuracy of the database.

There are, of course, limitations. The messages generally have to be fairly short, 160 characters or less (although messages can be split into two), and the messages are visually unexciting. Third-generation (3G) technology does permit good-quality pictures to be sent, but not everyone has a smartphone, and the extra cost of sending such large files may prove prohibitive to some firms. There is also the possibility of wear-off – as SMS marketing becomes more widespread, the initial novelty is likely to wear off, and it will become regarded as just another nuisance call. Poor targeting is likely to contribute to this, and SMS marketing is as prone to this as any other direct medium (McCartney 2003).

Think outside this box!

SMS is the defining communication medium of the early 21st century. Texting is almost an obsession among some young people: it has even been credited with reducing smoking among young people, because their hands are too busy to light a cigarette. Receiving a text message is exciting – it could be from a hot date, or from a friend in trouble, or from … a marketing company.

So is there a moral dimension here? Should companies be tapping into something as personal, and indeed as culturally embedded, as texting? If not, why not? Radio, television, cinema, newspapers, magazines and indeed the Internet would not exist in their present forms if it were not for advertising, so why not subsidise SMS the same way?

The key elements for success in SMS marketing are shown in Table 18.4.

SMS marketing is governed by the Mobile Marketing Association in the UK. This organisation was set up with the aim of preventing SMS marketing from suffering from the same excesses that have brought Internet marketing (and particularly spamming) into a degree of disrepute.

Table 18.4   Key elements for success in SMS marketing

Element	Explanation
Targeting	As with any other direct medium, targeting correctly is essential. Apart from wasted messages going to people who have no interest in the product, 'junk' messages only serve to annoy recipients.
Value added	The communication must be valuable to the recipient, in its own right. This means that it should go beyond a mere advertising plug, and provide real information or entertainment value. This is difficult in only 160 characters.
Interactive	The message should encourage recipients to respond, thus setting up a dialogue: this means that the company sending out the message will need people at the other end of the communication to text back to the subscribers.
Permission	Consumers must have a clear and easy way of opting out from receiving marketing communications to their mobiles (this is part of the New Electronic Communications Directive from the European Union).

Internet marketing

Much has been written about the Internet and its impact on marketing, particularly in the area of retailing: it is true to say that the Internet and e-commerce have changed the way firms do business in many areas. On the other hand, e-commerce still represents only a relatively small part of the world's business, and although the various aspects of the Internet that impinge on business have played a huge role in facilitating exchange, most traditional high street retailers do not need to become overly worried.

Think outside this box!

Because the Internet is virtually unregulated (because no government has yet worked out a way of doing so – but watch this space) it has been a medium for disseminating both the best and the worst of human communications: children who were separated from their parents in the 2004 tsunami in Asia were reunited through the Internet; charitable aims, enlightening messages, support for the lonely, help for the needy have all happened through the Internet. Like a bush telegraph for the global village, it keeps us all in touch.

On the downside, the Internet has been the medium for disseminating the worst pornography available, for showing beheadings and torture, for publishing malicious falsehoods and Nazi propaganda, in fact for showing the worst of humanity. In the past, advertisers have boycotted media such as soft-porn TV channels and malevolent magazines because they do not want their brand names to be associated with such communications. So what's happening with the Internet? Will we see advertisers deserting in droves, as a protest against the excesses of the medium? Or will we, instead, see advertisers jumping on the bandwagon, with the realisation that they are no longer bound by the fetters of government regulation?

From its early beginnings as a communications medium for academic and military uses, the Internet has grown to the point where the majority of firms have a website, and in most cases the websites allow at least some interactivity. Websites fall into two main categories: presence websites, which merely give information about the company and usually include contact telephone and e-mail addresses, and interactive websites, where customers can navigate around the site, obtain more information about the company and its products, and even place orders. As time goes on, and firms become more sophisticated in their use of the Internet, presence sites have all but disappeared in favour of the more complex, more expensive interactive sites.

Part of the problem in writing about the Internet is that the technology is progressing extremely rapidly, as are the computer skills of the general public. Communications technology is converging rapidly, so that the telephone, television, Internet, e-mail, SMS, fax and even radio are combining to offer seamless, interactive exchange of information anywhere in the world. Ultimately, the new technologies will need to be considered as a whole rather than as separate entities, but at present they are still operating independently to a large extent.

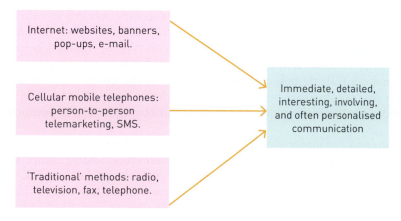

Figure 18.1   Electronic communications media

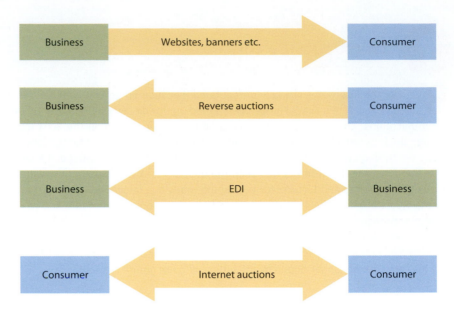

Figure 18.2   E-business relationships

In the business-to-business environment, many major firms have moved over to electronic data interchange (EDI) protocols to manage their relationships with both suppliers and customers. EDI involves setting up dedicated network connections with trading partners so that orders, invoices and even payments can be made electronically, without the use of paper invoices and orders and consequently with many fewer staff involved in the process.

The most prominent form of e-commerce is business-to-consumer marketing, however. It is here that some industries have been revolutionised: on-line travel booking is an obvious example, with low-cost airlines such as Ryanair and easyJet conducting virtually all their bookings on-line. The advantages are many for the companies concerned: the work of making the booking is shifted to the customer, the company's pricing is shifted to the computer, and even the cost of printing a ticket is borne by the customer. On other websites, it is possible to book hotel rooms, book bus and train tickets, arrange for transfers from airports, and so forth.

Consumer-to-business e-commerce also exists, on a relatively small scale: in this model, consumers group together to make offers to suppliers in a so-called 'reverse auction'. If the suppliers feel that the combined offer makes it worthwhile to meet the consumers' bid price, the deal goes ahead. This type of trading has had limited success, partly because of the effort of getting enough people together (even on-line) to make a realistic bid, and partly because of the uncertainty about whether the goods will eventually materialise. The majority of people appear to be prepared to pay more for the convenience and certainty of buying from a conventional retail outlet.

Consumer-to-consumer e-commerce is represented by firms such as eBay, the Internet auction site, on which consumers can sell second-hand goods, unwanted concert tickets and so forth. eBay has proved to be hugely successful, with millions of people worldwide logging on to buy or sell items (see end of chapter case study).

Website design

Websites can be designed professionally or can be created using specific software packages such as Wordpress. There are even website templates available which allow the most computer-illiterate person to create their own website.

Although a complete description of how to create a website is outside the scope of this book, there are certainly some features that should be included. These are as follows:

- Home page. This should be informative and clear, and should give a brief overview of what the firm has to offer customers. It should not be a hard sell or be mainly composed of sales pitches: facts will speak much better than superlatives, especially since visitors have been proactive in seeking out the website.
- About us. This should provide some information about the firm and its origins. The purpose of this section is to build credibility, and offer reassurance that the firm is a solid one that will not simply take people's money and disappear.
- Contact us. It should be as easy as possible for people to contact the firm, preferably by e-mail of course, but by telephone or snail-mail as well.
- Products/Services. Ideally, there should be a basic page giving a brief outline of individual products or services with a link to a page with more detailed information about the product.
- Pricing. For physical products this is straightforward, but for services it may be less so. It is better to provide some guidelines: for example, Pimlico Plumbers has very clear pricing on its website, based on an hourly rate which applies at different times of the day.
- Search box. The site should have a search facility whereby visitors can enter a search word or phrase which will take them to the appropriate part of the site. This can be a great time-saver for people.
- Shop. If the site is intended to makes sales directly, a shop is obviously essential. PayPal can be used for visitors to make purchases, but if the firm is a large one it will often have its own facilities for accepting credit and debit cards.
- Testimonials/reviews. In order to generate customer reviews, the site can contain a feedback form. Otherwise testimonials can be solicited from existing customers, perhaps using a social networking site such as LinkedIn.
- FAQs. Having answers to frequently-asked questions will almost certainly reduce the time spent handling queries by telephone. Telephone operators should record any questions that are not on the FAQ list but still get asked – otherwise the list is simply guesswork on the part of management.
- Press room. Any press releases should be posted on the website. Apart from ensuring that more of the firm's publics see the press release, there is also a strong possibility that a journalist researching a story might include some of the information.
- Event calendar. If appropriate, the site should publicise events such as seminars, exhibition attendance, product launches, or even salesforce activity. For some customers, knowing that salespeople will be in their area is a useful piece of information.
- Blog. Keeping people informed of latest developments and allowing them to comment makes the website more personal and engaging.
- Newsletter. This can be either a newsletter on the site (similar to a blog) or site visitors can be invited to sign up for an e-mail newsletter. This has the advantage that the firm can include special offers and discounts for loyal customers.

- Resources. The firm can offer expert advice on the website, for example on how to use the product or perhaps some market reports. This has two advantages: first, it provides interesting content that will engage visitors, and second, it establishes the firm as an expert in the field.
- Widgets. Widgets are pieces of code from other websites which add a specific function. Widgets might be Facebook badges, blog postings or tweets, photographs from the firm's Flickr account, and so forth. Widgets add value to the website in a very easily accessible manner.
- Site map. If the site is large a site map can help visitors find the information they need quickly and easily.
- Legal boilerplate. It is good practice to include a privacy policy and terms and conditions of business, as well as any statutory declarations that need to be made.

The website's functionality can be extended greatly by using third-party websites such as PayPal, which saves the company having to set up its own on-line payment system, or Google Maps, which can provide a map showing the location of the firm or its local branches. This approach is a great deal cheaper and more effective than developing the firm's own equivalent services.

Adoption of Internet marketing

Two factors are key in the growth of Internet marketing: its acceptance by consumers and its acceptance by marketers. Acceptance by consumers depends on a degree of computer literacy, access to computers, a belief that the companies on-line are honest and reputable, and reassurance about security of cash transactions on line.

Factors likely to impact on acceptance by the firm are as follows (Van Slyke and Belanger 2003):

1. Operational efficiency. If operational efficiency is likely to be improved by Internet marketing, it is more likely that the firm will go this route: for example, if the work of making bookings can be shifted to the customer, this will improve operational efficiency, which is a clear benefit for the firm.
2. Channel conflict. If other distribution channel members (e.g. retailers and wholesalers) feel threatened because the company is going direct to consumers via the Internet, this may inhibit adoption of the Internet as a medium for marketing.
3. New markets and competition. As new markets appear, they are likely to be Internet-driven: at the same time, if competitors are marketing on the Internet, there will be pressure for other firms to follow suit.
4. Financial investment. Setting up a website can be an expensive and time-consuming option (although equally, a small website can be set up relatively cheaply compared with many other marketing activities). Firms need to decide the level of investment that is appropriate to what the firm seeks to achieve.
5. Market changes. Consumer tastes and behaviours change, and undoubtedly there has been a revolution in the way consumers shop, at least for some items. For example, the past thirty years have seen a tremendous growth in air travel, particularly connected to foreign holidays. E-commerce has enabled people to book more of these trips on-line.

The rate at which firms become fully Internet-competent also depends on a range of factors, as shown in Table 18.5 (Doherty 1999).

Table 18.5   Factors in the rate of adoption of Internet marketing by firms

Factor	Explanation
Internal factors	These are the factors that arise from within the firm itself. This could include personnel, existing processes and procedures, current strategic aims, and so forth
Environmental factors	These result from influences outside the firm, over which the firm does not have direct control. Examples might be the degree to which competitors are using the Internet, or the extent to which potential customers might be using the Internet.
Comparative advantage	This is the extent to which using the Internet offers real advantages over existing methods of trading. If the Internet offers no real advantage (which is entirely possible), then there is no point in using it. For example, a company selling home improvements would find it difficult to do business solely via the Internet (although a website might be used to drive business to the company's offices, and might be used to offer basic price information and testimonials).

Figure 18.3   Adopting the Internet

As the industry progresses up the ladder, the emphasis shifts from evolutionary initiatives to revolutionary initiatives: the focus becomes longer-term, external and away from the 'bottom line' (the final profit figures) and towards the 'top line' (the company's strategic direction).

Companies that operate purely in cyberspace (i.e. companies that do not have a physical store chain) have had a somewhat patchy success rate. Some, such as Amazon.com, have survived and grown and have (eventually) shown a profit. Others have failed dismally, while yet others have been hugely successful (eBay among them). Some authors believed in the past that firms that have a physical presence as well as a cyber presence are likely to be the most successful (Fletcher et al. 2004). However, this view may be growing outdated as the Internet has become an integral part of people's lives.

INTERNATIONALISATION AND THE INTERNET

Internet-based companies face serious problems in the international context. Some of the problems are outlined in Table 18.6.

The Internet has gone through four stages of international development (Commonwealth of Australia 1999). These are as follows:

Wave One: The United States, Canada and the Nordic countries. These countries adopted the Internet from the start, in the 1980s, and are now the heaviest users of the technology.

Wave Two: The rest of the European Union, Australia, New Zealand, Japan, Republic of Korea, Taiwan, Singapore, Hong Kong and Israel. This wave was

Table 18.6 Problems of internationalisation and the Internet

Problem	Explanation and solution
Global from inception	The Internet is an inherently global medium, so firms have no opportunity to build expertise and a financial base in domestic markets before being forced into the global arena.
Rapid entry by 'me-too's	Internet-based firms find their systems and software are easily copied by firms in other countries. Also, foreign firms are often able to register foreign versions of the URL almost as soon as the company starts trading: it is virtually impossible to register the URL in all countries simultaneously.
Difficulty of meeting cultural differences	The Internet crosses cultural boundaries as well as national boundaries. This means that websites might be seen to be offensive in some cultures, or at least might be irritatingly irrelevant. Designing a site that offends no one is almost impossible.

characterised by high levels of private and public sector interest in developing broad information societies. There has been a high level of interest in consumer focus, and some of these countries (notably the UK and Germany) are virtually indistinguishable from first-wave countries in terms of Internet usage.

Wave Three: Developing countries across South East Asia, China, Brazil, Argentina, South Africa, Egypt, and small island states such as Tonga, Fiji, Barbados and French Polynesia. Characterised by high levels of interest in business applications of the Internet. In these countries, most people are too poor to be able to afford a private Internet connection

Wave Four: Least developed countries, or countries that deliberately avoid use of the Internet. These countries have unattractive investment environments, or attempts to ban the Internet for political, social, or religious reasons. For example, Facebook, YouTube, Twitter and 2600 other websites are banned in the People's Republic of China (though not in Macau or Hong Kong, the two Special Economic Areas).

BUYER BEHAVIOUR AND THE INTERNET

Buyer behaviour on the Internet has been the subject of considerable interest in recent years, but research goes out of date rapidly because of the rapid diffusion of the technology: for example, Monnier (1999) found that most surveys about the Internet showed that users were predominantly male, young and had above-average

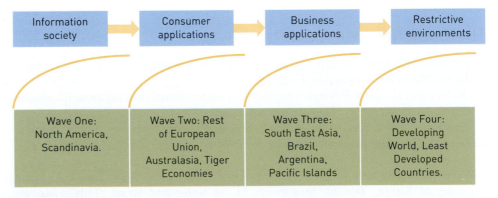

Figure 18.4 Global Internet adoption

levels of income and education. This profile has undoubtedly changed in the meantime, as access to the Internet has spread to other socio-economic groups: research conducted in 2003 by National Opinion Polls showed that Internet usage in the UK matched closely across the population spread in all age groups except the 55+ group, were virtually unaffected by gender differences, and showed relatively small differences in relation to income groups. These figures are now also clearly out of date: the Office for National Statistics found in 2012 that only 16% of the UK's adult population had never used the Internet, meaning (of course) that 84% had used it. In London, the usage rate was 88% of the adult population (ONS 2012). It seems safe to assume that children would be even greater users of the Internet.

For the purposes of understanding consumer behaviour on the Internet, there are three types of product: physical products, transaction-related products and virtual products (Craig et al. 2000). The characteristics of these in terms of behaviour are as follows:

- Physical products: The information search can be conducted on-line, but when it comes to actually making the purchase the customer either needs to go to a bricks-and-mortar store or the product needs to be delivered. Delivery may not always be easy or possible, depending on the product: for example, buying a motorbike on-line would almost certainly require the customer to collect the bike. Thus the final stage of the process depends on traditional marketing infrastructures.
- Transaction-related products: Products such as airline tickets and car hire can be researched and booked on-line, but the actual consumption of the product takes place off-line. The marketing infrastructure therefore still needs to operate on traditional lines – the airport check-in desk and aircraft will operate in the same way whether the customer bought the ticket on-line or not.
- **Virtual products**: Music, computer software, news services, stock market advice and so forth have no physical existence and can therefore be bought and delivered entirely on-line. Virtual products can easily reach global segments, because there is no need to consider the marketing infrastructure in the countries concerned: for example, when Amazon first started in the United States, the company had difficulty fulfilling orders from the UK because of the costs of shipping books across the Atlantic. This difficulty does not exist for on-line music retailers. Virtual products can easily be adapted to market segments and even individual customers.

Virtual products Anything that can be sold and delivered via the Internet.

Information is, of course, the key contribution the Internet makes. For virtual products, information actually is the product, but for transaction-related products the extra information enhances the product. For example, most airlines allow on-line customers to choose their seat on the aircraft at the time of booking and also have on-line check-in, and many hotels provide digital photographs of their rooms on-line. For physical products, the extra information improves decision-making and refines choice criteria.

Marketing in a changing world

As with any new medium, sooner or later someone finds a way to use it for criminal purposes. Phishing, fake websites, harvesting bank and credit card details, virus attacks on people's computers, all conspire to make people very wary of the Internet. As more and more people become afraid of using their computers,

(Continued)

(Continued)

and as more and more hackers and scammers join the ranks of the on-line community, legitimate companies will find it ever-more difficult to do business.

Provided banks and credit card companies continue to refund people who have been scammed consumers will feel confident in shopping on-line: however, recently banks have been taking a hard-line view on paying out, partly as a result of the global financial crisis and partly as a result of the sheer volume of claims. Now banks are increasingly taking the attitude that on-line fraud can only happen to people who are negligent with their card details – which, considering the skill of the con artists, may be a little harsh. After all, if someone calls you claiming to be from your electricity supplier and threatens to cut you off if you don't make an immediate credit card payment, you may well be so taken by surprise as to pay up. Once the caller has your card details, spending your credit limit takes only minutes.

Ultimately, the on-line community will have to learn to police itself, but since the Internet is worldwide and virtually uncontrollable, that time may be a long way off.

For companies supplying physical products on-line, there will always be a likelihood that people will carry out an information search on-line, but then buy the products from a bricks-and-mortar retailer. The reason for this is that nothing substitutes for a hands-on experience of the product, and in many cases the product needs a much closer examination than can be carried out on-line. In order to overcome this problem, on-line retailers need to offer something extra, either in terms of convenience or (more commonly) in terms of price. Given that the costs of running a website are likely to be much lower than the costs of running a bricks-and-mortar store, prices should be lower: however, in many cases the extra cost of delivering the goods eats into the overhead savings, so that firms find that their profit margins are squeezed.

McKinsey (2000) researched Internet users in order to identify segments of the market. The segments they identified were as follows:

- Simplifiers. These are experienced Internet users who seek convenience and low prices. They spend relatively little time on-line, but they account for half of all Internet purchases.
- Surfers. This is a small segment of people who enjoy novel approaches, and enjoy the control they have over the transaction process.
- Bargainers. This group are price-driven, and use the Internet to seek out the best deals.
- Connectors. These people are newcomers to the Internet who use it to connect to others via chat facilities, etc. Due to a lack of confidence in their own technical ability, they are looking for reassurance when using the Internet.
- Routiners. These users visit few sites, but use the sites intensively. They have a specific routine, perhaps for booking travel or for on-line banking.
- Sportsters. This group spend only a small amount of time on-line, visiting sites that focus on sports and entertainment.

Over time, Connectors are likely to become rare. There will be few people now who lack confidence in using the Internet for purchases.

Buyer behaviour itself differs on the Internet. Diffusion of innovation is likely to be faster, because the geographical proximity is less of an issue: especially in the case of virtual products, innovation adoption can (and does) proceed much faster than normal.

The evaluations a consumer has to make before buying are likely to be more complex, partly because there is simply more information available, and partly because the cues are different. For example, evaluating a hotel in another country might prove difficult if the consumer does not understand the local star rating system.

Country of origin effects are likely to be less important as cues because of increased exposure to a wider range of information from other countries. Finally, the role of opinion leaders is likely to diminish because of the proliferation of chat rooms, social networking sites and 'customer review' boxes on websites.

BARRIERS TO USE OF THE INTERNET

In the international context, there are several barriers that will limit growth of the Internet, at least in the short term. First, there is the language barrier. The Internet is heavily biased in favour of English: research by W3 Techs showed that in 2011 56% of websites were in English, with all other languages accounting for less than 7% each (W3 Techs 2012). Interestingly, the supposedly technologically advanced Japanese have only 4.4% of all websites in their own language – although this is probably more a reflection on the general popularity of the Japanese language than a statement about Japanese technology.

Second, information can become misrepresented because people from different cultures read icons and signs in different ways (see Chapter 7). A symbol such as a horse or a fish might have totally different meanings, depending on the cultural context of the observer.

Third, information may be less credible on the Internet, or it may acquire a spurious credibility: for example, information posted on forums or in chat rooms would not have the same credibility as a statement from a trusted friend (word of mouse versus word of mouth). On the other hand, some completely false information is posted on the Internet, but because it is well produced and well written it is often accepted as true by the less discerning surfers: in addition, the views of opinion leaders are more effective when they post information based on their own experiences (Huang 2010).

Other barriers include the technical capabilities of the consumers (which may be high in countries where most of the population is well-educated, but low in countries where education is at a lower level), and difficulties in maintaining cross-border differentials, especially in pricing. For example, second-market discounting (see Chapter 14) is extremely difficult: even if customers cannot actually buy the products at the lower price because the company refuses to ship to their country, they will still be able to see

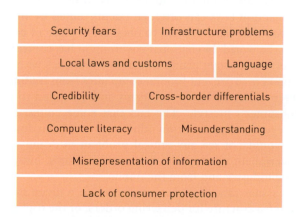

Figure 18.5   Barriers to Internet use: the brick wall

what people in other countries are paying, which leads to resentment. Equally, companies may not be able to do other than charge the same price across the board, which disadvantages poorer countries and may lead to losing market share to local competitors whose cost base is lower.

Internet sites also face local laws and customs: for example, comparative advertising (making comparisons between the company's products and its competitors) is illegal in Germany, advertising to children is illegal in Denmark, and English-language advertising is illegal in France. These restrictions only apply to websites based in those countries, however – foreign websites can still be accessed by Germans, Danes and French people. Local customs may also inhibit Internet use: Germans have proved to be highly resistant to credit cards, which means that buying on-line becomes difficult or impossible. A study by TGI Global showed that less than a third of German adults have a credit card, and less than one-fifth of Italians have one (compared with 62% of Britons and a massive 81% of French adults). This disparity undoubtedly has an effect on people's ability to buy on-line.

Think outside this box!

There seem to be so many problems with using the Internet, it's a miracle it ever got off the ground in the first place! How is it that a medium with so many barriers, so many negatives, has become so important in people's lives?

Could it be that part of the success is the complexity of the medium? Could it be that people actually like it because of the technology? Any sufficiently advanced technology is indistinguishable from magic, as Arthur C. Clarke once wrote: so does the Internet bring some magic into our lives?

Security issues also concern Web users, and have acted as an inhibitor in the past. More secure websites have certainly helped, as have guarantees from credit card companies that they will carry the losses resulting from fraudulent transactions, but many people are still fearful of losing money through fraud or simple error. Ordering the wrong goods, having one's credit card cloned, or simply being defrauded by a bogus website are all real problems (even though such events are rare).

Legal issues can also affect Internet adoption, both by consumers and by marketers. Consumer protection laws can often be circumvented by Internet-based firms, because the firm would be hard-pressed to obey every piece of consumer legislation in every country in the world. No national government has control over the Internet, so although a government might clamp down on companies within its own borders, it has little or no powers to prevent foreign companies from trading on-line. Personal information is often collected by on-line firms and compiled to provide a detailed picture of the consumer's lifestyle. The fact that some countries ban this type of activity will not prevent companies from other countries from doing it, and of course many companies would not see any ethical problem in doing so either. The only recourse for a government would be to ban some websites, but resistance to this is huge both from the industry and from the public.

Finally, logistics issues can affect Internet entry to a given market. If there is a poorly developed infrastructure for delivering orders, or the topography of the country is such that deliveries are difficult (for example, if the country is mountainous or homes are widely separated, as in outback Australia) there may well be problems with on-line ordering.

Chapter summary

Social media and digital marketing generally are in their infancy. The scenario is changing rapidly as new players enter the market, and as older business models are superseded. Partly this is driven by new technology: as computer and broadband speeds pick up, there are greater possibilities for information to be shared, both in terms of the type of information (video, sound, programs and so forth) and in the speed with which it can be disseminated.

Since communication is such an important part of marketing, it is therefore no surprise to find that marketers have latched onto the new technology and used it for their own purposes. However, digital marketing has another aspect – it is very much under the control of the users, who can make life very difficult indeed for firms that annoy them or behave in unacceptable ways.

Key points

- Digital marketing is an entirely different prospect from traditional marketing, and will therefore require a great deal of care in its use.
- Social media are run by the users – not by the marketers.
- SMS marketing can be extremely powerful because it goes direct to the individual.
- Good Web design is essential for any firm because it is often the first place customers go to find information about what the firm has to offer.
- Any organisation with a website is international – the design needs to reflect this.
- There are still barriers in place for using the Internet – it is unwise to assume that everyone is Net-savvy or even has access to it.

Review questions

1. What are the main differences between digital marketing and traditional marketing?
2. Why should you not send out a message to everyone in a Facebook group to which you belong?
3. How might you use social media to market a flying school?
4. If you were running a pizza delivery service, how might SMS marketing help you?
5. If you were running a website aimed at Germans or Italians, how might you overcome the problem of a lack of credit card penetration in those countries?
6. How would you attract Simplifiers to a website?
7. What steps might you take to reduce some of the negative connotations of the Internet?
8. How might you use social media to handle customer complaints?
9. How might success on a social media site be measured?
10. What are the key advantages of SMS marketing?

Case study revisited: Manchester United and Facebook

Manchester United's timeline on Facebook has a huge following. MUFC post photographs, articles and comments about the team's performance. Fans 'like' MUFC so that the articles automatically appear on their own Facebook pages, and many of them also click 'recommend', which causes the article to appear on their own timeline and those of their friends.

In this way, the content on the MUFC page proliferates to people who are not themselves fans of the football team, but who know someone who is. The opportunities for merchandising are obvious – if one knows that a friend is a fan of MUFC, the choice of birthday present becomes much easier.

Of course, Facebook is not without its drawbacks. MUFC's timeline often has spam appearing on it, which is irritating for fans as well as for the club. Also, people can post derogatory comments – either as a reaction to a poor performance on the pitch, or because they actually support another team. Also, the global nature of the fan base means that many comments are posted in languages other than English – and even using script that is non-European and therefore unreadable to many fans.

Most posts on the MUFC site are well received, however: the number of 'likes' frequently goes over 100,000, and MUFC is able to monitor which type of article or photograph is likely to be the most popular with fans. The cost of running the Facebook page is relatively low compared with other promotional media, not least because MUFC does not employ an army of people to respond to comments (unlike many other commercial organisations). Basically, MUFC allows any kind of comment and relies on the fans themselves to jump on anybody who acts inappropriately on the site.

Befriending a football team that one has not, technically, actually met may seem like an odd thing to do. But anyone who thinks that has clearly never been a true football fan!

Case study: eBay

In 1995, French-born computer systems developer Pierre Omidyar wanted to find some novel PEZ (candy) dispensers for his girlfriend, Pam, who was an avid collector of them. He placed an advertisement on the Internet, and was overwhelmed with offers – which sparked the idea of setting up an online car-boot sale. The idea grew into eBay, which is now the world's number-one e-commerce site, attracting 121,500 hits a minute and 175 million searches a day.

Part of eBay's success is that it makes shopping exciting. Goods are auctioned to the highest bidder, with strict time limits for bids: this means that a bidder might wait by the computer as the final minutes tick by, waiting to see whether the bid has been successful, and feeling elated if the bid is successful. Vendors can sell almost anything on eBay, except alcohol, drugs, credit cards, firearms, human body parts, lottery tickets, satellite descramblers, mailing lists and surveillance equipment. This list grows, as more and more bizarre items are offered – eBay monitors the site and withdraws anything that is illegal or unethical, but every so often something unacceptable will appear on the site. For example, a Taiwanese people trafficker tried to sell three Vietnamese girls on eBay, and an 18-year-old student tried to sell her virginity on the site (she eventually set up her own site, sold her virginity for £8400, and was arrested by Bristol police for soliciting).

There is a downside to eBay, however. People have been known to become addicted to the site, spending far more than they can afford on goods they don't need in order to experience the thrill of 'winning' an auction. There are rumours of eBay 'snipers' – people who use special computer programs to alert them when an auction is about to close, so that they can enter a last-minute bid which no one else has time to beat. There is even reputed to be a website called ebaywidow.com, on which a plea goes out from a woman whose husband has run up $20,000 of debt on eBay, but still cannot stop bidding. In fact this site does not exist – but eBay is the stuff of urban myth.

The site has attracted many users, most genuine, a few unscrupulous. Ticket touts have found that eBay is making serious inroads into their businesses, as people with spare tickets can cut out the middleman and sell on-line. Manchester United players are now forbidden to sign shirts after matches, because so many of them have turned up on eBay. eBay accounts for one-third of the UK's Internet traffic, and in 2004 150,000 Americans gave up their jobs to become full-time eBay traders.

Is there really a problem, though? Isn't eBay merely an extension of the old-style car boot sale, jumble sale, antiques fair, or auction room? Conducted on a worldwide basis, eBay gives everyone the chance to participate, and it makes trading easier. Perhaps a few people become over-involved in their search for a bargain, but this seems to be a small price to pay for a smooth system for exchanging unwanted goods.

From collecting PEZ dispensers to being multimillionaires, Pierre and his girlfriend, Pam, have little to complain about. With everyone from students to prime ministers buying and selling on eBay, it looks as if the boom is set to continue indefinitely.

Questions

1. How might eBay police what is allowed and not allowed on the site?
2. What threats might eBay pose to traditional marketers?
3. How might a commercial organisation use eBay to its own advantage?
4. What consumer needs does eBay fulfil?
5. How might traditional marketers meet the same needs as eBay?

Further reading

Direct and Interactive Marketing by Adrian Sargeant and Douglas C. West (Oxford: Oxford University Press, 2001) gives a very comprehensive overview of the subject.

A readable text by three of the acknowledged academic leaders in the field of direct marketing is *Exploring Direct and Customer Relationship Marketing*, 2nd edn, by Martin Evans, Lisa O'Malley and Maurice Patterson (London: Thomson Learning, 2004).

References

Commonwealth of Australia (1999) *Creating a Clearway on the New Silk Road: International Business and Policy Trends in Internet Commerce.* Canberra: Commonwealth of Australia.

Craig, C.S., Douglas, S.P. and Flaherty, T.B. (2000) *Information access and internationalisation – the internet and consumer behaviour in international markets.* Proceedings of the eCommerce and global business forum, 17–19 May, Santa Cruz, California. Accenture Institute for Strategic Change.

Doherty, N.F., Ellis-Chadwick F.E. and Hart, C.A. (1999) Cyber retailing in the UK: the potential of the Internet as a retail channel. *International Journal of Retail and Distribution Management*, 27 (1): 22-36.

Fletcher, R., Bell, J. and McNaughton, R. (2004) *International E-Business Marketing*. London: Thomson Learning.

Huang, Lei (2010) Social contagion effects in experiential information exchange on bulletin board systems. *Journal of Marketing Management*, 26 (3/4) 197-212.

McCartney, N. (2003) Getting the message across. *Financial Times IT Review*, 15 January.

McKinsey Marketing Practice (2000) All visitors are not created equally. www.mckinsey.com.

Monnier, P.D. (1999) *Cybermarketing: A Guide for Managers in Developing Countries*. Geneva: International Trade Centre.

Reed, Jon (2011) *Get Up to Speed with Online Marketing*. Harlow: FT Prentice Hall.

ONS (2012) www.ons.gov.uk/ons/rel/rdit2/internet-access-quarterly-update/2012-q2/stb-internet-access-2012-q2.html (accessed 23 January 2013).

Van Slyke, Craig and Belanger, France (2003) *E-Business Technologies: Supporting the Net-Enhanced Organisation*. New York: Wiley.

W3 Techs (2012) http://w3techs.com/technologies/overview/content_language/all (accessed 23 January 2013).

Woodcock, Neil, Green, Andrew and Starkey, Michael (2011) Social CRM as a business strategy. *Journal of Database Marketing and Customer Strategy Management*, 18 (1): 50-64.

More online

To gain free access to additional online resources to support this chapter please visit:
www.sagepub.co.uk/blythe3e

CHAPTER ⑲

Managing distribution and supply chains

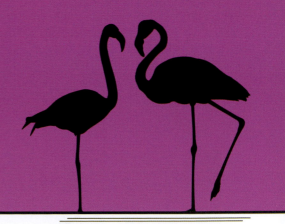

CHAPTER CONTENTS

LEARNING OBJECTIVES

After reading this chapter you should be able to:

- Explain the value of 'middlemen'.

- Describe the issues in deciding on market coverage.

- Describe ways of controlling distribution channels.

- Explain the difference between logistics and physical distribution.

- Explain the issues surrounding the calculation of service levels.

- Describe the drawbacks and advantages of just-in-time purchasing.

Introduction

The distribution of products is an essential part of the marketing mix, and getting the products into the right place at the right time and in the right quantities is the prerequisite for consumers to buy the products. Managing the channels of distribution by which products move from producer to consumer is a task that may fall to any or all of the members of the distribution chain: in some cases it is the manufacturers who call the tune, in other cases it is retailers or wholesalers.

Choosing the right distribution channel can also be a strategic issue: some distribution routes will provide competitive benefits, and of course different routes carry different risks. Choice of channel will depend in part on the segmentation of the market, as well as on the characteristics of the products and the state of the competition. Also, developing a new or unconventional channel of distribution can give the company a competitive edge that the product alone will not provide.

Preview case study: Giant Bicycles

In 1972, the Giant Manufacturing Company was first established in Taiwan, producing bicycles for the local market. In fact, the company was not giant at all at that time, but the name proved to be a prophetic one because within eight years Giant was the largest bicycle company in Taiwan, and was looking to expand internationally.

An obvious overseas market for Giant was The Netherlands, where everybody owns at least one bicycle and the entire country is networked by bicycle tracks. In 1986 Giant opened their first overseas sales office in Holland: in the following year the company opened up in the UK and the United States, and by 1991 had offices in six overseas countries including Japan and Australia. Their first overseas factory was opened in The Netherlands in 1996.

Giant has had notable successes on the racing circuit, and have its own race team: the team won the team prize in the Tour de France, and the World Cup, and the company expects to build on this success in the future. The rapid expansion of the company has not been without its problems, however: despite a huge investment in IT, and a commitment to 'the local touch', the company still faced an enormous problem in terms of logistics.

Apart from having to consider local needs and tastes (for example, Dutch cyclists predominantly use their bikes to commute to and from work, whereas Americans use their bikes for leisure and exercise), the company has been faced with the problem of shipping bikes worldwide from only three factories (in Taiwan, China and The Netherlands). Because of the wide range of cyclist needs (Dutch people are the tallest in the world: Japanese people are among the shortest) the company not only needs to produce a wide range of bikes, but also needs to ensure that stocks of bikes in the various retailers throughout the world can meet the demand. Giant makes over 3 million bicycles a year, but may need to deliver only one or two to a specific small retailer, perhaps in a remote area.

Functions of intermediaries

Although people often talk about 'cutting out the middleman' as a way of reducing prices, this actually does not work out in practice. Intermediaries provide important services in smoothing the path between producers and consumers, almost invariably reducing costs by increasing efficiency. For example, a can of tuna goes through numerous intermediaries on its way from fisherman to pantry. The canners, the exporters, the importers, the food brokers, the wholesalers and the retailers all add a small margin of profit at each stage, ending up at the point of sale for a cost of less than £1. It would clearly be inefficient for a wholesaler to deliver single cans to people's homes: still less would it be efficient for the fisherman to can his own fish and deliver to supermarkets. Intermediaries reconcile the needs of producers and consumers: producers need to manufacture a small range of products in large quantities, whereas consumers need to consume a wide range of products in small quantities. Figure 19.1 shows how a wholesaler might re-arrange shipments from producers into more convenient shipments for retailers.

Intermediaries do this in two ways: first, by breaking bulk deliveries into single units, and second, by assorting these units into a range of goods available off-the-shelf to consumers or even to the next intermediary. Using the example of the tuna

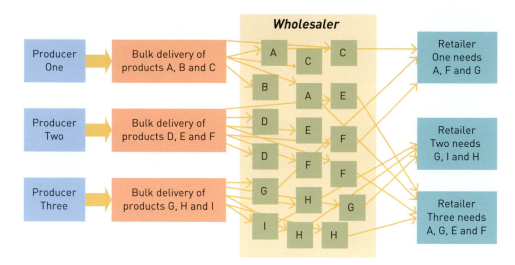

Figure 19.1   Bulk breaking and assortment

canneries, a delivery from the food importer of several tons of canned tuna might be broken down into separate cases of fish at the wholesaler: retailers are then able to buy a few cases of tuna, alongside cases of canned vegetables, cold meats and so forth to retail one can at a time to consumers.

The net result is a reduced number of transactions across the system as a whole, with a consequent rise in efficiency. The increased efficiency will almost always more than compensate for the intermediaries' profit margins.

Apart from improving efficiency, intermediaries improve accessibility to the product from consumers. In many cases, the products are actually made hundreds or thousands of miles from where they are consumed, so intermediaries are able to close the location gap and supply the goods at a more convenient place. There is also a time gap: the manufacturer may produce the goods during daylight hours, Monday to Friday, but the consumer may wish to buy the goods outside working hours, or at weekends. Retailers therefore stay open in the evenings and at weekends to meet this need.

Intermediaries provide ownership utility, in that the goods are available immediately from the intermediary's stocks. If goods were supplied direct from the factories, there would probably be a delay while goods are made (this is the case with many goods that are supplied directly from the producer to the consumer – as anyone who has ever bought a fitted kitchen knows).

Finally, intermediaries may provide specialist services such as after-sales, maintenance, installation, or even training in the use of the products. These services are often best performed by the firms that are closest to the consumers, in other words the retailers. Retailers provide information utility, in that they can usually answer questions about the products immediately before and after sales.

Distribution channels may be of any length, ranging from direct channels from producer to consumer (common in the home-improvements industry), through to the seven- or eight-member channels common in the food industry. The longer channels are often used by firms moving into foreign markets, and are often associated with lower-priced goods that are distributed in very large quantities.

The following factors determine the way distribution affects strategy:

1. Distribution adds value to the product by increasing utility (of place or of time).
2. The channel is the producer's main link to its ultimate consumers.
3. Choice of channel affects the rest of the marketing mix, so it affects overall strategy.

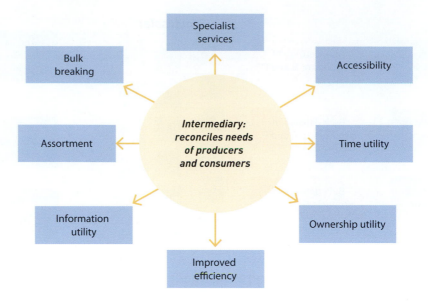

Figure 19.2   Functions of intermediaries

4. Building appropriate channels takes time and commitment (especially in a global context) so distribution decisions are difficult and expensive to change.
5. The distribution system itself often determines segmentation and targeting decisions. Conflicts may arise between the firm's strategic goals and those of the distributors, especially in global markets where timescales may differ.
6. Intermediaries in foreign countries may weaken the supplier's control over marketing decisions.

INTERMEDIARIES IN INDUSTRIAL CHANNELS

For manufacturers in B2B markets, distribution can be the make-or-break factor for the firm. Because industrial markets are often widespread geographically, manufacturers would have great difficulty in serving the markets directly.

Intermediaries in global B2B markets serve customers in the following ways:

1. Provide fast delivery. Local distributors will hold buffer stocks, so that end users will not be held up by (for example) a shortage of spare parts.
2. Provide a segment-based product assortment. Distributors such as motor-spares factors carry a wide range of stock appropriate to a specific industrial sector.
3. Provide local credit. Distributors may be able to provide credit facilities in the country in which they operate, whereas the producer may be unable to do this due to being in a different country.
4. Provide product information. Distributors can explain about the products in the local language, and with knowledge of local conditions.
5. Assist in buying decisions. Distributors can often give advice about several manufacturers' products, and can help in decision-making since they are likely to have knowledge of (for example) reliability and the availability of spare parts.
6. Anticipate needs. Because the distributors know the local market, they are often able to guess what customers might need and advise manufacturers accordingly.

Figure 19.3   Distributors' services to manufacturers

Because these advantages are apparent to the end customers, choosing the right distributor can mean the difference between success and failure for the manufacturer. However, distributors also serve manufacturers in the following ways:

1. Buy and hold stocks. Distributors are the customers of the manufacturers, because they actually buy the goods. This frees up working capital for the manufacturer.
2. Combine manufacturers' outputs. Customers almost always buy from several manufacturers. This means that they will be exposed to the firm's products whenever they buy from other manufacturers.
3. Share the credit risk. Although the manufacturer will offer credit to the distributors, this is less risky than offering credit to the hundreds of customers the distributor deals with – at the same time, the distributor is better-placed to assess the creditworthiness of the end customers.
4. Share the selling risk. The distributors have a stake in selling the products, since they have themselves made a commitment by buying the products in the first place. Obviously there is an assumption that the products are saleable, but in the event that the sales do not materialise both parties will share the loss.
5. Forecast market needs. Distributors are close to the market and are better placed to forecast what their customers will need.
6. Provide market information. Distributors are well-placed to feed back information about the market, about competitive activity, and so forth.

Channel strategy

Channel strategy is about choosing the right distributors. This will involve selecting the most effective distributors, the appropriate level of distribution intensity and the degree of channel integration.

Selecting the most effective distributors depends on market factors, producer factors, product factors and competitive factors. Market factors include buyer behaviour, much of which is about the expectations buyers have of where the product might be found. At the most obvious level, people do not expect to buy books at the greengrocer's, and

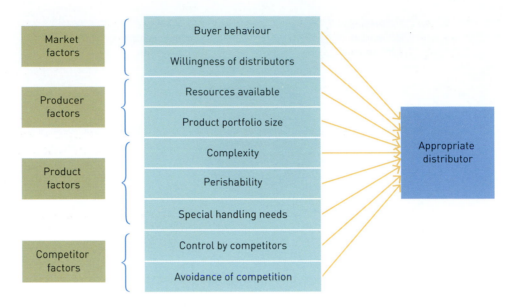

Figure 19.4   Choosing a distributor

yet Boots (the UK pharmacist) has been successful in selling computer equipment and cooking utensils. In some cases, the distribution network will be suited to the profile of the target audience, who have come into the shop for something else but buy the product on impulse: in other cases it will have been chosen because the shop sells similar products, and customers might reasonably expect to find the product category there.

Willingness of distributors to handle the product is also a market factor. Distributors may be unwilling to market the product for any number of reasons: they may feel that it would not sell in sufficient quantities to their customer base, it may be that the product does not sit well with the rest of their range, or they may feel that the profitability of the product is too low.

Think outside this box!

In marketing we are supposed to begin with the customer. If we begin with the customer, surely that means that retailers should be choosing suppliers, since retailers have the best knowledge of the customers and should therefore know what people want? In which case, retailers should be at the sharp end of new product development, hiring engineers and manufacturers to design and make the products, and booking out appropriate warehouse space and so forth.

In other words, if we are customer-centred, the present system is working backwards, isn't it? Perhaps we aren't as customer-centred as we like to pretend!

Producer factors include the resources the producer can bring to bear on the distribution problem. In some cases, producers do not have the resources to approach the market in the ideal manner, so they rely on the distributors to provide more of the necessary services to bring the product to market. For example, a coffee producer may not have enough money to establish its own brand in an overseas market, so it produces coffee for a supermarket as an 'own-brand'. The responsibility for establishing the brand then transfers to the supermarket, but of course the coffee producer will be paid proportionately less for the product. Likewise, a small exporter would not have the resources to establish an overseas salesforce, and might therefore recruit an agent in the foreign country: although the agent may work on commission, and therefore only be paid when he or she sells, the commission is likely to be higher than the cost of employing a salesforce directly and the firm will have much less control over how (and if) the product is marketed.

The product portfolio of the company may also have an effect. Single-product companies are unlikely to find it worthwhile to employ a direct salesforce: multiple-product companies need to consider the breadth of their distribution strategy.

Product factors might include complexity. If a product is complex, or needs to be tailored to individual customer requirements, direct distribution from producer to customer is more likely. This will allow the firm to discuss requirements and adjust the product: also, a high priced product will usually mean that the customer prefers to talk directly with the supplying company. Perishable goods usually require short distribution channels and minimal handling (which is a major problem for supermarkets), and products that require special handling may require direct distribution simply because distributors do not want the problem of handling the products.

Distribution channels are sometimes controlled or at least heavily influenced by competitors. The means by which channel control can be exercised are described later in the chapter – but if a competitor has seized control first, there may be a serious problem in obtaining distribution. In some cases, excessive control of a channel might be construed as a restrictive practice, and a company that is shut out of a market might be able to take the distributor to court, but this is hardly a good way to start a business relationship. Producers would be better-advised to seek a non-traditional outlet for their products.

Real-life marketing: Red Bull

Sometimes you just have to create your own channel. When Red Bull entered the UK market, the company wanted to target a young audience but found that the distribution networks were closed to them. Figuring that the product would appeal to a younger audience who would either be participating in sports, or would want to stay up late to party or study, Red Bull recruited a small army of students to act as part-time salespeople, calling on the places they liked to go themselves – night clubs and sports centres.

Since these places were seeking to attract a young audience, the part-time salespeople exerted a powerful influence: eventually Red Bull established its own warehouses in Britain (the company is Austrian in origin) but still used students as part-time workers in order to maintain the corporate image. More importantly, they acted as influencers, telling their friends about the product.

Red Bull now sells 3 billion cans of the drink a year. If you think you could do something similar, do this:

- Decide where you really want to sell the product, and focus on just those outlets.
- Decide who would be your best advocates for the product in those outlets, and recruit them.
- Stay committed to the distribution chain, even when other channels open up to you.

Table 19.1   Influences on channel design

Influence	Explanation
Competitors	In some cases, marketers will be looking for a different distribution route from that used by competitors: in other cases, they will need to follow a similar route because that is what customers expect. As a general rule, if the product can be differentiated from its competitors in a way that is not related to distribution, it should be distributed through the same channels as competitors in order to allow customers to compare the products: if there are no differentiating features between the product and its competitors, the distribution channel might be an effective way of competing.
Availability	In international markets, it is often the case that distribution can only be carried out through the one or two channels that are available; on the other hand, other channels may be available which are not common in the home country. Finally, competitors in the target country may already have tied up the existing distributors in exclusive contracts.
Culture	Culture affects the systems and negotiating tactics of distributors in foreign countries. Business culture varies considerably: for example, in Italy hypermarkets are rare, whereas in France they are commonplace. This is due to a cultural difference, in that Italians believe in supporting small local businesses that are often destroyed by hypermarkets, whereas French small businesses regard themselves as artisans and produce speciality products at premium prices.
Company objectives and resources	Some distribution decisions link to overall corporate strategy. For example, a company might seek to become pre-eminent in direct distribution worldwide (e.g. Avon Cosmetics). Corporate resources also have an effect: it may be impossible to distribute through all possible outlets simply because the company does not have the resources to produce the amount of stock required, or provide the credit needed by the retailers. In other markets, distributors need a great deal of support from suppliers: this can range from providing printed materials such as brochures, to providing on-line technical support through to full-scale training programmes.
Distribution strategy	The intensity of distribution (see next section), the competitive advantage being sought and the characteristics of the market will all affect distribution decisions.
Product characteristics	Some products, especially fragile or perishable products, demand very specific distribution techniques. For example, microlite aircraft are usually supplied in kit form from the factories for assembly at airfields. This means that local distributors need a high level of technical ability either to assemble the aircraft, or to advise would-be aviators who assemble their own planes.
Customers	Obviously, all distribution decisions have to be made in the light of what customers need and expect. If customers normally expect a product to be available from a particular type of outlet, there would have to be a compelling reason to distribute the product elsewhere. Such a compelling reason might be that the company sees a competitive advantage in not distributing the product on the same shelves as its competitors, of course.

Influences on channel design are shown in Table 19.1 (Czinkota and Ronkainen 2004).

In many cases firms might use different distribution routes for different customers. Some customers might be supplied direct, others might be supplied by agents, still others might be supplied via wholesalers and retailers. Many firms in B2B markets divide their customers into A-, B- and C-type customers. The As might represent the

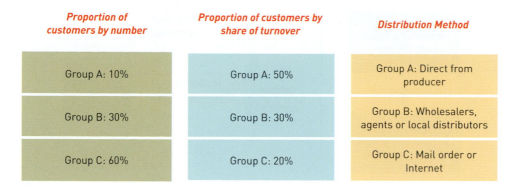

Proportion of customers by number	Proportion of customers by share of turnover	Distribution Method
Group A: 10%	Group A: 50%	Group A: Direct from producer
Group B: 30%	Group B: 30%	Group B: Wholesalers, agents or local distributors
Group C: 60%	Group C: 20%	Group C: Mail order or Internet

Figure 19.5   Different distribution routes

top 10% of customers, large firms perhaps accounting for 50% of the company's turnover. B-type customers might be medium-size companies accounting for 30% of sales, with the remainder being small firms that place only small orders. A-type customers might be dealt with directly, B-type customers through wholesalers or local distributors and C-type customers through mail order or the Internet.

This approach certainly applies the appropriate level of resources to each group of customers, but at the same time it may result in losing control of some customers who might be of strategic importance – for example small firms who have strong growth potential. There is also a potential 'turf war' problem if a small firm becomes larger (perhaps because the distributor did a good job in helping the firm) and, in moving from a B classification to an A classification, is immediately 'stolen' by the manufacturer.

Database marketing

Database marketing has been defined as:

> *An interactive approach to marketing that uses individually addressable marketing media and channels (such as mail, telephone and the salesforce) to provide information to a target audience, stimulate demand, and stay close to customers by recording and storing an electronic database memory of customers, prospects, and all communication and transactional data. (Stone et al. 1995)*

Database marketing is characterised by its two-directional, interactive nature. The database is used to send out information, but is then improved and refined by collecting the information which is returned from the recipients of the first contact. This is true even if the targeted individual does not respond at all: non-response demonstrates that this individual is either not interested in the offer, or did not receive it in the first place (perhaps because he or she has moved away, or even died).

The key to all direct marketing, and in particular the key to Internet-based direct marketing, is the creation of a suitable database. A database consists of two elements: a collection of customer data and a software program designed to manipulate the data. Databases can be sequential, relational or object-orientated: a sequential database contains a number of fields against which the data can be sorted. For example, a bank might keep customer files that contain the customer's name, address, account

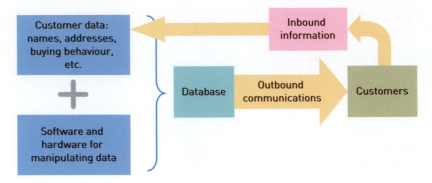

Figure 19.6   Database marketing

number, occupation category and income level. The bank would be able to sort customers against each of these criteria, and offer products that would be of most interest to the customer.

A relational database might be regarded as a set of tables that can be related to each other by the computer. The relationships do not have to be specified at the outset, so a relational database is much more flexible than a sequential database, but on the other hand tends to be slower to use and more expensive to set up. Table 19.2 shows the considerations that need to be taken into account when deciding whether to use a sequential database or a relational database.

Table 19.2   Sequential versus relational databases

Marketing requirements	Sequential or relational
Data requirements are clearly defined and unlikely to change	Sequential
Reporting requirements are likely to change	Relational
Market structure is complex and likely to change	Relational
Need to integrate with other systems	Relational
System is likely to be enhanced to include other applications in future	Relational
There is a need for quick development	Sequential
Initial cost is an important factor	Sequential
There is a requirement to add, modify or browse data on-line	Relational
There is a need for a user-friendly, flexible environment	Relational
The type of queries to be made are known, as are the type of reports required	Sequential
It is acceptable for selections and queries to be carried out by specialists	Sequential
There will often be long-batch processing runs	Relational
Queries need to be made on an ad-hoc basis	Relational

Object-orientated databases are a relatively new phenomenon. They operate on the basis of **polymorphism**, bundling together both code and data to create an 'object'. This object is able to carry out much of the routine cross-checking and validation which needs to be done in order to insert a new customer into the database.

Polymorphism Bundling data and code to create an object.

Real-life marketing: Integrate the database

Almost all firms keep customer details on computer. However, often different people within the organisation keep different sets of records: the accounts people might keep records of bad payers, the salespeople keep records of buyers' names and frequency of purchase, the warehouse keeps records of delivery addresses, and so forth.

Carphone Warehouse, the UK mobile telephone retailer, trains its salespeople to be consultative in their approach to customers, in other words to seek out solutions to customers' need problems. They also have the power to resolve complaints. They therefore needed to have instant access to customer details, but Carphone Warehouse found that often the same customer would appear in more than one place in the company's records. The company brought in Trillium software to integrate the database and 'de-dupe' customers appearing under more than one name (for example, as Alan Smith in one part of the site and as A. Smith in another).

The result was that staff now have all the customer's details available immediately, at the point of sale. This enables them to identify opportunities for cross-selling, and also to identify customer need more accurately.

If this situation sounds familiar to you, and you want to integrate your database, here are some ideas.

- Find out what information about customers exists within the firm, even if it is not on computer: some of your staff might be keeping paper records about some things.
- Combine the databases you do have and remove any duplications or obsolete addresses.
- Place password-enabled locks on anything confidential: you have a responsibility under the Data Protection Act.

The data needed to populate the database might come from a large number of sources. Typical sources might be:

- Company records. Companies keep records of the sales made, delivery addresses, and so forth (particularly in business-to-business marketing) but at a more subtle level, the records can be analysed to show the type of product each customer buys, and the frequency of purchase.
- Responses to sales promotions. A sales promotion not only tells the firm the name and address of a potential regular customer, it can also provide the firm with information about the customer's likes and dislikes, and (if the appropriate form is used), may even provide information about the customer's situation in terms of earnings, family size and so forth. The difficulty with collecting information in this way is that customers are likely to give misinformation if they perceive the questions as being intrusive.
- Warranty and guarantee cards. Returned warranty registrations provide information on the location of the end customers, and often give details about how the customer intends to use the product (this is especially true of computer users). Again, respondents might be less than truthful about how they intend to use the product, in case this affects the guarantee. Also, people frequently do not return warranty cards.
- Enquiries from potential customers. The fact that an enquirer does not buy the product is actually a useful piece of information. If marketers know why people

do not buy the product, they are able to consider ways of adapting the product or producing a different version in order to capture a new market segment.

- Exchange data with other organisations. This type of exchange is severely regulated by the Data Protection Act in the UK, and is restricted in many other countries by similar legislation. It is, however, permissible if customers have agreed to allow it. When companies exchange data, they are able to build up a fuller picture of the customer's needs and tastes, as well as obtaining details about new customers.
- Salesforce records. Salespeople frequently maintain detailed records of customers' details, such as customers' preferred ways of doing business, their personal details (names, number of children, etc.) and their attitude towards the company and competitors. This information is in addition to the basic information about what they buy, when and in what quantities. The problem for managers lies in finding ways to encourage the salesforce to give up this information.
- Application forms. Applications for credit cards, for membership of clubs or credit unions, or for loyalty schemes can provide detailed personal information. The drawback is that people occasionally lie on the forms in order to gain the benefits they are looking for from the membership, and also a form which is seen as intrusive might be off-putting for the applicant.
- Complaints. Customers who complain will often provide useful information on what is wrong with the product or the company. If a particular complaint arises frequently, this is an obvious indication: however, it is also useful to take details of dissatisfied customers because a pattern may emerge – the type of customer, the circumstances of use of the product, the way the complaint was handled, or the circumstances in which the product failed might all provide useful information. Equally, customers whose complaints are handled to their complete satisfaction often become more loyal than customers who did not have a complaint in the first place.
- Responses to previous direct marketing activities. Whether the response was positive or negative, the company can use the information to refine the existing database.
- Organised events. Exhibitions, trade fairs, or conferences can provide a list of interested potential customers. In-store tastings and special evening events can also be useful, since presumably those present are already interested in the general product area.
- Loyalty cards. Supermarket loyalty cards and frequent-flyer programmes provide extremely detailed information about customers' buying behaviour. This information can be analysed to give a very accurate portrayal of each customer: at first, supermarkets used this information to offer customers products they did not usually buy, but this approach turned out to be naïve since customers (for the most part) already knew about these products and did not want them. Subsequently, supermarkets realised that they would be more successful in notifying customers of special offers on products they were known to buy, but perhaps only occasionally.
- Surveys. It is important to note that, for ethical reasons, it must be made clear to people that they are participating in a survey which will lead to them being contacted by firms. This is different from a market research survey in which consumer attitudes are being sought out: using data of this sort for purposes for which it was not given is at least unethical, and in some countries illegal. However, there is no problem with asking people whether they intend to switch their mortgage to another bank, or whether they intend to change their car in the next year, provided it is clear that this will result in offers being made to respondents.

The type of information stored on a database is shown in Table 19.3.

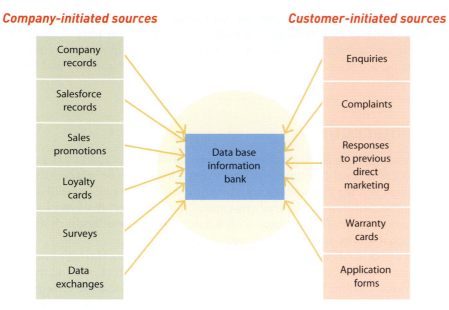

Figure 19.7   Sources of information

Table 19.3   Typical information stored on databases

Type of information	Explanation and examples
Customer and prospect information	Basic data about existing customers and future prospects would include contact details, personal characteristics (in consumer markets) or information on decision-makers and their buying criteria (for business-to-business markets).
Transaction information	Transaction information can be categorised under frequency (the number of times the customer buys), recency (the latest transaction carried out), amount (the quantity purchased) and category (the type of product being bought). More frequent customers are obviously valuable, but if the frequency rate is declining this may mean that the customer is buying elsewhere. Recency is useful because recent customers are more likely to recommend the product to others. Amount purchased is usually recorded in value terms: this is often regarded as the most important factor, but in fact the amount purchased needs to be measured against frequency of purchase and category. Category defines the type of product which is bought.
Promotional information	Databases should include information about the promotions that have been run, particularly when the promotion has been offered to different segments within the overall customer group. Knowing which customers respond best to particular types of promotion is invaluable information for the marketers.
Product information	Again, knowing which customers respond best to which type of product is invaluable for the marketers. Also, knowing which customers do not respond to a product may be helpful in developing new products.
Geodemographic information	Where possible, the database should contain information about people's incomes, family size, lifestyle and so forth. If the customer's postcode is available (which is almost certainly the case) a MOSAIC or ACORN analysis can be conducted to provide an approximation of the information, but detailed information can often be gleaned from the customers themselves.

The database is the starting-point for most direct marketing. Databases are used to identify customers for mailings or telephone campaigns, for improving customer relationship management, for managing distributors in the supply chain, for evaluating marketing activities, for identifying potential new target markets and for planning campaigns.

Direct marketing

Direct marketing is marketing without intermediaries. Direct marketers go straight from producer to final consumer, without using wholesalers or retailers to mediate between them and the customers – and therefore without having to build in a profit margin for the distributors. Naturally this means that the direct marketer has to fulfil all the functions normally associated with wholesalers and retailers, including delivery of the goods, after-sales service, promotion and so forth.

Because direct marketers deal with customers without going through intermediaries, they are normally much better placed to tailor the product offering than traditional marketers would be. They are also better placed to assess the effectiveness of their marketing activities, because the responses from customers are also direct.

The Direct Marketing Association defines direct marketing as follows:

Direct marketing is an interactive system of marketing which uses one or more advertising media to effect a measurable response and/or transaction at any location.

For the Direct Marketing Association, then, the key issue is the measurability of the activity.

An example of direct marketing is on-line marketing. Firms using the Internet to promote and sell products are, by definition, direct marketers. The growth in the use of the Internet for marketing purposes has been astronomical: buying goods on-line is becoming a significant proportion of total retail sales, and in some industries (notably the travel industry) on-line booking may eventually become the commonest way of buying travel.

Direct marketing is much more than a sub-section of the communication mix (Tapp 2004). Because direct marketing also encompasses fulfilment of orders, it in fact encompasses all marketing activities in some way, but does so on a direct basis.

THE BASIS OF DIRECT MARKETING

Direct marketing rests on four key issues (Holder 1998):

1. Targeting. Customers need to be identified and targeted accurately. For example, a direct mailing that is sent to people who have no need for the product is not only wasteful, it is also annoying for the recipients and therefore counter-productive in the long run.
2. Interaction. Getting a response from the customers is key to direct marketing's success. The responses may be in the form of a purchase, or in the form of a request for information, or in the form of supplying information: for the long-term management of databases, however, any responses from customers must be captured and recorded.
3. Control. Direct marketers have a great deal more control over events than do conventional marketers, simply because there are fewer organisations involved in providing value to the end consumer. It is also possible to pre-test almost every aspect of the direct provision.

4. Continuity. The aim in direct marketing is to use the information gathered to develop an ongoing, continuous relationship with the customer: each transaction should refine the firm's knowledge of the customer's needs and wants, and this knowledge should be reflected in future dealings.

Direct marketing is not a new activity: catalogues have been distributed almost since the invention of printing, and such institutions as mail order catalogues and book clubs have been around for over a hundred years. What has brought direct marketing to prominence in recent years is the dramatic fall in the cost of computers, and the parallel increase in their power, and hence the possibilities for developing sophisticated databases.

There are three categories of direct marketing: stand-alone, integrated and peripheral. Stand-alone direct marketing has no other means of managing the relationship with the customer. The UK's First Direct bank operates in this way: it has no branches, so customers can only access the bank via the telephone or (more recently) the Internet. The bank sends out information by post or on-line, and customers have their salaries paid directly into their accounts. There are limitations for the bank, of course: they deal only with private banking, not business banking, and there are products which they either do not supply or cannot supply as economically as can a bank with branches, simply because banking regulations require hard copies of some documents, and witnessed signatures for some others.

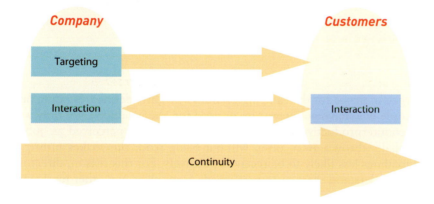

Figure 19.8   Issues in direct marketing

 Think outside this box!

Direct marketing seems to embody everything that people object to in business, and marketing in particular. Direct marketers send out mailings, they telephone people at home just as they are sitting down to dinner, they collect personal information about people and use it to sell to them. All in all, direct marketers sound like a real bunch of rascals.

So why do they carry on doing it? Is it some malevolence, some personality disorder, that makes them be such a pain to the rest of us? Or is it something else?

Is it, perhaps, that people respond to the offers? Perhaps people are (don't say it) actually *pleased* when someone contacts them to tell them about something they will like. Perhaps people like to be told that their usual ferry operator has a special deal on trips, or their local fast-food delivery service is giving away free pizzas, or their car dealer has a 0% finance deal on new cars.

It's all about the relevance of the offer, isn't it?

MANAGING DIRECT MARKETING

Direct marketing should be fully integrated with other marketing activities, particularly in the communications area. Building from the overall marketing strategy, the direct marketing element of the campaign needs to take account of the product positioning in the market, and the likely responses from competitors.

Ensuring that the messages from the campaign do not conflict with other marketing communications is not as simple as it might sound, because recipients of direct marketing communications consider the medium as well as the message. Indiscriminate mailings or telephone calls can lead potential customers to rank the communications along with junk mail and nuisance calls, so considerable care needs to be taken with both the style and the method of the communication.

Think outside this box!

We are told that people consider the medium as well as the message, but is this really so? Are TV advertisements really different from mailings? After all, a mailing is simply another communication, which can be read at leisure (or not at all), whereas a TV advert always seems to interrupt the programme at the point where it's just getting interesting (which is, of course, deliberate on the part of the TV company).

Presumably, then, mailings would be seen as a benign and pleasant way to receive information from companies, while TV and radio advertising would be an unpleasant and intrusive way.

Junk mail Poorly targeted direct mailings.

The target audience for the campaign should be tightly defined. Sending out mailings to people who have no interest in, or need for, the product is not only wasteful, it is also counterproductive. Poorly targeted mailings are perceived as '**junk mail**' and are usually thrown away, often without being read: this makes future, better-targeted mailings less likely to be received positively. For this reason, direct marketers need to understand their customers' needs as much as any other marketer needs to, but with the difference that direct marketers often have better information about customers than do other marketers. Segmentation can be carried out using the same categories as for other marketing activities, but a useful segmentation system for direct marketers is shown in Table 19.4.

The database of existing customers can be used to identify potential customers from bought-in or rented databases. The risk here is that our existing customers may not actually be the best customers: there may be a more lucrative group of people with whom we do not currently do business, perhaps because they are unaware of the firm and its products. There have certainly been cases where companies have underpriced their products, thus giving a 'cheap' image to more upmarket customers.

Having identified the groups to be targeted, a list can be developed either from the company's own database or from a rented database. Buying names from a rented database carries some risks: the list may not be 'clean', in other words some of the people on the list might have moved house, or died; other names on the list might be duplicated. This happens when an individual's address or name can be written in different ways: for example, an individual might be called Mr Alan James Fuller, Mr A.J. Fuller, Mr Alan J. Fuller, Al Fuller, and so forth. Computers are notoriously bad at picking up such variations. Similar problems arise in business-to-business markets, where standard industry classification numbers may not accurately describe the business the company is in, and companies sometimes change their names, merge with other companies, move headquarters and so forth.

Table 19.4   Segmentation in direct marketing

Criterion	Explanation
Competitors' customers	Sometimes these can be identified from lists of people who have indicated that they do not buy our products (perhaps as a result of an omnibus survey – but note the ethical warning issued earlier).
Prospects	People who have not previously purchased the product, but who qualify as having a need for the product and the means to pay for it. In general, prospects would be potential purchasers with a similar profile to our existing customers.
Enquirers	People who have contacted the organisation (for example, at an exhibition or trade fair) but have yet to make a purchase.
Lapsed customers	People who used to buy our products, but no longer do. These people are frequently the most cost-effective to target, because they already know the product and the company, and may have stopped buying for a reason that is easily addressed.
Referrals	People who have been recommended to the company by a friend or family member. Many companies run 'bring a friend' schemes to encourage referrals, often giving gifts to both the existing customer and the new customer.
Existing customers	People who currently buy the products, and can be encouraged (first) to continue to do so and (second) to buy more of the product.

Marketing in a changing world

Approaching potential consumers directly has always been part of the marketing scene – in fact, at one time it was pretty much the only way marketing happened, via street markets and one-man craft businesses such as blacksmiths and carpenters. Unfortunately, the rapid rise in direct mailings has led to protests from the public about too much mail, and clearly it is not in the industry's interests to send mailings to people who will never be customers.

The direct mail industry therefore set up the Mail Preference Service and the Telephone Preference Service. People who really do not want to get mail or telephone calls from companies can register – but what is the result? Those who do not register find themselves getting more and more calls and mail, because they are a dwindling pool of possible customers. At this point the government steps in and threatens to introduce legislation if the industry does not clean up its act, but in fact finds itself powerless to act – after all, how can they possibly stop someone's bank sending them information about a new type of account, or a new credit card?

Meanwhile the industry is under even more pressure from on-line and SMS spammers. These are almost entirely uncontrollable, despite the legislation, because they can operate from anywhere in the world. The latest scandal, about cold-calling people who have been mis-sold financial products, came to a head when two company directors were fined £440,000 for sending out 800,000 SMS messages a day. Since they were reputedly profiting by approximately £1 for every 100 messages sent, the fine was hardly a deterrent. Some Indian spammers have reputedly become multi-millionaires by selling the phone numbers of people who respond to such messages.

The problem for the honest companies is that the rogues are creating more and more restrictions, and greater and greater resistance to direct approaches. The solution is far from obvious.

The next stage in the process is to set the campaign objectives. These can be expressed financially, of course, and in most companies this is likely to happen, but marketers might consider setting marketing objectives such as response rates to mailings, acquisition or retention of customers, or communications objectives such as increasing awareness or reputation.

Acquiring new customers is almost always more expensive than retaining existing ones, so marketers might well look towards reducing customer churn (the rate at which customers leave and are replaced). Retaining customers also has the advantage that loyal customers are often prepared to recommend friends to use the product, are less likely to switch to competing brands and often buy new products from the same company (Stone et al. 1995). This is why companies adopting a relationship marketing approach (which has been closely associated with direct marketing) calculate the lifetime value of a customer rather than the immediate transaction value – a loyal customer is worth a great deal more to the firm than is an occasional customer.

Real-life marketing: Littlewood's

Littlewood's catalogue is an on-line and mail order company which was founded in the 1930s by John Moores. Moores was already a millionaire in 1932; having made his fortune from his Littlewood's football pool; he set himself the challenge of making another million, starting completely from scratch, from the catalogue business. He started with four staff and a rented office.

He recruited his first agents by sending a mailing out to his group of football pools gamblers. At the time, most working-class customers had no chance whatsoever of borrowing money, but the agents were creditworthy, so Moores sold to them on credit and they in turn gave credit to their customers. Since the customers were their friends, families and neighbours, the social bond ensured that they would get paid: they might have been prepared to cheat a large, faceless company, but they wouldn't rip off someone they knew.

This approach to direct marketing took off like a rocket – Littlewood's rapidly became one of the biggest catalogue retailers in the world, with thousands of distributors throughout the country. John Moores won his bet with himself, incidentally – he made his second million by 1936, no small achievement during a global depression.

If you want to be a millionaire within four years, here are the rules John Moores followed:

- Recruit agents from sources you can check up on.
- Only give credit to agents you know are creditworthy.
- Make full use of social networks, both to find customers and to recruit agents.
- Look for ways to remove the barriers that prevent people buying from you.

As we saw in Chapter 11, many firms concentrate too much on acquiring new customers at the expense of retaining existing ones: this has been called the 'leaky bucket' syndrome.

A retention objective often comes about as the result of a relationship marketing perspective. A 2% increase in customer retention has the same effect as a 10% reduction in overheads (Murphy 1997), because a loyal customer provides opportunities to persuade the customer to trade up to a more expensive version of the product, to sell the customer more products in the company's portfolio and to sell customers a replacement product when the existing one is likely to be coming towards the end of its useful life.

Direct marketing can be used as a sales promotion tool, sending special offers to people who are known to respond to them. For example, ferry companies and low-cost airlines send special offers by e-mail to frequent travellers: these are usually welcomed by the recipients, because they enjoy travel and welcome the opportunity to save money.

Distribution intensity

Producers also need to consider the intensity of their market coverage. In some cases, and for some products, the producer might be looking for as wide a coverage as possible – this would be the case for a mass-market product such as a chocolate bar or a coffee brand. Ideally, the producer would like the products to be available in as many outlets as possible, because sales are directly related to the number of outlets where the products are available. Since consumers probably have a wide range of products in the consideration set, another brand would almost certainly be an adequate substitute if the firm's brand is unavailable from the shop the consumer happens to be in at the time of purchase.

Selective distribution means that the producer uses a limited number of specialist outlets in a given area to stock the products. This type of distribution works best for **shopping products** such as hi-fi systems, bicycles, toys and so forth which need a specialist retailer who might be expected to offer expert advice. For this type of product, the manufacturer benefits by being able to concentrate on a few retailers, ensuring that they are trained in selling the product and (in particular) ensuring that the retailers understand the product's features and benefits so that they do not make promises that cannot be kept, and can provide suitable after-sales service. From the retailer's viewpoint, this arrangement also means that they can agree on an exclusive territory and thus reduce competition.

Shopping products Products that require an extensive information search and decision-making.

Exclusive distribution is an extreme form of selective distribution. Retailers or wholesalers are given the sole rights to sell the product within their area: in effect, this cuts out competition from other distributors as far as the individual product or brand is concerned. Exclusive agreements can work both ways: a retailer might seek the exclusive rights to a product, or the manufacturer might want to prevent the retailer from stocking competing brands. Some exclusive agreements can be against consumers' interests when they aim to reduce competition, however, so courts will occasionally overturn them if they are challenged by competitors or consumer groups.

 ## Think outside this box!

If consumers are kings, then presumably they are supposed to be given the greatest possible choice of goods to buy. If that's the case, why are exclusive agreements allowed at all? These agreements must *always* be in restraint of trade because they don't allow some people to have access to the goods!

Or is this a rather simplistic view of consumer needs? Most of us don't need to have Cartier jewellery displayed in Tesco, and those who can afford Cartier want to feel that it has come from an exclusive outlet. If some people feel that they do not want to mix with the riff-raff, why not indulge them? Isn't this one of the pleasures of being wealthy?

Selecting a distributor

Selecting a distributor may not always be an option: in many cases it is the distributors who have the power in the relationship, and who therefore choose which suppliers they want to do business with. However, there may be many circumstances in which the manufacturer (or importer) is in a position to choose between distributors, and in any case manufacturers should be prepared (in some circumstances) to avoid a market altogether rather than establish a relationship with a distributor which will generate problems in the longer term.

Moriarty and Kosnik (1989) developed a system for profiling potential partners. This is shown in Table 19.5.

Table 19.5   Partner profile

Characteristics	Weight (1–10)	Rating (1–10)	Total
Past performance			
Profitability			
Sales growth			
Market share			
Co-operation with other partners			
Experience with market/product			
Financial strength			
Capabilities			
Facilities			
Marketing/sales			
Design/technological			
Size of firm			
Language			
After-sales			
Knowledge of local business customs			
Reputation/relationships			
With suppliers			
With customers			
With financial institutions			
With government(s)			
Goals and strategies			
Short-term			
Long-term			
Compatibility			
Product lines			
Markets			
Style/personalities			

The weight refers to the importance placed on the characteristic by the company, and the rating relates to the actual performance by the prospective partner in regard to that rating. By multiplying one figure by the other an overall rating can be produced, against which the various alternative partners can be judged.

The partner profile chart is similar to the marketing audit in that it provides a 'snapshot' of the current situation regarding the prospective partner. It suffers from the same weaknesses as the marketing audit: it has a substantial degree of subjectivity despite appearing to be objective, and the situation may change over time (in fact, it may change before the assessment exercise has been completed). The major problem lies in collecting the necessary data to fill in the boxes, however: not all of it is likely to be available, and in particular there will be major gaps in the information when dealing across national borders, simply because the company is not in touch with local business information.

In international markets, similar organisational cultures are more important than similar national cultures when looking for business partners (Pothokuchi et al. 2002). This means that companies should look for distributors with a similar business philosophy, of a similar size and with compatible business objectives.

Once a distributor has been agreed on, it is difficult to change the decision. The distributor, not unnaturally, will feel aggrieved at any changes, having perhaps committed resources to the supplying firm. Likewise any new distributor is likely to be suspicious if the previous relationship broke down. In most cases, the agreement will be regulated by a contract or at least written agreement of some sort that outlines each party's rights and responsibilities. The key contract areas are shown in Table 19.6 (Fitzpatrick and Zimmerman 1985).

The type of relationship refers to whether the distributor will take title to the products or not. This means deciding whether the distributor will buy the goods from the supplier, or simply find orders for the supplier who will then collect the money from the end customer. In an international distribution agreement, this is important because the distributor will be in a much better position to assess the creditworthiness of local customers than will the supplier. The risk will therefore be a great deal less for the supplier, but of course the distributor will want to take a larger profit on the deal in exchange for carrying the risk. The second contract area describes the type of entity the supplier is dealing with. It is, in general, better to make distribution agreements with corporations rather than individuals because

Table 19.6 Agent/distributor agreements

Key contract areas	Key contract areas (continued)
Types of relationship	Terms/Conditions of sale
Corporation vs individuals	Facilities and personnel
Taxes	Inventory
Duration of agreement	Confidentiality
Termination of agreement	Proprietary information (trademarks, trade name, etc.)
Records and communication	Product sale or service agreement
Arbitration and governing law	Advertising and promotion
Payment and compensation	Other provisions

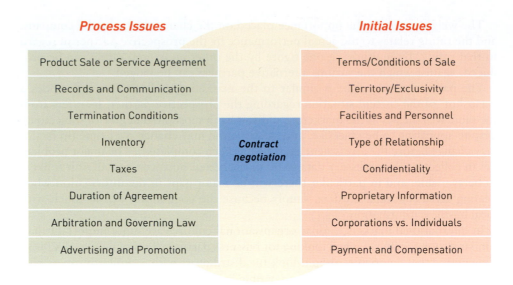

Figure 19.9   Distributor contracts

some countries regard individual agents or distributors as employees of the supplying company, which may mean liability under employment protection legislation (this is substantially the case in France, for example).

Taxation will arise in the country where the distributor is established, but there may be regulations about customs duties and VAT which might affect the overseas supplier. The distribution agreement should lay down who has the responsibility for dealing with these taxes.

The duration of the agreement should be limited, but should be sufficient to allow the distributor time to build a reputation. Too short an agreement will demotivate the distributor, which is not in anybody's interests: too long an agreement leaves the supplier at risk of being stuck with a distributor who is unable to deliver sales. Termination of the agreement will be governed by law in most countries: from the supplier's viewpoint, it would certainly be advisable to lay down standards of performance from the distributor, failure in which would lead to termination of the agreement. Again, in fairness to distributors the supplier should offer renewal agreements regularly, preferably well before the existing agreement runs out. Termination agreements should include clauses on how the termination is to be handled – what is to happen to unsold stocks, for example. Suppliers might well consider that it is worthwhile buying back any unsold stocks rather than have the distributor sell them off at a discount, potentially damaging the brand.

The product sale or service agreement identifies which products or services the distributor will be handling. This links with territory, because the supplier may prefer one distributor to handle some of its products in a given territory, while another distributor handles different products in the same territory. This may happen, for example, because the supplier produces a 'domestic' range and a 'professional' range of products. Each would be serving a different market, and therefore might require different distribution.

Arbitration and governing law refer to the ways in which disputes will be settled. Arbitration by a specified professional body is almost always cheaper and less damaging to the relationship than resorting to the law courts. In international agreements, it is usual to specify the country whose laws will be applied to any disputes between the parties. At one time, it became common in Eastern European countries to specify that contracts would be decided under English law, even when both parties to the contract were from the same Eastern European country: the reason for this was that fifty years or more of communism had left those countries with little or no effective commercial law.

The payment and compensation clause refers to the way commissions or profits will be divided between the parties. In many countries, anti-corruption laws mean that all transactions need to be traceable through clear accounting pathways.

Confidentiality agreements exist to protect the intellectual property rights of the supplier, and to preserve corporate information from being leaked out to competitors. Confidentiality clauses should outlive the overall agreement: a disgruntled distributor should not be in the position of being able to pass on company secrets to competitors after the agreement has terminated. The same applies to the distributor's use of trademarks, trade name and copyright.

> **Confidentiality agreement** A contract between two parties containing clauses to the effect that each will keep the other's secrets.

Records and communication need to be specified so that both parties can verify that business has been conducted fairly. Perhaps most importantly, the level and type of marketing activities to be undertaken by the distributor and the supplier need to be specified. Here a balance needs to be struck between the supplier's knowledge of the products and a desire to maintain brand values, and the distributor's knowledge of the local market and desire to meet and overcome local competition.

Here is a checklist for selecting and motivating distributors:

1. Ask potential customers to recommend possible distributors.
2. Determine which distributor fits the company's overall strategy the best. The goals of each should be compatible: an aggressive, high-growth strategy on the part of the supplier would not work well with a cautious, steady distributor.
3. Visit the distributor regularly. Apart from ensuring that the distributor is keeping to both the letter and the spirit of the agreement, visits enable the supplier to understand the market better, and work more closely with the distributor in developing the market.
4. Visit overseas customers with the distributor. Although some distributors might regard this with suspicion in the early stages of the relationship, visits are usually appreciated by the overseas buyers, and in the long run they help to support the distributor. They also enable the supplier to understand the market better.
5. Provide training and support. If possible, the distributor's staff should be given the opportunity to visit the supplier's factories or head office, perhaps for some formal training in the characteristics of the company's products. These exchanges will help both companies to understand each other's corporate culture.

Managing distribution channels

Channels can be led by any of the members. In some cases, manufacturers will have the power (especially when the manufacturer is large and the products have few close substitutes). In other cases wholesalers or importers will have the power, because they form the interface between manufacturer and retailer. In many cases, retailers hold the power because they are closest to the end consumers. Figure 19.10 depicts the continual tension between co-operation and conflict, in which power and leadership act as modifying influences, moving the balance between the two extremes.

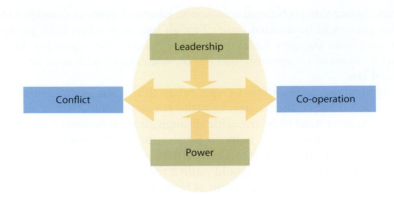

Figure 19.10   Factors in channel management

Channel co-operation is an essential part of the functioning of channels. Because each channel member relies on the other, members must co-operate if the goods are to flow freely along the channel. The problem is that conflict arises; although everyone agrees that co-operation is the best way forward for the overall success of the channel, each link in the channel has its own interests to consider, and short-term advantage might be gained at the expense of other members. Conflicts often centre around strategic non-compliance, perceptual disagreements and demarcation of decision-making responsibility (Moore et al. 2004). Power and conflict are equally important, but are exploited differently by managers (Gadde 2004).

Channel co-operation can be improved by using some or all of the following methods:

1. Channel members can agree on target markets, so that each member can direct their effort towards meeting the common goal.
2. Define the tasks each member will contribute. This minimises duplication of effort, and also prevents the end consumer being given conflicting messages.

In some cases channels can become highly integrated: this has been termed co-marketing (Marx 1995). Co-marketing involves sharing market information, and agreeing on strategic issues. Co-marketing can work extremely well if a condition of trust has been created between the channel members: however, there are some potential problems, as follows:

1. Channel members are likely to have relationships with other firms at the same time (because they are members of other channels). This can give rise to conflicts of interest.
2. Power in the channel is rarely equally-divided, so one member is likely to dominate the others, with potentially damaging consequences.
3. Expectations are sometimes not fulfilled, leading to disappointment and mistrust.

Sources of channel power are shown in Table 19.7 (Bitner 1992).

A power imbalance is not necessarily a barrier to entering a relationship, nor is it a bar to success for the relationship (Hingley 2005), but it clearly has an effect on the ways companies behave towards each other. Managing the channel in practice can be carried out either by co-operation and negotiation, or by coercion, with the most powerful member laying down the rules and compelling the others to follow.

Table 19.7   Channel power

Economic sources of power	Non-economic sources of power	Other factors
Control of resources. The degree to which the channel member has the power to direct goods, services or money within the channel.	Reward power. This is the power to provide benefits to channel members, for example to grant credit.	Level of power. The economic or non-economic sources of power are effective only if the members value them.
Size of company. The bigger the firm is compared with the other members, the more likely it is to be able to exercise economic power.	Expert power. This arises when the channel leader has a special expertise which the other members need.	Dependency of other channel members.
Referent power. This is the power that emerges when other members seek to copy the leader.		Willingness to lead. In some cases, only one firm is prepared to take the responsibility (and carry out the work) of co-ordinating and controlling the channel.
Legitimate power. This arises from a legal relationship. This could be contractual, or it could come about because one channel member has a substantial shareholding in another member firm.		
Coercive power. This exists when one channel member has the power to punish another channel member, for example by withholding stock.		

Attempts to control distribution channels by the use of power may well be looked on with disfavour by law courts, however, as they imply a restriction of trade. Table 19.8 shows the main channel management techniques.

Sometimes the simplest way to control a distribution channel is to buy out the members. This leads to vertical integration of the channel, an extreme example of which is the major oil companies, which carry out all the distribution functions from extraction of crude oil through to sales at petrol pumps.

Referent power Potential for control derived from a position of authority.

Legitimate power Potential for control derived from a legal or contractual position.

Coercive power Potential for control derived from the ability to punish the other party.

Logistics and the supply chain

Physical distribution is concerned with the movement of goods via road, rail, sea and air. Physical distribution is therefore about organising transportation to move goods in a timely and secure way from producer to consumer, taking all factors into account including budget.

Logistics, on the other hand, takes a holistic view of the process. A logistics approach to physical distribution considers the entire process of delivering value to customers, starting with raw materials extraction. Logistics takes the whole transport

Logistics The co-ordination of the supply chain to achieve a seamless flow from raw materials through to the consumer.

Table 19.8   Channel management techniques

Technique	Explanation	Legal position
Refusal to deal	One member refuses to do business with one or more other members. For example, a food wholesaler might refuse to supply private clubs on the grounds that this would be unfair on grocers and caterers.	In most countries suppliers do not have to sell their goods to anyone they do not wish to deal with. However, if the refusal to deal is based on a restriction of trade (for example, if a retailer is blacklisted for refusing to go along with a restrictive agreement) there may be grounds for a lawsuit.
Tying contracts	The supplier (sometimes a franchiser) demands that the channel member carries other products as well as the one the channel member wants to stock. If the supplier insists that the channel member carries the full range, this is called full-line forcing. For example, fast-food franchisees are usually required to buy all their supplies from the franchiser, and must carry the full range.	In the UK, most of these contracts would be illegal. They can be justified if, for example, only the supplier can provide goods of acceptable quality, or if the purchaser is free to carry competing products as well. Some agreements are accepted if the supplier is new to the market.
Restricted sales territories	Intermediaries are prevented from selling outside the area. Intermediaries usually prefer this arrangement, because it prevents other intermediaries from competing directly with them.	Courts have conflicting views about these arrangements. On the one hand, they do help weaker distributors, and can increase competition if other local dealers carry different brands: on the other hand, such agreements are a clear restraint of trade.

problem and integrates it into a smooth system for moving goods from where they are produced to where they are needed.

For example, until the early 1970s goods being moved internationally would be loaded onto lorries at the factory, driven to a sea port, unloaded into a warehouse, reloaded onto a ship, taken to the overseas port and unloaded into another warehouse, then reloaded onto lorries for delivery to distribution warehouses and, ultimately, to retailers. Loading cargo onto the ship (and off again at the other end) required eighteen men for each cargo hatch: eight on the quayside, eight on the ship and two winch operators. This did not include the ship's officers, who were needed to supervise the work.

During the 1970s the cargo container was developed. This allowed firms to fill the container at the factory, load the entire container onto a lorry (or train) for delivery to the ship, where it could be loaded onto the ship by (at some ports) one man in a specialised crane. The result of this has not only been a dramatic reduction in the number of dock workers needed, but also a dramatic reduction in the number of ships needed, since each ship spends only a few hours in port instead of the days formerly needed.

Logistics is central to supply chain management. Transport and warehousing links are the intermediate links in the supply chain, rather than the main concern, as they are in physical distribution orientation. It is in these areas that the most dramatic cost reductions can be made, with consequent increase in profit or reduction in price to the consumer (in either case, the competitive advantage improves).

Figure 19.11   Elements in logistics management

Co-ordinating the supply chain requires the following factors to be in place:

1. Data communication needs to be transparent, with all those involved being kept informed as to what is happening to the goods.
2. There must be a co-ordinating philosophy or set of rules to which all those involved should subscribe.

IT systems have enabled logistics co-ordinators to track consignments in real time wherever they are in the world. This enables effective use of resources: aircraft can always fly full, ships can be loaded swiftly and spend more time at sea, warehouses can be smaller because goods stay for shorter periods of time. For example, Chevron Oil introduced SAP logistics software in 1992 at a total cost of $160m. By 1997 the software had been responsible for reducing purchasing-related costs by 15%. In addition, purchase transactions were facilitated electronically instead of using paper transactions, which greatly improved the reliability of the process and improved response times (Brown 1997).

Another use of IT has been to minimise wasted journeys or part-full journeys. An example of how IT has been successful in this way is the Delego company of Sweden. Delego was started by two truck drivers who met by chance on a ferry from Denmark to Germany. Chatting to other drivers over a few beers, the two truckers realised that several of their erstwhile colleagues were travelling between the same two points, but with only half-full or even empty trucks. The two truckers planned a new system for organising part-loads, and eventually gave up their trucking jobs, borrowed some capital, and started the Delego website. The system works through the Internet: when a transport company has an empty or part-empty truck on a given route, the company enters its details on the Delego website (or by telephone), and Delego tries to match up the truck with a cargo, providing an estimate of the financial return for the trucker.

 Think outside this box!

Whenever firms talk about becoming more efficient they seem to regard job losses as inevitable. In fact, many go further – they actively try to get rid of staff. And yet business is about people. Without people nothing happens – and if people are not earning money, how are they going to buy the goods that the manufacturers produce?

Furthermore, if firms keep on firing their staff, the company is shrinking – yet isn't it part of the imperative for companies in a capitalist world that they should grow?

Or maybe it's about restructuring – shifting people from inefficient jobs into efficient ones, and from jobs that are basically 'make-work' into jobs that produce real value for everybody – company, customers and, yes, even the workers! One thing's for sure – continual changes in working practices make for interesting times.

Logistics has become widely adopted by global firms. Shipping and trucking companies are therefore redefining themselves as logistics facilitators. This means that such companies take responsibility for the whole process, moving goods from the factory gates to the final destination by whatever means are available. This leads to even greater savings for the businesses involved, since the process operates much more smoothly.

Logistics managers are responsible for some or all of the following interfaces:

1. Collaboration with physical distribution. Selecting transportation methods such as road, rail, sea or air.
2. Optimisation of the material flow within the work centre.
3. Planning and organising the storage area layouts, and the type of handling equipment involved.
4. Selection of suppliers for raw materials, price levels and specifications.
5. Selection of subcontractors to perform specific tasks.
6. Organising after-sales activities, including problem resolution with supplied products.
7. Verifying that sales forecasts accord with the real needs of the client.
8. Developing delivery schedules.
9. Developing packaging to meet the need for physical strength and security.

Not all elements of the logistical system are controllable by the logistics manager. Transport delays, changes in legislation requiring new documentation, the bankruptcy of distribution channel members, or even the weather can play havoc with the best-laid logistical systems. This means that even greater care should be taken with those elements that are controllable (see Table 19.9).

As with many other complex decisions, each element of the logistics system impacts on every other element. If the supplier fails to become reliable, the customer may have to bear the extra cost of holding large buffer stocks: additionally, if supplies fail, the customer may lose production or even customers. Clearly customers in many markets will favour reliable suppliers, and will even pay premium prices for this, so a good logistics system is likely to have pay-offs on the bottom line in terms of improved profits and possibly improved competitor advantage.

In practice, two main variables must be traded off against each other (see Figure 19.12). The first is the total distribution cost, which would generally be regarded as something that should be kept to a minimum. The second variable is the level of logistical service given to customers. As service improves, costs will rise, and there is likely to be a diminishing return for extra expenditure: in other words, there is a point at which further expenditure is unlikely to make a material improvement in service levels.

Firms need to trade off these cost and service level considerations in such a way as to maximise the firm's ability to achieve its strategic objectives. The total-cost approach to logistics management attempts to balance these by assuming that all logistical decisions impact on all other logistical problems, so management needs to look at the efficiency of the system as a whole rather than only concerning itself with individual elements of the structure. The interactions between the elements are described as cost trade-offs, because an increase in one cost may be matched by a decrease in another. Reducing overall costs is the aim of this approach, but there are difficulties.

For example, the separate elements of the logistical system will almost certainly be controlled by different firms, each with its own cost structure and strategic aims. Thus an increase in cost for one element of the system will not be offset by a reduction in cost elsewhere, since the gainer and the loser are actually different firms.

Table 19.9 Controllable elements in a logistics system

Element	Description
Customer service	Customer service is the product of all logistics activities. It relates to the effectiveness of the system in creating time and place utility. The level of customer service provided by the supplier has a direct impact on total cost, market share and profitability.
Order processing	This affects costs and customer service levels, because it is the starting point for all logistics activities. The speed and accuracy of order processing clearly affect customer service: this is particularly true in global markets, where errors or delays become multiplied by distance, and by the time which it takes to make corrections.
Logistics communications	The way in which information is channelled within the distribution system affects the smooth running of the logistics. For example, a good progress-chasing system will allow deliveries to be tracked and therefore customer reassurance will be greater.
Transportation	The physical movement of the goods is often the most significant cost area in the logistics process. It involves the most complex decisions concerning carriers and routes, and is therefore often most prone to errors and delays.
Warehousing	Storage space serves as the buffer between production and consumption. Efficient warehousing reduces transportation costs by ensuring that (for example) containers are shipped full, and transport systems are fully utilised.
Inventory control	This ensures that the correct mix of products is available for customers, and also ensures that stocks are kept at a reasonable level to avoid having too much capital tied up.
Packaging	The purpose of packaging is primarily to protect the contents from the environment and vice-versa. It also serves as a location for some shipping instructions, e.g. port of destination.
Materials handling	Picking stock to be included in an order is potentially a time-consuming and therefore expensive activity. Some warehouses have the capacity to automate the system, so that robots select the products and bring them to the point from which they will be shipped.
Production planning	Utilised in conjunction with logistics planning, production planning ensures that products are available in the right quantities and at the right times.
Plant and warehouse location	The location of the firm's facilities should be planned so as to minimise delivery times (and therefore minimise customer response times) as well as ensure that the costs of buying or renting space are minimised. This will often result in difficult decisions, since space near customers is likely to be more expensive than space in (for example) remote rural locations.

Even within a single firm, different departments will have their own budgetary constraints – managers may not be prepared to lose out so that someone else in the organisation can gain. Any attempt to organise the logistical system as a seamless whole must take account of these problems, which of course places a premium on supply chain integration.

In some cases, the business must maintain the highest possible service levels whatever the cost. For example, delivery of urgent medical supplies is not cost-sensitive, but it is highly service-sensitive. At the other extreme, delivery of paper for recycling is unlikely to be service-sensitive, but almost certainly will be cost-sensitive.

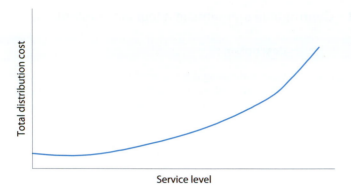

Figure 19.12   Logistics trade-offs

Determining the level of service is a complex problem because it is difficult to calculate the possible revenue gains from an improvement in customer service levels. This calculation needs to be made in the light of competitive pressures, customer preferences, industry norms and so forth. The cost element is much easier to calculate, and the net result needs to be a trade-off between the two elements. One study found that a 5% reduction in customer service levels resulted in a 20% decrease in sales (LaLonde et al., 1988).

MANAGING THE SUPPLY CHAIN

Supply chain management has been described as the integration of business processes from end user through original suppliers to provide products, services and information that add value for customers (Cooper et al. 1997). The critical element in managing the supply chain is to ensure that value is added for customers: in order to do this, the supply chain needs to be co-ordinated and to become as seamless as possible.

For business-to-business marketers this has two implications. First, it implies that the marketer needs to work at establishing relationships with both suppliers and customers, and in most cases will need to be prepared to change the firm's working practices in order to accommodate the needs of other firms in the supply chain. Second, it means that seeking new customers will mean fitting into an existing supply chain, where the rules and practices are already well established.

In order for relationships to work at optimum efficiency within the supply chain, the members need to share information about strategic plans, new product development, customer profiles and much else. For example, e-marketing firms need to integrate their internal and external supply chain activities as well as share strategic information if they are to succeed (Eng 2004). This information is commercially sensitive, so a great deal of trust is necessary. Goods flow down the supply chain, but information flows up it, enabling the various members of the chain to plan around the reality of existing market conditions. Effective supply chain management is a powerful tool for creating a competitive advantage for the following reasons (Quinn 2000):

1. It reduces costs.
2. It improves asset utilisation.
3. It reduces order cycle time, thus speeding up the delivery of customer satisfaction.

Effective supply chain management (SCM) can also shut out competitors by denying them access to sources of components or raw materials. For example, when CD

Table 19.10   Goals of supply chain management

Waste reduction	By minimising duplication, harmonising operations and systems, and by reducing inventories, waste is reduced. For example, harmonising materials handling equipment reduces the need for loading and unloading components and also creates economies of scale in purchasing equipment and containers.
Time compression	Improved information flows about market conditions enable supply chain members to predict demand more accurately and thus make response times quicker. Also, preferred-customer status within the supply chain means that each member responds more quickly to the needs of other members than to the needs of non-members. Reducing response times improves cashflow for all members because deliveries happen faster so invoices are paid sooner.
Flexible response	Ensuring flexibility in the supply chain means that all the members are able to adjust more quickly to changing market conditions. This can lead to major improvements in competitive advantage.
Unit cost reduction	Good supply chain management seeks to reduce unit costs, which will either allow the firms in the chain to make more money or will allow them to reduce the price to the end consumer, which again offers a competitive advantage. Cost is not necessarily the same as price: a customer operating a just-in-time manufacturing system may accept a slightly higher price for receiving small daily deliveries rather than paying a lower price for one large monthly delivery, because the savings in terms of holding stocks will outweigh the extra outlay.

players were first marketed the only sources of supply for the CD drives were three factories in Taiwan, all of which were under exclusive contract to Japanese electronics manufacturers. This effectively shut out European and US manufacturers until they could develop the manufacturing capacity themselves – a somewhat ironic position for the Europeans, since the technology was originally developed in the UK.

The goals of supply chain management are shown in Table 19.10.

If the supply chain is properly managed, it should create tangible benefits for customers in terms of reduced waste, more flexible and reliable deliveries and improved costs. For the members of the supply chain, it should increase security of supply, make planning easier, and reduce costs and competitive pressures. There have been many studies that have demonstrated the advantages of integrating the supply chain: Ferguson (2000) demonstrated that best-practice SCM companies have a 45% cost advantage over median supply chain competitors. On the other hand, supply chain glitches have been shown to cause an average 9% drop in the value of the company's shares on the day the problem is announced, and up to 20% decline in the six months following the announcement (Bowman 2001).

In global SCM there are four strategic marketing challenges (Flint 2004). These are:

1. Customer value learning. Finding out what customers regard as valuable is complex in the global environment, because supplying firms need to consider differing decision-making processes, differing decision-maker values, differing importance rankings of service versus physical attribute values, and so forth. The value chain may span several different cultures, so that each link in the chain must be considered separately as well as how it fits into the whole.
2. Understanding customer value change. Customers often change what they value as changing circumstances dictate. Because changes happen at different times in different countries, customer value is a moving target.

3. Delivering value in a world of uncertainty. Because change is constant, and may even be accelerating, it is virtually impossible to integrate the strategies of firms that are often thousands of miles apart and being pulled in different directions by local changes in the business environment.

4. The customer value process. In order to meet the problems raised by the first three challenges, marketers may need to shift from a functional towards a process orientation. This may be difficult, in that shareholders believe that they have invested in a company rather than in a supply chain, which makes it difficult for the process to be seamless.

These challenges will differ in importance from one firm to another, and the solutions will be widely varying, but these are not challenges a global firm can ignore. Success in integrating the supply chain provides an important competitive advantage, and given that globalisation also provides the best opportunities for minimising total costs managing the global supply chain effectively is a powerful route to growth.

ESTABLISHING AND MAINTAINING RELATIONSHIPS

Relationships exist not only between suppliers and purchasers, but also across several other categories of partner. Morgan and Hunt (1994) offered the following categorisation:

1. Supplier partnerships:

   - Goods suppliers
   - Services suppliers

2. Lateral partnerships:

   - Competitors
   - Non-profit organisations
   - Government

3. Buyer partnerships:

   - Intermediate customers
   - Ultimate customers

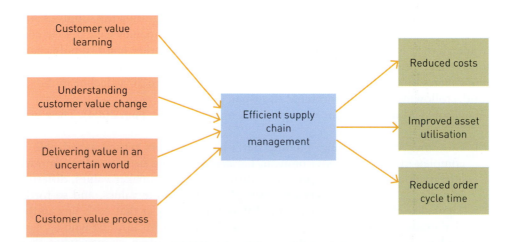

Figure 19.13   Supply chain management

4. Internal partnerships:

- Business units
- Employment
- Functional departments

From a marketer's viewpoint, the most important set of relationships here will be the buyer relationships, but this does not mean that the other relationships can safely be ignored. In terms of supply chain management, these relationships are important as they ensure that the firm's place in the supply chain and its ability to contribute effectively are assured. For Morgan and Hunt (1994), relationship marketing refers to all marketing activities directed towards establishing, developing and maintaining successful relational exchanges. This led them to develop the commitment-trust theory, which states that those networks characterised by relationship commitment and trust engender co-operation, a reduced tendency to leave the network, the belief that conflict will be functional rather than damaging, and reduced uncertainty.

All relationships (whether business or personal) are affected by the degree of trust that exists between the parties. Establishing a relationship of trust between businesses can be a complex affair, since many different individuals will need to be part of the process and consequently part of the outcome. There is more on this in Chapter 11.

Channel system orientation

In order to overcome some of the problems inherent in having a logistical system made up of several companies, supply chain management seeks to synchronise channel activities through a series of negotiations that divide up the overall profits between members. At least in theory, this should make all members better off,

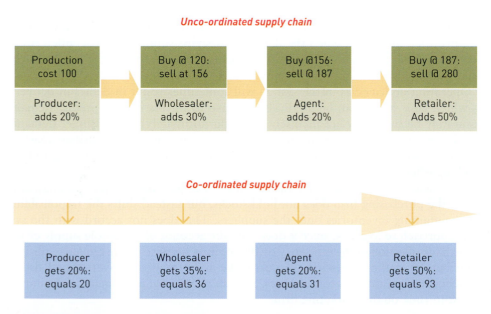

Figure 19.14   Profit sharing

since overall costs will fall and service levels will rise. In this scenario, relationships between the channel members must be seen as long-term, permanent, totally honest and highly co-operative if savings are to result.

Companies with effective logistics systems grow 8% faster than those without, realise a 7% price premium and are twelve times as profitable as firms with inferior service levels (Novich 1992). Setting the service level may or may not be a function of profitability: much depends on the strategic aim of the company involved. This means that it may be possible to help a partner firm to achieve a strategic aim in exchange for a concession on profitability.

Key elements in welding the channel into a single system are as follows:

1. Develop information systems that provide realistic sales forecasts for channel members.
2. Standardise packaging and handling systems (for example by using palletisation or containerisation).
3. Provide services (e.g. warehousing or data handling services) that improve efficiency for everyone (usually provided by the channel leader).
4. 'Pool' shipments to avoid the 'empty truck' problem.

Since the service level is often the only strategic advantage the channel has, there are obvious advantages in coming to an agreement and integrating the system. Unfortunately, such integration may take some years to achieve, since relationships of trust take time to establish. Supply chain management implies a greater degree of integration than does logistics management: SCM implies integration of all the business systems of the channel members, whereas logistics is only concerned with integrating the systems relating to the movement of goods.

Inventory management

Inventory management is the buffer in the logistical system. Inventories are essential in business-to-business markets because production and demand never quite match. This means that there are times when the producers need to stockpile product, and times when the demand outstrips supply and stockpiled products are released onto the market. This ensures a smooth flow of goods to the final users.

Operating deficiencies in the system will sometimes result in delays in delivery, in which case stocks can be used: also, industrial buyers cannot predict demand accurately because they are themselves relying (ultimately) on consumer demand, which is volatile. As we saw in Chapter 5, demand in business-to-business markets is much more volatile than that in consumer markets because of stocking and de-stocking effects.

There was an attempt by some firms to introduce just-in-time (JIT) purchasing in which the purchasing firm does not hold stocks, but instead shifts the responsibility for maintaining inventories onto the suppliers. This does not accord with the systems approach to logistics, since it does not take account of the whole supply chain. Some have questioned the efficiency of JIT recently because of the tendency for it to contribute to traffic congestion as trucks make more frequent deliveries, and also its tendency to increase costs for suppliers. See Table 19.11 for a summary of the impact of just-in-time on the marketing firm.

Table 19.11   Effects of JIT on marketing firms

Activity	Impact
Transportation	Because the number of shipments increases, the quantity ordered each time decreases. The shipments also need to meet the exact demands of the customer, and are non-negotiable, so the supplier must be flexible. In one study, 49% of companies using JIT said that the inability of suppliers to deliver to their specifications was a problem (Celley et al. 1986).
Field warehousing	Shipping over long distances may not be feasible because of the inherent unreliability of transportation, so smaller, more numerous warehouses will be needed. In addition, the use of third-party warehousing may be unsuitable because the customer will require absolute reliability: the supplier may not feel that a third party can be trusted sufficiently.
Field inventory control	Inventory levels of producers may need to be increased as customers will be totally unable to tolerate stockouts under any circumstances. Because of the need for 100% control of inventory, the producer may need to take over all the distribution functions.
Protective packaging	Packaging may be changed or even eliminated in some cases because the goods will be used immediately in production. This is a rare case where just-in-time might benefit the vendor.
Materials handling	There may be few changes here, but because the quantities delivered are much smaller, it may not be feasible to use (for example) containerisation as a way of reducing handling.
Order processing	The simplest way of dealing with this is electronically. The situation will inevitably become more complex as more frequent deliveries, at clearly-specified times, become necessary.

Think outside this box!

Just-in-time inventory management means arranging for components to arrive almost exactly at the moment when they are needed at the customer's factory. This obviously results in savings for the customer – but what about the supplier? Suppliers need to deliver small amounts frequently rather than large amounts periodically – so they use smaller vehicles, and more of them, and often park just outside the customer's gates until the exact minute for delivery.

Fine for the customer, of course, but wouldn't the supplier pass those costs on? Somebody has to keep the inventory – and somebody has to pay for it. Ultimately it's the end customer. And what about the impact on the environment? All those extra vehicles clogging the streets and parking spaces cannot be a good thing!

Yet *if all* firms could arrange the logistics in a JIT manner, wouldn't the flow of goods from raw materials to finished products be a real process, instead of a lot of starts and stops? Maybe JIT has something to offer after all!

Estimates of future sales are the key element in controlling the logistics system. These estimates need to be far more accurate than the general ones used for planning sales promotions or other long-term marketing plans: the logistics and inventory forecast needs to be flexible enough to operate on a day-to-day basis if necessary.

This requires some fairly sophisticated computer technology, which should be linked throughout the supply chain so as to enable firms further up the chain to predict demand. Falling inventory at the retailer means increased demand at the wholesaler, the manufacturer, the component supplier and the raw material supplier in that order, but delays in the system mean that increased demand at the retail level will perhaps take several months to filter through to the raw material level.

Managing logistics in international trade

Table 19.12 shows the commonest documents used in international trade. This comprehensive list of paperwork may not be necessary for all shipments. There is considerable duplication, in other words. Having said that, trucks travelling through Europe may need to carry large amounts of paperwork to satisfy the formalities at each border, once each truck has left the European Union. Standardising the documentation

Table 19.12   Trade documentation

Export document	Description
Ocean bill of lading	The contract between the shipper and the carrier. The bill of lading is a receipt given by the carrier (often issued by the ship's purser) which proves that the goods were loaded. It is often used as proof of ownership, so that it matches with the cargo unloaded, and can be bought and sold.
Export declaration	This includes complete particulars of the product and its destination, and is used to control exports and compile statistical information about exports.
Letter of credit	This is a financial document issued by the importer's bank, guaranteeing the exporter's payment subject to certain conditions (often the presentation of bill of lading to prove that the goods were shipped).
Commercial invoice	The bill for the goods from the seller to the buyer. Often used by customs officials to determine the true value of the goods.
Certificate of origin	This document assures the buyer that the goods have not already been shipped from a country with which, for example, a trade embargo applies. These certificates are often provided by a recognised chamber of commerce in the exporting country.
Insurance certificate	This assures the importer that insurance is in place to cover the loss of, or damage to, the goods in transit.
Transmittal letter	A list of the particulars of the shipment and a record of the documents being transmitted, together with instructions for disposition of documents.
Customs entry	This provides information about the goods, their origin, estimated value and destination. This is for the purpose of assessing customs duty.
Carrier's certificate and release order.	A document to advise customs of the details of the shipment, its ownership, port of loading and so forth. This certificate proves the ownership of the goods for customs purposes.
Delivery order	The consignee, or his customs broker, issues this to the ocean carrier as authority to release the cargo to the inland carrier. It includes all the data necessary to ascertain that the cargo may be released.

for trucks was a major issue within the EU in its attempts to maximise the free flow of goods throughout the Union, but of course the system is not perfect because member states are still permitted to ban imports from other member states if their governments believe that the imports represent a threat to human or animal life. This was the justification for the French ban on British beef imports during the late 1990s, and is the justification for the British ban on the import of live shellfish from the rest of the European Union. In the United States virtually all border controls between the states have been abolished, but differences in state taxation mean that some products (for example cigarettes) are still worth smuggling internally, and California maintains restrictions on imports of plants and fruit, for fear of importing an epidemic that would damage the state's lucrative fruit farming.

The most important document from the international marketer's viewpoint is the bill of lading, since this is proof of ownership. It is a document of possessory title, which means that only the holder of the bill of lading can collect the goods. There are exceptions to this general rule: if perishable goods arrive before the bill of lading has arrived (for example if the bill of lading has been posted but the goods were sent via airfreight) the shipper can release the goods to a third party on receipt of a letter of indemnity from the party collecting the consignment. Possession therefore passes when the bill of lading is transferred, but ownership only passes when the parties intend it to pass, as evidenced by the sales contract.

As receipts, bills of lading provide only prima facie evidence that a certain quantity was received on board, that packaging marks were in order and that the goods were apparently in good condition. Nevertheless it is up to the carrier to prove that the items stated were not put on board, or that they were loaded in good condition. Obviously, a ship's master is required to attest only that the goods appeared to be in good condition: with a few exceptions, the ship's officers are not expected to carry out detailed internal inspections of cargoes to investigate their inner qualities.

Think outside this box!

World trade is important. We can each make what we are good at making, and we can profit from ideas from other countries. Also, of course, more trade usually means less war – it is not a good idea to shoot the grocer. So why not just remove all trade restrictions immediately? Certainly there would be a painful period of re-adjustment, but after that, wouldn't life be so much easier? After all, poor countries frequently complain that they don't have fair access to rich markets while wealthier countries complain that they are paying too much for goods.

Or is free trade just a rich country's response? Do we only consider this approach because we know we have the economic power to clobber any opposition? A 10% drop in our standard of living during a period of readjustment would hardly be noticed – but in Mali or Ethiopia it would mean millions of deaths. So how *do* we control trade? Simply by more paperwork? Or by a controlled and calculated regime of duties and documents? And if so, who does the controlling and calculating?

Another problem in international transport is ensuring that everyone involved is clear about what is meant by specific terms. **Incoterms** refers to a set of words and phrases that have been agreed upon internationally to describe specific types of shipping conditions, so that importers and exporters know exactly who is paying for what.

Incoterms International Commercial Terms. A set of internationally agreed terms used in drawing up export contracts.

Transportation methods

Selecting a transportation method for a global market can be complex. As a general rule, the faster the shipment, the higher the cost, but standby air freight (in which the shipment is sent on the next available aircraft with spare capacity) can be relatively cheap, and when the cost of having capital tied up in goods in transit is also taken into account, can actually be cheaper than surface transportation. Obviously for perishable goods, or highly valuable goods such as computer chips, air freight is almost always cheaper, because there is less spoilage and the capital is tied up for a shorter period.

Five basic modes of transportation are used in business-to-business marketing. Goods are shipped by road, by rail, by air freight, by water, or in some cases by pipeline. Often combination systems are used, for example the ro-ro (roll-on, roll-off) ferries that transport lorries (or even just the trailers) across the English Channel, Irish Sea and North Sea routes.

Figure 19.15 shows the factors a marketing manager will typically take into account when choosing a transportation method. In most cases, each of the factors will trade off against each of the others in some way. For example, sea transport (or indeed inland waterway transport) will be substantially cheaper than air freight, but will also be much slower. Equally, the reliability of rail transport may compare unfavourably with road transport, but may protect the goods better.

In some circumstances accessibility is an issue. The city of Iquitos, in Peru, is only accessible by water or air – there are no rail or road links into the city. This obviously limits the choices somewhat. Less obviously, some towns in Australia which are accessible by rail may only see one freight train a week, and are much better served by road transport since Australian buses tow trailers for limited amounts of freight and usually offer a daily service.

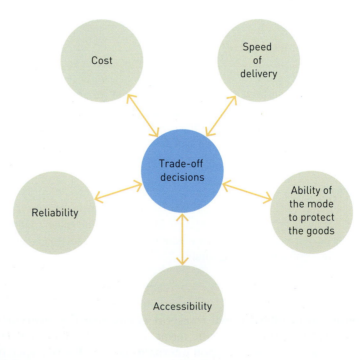

Figure 19.15   Trade-offs in transportation

Costs obviously vary in different countries. Inland waterways are widely used in Continental Europe, but are not commercially viable within the UK. Railway systems are heavily subsidised in Switzerland and the United States for environmental reasons, but not in the UK, where the system has deteriorated dramatically in the last fifteen years or so.

Sea freight includes scheduled services (**liners**), which operate according to a fairly strict schedule, visiting specific ports at specific dates, and **tramp** services, which sail once they have a full cargo for a specific destination. Liner services charge fixed rates, tramp ships (which are frequently modern, fast vessels) have variable rates that are almost always cheaper than the scheduled rates. Sea freight charges are based on either volume or weight, with extra charges for extra services, for example tallying cargo on and off (tallying means that a ship's officer counts the units of cargo as they are loaded).

Shipping agents will carry out all the functions of booking space on the ship and arranging for the loading of the cargoes: they are paid commission by the ship owners. The details of the shipment are contained on a standard shipping note (SSN) which advises the shipping company on what is to happen to the goods on arrival at the foreign port.

Airfreight used to be an expensive option, but is now much cheaper due to increased efficiency of aircraft and the introduction of standby airfreight. Speedy delivery means less stockholding, more rapid settlement of invoices, less insurance and therefore faster turnover of working capital. International airlines' cargo rates are fixed through IATA (International Air Transport Association) but carriers such as DHL are free to fix their own prices, and of course it is feasible to charter a cargo aircraft for a particularly large shipment. For air transport, the air waybill is the equivalent of the bill of lading, but it does not prove title to the goods. One of the problems with air transport, however, is that aircraft do not carry the standardised containers used by road and sea transport, so cargo has to be re-packed, increasing handling costs.

Road transport is usually very flexible in that goods can be collected and delivered door-to-door, a factor that offsets the sometimes high costs per mile (when compared with sea or even air). In combination with roll-on roll-off ferries, truckers can operate throughout Europe, much of the United States seaboards, the Far East and North Africa, but for longer distances containers are more useful. Many countries restrict cabotage (the collection of cargoes en route), so that a vehicle may make a delivery in one country and be unable to pick up a return cargo. Road cabotage has been abolished within the European Union, but still exists in most of Africa and non-EU countries.

Rail transport varies greatly between countries, largely due to the differences in rail and road infrastructure. In some countries (e.g. Germany) rail transport is well developed and competes well with road transport. In other countries (e.g. Thailand) the rail network is by no means national, but is effective and efficient over the routes it does cover. In yet other countries (e.g. the UK) the rail network is capable of carrying only a tiny fraction of the freight transport needs of the country, due to an aging and poorly maintained infrastructure and an emphasis on passenger transportation, which pushes the system close to capacity on many routes. The main drawback of rail transport in a small country like the UK is that the goods need to be loaded onto a lorry, unloaded onto a train, then reloaded onto a lorry at the other end. Normally it is simpler and quicker to drive the lorry directly to the customer's premises. Within continental Europe, the United States and Australia distances are great enough to make transferring cargoes worthwhile, although in all three cases the long-distance truck (or road-train, in Australia) are much more widely used.

Liner A ship or aircraft that operates on a regular route at fixed times.

Tramp ship A ship that does not follow set routes, but which sails when it has a cargo for a particular port.

Chapter summary

Intermediaries perform important functions, more than justifying their existence. Managing the supply chain is by no means simple, and it is not always the role of the manufacturer to do so – many supply chains are managed by wholesalers, retailers or other members, using negotiation, coercion or reward to make the system operate more smoothly. In an ideal world, the supply chain will take a logistics approach and will function as a single entity, but in practice this is difficult because each member of the chain is probably a member of several other chains as well, creating conflicts of interest.

Key points

- Cutting out the middleman raises costs.
- Market coverage may be intensive, selective or exclusive: this depends largely on the product category, but also on the target market.
- Relationships need to be long-term and based on trust.
- Direct and database marketing provide better control of what happens in the marketplace.
- Channels can be controlled by co-operation or by coercion.
- The level of service offered trades off against the overall cost.
- Good supply chain management can shut out competitors altogether.

Review questions

1. What is the difference between logistics and physical distribution?
2. Why do international agreements often specify the governing law of the contract?
3. Why would a firm prefer to limit the number of outlets its products are available from?
4. Refusal to deal is an example of which type of power?
5. How does culture affect choice of distributor in international markets?
6. What factors help in reconciling conflict and co-operation?
7. What are the key elements in developing a single channel system?
8. What factors might be relevant in determining which firm in the supply chain holds the power?
9. What factors might determine the level of service offered by the supply chain?
10. Why might companies with effective logistics systems experience greater growth than those without?

Case study revisited: Giant Bicycles

For Giant, the problem is complex. Worldwide distribution is difficult to arrange at the best of times, but given the huge variation in needs of customers, and the wide range of retail outlets which must be supplied, the company had a major logistics problem. Giant bikes are available on every continent, through over 10,000 retail outlets.

Giant therefore contacted Wincanton Group, a major European logistics company. Wincanton offers a full logistics service, including warehousing, intermodal transport (transport which involves different types of vehicle), customs clearance, document and records management, store services and even aircraft refuelling. Wincanton operates a fleet of vehicles, including lorries, barges and trains, and the company even manages sea ports and inland ports for barge transportation.

Wincanton's roots lie in the UK (it was originally a subsidiary of the dairy company that later became Cow and Gate), but its operations now cover almost the whole of Europe. The company handles logistics for major firms such as BMW, Tesco, Dow Chemicals, Electrolux and Hewlett–Packard, so shipping and storing bicycles presented no major problems.

Wincanton's success is due in no small measure to the company's innovative use of IT. Since Giant Bicycles also has a strong IT base, the companies were able to interface their systems and exchange data directly, greatly improving the efficiency of the overall system.

Giant Bicycles Ltd moved into the 21st century with more new products – an electrically assisted bicycle was introduced in 1999, followed by a range of models that are now available worldwide. The company's innovative Maestro suspension system has proved to be hugely popular, and the company also makes folding bicycles. However, no matter how many new models the company produces, and no matter how many markets it targets, Wincanton is confident in being able to provide the necessary logistical support.

Case study: C.A. Papaellina & Co. Ltd

Cyprus is an island in the Eastern Mediterranean, perhaps best known as a holiday destination. The party-and-package holiday resort of Ayia Napa, the Troodhos Mountains, the family resort of Paphos in the west, and the ancient Greek and Egyptian ruins on the island are world-famous. Cyprus has a considerable military presence also. Since 1974, the island has been divided between the Turkish Cypriots in the North, and the Greek Cypriots in the South, with the United Nations maintaining a truce between the two along the Green Line, which divides the town of Nicosia in two. The island's strategic situation, close to the Middle East, means that the British Army and the RAF maintain large bases on the island at Akrotiri and Dhekalia.

Cyprus has a small population (around 560,000 people) but up until the financial crisis had been economically highly successful, with a high standard of living and relatively low unemployment (around 12%, compared with over 20% for most other Mediterranean countries). Even though the country's banks were heavily exposed to Greek debt and were therefore badly affected by the economic crisis in Greece, the island represents a desirable, though small, market for most consumer goods. Cyprus is small: the Greek part of the island is less than 70 miles from end to end, and around 30 miles wide at the widest point.

C.A. Papaellina & Co. Ltd is one of the island's most important distributors. CAP was founded in 1930, and has since grown to the point where the company distributes into most of the retail outlets on the island. The company is well aware of the peculiarities of the Cypriot distribution system: for example, the island has many small street-corner kiosks, which sell everything from newspapers to bootlaces, as well as several huge hypermarkets (retail stores of over 5000 square metres selling area). CAP handles many international brands, such as Chanel, Davidoff, Jean Paul Gaultier, Kleenex, Lucozade, Ribena, Aquafresh, Maclean's, and even Tabasco Sauce. In 2002 the company opened its new pharmaceuticals centre, and in 2001 it signed a contract for new warehouse software worth CYP170,000 (approximately $300,000). This software was supplied by the UK software house, JBA Automated Systems of Durham, but the company now uses logistics software supplied by SAP. In 2010, CAP founded Health Line, which operates six Holland and Barratt health food stores on the island. In 2011 the company won the prestigious Investors in People Award in recognition of its exemplary staff management approach.

CAP is divisionalised into five separate areas. These are:

1. Personal care and household products.
2. Consumer healthcare products.
3. Paper products and foodstuffs.
4. Cosmetics and fragrances.
5. Pharmaceuticals.

CAP employs 150 people, runs its own salesforce, and supplies in every retail sector in Cyprus. This means that the firm is equally able to supply huge hypermarkets and corner kiosks – in itself, this presents considerable logistical and accounting problems. Using its own fleet of trucks and vans, the company distributes throughout the Greek portion of the island.

Because the Cypriot market is so small, distribution chains are short and are often integrated: CAP owns 30% of the AlphaMega Hypermarket in Nicosia, 100% of Beautyline (the cosmetics retail chain) and 100% of Demetrides and Papaellinas, the distributors for the Swiss pharmaceutical giant Novartis. CAP opened its own specialist pharmaceutical distribution centre, PharmacyLine, in March 2002. This distribution centre can carry out daily deliveries to every pharmacy in Cyprus, an important service considering that many medicines have extremely short shelf-lives, or may be in infrequent demand and therefore may not be stocked by the pharmacies.

Foreign companies appreciate the way CAP uses its intimate knowledge of the Cypriot market to facilitate distribution. For example, CAP has a re-labelling and re-packing unit in which imported products are re-labelled in Greek to meet local labelling requirements, and if necessary are also repackaged. CAP's knowledge of the local distribution systems means that the company is able to distribute in bulk to hypermarkets with the same ease with which its small vans distribute small quantities to kiosks: the mountainous topography of Cyprus, and its constant influx of foreign visitors, present special problems that only a local firm can solve.

Cyprus is a small island, dependent on foreign trade: the country has capitalised strongly on being a member of the European Union and the Euro. It can no longer be self-sufficient, but it has a large number of rich residents, so it imports most of what it needs from day to day, and exports some agricultural products and a lot of tourism. C.A. Papaellina is at the forefront of facilitating this exchange.

Questions

1. What advantages does Novartis gain from dealing through CAP?
2. Why might CAP have bought into retail outlets?
3. What specific problems might a confectionery manufacturer have when approaching the Cypriot market? How might CAP be able to help?
4. What are the major differences between supplying hypermarkets and supplying kiosks?
5. Why would competing manufacturers such as Chanel and Jean Paul Gaultier be prepared to use the same distributor?

Further reading

Martin Christopher, *Logistics and Supply Chain Management: Creating Value-Adding Networks*, 3rd edn (Harlow: Financial Times Prentice Hall, 2005). This is the latest edition of a leading text on logistics. It is easy to read, and is also full of examples and cases.

Michael Hugos, *Essentials of Supply Chain Management* (Hoboken, NJ: John Wiley, 2003). This is a more practice-orientated book, written by an American author who has very wide experience of distribution.

References

Bitner, M.J. (1992) Servicescapes: the impact of physical surroundings on customers and employees. *Journal of Marketing*, April: 57–71.

Bowman, Robert J. (2001) Does Wall Street really care about the supply chain? *Global Logistics and Supply Chain Strategies*, April: 31–5.

Brown, Eryn (1997) The best software business Bill Gates doesn't own: investors have scored big with enterprise software companies like SAP. How long can the good times roll? *Fortune*, 29 December. Retrieved from http://money.cnn.com/magazines/fortune/fortune_archive/1997/12/29/235908/ (7 June 2013).

Celley, A.F., Clee, W.H., Smith, A.W. and Vonderembese, M.A. (1986) Implementation of JIT in the United States. *Journal of Purchasing and Materials Management*, 22 (Winter): 13.

Cooper, M.C., Lambert, D.M. and Pugh, J.D. (1997) Supply chain management: more than a new name for logistics. *International Journal of Logistics Management*, 8 (1): 1.

Czinkota, M.R. and Ronkainen, I.A. (2004) *International Marketing*, 7th edn (Cincinnati, OH: Thomson–South-Western).

Eng, Teck-Yong (2004) The role of e-marketplaces in supply chain management. *Industrial Marketing Management*, 33 (2): 97–105.

Ferguson, Brad (2000) Implementing supply chain management. *Production and Inventory Management Journal*, March: 64.

Fitzpatrick, P.B. and Zimmerman, A.S. (1985) *Essentials of Export Marketing*. New York: AMACOM.

Flint, Daniel J. (2004) Strategic marketing in global supply chains. Four challenges. *Industrial Marketing Management*, 33 (1): 45–50.

Gadde, Lars-Erik (2004) Activity co-ordination and resource combining in distribution networks – implications for relationship involvement and the relationship atmosphere. *Journal of Marketing Management*, 20 (1): 157–84.

Hingley, Martin K. (2005) Power imbalance in UK agri-food supply chains: learning to live with the supermarkets? *Journal of Marketing Management*, 21 (1/2): 63–88.

Holder, D. (1998) The absolute essentials of direct marketing. IDM Seminar, Bristol.

LaLonde, B.J., Cooper, M.C. and Noordweir, T.G. (1988) *Customer Service: A Management Perspective*. Oak Brook, IL: Council of Logistics Management.

Marx, W. (1995) The co-marketing revolution. *Industry Week*, 2 October: 77–9.

Moore, Christopher M., Birtwistle, Grete and Burt, Steve (2004) Channel power, conflict and conflict resolution in international fashion retailing. *European Journal of Marketing*, 38 (7): 749–69.

Morgan, Robert M. and Hunt, Shelby D. (1994) The commitment–trust theory of relationship marketing. *Journal of Marketing*, 58 (July): 20–38.

Moriarty, Rowland T. and Kosnik, Thomas J. (1989) 'High-tech marketing: concepts, continuity, and change', *Sloan Management Review*, Summer.

Murphy, J. (1997) The art of satisfaction. *Financial Times*, 23 April.

Novich, N.S. (1992) How to sell customer service. *Transportation and Distribution*, 33 (January): 46.

Pothokuchi, V., Damanpour, F., Choi, J., Chen, C.C. and Park, S.H. (2002) National and organisational cultural differences and international joint-venture performance. *Journal of International Business Studies*, 33 (2): 243–65.

Quinn, F.J. (2000) A supply chain management overview. *Supply Chain Yearbook*, Jan: 15.

Stone, M., Davies, D. and Bond, A. (1995) *Direct Hit: Direct Marketing with a Winning Edge.* London: Pitman.

Tapp, Alan (2004) *Principles of Direct and Database Marketing.* Harlow: FT Prentice Hall.

More online

To gain free access to additional online resources to support this chapter please visit:
www.sagepub.co.uk/blythe3e

CHAPTER ⓴
Retail and wholesale marketing

CHAPTER CONTENTS

LEARNING OBJECTIVES

After reading this chapter, you should be able to:

- Explain the roles, responsibilities and rights of agents.

- Describe the differences between intermediaries who buy goods, and those who do not.

- Be able to decide when licensing and franchising agreements would be better than wholesaler–retailer distribution.

- Explain the relationships between wholesalers, retailers and consumers.

- Be able to decide on the appropriateness of service levels in retailing.

- Explain the key issues in deciding on the location of retail outlets.

Introduction

As we saw in Chapter 19, intermediaries perform vital functions in managing the delivery of goods and services from producer to consumer. In this chapter we will be looking at specific types of intermediary, the functions they perform, and the particular issues each has in performing profitably within the marketing function.

Intermediaries exist in many forms, from corner shops to multinational export houses, and perform many different functions. Choosing an appropriate intermediary is not necessarily a simple matter, especially as intermediaries frequently have more power in the supply chain than do producers, and can therefore pick and choose between suppliers.

Preview case study: Young's Home Brew

In 1968 Robert Young decided to establish a wholesale business specialising in home-brew kits. At the time, brewing beer and making wine at home were becoming popular hobbies: because beer brewed at home does not attract customs duty, people were attracted by the idea of producing their own alcoholic drinks at a fraction of the price it would cost in a supermarket. Also, people enjoyed experimenting with different flavourings – not to mention that home brew could be made much stronger than commercially produced wines and beers.

Based in the UK's Midlands area, Young's is well placed to deliver stock anywhere in the country, and prides itself on moving stocks quickly so that retailers and consumers have long use-by dates. This means that the products are less likely to go out of date on the retailer's shelves. Young's uses its own fleet of new trucks to deliver, offering next-day delivery of any of 2500 product lines.

Young's operates a telesales operation, which enables retailers to telephone in their orders, and has a retailer's area on its website to offer rapid advice and assistance to retailers. Perhaps unusually for a wholesaler, Young's also operates a frequently-asked-questions section on the website aimed at consumers. This area offers advice on common problems with home brewing and winemaking; as consumers write in with more questions, they will be posted on the website.

Technological advances in home brewing over the past thirty years mean that consumers can produce high-alcohol drinks: up to 40% alcohol is now possible, using high-resistance yeasts developed specially for the home-brewing trade. Young's offers advice to consumers and to the retail trade on dealing with new developments, and the company keeps ahead of the information flow by specialising – as a specialist wholesaler, Young's can be a centre of information as well as a dealer in home-brew products.

Categorising intermediaries

Intermediaries can be categorised in several different ways: one way is to divide them into those that take title to the products (buy the products from the producer or from another intermediary), and those that do not. Intermediaries that take title to the products can be considered as customers: they have specific needs which must be met by the producer, and will have similar decision-making procedures to those of any other B2B customer, with the exception that (in general) much more of the decision-making is devolved to the buyers, rather than to other members of the DMU.

Intermediaries that do not take title to the goods may require more support and management, because their commitment to the producer and the brand is less. In general, they are taking a much smaller risk, since they are not actually parting with any money to buy the goods themselves. These intermediaries are called agents, and they are subject to special rules of contract. An agent is usually appointed for a fixed period of time, under specific contractual arrangements, and has the role of obtaining orders for the product. Agency salespeople call on wholesalers and others, take orders and arrange delivery, usually on a commission-only basis.

Intermediaries that take title to the product divide into wholesalers, who only deal with other intermediaries, and retailers, who deal with the end consumers.

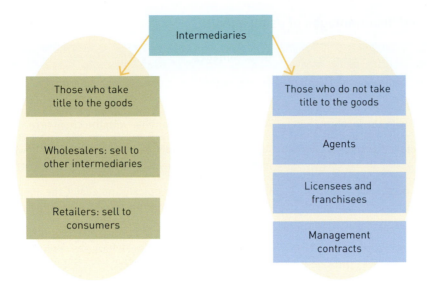

Figure 20.1 Categorising intermediaries

AGENTS

Agents are commonly used in international marketing, but are also used within national borders, typically by small firms that cannot afford to run a national sales-force or have only a few products. Although agency law differs from one country to another, there are some factors that all agency agreements will have in common. These are as follows:

- An agent cannot take delivery of the principal's goods at an agreed price and resell them for a higher price without the principal's knowledge and permission. In other words, the agent cannot make secret deals behind the principal's back.
- Agents must maintain strict confidentiality regarding their principal's affairs, and must pass on all relevant information.
- The principal is liable to third parties for wrongs committed by an agent 'in the course of his or her authority'. For example, if the agent fraudulently misrepresents the product, the principal is liable to the customer for any compensation. In effect, the agent is the principal as far as the customer is concerned: a company would not be allowed to disclaim liability if its agent had cheated a customer.

Within the European Union, agency law was harmonised in 1994 to include the following clauses to protect agents when their agreements are terminated:

- The agent will be entitled to full payment for any deal resulting from his or her work (even if it was concluded after the end of the agency).
- The agent will be entitled to a lump sum of up to one year's past average commission.
- The agent will be entitled to compensation (where appropriate) for damages to the agent's commercial reputation caused by an unfair termination of the agreement.

In some countries outside the European Union, agents are regarded as essentially employees of the client organisation, whereas in other countries they are regarded

Table 20.1   Advantages and disadvantages of using agents

Advantages	Disadvantages
Operations are subject to direct control by the client.	Agents require considerable support from the client company.
Agents are usually very familiar with the local market.	Agents may not be familiar with the client firm.
Agents have appropriate contacts for arranging after-sales service, etc.	Agents act independently, so may set up deals with firms with whom they have a special arrangement.
Financial risk is low – no sales, no costs.	Unless sales happen quickly and easily, the agent might decide to concentrate efforts on a different client firm.
Agents usually act for other firms as well, so may be able to create marketing synergies.	Because agents usually work for several firms, they may have conflicts of interest.
The lack of long-term commitment on the part of the client means that it is easy to withdraw from the arrangement.	The lack of long-term commitment may reduce the incentive to sell.

Brokers Intermediaries who bring buyers and sellers together but do not themselves handle goods.

Factors Intermediaries who hold stocks of product but do not take title to the goods.

Del credere **agents** Intermediaries who do not take title to the goods, but who do accept the credit risk from customers.

as independent and self-contained businesses. If a company is considering employing an agent in a foreign country, it is certainly advisable to check the legal position of agents – it is unlikely to be the same as that obtaining within the EU.

Table 20.1 shows the advantages and disadvantages of using agents.

Agents fall into three categories: **brokers**, who simply bring buyers and sellers together; **factors**, who hold stocks of the goods on behalf of the client company and who may have discretion to negotiate prices; and *del credere* **agents** who also accept responsibility for bad debts. *Del credere* agents offer an extra level of security, particularly in overseas markets, for two reasons: first, they are better able to assess the creditworthiness of customers, and second, they are less likely to be tempted to sell to someone who is not creditworthy: an agent who has no responsibility for credit is likely to sell to anyone who is prepared to place an order.

In the main, agents are effectively salespeople who act for several firms at once. A manufacturer's agent usually specialises in particular categories of buyer: some call on food wholesalers, some on novelty-goods wholesalers, and so forth. A manufacturer's agent might carry products from a dozen different manufacturers, increasing the efficiency of each call.

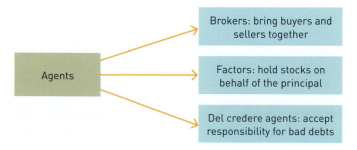

Figure 20.2   Categories of agent

Think outside this box!

There seems to be a lot of trust involved in hiring an agent. After all, as principal the company is bound by any agreement the agent makes, and is responsible (ultimately) for anything the agent does or says. Added to that, agents seem to have all sorts of rights in law – so why bother with an agent at all?

Taking on an agent might seem to be the simplest route to internationalising: a local person, who has the contacts and the local knowledge, can just be plugged into the firm's existing systems. But isn't this just a short cut, and what's more one that will lead to problems later? Taking a short cut down a dark alleyway at dead of night might save some effort – but it's no use if you get mugged halfway through!

LICENSING AND FRANCHISING

In some cases firms will own intellectual property (brands, patents, registered trade marks or specialist knowledge) but lack the resources to exploit them effectively. For example, a firm may have a patented product with global potential, but lack the necessary financial or organisational resources to set up a global marketing operation before the patent expires or is rendered obsolete by technological advances elsewhere. In these circumstances, the firm might arrange a licensing agreement or a **franchise** agreement with other firms, either at home or abroad, under which the licensee is allowed to exploit the intellectual property in exchange for a fee or a royalty.

Licensing is appropriate in the following circumstances:

- Where it is not feasible to set up business in a particular foreign country (perhaps because of local laws preventing foreign businesses form entering the market) but where intellectual property such as patents are protected.
- Where the cost of shipping goods to the foreign market would be prohibitive.
- Where the target market is particularly patriotic, so that 'home-produced' products will sell better than imports. This is often the case in France, and in Australia.
- The licensee will have to purchase materials or components from the licensor. This gives a substantial degree of control over the process, and also ensures that the licensor knows exactly how much of the product is being sold.
- The licensor is already over-stretched in terms of the markets it is already selling to.

Franchising An agreement to use a firm's business methods and intellectual property in return for a fee and a royalty.

The main categories of licence are shown in Table 20.2.

Licensing is often used in cases where the product is perishable or fragile: for example, Pilkington Glass made more money from licensing their intellectual property in the float-glass technique than they did from actually making glass. This is because it is extremely difficulty to ship glass over long distances. Although the patents on float glass are now expired, Pilkington still maintain a very active research and development programme so that they can create new intellectual property and retain control of their licensees.

The advantages and disadvantages of licensing agreements are shown in Table 20.3. Licensing contracts are complex, and need to cover specific elements, as follows:

- Fees and royalties.
- Geographical area covered by the agreement.
- Permissible selling prices.

- Quality control arrangements.
- Frequency of payments.
- Confidentiality requirements.
- Procedures for settling disputes, and which country's law should apply to the agreement.
- Minimum production levels.
- Termination and renewal arrangements.

Table 20.2   Categories of licence

Category	Explanation
Assignments	The licensor hands over all its intellectual property rights to the licensee in exchange for a royalty. The licensee can then use the information in any way.
Sole licence	The licensor retains the rights to the patents, brands etc. but agrees not to extend licences to anyone other than the licensee during the period of the agreement.
Exclusive licence	The licensor agrees not to use the patents, trade marks etc. for its own business during the life of the agreement. This means that the licensee has the sole use of the intellectual property for a specified period, which is of course a favourable position for the licensee.
Know-how licence	These cover confidential but not patented (and perhaps non-patentable) intellectual property. This may be a process, or a specific way of exploiting knowledge that is in the public domain.

Table 20.3   Advantages and disadvantages of licensing

Advantages	Disadvantages
No capital investment for the licensor.	May be difficult to verify sales figures.
Can be undertaken by small firms.	Lower revenues to the licensor.
Immediate access to local expertise.	Licensee acquires know-how and may set up in competition once the agreement expires.
No import tariff or transportation costs.	Quality levels may not be maintained.
Materials and components might be sold to the licensee.	Complex contractual arrangements may be necessary.
Licensor usually receives an initial lump sum payment, which helps defray the development costs.	Many possibilities for conflict and misunderstanding.
Risk of failure shared with licensee.	Licensee might not fully exploit the local market.
Allows entry to markets which might otherwise be closed to foreign firms.	Licensee's firm could become insolvent and cease production, causing damage to the brand in the foreign country.
No export knowledge required.	Licensee might be less competent either as a producer or as a marketer than at first appeared.
Provides income to help offset future research and development expenditure.	

- Ownership of new inventions resulting from the licensor's work.
- Licensee's capacity to become involved with competing products.
- Licensee's capacity to subcontract.
- Support services to be provided by the licensor (for example, training and technical support).

A variation in licensing is franchising. Franchising is commonly used when a company has the rights to a brand name or a business format: it is commonly used in services market where patents do not apply. A large number of well-known service businesses are franchises: Subway sandwich shops, Holiday Inn hotels, Dyno-Rod drain-cleaning services, and many others are franchises.

The franchisee is entitled to use the brand name, business systems, trade marks and indeed the entire business format within a given locality in exchange for paying a lump sum up front followed by a regular royalty based on turnover. In most cases, the franchisee also has to buy its supplies from the franchisor: in effect, the franchisor retains complete control over the running of the business, and especially over the marketing of the brand, but the franchisee bears most of the risks of failure.

Franchisees are independent self-employed businesses, not employees of the franchisor, and rarely have any right of redress against the parent company in the event of the business collapsing. Franchise agreements usually contain very detailed rules about how the business is to be run: these rules are intended to preserve the brand values, and protect other franchisees from encroachment either by expansion outside the designated territory, or by differentiating one outlet from another in order to poach business. In effect, franchisees are prevented from competing against each other.

Most franchise agreements, therefore, are loaded heavily in favour of the franchisor. The reason franchisees are still prepared to take them on is that franchises

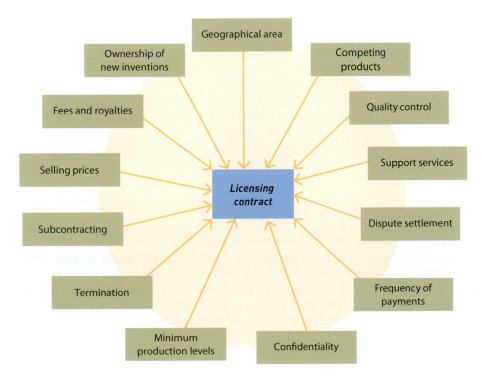

Figure 20.3   Elements in licensing contracts

rarely go bankrupt. The failure rate is extremely small compared with other businesses, because the franchisee is buying into an already-established brand and has the training and back-up of the parent company.

Real-life marketing: Franchise your format

If you have a good business model, you could expand a lot faster if you do what Holiday Inns did. Holiday Inns are an international chain of hotels, nine out of ten of which are franchised and are therefore independently owned and operated. The first Holiday Inn opened in 1952, and in the next fifty years or so the chain expanded to the point where in the early years of the 21st century it comprised more than 1500 hotels worldwide, with 284,000 rooms. Because the hotels are franchised, the hoteliers who own them benefit from a centralised reservation system, and from a brand that prides itself on a friendly approach and what Holiday Inns calls a 'can-do' service, by which it means that whatever a guest needs, the hotel staff will do their best to provide it.

The hotel chain has an internationally consistent image, which reassures customers that they will get the same level of service in a Holiday Inn whether they are in Singapore or Sacramento: this can be particularly important for business travellers, who have enough to think about without having to consider choosing a hotel and finding out which services are available and which are not in each case.

Franchising enabled Holiday Inns to create an international hotel network at a speed that would have been impossible if the parent company had tried to set up a new hotel in each location directly. Local franchisees were able to cut through red tape, and establish a presence in local markets, at a rate that could not be equalled by an incoming firm.

Marketing is centrally administered, in order to keep the brand values consistent across all the countries the chain operates in. At the time of writing 238 hotels were being built, and more will be added as the century progresses.

If you think you have a robust, proven business format, this is what you need to do to franchise it.

- Your business model must be proven to work. In other words you must have been running it as a business for long enough to get the bugs out of the system.
- You will need to let the earlier franchisees have a more generous deal than the later ones. You are still an unknown quantity, and they will have to sell the idea to their bank managers.
- You will need a very clear manual, covering all eventualities. Franchisees will need this as well as thorough training, but the manual also helps to maintain your brand values, and acts as a referee in the case of any disputes with franchisees.
- You will have to provide a lot of support in the early stages, but this will pay off in the longer term.

MANAGEMENT CONTRACTS

In some cases, particularly in international marketing, a firm might agree to provide a team of expert managers to help set up an enterprise in the foreign country. Typically the management team will set up the new business, train local personnel in running it and eventually hand over the enterprise as a going concern to the foreign company. This is called a turnkey contract, and is often used for such major enterprises as hydro-electric generating systems or heavy industrial complexes such as car factories. During the 1960s and 1970s, Fiat set up several car factories in Eastern Europe, passing on obsolete Fiat technology and designs (which were still far ahead of anything available in the East).

The advantage for the supplying firm is that there is very little risk attached, and the returns can be predicted very accurately: problems include the potential for disagreement with the foreign company, and in some cases of course the supplying firm will be setting up a competitor in business. Disagreements might include arguments about best working practices, and about training: it is easy for the supplying company to claim that the staff are untrainable, and for the commissioning company to claim that the training programme is at fault, for example.

For the commissioning company, the main advantage is that they obtain a working installation far more quickly than would be the case if they had to begin building expertise from scratch: new technology can be acquired quickly, although the commissioning company is often reliant on the goodwill of the supplying company for providing the appropriate level of training. Also, the arrangement might end up more expensive than simply hiring appropriately qualified consultants to carry out the work.

Wholesalers

Wholesalers are organisations that take title to the goods, but who sell only to other intermediaries. They carry out the following functions, which are of importance to manufacturers:

- Negotiate with suppliers (manufacturers, importers, other wholesalers, etc.)
- Carry out some promotional activities, within the trade. Some wholesalers have their own salesforces, and they also carry out some sales promotion, advertising and publicity.
- Warehousing, storage and product handling.
- Transport of local and sometimes long-distance shipments.
- Inventory control: some even do this on behalf of the retailer, at the retailer's premises.
- Credit checking and credit control.
- Pricing and collection of pricing information, particularly about competitors.
- Act as a channel of information up and down the supply chain.

These are all functions which the manufacturer would have to carry out on an individual basis if the wholesaler were not available to do them.

The wholesalers also provide services to retailers, as follows:

- Information-gathering and dissemination.
- One-stop shopping for a wide range of products from a wide range of manufacturers.
- Facilities for buying relatively small quantities.
- Fast deliveries, often on a cash-and-carry basis.
- Flexible ordering – amounts can be varied as consumer demand fluctuates.

For most retailers, it is clearly much more economical to use a wholesaler than to buy direct from the manufacturer. Only if a retailer is big enough (e.g. a major supermarket chain) to order economic quantities from a manufacturer will it be worthwhile to do so, and in most cases such large retailers operate their own warehouse and central bulk-breaking facilities in any case, in effect carrying out the wholesaler's job in-house.

There are many different types of wholesaler, as listed in Table 20.4.

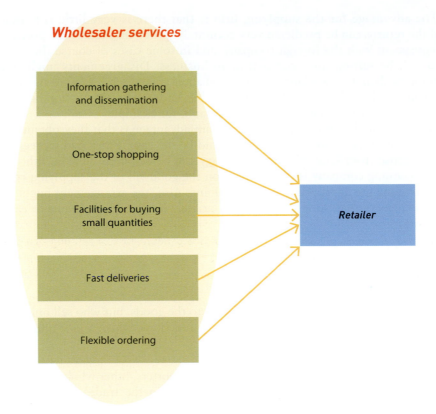

Figure 20.4   Wholesalers' services to retailers

Retailers

Retailers deal with any sales that are for the customer's own use, or for the use of family and friends. In other words, any purchases that are not for business needs are the domain of the retailer.

Therefore, a retailer is not necessarily a High Street shop, or a market trader; mail order catalogues, TV phone-in lines, even door-to-door salesmen are all retailers. The Tupper Corporation (which sells Tupperware on the **party plan**) is as much a retailer as Aldi, Makro, or Coles, even though the product is sold in the customer's own home.

Traditionally most retail outlets have been in city centres or suburban High Streets. Partly this was for convenience, so that shoppers had a central area to visit for all their shopping requirements, and partly it was due to planning regulations that zoned most retail shops in traditional retail areas, away from industrial parks and housing estates.

Within the last twenty years out-of-town hypermarkets and shopping parks have been growing up. This is in response to the following factors:

- Greater car ownership means an increase in **outshopping** (shopping outside the area where the consumer lives).
- High city-centre rents and property taxes make out-of-town sites more attractive for retailers.
- Town planners have used retail parks as a way of regenerating decaying industrial sites on the edges of towns.

Party plan A direct-marketing tool in which the salesperson holds private presentations for groups of friends in a private home.

Outshopping Shopping outside the area in which one lives.

Table 20.4 Types of wholesaler

Wholesaler	Description
Merchant wholesaler	These firms buy in goods and sell directly to retailers, usually delivering the goods and having a salesforce calling on retailers in their geographical area.
Full-service merchant wholesaler	These provide a wide range of services for retailers, including shop design, sales promotion, advertising, coupon redemption, own-brand products, management support and so forth. For example, Spar is a grocery wholesaler that supplies small corner grocery shops throughout the UK and parts of the rest of Europe. Each shop is individually owned and managed, but carries the Spar logo and stocks Spar own-brand products (the Happy Shopper brand).
General-merchandise wholesalers	These wholesalers carry a wide product mix, but have little depth. They deal mainly with small grocery shops and general stores, operating as a one-stop shop for this type of retailer. Cash-and-carry warehouses are a good example, where the retailer collects the stock and takes it away using his or her own transport.
Limited-line wholesalers	These outlets offer only a limited range of products, but stock them in depth. They are often found in industrial markets, selling specialist items such as building materials and equipment: they are often able to offer specialist advice and expertise in the field.
Speciality-line wholesalers	Speciality line wholesalers carry a very narrow range, perhaps concentrating on only one type of product. They are typically found in industries where the products require special handling, or require specialist expertise in the buying or marketing of the product. For example, there are wholesalers who specialise only in coffee. In many cases, they sell only to other wholesalers.
Rack jobbers	These are wholesalers who maintain their own stands or displays in retail outlets. The wholesaler takes responsibility for stocking and maintaining the stand, the retailer collects the money from consumers and keeps a share of the proceeds. This saves the retailer's working capital, and in some cases removes the need for expertise in buying the stock: for example, rack jobbers might put a stand selling cosmetics in a clothing shop.
Limited-service wholesalers	These take title to the goods, but do not actually take delivery, store inventory, or monitor demand. An example might be a coal wholesaler who orders from an importer or from a coal mining company, and arranges delivery direct to a coal merchant without actually storing the coal.
Cash-and-carry wholesaler	This is a category of general-merchandise wholesaler: the wholesaler acts like a giant supermarket where retailers come and choose goods, using their own transport to take the goods away.
Drop shipper (or desk jobber)	This is similar to a limited-service wholesaler. Drop shippers have a salesforce that obtains orders from retailers: the orders are passed directly to manufacturers, who then arrange delivery direct to the retailer.
Mail-order wholesalers	In some industries, orders can be taken and goods despatched through the post or via the Internet. Mail-order wholesalers produce catalogues to sell to retailers.

Such out-of-town sites have not necessarily damaged all town-centre retailers, although there has been a shift in the composition of city-centre retail districts. For example, food retailers have largely gone from central sites in major cities, except for delicatessens and speciality food outlets. In the United Kingdom, the supermarket chain Tesco has recently begun to reverse this trend with the establishment of its Metro stores in city centres, closely followed by arch-rival Sainsbury's Central stores. These stores carry a limited range of products, usually in smaller pack sizes, and aim at office workers shopping in their lunch hours, students or convenience shopping.

Marketing in a changing world: The death of the High Street?

At the beginning of 2013 things looked bleak for the British High Street. Despite the fact that the country was beginning to creep out of the financial crisis, three major High Street store chains closed their doors. HMV, the oldest music retailer in Britain, called in the administrators. Jessop's camera shops closed down. Finally, the Blockbuster chain of DVD rental shops closed.

So what killed them? Was it the Internet? No, not really – on-line shopping still accounts for less than 10% of retail. Was it government and local government taxation? Well, that didn't help, but all other retailers are in the same boat and they seem to have survived.

Perhaps it was more that these were businesses that had not moved with the times. Blockbuster would hardly be able to survive when people can download movies or simply watch them on Sky Movies for less than it costs to rent a DVD. And people don't buy cameras from a specialist shop any more, since the technology has moved on and a good digital camera, foolproof and cheap, can be bought from any large supermarket. And HMV missed the boat – apart from music downloads, the stores were probably uncompetitive anyway.

Perhaps the issue is that there are companies that have become complacent, or have outlived their usefulness, but it takes a recession to give them the final push.

Here are some descriptions of different types of retail outlet.

Convenience stores, or corner shops, offer a range of grocery and household items. These local shops often open until late at night. They are usually family-run, often belong to a trading group such as Spar, Circle K and 7-Eleven, and cater for last-minute and emergency purchases. In recent years, the Circle K and 7-Eleven franchises have expanded internationally from the United States and are making inroads into the late-night shopping market. Convenience stores have been under threat from supermarkets as later opening has become more common, and as the laws on Sunday trading in many countries have been relaxed.

Supermarkets are large self-service shops, which rely on selling at low prices. Typically they are well-laid-out, bright, professionally run shops carrying a wide range of goods.

Hypermarkets are even bigger supermarkets, usually in an out-of-town or edge-of-town location. A typical hypermarket would carry perhaps 20,000 lines. The true hypermarket sells everything from food to TV sets.

Department stores are located in city centres and sell everything. Each department has its own buyers, and functions as a separate profit centre. Examples are Harrods of London, El Corte Ingles in Spain and Clery's in Dublin. Within department stores, some functions are given over to **concessionaires**, who pay a rental per square foot plus a percentage of turnover to set up a store-within-a-store. Miss Selfridge, Brides and Principles all operate in this way within department stores. The trend is towards allowing more concessionaires, and around 70% of Debenham's floor space is allocated this way.

Variety stores offer a more limited range of goods, perhaps specialising in clothes (e.g. Primark) or in housewares (e.g. Lakeland).

Discounters (sometimes called baby sharks) are grocery outlets offering a minimum range of goods at very low prices. Often the decor is basic, the displays almost non-existent, and the general ambience is one of pile-it-high-and-sell-it-cheap. Lidl, Aldi and Kwik Save are examples of this approach; such stores typically only carry 700 lines or so.

Niche marketers stock a very limited range of products, but in great depth. Examples are Sock Shop and Tie Rack. They frequently occupy tiny shops (even kiosks at railway stations) but offer every possible type of product within their very narrow spectrum. Niche marketers were the success story of the 1980s, but declined somewhat during the 1990s. There are plenty of nichers still around, however.

Discount sheds are out-of-town DIY and hardware stores. They are usually businesses requiring large display areas, but with per-square-metre turnovers and profits that do not justify city-centre rents. Service levels are minimal, the stores are cheaply constructed and basic in terms of decor and ambience, and everything is geared towards minimising the overhead.

Catalogue showrooms have minimal or non-existent displays, and are really an extension of the mail order catalogue. Customers buy in the same way as they would by mail order, by filling in a form, and the goods are brought out from a warehouse at the rear of the store. These outlets usually have sophisticated electronic inventory control.

Concessionaires Firms that rent space in department stores, paying a rental and usually a commission on sales.

Discounters Retailers that carry a limited range of stock at low prices.

Discount sheds Out-of-town stores offering a wide range of products at low prices.

Catalogue showrooms Retailers that have a bricks-and-mortar presence but use a brochure to display the goods rather than display shelves.

Shopping behaviour

People have many motives for shopping, going beyond a simple need to obtain goods and services. These can be divided into social motives and personal motives, each of which determine the choice of retailer, the time spent shopping and much of the effort that is expended.

Social motives include the following:

- Social experience outside the home. These include talking to shop assistants, going shopping with a friend or friends, or getting out of the house for a while.
- Communication with others having a similar interest. Whether shopping for clothes or computers, people enjoy taking a friend along, especially if the friend has a specific expertise that can be used.
- Peer group attraction. Going to specific shops means mingling with people from a similar social background. This is reassuring in terms of self-image.
- Status and authority. Being a customer is a pleasant experience – the shop assistants (if they are well-trained) are attentive and interested in the customers' needs, which means that customers enjoy the warm glow of being looked after.
- Pleasure of bargaining. In some situations in every country, bargaining is acceptable, and in some countries it is normal practice almost everywhere. The bargaining process is enjoyable because it has the elements of power, of exercising skill, and of getting a bargain.

Personal motives include the following:

- Role playing. Playing the part of the customer is a pleasant experience: some people even adopt a new persona when shopping, in order to enhance their own self-esteem.
- Diversion. Looking at new products is an entertainment in itself, and browsing around the shops can be a relaxing way of spending some time.
- Self-gratification. Meeting one's own needs buy buying goods relieves the tensions set up by lacking something that is regarded as essential.
- Learning about new trends. Learning is, in itself, a pleasurable thing. Being the first to know about new products is important for some people's self-esteem.
- Physical activity. Often people have sedentary lives: going for a walk round the shops can relieve this. Often people experience this motivation when on holiday – relaxing on the beach or by the pool quickly becomes boring.
- Sensory stimulation. Simply exposing one's senses to new sensations is pleasurable, and shopping fulfils this role admirably.

Shoppers can be categorised according to their shopping behaviour, as shown in Table 20.5.

Table 20.5　Shopper profiles

Profile	Explanation
Yesteryears	Approximately 17% of shoppers fit this profile. Yesteryears are insecure, conservative, somewhat anti-social and are risk avoiders. They are typically older females, and are looking for low prices, guarantees, convenient retailer location and speedy service. They are light consumers who like chain stores and discount stores.
Power purchasers	Representing about 15% of shoppers, this group are self-indulgent variety seekers. They are risk-takers and big spenders, and tend to be young. They are looking for friendly salespeople, easy-to-find merchandise, high quality, fast service, and are brand-conscious. They are very heavy consumers, and like department stores, chain stores and speciality shops.
Fashion foregoers	These are fashion laggards, and are unconcerned about image or style. They tend to be mundane and anti-social, and are typically single men living alone. They look for low prices, ease of finding merchandise, convenient location and a wide selection of products. They are light consumers who shop infrequently, and they like DIY outlets. They represent around 16% of shoppers.
Social strivers	This group are style-conscious fashion experimenters who like shopping, are social people and are brand-aware. They are young, female, often somewhat down-market, and are heavy consumers. They like guarantees, friendly salespeople, a wide selection of goods, and high quality. Typically they shop anywhere and everywhere (except DIY stores) and shop as often as possible. Because of this, they represent 20% of shoppers.
Dutifuls	These people are sacrificial, practical risk avoiders and represent 16% of the country's shoppers. They are comparison shoppers (they like to shop around). Typically, they are downmarket midlife households or down/middle market older households. They look for low prices, guarantees, ease of finding merchandise, convenient location, friendly salespeople and speed of service. They shop relatively infrequently, and are light consumers.
Progressive patrons	These are self-confident, artistic, variety-seeking, open-minded, risk-taking, innovative and imaginative people. They are often male, but may also be middle to upmarket midlife families. They look for ease of finding merchandise, high quality, wide selection, and specific brands. They are very heavy consumers, and like speciality stores, catalogue outlets, convenience stores, and DIY outlets. They account for the remaining 16% of shoppers.

Choice of retailer is determined by the proximity of the store (the closer, the better), the store design and physical facilities, the merchandise on offer, advertising and sales promotion activities, store personnel, customer service and the other clients. This last is an interesting example of a factor over which the store does not have direct control, but it clearly has an influence on the image of the store, and the shopping experience. A store with an upmarket clientele and image will attract people who associate themselves with that image: a store with a downmarket image and a disreputable clientele will repel more upmarket clients.

Non-store retailing

Non-store retailing includes door-to-door selling, vending machines, telemarketing (selling goods by telephone), mail order, in-home selling and catalogue retailing.

Door-to-door selling has suffered a decline in recent years, largely because of the changing role and working patterns of women. Forty years ago most married women would be at home during the day, so that door-to-door selling of everything from brushes to kitchen knives was a viable option for companies. Low overheads for the firm coupled with convenience for the housewife meant that door-to-door salesmen could count on a reasonable success rate, with few empty houses. By the 1990s, however, most women worked outside the home so houses were empty during the day, and calling in the evenings was perceived as intrusive by most householders – it would be difficult to imagine householders giving a warm welcome to a knife salesman turning up on doorsteps at nine o'clock at night, for example.

A more acceptable form of in-home selling is the party plan. Pioneered by firms such as Tupperware, party plan selling involves a local agent for the firm, who recruits homeowners to run a 'party' for friends and work colleagues. The party will involve the usual food, drink and conversation, but will also be centred around a demonstration of the firm's products. The party organiser will be given a commission (often in the form of free product, but sometimes in cash) for his or her efforts in organising the party. Party plan retailing seems to be a predominantly female activity.

Real-life marketing: Party time!

Many firms sell their products via party plan – everything from sex aids to kitchen utensils is sold in people's own homes. Perhaps one of the most successful areas, though, is cosmetics. Firms like Moor@ Home, which sells products extracted from lowland moors (essentially, mudpacks and similar skin treatments), and Oriflame, the Swedish cosmetics company, are cashing in on the boom in party plan.

Party plan makes a good choice for selling cosmetics because it allows the customers to try products out in a private atmosphere, but with friends presents to give feedback. Women particularly seem to find party plan attractive: virtually all party plan companies direct their activities at women, perhaps because women tend to see shopping as a social activity, whereas most men view shopping as a solitary pursuit, usually connected with utilitarian needs.

(Continued)

(Continued)

One of the big advantages of party plan is that you can start small. If you are in the business of making jewellery in your spare time, for example, having a party to show it to people is a simple way to go and it's cheap to set up. If you think this might be for you, here are some rules:

- Ensure that your party hosts (or hostesses) are well-motivated, and make it as easy as possible for them to run the party.
- Pay hosts with product – and make sure the guests get something special, too.
- Go to the party yourself, or (if the idea gets bigger) use trained salespeople.
- Build in plenty of fun to the events – it's supposed to be a party.
- Go to some parties organised by other party plan companies so that you can see how it works in practice.
- Recruit guests from one party to organise the next ones.

E-commerce refers to retailing over the Internet. At first, Internet transactions were dominated by business-to-business marketing, but in recent years on-line retailing has taken off as more people have become Internet-literate. Currently, Internet-based retailing accounts for around 10% of all retailing, and current thinking is that this will increase over time. Almost anything can be bought on-line, from clothing to central heating boilers, and in many cases the products are sold at much lower prices than would be the case in a traditional bricks-and-mortar retailer.

There are, however, drawbacks from the consumer's viewpoint. It is not possible to rummage through a rack of clothing, for example, and it is often difficult to get advice – good salespeople are very helpful with decision-making, and it is hard to achieve this on-line. There are fears about security of payment, as well, and in some cases having to be home to receive deliveries may not be convenient.

Perhaps most importantly, though, on-line shopping lacks the social element that is so important in motivating shoppers. Many people, perhaps most people, see shopping as an entertainment: one has only to see how many people enjoy visiting local shops and marketplaces when they are on holiday to realise that. One cannot ask one's best friend's opinion about new clothes on-line, nor can one find the perfect gift for Uncle Albert; haggling in a Moroccan market is good fun, too. On-line retailing is geared (at present) to people who know exactly what they want and how much they want to pay.

Bricks-and-mortar retailers have not been slow to see the potential threat from e-commerce. Most supermarkets and many other retailers now have on-line ordering of their own, and can offer the option of delivery or collection (which a purely Internet-based retailer cannot do). Competition is strong: on-line supermarkets such as Ocado have sprung up to challenge the mainstream supermarkets.

Tools of non-store retailing

DIRECT MAIL

Direct mail is material sent via the postal service to the recipient's home or business premises. The purpose is to generate a response or a transaction: the mailing may contain information, may request information, or may make a proposition for an exchange (offer something for sale, in other words). In some cases the mailing is

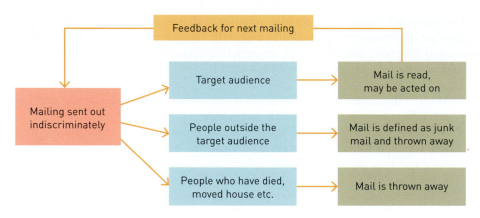

Figure 20.5   Targeting mailings

intended to maintain a relationship with the customer – many banks send out information about new services, or changes to existing services, simply in order to make sure that customers do not suddenly have a nasty surprise when they try to carry out a transaction.

Direct mail is often equated with junk mail. There is, however a distinction: junk mail is indiscriminate, untargeted mailings, whereas direct mail is (or should be) carefully targeted. Although no company wants to waste money sending offers to people who will not respond, sometimes firms lack the sophistication to be able to target mail accurately. Also, firms often use outdated mailing lists, sending out mailings to people who have moved house or died, or whose circumstances have changed.

Apart from the waste, there is also the risk of damaging the brand by the use of poorly targeted and indiscriminate mailings. Since people have a negative view of junk mail, there is a very real danger of transferring that negativity to the brand – people might feel less well disposed towards a company that is perceived as harassing them.

Of course, there will always be a certain amount of room for error – direct mail companies cannot be completely up-to-date. For example, someone who was very interested in the possibility of buying seeds for his or her allotment six months ago might have had to give up gardening for health reasons and will therefore have no interest in seed catalogues. Likewise, people move house on average every seven years, which of course means that some people move house much more frequently than this. Mailings sent to these addresses are wasted unless the new owner sends them on.

Within the UK, approximately 100 million pieces of mail are returned each year marked 'Return to Sender' or 'Gone Away'. This represents over £4 million in wasted postage, and around £200 million in wasted mailings. This does not take account of the (perhaps larger) number of mailings which are simply thrown away. Much of this wastage could be reduced: agencies exist to clean mailing lists. One such agency, ReAD, claims to identify over 94% of gone aways and 80% of deceased people, by comparing records with the Register of Births, Deaths and Marriages and by examining records at the Land Registry (Reed 1996). Cleaning the in-house database should be even easier: if a target customer has failed to respond to a certain number of mailings, he or she could be struck off the list or perhaps even contacted by telephone to check that he or she is still a potential customer for the product.

The major advantage of direct mail retailing is that it is relatively cheap compared with other communications methods, especially considering that it is (or should be) accurately targeting the most likely prospective customers. Managers of direct mail should ask the following questions (Bird 2000):

1. Who is the target market? In other words, who are the people the mailing is intending to influence, persuade or inform?
2. What response is required? What is it that we would like these people to do? Are we expecting them to make a purchase, or merely to make an enquiry? Are we expecting them to keep the information for future use, or make use of it immediately?
3. Why should they act on what we are sending them? What reasons for action are we giving them? What's in it for them?
4. Where are the target audience? What addresses do we have for the target audience, and would it be better to contact them at work, or at home? Where in the country do they live, and how does that affect their propensity to respond?
5. When is the best time to reach them? Should we aim for the mailing to arrive at the weekend, when people might be expected to have the time to read it and act on it, or should we aim for a weekday, when our offices are open and they will be able to respond? For business people, the best days to receive mailings are likely to be Tuesdays, Wednesdays or Thursdays because Mondays and Fridays tend to be dominated by starting and finishing the week's work.

Managing direct mail also means handling the logistics of the exercise: allowing plenty of time to design a mailing that will appeal to the target audience, allowing sufficient resources for stuffing envelopes, and (often omitted) ensuring that the organisation has sufficient resources in place to handle any reasonable level of responses. Some organisations have become extremely sophisticated in handling these issues: many will test different types of mailing to determine the appropriate style. This is done by designing different mailings (changing headings, illustrations, type of copy, mechanics and so forth) and coding the reply coupons so that the level

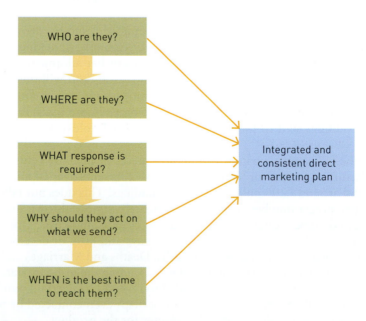

Figure 20.6 Planning direct mailing

Table 20.6   Direct mail in Europe

Country	Items of direct mail per head of population
Belgium	107
Netherlands	97
Finland	97
Austria	90
UK	79
Germany	78
Sweden	75
France	70
Denmark	45
Ireland	30
Italy	26
Spain	22

of response from each mailing can be measured. The various designs are then sent out to representative samples of the target group, and the subsequent responses are checked against the codes.

Direct mail is big business throughout Europe, and despite the problems of poor targeting and consequent low response rates (3% is regarded as typical), the medium does work. Even a 3% response rate is a vast improvement on the response rates to, for example, television advertising. Table 20.6 shows the annual figures for European direct mail. There is, of course, a large discrepancy between the country with the highest amount of direct mail (Belgium) and the country with the small- est amount (Spain). This is probably a reflection on the different infrastructures of these countries: Belgium has a largely urban population, and a well-developed and reliable postal service, whereas Spain has a largely rural population and a somewhat less reliable postal service. There is a slightly lower literacy rate for Spain (97% compared with 98% for Belgium) but this is unlikely to have had any real effect.

Overall, direct mail is an effective way of communicating directly with a target audience. The key to success for managers is to ensure a good database, and conse- quently an accurate mailing list.

Telemarketing

Telemarketing is the name given to direct marketing through the telephone system. In general, it refers to communication via landline: SMS marketing (sending text messages to mobile telephones) is generally regarded as a separate form of market- ing, because it is less interactive: there is more on SMS in Chapter 18.

Telemarketing falls into two main categories: inbound telemarketing, in which a call centre receives calls from people responding to advertisements or other

Telemarketing Selling or researching via the telephone.

marketing communications, and outbound telemarketing in which the call centre personnel initiate the calls.

Telemarketing is versatile, and has the advantage of being immediately interactive – the prospect and the telemarketer can develop a conversation instantly. The main drawback is that customers often see it as intrusive (at least as far as outbound telemarketing is concerned) and the UK's Telephone Preference Service, which circulates lists of people who do not wish to be telephoned by telemarketers, has experienced a large increase in subscribers in recent years. Legislation in the United States introduced a Federal Trade Commission Do-Not-Call list, which allows consumers to register their names and telephone numbers on a list of people who do not want to receive unsolicited telephone calls. The Do-Not-Call list was overwhelmed by requests from consumers within the first few days of its existence: if companies continue to call people on the list, the firms are liable for fines of up to $11,000 per violation. Similar legislation is currently going through the European Union system, and is likely to be in force in EU member states in the near future. The legislation in the United States covers calls from outside the US, provided the calls are being made on behalf of a US company, but the European legislation does not seem to similarly cover this eventuality at the time of writing.

In some ways these do-not-call lists might seem to be a problem for telemarketing companies, but in fact they simplify matters in the long run by eliminating people who would otherwise put the phone down, or (worse) be abusive to the telesales staff. From the viewpoint of a telemarketer, being able to talk to someone who is prepared to listen is a major advantage. Also, the legislation does not cover companies with whom the consumer already has a relationship. This has to be an exception, otherwise it would be impossible for a firm to telephone a customer (for example) to say that his or her order has arrived, or for a bank to call a customer to warn of an excess overdraft situation.

Think outside this box!

People often seem to regard companies as somehow being the enemy. Why should this be? If it were not for companies, we would have no clothes to wear, no food to eat, no houses to live in, and no jobs to go to. Companies are actually just groups of people, all trying to provide something we will like enough to give them our hard-earned cash – so shouldn't we be helping them as much as possible?

Or could we argue that, by saying we don't want any phone calls, we are actually helping by preventing those companies from wasting their time? On the other hand, might we not be missing out on offers that would really help us out?

Telemarketing is, in common with other 21st century communications media, technology-driven. Apart from the storage of large databases that can be made available to call-centre staff, computers can do much of the dialling. Rather than telesales operators pushing buttons to dial the numbers, predictive dialling systems are used to call up large numbers of people. The computer makes the outbound calls, only passing on the call to an operator when a person answers. This cuts out a lot of wasted time calling answering machines, fax machines and empty houses, although it does put a lot of extra pressure on the telesales staff, who often work under heavy pressure anyway. Automated systems can also arrange for automatic call-backs to customers at a later date, connecting to the same telesales operator and calling up the relevant information on the operator's screen.

Outbound telemarketing is useful for the following activities:

- Direct selling. Telemarketing is often used to service smaller accounts in the business-to-business environment, where the cost of sending a salesperson is not justified by the size of the business. Telesales cannot really replace a face-to-face call where the product is new or complex, because nothing really replaces the kind of detailed discussions that can take place between a salesperson and a buyer, but telesales are certainly capable of dealing with re-ordering situations, or with interim calls between sales visits.
- Supporting the salesforce. Telemarketers can contact buyers between salesperson visits, or to inform buyers of the impending visit of a salesperson, or to make and confirm appointments. Inbound telemarketers perform the same function, but the process is instigated by the customer in those circumstances.
- Generating and screening leads. Telemarketers can establish an initial contact with a prospective customer, and set up an initial visit from the salesperson. Outbound telemarketers can also check on leads that have come in as a result of exhibition attendance or magazine advertising, and can qualify the lead (i.e. ensure that the person has a need for the product and the means to pay for it).
- Marketing database building and updating. Checking that the details on the company database are still relevant and correct is a useful task for telemarketers. Also, if the database has come from a source such as an industry directory, a telemarketing call might need to be made to fill in gaps in the information supplied.

Inbound telemarketing does not suffer from the same restrictions and problems as outbound telemarketing. Inbound calls are those initiated by the customer, perhaps as a result of visiting a website or seeing an advertisement. Telephoning a call centre is a quick and flexible way for most people to do business, and provided the call centre staff are trained properly and have the time to deal with the call fully, the chances of making a sale are strong.

The main advantage of telemarketing is that it has many of the advantages of face-to-face selling but is orders of magnitude cheaper. It has the same flexibility and immediacy, and much of the same personal elements, but a telephone call is likely to cost around £5 at most whereas a personal sales call is likely to cost £150 or more. Telemarketing can have any of the following roles in the selling process:

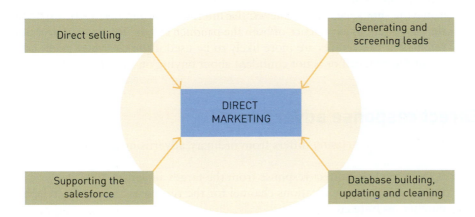

Figure 20.7 Outbound telemarketing

- Primary role. Here the telemarketing exercise is also the selling (telesales) exercise. The telemarketer is expecting to obtain an order as a result of the telephone call. Using telemarketing as the primary sales method will only work if the selling process is essentially routine (not a problem-solving role, but an explanation of features and benefits), the price of the product being sold is relatively low, the products are not technical, and there is a widely spread customer base.
- Supporting role. Telemarketing helps (as explained earlier) in situations where some face-to-face contact is indicated, but telemarketers can carry out some routine aspects of the process such as making and confirming appointments, or carrying out follow-up and after-sales calls.
- Combination role. In some cases, and for some products, telemarketing can take the primary role while still acting in a supporting role for other sales. For example, a field salesforce might have responsibility for selling major capital equipment to firms, using the telemarketing people to support them in this, but subsequently telemarketing people might handle sales of peripherals and consumables. In some cases, for example the computer industry, the sale of a new computer system to a company might be enhanced by offering rapid telephone ordering of printer cartridges, special paper, CD-RW discs, and so forth.
- No role. Some selling situations, notably key-account selling, allow no real role for telemarketing. Apart from a purely 'secretarial' role of confirming appointments, telemarketing is unlikely to work in a key-account scenario.

The main disadvantages of telemarketing, which may preclude it from consideration, are as follows:

- It does not have the same power as a personal visit. Around 70% of communication is non-verbal: facial expressions, body language, physical appearance and the ability to show samples or photographs of the product are much more powerful than any purely verbal presentation.
- It is easier for a customer to reject a telephone call: being rude to someone face-to-face is a great deal harder than simply putting the telephone down.
- Telephone selling is often regarded as an invasion of privacy, so a telemarketing call starts off on the wrong basis.
- Labour costs are higher than for direct mail (though the impact is likely to be higher).
- There is growing pressure on the industry in terms of government regulation. This will inevitably lead to restriction, Do-Not-Call lists, and possibly even the outright banning of outbound telemarketing.
- The Internet represents a cheaper, more consumer-friendly and faster method of achieving similar results. However, the Internet is more likely to be used when the customer has experience of both the product and the Internet: conventional retailers or call centres are more likely to be used if the customer needs advice about the product, or is not confident about buying on-line (Rhee 2010).

Direct response advertising

Direct-response advertising Messages inserted in a medium with the intention of generating a dialogue with potential consumers.

Direct response advertising differs from ordinary advertising as follows:

1. It seeks to elicit a direct response from the target audience.
2. It provides a communications channel for the responses (a coupon, telephone number, website etc.)
3. It has a strong call-to-action in the advertisement (for example, it will say 'Call this number now').

Figure 20.8   Direct response advertising

The purpose of direct advertising is to use the mass media to reach a wider audience than would be possible with, for example, a mailing. Also, direct advertising can be used in circumstances where direct mailing could not be used – typically, when there is no mailing list available. Direct response advertising can appear in print media, billboards, or broadcast media (though direct response television is more common than direct response radio).

A typical print-based direct response advertisement will incorporate the telephone number or Web address into the advertising itself, although many advertisements still add the telephone number only at the end, almost as an afterthought. The number should be a free number, or at least a local-rate number: the fewer obstacles in the way of responding, the better.

Direct response television (DRTV) demands considerable creativity on the part of the marketer, and also requires fairly frequent repetition of the advertisements. Because there is no hard copy, the target audience need either to be able to remember the contact details (which is unlikely unless the telephone number or address is very easily memorable) or enough time to write the details down. The advertisements vary in length worldwide: in the UK, the standard 30-second advertisement is usual, although sometimes the advertisements are 60 seconds or even 120 seconds during off-peak times. Shorter slots are rarely used because of the need to ensure that people have enough time to act on the call-to-action, and enough time to write down telephone numbers and so forth.

In other countries, longer time slots may be available: in the United States, the infomercial (a half-hour programme about the product) is common on some cable stations, and in Spain it sometimes seems as if the entirety of TV advertising consists of direct response advertising.

Digital TV has made a substantial difference in the way people interact with direct response advertising. Because digital TV has a degree of interactivity built in, people are able to press the red button on their remote control handsets to find out more about products, and even to order a brochure or free sample. Eventually, digital TV will be even more interactive: there are currently three modes in which this could happen. First, the viewer has the single mode in which he or she can switch between the normal TV programming and the interactive mode. This is the system that allows viewers to access a purchase site after seeing the advertisement. Second, there is the simultaneous mode, in which the viewer can split the screen or use a picture-in-picture (PIP) window, either to continue watching the programme while interacting with the site through the PIP window, or using the PIP window to keep up with the show while using the main screen to choose products. This is particularly useful if one member of the family wants to follow up on the product but the others would prefer to watch the programme. The third model is the pause mode, in which the programme is downloaded to a hard disc so that the viewer can pause the programme while interacting with the advertising, then return to the programme afterwards. This system allows viewers to customise their viewing, downloading programmes of interest and watching them later (much the same as using a VCR or DVD recorder, but faster and simpler).

DRTV is undoubtedly going to grow in importance in the next few years. In the UK, digital TV became the broadcasting standard in 2012, at which time the analogue signal stopped altogether (as happened in 1985 with the old 405-line broadcasting standard in the UK) and any remaining TVs that have not been converted will be scrapped.

A wide range of products can be sold using DRTV, but the following criteria are useful in ensuring success in selling off the screen:

1. If the product is one that benefits from a demonstration, for example exercise equipment or clothing.
2. If the product has mass consumer appeal (since television is a mass medium) or if it has appeal to a specific group of people who might be expected to watch a specialist cable channel (for example, history books might sell well to people who watch the History Channel).
3. The advertising itself must be engaging and interesting (see Chapter 15 on zipping and zapping).
4. The company needs an efficient inbound telemarketing operation to be able to respond to calls. This is especially important since the calls will tend to bunch up immediately after the advertisement is aired: the call centre might be overwhelmed for ten or fifteen minutes, then be idle until the advertisement airs again.

Direct response radio advertising is less common than DRTV. The problem of delivering a response channel is much greater, because of the lack of visual clues or the permanency that comes from print media. Radio advertising therefore needs to be more creative in finding ways to make telephone numbers (or even websites) memorable. Sometimes this is done by using a memorable telephone number that fits the advertising platform, sometimes it is done by linking the telephone number to a catchy jingle. The key to this is repetition – interested customers are not likely to have a pen handy to write down the numbers, especially considering that many people only listen to commercial radio when they are driving.

The main advantage of direct radio is, of course, cost. Radio advertising is far cheaper than TV advertising, and reaches a wider audience than press advertising: it also has the advantage that the advertising is difficult to zip or zap (see Chapter 15). It is probable that direct radio advertising is currently an under-used medium.

Catalogue retailing

Catalogues have proved to be an enduring form of direct market in several countries. Catalogues are distributed to consumers and agents, and orders are placed by mail: goods are then delivered either through the post, or via parcel delivery services.

The United States had the first mail order catalogues during the 19th century, serving remote farms and communities: the steadily spreading rail network made catalogue shopping possible, and the idea caught on in other countries. The drivers for catalogue shopping are as follows:

1. Availability of credit. In many cases, people from poorer backgrounds (especially people who are unemployed) have little or no access to credit. The local catalogue agent (a friend or neighbour) who is creditworthy takes on the credit risk, offering credit in turn to the end consumer. The agent earns commission, and is less exposed to the credit risk than the company would be, because he or

she has a social link with the end consumer. This has been an important driver in the growth of the UK catalogue industry, although as credit has become more readily available to people at all levels of society, the availability of credit has become less important.

2. Convenience. In circumstances where people live a long way from shops (as was the case in the early days in the United States, and is still to an extent the case), or when shopping hours are restricted (as was the case in Germany) catalogue shopping presents an attractive alternative. Catalogues might also present a useful alternative for people who find it difficult to get to the shops, either because they have small children or because they are housebound through illness or disability.

3. Range of goods. Many catalogues have an extremely wide range of products, meaning that people can quickly find exactly what they need.

Many catalogues operate alongside retail operations: firms such as Next, essentially a store retailer, can run a catalogue operation alongside the store. Likewise, firms like Argos (which is essentially a catalogue retailer) run stores in which the catalogue is the starting-point for buying. Customers enter the store, find the goods in the catalogue, fill in a form and then collect the goods from a counter at the back of the store. The advantage of this system is that there is no need to wait for delivery (or pay for it), and customers can browse the catalogue at home before visiting the store (or perhaps asking a friend to collect the goods).

The UK, Germany and the United States are the three countries that make most use of catalogue buying. In each country the market accounts for approximately 4% of retail sales, which represents a substantial amount of business, but hardly threatens traditional High Street retailers.

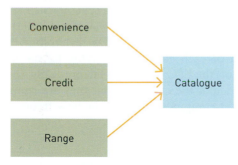

Figure 20.9   Advantages of catalogue marketing

Changes in retailing

Because consumer needs change rapidly, there are fashions in retailing (the rise and fall of niche marketing demonstrates this). Being responsive to consumer needs is, of course, important to all marketers but retailers are at the 'sharp end' of this process, and need to be able to adapt quickly to changing trends. The following factors have been identified as being crucial to retail success:

- *Location.* Being where the consumer can easily find the shop – in other words, where the customers would expect such a shop to be. A shoe shop would typically be in a high street or city-centre location, whereas a furniture warehouse would be typically out of town.

- *Buying the right goods in the right quantities* to be able to supply what the consumer wants to buy.
- *Offering the right level of service.* If the service level is less than the customer expects, he or she will be dissatisfied and will shop elsewhere. If the service level is too high, the costs increase and also the customer may become suspicious that the prices are higher than they need be. Discount stores are expected to have low service levels, and consumers respond to that by believing that the prices are therefore lower.
- *Store image.* If the shop and its goods are upmarket, so must be the image in the consumer's mind. As with any other aspect of the product, the benefits must be as expected, or post-purchase dissonance will follow.
- *Atmospherics.* This is the physical elements of the shop design that encourage purchase. Use of the right colours, lighting, piped music and even odours can greatly affect purchasing behaviour (Bitner1992). For example, some supermarkets use artificially generated smells of fresh bread baking to improve sales of bakery goods. Aromas in retail shops can create a sense of place and familiarity, and it is even possible to create a 'corporate odour' (Davies et al. 2003).
- *Product mix.* The retailer must decide which products will appeal to its customers. Sometimes this results in the shop moving away from its original product range into totally unrelated areas.

Recent trends in retail include the greater use of EPOS (electronic point-of-sale) equipment and laser-scanners to speed checkout queues through (and, incidentally, to save staffing costs), and the increasing use of loyalty cards. These cards give the customer extra discounts based on the amount spent at the store over a given period. The initial intention is to encourage customers to buy at the same store all the time in order to obtain the discounts, and in this sense the cards are really just another sales promotion. This type of loyalty programme, involving economic benefits, does have a positive effect on customer retention. The schemes also tend to help in terms of increasing the retailer's share of the customers (Verhoef 2003).

There is a further possibility inherent in EPOS technology, however. It is now possible to keep a record of each customer's buying habits and to establish the purchasing pattern, based on the EPOS records. Theoretically, this would mean that customers could be reminded at the checkout that they are running low on certain items, since the supermarket computer would know how frequently those items are

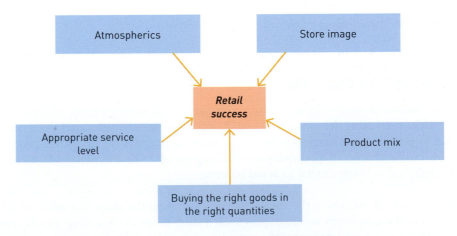

Figure 20.10   Factors in retail success

usually bought. The phrase Domesday marketing has been coined by Professor Martin Evans to describe this; whether it could be seen as a useful service for consumers, or as an unwarranted invasion of privacy, remains as a topic for discussion (Evans 1994). EPOS systems in the UK were redesigned in 2004 to allow for the introduction of chip-and-pin credit cards. These have been used in France and Spain for many years to reduce credit card fraud and reduce time spent at the checkouts.

Think outside this box!

Most of what we do is recorded on computer somewhere – in fact, firms and government departments know a great deal more about us than we like to think. If the police or the tax authorities really want to know about our expenditure and lifestyles, they can find out very quickly and easily – almost at the touch of a button, in fact.

So how does that make you feel? In George Orwell's book *1984* he described a society where everyone was under surveillance all the time by the dictator, Big Brother. The TV show *Big Brother* has shown how people crack under the strain of being watched all the time – and yet we are quite happy to hand over our loyalty card at the supermarket and have all the details of our purchases recorded, including our credit card number, home address, and even e-mail address and telephone number. Big Brother knows what you bought – even those personal items that you wouldn't want your mother to know you buy! All in the name of providing a better service.

But does it matter? We live in a goldfish bowl anyway – privacy is dead! At least the supermarket only wants this information so they can tell us about good deals on stuff we might want to buy: it isn't the Secret Service after us for imaginary crimes against the state. So why not let everybody know everything, and have done with it?

Forms of ownership in retail are also diverse. Although most retail outlets are still owner-managed and independent (around 62% of UK retailers fall into this category), the sales volume for independents is well behind that of the majors. Independents account for less than 30% of UK retail sales, and much of this is concentrated in the CTN (confectionery, tobacco, news) sector. This sector continues to survive because it offers more personal service and more flexible opening hours, although this advantage has been eroded markedly by major supermarket chains, who now offer very extended (even 24 hour) opening times.

A second category of ownership is the corporate chain. This has multiple outlets under common ownership, and is the usual form of ownership for major supermarkets, High Street clothing chains such as Next, and pharmacies such as Boot's. Many of these chains are long-established, and have built their success on their skills in purchasing rather than on selling. Most of the major chains operate centralised purchasing so that they are able to gain maximum bulk discounts from suppliers, and have maximum control over the supply chain. Some, such as Marks & Spencer, commission small manufacturers to produce items exclusively for the chain. This maximises the control the retailer has over the supply chain.

Although some of these chains allow a degree of local flexibility in purchasing (for example, Tesco allow its Welsh, Scottish and Irish branches to stock a small range of locally produced goods to capitalise on the patriotic feelings of its customers), their main strength comes from bulk purchasing. Many of them offer extensive ranges of own-brands (products which carry the retailer's name rather than the manufacturer's). These own-brands compete with manufacturer's brands, although a recent piece of research has indicated that they often help to increase sales of manufacturers' brands. At the same time, the evidence is that heavy own-brand users contribute less to store profits than other shoppers (Ailawadi and Harlam 2004).

The third type of ownership is the contractual system, whereby independent retailers band together, either as a co-operative between the retailers, or as a system sponsored by a wholesaler (such as the Spar system discussed earlier). The advantage is that the group can still benefit to some extent from bulk buying, but this is mitigated somewhat by the costs of running the group and inherent inefficiencies in having a large number of independent managers, each of whom has his or her own ideas about running the business. The lack of a consistent brand image is a major problem for these chains: some of the stores are indistinguishable from mainstream supermarkets, while others show the lack of investment that is often the hallmark of small businesses.

Franchising has been discussed earlier in terms of service industries such as fast food and hotel services, but it also exists in retailing. Benetton is the prime example: most Benetton retailers are franchises, and thus many of the risks are passed on to the retailer. Benetton franchisees in Germany have raised objections to Benetton's infamous advertising campaigns, because they found that the campaigns were losing them business; from Benetton's viewpoint, this was simply part of a normal business risk, but the risk was being borne by the franchisees since Benetton continued to show profits in other countries without any difficulty.

SERVICE LEVELS

In common with other service industries, retailers need to set a service level which their customers will find acceptable. There is, of course, a trade-off in terms of cost – the higher the service level, the greater the cost. The service level varies considerably from retailer to retailer, but broadly comes down to the categories in Table 20.7.

Table 20.7   Service levels

Service level	Explanation
Full service	Full-service retailers pay close personal attention to the customer, offer a range of account and delivery services, and charge premium prices as a consequence. Such stores as Harrod's, Cartier and Tiffany's are in this category.
Limited service	These stores do not offer the full 'red carpet' service, but do offer extras such as credit facilities, technical advice, or home delivery. The driver for deciding the service level is what the consumer must have: for example, a computer retailer must offer technical advice because few consumers would be sufficiently IT-literate to be aware of the latest technology.
Self-service	Typical of supermarkets, self-service offers the minimum service level possible, in exchange for low prices. The customer performs most of the in-store functions, selecting goods and taking them to a checkout to pay. Having said that, many supermarkets offer a little more than the minimum (for example offering to wrap cut flowers, or offering a home delivery service for larger orders). Lidl is an example of a 'no-frills' self-service store, whereas Tesco offers small extras that make shopping easier.

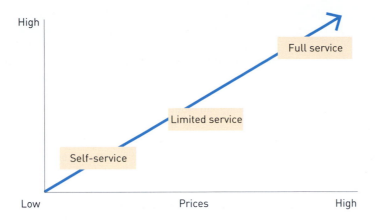

Figure 20.11 Service levels and price

MERCHANDISE LEVELS

There are two dimensions of range for retailers: breadth of range, which means the variety of different product lines stocked, and depth of range, which refers to the amount of choice within the product line. Department stores represent the greatest breadth of range, aiming to offer everything from clothing to food to electrical goods to hairdressing under one roof. The original aim of a department store was to ensure that customers would not need to go anywhere else to do their shopping – a revolutionary concept in the 19th century when the first stores were opened.

Depth of range usually means that the retailer specialises in a particular type of product, and stocks every conceivable variant on the product. Niche retailers such as Tie Rack and Knickerbox are examples of this.

In recent years, shopping malls have largely replaced department stores. The advantage of the shopping mall is that it allows specialist retailers (who stock a deep range of products) while at the same time offering the main advantage of department stores, which is the breadth of range. Because many of the niche retailers are also chain stores, they can take advantage of bulk buying in a way that traditional department stores are unable to do. The result of this is that some department stores and department store chains are closing their doors. Most spectacular of these in recent times was the Allders department store chain, which went into administrative receivership in February 2005 with the loss of hundreds of jobs.

Real-life marketing: Tie Rack

Retailers often like to think big – big stores can carry a wider range of stock and admit more customers, but sometimes it pays to think small. In 1981, the first Tie Rack store opened its doors. The concept was simple: using extremely small outlets in railway stations and airports, within department stores, and in shopping arcades, the company aimed to specialise only in neckwear. Tie Rack sold every type of tie and scarf, and nothing else.

(Continued)

(Continued)

Ties have the advantage of being small and high-priced. This meant that even a small shop could carry a very large range – much more than would be available in most general fashion outlets. Overheads, on the other hand, were extremely low. Locating the stores in railway stations and airports was a stroke of genius – per square foot, these locations are expensive, but there is a very high footfall of relatively well-off people who often have time to kill while waiting for their train or plane.

The success of the chain means that, as of 2012, it operates in 24 countries, through 330 outlets (most of which are tiny, in retail terms) and has amalgamated with Frangi SpA, the Italian fashion company.

If you have a small but high-priced product, this might be a way forward for you, too. In practice:

- Think outside the box – you should be doing this anyway, as a good marketer.
- Look for a potential resource that is currently underused or is being ignored altogether.
- Specialise. For small firms, the only way to compete against large firms is to specialise in something, because they are trying to be all things to all people.
- Don't compete head-on with the big retailers – they can squash you flat!

Strategic decisions in retailing

Location is a key decision in retailing, because the whole point of being a retailer is to place the goods at the most convenient point possible for the consumers to make their purchases. If the wrong location is chosen, the store will not generate enough trade to remain viable (Anderson 1993). In addition to lost business, relocation costs can represent a very substantial drain on capital, since the cost of fitting out a store can be extremely high.

The location decision hinges on two key factors: catchment area and the type of goods being sold. Catchment area refers to the radius around the store within which customers might reasonably be expected to travel, and an astute retailer will look towards investigating the profile of the customers within that area. A useful tool for doing this is a geodemographic rating tool such as ACORN or MOSAIC, which gives a fairly detailed description of the type of people living within the area. Catchment area analysis should also look at competition already in the area, and potential competitive responses. Stores do not necessarily avoid areas where there are many competitors, of course – it is equally valid to go to an area where there are already successful businesses, because splitting the market may still provide the store with enough business to be profitable, and the presence of competitors indicates that there is business to be done.

The second main factor in location decisions is type of goods. Some goods require a city-centre location, others do better in out-of-town locations. Fashion retailers tend to congregate in city centres, because fashion retailing tends to be a social event as much as a utilitarian, practical exercise. A day out in town is an appealing prospect for many consumers, because of the hedonic aspects of shopping. Convenience goods need to be readily available near to where the consumers live or work: shopping goods can be less conveniently situated because people are prepared to spend more time in travelling and searching.

Another factor is the cost of premises. For bulky goods such as consumer appliances (washing machines, fridges etc.) the high cost of city-centre premises means that retailers have difficulty in displaying a wide enough range of goods. Most such products are infrequently bought, so people are prepared to travel outside the city centre: edge-of-town retail parks, with their lower rents and easy car parking are the obvious site for such products.

Table 20.8 Location-decision factors

Factor	Explanation
Population	This refers to the size of the population, the age profile, income, housing type, unemployment level, lifestyle and ethnic mix.
Accessibility	This refers to pedestrian flow (also called footfall), public transport, car access, parking, visibility, staff access and delivery access.
Competition	The existing activity of competitors, the saturation level of competition, the cash turnover, the age of the outlets, the trade areas, the design and facilities offered by competitors, and the future potential for competitive activity all need to be taken into account.
Costs	The costs of acquiring a site, the development of the site, shop fitting, rent and local property taxes, maintenance of premises, security, staffing and delivery costs come under this heading.

Another classification of location-decision factors was offered by McGoldrick in 1992. This is shown in Table 20.8.

Locations can be classified as follows:

- City centre. City centres are usually the focal point for office development and transport connections, so they offer a large footfall. At ground level, most city centres are dominated by retail outlets, but such sites are expensive in terms of rent and taxes so they tend to be dominated by high-margin products such as fashion, jewellery and financial services. City centre locations are often called prime or primary locations.
- Suburban. Suburban locations are predominantly in residential areas. Often called secondary shopping centres, these parades of shops may run for whole streets in suburban locations, or may be a small row of six or seven convenience stores.
- Out of town. Edge of town or out-of-town retail parks have sprung up in the last thirty years or so, often near to major trunk roads. They take advantage of low rents and (in some cases) subsidies from local government departments, especially when they occupy 'brownfield' sites formerly used for industry. During the 1990s the concept was expanded to include the idea of an out-of-town shopping and entertainment complex (for example the MacArthur Glen

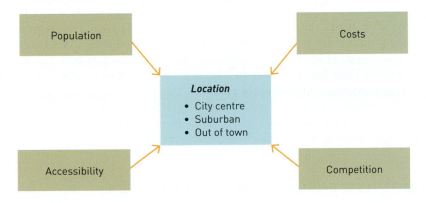

Figure 20.12 Location factors

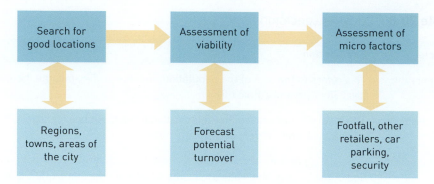

Figure 20.13 Location-decision process

centres), which include cinemas, restaurants and even bowling alleys. These centres are often some distance from major cities (the MacArthur Glen complex at Sarn Park is about half-way between Cardiff and Swansea, in a rural area just off the M4 motorway).

The location-decision process follows three stages:

1. Search for good locations. The retailer needs to decide which regions, towns, or areas of the city to locate in. Areas can be defined by socioeconomic categories, and retailers can establish retail spend potential by using geodemographic profiling.
2. Assessment of viability. Forecasting turnover using multiple regression techniques may be a possibility for comparing different locations. Often, such techniques give a spurious credibility to the results, when in fact most of the information included in the calculation is subjective. For example, a firm may decide that being near to a competitor is a good thing because the management believe they have a better selling proposition: on the other hand, if the competitor's selling proposition is actually better in the eyes of consumers, the store would be better locating elsewhere.
3. Assessment of micro factors. Issues such as footfall, presence of other retailers who are not competitors but who might attract customers, nearness of car parks and ease of parking, and security levels might all be taken into account. The site itself (which may well be an existing building) needs to be assessed in terms of ease of access for deliveries, length and terms of the lease, planning permission issues, and even local environmental factors. For example, one major food retailer fell foul of the health inspectors during 2004 because of a rat infestation of epidemic proportions. The store owners had failed to take account of their location next to a large river, which of course is a breeding-ground (and major highway) for rats.

Having selected a location, the retailer needs to consider competitive factors and competitive positioning within the chosen marketplace.

Competitive positioning for retailers

A key aspect of positioning is the store image and atmosphere. The shop front, the interior décor, the lighting, the display units, and the fixtures and fittings all

Table 20.9 Elements in store image

Element	Explanation
Sight	Lighting and colour are the two chief elements in sight. Most supermarkets now use green around the vegetable section, because this gives an impression of coolness and freshness: yellow appears bright and sunny, but also induces anxiety which may make shoppers hurry past that part of the store.
Scent	Many supermarkets have in-store bakeries which generate the smell of fresh bread, but those that do not have space for a bakery will sometimes use aerosol scents to generate the same aroma. Another ploy is to have a hot-chicken counter: these counters are not especially profitable in themselves, but they do generate smells that encourage shoppers to buy more food.
Sound	Many stores have background music playing, because research shows that music tends to make shoppers spend more time in the store (and consequently spend more money). Also, a silent atmosphere can seem unfriendly and unsettling for shoppers.
Other sensory experiences	Tactile factors such as the feeling of walking on carpet, the use of natural materials in display areas, and the provision of comfortable seating (depending on the store) all affect the shopping experience. Some stores (e.g. bookshops, women's fashion shops) provide seating – the bookshops do so to allow customers to browse books more easily, women's fashion stores often provide seating for accompanying partners.
Other shoppers	The degree of crowding in the store and the behaviour of other customers are important parts of the shopping experience, but are less controllable by the retailer. The store should not be overcrowded, but neither should it be empty: also, customers prefer to shop where they feel that similar people to themselves shop. Wealthier customers prefer not to shop at the same stores as poorer people, and vice versa; young people prefer to buy their clothes at stores where other young people shop.

contribute to the overall impression customers have of the store. The elements that go to make up the overall perception of the store are listed in Table 20.9.

LAYOUT AND DISPLAY STRATEGIES

Store layout and display affects customer perception of the store as well as their buying behaviour within the store. Store layouts conform to one of three main types, as shown in Table 20.10 (McGoldrick 1990). Hypermarkets and other large stores might use a combination of these layouts, using a grid layout for FMCG (fast-moving consumer goods) lines, and a free-flow layout for shopping goods or gift items.

Products can be displayed in one of five basic formats (Rosenbloom 1981). These are:

1. Open display. The goods are displayed on racks or counters where customers can pick them up and examine them. This type of display maximises customer involvement with the product and encourages trial, but can clearly lead to deterioration of the products due to excessive handling (shop soiling).
2. Theme display. The retailer may decide to base a display around a theme – summer holidays, Mother's Day, Easter, gardening, etc. These displays are intended to be eye-catching and to give customers a reminder of the various items they will need to enjoy the forthcoming event.
3. Lifestyle display. Here the display revolves around a particular lifestyle or life stage – a furniture shop might display the products in a room setting, for example.

Table 20.10   Store layouts

Layout	Description
Grid pattern	Aisles are arranged systematically so that customers walk in straight lines past the displayed merchandise. This layout is typical of supermarkets. This layout makes it easy for customers to find what they are looking for: supermarkets typically label each aisle so that shoppers can go straight to the goods they need.
Free flow	Displays are laid out in an irregular pattern, making a more interesting store layout for browsing. Free flow layouts encourage customers to wander around and browse the products on display: they are not conducive to quick decision-making.
Boutique layout	Boutique layout separates the store into separate, smaller sections. This layout might be used in a fashion shop, where different types of clothing might be displayed in different sections – the impression is of a set of small stores within the larger store.

4. Co-ordinated display. This is similar to theme displays and lifestyle displays – for example, a display might revolve around physical fitness, with mannequins dressed in sports clothes, accompanied by exercise equipment or sports equipment.
5. Classification dominance display. Here the retailer groups similar products together to give the impression that the store specialises in that category of product.

Retailing has gone through many changes in the last hundred years or so, but the end result is that retailers frequently have the strongest influence in the distribution channel because they are, by definition, closest to the consumers. As retailers have grown in size, they have been able to exert much greater influence on producers, telling them what to produce, and when to produce it; retailers have even been able to specify the sizes, colours and quality of agricultural produce.

Perhaps the biggest revolution in retailing will come from the Internet. As we saw in Chapter 18, more and more products are being bought on-line, and traditional bricks-and-mortar retail outlets need to take this into consideration. The most successful retailers on-line appear to be the 'clicks and mortar' outlets that combine a website with a physical High Street shop. This allows customers to check on the website whether the shop stocks the product category, but to visit the shop to see the actual product; likewise, consumers can see the product in the shop, go home to think about it, then order on-line. Having a physical presence improves the trust level between consumer and retailer, and reassures the customer that there will be a line of recourse if anything goes wrong with the purchase.

Chapter summary

Wholesalers, agents, retailers and other intermediaries perform useful functions in ensuring that the right products reach the right customers at the right time and in the right condition. Their activities account for the major part of the cost of goods in most cases, but without them there would be great inefficiencies and duplicated effort in the supply chain.

The result of their proximity to customers is improved fit between need and supply, and also an increase in power in the supply chain, with wholesalers and retailers generally having more bargaining power than manufacturers. Although consumers have the ultimate power (simply by choosing to spend their money elsewhere) their spokesperson is the retailer, who gauges consumer need and translates this into purchases from wholesalers and manufacturers.

Key points

- Agents are, for all practical purposes, the principal. The principal is bound by any acts of, or agreements made by, its agents.
- Intermediaries do not necessarily buy the products they handle.
- Licensing is most appropriate if products are perishable or fragile.
- Not all retailers have shops: a retailer is any firm that sells direct to consumers.
- Service levels have to be traded off against costs, and ultimately against prices.
- Location decisions are based on population, accessibility, competition and costs.

Review questions

1. What is the difference between a licensee and a franchisee?
2. How might an Internet retailer set up a bricks-and-mortar store?
3. What factors might a retailer take into account when deciding on service levels?
4. Why might a wholesaler provide a support service for consumers?
5. How might a discount grocery store decide on where to locate new stores?
6. What type of store layout would you expect in an electronic goods retailer?
7. How might a retailer encourage lower-income shoppers?
8. What advantages might there be for a wholesaler in becoming a full-service wholesaler?
9. What are the advantages and disadvantages of outbound telesales?
10. What are the limiting factors on Internet-based retailing?

Case study revisited: Young's Home Brew

Home brewing has gone through a number of stages: from its beginnings, when people made wines from fruits and even vegetables, through a period when some fairly lethal concoctions were produced, to a stage where home-made wines and beers are often of much higher quality than those produced commercially. Home wine-makers use fewer chemicals and additives, and are in control of the process: and of course the cost is a fraction of what they would pay in a pub or even in a supermarket. For example, 40 pints of beer costs around £15 to brew at home, compared with a cost of around £120 across the bar of a pub.

Young's therefore has a strong, mature market, but one that is changing as technology improves. As the acknowledged experts in the home-brewing field, Young's has a role in keeping ahead of the game and keeping retailers and consumers informed of new developments.

Young's deals with a product that is somewhat perishable (though not in the category of, for example, fresh greengrocery). This means that its inventory control has to be of a high standard: rotating stock to ensure that older stock is shipped out before it reaches its use-by date, and ensuring that stock is stored in optimum conditions are just two of the problems Young's faces.

Young's is probably a prime example of the advantages of specialising. Because the firm has developed a strong expertise in its field (and shows great enthusiasm for the products themselves) Young's has gained an unequalled reputation in the home-brewing business. Despite operating in a small niche market, it has become highly successful. By moving beyond simply providing products, and providing information as well, Young's has established itself as the UK's primary wholesaler in home-brew.

Case study: IKEA

Imagining a furniture store that is bigger than several football pitches is one thing: imagining a furniture store that attracts more visitors than any tourist attraction in the UK is another. Yet IKEA has achieved that remarkable distinction – and all based on cheap, well-designed, flat-pack furniture, and an understanding of what customers want.

IKEA first started in 1943 in a little village in Sweden, when a 17-year-old Ingvar Kamprad was given some money by his father, for doing well at school. Ingvar used the money to start a small business, selling pens, wallets, picture frames and indeed anything else he could find a market for. In 1953 Ingvar opened his first furniture showroom. Within forty years IKEA had expanded throughout Europe, had established its own railway company for transporting furniture, and had manufacturers ranging from woodworkers to shopping-trolley manufacturers working on its innovative furniture designs.

The success of IKEA is based on a number of factors. First, the attitude towards staff. Members of staff are called co-workers, and they are empowered to deal with customer problems as they arise – they do not need to seek approval for offering a reduction on damaged stock, for example. In 1999, the company held a Big Thank You day, in which the entire day's sales takings were divided equally among the co-workers, which meant that some staff had a bonus equivalent to a month's pay. Second, the design of the furniture. IKEA's furniture is largely Scandinavian and has the typical clean lines and functionality of Swedish design. Third, virtually everything IKEA sells packs small enough to fit into the average hatchback car, and even the larger items will easily fit onto a roof rack (this idea was introduced into the company in 1955 when an IKEA co-worker took the legs off a table in order to fit it into a car). Fourth, IKEA has a unique self-service system that guides customers around the store.

When customers enter an IKEA store they begin by going around the showroom area. In this area furniture is displayed in room settings and in 'category' settings (for example, a group of different chairs might be displayed next to an office layout). The route around the showroom is indicated by arrows on the floor, but of course customers are able to follow any route they prefer. Occasionally there are displays of small items which customers are at liberty to pick up, but the main items of furniture are stored elsewhere, so customers are invited to pick up notepads, pencils and paper tape measures so that they can check each item of furniture and note its catalogue number. Having made a selection, customers proceed to two areas: the Marketplace area, where smaller items are available to place in shopping baskets, and the Warehouse area, where the flat-pack furniture is kept. Customers check the catalogue reference against their selection, take the flat-pack to the checkouts, pay and leave. Beyond the checkouts there is a cafeteria which sells low-priced meals (including Swedish meatballs, of which IKEA is the largest outlet in the UK), and even Swedish delicatessen specialities to take home.

IKEA's innovative approach to furniture retailing extends to its special children's furniture, designed to be fun as well as practical: a system that has a bunk bed built above a wardrobe and desk has a slide to get down from bed in the morning, for example. Enjoyable shopping is certainly at the heart of IKEA's philosophy. The cafeterias are pleasant, peaceful and spacious and geared around the idea that a visit to IKEA is a day out in itself, not simply a way of buying furniture. Children can play on the furniture in the children's section, and adults can enjoy lingonberry juice and meatballs in the cafeteria. Staff are helpful and friendly, and for the opening week of the stores the company hires entertainers (street performers, clowns, musicians and so forth) to liven up the store and the car parks. To be able to position a furniture store against theme parks as 'day-out' destinations is no mean feat – but IKEA seems to have achieved this admirably.

Questions

1. What is the balance between hedonism and utilitarianism in IKEA stores and products?
2. What needs does IKEA meet in its customers?
3. IKEA seems to have a carefully prescribed route around the store. Why might this be?
4. Why might IKEA be so generous to its staff?
5. Why put a cafeteria and delicatessen beyond the checkouts?

Further reading

There are a great many practitioner-type books available on retailing, but relatively few on wholesaling.

Among the more 'academic' books on retailing, *Retailing – An Introduction* by Roger Cox and Paul Brittain (Harlow: Prentice Hall, 2004) offers a very readable, but academically rigorous, text. One author is a very experienced retail practitioner, the other is a respected academic, so the balance is a good one and the subject is approached well from both perspectives.

Regarding wholesaling, there are very few books on the topic at all, and most of these are economic analyses of the availability of wholesalers in different industries. The few 'how-to' books on wholesaling that exist are seriously out of date, and most are out of print.

References

Ailawadi, Kusum L. and Harlam, Bari (2004) An empirical analysis of the determinants of retail margins: the role of store brand share. *Journal of Marketing*, 68 (1): 147–55.

Anderson, C.H. (1993) *Retailing*. St Paul, MN: West Publishing.

Bird, D. (2000) *Commonsense Direct Marketing*. London: Kogan Page.

Bitner, M.J. (1992) Servicescapes: the impact of physical surroundings on customers and employees. *Journal of Marketing*, April: 57–71.

Davies, Barry J., Kooijman, Dion and Ward, Philippa (2003) The sweet smell of success: olfaction in retailing. *Journal of Marketing*, 19: 611–27.

Evans, Martin (1994) Domesday marketing. *Journal of Marketing Management*, 10 (5): 409–31.

McGoldrick, P. (1990) *Retail Marketing*. Maidenhead: McGraw–Hill.

Reed, D. (1996) Direct flight. *Marketing Week*, 1 November, pp. 45–7.

Rhee, Eddie (2010) Multi-channel management in direct marketing retailing: traditional call center versus Internet channel. *Journal of Database Marketing and Customer Strategy Management*, 17 (2): 70-7.

Rosenbloom, B. (1981) *Retail Marketing*. New York: Random House.

Verhoef, Peter C. (2003) Understanding the effect of customer relationship management efforts on customer retention and customer share development. *Journal of Marketing*, 67 (4): 30–45.

More online

To gain free access to additional online resources to support this chapter please visit:
www.sagepub.co.uk/blythe3e

CHAPTER ⑳ 21
Services marketing

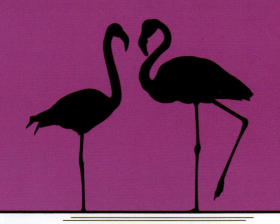

CHAPTER CONTENTS

LEARNING OBJECTIVES

After reading this chapter you should be able to:

- Explain the role of service in increasing customer loyalty.

- Explain how the purchase of services differs from that of physical products.

- Describe how risk increases in service purchases.

- Explain how failures occur in service provision, and outline ways of dealing with them.

- Show how consumers can also be producers.

- Explain the role of physical evidence in improving future business.

Introduction

Although the original idea of including people, process and physical evidence in the marketing mix came about because of a need to account for services marketing, all marketers need to understand the role of these three extra Ps in making products more attractive to consumers.

Business is not conducted by companies: companies are a legal fiction, without any real existence except through their employees. Business is conducted by *people*, and the relationships between the individuals concerned are probably the most important factor in many business transactions. The process of purchase and supply of products is also important in terms of assessing value for money, providing convenience and (often) differentiating one product from another. Physical evidence is what we use to confirm our possession of the product – think how often people use the phrase 'Nothing to show for it!'

Ultimately these three elements can be all that differentiates one product from another.

Preview case study: easyJet

EasyJet, the low-cost, no-frills airline, has been the subject of many case studies and is widely-used as an example of how an innovative approach to marketing can produce tremendous competitive advantage. This does not mean that things have always gone smoothly for the airline – in fact, at one point it looked as if the company was going to become a victim of its own success!

The demand for cheap flights, and the availability of new routes, were growing faster than the airline's ability to buy or lease aircraft. EasyJet could not afford to relax on opening up new routes, because a failure to seize opportunities in that regard would have left the routes open for competitors, of which many had grown up since the early days when Ryanair and easyJet were the only two budget airlines in Europe. Also, passenger numbers were growing so fast that easyJet's prices were rising: unless one booked very early indeed, the aircraft would be filling fast and the computer system would raise the air fare, thus destroying the company's main selling point.

The choices were simple: either the company would have to raise fares across the board and use the money to fund new aircraft (thus destroying the firm's only competitive advantage), or it would have to find ways to make the existing aircraft work harder. EasyJet chose the latter course.

Aircraft suffer from some limitations. They fly at the speed they fly: although it is possible to speed up a little, the cost in fuel outweighs the savings made. They have a fixed number of seats: unlike buses or trains, passengers cannot stand in the aisles. They cannot tow trailers, or have extra carriages put on, or in any way expand their capacity. Many airports nowadays do not operate on a 24-hour basis, because of environmental and noise considerations, so short-haul aircraft are effectively grounded overnight. The only slack in the system that easyJet could identify was the turnround time on the ground: the less time spent on cleaning and servicing the aircraft ready for its next batch of passengers, the more time it could spend in the air.

EasyJet called in the consultants, but rather than hire time-and-motion consultants, the airline brought in a group that specialises in developing innovative corporate cultures. For the next three months the consultants interviewed all the people involved in turning round the aircraft – the baggage handlers, the caterers, refuelling companies, airport staff, easyJet front-line staff, ground engineers, pilots, cabin crew, even the cleaning contractors. The consultants were then in a position to set up the right conditions for people who actually do the job to pool their ideas.

Service products

For many marketers, the difference between service products and physical products is negligible, in marketing terms. The reason for this is that a service is also a bundle of benefits, and it is not hard to imagine circumstances where a service can provide the same benefits as a physical product. For example, someone who needs cheering up might eat a bar of chocolate (a physical product) or might watch a DVD of a favourite comedy show (a service product). A man wanting to impress his girlfriend might buy her a gift, or take her out to the theatre – the benefit to the customer is the same.

As we saw in Chapter 1, there is a debate among academics about service-dominant logic (Vargo and Lusch, 2004). Service-dominant logic suggests that all marketing is

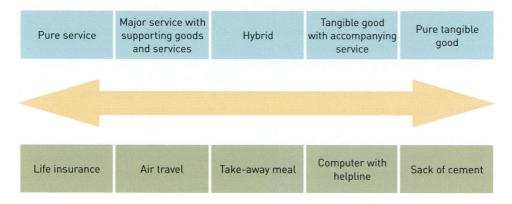

Figure 21.1   Services versus tangible products

service marketing because people are buying a service to which they contribute. People do not buy a car, they buy a transportation service to which they provide part of the input. This way of looking at things means that car manufacturers would define their competition to include railways, buses and airlines. It also may have implications for product design, so that the consumer is able to provide an enhanced service by making better use of the product.

Even for more traditional marketers, categorising products as either service products or physical products is somewhat misleading. Almost all physical products contain an element of service, and almost all services contain physical elements – and many companies find that the best way of differentiating their products from those of competitors is to include some extra service elements, especially in business-to-business markets (Raddats and Easingwood 2010). In effect, all products are on a continuum between the purely physical product (for example a bag of cement) to the purely service (life insurance). Even at these extremes there are no pure products: a bag of cement still has to be stocked by a builders' merchant, and an insurance policy still has a physical document to prove that it exists. It may therefore be more accurate to talk about service elements rather than service products. The factors distinguishing service elements are as follows:

- They are intangible. Service elements do not have any physical existence: the well-being one feels from spending time at the gym cannot be touched, sold, stored or given away to anyone else, but it is real nonetheless.
- Production and consumption occur at the same time. The airline passenger enjoys the flight at the same time as the aircraft flies: the theatregoer enjoys the play at the same time as the actors perform.
- Services are perishable. Once the aircraft takes off, any empty seats cannot be sold, or stockpiled for later. If a restaurant is empty, the staff still have to be paid, and their time cannot be saved up for busy times.
- Services cannot be tried in advance. It is not possible to try out a haircut before the hairdresser starts cutting, nor can one eat a meal in a restaurant before ordering it.
- Services are variable, even from the same supplier. Sometimes the chef has a bad day, or the waiter is in a bad mood: on the other hand, sometimes a chef has an inspired day which transforms the food.

Each of these factors creates its own marketing problems. The **intangibility** of the product means that customers are, in effect, buying a promise: it is difficult for them

Intangibility The inability to touch a service.

to judge the product, and may even be difficult to judge it after it has been consumed (Choi and Scarpa 1994; Zeithaml and Bitner 1996). Intangibility therefore creates greater risk (there is more on this later).

Because consumption and production occur at the same time, the consumer is present for much of the production process, which means that there is much more contact between producer and consumer than would be the case with a physical product. This allows the service provider much greater opportunities to tailor the product to the customer.

Perishability Services are perishable because they cannot be stockpiled.

The **perishability** of services has implications for pricing and promotion. The supplier must try to alter either the supply side or the demand side of the process in order to match production and consumption. Altering the supply side may mean employing part-time staff, working flexibly and in general adding and subtracting people and equipment in order to meet a fluctuating demand. Evening out demand is often simpler – airlines offer cheap seats off-season, bars operate 'happy hours' for quiet parts of the day, restaurants offer 'early bird' meals early in the evening. Discount days for some groups of consumers (e.g. students and retired people) enable retailers to fill the store on quiet days, and so forth: there is more on this in Chapter 14.

Variability In services, the difference between one service and the next, even from the same supplier.

Finally, the **variability** of services can be an asset or a liability. In some cases, variability is not good: restaurants rely on producing food of a consistent quality in order to maintain a reputation: this is difficult to do, since cooking is essentially a creative process. Fast-food restaurants overcome this by standardising and de-skilling the process as much as possible, and employing low-skill low-wage workers to produce the food. Automating as much of the service as possible also helps.

Real-life marketing: Be consistent

You're probably familiar with the way that the fast-food industry has deskilled cooking so that untrained people can produce a basic meal (like burgers or pizza) more or less on demand. But the concept can be applied to other service industries.

Etap Hotels is a French chain (part of the Accor group) which has deskilled the hotel business. Etap hotels are noticeable for their lack of staff. Bookings and cancellations are made on-line or via automated telephone exchanges, and late-arriving travellers can use their credit cards to pay for a room, using a machine rather like a cashpoint to generate a code number to access the room. The same machine accepts identification for a pre-booked room, so the reception function has been automated too. The rooms themselves are basic, easy to clean, and require minimal checking. The TV remote is bolted to the bed, and nobody checks on how many people use the room. In other words, there isn't much to steal and there's nothing to break, so rooms can be serviced rapidly by unskilled people.

Customer satisfaction is high because a clean room for a low price is what many travellers need – the no-frills approach is very popular in a country where hotel rooms are variable, to say the least.

If you think you could deskill your business, here's a checklist:

- Pass as much as possible of the booking system to the customer, using the Internet or automated systems.
- Remove direct human contact as much as possible, because that's the point where the variability will happen.
- Standardise as much as possible in pricing, systems and routines. This removes the need for people who can make decisions.
- Deskill everything so that the variance caused by different skill levels is removed.
- Keep the choices limited. The fewer choices on your range of services (whether it's a menu or a travel itinerary) the less chance there is of getting the order wrong, and the greater the economies of scale.

An alternative approach is to employ educated, well-trained people and empower them to vary the service in order to meet the needs of the customers. In these circumstances, variability is seen as an asset to the business, because the service can be tailored to the individual customer's needs. Top-class hotels operate in this way, allowing desk staff to deal with customer complaints, solve customer problems and make adjustments to the customer's experience of the hotel on an ad hoc basis, without having to refer to senior managers.

Kotler (2003) suggested five categories of product, expressed as combinations of physical product and services:

1. Pure tangible good. This includes products such as paper, salt, or computer discs, which have almost no service attached to them.
2. Tangible good with accompanying service. This would include highly technical products which are dependent on installation, servicing, planning, training or maintenance.
3. Hybrid. This would be an equal offering of tangible and intangible benefits. In this case, the service portion of the product is as important as the tangible portion.
4. Major service with supporting goods and services. In this case, the important part of the product is the service element, but some physical goods and supporting services are required. Airline passengers, for example, are mainly buying transport services but they also need some tangibles such as food and seating, and some support services (travel agents, etc.) are also needed.
5. Pure service. Here the product is almost entirely intangible, for example consultancy services or accounting services.

From the customer's viewpoint, buying a service is much more risky. Services are variable and cannot be tested, so the consumer has to take a great deal on trust: physical products can be returned if they prove to be faulty, but a bad haircut cannot be returned, and it may even prove problematical to avoid paying for it. Even a minor defect in a stereo system would justify returning it: an uncomfortable tram ride with a bad-tempered conductor will not result in a refund of the fare.

Because of this, consumers will need to spend more time on information-gathering, are likely to rely more heavily on word-of-mouth communications, and will want to know more about the qualifications and experience of the service provider. For example, someone looking for a hairdresser might want to know about the

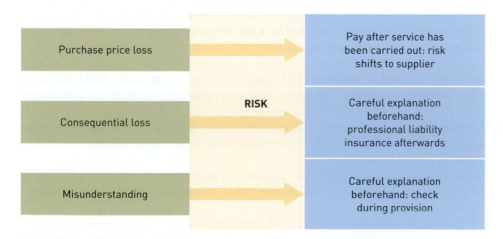

Figure 21.2 Risk in service purchases

experience and qualifications of the stylist, whereas few people would care about the engineering qualifications of Sony's chief designer.

Most of the risk attached to buying a physical product is limited to the purchase price, unless of course the product is defective in a way that causes injury or property damage. Products with a high service element carry additional risks, however, as follows:

1. Consequential loss. These arise when a poorly performed service causes loss to the customer. For example, a chartered accountant who fails to file a client's tax return on time might cause the client to be fined by the tax authorities, and perhaps be ordered to pay interest and surcharges. For this reason, service providers are usually careful to explain the risks beforehand, to put disclaimers into their contracts, and to carry professional liability insurance. Customers can take legal action if they have suffered consequential losses as a result of a poorly executed service.

2. Purchase price risk. This is the risk that the customer will lose the money paid for the service. In fact, this risk is lower for consumers in some service situations, because the service is only paid for after it has been consumed: in theory, a customer can refuse to pay for a meal that is not of the right quality. In practice, few people actually do this, but it is advisable for the supplier to check that everything is satisfactory during the service provision. This is why waiters will check that food is satisfactory while the diners are still eating, and why service stations call car owners if they find that extra work needs to be done. This type of check has two advantages for the supplier: first, it enables any problems to be corrected early, and second, it makes it much harder for the customer to claim that the service was faulty in order to avoid paying.

3. Misunderstanding. Sometimes a customer does not understand the full implications of the service. For example, the client of a lawyer is unlikely to understand all the legal issues involved in the case (which is why he or she has hired a professional in the first place). The client may not understand the ramifications of (for example) conceding a point to the opposing lawyer.

Service purchasing therefore follows a somewhat different sequence from that of purchasing a physical good, as shown in Figure 21.3.

Because customers are buying a promise, they are much more likely to use indirect measures of quality when choosing a service. This means that they are likely to assume that the food will be better at a more expensive restaurant, that the hairdressing salon in the town centre will be better than the suburban one, and that the lawyer with the expensively fitted offices will be more likely to win the case. These assumptions are, of course, irrational.

Involvement is also likely to be greater in service industries because of the additional risks involved. Customers tend to have favourite restaurants, hairdressers and family solicitors: even when problems become apparent, customers are reluctant to switch bank accounts, whereas they are prepared to switch brands of tuna in order to save a few pence. Note that the same customers who switch brands easily when buying physical products are likely to remain loyal to the same supermarket, which is after all a service provider.

In services markets there is more emphasis on Booms and Bitner's people, process and physical evidence (Booms and Bitner 1981). These have the following effects:

- People. Because most services are produced with the buyer present, there is usually direct contact between the producer and the consumer. Consumers need to relate to their hairdressers, lawyers and aircraft cabin crew, and the

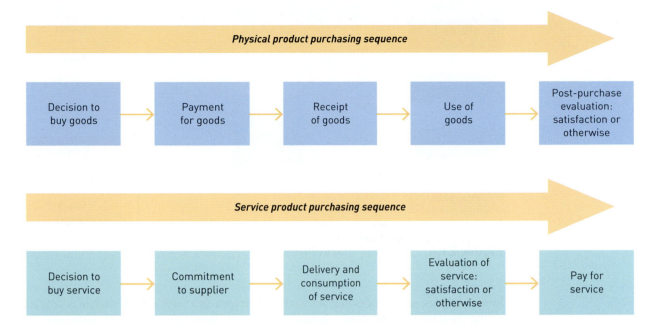

Figure 21.3   Service purchasing versus physical product purchasing

personalities of the providers affect the total experience. These front-line peo-ple who actually deliver the service have been called 'part-time marketers' (Gummeson 1991), and they often outnumber the full-time marketers in the marketing department.

- Process. Due to the customer's presence, the process becomes part of the total experience. There is a great deal of difference between a pizza served in an expensive restaurant and a pizza delivered by a local takeaway, but the differ-ence is far more apparent in the process than it is in the physical product.
- Physical evidence. This usually refers to the tangibles that accompany a service product: the glossy brochure, the décor of the shop or offices, the appearance of the person after the hairdo is completed, and so forth. Since virtually all products contain elements of both services and physical products, the tangible part of the product may constitute the major part of what the customer is pay-ing for – a take-away meal is an example here.

In many ways, marketing techniques for services are very similar to those for physical products, but it is important to remember that (from the consumer's viewpoint at least) the risks are greater, and therefore the decision process will be longer, and will rely on different criteria from those used for a physical product.

Marketing of services

The distinction between physical products and services is becoming more blurred as time goes on, because marketers of physical products are using service attributes to augment their products, and service marketers are including more physical evidence in their offerings for the same reason.

Clearly people, process and physical evidence rise in importance as products move closer to the 'service' end of the spectrum. Most services involve direct input by

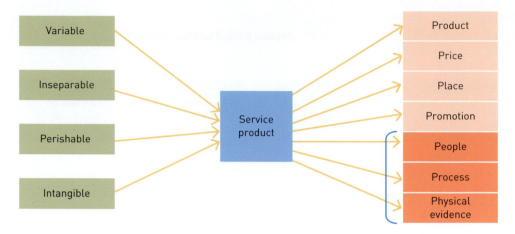

Figure 21.4   Services marketing

human beings, so the personal interaction between provider and customer is crucial to the customer's experience. An unfriendly taxi-driver, an irritating hairdresser, or a careless air hostess can damage the customer's experience of the service even when the practical aspects (the taxi journey, the hairstyle, or the flight) are all perfect.

Some service industries encourage strong customer loyalty. These are typically personal services such as hairdressing and beauty therapy, food and beverage services such as pubs and restaurants, and some technical services such as car maintenance and computer technical support services. Banks often engender strong customer loyalty, in part because people find it difficult to switch banks: transferring standing orders and direct debits is time-consuming, and many people feel that a long-term relationship with a bank is more likely to lead to preferential treatment in case of an unexpected overdraft or loan situations arising. Loyalty here is generated through the negative stimulus of high switching costs.

Think outside this box!

There is a lot of talk about loyalty, customer relationships and so forth. But do we really want this, as consumers? What's in it for us? Do we really *want* to have a relationship with the bank manager, or go on a nice holiday with our insurance company?

Wouldn't we rather they just served us in a friendly and efficient manner when we need them, and then get back in the box and leave us alone until the next time? On the other hand, perhaps it's rather comforting to know that the bank is thinking about us when we're gone!

On the other hand, some services do not automatically engender customer loyalty. Taxis and buses are prime examples; although someone might use the same taxi firm when travelling from home, this is unlikely to be the case for someone arriving at an airport or train station. At these times, one simply takes the first available taxi. It would be extremely rare for someone to have a regular taxi driver, although most people will use the same hairdresser on each visit. Other services such as airlines

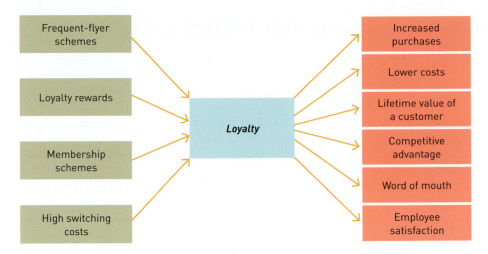

Figure 21.5   Benefits of loyalty

need to work hard to encourage loyalty, primarily through their use of frequent-flyer programmes. Most airline passengers are simply looking for the lowest fare between their chosen departure point and destination; apart from business travellers, who often travel the same route anyway, loyalty is low.

If loyalty can be generated, the benefits for the organisation are considerable. There are six main benefits, as follows:

1. Increased purchases (Reichheld and Sasser 1990). Customers tend to increase their purchases year-on-year with firms with whom they have a relationship. Of course, there must be a limit to this, but it is logical to assume that people are more likely to spend money with firms in whom they trust.
2. Lower cost. Attracting new customers is always more expensive than retaining existing ones.
3. Lifetime value of a customer. As we saw in Chapter 11, customer value should be measured in terms of how much the customer spends in a lifetime, rather than in a single transaction.
4. Sustainable competitive advantage. The intangible aspects of a service relationship are difficult to copy: a loyal group of customers are, by definition, difficult for a competitor to lure away (Roberts et al. 2003).
5. Word of mouth. This is much more important in services marketing because of the intangibility of services. It is not possible, in most cases, to try out a service before purchase, so people rely heavily on the recommendations of friends. Firms with large numbers of loyal customers are more likely to benefit from this.
6. Employee satisfaction. Staff are more likely to stay with a firm that has a large group of loyal customers. Because staff in service industries are close to the customers, they are subject to direct customer feedback: praise is welcome, but regular complaints will demoralise staff and make them doubt whether they are working for a good company.

Lowering the rate of customer churn (plugging the holes in the leaky bucket – see Chapter 11) causes a substantial rise in overall profits (Reichheld and Sasser 1990). Reducing risk is one way of avoiding the loss of customers, since risk is generally higher in services purchase.

Marketing in a changing world: Airlines and the environment

Air travel has increased dramatically in the past thirty years or so, since the deregulation of air travel. There have been several other drivers, too: greatly increased standards of living, time pressures on the travelling public, improved efficiency of aircraft in terms of reliability, lower costs all round, a fashion for travelling to exotic places – especially among young people – and a more global perspective among the world's population. Not to mention a shift towards experiences rather than more possessions – many people have everything they want in material terms, so instead want to spend money on experiences.

Environmentalists have jumped on this, of course, pointing out that air transport is the fastest-growing contributor to greenhouse gas emissions. This has led to a number of pressures on aircraft manufacturers and airlines: manufacturers seek to develop more efficient aircraft, airlines aim to fly aircraft as full as possible (this makes economic sense anyway). Various governments have imposed extra taxation burdens on airlines, and campaigners have tried to prevent new airports being built and old ones expanded.

Airlines make a wonderful target, of course, because they are in the luxury business. Flying is something we can do without. Environmentalists don't like to point out that agriculture is a big contributor to greenhouse emissions, and in particular the beef and dairy industry. The gases emitted by ruminating cows account for a large portion of agricultural greenhouse gases. Likewise, electricity generation accounts for a lot of greenhouse gas – and no one wants to think too hard about that one, either.

In fact air transport only contributes around 2–3% of greenhouse gas emissions. Airline bosses have tried to point this out, and fight against what they see as unfair discrimination, but with little success. It seems as if people like to pick and choose which environmental issues they will pick up on, and which they will pretend aren't happening!

People

Company employees can be divided into four main groups (Judd 1987):

Contactors Staff who have daily contact with customers.

1. **Contactors**. These people have frequent and regular contact with customers. They are typically heavily involved with marketing activities: they are salespeople, telesales operators, and customer service people. Because they are dealing with customers on a day-to-day basis, they need to be trained in customer relations and should be motivated to deal with customers. They should also be recruited on the basis of their ability to deal with people.

Modifiers Staff who have some contact with customers for specific purposes.

2. **Modifiers**. These people deal with customers regularly, but have no direct marketing role. They are receptionists, truck drivers, switchboard operators, and (sometimes) warehouse personnel or progress chasers. They need a clear view of the organisation's marketing strategy, and to be aware of their own role within it. Modifiers need good people skills, and training and monitoring of performance regarding their customer contacts.

3. Influencers. These people are involved with the traditional elements of the marketing mix, but have little or no contact with customers. Influencers need to be evaluated and rewarded according to customer-orientated performance standards.

Isolateds Staff who have no relationship with customers.

4. **Isolateds**. Isolateds have no customer contact and very little to do with conventional marketing functions. Examples are accountants, personnel people and office cleaners. Although they need to be alerted to the idea that their efforts are important in supporting the other staff, they do not need any specific training for dealing with customers. In essence, their role is to create the right conditions under which the customer-focused staff can do their jobs.

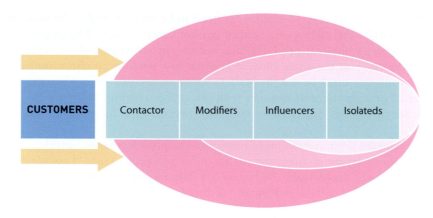

Figure 21.6 Employees and customers

Of course, everyone goes home at the end of the day and talks to family and friends about the firm, and as such everyone in the firm bears some responsibility for the corporate image and for marketing (see Chapter 16). Creating shared values and especially creating a feeling of corporate justice (that one is working for a fair-minded company) affect how employees deal with customers. This in turn affects customers' perception of the organisation (Maxham and Netemeyer 2003).

In practice, no matter how hard companies try to deliver the perfect service, the natural variability of employee performance will mean that there will always be some occasions on which the service falls below standard. This means that firms need to concentrate on recovering from service mistakes when they do occur (Rasmusson 1997). The first step in this is to empower front-line employees.

Think outside this box!

Companies expect more and more of their employees nowadays. Not so many years ago, people had nine to five jobs – they would sit at their desks, or on the production line, from nine in the morning until five in the afternoon, then get paid on Friday. Some people did exactly the same job for fifty years and ended up with a gold watch at the end of it – but not any more! Employers expect people to be able to multitask, to switch jobs with each other, and to take on an ever-wider range of tasks.

Empowerment seems to be following along the same lines – employers expecting people to take on responsibility for customer satisfaction as well as carry out their normal jobs! On the other hand, maybe customer satisfaction is what all our jobs are about, at the end of the day, and empowerment just recognises that fact!

Empowerment means giving employees the authority to sort out problems without having to refer to management. This approach to managing people makes the employees responsible for their own actions, and more importantly makes them responsible for controlling the service delivery. The purpose of the exercise is to ensure that problems are dealt with as soon as they happen, without the customer having to wait for a decision from management. Because many services are carried out on a one-to-one basis, managers would find it difficult or impossible to supervise

Empowerment Giving staff the ability to resolve customer problems without recourse to higher management.

every aspect of the process, so employees need to be empowered if the system is to operate smoothly: the efforts of a factory worker can be checked by examining the tangible output (a physical product), but because production and consumption of services take place at the same time, it is often not possible to check outputs and therefore the onus must be on the staff member to act professionally, and on the employer to provide the staff member with the authority to do so.

There are three basic objectives of staff empowerment, as follows:

1. To make the organisation more responsive to pressures from outside.
2. To remove layers of management in order to reduce costs. Less supervision means fewer supervisors: managers are left free to coach and support staff rather than direct them, which also reduces workload and stress for managers.
3. To create employee networks. This encourages collaboration, teamwork and horizontal communication, which in turn tends to improve employee motivation.

The basic empowerment options are as shown in Table 21.1.

For most staff, empowerment is a powerful motivator because it increases job satisfaction: if they are not empowered, staff can feel like small cogs in a very large machine, especially in modern global organisations. Being part of a smaller, empowered team brings the workplace down to a human scale.

There are, of course, trade-offs in staff empowerment. These are illustrated in Figure 21.7.

Purely from the viewpoint of how the customers will be treated, the deciding factors in empowerment are the competitive environment and the relative importance

Table 21.1   Options for empowering staff

Option	Explanation
Encourage employees to contribute ideas	This needs to go beyond simply putting up a suggestion box. Some firms (notably Ford) pay substantial cash rewards to employees who think of money-saving ideas for the company.
Establish work teams	Work teams are allowed to share and manage their own work, which enables them to help each other and establish quality controls within the group. This is seen by most employees as less threatening than management controls.
Empower staff to change strategic parameters	This allows employees to take responsibility for the overall outcome, rather than simply having responsibility for their own actions.

	High customer contact	*Low customer contact*
Highly-structured, rigid competitive environment with little change	Limited empowerment	No empowerment
Unstructured, rapidly-changing competitive environment	High empowerment	Limited empowerment

Figure 21.7   Trade-offs in staff empowerment

of close linkages with the customers. If there is little customer contact, there is little need for staff empowerment, and none at all if the competitive environment is rigid and unchanging. On the other hand, if there is high customer contact empowerment will need to be in place, and staff will need to be highly-empowered if they have to deal with an unstructured, rapidly changing environment.

Problems can arise from empowerment. Some people are risk-averse, and therefore reluctant to assume the responsibility that goes with empowerment: managers might overcome this by giving extra support to these staff, and by putting in reward systems for correct decisions. There should not be a culture of blame: punishing staff for making wrong decisions is a sure way of ending up with staff who make no decisions at all, which is of course the worst outcome. Problems arise from the following areas:

1. When the empowerment is taken away as soon as the most important and interesting decisions have been made.
2. When the parameters are not clear, so that employees become afraid of making wrong decisions.
3. When communication is poor, both between managers and staff and within the staff teams.

When setting parameters, clear guidelines should be given: at the same time staff should not be overly burdened with fixed rules, because the whole point of empowerment is to enable staff members to act when something unexpected occurs. If all the possible circumstances could be outlined in advance, presumably they could be prevented from happening.

Murphy (2001) points out that empowerment does not always benefit employees. Many find it threatening, and others see it as a way for management to abdicate responsibility without paying the staff any extra for doing what they see as a management job. Staff who become alienated from the process (either because they feel they have been given extra responsibility without being given extra pay, or because the empowerment is too restricted to be of any use) may act in ways that are detrimental to the firm or to customer relations. For example, an employee might be over-generous to a favourite customer, or neglect a customer who is regarded as a nuisance.

Here is a checklist for successful empowerment of employees:

1. Employees need to be selected, trained and nurtured with empowerment in mind.
2. Employees should be given clear guidelines without being bound by rules that cannot, in any case, cover every eventuality.
3. Empowerment works best when combined with a team approach: the support of other members of the team offers invaluable reassurance.
4. Rewards must reflect the contribution the employee makes.
5. There should not be a culture of blame. Failure should be seen as an opportunity to learn, not as a matter for punishment.

The concept of empowerment implies that power is being devolved from senior managers to junior staff: this may be unhelpful. It may be better to think of empowerment as being about encouraging staff to use their initiative: it does, in any case, require skilful management.

Team-building is itself a marketing task. Individual contributions to the team's efforts are almost always determined by the needs of the individual employee – the need for promotion, for personal development, for job satisfaction, or for the esteem of the group (Cummings 1981). Successful teams need shared objectives, preferably

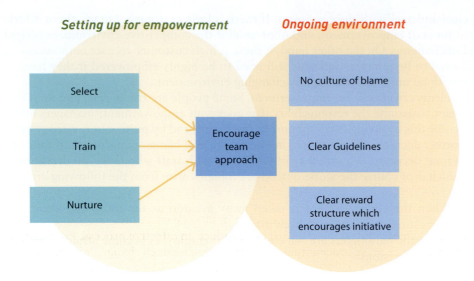

Figure 21.8   Successful empowerment

agreed within the group rather than imposed from outside. Belbin (1981) suggests that teams should be able to perform the following tasks between them:

1. Create useful ideas.
2. Analyse problems effectively.
3. Get things done.
4. Communicate effectively.
5. Have leadership qualities.
6. Evaluate problems and options logically.
7. Handle technical aspects of the job.
8. Control their work.
9. Report back effectively either verbally or in writing.

Leaders should be able to shape and share a vision that gives a point to the work of others (Handy 1989).

Process

A process is a series of actions taken in order to convert inputs to something of greater value (Finlay 2000). If the process does not create greater value, it is neither efficient nor effective: a dysfunctional process can actually reduce value. For example, a chef might take basic ingredients such as flour, eggs, apples and so forth and create a pie, adding to the value of the ingredients. A great chef can take the same ingredients and create a work of art: a bad chef might take the already-valuable ingredients and create an inedible mess.

In marketing, every process combines the following basic resources:

1. Basic assets. These are the tangible and intangible assets of the business: they appear on the balance sheet, and include tangible assets such as plant and equipment, cash in hand, work in progress, buildings, and fixtures and fittings. Intangible assets include the reputation of the firm, the reputation of its brands, and a factor that accountants call 'goodwill', which acts as a catch-all for any other intangible assets.

2. Explicit knowledge. This is knowledge that can be written down or otherwise recorded. It includes patents, market research, customer databases and so forth.

3. Tacit knowledge. This is knowledge that is difficult or impossible to write down, because it resides mainly in the heads of employees. Skilled workers or professionals within the firm may have industry-specific skills which cannot easily be replaced. Consider a restaurant that intends to specialise in Tibetan food: finding a Tibetan chef might be a difficult task if the existing chef decides to leave. Equally, a skilled buyer or corporate lawyer would be difficult to replace.

4. Procedure. This is the mechanism by which the basic assets, explicit knowledge and tacit knowledge are brought together to create a process.

Procedure is often mistaken for process, but in fact the two differ: a good procedure that lacks the necessary staff skills will not produce an effective process, for example. Unfortunately, because procedure is easy for management to change, it is the element that changes most often. Changing the procedure means that staff have to re-adjust and re-order their knowledge, so there is inevitable disruption to the process and wasted time and effort.

When processes are linked together to deliver a set of benefits to customers they become part of the firm's overall capability. A capability should be more than the sum of the individual processes, but this will not happen if the processes are not linked correctly or if they are mutually damaging in some way (Stalk et al. 1992).

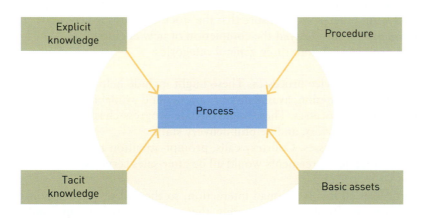

Figure 21.9 Developing processes

Think outside this box!

Surely one of the problems companies have is controlling the processes. Employees will cut corners, figure out new ways to do things, and try to make things easier for themselves and (sometimes) the customers as well. Not to mention that middle managers are actually expected to change things and adapt to changing circumstances.

If so, how can processes ever realistically be combined to create capabilities? Or are we actually saying that the ability to create and adapt is also part of a process, and consequently part of a capability the firm has?

In services markets, the consumers can sometimes be seen as a co-producer of the service. For example, live theatre clearly has serious drawbacks over television: it cannot hope to provide the same level of special effects and scenes, and the actors' performances may not always be perfect (whereas on TV an imperfect performance is simply re-shot). Additionally, going to the theatre involves booking seats, going out in the cold and finding one's way to the theatre, sitting in what are often uncomfortable seats, not being able to have a drink or a snack during the performance, and not being able to press the pause button. The theatre does not allow one to change channels if the play is boring, it does not allow one to turn up the volume if the actors are speaking too quietly, and it does not allow one to watch the play wearing a dressing-gown. For these experiences, people pay for a ticket – so what is the attraction? The main attraction is that there is an atmosphere in the theatre, generated by the presence of an audience – the other consumers. A half-empty theatre seems bleak; a theatre full of people responding to the show helps generate a response in the person watching the play.

Developing services processes

As with any other question in marketing, the starting-point for developing a service process is the customers' needs. In some cases the needs can be presented as a hierarchy – for example, an airline's maintenance depot may not require new engines to be delivered urgently, but probably would need spare parts to be delivered quickly, as a grounded aircraft is an expensive item. The aero engine manufacturer would therefore see the supply of engines as being less important than the supply of spare parts, and would then seek to ensure that the stock of spares is kept up to an appropriate level even if this delayed the completion of new engines.

Service processes fall into three general categories:

1. Before-sales service processes. These might include helpful sales staff, readily-available information, availability of samples and availability of supplies.
2. During-sales processes. These might include progress-chasing of orders, prompt and reliable delivery, and helpful delivery staff.
3. After-sales processes. Courtesy calls, prompt attention to complaints, warranties and service agreements would all be after-sales services.

These processes all involve human interaction, so they all provide opportunities to improve customer loyalty. Unfortunately, they are also easy to copy, and not very difficult to exceed, so it may be difficult to maintain competitive advantage. Also, there is a trade-off between service level and cost: some firms have been successful by cutting back dramatically on service and reducing prices accordingly. Retailers, low-cost airlines and fast-food restaurants offer minimal service, but have streamlined processes that reduce cost and deliver the core product efficiently. In some cases, the streamlined process might actually be preferable to the more staff-intensive process it replaces – many people find that booking flights on the Internet is a great deal easier than going through a travel agent.

Setting the right level of service can therefore be a source of competitive advantage. The emphasis here is on setting the right level – too high a level of service, and the price will have to rise or the profits will have to fall. Too low a level, and many customers will go elsewhere. Many firms still try to provide a high level of service for a low price – often at the expense of their employees – but this can only be done by shaving profits or otherwise acting in ways that reduce longer-term competitiveness. Note that segmentation still applies: some people are happy to pay for an enhanced service, while others prefer to buy the cheapest. Indeed, individuals often shift between the two levels, depending on the occasion – a couple going out to dinner for their 25th wedding anniversary will not eat at the same restaurant they might go to for a quick lunch during the working week.

Processes can be considered as structural elements that can be used to deliver a strategic position. A process-orientated approach to strategy involves the following steps (Shostack 1987):

1. Break down the process into logical steps to make control easier.
2. Take the more variable processes into account: variability leads to different outcomes at different times because of variations in the judgement of the people delivering the service, or because of human error, or because of customer choice. Naturally this problem is made worse by staff empowerment, especially if the boundaries are not clearly drawn.
3. Set tolerance standards which recognise that service processes do not always run smoothly, but rather function within a performance band. For example, it would be uneconomic (if not outright impossible) to ensure that no one queues for longer than two minutes in a supermarket, but it should be possible to set a target such as 95% of customers will queue for less than two minutes.

Service processes have aspects of both complexity and divergence. Complexity is about the number of stages the process has to go through, and the number of separate processes involved; divergence is about the variability of the stages, and the consequent variability of the outcomes.

An airline is an example of a complex service. Several hundred different tasks need to be undertaken, and dozens of entirely separate service processes need to be co-ordinated for the passengers to reach their destinations. First, a travel agent (or a website) needs to sell the ticket, which means ensuring that the passenger is on the

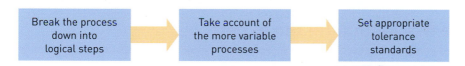

Figure 21.10   Process-orientated approach to strategy

	High divergence	*Low divergence*
High complexity	Unstable, unreliable, high-cost service	Stable, reliable, high-cost service
Low complexity	Variable, customised, simple to provide service	Simple, reliable easily-provided, cheap service

Figure 21.11   Complexity versus divergence

right plane at the right time, leaving from the right airport and arriving at the right airport. Second, the aircraft needs to be correctly serviced and fuelled – services often carried out by separate companies. Food for the passengers needs to be provided by yet another service company. Both airports (and any intermediate airports, if the journey is a long one) need to be prepared to handle the aircraft and its passengers, and several air traffic control agencies in different countries need to become involved. Alcoholic drinks, in-flight entertainment, in-flight magazines and (on long-haul aircraft) in-flight packs of earplugs, headrests, eyeshades and so forth also need to be provided. Even at the airports several companies will be involved in the process – airport caterers, bookstores, travel goods shops, duty-free shops, baggage handlers, car parks, taxi firms and bus companies might be involved.

On the other hand, the service is not very divergent. Apart from the differences between flying economy, business class or first class the experience is much the same for all passengers. Caterers go to great efforts to ensure that all meals are standardised, flight attendants go to equal efforts to treat everyone with the same degree of formality and friendliness (and of course are in uniform), and obviously all the passengers depart from, and arrive at, the same airports. The entire process is so formulaic that frequent flyers find it difficult to remember which airline they are flying with, because each one treats its customers virtually identically.

By contrast, hairdressers exhibit almost exactly the opposite characteristics. In most hair salons, the client will only be attended by one or two of the staff, in a process that does not involve any other companies apart from the salon's suppliers of hair products, electricity, and so forth. The end result, however, varies considerably – if the salon is any good, each customer is dealt with as an individual and receives an individual hairstyle based on the client's physical features, age, lifestyle and so forth. On the other hand, things can go wrong more often in a hairdressing salon than on an aeroplane – there are perhaps too many variables in the equation, not least of which are the characteristics of clients' hair.

Real-life marketing: Be the expert

You've heard the expression that the customer is always right – but is that really true? At the beginning of the 1960s Britain was a dynamic place. One of the areas in which Britain was booming was in fashion – and hairdressing was no exception.

A young hairdresser called Vidal Sassoon was about to revolutionise thinking in the hair business. Before Sassoon, the client was queen: hairdressers did clients' hair exactly in the way they were told to, hardly even daring to offer advice. Hair was typically curled and bouffed to create almost hat-like effects. Sassoon developed an entirely new way of cutting hair, using fingers and scissors, rather than combs, razors and scissors. Haircuts became precise, and hairstyles became geometrical –he simply allowed the hair to fall naturally, perhaps blow-drying it to create movement.

The second innovation on Sassoon's part was that he would not follow orders from the clients. Sassoon's argument was that he was the expert in hairdressing, and therefore he was in the best position to decide what style would suit the customer and how the look would be achieved. He also offered only a small range of hairstyles – almost in the same way as clothes designers offer collections. The outcome of a visit to a Sassoon salon was, and still is, a fairly standardised 'look' which others can recognise as a Sassoon cut. By limiting divergence, Sassoon established a brand.

To become the expert in practice, you should do the following:

- Really be the expert – know your business inside out and backwards.
- Be firm but polite. Don't allow anyone to leave the premises with something you're not happy with – any more than a chef will allow food out of the kitchen if it's not as it should be.
- Always get the customer on board. Don't be confrontational, be consultative.

A hairdressing salon represents a process that is divergent, but not complex. Each customer will have different hair and facial features so will need a different hairstyle, but the service is provided by one, or at most two, people. Most services fall somewhere between airlines and hairdressing, but the complexity and divergence of the service can often be adjusted to establish a competitive position. The possible effects of adjusting these factors are as follows:

- Reducing divergence will reduce costs, improve productivity and make distribution easier. A typical example would be a fast-food restaurant, which offers a limited menu of standardised food at low cost.
- Increased divergence allows greater customisation, greater flexibility and (usually) premium pricing. High divergency is found among niche businesses and small, flexible businesses such as bespoke tailors.
- Reduced complexity usually means specialising in a basic, no-frills service offered by one firm, offering the core benefits of the product.
- Increased complexity increases customer choice by offering a wider range of products, but it also offers a wider range of separate features within the main product on offer. An example might be a computer retailer, which offers free delivery, on-site maintenance and on-line technical support: each of these separate processes adds to the core service of selling the computer, and each is almost certainly offered by a company other than the retailer through a totally separate service process.

Low and high complexity may not always be apparent from the consumer's viewpoint, however. Divergence will always be apparent, because it is the degree to which the outcomes vary for each consumer.

Physical evidence

The intangibility of most of the benefits of a service means that consumers do not have any evidence that the service ever took place. The evidence might be useful to show to other people (a certificate from a training course, a life insurance policy to show to a bank) or it might be simply something to act as a reminder of the pleasure the consumer obtained from the service (a souvenir of a holiday, a menu from a restaurant, a travel kit from an airline). Physical evidence might also be used as a way of assessing the quality of a product before committing to a purchase (the bank branch's décor, or the menu in the window of a restaurant).

Think outside this box!

It's commonly said that you can't judge a book by the cover – yet apparently we are expected to believe that we can judge a bank by its décor. Are we really as naïve as that? Do people seriously think that reading the menu gives any idea of the quality of the food?

There again, what else do we have to go on? We can hardly go into the restaurant and taste the food first! Maybe restaurants should try this as an experiment – let people have a small taste of the food before they commit to buying a meal. This is, after all, what happens in Spain, in many tapas bars.

Some people might think that banks would be better spending their money on reducing their charges or improving their service – but the evidence is that having a smart interior really does affect people's decisions about where to bank. So maybe we really *are* judging the book by the cover!

In some cases the physical element of the product itself is sufficient to act as physical evidence. A meal in a restaurant fulfils this: the food, the surroundings, the quality of the crockery and cutlery all convey evidence about the quality of the experience, even though the greater part of the bill will be absorbed by the chef's time in cooking the food and the waiter's time in delivering it (not to mention the washing up). In other cases, for example life insurance or other financial services, the physical evidence is likely to be much less or lacking altogether, in which case the firm may need to produce something that will provide evidence, for example a glossy brochure or policy document. For practical and legal purposes, most insurance documents could be printed on one or two sheets of paper, but for marketing purposes the document needs to be much more substantial.

There are four generic ways to add value through physical evidence:

1. Create physical evidence that increases loyalty.
2. Use physical evidence to enhance brand image.

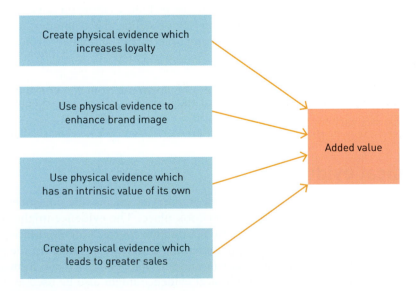

Figure 21.12   Adding value through physical evidence

3. Use physical evidence that has an intrinsic value of its own, e.g. a free gift.
4. Create physical evidence that leads to further sales.

Airlines use their frequent-flyer programmes to increase loyalty: the physical evidence of the flights taken is the regular newsletter which is sent out and the plastic card the frequent flyer uses to gain access to the executive lounges at airports en route. Some airlines (KLM for example) also issue special plastic baggage tags, which let the baggage handlers know they are dealing with a very important suitcase: what effect this has on the baggage handlers is debatable, but the effect on the customer is a feeling of importance. At each level of membership of KLM's frequent flyer programme (Blue Wing, Silver Wing and Gold Wing) the colour of the card changes, as do the benefits to which the holder is entitled. These physical elements of the service are intended to encourage the customer to fly more often with KLM: failure to fly a set number of times a year with the airline will result in a downgrade to a lower level. An intangible benefit of membership for the customer is the occasional free flight – membership points can be exchanged for free flights at a set rate per distance travelled, or for upgrades into business class.

Brand image can be enhanced by using physical evidence that fits in with the brand's essential qualities. For example, an insurance company that wishes to convey a solid, respectable image will produce a glossy policy document full of high-flown legal phrases and reassuring photographs of solid corporate headquarters. A company aiming to convey a more down-to-earth, welcoming image might produce a policy couched in simple language, with photographs of smiling staff and policyholders. Physical evidence need not always be up-market: most low-cost airlines emphasise the cost-cutting aspects of their businesses by requiring passengers to print off their own tickets on their computers, or by having no tickets at all. This is about as basic as physical evidence can get, but it does emphasise the point that the airline does not waste passengers' money on anything that is not absolutely necessary.

Physical evidence that has an intrinsic value of its own would include free gifts: this is a common ploy in the financial services industry. Clocks, pen sets, DVD players, radio alarm clocks and so forth are often given out to people who take out insurance policies or pension plans. Clearly very few people would take out an insurance policy simply to win a carriage clock, but the existence of the clock on the policyholder's mantelpiece is good evidence of the existence of the policy.

Physical evidence that leads to further business might include reminder cards sent out by garages to let drivers know that their cars are due for a service. Dentists, opticians, hairdressers and some hospitals use reminders like this to tell people they need check-ups: the physical evidence of the previous visit serves to generate more business. Some business gifts fulfil a similar function: a desk calendar, notepad or pen given away at the conclusion of a sale may serve as a reminder when a future need arises.

Chapter summary

Although people, process and physical evidence are often associated with service industries, the fact is that every product involves some service elements. Business is not conducted by companies: it is conducted between human beings, carrying out processes that improve the lives of other human beings. In some cases, they will also need to provide some kind of proof that the service has been carried out – hence the physical evidence aspect.

Key points

- Service industries often command greater loyalty than do industries that deal with physical products. This is because of the higher risk to the consumer of buying services.
- Services purchasing follows a somewhat different route from purchasing physical products.
- Risk is higher for all concerned in services marketing.
- There will always be some failures in providing services.
- For empowerment to work, there should be clear guidelines, a no-blame culture and clear rewards for success.
- Process combines basic assets, explicit knowledge, tacit knowledge and procedure.
- Consumers can be seen as co-producers of services in many cases.
- Services are characterised in two dimensions: complexity and diversity.
- Physical evidence can be used to increase loyalty, enhance brand image, increase value and increase future sales.

Review questions

1. What mechanisms might a restaurant chain use to improve customer loyalty?
2. What are the main factors in risk for customers of service firms?
3. What are the main differences between services and physical products?
4. What are the key differences between contactors, modifiers, influencers and isolateds?
5. How might physical evidence be used to increase loyalty?
6. How might improved service provision help sales of physical products?
7. What are the advantages of empowering staff?
8. What differences in decision-making might consumers exhibit when purchasing services?
9. How might a firm minimise the effects of variability in service provision?
10. What factors combine to produce service process?

Case study revisited: easyJet

One of the early discoveries by the consultants was that people carrying out the various tasks did not understand how their processes fitted with other people's activities, because they had little or no idea of what the other teams actually did. Worse, they did not understand how each job was reliant on every other job. The consultants arranged for cross-disciplinary groups to meet and explain each other's jobs. The result of this was some creative ideas for cutting ground time. For example, ground engineers normally wait until all the passengers have disembarked before coming on board to discuss servicing needs with the pilots: this inevitably causes delays as it can take ten minutes or more for passengers to collect their hand baggage and leave the plane. Discussions within the focus groups led to the idea of supplying ground engineers with headsets so that they could talk to the pilots from the tarmac while the passengers disembark, getting most questions out of the way before needing to board the aircraft. Another innovation is for the cabin crew to begin cleaning the cabin before the aircraft arrives – the cabin crew collect unwanted magazines and newspapers and any obvious rubbish while the aircraft is in its final approach and the seatbelt sign is on.

Ideas were disseminated by videoing the sessions and allowing staff to see what the groups discussed. Ideas continue to flow from the staff, because they have developed an innovative culture. After all, who can understand the job better than those who do it all day, every day?

The net result of the exercise is that average turnround times are down from 50 minutes to 33 minutes, and in one notable case an aircraft was turned round in only 7 minutes. This may not seem a lot, but if an aircraft makes an average of four return flights a day, over an hour per day will be saved in downtime. Over a working year, this equates to more than 60 return flights from Luton to Nice – which is equivalent to over a million pounds per aircraft in extra sales revenue.

Case study: PayPal

One of the barriers to doing business on the Internet is the security of payments. After all, when one buys something on-line, the vendor might be anywhere in the world: if anything goes wrong with the product or its delivery, or even if a simple mistake has been made, it might be impossible to visit the vendor's premises to get a refund. In a worst-case scenario, the vendor may not exist at all, and certainly in the early days of Internet retailing there was a high level of fraud.

Even when the vendor is wholly trustworthy, many people are nervous about entering their credit card details into a website. After all, there are some very clever hackers out there, and horror stories abound about the dangers of identity theft, fraudulent transactions on credit cards and employees selling credit card details to criminals. For

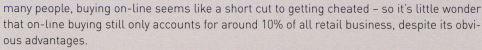

many people, buying on-line seems like a short cut to getting cheated – so it's little wonder that on-line buying still only accounts for around 10% of all retail business, despite its obvious advantages.

PayPal was created in 2000 by merging two other companies that had been set up in the late 1990s to process on-line payments. The company operates as a buffer between the retailer and the customer, ensuring that the payments are totally secure: PayPal charges retailers a small fee for processing payments, in the same way as credit card companies do, so that consumers pay the advertised price for products and are thus not encouraged to use other methods of payment. The procedure is simple – a customer making a purchase is directed to the PayPal site, makes the payment by credit or debit card, and has the order confirmed immediately.

Initially, PayPal hoped that it would earn enough from interest payments on cash held on account that it would not need to charge fees: however, this model proved flawed, partly because vendors withdrew their payments almost immediately and partly because many purchasers paid by credit cards, on which PayPal had to pay a commission to the credit card company. Adjustments to the fee structure made the model more viable. At the same time, the rapid growth of eBay opened up a lucrative extra market for PayPal. eBay vendors are often individuals or small firms who are unable to accept credit card payments. Since one of the strengths of the Internet as a retailing outlet is that payments do not require cash, there was a major barrier to doing business on eBay. PayPal filled the gap neatly because the company could accept credit card payments and pass on the payment direct to the individual's PayPal account and thence to his or her bank account.

Such was the synergy between PayPal and eBay that eBay bought PayPal for $1.5bn in 2002. This was a wonderful outcome for the original founders, of course – making that kind of money in only four or five years is something of a dream come true – but it was also money well spent for eBay. PayPal is not exclusively used for eBay transactions, but it certainly makes them a lot easier, and owning PayPal means that eBay has control of the entire cashflow.

There are other payment methods, of course, and many people now buy their airline tickets, rail tickets, pizza deliveries, clothing and even groceries on-line using credit cards. Yet PayPal fills a neat gap – buffering against fraud, and enabling even the smallest transactions to be fulfilled.

Questions

1. How does PayPal minimise variability in its service provision?
2. How does PayPal reduce risk in financial services?
3. What difficulties in consumer decision-making does PayPal address?
4. What are the benefits to businesses of using PayPal's service?
5. What is the role of physical evidence in PayPal's service?

Further reading

Principles of Services Marketing, 6th edn by Adrian Palmer (Maidenhead: McGraw–Hill, 2011) is a well-established, readable and comprehensive textbook. This book has become established as the leading text in the field.

Services Marketing, by Valarie Zeithaml and Mary Jo Bitner is an American text with a good pedigree. Zeithaml and Bitner almost invented services marketing between them, so the text is certainly definitive, but of course uses American examples and contexts, which are not always familiar to non-Americans. It is now in its sixth edition, with co-author Dwyne D. Gremler (New York: McGraw-Hill, 2012).

References

Belbin, R.M. (1981) *Management Teams: Why They Succeed or Fail*. London: Heinemann.

Booms, B.H. and Bitner, M.J. (1981) Marketing strategies and organisation structures for service firms. In J. Donnelly and W.R. George (eds), *Marketing of Services*. Chicago, IL: American Marketing Association.

Choi, C.J. and Scarpa, C. (1994) A note on small vs. large organisations. *Journal of Economic Behaviour and Organisation*, 24: 219–24.

Cummings, T.G. (1981) Designing effective work groups. In P.C. Nystrom and W.H. Starbuck (eds), *Handbook of Organisational Design*. Oxford: Oxford University Press.

Finlay, P. (2000) *Strategic Management: An Introduction to Business and Corporate Strategy*. Harlow: FT Prentice Hall.

Gummeson, E. (1991) Marketing orientation revisited: the crucial role of the part-time marketer. *European Journal of Marketing*, 25 (2): 60–75.

Handy, C. (1989) *The Age of Unreason*. London: Hutchinson.

Judd, V.C. (1987) Differentiate with the 5th P: People. *Industrial Marketing Management*, 16: 241–7.

Kotler, Philip (2003) *Marketing Management*. Upper Saddle River, NJ: Prentice Hall.

Maxham, James G. III and Netemeyer, Richard G. (2003) Firms reap what they sow: the effect of shared values and perceived organisational justice on customers' evaluation of complaint handling. *Journal of Marketing*, 67 (1): 46–62.

Murphy, J.A. (2001) *The Lifebelt: The Definitive Guide to Managing Customer Retention*. Chichester: John Wiley.

Raddats, Chris and Easingwood, Chris (2010) Services growth options for B2B product-centric businesses. *Industrial Marketing Management*, 39 (8): 1334-5.

Rasmusson, Erika (1997) Winning back angry customers. *Sales and Marketing Management*, Oct: 131.

Reichheld, F.F. and Sasser, W.E. Jr (1990) Zero defections, quality comes to services. *Harvard Business Review*, 68 (5): 105–11.

Roberts, K., Varki, S. and Brodie, R. (2003) Measuring the quality of relationships in consumer services: an empirical study. *European Journal of Marketing*, 37 (1/2): 169–96.

Shostack, G.L. (1987) Service positioning through structural change. *Journal of Marketing*, 51 (Jan): 34–43.

Stalk, G., Evans, P. and Shulman, L. (1992) Competing on capabilities. *Harvard Business Review*, 70 (2): 57–69.

Vargo, Stephen L. and Lusch, Robert F. (2004) Evolving to a new dominant logic for marketing. *Journal of Marketing*, 68 (Jan.): 1–17.

Zeithaml, V.A. and Bitner, M.J. (1996) *Services Marketing: Integrating Customer Focus Across the Firm*. New York: McGraw–Hill.

More online

To gain free access to additional online resources to support this chapter please visit:
www.sagepub.co.uk/blythe3e

Glossary

Above the line	Advertising for which the advertising agency obtains a commission from the media.
Achievers	People who seek respect by buying appropriate products.
ACORN	A geographical segmentation method: A Classification Of Residential Neighbourhoods.
Actual state	The situation the individual is currently experiencing.
Adapter	A company that produces new products, superior to those produced by the market leader.
Advertising	A paid message inserted in a medium.
Advertising research	Investigations into the effectiveness and potential effectiveness of marketing communications.
Advertorials	Advertisements that are written in the style of editorials (not to be confused with press releases).
Affect	The emotional component of attitude.
Affective	Relating to emotional factors.
Aftermarket	See MRO.
Aggressive	Someone who usually moves against people and controls fear and emotions in a quest for success, prestige and admiration.
Alliteration	Using similar sounds in a slogan to aid memory.
Ambient advertising	Advertising that becomes part of the environment.
Ambiguity	The degree to which stimuli can be interpreted in different ways.
Anthropology	The study of culture.
Aspirational groups	Groups an individual would like to be a member of.
Assonance	Repetition of vowels in a slogan to aid memory.
Assortment adjustment	Changing the proportions of products owned in order to increase satisfaction.
Assortment depletion	Using up resources or wearing out products.
Attitude	A learned tendency to respond in a consistent manner to a specific stimulus or object.
Audience fade-out	The tendency for TV viewers to leave the room or lose concentration when the commercial breaks occur.
Automatic group	A group to which one belongs by virtue of birth. Also called category group.
Backward conditioning	The unconditioned stimulus comes before the conditioned stimulus.
Banners	Advertising messages on websites.
Barrier to entry	A factor that prevents a firm from entering a specific market.
Belief	An understanding that an object possesses a particular attribute.
Belongers	People who seek to join groups in society.
Below the line	Promotional tools for which the advertising agency charges the client.
Benchmarking	Setting performance parameters by comparing performance with that of the best of the competing firms.
Bias	Errors in research results caused by failures in the research design or sampling method.
Boundary scanning	The practice of monitoring the interfaces between the firm and its public.

Boycott	To avoid buying a company's products.
Brainstorming	Generating new product ideas by group discussion.
Brand	The focus of marketing activities.
Brand audit	The process of determining whether a specific brand is being marketed effectively.
Brokers	Intermediaries who bring buyers and sellers together but do not themselves handle goods.
Buyback	An agreement on the part of a supplier to accept payment in finished products.
Buyer	The person who negotiates the purchase.
Cash Cow	A product with large share of a mature market.
Catalogue showrooms	Retailers that have a bricks-and-mortar presence but use a brochure to display the goods rather than display shelves.
Categorical plan	An approach to valuing suppliers based on salient performance factors.
Categorisation	Filing information alongside similar information in the memory.
Central route	Cognitive approach to changing behaviour.
Chunking	The mental process whereby information is stored alongside connected information.
Classical conditioning	The instilling of automatic responses in an individual by repetition of stimulus and reward.
Cloner	A company that produces copies of products sold by the market leader.
Closed questions	Enquiries to which there will be only a small range of possible answers, usually yes or no.
Closing techniques	Those questions and behaviours that end the sales presentation and elicit a decision from the buyer.
Clutter	Excessive advertising.
Coercive power	Potential for control derived from the ability to punish the other party.
Cognition	The rational component of attitude.
Cognitive	Relating to rational factors.
Cognitive effort	The degree of effort the consumer is prepared to put into thinking about the product offering.
Cognitive structure	The way information is fitted into the existing knowledge.
Commission	Performance-related payments made to salespeople.
Comparative advantage	The degree to which one country is better at producing certain goods rather than another.
Compatibility	The degree to which a product fits into the adopter's life.
Compensatory	Of a heuristic, one that allows negative features to be offset against positive features.
Competitor orientation	The belief that corporate success comes from understanding competitors.
Complexity	The degree to which the product is difficult to understand.
Compliant	Someone who moves towards people, has goodness, sympathy, love, unselfishness and humility.
Compulsive consumption	An obsessive need to buy and use products.
Conation	Intended behaviour.
Concept testing	A market research exercise in which feedback is obtained on the basic idea for a new product.
Concessionaires	Firms that rent space in department stores, paying a rental and usually a commission on sales.
Conclusive research	Investigations intended to provide answers to problems.
Conditioned response	A response that results from exposure to a conditioned stimulus.
Conditioned stimulus	A stimulus offered at the same time as an unconditioned stimulus, with the intention of creating an artificial association between it and the unconditioned response.
Conditions	Situations that make a sale impossible.
Confidentiality agreement	A contract between two parties containing clauses to the effect that each will keep the other's secrets.

Confirming houses	An organisation that handles the mechanics of exporting and importing on behalf of manufacturers or buyers.
Conjunctive	Heuristics that are considered together.
Connotative	Having the same meaning for everybody.
Consideration set	The group of products that might be capable of meeting a need.
Consumer	One who obtains the benefits from a product.
Consumerism	The set of organised activities intended to promote the needs of the consumer against those of the firm.
Contactors	Staff who have daily contact with customers.
Continuous innovation	Incremental improvements in an existing product.
Convenience sampling	Selecting respondents by availability, without regard to the characteristics of the respondents.
Convenience stores	Stores located in residential areas which stock frequently purchased items.
Core competences	The central, most important aspects of the company's abilities.
Corporate reputation	The overall image of the organisation.
Cost-plus pricing	Setting prices by calculating the outlay on producing the items, and adding on a profit margin.
Cost-ratio plan	A method of evaluating suppliers based on the costs of doing business with them.
Counterpurchase	An agreement on the part of a supplier to accept payment in kind, or to spend the proceeds of the sale in the country in which the sale is made.
Countertrading	Bartering of goods in international markets.
Cross-selling	Selling new product lines to an existing customer.
Cue	An external trigger that encourages learning.
Culture	The set of shared beliefs and behaviours common to an identifiable group of people.
Customary pricing	The price a product has always been sold for.
Customer	One who decides on payment for a product.
Customer intimacy	The degree to which a firm is close to its customers.
Customer orientation	The belief that corporate success comes from understanding and meeting customer needs.
Customer research	Investigations into the behaviour of purchasers of a product.
Customer size specialist	A company that specialises in dealing with customers of a specific size.
Customer-specified innovation	New product ideas that are generated by customers.
Cut-off	A filtering device that involves deciding the outer limits of acceptability for a given product's characteristics.
Database marketing	Using a list of customers or potential customers stored on a computer to drive the marketing effort.
Decider	The person who has the power to agree a purchase.
Decision tree	A diagrammatic representation of the route a manager must take to reach a decision.
Decision-making unit (DMU)	A group of people who, between them, decide on purchases.
Del credere **agents**	Intermediaries who do not take title to the goods, but do accept the credit risk from customers.
Delphi	A system of research under which opinions are sought iteratively from experts.
Demand pricing	Calculating price according to what consumers are prepared to pay.
Demographics	The study of the structure of the population.
Denotative	Having a unique meaning for an individual.
Deontology	The belief that actions can be judged independently of outcome.
Dependent variable	The stimulus that is applied to generate a response.
Desired state	The situation the individual wishes to be in.
Detached	Someone who moves away from people, is self-sufficient and independent.
Dichotomous question	An inquiry that can only be answered 'yes' or 'no'.
Differentiation	Factors that distinguish one product from another.

Direct response	A type of advertising campaign that contains a method for the consumer to contact the supplier immediately and directly.
Direct-response advertising	Messages inserted in a medium with the intention of generating a dialogue with potential consumers.
Discontinuous innovation	A new product that significantly changes consumers' lifestyles.
Discount sheds	Out-of-town stores offering a wide range of products at low prices.
Discounters	Retailers that carry a limited range of stock at low prices.
Discrimination	The ability to distinguish between similar stimuli.
Dissociative group	A group to which one would not wish to belong.
Dissonance	The emotional state created when expectations do not match with outcomes.
Distribution research	Investigations into the effectiveness of different outlets for products.
Dodo	A product with a small share of a shrinking market.
Dog	A product with a small share of a mature market.
Dramaturgical analogy	The view that life is essentially theatrical in nature.
Drive	The force generated in an individual as a result of a felt need.
Dumping	Disposing of products in a foreign market at prices below the cost of production.
Dynamically continuous innovation	A product that is a substantial shift in technology but does not change people's lives.
Eclectic	All-encompassing, taking account of all factors.
Economic choice	The inability to spend the same money twice.
Economics	The study of supply and demand.
Economies of scale	Cost savings resulting from large production runs.
Elaboration	The structuring of the information within the brain, and adding to it from memory in order to form a coherent whole.
Elasticity of demand	The degree to which people's propensity to buy a product is affected by price changes.
Empowerment	Giving staff the ability to resolve customer problem without recourse to higher management.
End-of-pipe solution	Cleaning up pollution after it has been created rather than re-engineering the process so that pollution is not produced.
End user	The person or company who uses the product, without selling it on or converting it into something else.
End-use specialist	A firm that specialises in supplying all the needs of a specific group of customers, who use a product in a specific way.
Environment research	Investigations into the external factors that impinge on the organisation's activities.
Environmental scanning	Continuous monitoring of external factors that might impinge on the organisation's activities.
Ethics	A set of rules for good behaviour.
Ethnicity	Cultural background.
Ethnocentrism	The belief that one's own culture is superior to others.
Experiment	A research technique in which a controlled situation is used to determine consumer response to a given stimulus.
Exploratory research	Investigations intended to identify problems.
Export agent	A person or company that takes responsibility for organising the export of goods without taking title to the goods.
Export house	An organisation that buys goods for sale abroad.
Extended problem-solving	Non-routine purchasing behaviour.
Extension	Increasing the number of products owned.
External environment	Factors that operate outside the organisation.
External search	Looking for information in places other than memory.
External validity	A condition where a research exercise would generate the same results if it were repeated elsewhere.
Extinction	The gradual weakening of conditioning over time.

Factors	Intermediaries who hold stocks of product but do not take title to the goods.
Familiarity	The degree to which an object is known.
Field research	Investigations carried out in the marketplace.
Financial risk	The danger of losing money as the result of a purchase.
First-time prospects	Potential customers with whom the company has never done business before.
Focus group	Respondents brought together to discuss a research question in a controlled and structured manner under the guidance of a researcher.
Foregrounding	Bringing an advertising slogan to the forefront of customer's mind.
Formal group	A group with a known, recorder membership list.
Formal structure	The official relationships between members of an organisation.
Forward conditioning	The conditioned stimulus comes before the unconditioned stimulus.
Franchising	An agreement to use a firm's business methods and intellectual property in return for a fee and a royalty.
Frequency	Number of times each consumer is exposed to the communication.
Functional risk	The risk that a product or service will not provide the expected benefits.
Gatekeeper	The person who controls the flow of information.
Generalisation	The tendency for the individual to react in several ways to the conditioned stimulus.
Generally concerned	One who believes that the environment is important, but does little to change his or her behaviour accordingly.
Geocentrism	Viewing corporate activities in a global manner.
Geographical proximity	The closeness of the market in physical terms.
Global customers	Firms that are willing to purchase products outside their domestic markets and tend to have global control of purchasing from headquarters.
Globalisation	The view of the world as a single market and single source of supply.
Goal	An objective.
Green activist	One who is proactive in espousing an environmentally friendly lifestyle.
Green customer	One whose purchases are influenced by environmental concerns.
Green thinker	One who believes in being environmentally friendly.
Grey market	(1) Re-import of brands from markets where the prices are lower. (2) Older consumers.
Hedonic needs	Needs that relate to the pleasurable aspects of ownership.
Heuristic	A decision-making rule.
High-context culture	A culture that is homogeneous and has rigid rules.
Homophilous influence	The love of being like everyone else.
House journal	A medium for disseminating information within an organisation.
Icebreaker	A statement or question used at the beginning of a sales presentation with the intention of establishing a rapport with the buyer.
Ideal self	The person we wish we were.
Identifiers	The major variables in segmentation, which can be listed without carrying out extensive research.
Image	The overall impression a company or brand has in the eyes of its publics.
Image building	A type of campaign that is conducted for the purpose of conveying a specific perception of a product in the minds of customers.
Imitator	A company that makes somewhat differentiated products which are similar to those produced by the market leader.
Import house	An organisation that buys goods in from abroad.
Impulse purchases	Purchases made without apparent conscious thought.
Incoterms	International Commercial Terms. A set of internationally agreed terms used in drawing up export contracts.
Independent variable	The response resulting from a dependent variable.
Influencer	The person who has the ability to sway the judgement of a decider.

Influencers	Staff who can affect the way customers are treated even though they have no direct access to them.
Infomercial	A feature-length TV programme about a product.
Informal group	A group that does not have a fixed membership list or known rules.
Informal structure	The unofficial relationships between members of an organisation.
Infrastructure	The physical resources available to the firm for logistical processes.
Initiator	The person who first recognises a problem.
Inner directed	Motivated by forces originating within the individual.
Innovation cost	The expenditure of money and effort resulting from adopting a new product.
Intangibility	The inability to touch a service.
Internal ad hoc data	Information supplied by systems within the organisation for a specific purpose.
Internal continuous data	Information supplied by systems within the organisation on a constant basis.
Internal environment	Factors that operate within the organisation.
Internal marketing	The practice of creating goodwill among employees.
Internal validity	A condition where a research exercise provides evidence that supports what the exercise was intended to discover.
Intranet	A computer-mediated system for internal communications within an organisation.
Involvement	Emotional attachment to a product.
Isolateds	Staff who have no relationship with customers.
Judgement sampling	Selecting respondents according to criteria established by the researcher.
Junk mail	Poorly targeted direct mailings.
Just in time	A supply chain management system in which the purchaser does not maintain an inventory, but instead switches responsibility for this to the supplier.
Key account	A customer or potential customer with strategic importance to the firm.
Key-account manager	Someone charged with the task of managing the relationship with a strategically important customer.
Law of primacy	The law that states that early learning about an object will colour future experiences of the object and future interpretations of that experience.
Leads	People who are prepared to hear what a salesperson has to say.
Least dependent person	The individual with the most power in a group.
Legitimate power	Potential for control derived from a legal or contractual position.
Lexicographic	A hierarchy of heuristics.
Licensing	An agreement to use a firm's intellectual property in exchange for a royalty.
Limited problem-solving	Routine purchasing behaviour.
Liner	A ship or aircraft that operates on a regular route at fixed times.
Livery	Painting a public-transport vehicle in corporate colours or advertising.
Lobbying	Making representations to politicians with the aim of changing legislation.
Logistics	The co-ordination of the supply chain to achieve a seamless flow from raw materials through to the consumer.
Longitudinal study	Research that is carried out over a lengthy time period.
Looking-glass self	The way we think other people see us.
Low-context culture	A culture that is heterogenous and has tolerant rules.
Loyalty	The tendency to repeat purchase of a brand.
Macro environment	Factors that affect all the firms in an industry.
Margin	Gross profit calculated as a proportion of the price a product is sold for.
Market challenger	A company that seeks to grow at the expense of the market leader.
Market follower	A company that follows the lead of the main company in the market.
Market research	Investigations intended to improve knowledge about customers and competitors.
Market segment	A group of people having similar needs.

Marketing information system	Mechanisms for providing a constant flow of information about markets.
Marketing orientation	The belief that corporate success comes from understanding the relationships in the market.
Marketing research	Information-gathering for the purpose of improving the organisation's effectiveness.
Mark-up	Gross profit calculated as a proportion of the price paid for an item.
Maturation	The development of the organism over time.
Mechanics	In sales promotion, the activities the customer must undertake.
Memory	The mechanism by which learned information is stored.
Merchandiser	A type of salesperson who has the responsibility of establishing and maintaining in-store displays.
Message intrigue	The increased interest developed by ambiguous communications.
Metaphor	A sign that relates to an object.
Micro environment	Factors that affect one firm only.
Micromarketing	Tailoring a product to a specific customer's needs.
Missionary	A salesperson who does not sell directly, but who has the task of 'spreading the word' about a product to people who influence purchase.
Modified rebuy	A repeat purchase where some changes have been made.
Modifiers	Staff who have some contact with customers for specific purposes.
Monopolistic competition	A situation in which one company exercises strong influence in the market, but other companies still enter the market and compete effectively.
Monopoly	A situation in which one company controls the market.
Mortality	The tendency for respondents to disappear over time.
Motivation	The force that moves an individual towards a specific set of solutions.
MRO	Maintenance, repair and overhauling company.
Multibuys	A sales promotion in which customers are offered extra packs of product when they buy one or more packs.
Multinational global customers	Customers who source products globally, and also use the products globally.
Mystery shoppers	A marketing research technique whereby the researcher pretends to be a customer.
Myths	Heroic stories about a product.
Narrowcast	Accurate targeting of audiences in broadcast media.
National global customers	Customers who source products globally but use them only within their national borders.
Need	A perceived lack of something.
New task	A purchase that has no precedent.
Niche marketer	A firm that is content with a small segment of the market.
Niche marketing	Serving a small segment.
Non-compensatory	Of a heuristic, one that does not allow a positive feature to offset a negative feature.
Non-universal ownership	Not owned by people who are not members of the group.
Normative compliance	The pressure to conform to group norms of behaviour.
Novices	Customers who have purchased the product for the first time within the last 90 days.
Objections	Questions raised by a prospect in the course of a sales presentation.
Objective	Not subject to bias from the individual.
Observability	The degree to which the product can be seen by others.
Odd–even pricing	Using '99p' or '95c' endings on prices.
OEM	Original-equipment manufacturer.
Oligopoly	A situation in which a group of companies control the market between them.
Open questions	Enquiries to which there might be a wide range of possible answers.
Operant conditioning	The instilling of automatic responses via the active participation of the individual.
Optimum stimulation level (OSL)	The level at which the gap between the desired state and the actual state has not yet become unpleasant.

Organismic organisations	Organisations that do not have a fixed structure: they adapt according to the task facing the organisation.
Outbound logistics	Controlling the flow of the product from the organisation to its customers.
Outer directed	Taking one's cue from the behaviour of others.
Outshopping	Shopping outside the area in which one lives.
Panel	A permanently established group of research respondents.
Party plan	A direct-marketing tool in which the salesperson holds private presentations for groups of friends in a private home.
Penetration pricing	Setting low prices in an attempt to capture a large market share.
People	The individuals involved in providing customer satisfaction.
Perceived cost of search	The degree to which an individual believes that an information search will be too arduous or expensive.
Perception	The process of building up a mental map of the world.
Perceptual map	The individual's view of competing products.
Perfect competition	A state of affairs where everyone in the market has perfect knowledge and no one buyer or seller can influence the market.
Peripheral route	Affective approach to changing behaviour.
Perishability	Services are perishable because they cannot be stockpiled.
Personal sources	The means–end knowledge stored in an individual's memory.
Physical distribution	The movement of products along the value chain from producer to retailer and ultimately to the consumer.
Physical evidence	The tangible proof that a service has taken place.
Physical risk	The danger of physical harm as the result of a purchase.
Piggy-backing	Attaching one product to another for the purposes of sales promotion.
Place	The location where the exchange takes place.
Polycentrism	Viewing corporate activities as emanating from centres in a number of countries.
Polymorphism	Bundling data and code to create an object.
Pop-ups	Advertising messages that appear on websites.
Positioning	Placing the product in the appropriate location in the consumers' perceptual maps.
Post-purchase evaluation	The process of deciding whether the outcome of a purchase has been appropriate or not.
Predatory pricing	Pricing at extremely low levels (sometimes below the cost of production) with the intention of damaging competitors or forcing them to leave the market.
Preliminary research	Investigations intended to outline the dimensions of a problem.
Presence website	A website that is not interactive but directs customers to another medium.
Press releases	News stories about the organisation.
Price	The exchange that the customer makes in order to obtain a product.
Primary data	Information collected first-hand for a specific purpose.
Primary group	The group of people who are closest to the individual.
Primary research	Research that is carried out from scratch for a specific project.
Private responses	Complaints made to friends or family about a product or company.
Problem Child	A product with a small share of a growing market.
Process	The set of activities that together produce customer satisfaction.
Procurement	Obtaining goods to be used in production or running the organisation.
Product	A bundle of benefits.
Product champion	An individual who has or is given the role of guiding a new product through the development process.
Product differentiation	A type of campaign that emphasises the differences between a product and competing products.
Product life cycle	The process of launch, growth, maturity and decline which products are thought to go through.

Product orientation	The belief that corporate success comes from having the best product.
Product placement	The use of branded products in TV programming or movies.
Product portfolio	The range of goods offered by a firm.
Product research	Investigations intended to generate knowledge that can be used to inform new product development.
Production orientation	The belief that corporate success comes from efficient production.
Product-line pricing	In circumstances where sales of one product are dependent on sales of another, calculating both prices to take account of the price of each product.
Project teams	Groups of people with the responsibility for guiding products through the development process.
Projective technique	A research method that invites respondents to say what they think another person might answer to a specific question or problem.
Promotion	Marketing communications.
Prospects	People who have a need for a product and the means to pay for it.
Psychological proximity	The degree to which countries are culturally close to each other.
Psychology	The study of thought processes.
Psychology of complication	The desire to make one's life more complex and therefore more interesting.
Psychology of simplification	The desire to make one's life simpler and therefore less demanding.
Psychosocial risk	The danger of looking foolish as a result of a purchase.
Public relations	The practice of creating goodwill towards an organisation.
Publics	The groups of people with whom the organisation interacts.
Pull strategy	Promoting to end users in order to 'pull' products through the distribution channel.
Push strategy	Promoting to channel intermediaries in order to 'push' products through the distribution channel.
Qualitative data	Information that cannot be expressed numerically.
Quantitative data	Information that can be expressed numerically.
Quota sampling	Selecting respondents according to a set of prearranged parameters.
Reach	Number of potential consumers a communication reaches.
Real self	The objective self that others observe.
Recession	A situation in which gross national production falls for three consecutive months.
Redundancy	In communications, sending a message by more than one route, to ensure a correct delivery.
Reference group	A group from which one takes behavioural cues.
Referent power	Potential for control derived from a position of authority.
Registration	A system for protecting the brand name.
Regression effect	The tendency for extremes to move towards the middle in longitudinal studies.
Reinforcement	Increasing the strength of learning by rewarding appropriate behaviour.
Relationship marketing	The practice of concentrating on the lifetime value of customers rather than their value in the single transaction.
Relative advantage	The degree to which a new product is better than the one it replaces.
Replenishment	Replacing products that have been worn out or used up.
Research plan	An outline of the steps that must be taken in gathering information systematically.
Reseller organisation	A firm that buys goods in order to sell them on to other firms or consumers.
Response	The reaction the consumer makes to the interaction between a drive and a cue.
Retention	The stability of learned material over time.
Role	The position one has in the group.
Rookie	A new sales recruit.
Roughs	Draft advertising materials produced for a client's approval.
Sales cycle	The series of activities undertaken by salespeople.
Sales orientation	The belief that corporate success comes from having proactive salespeople.

Sales presentation	A structured interview in which a salesperson ascertains a customer's needs and offers a solution that will meet those needs.
Sales research	Investigations into aspects of the personal selling function, including the performances of individual salespeople.
Salient belief	An understanding that an object possesses a relevant attribute.
Sampling	Selecting appropriate respondents for research.
Scamps	See Roughs.
Screening	Selecting new product ideas for further development.
Second lifetime value	The value of a former customer who has been won back to the firm's products.
Second-market discounting	Charging lower prices in some markets or some market segments than in others.
Secondary data	Information collected second-hand: information that was originally collected for a different purpose from that for which the researcher now wants to use it.
Secondary group	A group to which one belongs but which one does not relate to on a regular basis.
Secondary research	Research that has already been carried out (often by someone else for another purpose) and is available to the researcher for the current project.
Segmentation	Dividing the market into groups of people with similar needs.
Selectivity	Selecting from external stimuli.
Self-concept	One's view of oneself.
Self-image	The subjective self: the person we think we are.
Semiotics	The study of meaning.
Shelf price	The cost of a product when it is on the shelf, not including delivery costs etc.
Shopping products	Products that require extensive information search and decision-making.
Signal	A feature of the product or its surrounding attributes which conveys meaning about the product.
Simultaneous conditioning	The conditioned stimulus and the unconditioned stimulus are offered at the same time.
Simultaneous engineering	Carrying out development processes in parallel rather than sequentially in order to reduce time to market.
Situational factors	Elements of the immediate surroundings that affect decision-making.
Situational sources	Sources of involvement derived from immediate social or cultural factors.
Skimming	Pricing products highly at first, but reducing the price steadily as the product moves through its life cycle.
SMS	Short Message Service, or texting on cellular telephones.
Societally conscious	Cause-oriented people who become involved in charitable work.
Socio-cultural	Appertaining to the social effects of buying or not buying a product.
Sociology	The study of behaviour in groups.
Sophisticates	Customers who have purchased the product before and are ready to rebuy or have recently repurchased.
Spam	Unwanted commercial e-mails.
Species response tendencies	Automatic behaviour as a result of instinct rather than learning.
Specific-customer specialist	A company that specialises in dealing with a narrow range of customers.
Spin-doctoring	Attempts to cover up bad news by slanting it in a way that puts the organisation in a favourable light.
Sponsorship	Payment to a cause or event in exchange for publicity.
Stakeholders	People who are impacted by corporate activities.
Stars	Products with a large share of a growing market.
Straight rebuy	A repeat purchase with no modifications.
Strap line	The slogan at the end of an advertisement.
Structured observation	A marketing research technique that involves directly watching consumer behaviour.
Subjective	Appertaining to the individual; influenced by or derived from personal taste or opinion.
Subjectivity	The unique world-view within the individual.
Sugging	Selling under the guise of market research.
Survivors	Those people who struggle to maintain any kind of lifestyle.

Sustainers	People who have very limited incomes, but can still maintain a basic standard of living.
Switching cost	The expenditure of money and effort resulting from changing from one product to another.
System selling	Marketing on a one-to-one basis by a team of salespeople.
Targeting	Choosing which segments to service.
Tariff barriers	Customs duties that make a product less competitive in an overseas market.
Teaser campaign	An advertising campaign in two stages: the first stage involves a message which in itself is meaningless, but which is explained by later advertisements in the second stage.
Technophobe	Someone who does not like new products.
Technophone	Someone who has an interest in new technology.
Telemarketing	Selling or researching via the telephone.
Teleology	The belief that acts can be judged by their outcomes.
Telephone selling	The practice of using telephone communications as a personal selling medium rather than face-to-face meetings.
Telesales	Selling over the telephone.
Territory	The geographical area or group of potential customers allocated to a salesperson.
Test marketing	Offering a product to a small group of consumers in order to judge the likely response from a large group of consumers.
Third-party responses	Complaints made via lawyers or consumer rights advocates.
Time series	Analysis that shows how the situation has progressed over a period, carried out in order to predict likely future trends.
Trade association	A group of companies in the same industry, set up to look after the collective interests of the group.
Trade up	Buying the more expensive model.
Tramp ship	A ship that does not follow set routes, but which sails when it has a cargo for a particular port.
Transfer pricing	Internal pricing in a multinational company.
Trialability	The degree to which the product can be tried out before adoption.
Triangulation	Using more than one research method to answer the same question in order to reduce the chances of errors.
Turnkey contract	An agreement whereby one firm establishes an entire business in a foreign country and subsequently hands over the business to another firm, in exchange for a fee and occasionally royalties.
Unconditioned response	The existing automatic response of the individual to an unconditioned stimulus.
Unconditioned stimulus	A stimulus that would normally produce a known reaction in an individual: this stimulus is offered as part of the conditioning process.
Unique selling proposition (USP)	The factors that distinguish a product from its competitors.
User	The person who uses the product.
Utilitarian	Appertaining to the practical aspects of ownership.
Value	The benefit a customer obtains from a product.
Value analysis	A method of evaluating components, raw materials and even manufacturing processes in order to determine ways of cutting costs or improving finished products.
Value breakdown	A situation in which the service offered by a producer does not materialise.
Value chain	The firms involved in the process of turning raw materials into products.
Value chain analysis	Assessment of ways in which organisations add value to the products they handle.
Value network	The group of organisations that collectively add value to raw materials.
Value-based marketing	Marketing whose end goal is raising the share value of the company.
Variability	In services, the difference between one service and the next, even from the same supplier.

Vertical integration	A situation in which one company controls or owns suppliers and customers throughout the supply chain.
Virtual products	Anything that can be sold and delivered via the Internet.
Visible	Able to be seen by others.
Voice responses	Complaints made directly to the supplier.
Wall newspaper	A poster giving information to employees.
Want	A specific satisfier for a need.
War Horse	A product with a large share of a shrinking market.
Website	A page on the Internet designed for and dedicated to an organisation or individual.
Weighted-point plan	A method of evaluating suppliers based on factors that are of greatest importance to the company.
Worst self	The negative aspects of one's personality; the aspects we wish to overcome in ourselves.
Zapping	Using the TV remote control to avoid advertising messages.
Zipping	Using the fast-forward function to skip past TV advertising in a recorded programme.

Index